Lecture Notes in Computer Science 11751

More information about this series at http://www.springer.com/series/7412

Elisa Ricci · Samuel Rota Bulò ·
Cees Snoek · Oswald Lanz ·
Stefano Messelodi · Nicu Sebe (Eds.)

Image Analysis and Processing – ICIAP 2019

20th International Conference
Trento, Italy, September 9–13, 2019
Proceedings, Part I

 Springer

Editors
Elisa Ricci ⓘ
University of Trento
Povo, Italy

Samuel Rota Bulò ⓘ
Mapillary Research
Graz, Austria

Cees Snoek ⓘ
University of Amsterdam
Amsterdam, The Netherlands

Oswald Lanz ⓘ
Fondazione Bruno Kessler
Povo, Italy

Stefano Messelodi ⓘ
Fondazione Bruno Kessler
Povo, Italy

Nicu Sebe ⓘ
University of Trento
Povo, Italy

ISSN 0302-9743   ISSN 1611-3349   (electronic)
Lecture Notes in Computer Science
ISBN 978-3-030-30641-0   ISBN 978-3-030-30642-7   (eBook)
https://doi.org/10.1007/978-3-030-30642-7

LNCS Sublibrary: SL6 – Image Processing, Computer Vision, Pattern Recognition, and Graphics

This Springer imprint is published by the registered company Springer Nature Switzerland AG
The registered company address is: Gewerbestrasse 11, 6330 Cham, Switzerland

Preface

The International Conference on Image Analysis and Processing (ICIAP) is an established scientific meeting organized biennially and promoted by the Italian Association for Computer Vision, Pattern Recognition and Machine Learning (CVPL; ex-GIRPR) of the International Association for Pattern Recognition (IAPR). The conference traditionally covers topics related to computer vision, pattern recognition, and image processing, addressing both theoretical and applicative aspects.

The 20th International Conference on Image Analysis and Processing (ICIAP 2019), held in Trento, Italy, September 9–13, 2019 (https://event.unitn.it/iciap2019), was organized jointly by University of Trento and Fondazione Bruno Kessler.

The conference was located in the city center, at the Faculty of Law of University of Trento, nearby Piazza Duomo, namely the historical, main square of the city. ICIAP 2019 was endorsed by the International Association for Pattern Recognition (IAPR). This year the conference was co-located with the 13th International Conference on Distributed Smart Cameras (ICDSC 2019) (https://event.unitn.it/icdsc2019/), and a joint keynote speech and oral session was organized.

ICIAP is traditionally a venue to discuss image processing and analysis, computer vision, pattern recognition and machine learning, from both theoretical and applicative perspectives, promoting connections and synergies among senior scholars and students, universities, research institutes, and companies. ICIAP 2019 followed this trend, and the program was subdivided into nine main topics, covering a broad range of scientific areas, which were managed by two area chairs per each topic. They were: Video Analysis and Understanding, Pattern Recognition and Machine Learning, Deep Learning, Multiview Geometry and 3D Computer Vision, Image Analysis, Detection and Recognition, Multimedia, Biomedical and Assistive Technology, Digital Forensics, and Image Processing for Cultural Heritage.

ICIAP 2019 received 207 paper submissions from all over the world, including Algeria, Austria, Belgium, Brazil, Bulgaria, Canada, China, Czech Republic, Denmark, Egypt, Finland, France, Germany, Greece, India, Israel, Italy, Japan, Korea, Morocco, Mexico, Pakistan, Poland, Romania, Russia, Saudi Arabia, Slovenia, Spain, Sweden, Switzerland, Tunisia, Turkey, the United Kingdom, and the USA. To select papers from these submissions, 21 expert researchers were invited to act as areas chairs, together with the international Program Committee and an expert team of reviewers. A rigorous peer-review selection process was carried out where each paper received at least two reviews. This ultimately led to the selection of 117 high quality manuscripts, presented during the conference in the form of 18 orals, 18 spotlights, and 81 posters, with an overall acceptance rate of about 56%. Among oral papers selected at ICIAP 2019, four were selected as Brave New Ideas Paper, i.e. papers exploring highly innovative ideas, visionary applications, and theoretical paradigm shifts in the area of computer vision, pattern recognition, machine learning, multimedia analysis, and image processing. The ICIAP 2019 proceedings are published as volumes of the *Lecture Notes in Computer Science* (LNCS) series by Springer.

The program included four invited talks by experts in computer vision, pattern recognition, and robotics: Davide Scaramuzza, University of Zurich and ETH Zurich (Switzerland), Tal Ayellet, Technion Israel of Technology (Israel), Emanuele Rodolà, Sapienza University of Rome (Italy), and Alessandra Sciutti, Italian Institute of Technology (Italy), who addressed very interesting and recent research approaches and paradigms such as deep learning, 3D modeling and reconstruction, visual robot navigation, semantic scene understanding, human-robot interaction, visual cognition, computer graphics, and image enhancement. ICIAP 2019 also included several tutorials on topics of great relevance for the community: Vision, Language and Action: from Captioning to Embodied AI, Lorenzo Baraldi and Marcella Cornia (University of Modena Reggio Emilia); Transferring Knowledge Across Domains: an Introduction to Deep Domain Adaptation, Massimiliano Mancini (Sapienza University of Rome, FBK and Italian Institute of Technology) and Pietro Morerio (Italian Institute of Technology); High-Dynamic-Range Imaging: Improvements and Limits, Alessandro Rizzi (University of Milano); Anomaly Detection in Images, Giacomo Boracchi (Politecnico Milano) and Diego Carrera (ST Microelectronics); Fingerprint Presentation Attacks Detection: Lessons Learned and a Roadmap to the Future, Gian Luca Marcialis (University of Cagliari); and Probabilistic and Deep Learning for Regression in Computer Vision, Stephane Lathuilière (University of Trento) and Xavier Alameda-Pineda (Inria Grenoble). ICIAP 2019 also hosted the presentation of the results of the Challenge DAFNE (Digital Anastylosis of Frescoes challeNgE), an international competition in the artistic heritage sector designed to provide virtual solutions that ultimately add to the fresco restorer's toolkit.

ICIAP 2019 also hosted five satellite events: four workshops and one industrial session. The workshops were: BioFor Workshop on Recent Advances in Digital Security: Biometrics and Forensics, organized by Daniel Riccio, Francesco Marra, Diego Gragnaniello (University of Naples Federico II, Italy) and Chang-Tsun Li (Deakin University, Australia); the First International Workshop on eHealth in the Big Data and Deep Learning Era, organized by Tanmoy Chakraborty (Institute of Information Technology Delhi, India), Stefano Marrone (University of Naples "Federico II", Italy) and Giancarlo Sperl (CINI - ITEM National Lab, Naples, Italy); Deep Understanding of Shopper Behaviours and Interactions in Intelligent Retail Environment, organized by Emanuele Frontoni (Università Politecnica delle Marche), Sebastiano Battiato (University of Catania, Italy), Cosimo Distante (ISASI CNR, Italy), Marina Paolanti (Università Politecnica delle Marche, Italy), Luigi Di Stefano (University of Bologna, Italy), Giovanni Marina Farinella (University di Catania, Italy), Annette Wolfrath (GFK Verein, Germany) and Primo Zingaretti (Università Politecnica delle Marche, Italy) and the International Workshop on Pattern Recognition for Cultural Heritage (PatReCH 2019), organized by Francesco Fontanella, Mario Molinara (University of Cassino and Southern Lazio, Italy) and Filippo Stanco (University of Catania, Italy). The Industrial Session was organized with the purpose of bringing together researchers and practitioners in industrial engineering and computer science interested in industrial machine vision. The session was organized by Luigi di Stefano, Vittorio Murino, Paolo Rota, and Francesco Setti. In the industrial session we hosted several companies as well as start-ups to show their activities while assessing them with respect to the cutting-edge research in the respective areas. The papers from the workshop and the industrial session were all collected in New Trends in Image Analysis and Processing – ICIAP 2019. We thank all the workshop and industrial session organizers and tutorial speakers who made possible such an interesting pre-conference program.

Several awards were conferred during ICIAP 2019. Two student support grants were provided by the International Association for Pattern Recognition (IAPR). The Eduardo Caianiello Award was attributed to the best paper authored or co-authored by at least one young researcher (PhD student, Post Doc, or similar). A Best Paper Award was also assigned after a careful selection made by an ad hoc appointed committee. The award was dedicated to Prof. Alfredo Petrosino, an eminent scientist and one of the most active members of the Italian Chapter of the IAPR, who passed away this year. During the conference an important moment was dedicated to commemorate the memory of Prof. Petrosino who will be greatly missed.

The organization and the success of ICIAP 2019 was made possible thanks to the cooperation of many people. First of all, special thanks should be given to all the reviewers and the area chairs, who made a big effort for the selection of the papers. Second, we also would like to thank the industrial, special session, publicity, publication, and Asia and US liaison chairs, who, operating in their respective fields, made this event a successful forum of science. Special thanks go to the workshop and tutorial chairs, as well as all workshop organizers and tutorial lecturers for making the conference program richer with notable satellite events. The communication services department of UNITN that supported all the communication, the registration process, and the financial aspects of the conference, among many other issues, should be acknowledged for all the work done. Last but not least, we are indebted to the local Organizing Committee (mainly colleagues from MHUG, University of Trento, and FBK-TeV) who covered almost every aspect of the conference when necessary and the day-to-day management issues of the ICIAP 2019 organization. Thanks very much indeed to all the aforementioned people, as without their support we would not have made it. We hope that ICIAP 2019 met its aim to serve as a basis and inspiration for future ICIAP editions.

August 2019

Elisa Ricci
Samuel Rota Bulò
Cees Snoek
Oswald Lanz
Stefano Messelodi
Nicu Sebe

Organization

General Chairs

Oswald Lanz   Fondazione Bruno Kessler, Italy
Stefano Messelodi   Fondazione Bruno Kessler, Italy
Nicu Sebe   University of Trento, Italy

Program Chairs

Elisa Ricci   University of Trento and Fondazione Bruno Kessler, Italy
Samuel Rota Bulò   Mapillary Research, Austria
Cees Snoek   University of Amsterdam, The Netherlands

Workshop Chairs

Marco Cristani   University of Verona, Italy
Andrea Prati   University of Parma, Italy

Tutorial Chairs

Costantino Grana   University of Modena e Reggio Emilia, Italy
Lamberto Ballan   University of Padova, Italy

Special Session Chairs

Marco Bertini   University of Florence, Italy
Tatiana Tommasi   Italian Institute of Technology, Italy

Industrial Chairs

Paul Chippendale   Fondazione Bruno Kessler, Italy
Fabio Galasso   OSRAM, Germany

Publicity/Web Chairs

Davide Boscaini   Fondazione Bruno Kessler, Italy
Massimiliano Mancini   Sapienza University of Rome, Fondazione Bruno Kessler and Italian Institute of Technology, Italy

Publication Chair

Michela Lecca   Fondazione Bruno Kessler, Italy

Local Chairs

Fabio Poiesi   Fondazione Bruno Kessler, Italy
Gloria Zen   University of Trento, Italy
Stéphane Lathuillère   University of Trento, Italy

Asia Liaison Chair

Ramanathan Subramanian   University of Glasgow, Singapore

USA Liaison Chair

Yan Yan   Texas State University, USA

Steering Committee

Virginio Cantoni   University of Pavia, Italy
Luigi Pietro Cordella   University of Napoli Federico II, Italy
Rita Cucchiara   University of Modena and Reggio Emilia, Italy
Alberto Del Bimbo   University of Firenze, Italy
Marco Ferretti   University of Pavia, Italy
Gian Luca Foresti   University of Udine, Italy
Fabio Roli   University of Cagliari, Italy
Gabriella Sanniti di Baja   ICAR-CNR, Italy

Invited Speakers

Davide Scaramuzza   University of Zurich and ETH Zurich, Switzerland
Tal Ayellet   Technion Israel of Technology, Israel
Emanuele Rodolà   Sapienza University of Rome, Italy
Alessandra Sciutti   Italian Institute of Technology, Italy

Area Chairs

Video Analysis and Understanding

Andrea Cavallaro   Queen Mary University of London, UK
Efstratios Gavves   University of Amsterdam, The Netherlands

Pattern Recognition and Machine Learning

Battista Biggio   University of Cagliari, Italy
Marcello Pelillo   University of Venice, Italy

Deep Learning

Marco Gori   University of Siena, Italy
Francesco Orabona   Boston University, USA

Multiview Geometry and 3D Computer Vision

Andrea Fusiello   University of Udine, Italy
Alessio Del Bue   Istituto Italiano di Tecnologia, Italy
Federico Tombari   Technische Universität München, Germany

Image Analysis, Detection and Recognition

Barbara Caputo   Politecnico di Torino and Italian Institute of
                           Technology, Italy
Jasper Uijlings   Google AI, USA

Multimedia

Xavier Alameda-Pineda   Inria, France
Francesco De Natale   University of Trento, Italy

Biomedical and Assistive Technology

Giovanni Maria Farinella University of Catania, Italy
Roberto Manduchi   University of California Santa Cruz, USA

Digital Forensics

Giulia Boato   University of Trento, Italy
Fernando Pérez-González   University of Vigo, Spain

Image Processing for Cultural Heritage

Andreas Rauber   TU Wien, Austria
Lorenzo Seidenari   University of Florence, Italy

Brave New Ideas

Michele Merler   IBM T. J. Watson Research Center, USA
Concetto Spampinato   University of Catania, Italy

Program Committee

Aladine Chetouani	Université d'Orléans, France
Albert Ali Salah	University of Utrecht, The Netherlands
Alberto Pedrouzo Ulloa	University of Vigo, Italy
Aleksandr Ermolov	University of Trento, Italy
Alessandro Ortis	University of Catania, Italy
Alessandro Piva	University of Florence, Italy
Alfredo Petrosino	Uniparthenope, Italy
Aliaksandr Siarohin	University of Trento, Italy
Anders Hast	Uppsala University, Sweden
Andrea Pilzer	University of Trento, Italy
Andrea Simonelli	Mapillary Research, Austria
	Fondazione Bruno Kessler and University of Trento, Italy
Andrea Torsello	Ca' Foscari University, Italy
Angelo Marcelli	University of Salerno, Italy
Antonino Furnari	University of Catania, Italy
Beatrice Rossi	ST Microelectronics, Italy
Benedetta Tondi	University of Siena, Italy
Bogdan Smolka	Silesian University of Technology, Poland
Brian Reily	Colorado School of Mines, USA
Carla Maria Modena	Fondazione Bruno Kessler, Italy
Carlo Colombo	University of Florence, Italy
Carlo Sansone	University of Salerno, Italy
Cecilia Pasquini	University of Innsbruck, Austria
Christian Riess	Friedrich-Alexander University Erlangen-Nuremberg, Germany
Christian Micheloni	University of Udine, Italy
Dan Popescu	CSIRO, Australia
Daniel Riccio	University of Naples Federico II, Italy
David Fofi	Université Bourgogne Franche-Comte, France
Davide Boscaini	Fondazione Bruno Kessler, Italy
Désiré Sidibé	Université de Bourgogne, France
Diego Carrera	Politecnico di Milano, Italy
Edoardo Ardizzone	University of Palermo, Italy
Eleonora Maset	University of Udine, Italy
Elisabetta Binaghi	University of Insubria, Italy
Enver Sangineto	University of Trento, Italy
Eyasu Zemene	Qualcomm, USA
Fabio Ganovelli	ISTI-CNR, Italy
Fabio Bellavia	University of Florence, Italy
Fabio Poiesi	Fondazione Bruno Kessler, Italy
Federica Arrigoni	University of Udine, Italy
Federico Becattini	University of Firenze, Italy
Federico Iuricich	Clemson University, South Carolina, USA

Filippo Stanco	University of Catania, Italy
Florian Bernard	Max Planck Institute, Germany
Francesco Banterle	CNR Pisa, Italy
Francesco Camastra	University of Naples Parthenope, Italy
Francesco Isgro	University of Naples, Italy
Francesco Turchini	University of Florence, Italy
Gianluigi Ciocca	University of Milano-Bicocca, Italy
Giosuè Lo Bosco	University of Palermo, Italy
Giovanni Fusco	Smith-Kettlewell Eye Research Institute, USA
Giovanni Gallo	University of Catania, Italy
Giuseppe Boccignone	University of Milan, Italy
Gloria Zen	University of Trento, Italy
Huiyu Zhou	University of Leicester, UK
Irene Amerini	University of Florence, Italy
Ismail Elezi	Ca' Foscari University of Venice, Italy
Levi Osterno Vasconcelos	Istituto Italiano di Tecnologia, Italy
Lorenzo Baraldi	University of Modena and Reggio Emilia, Italy
Lorenzo Porzi	Mapillary Research, Austria
Loretta Ichim	Polytechnic University of Bucharest, Romania
Lucia Maddalena	National Research Council, Italy
Luigi Di Stefano	University of Bologna, Italy
Luisa Verdoliva	University Federico II of Naples, Italy
Manuele Bicego	University of Verona, Italy
Marcel Worring	University of Amsterdam, The Netherlands
Marco Fiorucci	Italian Institute of Technology, Italy
Marco La Cascia	University of Palermo, Italy
Maria De Marsico	Sapienza University of Rome, Italy
Maria Giulia Preti	EPFL, Switzerland
Massimiliano Mancini	Sapienza University of Rome, Fondazione Bruno Kessler and Istituto Italiano di Tecnologia, Italy
Massimo Tistarelli	University of Sassari, Italy
Massimo Piccardi	University of Technology Sydney, Australia
Michal Kawulok	Silesian University of Technology, Poland
Michele Nappi	University of Salerno, Italy
Modesto Castrillon-Santana	University of Las Palmas de Gran Canaria, Spain
Mohamed Lakhal	Queen Mary University of London, UK
Pablo Mesejo	Universidad de Granada, Spain
Paolo Napoletano	University of Milano-Bicocca, Italy
Paul Gay	Insa-Rouen, France
Pier Luigi Mazzeo	CNR, Italy
Pietro Pala	University of Florence, Italy
Simone Marina	University of Florence, Italy
Richard Jiang	Lancaster University, UK
Richard Wilson	University of York, UK
Ruggero Pintus	Center for Advanced Studies, Research and Development in Sardinia, Italy

Samuele Salti	University of Bologna, Italy
Sebastiano Battiato	Università di Catania, Italy
Sebastiano Vascon	Ca' Foscari University of Venice & European Centre for Living Technology, Italy
Silvia Biasotti	CNR-IMATI, Italy
Simone Bianco	Università degli Studi di Milano-Bicocca, Italy
Sinem Aslan	Ca' Foscari University of Venice, Italy
Stefano Berretti	University of Florence, Italy
Stefano Tubaro	Politecnico di Milano, Italy
Stuart James	Italian Institute of Technology, Italy
Subhankar Roy	University of Trento, Italy
Swathikiran Sudhakaran	Fondazione Bruno Kessler, Italy
Thi-Lan Le	International Research Institute MICA, Vietnam
Walter Kropatsch	TU Wien, Austria
Yahui Liu	University of Trento, Italy
Yiming Wang	Italian Institute of Technology, Italy

Endorsing Institutions

International Association for Pattern Recognition (IAPR)
Italian Association for Computer Vision, Pattern Recognition
    and Machine Learning (CVPL)
Springer

Institutional Patronage

University of Trento, Italy
Fondazione Bruno Kessler, Italy

Contents – Part I

Pattern Recognition and Machine Learning

Deep Learning

Multiview Geometry and 3D Computer Vision

Contents – Part II

Multimedia

Biomedical and Assistive Technology

Video Analysis and Understanding

Video-Based Convolutional Attention
for Person Re-Identification

Marco Zamprogno$^{(\boxtimes)}$, Marco Passon$^{(\boxtimes)}$, Niki Martinel$^{(\boxtimes)}$, Giuseppe Serra$^{(\boxtimes)}$,
Giuseppe Lancioni$^{(\boxtimes)}$, Christian Micheloni$^{(\boxtimes)}$, Carlo Tasso$^{(\boxtimes)}$,
and Gian Luca Foresti

Università degli Studi di Udine, Udine, UD, Italy
{zamprogno.marco,passon.marco,lancioni.giuseppe}@spes.uniud.it
{niki.martinel,giuseppe.serra,christian.micheloni,carlo.tasso}@uniud.it

Abstract. In this paper we consider the problem of video-based person re-identification, which is the task of associating videos of the same person captured by different and non-overlapping cameras. We propose a Siamese framework in which video frames of the person to re-identify and of the candidate one are processed by two identical networks which produce a similarity score. We introduce an attention mechanisms to capture the relevant information both at frame level (spatial information) and at video level (temporal information given by the importance of a specific frame within the sequence). One of the novelties of our approach is given by a joint concurrent processing of both frame and video levels, providing in such a way a very simple architecture. Despite this fact, out approach achieves better performance than the state-of-the-art on the challenging iLIDS-VID dataset.

Keywords: Video-based person re-identification · Visual attention · Convolutional attention · LSTM · iLIDS-VID

1 Introduction

Given an image or video of a person taken from one camera, the Re-Identification task (ReID) is the process of re-associating the person by analyzing images or videos taken from a different camera with non-overlapping field of view. Although humans can easily re-identify others by leveraging descriptors based on the person's face, height, clothing, and walking pattern, ReID is a difficult problem for a machine to solve, since it should deal with features between cameras like different lighting conditions, different point of views or person occluded by objects or other people.

Traditionally many attempts to explore the problem has been proposed for still images (*e.g.*, [1–6]), while recently some research groups have experimented

---

M. Zamprogno and M. Passon—Equally Contributed.

© Springer Nature Switzerland AG 2019
E. Ricci et al. (Eds.): ICIAP 2019, LNCS 11751, pp. 3–14, 2019.
https://doi.org/10.1007/978-3-030-30642-7_1

approaches based on video images (*e.g.*, [7]). Using videos for Re-Identification provides several advantages over still images. The video setting is a more natural way to perform Re-Identification, as a person will normally be captured by a video camera producing a sequence of images rather than a single still image. Given the availability of sequences of images, temporal information related to a person motion may help to disambiguate difficult cases that arise when trying to recognize a person in a different camera. Furthermore, sequences of images provide a larger number of samples of a person appearance, thus allowing a better appearance model to be built. On the other hand, this large set of information needs to be treated properly.

To address this challenge, in this paper we propose an approach to the problem of video-based person re-identification that is characterized by two main aspects. First, we propose a deep neural network architecture based on a Siamese framework [8] which evaluates the similarity of the query video to a candidate one. Second, we introduce a novel spatio-temporal attention mechanism with the aim to select relevant information from different areas of the frames of the input video, and from their evolution over time. Attention mechanisms have been largely exploited in a variety of different implementations and in many different domains of Deep Learning such as Natural Language Processing [9] and Computer Vision [10]. The intuition behind Attention in Computer Vision is to mimic the human visual process. Humans give different importance to different areas in an image as they are able to focus on 'hot' areas and neglect others [11]. This improves greatly the ability to recognize structures and patterns in otherwise flat data. Nevertheless there are relatively few attempts to use Attention in the field of Automatic Re-Identification. [12] proposes integrating a soft attention based model in a Siamese network to focus adaptively on the important local regions of an input image pair. [13] uses a spatial pyramid layer as the component attentive spatial pooling to select important regions in spatial dimension. [10] proposes a spatial attention module focused on recognizing the skeleton to identify the poses, and then a temporal module to recognize the actions.

Unlike other approaches, which use at least two separate modules to identify spatial and temporal features, we use a joint module to identify both at the same time. This allows us to define a simpler architecture which provides state-of-the-art performance on the well-known iLIDS-VID dataset.

2   Related Work

The interest for video-based Person Re-Identification has increased significantly in recent years [14]. The aim of the first works was to manually extract feature representations invariant to changes in poses, lighting conditions, and viewpoints. Using these features, they proposed distance metrics to measure the similarity between two images. In particular, one of the first studies computes the spatio-temporal stable region with foreground segmentation [15]; while [16] employs more compact spatial descriptors and color features, constructed by using the manifold geometry structure in video sequences.

With the advent of Deep Learning approaches, Convolutional Neural Networks (CNNs) have been introduced in visual recognition tasks yielding to considerable improvements in the performance [17] with respect to more classical solutions [18]. In fact, CNNs are able to extract different features from a given image, representing them as a set of output maps avoiding manual effort in feature engineering. Image-based Automatic Person Re-Identification is one of the fields in which CNNs achieved remarkable results [19–24].

However, considering that Person Re-Identification is usually done in settings that involve, for example, surveillance cameras, it is easy to argue that image-based person re-identification is no more an adequate schema to address current needs.

This led to most recent works that began exploring video-based person re-identification [8,13,25–30], a setting closer to real-world applications. Videos have the advantage to contain temporal information that is potentially helpful in differentiating between persons. For example, in [8], the proposed CNN model extracts features from subsequent video frames that are fed through a recurrent final layer in order to combine frame-level features and video-level features.

Not all the parts of an image or of a video are equally important and humans place more focus only on some of them, assigning little to no importance to the rest. This attention mechanism has been adopted in a variety of applications, such as machine translation [31], action recognition [32], image recognition [33] and caption generation [34]. Recently, Attention models [10,32] have been proposed for video and image understanding. These models assign weights to different parts of each frame, making some of them more important than others. In particular, [12] proposes integrating a spatial attention based model in a siamese network to adaptively focus on the important local parts of an input image pair.

With respect to the existing literature, [29] and [35] are the most similar to our approach. [29] uses a Recurrent Neural Network (RNN) to generate temporal attentions over frames so that the model can focus on the most discriminative ones in a video. [35] instead directly calculates the attention scores on frame-based features, using a simple architecture with two separate temporal and spatial modules. Our approach exploits a single attentive module to extract both temporal and spatial features from frames at the same time, resulting in an even simpler architecture that provides state-of-the-art performance.

3   The Proposed Approach

The proposed approach (see Fig. 1) is based on a Siamese network [8]. This schema is composed by two identical networks, or branches, in which the first is fed with the query video and the second with the candidate video to be compared. Each branch includes a sequence of modules that will be described in details in next sub-sections. The parameters of the two branches are shared. The output of the Siamese network is a value that represents the similarity of the two input video sequences in terms of the distance between their respective features vectors, which should be close to zero if they belong to the same person, close to one otherwise.

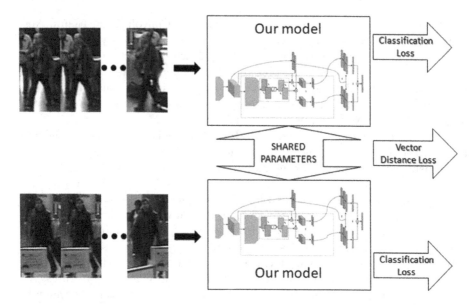

Fig. 1. Siamese network scheme. Each network receives as input a person image sequence to classify. The loss is calculated as the sum of the classification error of each network, plus the Euclidean distance between the two descriptive vectors, which should be close to zero if the two sequences belong to the same person, or close to one if they belong to different people.

3.1 Spatio-Temporal Attentive Module

The Spatio-Temporal Attentive Module is the core module of the proposed architecture. It aims to identify the portions of a frame which an human eye would normally focus on. Those areas should contain relevant spatial information, and we want to exploit them to improve the re-identification performance. Since the input frames are enhanced with the temporal information of the optical flow, both spatial and temporal features will be exploited by this network.

Inspired by [11], we propose to use a particular combination of convolutional network and LSTM, called Attentive ConvLSTM, capable of working on spatial features, in which the internal state of the network is given by the standard LSTM state equations where the matrix products between weights and inputs are replaced by convolutional operators. The ability to work with sequences is exploited to process input spatial features iteratively. The general idea of how this module works is shown in the bottom part of Fig. 2.

Our aim is to exploit attentive maps to better identify relevant features of frames and provide state-of-the-art performance while using a simple network. The architecture of each branch (see Fig. 2) is based on an initial convolutional network to reduce the image size, an attentive model to generate attentive maps, a fully connected layer to extract significant features from the original frames, and a final part where the features are combined.

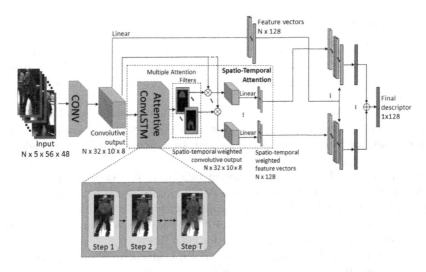

Fig. 2. Detailed Network scheme. The main blocks are the initial convolutional network, the Spatio-Temporal Attention Module, and the final part which performs averaging and normalization. The bottom part gives an idea of the multiple refining steps.

More in details, the architecture consists of an ConvLSTM to recurrently processes attentive features at different locations of the frame, focusing on different regions of the tensor. A stack of features $\mathbf{X}$ is repeatedly given in input to the LSTM, which sequentially updates an internal state based on three sigmoid activators. Update is performed by two blocks: the Attentive Model, and the ConvLSTM. The Attentive Model generates an attention map using a convolutional layer that takes as input the original $\mathbf{X}$ and the previous hidden state, followed by a `tanh` activation function and another convolutional layer, and finally normalized with a `softmax` operator. The resulting output represents a normalized spatial attention map, which is then applied to the original $\mathbf{X}$ with an element-wise product, resulting in the filtered $\mathbf{X}'$. In ConvLSTM, each of the three sigmoid activators is given in input the sum of two different convolutive layers, the first taking as input $\mathbf{X}'$ and the second taking as input the previous hidden state, and a bias. The output of the first sigmoid is then multiplied element-wise with the previous $\mathbf{X}'$, the output of the second sigmoid is multiplied element-wise with the state of the LSTM memory cell, and the two resulting outputs are summed together and fed to a `tanh` activator. The result is multiplied element-wise with the output of the third sigmoid, and the resulting tensor is the new hidden state.

The Spatio-Temporal Attentive Module takes in input an image and produces in output multiple attentive maps, using an iterative refinement in T steps (based on our preliminary experiments, we set $T = 10$). We then apply those maps to the original input and obtain multiple different filtered outputs. Ideally, each filter should focus on a different spatio-temporal feature of the frame.

3.2   Architecture Details

The starting input (see Fig. 2) consists of video sequences composed by a batch of N frames, each frame has size 56×48, with 3 channels for the YUV, plus 2 for the vertical and horizontal components of the optical flow, for a total of 5 channels.

The input is first processed through a convolutional network which consists of 3 stages, each composed by convolution, max-pooling, and nonlinear activations. Each convolution filter uses 5×5 kernels with 1×1 stride and 4×4 zero padding. This outputs a batch of size $N \times 32 \times 10 \times 8$.

At this point, the model branches in two lines: the same input is passed to the Spatio-Temporal Attentive Module previously described, and to a fully connected layer preceded by a dropout applied with $p = 0.6$ probability. The first aims to output multiple spatio-temporal-filtered feature vectors for each frame, and the second a general feature vector for each frame.

Spatio-Temporal Attention generates multiple attentive filters. Each of these filters has size 10×8, is first normalized with a sigmoid between 0 and 1, and then applied with an element-wise multiplication to the original output of the first convolutional network, obtaining multiple blocks weighted with a different filter with the same dimension of the input, $N \times 32 \times 10 \times 8$; each of these blocks focus on a specific zone of the frames. A final fully connected layer generates, for each block, a batch of spatio-temporal-weighted feature vectors of size $N \times 128$. This final layer is also preceded by a dropout with $p = 0.6$. In our model, since we generate 3 filters, we obtain 3 spatio-temporal-weighted feature vectors.

The two branches of the network are then merged together, and the general feature vectors are concatenated with each of the spatio-temporal weighted feature vectors, resulting in 3 combined-feature vectors of size $2N \times 128$. Finally, each of these batches is averaged, normalized using L2 normalization, and lastly summed together, obtaining a final feature descriptor of size 1×128.

4   Experimental Results

Our approach has been tested and evaluated on the public iLIDS-VID benchmark [27], since it is a challenging dataset that contains many occlusions, severe illumination changes and background clutters. It is also widely used in literature and it is then easier to fair compare our results. The iLIDS-VID dataset consists of videos of 300 distinct people. For each person there are two different video sequences, captured by two non-overlapping cameras. The video sequences have a varying number of frames, with the shortest sequence having 23 frames long and the longest having 192 frames, averaging at 73 frames.

4.1   Experimental Setup

To be comparable with literature, we follow the experimental setup proposed by [8]. The dataset is randomly split in two: 50% of the people form the training set and 50% the test set. During the execution of the experiments, a different train/test split is computed for every repetition and the final results are then averaged. The network is trained for 1500 epochs using Stochastic Gradient Descent algorithm. One epoch consists in showing the Siamese network an equal number of positive sequence pairs and negative pairs, sampled randomly from all the persons in the training set, alternatively.

A positive sequence pair consists of two full sequences of arbitrary length, recorded by two different cameras, showing the same person. Analogously, a negative sequence pair shows two different persons. During the training phase, the length of the sequences is set to 16, that is, 16 consecutive frames belonging to a person are randomly sampled and used during this phase. As in [27], the first camera is the probe and the second the gallery.

All the images in the dataset go through a preprocessing step where they are converted from the RGB to the YUV color space and each color channel is normalized in order to have zero mean and unit variance. The three color channels are expanded with two more channels corresponding to the horizontal and vertical component of the optical flow computed between each pair of consecutive frames using Lucas-Kanade algorithm [36]. The two optical flow channels are normalized to bring them within the $[-1, 1]$ range.

Data augmentation is applied to each sequence during the training phase in order to increase the diversity of the training sequences. Each frame in the sequence undergoes cropping and mirroring, the same transformation is applied in the same way to all the frames belonging to the same sequence.

The testing phase is performed considering a video sequence belonging to the first camera as probe and a video sequence belonging to the second camera as gallery. In this phase, we use up to 128 frames to form a sequence. The frames are always the starting frames for the probe, and the ending frames for the gallery. If this is not possible, because a person's sequence does not have enough frames, we consider all the available frames.

All tests are performed 10 times with different seeds, each time presenting the model different people for training and testing.

4.2   Results

First we compared the results of our model when using different numbers of filters for the Spatio-Temporal Attention Module, as shown in Table 1. We found that performance increases when generating more filters, but with four or more the model saturates and the performance starts decreasing.

Second, we present experimental results with 3 filters on sequences of varying lengths between 2 and up to 128 frames, and the results are shown in Table 2. Note that if a person's sequence does not have enough frames, we still consider all the available frames and that in all cases the training has been performed using a fixed length sequence of 16. As one could expect, it is confirmed that the performance increases as the number of frames in sequence of frames grows, as also noted by [8]. Since the average sequence length in the dataset is 73,

Table 1. Average results obtained using an increasing number of filters.

#filters	Rank-1	Rank-5	Rank-10	Rank-20
Average results using different number of filters				
0	60.5	84.8	93	96.9
1	59.4	85.7	93.2	97.4
2	63	**87.7**	93.9	97.3
3	**63.3**	87.4	**94**	**97.8**
4	59.6	87.2	93.9	97.7

the performance does not increase much between 64 and 128, because most sequences are not long enough to benefit from the additional length.

Table 2. Average results with different sequence lengths (expressed in frames).

Length	Rank-1	Rank-5	Rank-10	Rank-20
Average results with different sequence lengths				
2	16.7	37.7	50.9	64.6
4	22.7	46.9	60.3	72.6
8	31.7	59.3	71.3	84.2
16	43.8	72.6	83.9	91.4
32	53.9	80.7	89	95.3
64	61	85.6	92.5	96.7
128	63.3	87.4	94	97.8

Finally, we present the comparison of our model with the state-of-the-art in Table 3. Despite beeing a simple architecture, our solution outperforms other methods proposed in the literature on 2 metrics out of 4. Note that [35] claim better results on their paper, but, in order to provide a fair comparison, we re-ran their provided code on our dataset splits. In addition, for the sake of completeness we report the performance of [37] as well, even if their testing protocol is not directly comparable with the others, as they always use all the available frames.

The simplicity of our architecture comes from the choice of making the spatial and temporal module work jointly. In fact their output is merged in order to, hopefully, get the best of the two and select only the most relevant information obtained by their combination.

Table 3. Comparison with state-of-the-art methods.

iLIDS-VID				
Methods	Rank-1	Rank-5	Rank-10	Rank-20
Proposed Approach	**63.3**	**87.4**	94	97.8
Rao et al. [35]	62.2[a]	86.8	**94.8**	97.8
Xu et al. [38]	62	86	94	**98**
Zhang et al. [39]	60.2	85.1	-	94.2
McLaughlin et al. [8]	58	84	91	96
Zhengl et al. [40]	53	81.4	-	95.1
Yan et al. [28]	49.3	76.8	85.3	90.1
Liu et al. [37]	68[b]	86.8	95.4	97.4

[a]These results were obtained in our tests on the code provided, and are substantially lower than claimed in the paper
[b]Results are shown for completeness, but are not directly comparable

5 Conclusions

We described a novel architecture which exploits a single attentive network to extract both spatial and temporal features to perform video-based person Re-Identification, providing state-of-the-art performance on the recent challenging iLIDS-VID dataset.

While the improvement obtained is not groundbreaking, the experiments confirm that employing a joint spatial and temporal attention mechanism can help pushing higher the performances in the field of person Re-Identification using only simple neural networks.

Our experiments confirms that using a longer sequence of frames brings to better performance. Analogously, one may think that using an higher number of filters will always lead to better results; however this is true up to a certain point: our experiments shows that using 3 attentive filters is better than using none, but going above this number leads to a degradation in performance.

Future work will validate the results obtained in this study performing the reported experiments on other datasets.

Acknowledgements. This project was partially supported by the FVG P.O.R. FESR 2014-2020 fund, project "Design of a Digital Assistant based on machine learning and natural language, and by the "PREscriptive Situational awareness for cooperative autoorganizing aerial sensor NETworks" project CIG68827500FB".

References

1. Martinel, N., Micheloni, C., Piciarelli, C.: Distributed signature fusion for person re-identification. In: International Conference on Distributed Smart Cameras, pp. 1–6 (2012)

2. Martinel, N., Dunnhofer, M., Foresti, G.L., Micheloni, C.: Person re-identification via unsupervised transfer of learned visual representations. In: International Conference on Distributed Smart Cameras, pp. 1–6 (2017)
3. Lisanti, G., Martinel, N., Del Bimbo, A., Foresti, G.L.: Group re-identification via unsupervised transfer of sparse features encoding. In: International Conference on Computer Vision, pp. 2449–2458 (2017)
4. Martinel, N., Foresti, G.L., Micheloni, C.: Unsupervised hashing with neural trees for image retrieval and person re-identification. In: International Conference on Distributed Smart Cameras (2018)
5. Martinel, N.: Accelerated low-rank sparse metric learning for person re-identification. Pattern Recogn. Lett. **112**, 234–240 (2018)
6. Lisanti, G., Martinel, N., Micheloni, C., Del Bimbo, A., Luca Foresti, G.: From person to group re-identification via unsupervised transfer of sparse features. Image Vis. Comput. **83**(84), 29–38 (2019)
7. Zheng, L., Yang, Y., Hauptmann, A.G.: Person re-identification: Past, present and future, CoRR, vol. abs/1610.02984 (2016)
8. McLaughlin, N., Martinez del Rincon, J., Miller, P.: Recurrent convolutional network for video-based person re-identification. In: Proceedings of the IEEE Conference on Computer Vision and Pattern Recognition, pp. 1325–1334 (2016)
9. Passon, M., Comuzzo, M., Serra, G., Tasso, C.: Keyphrase extraction via an attentive model. In: Italian Research Conference on Digital Libraries (2019)
10. Song, S., Lan, C., Xing, J., Zeng, W., Liu, J.: An end-to-end spatio-temporal attention model for human action recognition from skeleton data. In: Thirty-First AAAI Conference on Artificial Intelligence (2017)
11. Cornia, M., Baraldi, L., Serra, G., Cucchiara, R.: Predicting human eye fixations via an lstm-based saliency attentive model. IEEE Trans. Image Process. **27**(10), 5142–5154 (2018)
12. Liu, H., Feng, J., Qi, M., Jiang, J., Yan, S.: End-to-end comparative attention networks for person re-identification. IEEE Trans. Image Process. **26**(7), 3492–3506 (2017)
13. Xu, S., Cheng, Y., Gu, K., Yang, Y., Chang, S., Zhou, P.: Jointly attentive spatial-temporal pooling networks for video-based person re-identification. In: Proceedings of the IEEE International Conference on Computer Vision, pp. 4733–4742 (2017)
14. Vezzani, R., Baltieri, D., Cucchiara, R.: People reidentification in surveillance and forensics: a survey. ACM Comput. Surv. **46**, 29:1–29:37 (2013)
15. Gheissari, N., Sebastian, T.B., Hartley, R.: Person reidentification using spatiotemporal appearance. In: 2006 IEEE Computer Society Conference on Computer Vision and Pattern Recognition (CVPR 2006), vol. 2, pp. 1528–1535 (2006)
16. Truong Cong, D.N., Achard, C., Khoudour, L., Douadi, L.: Video sequences association for people re-identification across multiple non-overlapping cameras. In: Foggia, P., Sansone, C., Vento, M. (eds.) ICIAP 2009. LNCS, vol. 5716, pp. 179–189. Springer, Heidelberg (2009). https://doi.org/10.1007/978-3-642-04146-4_21
17. Krizhevsky, A., Sutskever, I., Hinton, G.E.: Imagenet classification with deep convolutional neural networks. In: Advances in Neural Information Processing Systems, pp. 1097–1105 (2012)
18. Rani, A., Foresti, G.L., Micheloni, C.: A neural tree for classification using convex objective function. Pattern Recogn. Lett. **68**, 41–47 (2015)
19. Qian, X., Fu, Y., Jiang, Y.-G., Xiang, T., Xue, X.: Multi-scale deep learning architectures for person re-identification. In: Proceedings of the IEEE International Conference on Computer Vision, pp. 5399–5408 (2017)

20. Ustinova, E., Ganin, Y., Lempitsky, V.: Multi-region bilinear convolutional neural networks for person re-identification. In: IEEE International Conference on Advanced Video and Signal Based Surveillance, pp. 1–6 (2017)
21. Varior, R.R., Shuai, B., Lu, J., Xu, D., Wang, G.: A siamese long short-term memory architecture for human re-identification. In: European Conference on Computer Vision, pp. 135–153 (2016)
22. Xiao, T., Li, H., Ouyang, W., Wang, X.: Learning deep feature representations with domain guided dropout for person re-identification. In: Proceedings of the IEEE Conference on Computer Vision and Pattern Recognition, pp. 1249–1258 (2016)
23. Zhang, L., Xiang, T., Gong, S.: Learning a discriminative null space for person re-identification. In: Proceedings of the IEEE Conference on Computer Vision and Pattern Recognition, pp. 1239–1248 (2016)
24. Hadsell, R., Chopra, S., LeCun, Y.: Dimensionality reduction by learning an invariant mapping. In: 2006 IEEE Computer Society Conference on Computer Vision and Pattern Recognition (CVPR 2006), vol. 2, pp. 1735–1742 (2006)
25. Li, Y., Zhuo, L., Li, J., Zhang, J., Liang, X., Tian, Q.: Video-based person re-identification by deep feature guided pooling. In: Proceedings of the IEEE Conference on Computer Vision and Pattern Recognition Workshops, pp. 39–46 (2017)
26. Liu, K., Ma, B., Zhang, W., Huang, R.: A spatio-temporal appearance representation for video-based pedestrian re-identification. In: Proceedings of the IEEE International Conference on Computer Vision, pp. 3810–3818 (2015)
27. Wang, T., Gong, S., Zhu, X., Wang, S.: Person re-identification by video ranking. In: Fleet, D., Pajdla, T., Schiele, B., Tuytelaars, T. (eds.) ECCV 2014. LNCS, vol. 8692, pp. 688–703. Springer, Cham (2014). https://doi.org/10.1007/978-3-319-10593-2_45
28. Yan, Y., Ni, B., Song, Z., Ma, C., Yan, Y., Yang, X.: Person re-identification via recurrent feature aggregation. In: ECCV, pp. 701–716 (2016)
29. Zhou, Z., Huang, Y., Wang, W., Wang, L., Tan, T.: See the forest for the trees: joint spatial and temporal recurrent neural networks for video-based person re-identification. In: CVPR, pp. 4747–4756 (2017)
30. Zhu, X., Jing, X.-Y., You, X., Zhang, X., Zhang, T.: Video-based person re-identification by simultaneously learning intra-video and inter-video distance metrics. IEEE TIP 27(11), 5683–5695 (2018)
31. Bahdanau, D., Cho, K., Bengio, Y.: Neural machine translation by jointly learning to align and translate, arXiv preprint arXiv:1409.0473 (2014)
32. Sharma, S., Kiros, R., Salakhutdinov, R.: Action recognition using visual attention, arXiv preprint arXiv:1511.04119 (2015)
33. Ba, J., Mnih, V., Kavukcuoglu, K.: Multiple object recognition with visual attention, arXiv preprint arXiv:1412.7755 (2014)
34. Xu, K., et al.: Show, attend and tell: Neural image caption generation with visual attention. In: International Conference on Machine Learning, pp. 2048–2057 (2015)
35. Rao, S., Rahman, T., Rochan, M., Wang, Y.: Video-based person re-identification using spatial-temporal attention networks (2018)
36. Lucas, B.D., Kanade, T.: An iterative image registration technique with an application to stereo vision. In: IJCAI, pp. 674–679 (1981)
37. Liu, Y., Yan, J., Ouyang, W.: Quality aware network for set to set recognition, CoRR, vol. abs/1704.03373 (2017)
38. Yi, D., Lei, Z., Liao, S., Li, S.Z.: Deep metric learning for person re-identification. In: ICPR, pp. 34–39 (2014)

39. Zhang, W., Hu, S., Liu, K.: Learning compact appearance representation for video-based person re-identification. IEEE Trans. Circ. Syst. Video Technol. (2017). abs/1702.06294
40. Zheng, L., et al.: MARS: a video benchmark for large-scale person re-identification. In: Leibe, B., Matas, J., Sebe, N., Welling, M. (eds.) ECCV 2016. LNCS, vol. 9910, pp. 868–884. Springer, Cham (2016). https://doi.org/10.1007/978-3-319-46466-4_52

A New Descriptor for Keypoint-Based Background Modeling

Danilo Avola[1]([✉]), Marco Bernardi[1], Marco Cascio[1], Luigi Cinque[1], Gian Luca Foresti[2], and Cristiano Massaroni[1]

[1] Department of Computer Science, Sapienza University,
Via Salaria 113, 00198 Rome, Italy
massaroni@di.uniroma1.it
[2] Department of Mathematics, Computer Science, and Physics,
University of Udine, Via Delle Scienze 206, 33100 Udine, Italy
{avola,bernardi,cascio,cinque}@di.uniroma1.it,
gianluca.foresti@uniud.it

Abstract. Background modeling is a preliminary task for many computer vision applications, describing static elements of a scene and isolating foreground ones. Defining a robust background model of uncontrolled environments is a current challenge since the model must manage many issues, e.g., moving cameras, dynamic background, bootstrapping, shadows, and illumination changes. Recently, methods based on keypoint clustering have shown remarkable robustness especially in bootstrapping and camera movements, highlighting however limitations in the analysis of dynamic background (i.e., trees blowing in the wind or gushing fountains). In this paper, an innovative combination between the RootSIFT descriptor and an average pooling is proposed in a keypoint clustering method for real-time background modeling and foreground detection. Compared to renowned descriptors, such as A-KAZE, this combination is invariant to small local changes in the scene, thus resulting more robust in dynamic background cases. Results, obtained on experiments carried out on two benchmark datasets, demonstrate how the proposed solution improves the previous keypoint-based models and overcomes several works of the current state-of-the-art.

Keywords: Background modeling · Foreground detection · Keypoint clustering · Dynamic background · RootSIFT

1 Introduction

In computer vision community, the background modeling has always been a field of great interest. This is because it can be a main prerequisite for many smart applications, ranging from active video surveillance to optical motion capture. Due to many dynamic factors of the scene, background modeling is a very complex task. For example, creating the model when there are foreground elements within the scene (i.e., bootstrapping), managing natural light changes

© Springer Nature Switzerland AG 2019
E. Ricci et al. (Eds.): ICIAP 2019, LNCS 11751, pp. 15–25, 2019.
https://doi.org/10.1007/978-3-030-30642-7_2

over time, or handling the movement performed by parts of the scenery (i.e., dynamic background) are all critical aspects in defining a robust background model of uncontrolled environments.

Over the years, different solutions have been proposed both for gradually light changes, such as the adaptive model based on self-organizing feature maps (SOFMs) presented in [22], and for bootstrapping problem, by using keypoint clustering methods [5–7]. The last cited works have introduced a new background modeling technique, based on the most interesting points of an image, able to manage efficiently video sequences acquired by moving video cameras. Typically keypoint-based methods are structured as follows: first, the background model is defined using keypoints and related descriptors detected by a feature extractor; then the keypoints of the model are tracked across consecutive frames, through a feature matching phase, to tell apart background keypoints from the foreground ones; finally, the Density-Based Clustering of Application with Noise (DBSCAN) is applied to extract foreground keypoint clusters, which represent the foreground element regions inside the scene. Despite their great results, the aforementioned works cannot bear scenarios consisting of dynamic elements (i.e., trees blowing in the wind or gushing fountains), that is because the common descriptors of the keypoints are too sensitive to all variations that can occur in an uncontrolled environment.

This paper, extending the pipeline of the adaptive bootstrapping management (ABM) proposed in [5], introduces an innovative strategy to improve the feature matching phase accuracy in keypoint-based methods for dynamic background modeling. Once the keypoints are extracted with the A-KAZE algorithm [1], descriptors are computed combining the RootSIFT [2] with an average pooling, applied on different patches obtained from a neighbourhood of each keypoint. Compared to renowned descriptors, such as A-KAZE, this combination results invariant to small local changes caused by moving background. Moreover, in the feature matching step, the Hamming distance is replaced by the Bhattacharyya distance, since the latter is more suitable to measure the closeness between our new descriptors, compared to the former, which is applicable only between binary descriptors (i.e., A-KAZE, ORB [26], and others). Experiments on the Scene Background Modeling.NET (SBMnet) [18] dataset have shown how the proposed model provides good performance, in terms of background reconstruction, in very challenging video sequences. Finally, including a foreground detection module, inspired by the work proposed in [7], additional tests on the Freiburg-Berkeley Motion Segmentation Dataset (FBMS-59) [24] dataset have also shown that our solution can be integrated into a moving object detection pipeline obtaining excellent results.

The rest of paper is organized as follows. In Sect. 2, a brief overview of the state-of-the-art on background modeling is presented. In Sect. 3, the proposed method is described in detail, presenting both our descriptor for background modeling and the distance metric used in the feature matching phase. Section 4 contains the experimental results on the SBMnet and FBMS-59 datasets. Finally, Sect. 5 concludes the paper.

2   Related Work

In recent years, the background modeling has been extensively studied, often integrating it as prerequisite for other tasks, such as foreground detection or image segmentation. A valid example is reported in [31], where a spatio-temporal tensor formulation and a Gaussian Mixture Background Model are fused to perform a hybrid moving object detection system. In [21], a hierarchical background model for video surveillance using PTZ camera is presented, obtained by separating the range of continuous focal lengths of the camera into several discrete levels and partitioning each level into many partial fixed scenes. Then, each new frame acquired by the PTZ camera is related to a specific scene using a fast approximate nearest neighbour search. Another interesting model is used to implement the change detection method proposed in [29], where a pixel representation is characterized in a non-parametric paradigm by an improved spatio-temporal binary similarity descriptors. This model is also used after in [10] to guide the training of a Convolutional Neural Network (CNN) in performing a foreground segmentation. In [27], the background model is built using appearance features, obtained by considering each pixel neighborhood, and the foreground is separated from the background classifying each pixel using its associated feature vectors and a Support Vector Machine (SVM). Two different models are proposed in [12] to segment background and foreground dynamics, respectively, where the first one is based on the Mixture of Generalized Gaussian (MoGG) distributions and the second one combines multi-scale correlation analysis with a histogram matching. In [15], a pre-trained CNN model is used to create the background model, extracting features from a cleaned background image, without moving objects. The foreground detection is performed comparing the features of the previous model with the features extracted from each frame of the video sequence using the previous CNN. In [32], a dual-target non-parametric background model, able to work with different scenarios and simultaneously distinguish background and foreground pixels, is introduced. Moreover, a novel classification rule is presented: for the background pixels, the method controls the updating of neighbouring pixels to obtain a complete silhouette of static or low-speed moving objects; instead, for the foreground pixels, it controls the current pixel updating to decrease false detection caused by improper background initialization or frequent background changes. To conclude, an innovative solution is presented in [7], where a model-based on clustering of keypoints is used with a spatio-temporal tracking to distinguish the candidate foreground regions that contain moving objects. To follow, a change detection step is locally applied into candidate foreground regions to obtain the moving object silhouettes. Our solution can be perfectly integrated within the pipeline proposed in the latter cited work, replacing the original model and reducing false positives in the foreground detection stage.

3 Proposed Method

In this section, the proposed solution to perform dynamic background modeling, extending the pipeline of the ABM method, is described.

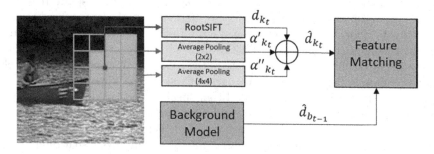

Fig. 1. An overview of the proposed solution used to improve the ABM method.

3.1 ABM Method

The original ABM method, taking a video sequence as input, is mainly composed of the following steps:

- using the A-KAZE feature extractor, a keypoint set K_{b_t} and a descriptor set D_{b_t} are computed on the first frame f_0;
- the background model is initialized using K_{b_t} and D_{b_t};
- for each frame f_t of the video sequence, with $t > 0$:
  - keypoints K_t and descriptors D_t are extracted from f_t;
  - the candidate foreground keypoint set K_{F_t} and the background keypoint set K_{B_t} are estimated using a feature matching operation between D_{b_t} and D_t, based on Hamming distance;
  - the set C_t of clusters, representing the foreground element regions, is computed using DBSCAN and K_{F_t};
  - the background model is updated using the keypoints in K_{B_t} and their descriptors.

The choice of using A-KAZE feature extraction method derives from both its good performance in terms of speed and accuracy [1], and its great results obtained in several other fields, including object detection [4,8,11] and mosaicking [3,9,30]. The DBSCAN algorithm is preferred over other standard clustering algorithms, like K-Means, because it does not require a priori knowledge of the cluster number.

3.2   Proposed Descriptor

In our solution, a new descriptor is proposed to be used both in background model initialization and in feature matching phase, instead of relying on A-KAZE descriptor as in the ABM method (although A-KAZE is used to extract the keypoints). This new descriptor is obtained combining RootSIFT and average pooling operations, as shown in Fig. 1. For each keypoint k_t extracted in the frame f_t (or k_b, if we consider the background model keypoints), the RootSIFT is used to extract the d_{k_t} descriptor vector. RootSIFT feature extractor extends SIFT descriptors, using an L1-normalization and applying the square-root of each element in the SIFT vector. Afterwards, a neighbourhood Ψ_{k_t} of size 8×8 pixels is taken from each keypoint k_t, considering the pixels outside the image as zero value if the keypoint is placed at the border. Two average pooling operations are applied on Ψ_{k_t}, where the first one uses a filter size of 2×2, whereas the second one uses a size of 3×3. All the operations use a stride of 1, and their results are scaled using the L1-normalization. The outputs are represented by two feature vectors called α'_{k_t} and α''_{k_t}, respectively. Finally, the d_{k_t}, α'_{k_t} and α''_{k_t} vectors are concatenated in a single descriptor, called $\hat{d}_{k_t}$ (or $\hat{d}_{b_{t-1}}$ for $k_b \in K_{b_{t-1}}$).

In the ABM feature matching module, the previous Hamming distance, used for comparing the A-KAZE binary descriptors, must be replaced by another suitable metric. Our choice fell on Bhattacharyya distance where, given two different keypoints $k_t \in K_t$ and $k_b \in K_{b_{t-1}}$ and their descriptors $\hat{d}_{k_t}$ and $\hat{d}_{b_{t-1}}$, the similarity between k_t and k_b is measured as follows:

$$dist(k_t, k_b) = \sum_{i=0}^{n-1} \sqrt{\hat{d}_{k_t}(i)\hat{d}_{b_{t-1}}(i)}. \tag{1}$$

Performing these changes, our modified ABM method can handle small variations caused by dynamic backgrounds, focusing only on significant movements, typically associated to the foreground elements. In this way, robustness is ensured on bootstrapping and moving camera problems, as well as A-KAZE descriptors.

3.3   Foreground Detection

As described in the introduction, in this work, a customized version of the foreground detection stage, presented in [7], is integrated to identify moving objects within scenes. For each frame f_t of the video sequence, this stage performs a change detection algorithm between the candidate foreground areas A_{f_t} and the background model. The final result is represented by a binary image, called I_{mask_t}, containing the mask of identified foreground element silhouettes in f_t. The change detection can be summarized in these main steps:

– The background model representation I_{b_t} (i.e., the obtained image representing the reconstruction of the background at time t, without foreground elements) and f_t are converted to grayscale;

- initially, a mean filter of size 3×3 and a stride of 3 are applied both in I_{b_t} and f_t;
- the differences between the average values obtained by filters at the same location in I_{b_t} and f_t are computed;
- for each 3×3 filter region, if the difference value exceeds the threshold τ_1 and some pixels of the filter interpolate with a foreground cluster $a \in A_{f_t}$, it means that something between f_t and I_{b_t} is changed and further analysis must be performed in that region:
  - within the analysed 3×3 region, the difference between the pixel values of f_t and I_{b_t} is performed;
  - if the difference at position (h, w) exceeds the threshold τ_2, then $I_{mask_t}(h, w) = 1$, otherwise $I_{mask_t}(h, w) = 0$.
- else, for each pixel with coordinates (h, w), included in the considered 3×3 region, $I_{mask_t}(h, w) = 0$;
- once all the regions are analysed, to reduce the noise in I_{mask_t}, an opening morphological operation is performed.

The two thresholds τ_1 and τ_2 are set to 15 and 30, respectively, based on empirical tests performed on the FBMS-59 dataset video sequences. Through this foreground detection pipeline, the proposed model can be used effectively to separate the background from the moving objects present in the scene.

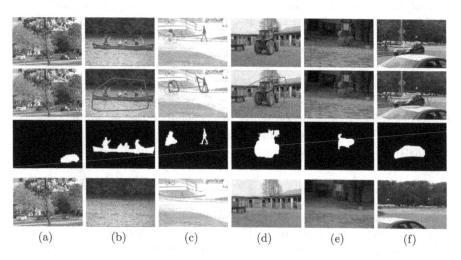

(a)   (b)   (c)   (d)   (e)   (f)

Fig. 2. Examples of moving object detection and background updating. The video sequences from the column (a) up to the column (c) belong to the SBMnet dataset. The other sequences belong to the FBMS-59 dataset. For each column (from the top to the bottom), the first picture is the generic frame, the second is the keypoint clustering stage, the third is the moving object mask, and the last is the background updating. From the first column up to the last one the following videos are shown: fall, canoe, pedestrians, cars4, dog, and farm01.

4   Experimental Results

This section reports the experimental results obtained on SBMnet and FBMS-59 datasets. The first one was used to prove the robustness of the proposed solution in dynamic background and very short scene reconstruction. The second one was used to perform a comparison with selected key works of the current literature in foreground detection task.

4.1   SBMnet Dataset

The SBMnet dataset provides several sets of videos focused on the following challenges: Basic, Intermittent Motion, Clutter, Jitter, Illumination Changes, Background Motion, Very Long and Very Short. To show the improvements with respect to the previous ABM method, in this paper, we focused mainly on the Background Motion and Very Short categories. The visual representations of some results, obtained on key videos of these two categories, are shown in Fig. 2 from column (a) to (c). It should be noted that the proposed method is able to distinguish the foreground (for example the car or the canoe) from movements performed by the dynamic background (i.e., the water and trees blowing in the wind). In Tables 1 and 2, the experimental results and comparisons, with some key works in the current literature, on both selected categories are reported.

   Based on the protocol proposed in [23], the following metrics were used: the Average Gray-level Error (AGE), the Percentage of Error Pixels (pEPs), the Percentage of Clustered Error Pixels (pCEPs), the Multi-Scale Structural Similarity Index (MS-SSIM), the Peak-Signal-to-Noise-Ratio (PSNR), and the Color image Quality Measure (CQM). Considering the background motion category, the proposed solution outperforms the previous ABM method, in terms of pEPs, PSNR, and MSSIM metrics. This means that our reconstruction contains few noisy points distributed within the whole image. For the veryShort category, we improve the performance on the AGE metric, with respect to the ABM method, while the average measures of the other metrics are very close to the state-of-the-art results.

Table 1. Results and comparison of the proposed method on background reconstruction using the Motion Background category.

Methods	Average AGE	Average pEPs	Average pCEPs	Average MSSSIM	Average PSNR	CQM
Our	9.9163	0.1337	0.0364	0.8747	26.5743	27.2464
ABM [5]	9.9952	0.1316	0.0292	0.8662	26.3616	27.5133
AAPSA [14]	11.1404	0.1488	0.0381	0.8422	24.4876	25.4679
BE-AAPSA [25]	9.3755	0.1266	0.0259	0.8766	26.0041	26.9062
LaBGen-P-Semantic (MP+U) [20]	8.7583	0.1152	0.0189	0.8805	27.0334	28.1119
DECOLOR [33]	10.5910	0.1403	0.0351	0.8535	24.2455	25.1072

Table 2. Results and comparison of the proposed method on background reconstruction using the Very Short category.

Methods	Average AGE	Averege pEPs	Average pCEPs	Average MSSSIM	Average PSNR	CQM
Our	7.8508	0.0867	0.0430	0.9054	25.0245	25.9079
ABM [5]	7.7572	0.0664	0.0238	0.9101	26.2541	27.0108
AAPSA [14]	9.2952	0.0860	0.0438	0.8870	22.7636	23.7275
BE-AAPSA [25]	8.0857	0.0832	0.0429	0.8921	25.6458	26.5128
LaBGen-P-Semantic (MP+U)[20]	4.5450	0.0245	0.0056	0.9629	31.4073	32.0297
DECOLOR [33]	8.9984	0.1058	0.0809	0.9475	27.5064	28.2282

4.2   FBMS-59 Dataset

The FBMS-59 dataset is an extensive benchmark for testing feature based motion segmentation algorithms. The visual representations of the results, obtained on several video sequences, are shown in Fig. 2 from the column (d) to column (f). As can be observed, the proposed model perfectly reconstructs the background and, then, isolates the foreground element silhouettes. In Table 3, the comparisons, in terms of precision, recall, and F1-measure, between the proposed solution and key works of the current state-of-art are reported. Instead, in Table 4 additional results on video sequences not tested by the mentioned key works are also reported to provide a further term of comparison for future works. Anyway, the overall results highlight how our approach achieves good performance with respect to the ongoing literature, even overcoming the keypoint-based method proposed in [5]. The obtained high recall values prove that our method is able to capture most of the foreground object pixels, thus resulting suitable for person re-identification or surveillance applications. Especially the latter requires greater precision in estimating the silhouette of foreground objects, probably belonging to intruders, accepting false positives as a compromise.

Table 3. Comparison with key works of the current literature on the FBMS-59 dataset.

	people1			people2			cars6			tennis		
	Prec	Rec	F1	Prec	Rec	F1	Prec	Rec	F1	Prec	Rec	F1
Proposed method	0.801	**0.950**	0.871	0.834	0.980	0.899	0.786	0.949	0.860	0.793	**0.989**	**0.891**
Avola et al. [7]	0.765	0.917	0.840	N.A	N.A	N.A	0.785	0.910	0.840	N.A	N.A	N.A
Kwak et al. [19] - with NBP	0.950	0.930	**0.940**	0.850	0.760	0.828	N.A	N.A	N.A	N.A	N.A	N.A
Kwak et al. [19] - without NBP	0.910	0.760	0.828	0.910	0.220	0.286	N.A	N.A	N.A	N.A	N.A	N.A
Elqursh et al. [16] - 1	0.940	0.850	0.893	0.840	**0.990**	0.909	N.A	N.A	N.A	0.860	0.920	0.890
Elqursh et al. [16] - 2	**0.970**	0.880	0.923	0.850	0.970	0.906	N.A	N.A	N.A	**0.900**	0.810	0.850
Ferone et al. [17]	0.958	0.923	**0.940**	**0.931**	0.971	**0.950**	**0.866**	0.964	**0.913**	N.A	N.A	N.A
Brox et al. [13]	0.890	0.775	0.829	N.A	N.A	N.A	0.824	**0.994**	0.901	N.A	N.A	N.A
Zhou et al. [33]	0.936	0.933	0.934	0.925	0.965	0.945	0.837	0.984	0.905	N.A	N.A	N.A
Sheikh et al. [28]	0.780	0.630	0.697	0.730	0.830	0.777	N.A	N.A	N.A	0.270	0.830	0.400

Table 4. Additional experiments on FBMS-59 dataset.

	dog			farm01			cars4		
	Rec	F1	Prec	Rec	F1	Prec	Rec	F1	Prec
Proposed method	0.747	0.965	0.842	0.832	0.773	0.802	0.602	0.941	0.734

5 Conclusion

This work presents an innovative combination of the RootSIFT descriptor and an average pooling for real-time dynamic background modeling and foreground detection. Unlike the previous keypoint-based method, the proposed solution is invariant to small local changes caused by dynamic background. The method provides remarkable results, with respect to different key works of the current state-of-the-art, in both background reconstruction challenges and foreground detection challenges.

Acknowledgement. This work was supported in part by the MIUR under grant "Departments of Excellence 2018–2022" of the Department of Computer Science of Sapienza University.

References

1. Alcantarilla, P., Nuevo, J., Bartoli, A.: Fast explicit diffusion for accelerated features in nonlinear scale spaces. In: British Machine Vision Conference (BMVC), pp. 1–12 (2013)
2. Arandjelović, R., Zisserman, A.: Three things everyone should know to improve object retrieval. In: IEEE Conference on Computer Vision and Pattern Recognition (CVPR), pp. 2911–2918 (2012)
3. Avola, D., Cinque, L., Foresti, G.L., Martinel, N., Pannone, D., Piciarelli, C.: A UAV video dataset for mosaicking and change detection from low-altitude flights. IEEE Trans. Syst. Man Cybern. Syst., 1–11 (2018). https://ieeexplore.ieee.org/document/8303666
4. Avola, D., Foresti, G.L., Martinel, N., Micheloni, C., Pannone, D., Piciarelli, C.: Aerial video surveillance system for small-scale UAV environment monitoring. In: IEEE International Conference on Advanced Video and Signal Based Surveillance (AVSS), pp. 1–6 (2017)
5. Avola, D., Bernardi, M., Cinque, L., Foresti, G.L., Massaroni, C.: Adaptive bootstrapping management by keypoint clustering for background initialization. Pattern Recogn. Lett. **100**, 110–116 (2017)
6. Avola, D., Bernardi, M., Cinque, L., Foresti, G.L., Massaroni, C.: Combining keypoint clustering and neural background subtraction for real-time moving object detection by PTZ cameras. In: International Conference on Pattern Recognition Applications and Methods (ICPRAM), pp. 638–645 (2018)
7. Avola, D., Cinque, L., Foresti, G.L., Massaroni, C., Pannone, D.: A keypoint-based method for background modeling and foreground detection using a PTZ camera. Pattern Recogn. Lett. **96**, 96–105 (2017)

8. Avola, D., Foresti, G.L., Cinque, L., Massaroni, C., Vitale, G., Lombardi, L.: A multipurpose autonomous robot for target recognition in unknown environments. In: IEEE International Conference on Industrial Informatics (INDIN), pp. 766–771 (2016)
9. Avola, D., Foresti, G.L., Martinel, N., Micheloni, C., Pannone, D., Piciarelli, C.: Real-time incremental and geo-referenced mosaicking by small-scale UAVs. In: Battiato, S., Gallo, G., Schettini, R., Stanco, F. (eds.) ICIAP 2017. LNCS, vol. 10484, pp. 694–705. Springer, Cham (2017). https://doi.org/10.1007/978-3-319-68560-1_62
10. Babaee, M., Dinh, D.T., Rigoll, G.: A deep convolutional neural network for video sequence background subtraction. Pattern Recogn. **76**, 635–649 (2018)
11. Bedruz, R.A.R., Fernando, A., Bandala, A., Sybingco, E., Dadios, E.: Vehicle classification using AKAZE and feature matching approach and artificial neural network. In: TENCON 2018–2018 IEEE Region 10 Conference, pp. 1824–1827 (2018)
12. Boulmerka, A., Allili, M.S.: Foreground segmentation in videos combining general gaussian mixture modeling and spatial information. IEEE Trans. Circuits Syst. Video Technol. **28**(6), 1330–1345 (2018)
13. Brox, T., Malik, J.: Object segmentation by long term analysis of point trajectories. In: Daniilidis, K., Maragos, P., Paragios, N. (eds.) ECCV 2010. LNCS, vol. 6315, pp. 282–295. Springer, Heidelberg (2010). https://doi.org/10.1007/978-3-642-15555-0_21
14. Chacon-Murguia, M.I., Ramirez-Quintana, J.A., Ramirez-Alonso, G.: Evaluation of the background modeling method auto-adaptive parallel neural network architecture in the SBMnet dataset. In: International Conference on Pattern Recognition (ICPR), pp. 137–142 (2016)
15. Dou, J., Qin, Q., Tu, Z.: Background subtraction based on deep convolutional neural networks features. Multimedia Tools Appl. **78**, 14549–14571 (2018)
16. Elqursh, A., Elgammal, A.: Online moving camera background subtraction. In: Fitzgibbon, A., Lazebnik, S., Perona, P., Sato, Y., Schmid, C. (eds.) ECCV 2012. LNCS, vol. 7577, pp. 228–241. Springer, Heidelberg (2012). https://doi.org/10.1007/978-3-642-33783-3_17
17. Ferone, A., Maddalena, L.: Neural background subtraction for pan-tilt-zoom cameras. IEEE Trans. Syst. Man Cybern.: Syst. **44**(5), 571–579 (2014)
18. Jodoin, P., Maddalena, L., Petrosino, A., Wang, Y.: Extensive benchmark and survey of modeling methods for scene background initialization. IEEE Trans. Image Process. **26**(11), 5244–5256 (2017)
19. Kwak, S., Lim, T., Nam, W., Han, B., Han, J.H.: Generalized background subtraction based on hybrid inference by belief propagation and bayesian filtering. In: IEEE International Conference on Computer Vision (ICCV), pp. 2174–2181 (2011)
20. Laugraud, B., Piérard, S., Van Droogenbroeck, M.: LaBGen-P-Semantic: a firststep for leveraging semantic segmentation in background generation. J. Imaging **4**(7), 86 (2018)
21. Liu, N., Wu, H., Lin, L.: Hierarchical ensemble of background models for PTZ-based video surveillance. IEEE Trans. Cybern. **45**(1), 89–102 (2015)
22. Maddalena, L., Petrosino, A.: A self-organizing approach to background subtraction for visual surveillance applications. IEEE Trans. Image Process. **17**(7), 1168–1177 (2008)
23. Maddalena, L., Petrosino, A.: Towards benchmarking scene background initialization. In: Murino, V., Puppo, E., Sona, D., Cristani, M., Sansone, C. (eds.) ICIAP 2015. LNCS, vol. 9281, pp. 469–476. Springer, Cham (2015). https://doi.org/10.1007/978-3-319-23222-5_57

24. Ochs, P., Malik, J., Brox, T.: Segmentation of moving objects by long term video analysis. IEEE Trans. Pattern Anal. Mach. Intell. **36**(6), 1187–1200 (2014)
25. Ramirez-Alonso, G., Ramirez-Quintana, J.A., Chacon-Murguia, M.I.: Temporal weighted learning model for background estimation with an automatic re-initialization stage and adaptive parameters update. Pattern Recogn. Lett. **96**, 34–44 (2017)
26. Rublee, E., Rabaud, V., Konolige, K., Bradski, G.: ORB: an efficient alternative to sift or surf. In: 2011 International Conference on Computer Vision, pp. 2564–2571 (2011)
27. Sajid, H., Ching, S., Cheung, S., Jacobs, N.: Appearance based background subtraction for PTZ cameras. Sig. Process. Image Commun. **47**, 417–425 (2016)
28. Sheikh, Y., Javed, O., Kanade, T.: Background subtraction for freely moving cameras. In: IEEE International Conference on Computer Vision (ICCV), pp. 1219–1225 (2009)
29. St-Charles, P., Bilodeau, G., Bergevin, R.: Subsense: a universal change detection method with local adaptive sensitivity. IEEE Trans. Image Process. **24**(1), 359–373 (2015)
30. Tengfeng, W.: Seamless stitching of panoramic image based on multiple homography matrix. In: IEEE Advanced Information Management, Communicates, Electronic and Automation Control Conference (IMCEC), pp. 2403–2407 (2018)
31. Wang, R., Bunyak, F., Seetharaman, G., Palaniappan, K.: Static and moving object detection using flux tensor with split gaussian models. In: IEEE Conference on Computer Vision and Pattern Recognition Workshops (CVPRW), pp. 420–424 (2014)
32. Zhong, Z., Wen, J., Zhang, B., Xu, Y.: A general moving detection method using dual-target nonparametric background model. Knowl. Based Syst. **164**, 85–95 (2019)
33. Zhou, X., Yang, C., Yu, W.: Moving object detection by detecting contiguous outliers in the low-rank representation. IEEE Trans. Pattern Anal. Mach. Intell. **35**(3), 597–610 (2013)

Emotional State Recognition with Micro-expressions and Pulse Rate Variability

Reda Belaiche[1]([✉]), Rita Meziati Sabour[1], Cyrille Migniot[1], Yannick Benezeth[1], Dominique Ginhac[1], Keisuke Nakamura[2], Randy Gomez[2], and Fan Yang[1]

[1] ImViA EA 7535, Univ. Bourgogne Franche-Comté, Dijon, France
{reda.belaiche,rita.meziatisabour,cyrille.migniot,
yannick.benezeth,dominique.ginhac,fan.yang}@u-bourgogne.fr
[2] Honda Research Institute Japan Co., Ltd., 8-1 Honcho, Wako-shi, Saitama, Japan
{keisuke,r.gomez}@jp.honda-ri.com

Abstract. Machine learning has known a tremendous growth within the last years, and lately, thanks to that, some computer vision algorithms started to access what is difficult or even impossible to perceive by the human eye. It is then natural that scientists began looking for ways to probe humans' emotions and their psyche with this technology. In this paper, we study the feasibility of recognizing and classifying the abstract concept of *emotional states* from videos of people facing a regular RGB camera. We do so by using the barely perceptible micro facial expressions humans cannot control, as well as the spontaneous variations of the pulse rate that we estimated using remote photoplethysmography. We compare these two modalities and our experimental results show that it is possible to classify emotional states from these implicit information gathered from regular cameras with encouraging performances.

Keywords: Affective computing · Facial expressions · LBP ·
Pulse rate variability · Remote photoplethysmography

1 Introduction

People's general emotional state and mood have been much studied topics in the fields of psychology and medicine. It has been proved that a person's emotional state can impact their reaction time and learning ability in the short term, and even their health in the long run [1,2]. Being able to automatically predict a person's emotional state offers various real-world applications [3,4] such as neuromarketing [5] or automobile drivers' monitoring [6]. Contrary to simple emotions, emotional states are complex states of the human mind that are provoked by their surroundings or internal thoughts over a certain period of time. To recognize a person's emotional state, computer scientists researched many cues: gestures, voice intonations, and also macro facial expressions variations

E. Ricci et al. (Eds.): ICIAP 2019, LNCS 11751, pp. 26–35, 2019.
https://doi.org/10.1007/978-3-030-30642-7_3

over time. More recently, the scientific community started to gain interest in the exploration of micro-expressions [7].

Facial expressions offer very important benchmarks in every day's social interactions. Most people are familiar with macro facial expressions, however, few people are aware of the existence of micro facial expressions [7,8], and even fewer know how to detect and recognize said micro-expressions. Initially discovered by Haggard and Isaacs [9], micro-expressions are a type of involuntary facial expressions that are extremely fast and of very low intensity. Their duration is within 1/4 s, which makes their localization and analysis rather complicated tasks. Micro-expressions can occur in two situations: conscious suppression and unconscious repression. Conscious suppression happens when a person intentionally tries to stop themselves from showing their true emotions or tries to hide them. Unconscious repression occurs when the subject himself does not realize their true emotions. In both cases, micro-expressions betray the subject's real emotions independently from his awareness of their existence.

Another avenue of research in emotion recognition is based on the analysis of physiological signals such as skin temperature, electrodermal activity or electromyography. Among many physiological features, the variations in the cardiac rhythms are an interesting indicator of the autonomic function [10]. In fact, the heart beating rate continuously fluctuates. The *Heart Rate Variability* (HRV) is conventionally defined as the time intervals between successive beats and is usually estimated from Electrocardiogram recordings. In the last decades, non-contact methods to evaluate the cardiac activity have been developed. One particular method is *Remote Photopletysmography* (RPPG) [11,12], which enables to estimate the pulse rate from a video. The basic principle of RPPG stems from reflective photoplethysmography where the light reaching a camera is modulated by the blood pulsations of the skin. The rhythmic beating of the heart results in the pulsating blood volume alterations, which in turn lead to minute changes in the skin color that can be quantified using different signal processing techniques to generate a cardiac signal. From an RPPG signal, the *Pulse Rate Variability* (PRV) can be estimated by calculating the pulse-to-pulse time intervals. Both HRV and PRV describe changing heart beat rhythms, and multiple researches have demonstrated similarity between PRV and HRV [13,14]. Therefore, the PRV can also be an indicator of the autonomic activity [15].

In this paper, we explore the feasibility of classifying and predicting a person's emotional state, based on two kinds of hidden information only perceptible to computer vision algorithms. This is realized through facial expression recognition and its recent extension to micro-expression recognition on one hand, and the analysis of the remotely measurable PRV on the other hand. These two approaches are quite complementary since *Micro/Macro-Facial Expressions* (M/M-FEs) describe the pixel content of the whole image at small intervals of time, while PRV processes the signal given by the color changes in pixels over a longer duration. In this work, we use the $CAS(ME)^2$ dataset [16], in which the subjects were exposed to different kinds of excitation videos to induce different reactions while they themselves were filmed. The main objective of this dataset is to facilitate the development of algorithms for micro-expressions spotting from long video streams and to the best of our knowledge, this is the first study where physiological signals are estimated from this dataset. The two modalities explored are also the only ones we can use on that dataset.

The paper is organized as follows: we describe M/M-FEs and PRV-based feature extraction methods used for this study in Sect. 2. Experiments are presented and discussed in Sect. 3 and a conclusion is given in Sect. 4.

2   Feature Extraction Methods

In order to recognize emotional states, we have to go through two steps: feature extraction (M/M-FEs and PRV) and classification. In this section, we present the estimation of M/M-FEs and PRV-based features.

2.1   M/M-FEs-based Feature Extraction

We use the *Local Binary Pattern Three Orthogonal Planes* (LBP_TOP) operator, which is the baseline descriptor used as reference in most papers studying micro-expressions [16,17] to describe M/M-FE videos. The LBP operator is a type of visual descriptor that was originally designed for texture description [18]. The general idea is to threshold a small area around each pixel in order to build a binary code. This code is obtained by comparing neighbour pixel values with the center pixel: values superior or equal to the center pixel's value get assigned a 1 while smaller values get assigned a 0. The choice of the surrounding area directly affects the kind of edges it is possible to detect in an image. For pixel neighborhoods referring to N sampling points on a circle of radius R, we generally use the notation $LBP_{N,R}$, whose value for a pixel c can be given by:

$$LBP_{N,R} = \sum_{p=0}^{N-1} t(g_p - g_c)2^p. \tag{1}$$

Here g_c represents the gray value of the center pixel c while g_p represents the gray values of equally spaced pixels on a circle of radius R, t defines a thresholding function $t(x) = 1$ if $x \geq 0$ and $t(x) = 0$ otherwise. The feature vector representing an input image is calculated by extracting the histogram distribution of the LBP. We can consider LBP as texture primitives that include different types of curved edges, spots, flat areas, and so on. For an efficient facial representation, images usually get divided into local blocks from which we extract the LBP histograms and concatenate them into an enhanced feature histogram [19]. Local texture can then be described using said histograms of the binary values for a block in the image. The conventional LBP only serves for spatial data in 2D images. To describe data in the 3D spatio-temporal domain, the basic LBP is extracted from the three planes XY, XT and YT for each pixel as shown in Fig. 1. The resulting three histograms are then concatenated into a feature vector describing the video.

LBP_TOP can only describe a single M/M-FE. The method to describe a whole video containing several M/M-FEs is explained in Sect. 3.2.

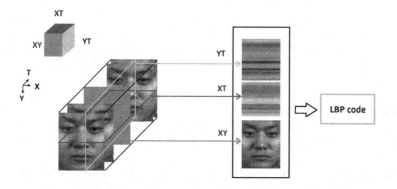

Fig. 1. Illustration of a spatiotemporal volume of a video [16]

2.2 PRV-Based Feature Extraction

Three main steps are followed to obtain the PRV signal as summarized in Fig. 2: face detection and tracking, RPPG pulse extraction and PRV estimation. First, the Viola-Jones face detection algorithm is used to detect the region of interest (ROI) for each video frame. The location of the ROI is then tracked and predicted with a linear Kalman filter. Next, the skin is detected by using the method Conaire *et al.* proposed in [20], allowing to select pixels that are spatially averaged. This yields to a unique RGB triplet for each frame. The triplets are then concatenated to form the RGB temporal traces.

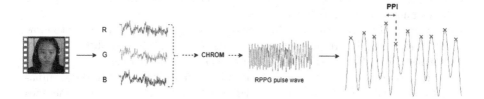

Fig. 2. Framework to obtain a PRV signal using RPPG

The second step consists in computing the pulse signal from the RGB traces. Many advanced and complex techniques have been proposed recently [11,21]. In this work, we use the chrominance algorithm proposed by De Haan *et al.* [22], and denoted as CHROM in Fig. 2. The principal advantage of this method lies in its computational simplicity, owing to its analytic formulation. After normalizing the RGB traces (let R_n, G_n and B_n be the relative normalized traces), two orthogonal chrominance signals X_s and Y_s are built as: $X_s = 3R_n - 2G_n$ and $Y_s = 1.5R_n + G_n - 1.5B_n$. X_s and Y_s are then band-pass filtered with a Butterworth filter (cut-off frequencies of 0.7 and 3.5 Hz) to give two signals X_f and Y_f. The pulse signal S is then obtained as: $S = X_f - \alpha Y_f$, where $\alpha = \frac{\sigma(X_f)}{\sigma(Y_f)}$, and $\sigma(.)$ is

the standard deviation operator. Including the ratio α minimizes disturbances
due to motion, since they alter the amplitudes of the chrominance signals X_s
and Y_s in the same way while the cardiac pulse signal does not. The third step
is to interpolate and resample (we used a sampling rate of 125 Hz) the RPPG
pulse wave in order to increase the time domain resolution and to facilitate
peak detection. *Pulse-to-Pulse Interval* (PPI) time series is then measured to
constitute the PRV signal.

From the PRV signal we extract time-domain, frequency-domain and statistical features, which are defined as follows:

- **time-domain:** features that are computed in this study are the standard
  deviation of the pulse-to-pulse intervals (SDPP) and the square root of the
  mean squared of successive differences (RMSSD) of the PPI series. SDPP is
  the square root of PPI variance, and reflects the effect of all the components
  that induce the pulse variability during the video recording. RMSSD describes
  the evolution of consecutive pulse-to-pulse time intervals and reflects the high-
  frequency component of the PRV. SDPP and RMSSD are obtained as:

$$SDPP = \sqrt{\frac{1}{N}\sum_{i=1}^{N}(PP_i - \overline{PP})^2} \qquad (2)$$

$$RMSSD = \sqrt{\frac{1}{N-1}\sum_{i=2}^{N}(PP_i - PP_{i-1})^2} \qquad (3)$$

  where N is the total number of PP intervals, PP_i is the ith PPI and $\overline{PP}$ is
  the mean value of the PPI series.
- **frequency-domain:** the density spectrum analysis of the PRV gives the low
  (LF) and high (HF) frequency components of the pulse variability. Since the
  interpretation of the role of the LF component in describing the autonomic
  function is complex, as it reflects both the sympathetic and the parasympa-
  thetic activities; we focused on the HF component. The HF range includes
  frequencies between 0.15 Hz and 0.4 Hz, and represents the PNS activity.
- **statistical analysis:** the TIPP describes a tiangular iterpolation of the PPI
  histogram. It is the width of the triangular function that best fits the PPI
  histogram.

3 Experiments and Discussion

3.1 Dataset Presentation

The number of scientific papers dealing with the automatic analysis of micro-
expressions is rather limited. One of the reasons for it can be attributed to the
lack of datasets containing real micro-expressions. Fortunately, this is beginning
to change and recently a new dataset for facilitating the study on spontaneous

micro-expressions spotting and recognition has been made public. This dataset, named $CAS(ME)^2$ [16], is the first dataset that can be used for the study of facial micro-expressions, and offers at the same time the possibility to estimate, by video analysis, physiological parameters such as PRV. Indeed, the videos are sufficiently long and with no inter-frame compression, allowing to use RPPG techniques.

22 participants in total were filmed while watching 3 different kinds of excitation videos (disgust, anger and happiness). Each candidate was asked not to show his emotions. This was done to minimize the number of easily noticeable macro-expressions and to maximize the number of micro-expressions they would show. The dataset was originally proposed for automatic M/M-FE spotting and recognition, and while micro-expressions spotting has been getting good results [23], their recognition still presents many challenges.

$CAS(ME)^2$ offers 2 kinds of annotations for M/M-FEs. The first one is done according to the facial muscle movements based on the *Action Units* (AU) following the Facial Action Coding System (FACS) proposed by Ekman. The second annotations are based on the self-reported emotions from the candidates. These two annotations are not in agreement for all the videos. Furthermore, in some cases, the emotional type of the elicitation video and the annotations based on AU are sometimes contradictory (some subject would show a negative facial expression in front of a happiness-inducing video). 24.05% of the facial expressions are classified as *others* (*i.e.* where related AU are not discriminative). Some subjects would also show contradictory facial expressions on the same video. These observations encouraged us to propose for the first time the use of the emotional type of elicitation videos, also called excitation videos, of $CAS(ME)^2$ as our ground truth. We work under the assumption that the emotional state of the person watching a video would be equivalent to the emotion that video was made to induce. Our motivation behind this decision is to use a labeling that would be more straightforward and less inclined to cause confusion.

In total, the number of available videos is 62, with 14 videos provoking happiness, 24 for disgust and 24 for anger. The video length ranged from 1 min (1800 frames) to approximately 2 min and 30 s (4500 frames).

3.2 Model Validation Protocol

The modalities we concentrate on were tested on the same videos following the *Leave One Subject Out* (LOSO) cross-validation protocol: one subject's data is used as a test set in each fold of the cross-validation. This is done to better reproduce actual use conditions where the encountered subjects are alien to the model when it was trained. Older studies would use k-fold cross-validation; however, this would result in a severe case of overfitting as the accuracies on the test sets would be much higher than with LOSO. This can be attributed to the fact that samples from the same subject would be present in both the training and testing sets. Considering the fact that the same subject can show the exact same expression many times (which may cause occurrences of the same expression from that subject to belong to the training and the test sets at the same time), and that some subjects can be more inclined to show a specific type of emotion more often, using the LOSO protocol seems to be the most rigorous option.

3.3   Recognition with M/M-FEs and PRV

After extracting the M/M-FEs' features with LBP_TOP, a simple majority vote is applied on the different results of each M/M-FE in a video to get the person's general feeling over an extended period of time. The winning class would be used to represent a person's emotional state for the whole video.

The overall classification then needs four SVMs with *Radial Basis Function* (RBF) kernels: one that was trained on the three classes, and three that were trained on each possible pairing of two classes from the three initial ones. The 2-class SVMs were used when we had a perfect equality between 2 classes using the 3-class emotional state classifier. The parameters for the spatio-temporal radii of LBP were equivalent to the ones used in [16]. Concerning the PRV, the features were obtained from the extracted PRV waveforms of each video, and concatenated to form (SDPP, RMSSD, HF, TIPP) vectors. Emotional state classification was then realised based on these values using a non-linear SVM, with an RBF kernel.

PRV-based features encapsulate slow changes in the heart rate. As a consequence, the entire videos are needed to obtain meaningful PRV information. This is not the case of M/M-FEs, which appear for very small durations (between $1/2$ and 4 s for macro and less than $1/4$ s for micro-expressions). Besides, each video contains different M/M-FEs, which impelled us to apply an aggregation process in order to describe the videos.

3.4   Results and Discussion

The final results of emotion classification using macro and micro-expressions and the pulse rate variability are given by Table 1. Confusion matrices give the rate of successful and unsuccessful predictions of the emotional states in order to estimate to what point a classifier confuses two classes. Accuracy rates describe how reliable the classifiers are at predicting emotional states correctly. The voting process on M/M-FEs had an overall accuracy of 42.74% while PRV's accuracy was 59.79 %. If we compare the results of LBP_TOP on excitation videos (for the emotional state) and its original use for labels based on AU, we can see that with 40.95% [16] on the 4 AU-based classes and 42.74% on the excitation video-based labeling, the scores are comparable.

The observed results are interesting since PRV performances surpass those of M/M-FEs, which is quite surprising as $CAS(ME)^2$ was originally made for M/M-FEs recognition but not for PRV estimation. Besides, the dataset does not propose videos with a reference neutral emotional state, preventing us from normalizing the PRV-based features as is usually done to mitigate the impact of the user-dependence effect [24].

Table 1. Emotional state classification confusion matrix and accuracies for M/M-FEs and PRV. Present excitation emotions in $CAS(ME)^2$ are Disgust, Anger and Happiness. Results are expressed in percentage (%)

True	M/M-FEs			PRV		
	Predicted					
	Disgust	Anger	Happiness	Disgust	Anger	Happiness
Disgust	57.4	40.4	2.1	75.0	4.0	21.0
Anger	44.7	55.3	0.0	0.0	75.0	25.0
Happiness	56.7	43.3	0.0	35.0	20.0	45.0
Accuracy	**42.74**			**59.79**		

A possible explanation for the discrepancy of the results obtained with the two modalities could be that M/M-FEs adequately describe sudden changes in emotions, contrary to PRV features that cannot describe these rapid variations in emotions. The difference in temporality between these two modalities is quite obvious; however, it suggests that the use of M/M-FEs for the description of emotions felt over long periods, *e.g.* as in [25], might not be the most appropriate modality. Moreover, the relationship between the emotional states and the occurrences of M/M-FEs is actually rather complex. An interesting illustration of this hypothesis is that we observed cases of contradictory facial expressions on the same video.

4   Conclusion

From simple videos it is possible to extract analytical and physiological features, including M/M-FEs and PRV. Our results show that PRV can be an interesting feature to estimate emotional states with a classification accuracy of about 60%. Although M/M-FEs yielded lower results, ways of improvement have to be delved into. We emphasize with this work that the use of M/M-FEs for the description of emotions must be considered carefully. Mainly because of the intricate relationship between the experienced emotion and its display medium. If both modalities are interesting for studies on emotion recognition, their complementarity will undoubtedly allow for a better apprehension of the complexity of the emotions felt and displayed.

Future works could include the use of other datasets that would take advantage of the complementarity of these two promising modalities with stimulus of various durations. Concerning PRV extraction, having neutral emotional state sequences would allow normalizing our features to mitigate the impact of the user-dependence. Eventually, we also plan a fusion of M/M-FEs and PRV features for emotional state prediction and to investigate the use of M/M-FEs features to alleviate the intra-user dependence of PRV features.

References

1. Rothman, A.J., Salove, P., et al.: Emotional states and physical health. Am. Psychol. **55**(1), 110 (2000)
2. Tyng, C.M., Hafeez, U.A., et al.: The influences of emotion on learning and memory. Front. Psychol. **8**, 1454 (2017)
3. Chen, Y.-L., Chang, C.-L., Yeh, C.-S.: Emotion classification of youtube videos. Decis. Support Syst. **101**, 40–50 (2017)
4. Bargal, S., et al.: Emotion recognition in the wild from videos using images. In: Proceedings of the 18th ACM International Conference on Multimodal Interaction (2016)
5. Vecchiato, G., Astolfi, L., Fallani, F.D.V.: On the use of EEG or MEG brain imaging tools in neuromarketing research. Comput. Intell. Neurosci. **2011**, 3 (2011)
6. Nass, C., Jonsson, M., Harris, H.: Improving automotive safety by pairing driver emotion and car voice emotion. In: Extended Abstracts on Human Factors in Computing Systems (2005)
7. Ekman, P., Friesen, W.V.: Nonverbal leakage and clues to deception. Psychiatry **32**(1), 88–106 (1969)
8. Ekman, P.: Telling Lies: Clues to Deceit in the Marketplace, Politics, and Marriage (Revised Edition). WW Norton & Company, New York (2009)
9. Haggard, E.A., Isaacs, K.S.: Methods of Research in Psychotherapy. Springer, New York (1966). https://doi.org/10.1007/978-1-4684-6045-2
10. McCraty, R., Atkinson, M., Tomasino, D.: Science of the Heart - Exploring the Role of the Heart in Human Performance, Institute of HeartMath (2001)
11. Sun, Y., Thakor, N.: Photoplethysmography revisited: from contact to non contact, from point to imaging. IEEE Trans. Biomed. Eng. **63**(3), 463–477 (2016)
12. McDuff, D.J., Estepp, J.R., Piassecki, A.M., Blackford, E.B.: A survey of remote optical photoplethysmographic imaging methods. In: Proceedings of the Annual International Conference of the IEEE Engineering in Medicine and Biology Society (2015)
13. Gil, E., Orini, M., Bailon, R., et al.: Photoplethysmography pulse rate variability as a surrogate measurement of heart rate variability during non-stationary conditions. Physiol. Measur. **31**(9), 1271 (2010)
14. Schafer, A., Vagedes, J.: How accurate is pulse rate variability as an estimate of heart rate variability? a review on studies comparing photoplethysmographic technology with an electrocardiogram. Int. J. Cardiol. **166**(1), 15–29 (2013)
15. Nitzan, M., Babchenko, A., Khanokh, B., Landau, D.: The variability of the photoplethysmographic signal - a potential method for the evaluation of the autonomic nervous system. Physiol. Measur. **19**(1), 93 (1998)
16. Qu, F., Wang, S.J., Yan, W.J., et al.: CAS(ME)^2: a database for spontaneous macro-expression and micro-expression spotting and recognition. IEEE Trans. Affect. Comput. **9**(4), 424–436 (2017)
17. Pfister, T., Li, X., Zhao, G., Pietikainen, M.: Recognising spontaneous facial micro-expressions. In: IEEE International Conference on Computer Vision (2011)
18. Ojala, T., Pietikäinenand, M., Mäenpää, T.: Multiresolution gray-scale and rotation invariant texture classification with local binary patterns. IEEE Trans. Pattern Anal. Mach. Intell. **7**, 971–987 (2002)
19. Ahonen, T., Hadid, A., Pietikainen, M.: Face description with local binary patterns: application to face recognition. IEEE Trans. Pattern Anal. Mach. Intell. **12**, 2037–2041 (2006)

20. Conaire, C.O., O'Connor, N.E., Smeaton, A.F.: Detector adaptation by maximising agreement between independant data sources. In: IEEE Conference on Computer Vision and Pattern Recognition (2007)
21. Poh, M.Z., McDuff, D.J., Picard, R.W.: Advancements in noncontact, multiparameter physiological measurements using a webcam. IEEE Trans. Biomed. Eng. **58**(1), 7–11 (2011)
22. De Haan, G., Jeanne, V.: Robust pulse-rate from chrominance-based rPPG. IEEE Trans. Biomed. Eng. **60**(10), 2878–2886 (2013)
23. Han, Y., Li, B., Lai, Y.K., Liu, Y.J.: CFD: a collaborative feature difference method for spontaneous micro-expression spotting. In: 25th IEEE ICIP (2018)
24. Benezeth, Y., Li, P., Macwan, R., et al.: Remote heart rate variability for emotional state monitoring. In: IEEE International Conference on Biomedical and Health Informatics (2018)
25. Li, X., Hong, X., Moilanen, A., et al.: Towards reading hidden emotions: a comparative study of spontaneous micro-expression spotting and recognition methods. IEEE Trans. Affect. Comput. **9**(4), 563–577 (2018)

Deep Motion Model for Pedestrian Tracking in 360 Degrees Videos

Liliana Lo Presti$^{(\boxtimes)}$ and Marco La Cascia

University of Palermo, Palermo, Italy
`liliana.lopresti@unipa.it`

Abstract. This paper proposes a deep convolutional neural network (CNN) for pedestrian tracking in 360° videos based on the target's motion.

The tracking algorithm takes advantage of a virtual Pan-Tilt-Zoom (vPTZ) camera simulated by means of the 360° video. The CNN takes in input a motion image, i.e. the difference of two images taken by using the vPTZ camera at different times by the same pan, tilt and zoom parameters. The CNN predicts the vPTZ camera parameter adjustments required to keep the target at the center of the vPTZ camera view.

Experiments on a publicly available dataset performed in cross-validation demonstrate that the learned motion model generalizes, and that the proposed tracking algorithm achieves state-of-the-art performance.

Keywords: Tracking · CNN · Motion · 360° video

1 Introduction

Pedestrian tracking has been largely studied in computer vision both with fixed zoom static/mobile cameras [1–3], Pan-Tilt-Zoom (PTZ) cameras [4–6] and in camera networks [7–10]. In particular, tracking algorithms for PTZ cameras aim at controlling the camera so that the target always appears at the center of the camera view, eventually zooming in or out if necessary. In these algorithms, the camera control procedure poses several issues, and greatly limits the reproducibility and comparison of the tracking algorithms.

In the last years, 360° videos are emerging as a new technology enabling novel multimedia and Virtual Reality applications [11,12]. Such videos are collected by cameras including two or more optical sensors acquiring images from different viewpoints. The acquired images are then stitched in order to create a spherical view stored, in general, as equirectangular image (see Fig. 1). In an equirectangular image, coordinates of each pixel represent polar and azimuth angles of the corresponding point onto the spherical surface.

Only recently, in [13–15], it has been recognized the possibility of adopting 360° cameras for surveillance purposes. These papers have proposed using

© Springer Nature Switzerland AG 2019
E. Ricci et al. (Eds.): ICIAP 2019, LNCS 11751, pp. 36–47, 2019.
https://doi.org/10.1007/978-3-030-30642-7_4

360° videos to simulate vPTZ cameras, thus enabling the evaluation and comparison of algorithms for PTZ cameras.

Tracking in 360° videos is challenging in several respects. First, performing tracking directly onto equirectangular images is difficult because the target appearance would depend on the location of the target on the equirectangular image itself, and the image sphericity must be taken into account during tracking. Second, even considering vPTZ cameras as in [15], prediction of the best zoom factor to track the target over time is challenging, especially with occlusions and abrupt changes of direction/velocity of the target. Finally, in contrast to PTZ cameras, where optical zoom allows the acquisition of high quality images of the target, in vPTZ cameras only a digital zoom is available, which limits the quality of the target images during tracking when zooming in is required.

In this paper, we present a novel pedestrian tracking algorithm for 360° videos based on deep CNN. Deep learning based approaches have already been proposed for visual tracking. In some approaches [16–18], CNN are used to extract an appearance representation of the target. In other approaches, target re-identification is performed by learning a similarity metric by means of Siamese networks [19–21]. At the best of our knowledge, no deep learning based approach has been proposed yet for visual tracking in 360° videos.

We propose to track pedestrians by vPTZ cameras controlled based on the pedestrians' motion. Motion dynamics are modeled by a deep CNN trained to regress the adjustments of the pan, tilt and zoom parameters required to maintain the target at the center of the vPTZ camera view. To clarify, let us assume that at time t the parameters of the vPTZ camera to acquire the target image I_t are (p_t, t_t, α_t), namely pan, tilt and field of view (FOV) angles respectively. In our approach, we use these same parameters to acquire an image I_{t+1} at time $t+1$ by our vPTZ camera. The difference between I_{t+1} and I_t is used to measure the pedestrian motion and is fed in input to a CNN to predict the parameter variations $(\Delta p_t, \Delta t_t, \Delta \alpha_t)$ required to maintain the target at the center of the vPTZ camera view. Our tracking algorithm includes a re-identification strategy used whenever an occlusion arises and no motion information is available.

The main contributions of this paper are summarized as follows:

1. We present a deep learning based approach for tracking in 360° videos;
2. We model motion dynamics by means of a CNN trained on difference images (motion images); we do not use the CNN to model the target appearance nor to learn a similarity metric. Instead, we train a single motion model that we use to track our targets (targets are not included in the training set);
3. We propose a novel and compact deep CNN for visual tracking. The network, with less than 200 K parameters, is used to regress the vPTZ camera parameter variations from difference images of size 64×128 pixels;

Experiments in cross-video validation show that our approach is viable and allows to achieve state-of-the-art performance on a publicly available dataset.

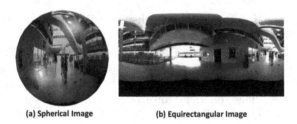

(a) Spherical Image   (b) Equirectangular Image

Fig. 1. Spherical and Equirectangular Images: (a) example of spherical image acquired by a 360° camera (i.e., a camera including at least two optical sensors); (b) the corresponding equirectangular image whose rows and columns represent polar and azimuth angles respectively.

2   Related Work

By analogy with tracking-by-detection techniques, first deep learning approaches for tracking trained a model online to adapt it to the target appearance changes.

In [16], to limit the computational burden of training the model online, the retraining is performed only when the target appearance largely changes.

To skip the training procedure, in [18], convolutional filters are derived from the first target template and used to discriminate between target and background. In this way, the method does not online train a CNN. The core idea of the work in [17] is that the target can share features (domain shared features) with other objects, but can also have some specific and peculiar features (domain specific features). The former can be modeled offline, the latter must be learned online. By these motivations, the method fuses offline and online trained convolutional layers while tracking the target in a video, limiting the cost of the online training of the network.

Works in [19,20] propose to use offline trained networks for visual tracking. Such methods use Siamese network, that is two branches convolutional neural network able to process pairs of images. The method in [19] uses the Siamese network as a matching function. The first branch of the network processes the first target template, while the second branch processes, one-by-one, several target image candidates. The image candidate with the best match is selected has the new target location. The main limitation of this work is that it needs to process multiple image candidates to locate the target. To overcome such limitation, the method in [20] adopts a Siamese network trained to regress the new target bounding box on a larger search area.

In contrast to these methods, in this paper we do not learn a similarity metric nor we attempt to model the target appearance by deep features or deep models. Instead, we use a deep CNN to model motion dynamics. The network is trained offline, and no model adaptation is required during the target tracking.

In this sense, our network is related to LikeNet [21], a Siamese network that computes a pixel-wise distribution over motion classes. The network receives as input the target template and a target candidate shifted by a specific motion

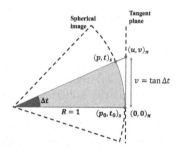

Fig. 2. From Spherical coordinates to tangent plane coordinates: the image shows a section of the sphere. We set a coordinate system $(u, v)_\pi$ on the plane with origin in the tangent point $(p_0, t_0)_S$. The point $(p, t)_S$ on the sphere is projected to $(u, v)_\pi$. The coordinate v can be easily calculated from the angle difference $\Delta t = t - t_0$.

vector. The similarity provided by the network is interpreted as the probability associated to the motion vector used to generate the target candidate. Our network takes in input only a difference image to predict the pan, tilt, FOV angle variations required to control the vPTZ camera.

There are no many works on visual tracking in 360° videos. In [13], the authors propose simulating a PTZ camera from spherical videos acquired offline. Experiments with the Camshift algorithm [22] are presented to test the use of such vPTZ cameras. Despite authors of [13] claim that their framework can simulate zoom in and out, experiments were run with a fixed zoom factor.

In [14], the authors propose a method to predict the adjustments of the pan, tilt and zoom parameters from motion templates computed on the first image of the target. The method assumes that a weighted sum of these motion templates can approximate the actual target's motion, and that the same weights can be used to compute the parameter adjustments from the parameters used to generate the motion templates. Weights are estimated by minimizing the approximation error in a least square sense.

In [15], a tracking-by-detection algorithm is proposed to track pedestrian by vPTZ cameras. At each time, a detector is used to locate pedestrians in the image acquired by the vPTZ camera. An adaptive appearance model is used to establish correspondences of the detection to the target; the center of the selected detection on the vPTZ camera plane is used to re-estimate the pan, tilt, zoom parameters required to control the virtual camera. The approach uses a gnomonic transformation [23] and its inverse to transform camera plane coordinates to spherical coordinates and conversely.

Similarly to the work in [13–15], we use vPTZ cameras to track pedestrians. The tracking problem is formulated as the estimation of the parameter variations needed to foveate the vPTZ camera on the target.

3   Equirectangular Images and Virtual PTZ Cameras

Tracking a point (p_0, t_0) on a spherical image corresponds to control a vPTZ camera whose pan and tilt angles are respectively p_0 and t_0. In this sense, the tangent plane to the sphere in (p_0, t_0) represents the camera plane, and the FOV angle defines the extension of the spherical surface to project onto the vPTZ camera plane.

As detailed in [15], simple geometrical transformations [23] allows to map the spherical image onto the virtual camera plane. In this section, we present a much simpler approach to map spherical coordinates onto the tangent plane.

3.1   From Spherical Image to vPTZ Camera Plane

Pixel coordinates (x_r, y_r) on the equirectangular image represent normalized values of polar and azimuth angles of the corresponding point on the sphere surface. The angles can be recovered from the pixel coordinates by a simple re-scaling such that the polar angle t_0 ranges in $[0, 180°]$, while the azimuth angle p_0 ranges in $[0, 360°]$.

Our goal is that of projecting the spherical surface centered in (p_0, t_0) and with angular extension equals to α_0 onto a tangent plane π.

As illustrated in Fig. 2, we set a coordinate system (u, v) on the plane π with origin on the tangent point (p_0, t_0). Given a spherical point (p, t), the corresponding point (u, v) on the plane π can be found as:

$$u = \tan(p - p_0); \qquad (1)$$
$$v = \tan(t - t_0). \qquad (2)$$

Reasoning in a similar way, given the angular extension α_0 of the spherical surface to project, the projected area will have coordinates on the tangent plane varying in $[-2\tan\frac{\alpha_0}{2}, 2\tan\frac{\alpha_0}{2}]$.

Finally, we transform the coordinates (u, v) into an image coordinate system (x, y) by translating and re-scaling the points such that $x \in [0, w[, y \in [0, h[$ where w and h are the width and the height of the vPTZ camera image.

By simple algebraic manipulation, it is possible to recover equations for the inverse mapping (from image coordinates (x, y) to the spherical surface (p, t)).

4   Tracking with Virtual PTZ Cameras

Our algorithm aims at estimating the vPTZ camera parameter adjustments required to keep the target at the center of the camera view. Let us assume that, at time t, the vPTZ camera parameters are (p_t, t_t, α_t). Our algorithm computes a motion image to measure the movements of the target and uses a CNN to predict the parameter variations $(\Delta p, \Delta t, \Delta\alpha)$. At the next iteration, the camera parameters will be adjusted to $(p_t + \Delta p, t_t + \Delta t, \alpha_t + \Delta\alpha)$ and the procedure re-iterated. In the following, we provide details about the motion image calculation, the proposed CNN and the strategy adopted to train the model.

4.1 Motion Images

Given two spherical images S_t and S_{t+1} acquired at time t and $t+1$ respectively, and the parameters (p_t, t_t, α_t) of the vPTZ camera at time t, we define I_t and I_{t+1} as the images acquired by the vPTZ camera from the two spherical images S_t and S_{t+1} as described in Sect. 3.

We define the motion image MI_t as:

$$MI_t = I_{t+1} - I_t \tag{3}$$

Figure 3 shows examples of motion images, where the pixel intensity values have been normalized to range in $[0, 255]$. As shown in the figure, motion images can visually represent the target's motion dynamics. Since the two images I_t and I_{t+1} are generated by the same (p_t, t_t, α_t) parameters, the image difference operator has the effect of suppressing the background and highlighting the changes in the scene mainly due to the target's motion. Depending on the velocity and direction of the target's movements, the motion image presents borders whose thickness and structure is correlated somehow with the parameter variations that are necessary to control the vPTZ camera and track the target.

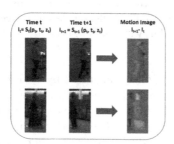

Fig. 3. Motion Images: on the left, pairs of images acquired by our vPTZ camera with the same parameters (p, t, z) but at different time instants; on the right, the normalized motion images computed as difference between the most recent image and the less recent one. In both cases, the motion images highlight the need of: increasing the pan parameter in the top row, decreasing the pan parameter in the bottom row.

4.2 Modeling Motion in 360° Videos

We want to model the target's motion by means of a convolutional neural network that is able to regress the parameter variations of a vPTZ camera from motion images. We expect that, during training, our neural network learns a relation between the border thickness and structure depicted in the motion images and the parameter variations. Ideally, we need to generate a training set of pairs of motion images and parameter variations, $\{MI_t, (\Delta p_t, \Delta t_t, \Delta \alpha_t)\}_t$.

Whilst very intuitive, the use of motion images to regress such parameter variations is not straightforward. Indeed, the same parameter variations can led to different motion images. As an example, let us consider the images shown in

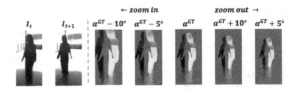

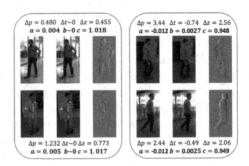

Fig. 4. The shown motion images are characterized by the same parameter variations despite their appearance greatly changes.

Fig. 5. Normalizing the parameter variations by the initial FOV angle: each block shows motion images characterized by different parameter variations (reported on top and on bottom of the images) but with similar normalized values (a, b, c) (in bold font).

Fig. 4. On the left, we show images acquired by a vPTZ camera at time t and $t+1$ with the same parameters. On the right, we show the corresponding motion images obtained by perturbing the FOV angle (α^{GT}) with $\pm10°$, $\pm5°$. Despite the actual parameter variations required to track the target are the same, the shown motion images greatly differ one each other. In particular, lower is the value of the FOV angle, higher is the border thickness in the motion image. This suggests that the parameter variations should be put in relation with the initial FOV angle. To account for this issue, in our training schema, we generate a training set $\{MI_t, (a, b, c)\}_t$ where $a = \frac{\Delta p_t}{\alpha_t}$, $b = \frac{\Delta t_t}{\alpha_t}$ and $c = \frac{\alpha_{t+1}}{\alpha_t}$. Figure 5 shows examples of motion images with similar values of (a, b, c).

At test time, we use our CNN to regress (a, b, c). Later on, by using the currently estimated value of p_t, t_t, α_t and by inverse formulas, we calculate from (a, b, c) the values of $p_{t+1}, t_{t+1}, \alpha_{t+1}$.

Our training procedure is fully supervised. To generate the training set, we used the tracks of pedestrians for which we knew the parameters (p_t, t_t, α_t) for each t. We computed motion images of consecutive frames (namely frames with time delay equals to 1) as described in Sect. 4.1. To augment the training data, we also included motion images computed with different time delays. Furthermore, we included images obtained by perturbing the initial FOV angle α_t with values sampled by a Normal distribution.

4.3   Modeling Motion by Convolutional Neural Network

We designed a deep convolutional neural network to regress, from motion images, the corresponding values (a, b, c) needed to calculate the vPTZ camera parameter variations. The network is shown in Fig. 6. To limit the number of parameters, we used 3×3 convolutional kernels in each layer. To progressively reduce the feature map size, we did not use any padding when applying the convolutional operator. We used a max-pooling layer any two convolutional layers. Overall, our network is composed of 7 convolutional layers, 3 max-pooling layers and 2 fully connected layers.

In all layers, we use a ReLU activation function and, for regularization purposes, we add Dropout layers after each ReLU activation function with a probability of 0.2 after convolutional layers, and 0.5 after dense layers.

Since we are interested in regression, the output layer uses a linear activation function. We trained the model by adagrad, in order to adapt the learning rate during the minimization of the mean-squared error.

With an input of size 64×128, the network counts less than 200K parameters, which made feasible training the model on a TitanX GPU.

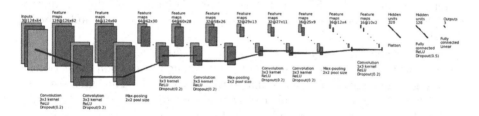

Fig. 6. Proposed Deep Convolutional Neural Network: the network is composed of 7 convolutional layers, 3 max-pooling layers and 2 fully connected layers. All kernels have size 3×3 and all layers, but the last, adopt a ReLU activation function. The output layer is composed of 3 neurons to regress the values (a, b, c).

4.4   Dealing with Occlusions and Absence of Motion

Our technique is able to predict the vPTZ camera parameter variations to track a moving target. However, to be able to use our model within a tracking algorithm it is necessary to account for two cases: (1) absence of motion; (2) occlusions.

The former case can be easily detected by measuring the motion image entropy: low values of the entropy indicates that the motion has little importance. Hence we set a threshold T_M on the entropy to detect the absence of motion. In such case, the parameters of the vPTZ camera are not modified.

In case of occlusions, the motion image can be useless to track the target, especially when the occluding object is closer to the camera than the target. We use a descriptor of the target's appearance to detect such cases. We extract the descriptor from the first detection of the target. When the appearance similarity of the target and the candidate target is below a threshold T_A, then it is not possible to use our deep motion model. Instead, we use CamShift [22] to re-identify the target as soon as the occlusion ends; to limit the cases when the target exits the FOV without being re-identified by CamShift, we use a FOV angle of 90°. As soon as the appearance similarity is higher than T_A, the algorithm switches tracking mode, and uses the proposed deep motion model to track the target.

We described the target's appearance by means of a 2D color histogram of the hue and saturation values. To establish matches between the descriptors, we adopted the histogram intersection similarity metric.

5   Experimental Results

We performed experiments on the publicly available dataset in [13]. The dataset provides 6 fully annotated tracks of different pedestrians. The tracks are split in 3 scenarios each including 3, 2 and 1 pedestrian track respectively. The average number of frames in the 6 tracks is about 650.

In the videos, pedestrians move randomly – alone or in groups – around the camera. All videos are characterized by strong illumination artifacts and cluttered background (see Fig. 1(b)). The scenarios are especially difficult due to the high number of occlusions and the abrupt changes of direction and velocity of the targets.

We performed experiments in cross-scenario validation: at each iteration, a scenario was used for test purposes and the remaining two to train the network. On average, the number of training images was about 109K. The batch size was set to 128 and the maximal number of epochs to 300. We used the 5% of the training data as validation set and adopted early stopping to select the model with the lowest validation loss considering a patience parameter of 50.

We have considered to evaluate our technique with the metrics described in [13]. However, we noted that the Target to Center Error (TCE) in [13] is not appropriate to measure the performance of tracking algorithms that use vPTZ cameras. Indeed, the TCE is expressed in pixels and the error is measured on the vPTZ camera plane, whose dimensions ($W \times H$) can be arbitrarily set. As an example, in [13] the size of the vPTZ camera plane was set to 640×480 while, in our implementation, the image size was set to 64×128. Furthermore, such error measurement greatly depends on the zoom factor. Hence, it seems reasonable to measure the error directly on the spherical surface. For these reasons, we assess our tracker performance by computing the mean absolute error (MAE) of the estimated pan, tilt and FOV angles for the valid detection. A detection is valid if the estimated target location (on the spherical surface) is inside the true FOV angle derived from the ground-truth. All non valid detections contribute to the track fragmentation (TF) error, which represents the average percentage of erroneous detections of the target.

We compare our technique against the baseline method suggested in [13], namely CamShift [22], and we used the implementation available in the OpenCV Library. When using CamShift, we track pedestrians in the HSV color space by setting a FOV angle equals to 90°. To deal with occlusions, our algorithm uses the same Camshift implementation. In particular, the adopted 2D histogram had 16×16 bins for the hue and saturation channels of the image. The thresholds to detect absence of motion and occlusions were set to $T_M = 1$ and $T_A = 0.7$. We have experimented making the threshold T_A dynamic by decreasing it of the 5% every time the algorithm uses CamShift, and setting T_A back to 0.7 when the algorithm uses the deep motion model.

Table 1 reports the results of our experiments. The first line shows the performance of the model when only the CNN is used. In practice, the TF is very high due to the fact that, when an occlusion arises, the tracker drifts and follows the occluding object. Nonetheless, for the valid detections, the MAE over the pan, tilt and FOV angles are of few degrees. When using CamShift to re-identify the target at the end of the occlusion, the TF decreases of about the 23.53%. In our experiments, we did not use an adaptive appearance descriptor and, in the long time, the adopted descriptor is not useful anymore to re-identify the target. This explains why, in our experiments, the TF remains high whilst much lower than the one achieved by using only CamShift (third row of the table). CamShift suffers from the fact that the appearance descriptor is not adapted over time. The MAE of the FOV angle is much higher with CamShift due to the fact that the algorithm tends to drift and, whilst we limited the size of the detected bounding box to up ± 3 times the size of the first target's bounding box, the detected area tends to grow over time. We also compare our method to the tracking-by-detection technique proposed in [15] and to the method in [24], which uses particle filtering to track the target. The track fragmentation of this last method is comparable to that of the CamShift algorithm but higher than that achieved using also our CNN model.

Overall, these results show the viability of the proposed method but highlight the need of a stronger technique for person re-identification.

Table 1. Experimental Results: MAE stands for Mean Absolute Error, p, t, α indicates pan, tilt and FOV angles respectively, TF stands for Track Fragmentation

Method	$MAE(p)$	$MAE(t)$	$MAE(\alpha)$	TF
CNN [ours]	1.94°	1.29°	4.12°	67.84%
CNN + CamShift [ours]	2.55°	4.11°	11.82°	51.88%
CamShift [22]	3.86°	4.68°	36.11°	64.43%
TbyD [15]	2.43°	3.44°	15.26°	70.45%
PF [24]	3.14°	2.79°	9.85°	59.85%

6   Conclusions and Future Work

In this paper, we presented a tracking algorithm for 360° videos that simulates a vPTZ camera to foveate frame-by-frame on the target. The algorithm adopts a deep CNN to model the dynamics of the target's motion, and uses such model to predict the pan, tilt and FOV angle variations required to keep the target at the center of the vPTZ camera view. The proposed CNN has a limited number of parameters, receives in input a motion image and predicts values of the parameter changes normalized with respect to the FOV angle of the current frame.

Experimental results show that the adopted convolutional model is able to predict the parameter variations in absence of occlusions. To deal with occlusions, we use CamShift to re-identify the target. Experiments show the weakness of the adopted appearance model.

In future work, we will modify our model to enable the prediction of when and where an occlusion is going to arise. We will consider the possibility to extend our algorithm to multi-target tracking to improve re-identification and occlusion handling, and we will investigate tracking on the spherical views by using spherical CNN.

References

1. Hare, S., et al.: Struck: structured output tracking with kernels. IEEE Trans. Pattern Anal. Mach. Intell. (PAMI) **38**(10), 2096–2109 (2016)
2. Zdenek, K., Mikolajczyk, K., Matas J.: Tracking-learning-detection. IEEE Trans. Pattern Anal. Mach. Intell. **34**(7), 1409–1422 (2012)
3. Zhang, J., Lo Presti, L., Sclaroff, S.: Online multi-person tracking by tracker hierarchy. In: Proceedings of Advanced Video and Signal-Based Surveillance (AVSS), pp. 379–385. IEEE (2012)
4. Micheloni, C., Rinner, B., Foresti, G.L.: Video analysis in pan-tilt-zoom camera networks. IEEE Signal Process. Mag. **27**(5), 78–90 (2010)
5. Kang, S., Paik, J.K., Koschan, A., Abidi, B.R., Abidi, M.A.: Real-time video tracking using PTZ cameras. In: Proceedings of Quality Control by Artificial Vision, vol. 5132, pp. 103–112 (2003)
6. Bagdanov, A.D., et al.: A reinforcement learning approach to active camera foveation. In: Proceedings of Workshop on Video Surveillance and Sensor Networks. ACM (2006)
7. Song, B., et al.: Tracking and activity recognition through consensus in distributed camera networks. IEEE Trans. Image Process. **19**(10), 2564–2579 (2010)
8. Lo Presti, L., Sclaroff, S., La Cascia, M.: Object matching in distributed video surveillance systems by LDA-based appearance descriptors. In: Foggia, P., Sansone, C., Vento, M. (eds.) ICIAP 2009. LNCS, vol. 5716, pp. 547–557. Springer, Heidelberg (2009). https://doi.org/10.1007/978-3-642-04146-4_59
9. Lo Presti, L., Sclaroff, S., La Cascia, M.: Path modeling and retrieval in distributed video surveillance databases. IEEE Trans. Multimedia **14**(2), 346–360 (2012)
10. Ristani, E., Solera, F., Zou, R., Cucchiara, R., Tomasi, C.: Performance measures and a data set for multi-target, multi-camera tracking. In: Hua, G., Jégou, H. (eds.) ECCV 2016. LNCS, vol. 9914, pp. 17–35. Springer, Cham (2016). https://doi.org/10.1007/978-3-319-48881-3_2
11. Hosseini, M., Viswanathan, S.: Adaptive 360 VR video streaming: divide and conquer. In: IEEE International Symposium on Multimedia (ISM). IEEE (2016)

12. Su, Y., Grauman, K.: Making 360° video watchable in 2D: learning videography for click free viewing. In: International Conference on Computer Vision and Pattern Recognition (2017)
13. Chen, G., et al.: Reproducible evaluation of Pan-Tilt-Zoom tracking. In: ICIP (2015)
14. Greco, L., La Cascia, M.: 360° tracking using a virtual PTZ camera. In: Battiato, S., Gallo, G., Schettini, R., Stanco, F. (eds.) ICIAP 2017. LNCS, vol. 10484, pp. 62–72. Springer, Cham (2017). https://doi.org/10.1007/978-3-319-68560-1_6
15. Monteleone, V., Lo Presti, L., La Cascia, M.: Pedestrian tracking in 360 video by virtual PTZ cameras. In: RTSI. IEEE (2018)
16. Li, H., Yi, L., Porikli, F.: Deeptrack: learning discriminative feature representations online for robust visual tracking. IEEE Trans. Image Process. **25**(4), 1834–1848 (2016)
17. Nam, H., Bohyung, H.: Learning multi-domain convolutional neural networks for visual tracking. In: Proceedings of Computer Vision and Pattern Recognition. IEEE (2016)
18. Zhang, K., et al.: Robust visual tracking via convolutional networks without training. IEEE Trans. Image Process. **25**(4), 1779–1792 (2016)
19. Tao, R., Gavves, E., Smeulders, A.: Siamese instance search for tracking. In: Proceedings of Computer Vision and Pattern Recognition. IEEE (2016)
20. Held, D., Thrun, S., Savarese, S.: Learning to track at 100 FPS with deep regression networks. In: Leibe, B., Matas, J., Sebe, N., Welling, M. (eds.) ECCV 2016. LNCS, vol. 9905, pp. 749–765. Springer, Cham (2016). https://doi.org/10.1007/978-3-319-46448-0_45
21. Ahmadi, A., Ioannis, M., Ioannis, P.: LikeNet: a siamese motion estimation network trained in an unsupervised way. In: BMVC, p. 296 (2018)
22. Comaniciu, D., Ramesh, V., Meer, P.: Real-time tracking of non-rigid objects using mean shift. In: Computer Vision and Pattern Recognition, vol. 2, pp. 142–149. IEEE (2000)
23. Snyder, J.P.: Map Projections-A Working Manual. U.S. Geological Survey Professional Paper 1395. Washington, DC: U.S. Gov. Printing Office, pp. 164–168 (1987)
24. Monteleone, V., Lo Presti, L., La Cascia, M.: Particle filtering for tracking in 360 degrees videos using virtual PTZ cameras. In: Image Analysis and Processing (ICIAP) (2019)

Comparisons of Visual Activity Primitives for Voice Activity Detection

Muhammad Shahid[1], Cigdem Beyan[1], and Vittorio Murino[1,2(✉)]

[1] Pattern Analysis and Computer Vision, Istituto Italiano di Tecnologia,
Genova, Italy
{Muhammad.Shahid,Cigdem.Beyan,Vittorio.Murino}@iit.it
[2] Department of Computer Science, University of Verona, Verona, Italy

Abstract. Voice activity detection (VAD) with solely visual cues have usually performed by detecting lip motion, which is not always feasible. On the other hand, visual activity (e.g., head, hand or whole body motion) is also correlated with speech, and can be used for VAD. Convolutional Neural Networks (CNNs) have demonstrated significantly good results for many applications including visual activity-related tasks. It can be possible to exploit CNN's effectiveness to visual-VAD when whole body visual activity is used. The way visual activity is represented (called visual activity primitives) to be given to a CNN as input, might be important to perform an effective VAD. Some primitives might result in better detection and provide consistent VAD performance such that the detector works equally well for all speakers. This is investigated, for the first time, in this paper. Regarding that, we compare visual activity primitives quantitatively in terms of the overall performance and the standard deviation of the performance, and qualitatively by visualizing the discriminative image regions determined by CNN trained to identify VAD classes. We perform a data-driven VAD with a person-invariant training i.e., without using any labels or features of the test data. This is unlike the state-of-the-art (SOA), which realizes a person-specific VAD with hand-crafted features. Improved performances with much lower standard deviation as compared to SOA are demonstrated.

Keywords: Voice activity detection · Visual activity ·
Dynamic images · Optical flow · Social interactions

1 Introduction

Voice Activity Detection (VAD) consists in automatically detecting "Who is Speaking and When" in an audio/video recording. Automatic VAD contributes various applications of human-human interaction analysis, human-computer

---

M. Shahid and C. Beyan—Equally contributed.

© Springer Nature Switzerland AG 2019
E. Ricci et al. (Eds.): ICIAP 2019, LNCS 11751, pp. 48–59, 2019.
https://doi.org/10.1007/978-3-030-30642-7_5

(robot) interaction and also many industrial applications. As an example, for analysis of human-human interactions, VAD can be used to extract speaking turn-based nonverbal features (e.g., the length of the speech, the length of the overlapping speech, etc.), which later on can be used to detect personality traits (e.g. [17]), dominance (e.g., [15]) or emergent leaders (e.g., [1]). Performing an accurate VAD can allow a robot (or a computer) to reply to a specific interlocutor when there is more than one person in a human-robot interaction environment [5]. Video conferencing systems can utilize VAD to present the video of the speaking person only during multi-person meetings. Additionally, an effective VAD can improve video navigation and retrieval, speaker model adaptation to enhance speaker recognition, and speaker attributed speech-to-text transcription [9].

Traditionally, VAD is performed by processing audio only, which is typically called speaker diarization [21]. On the other hand, multimodal approaches, normally referred to as active speaker detection [6,22], have become popular, mostly adopting video and audio modalities. Multimodal approaches have either modelled the speech and visual cues such as facial, body cues jointly (e.g., [6]) or have performed audio speaker diarization while video has used to track/localize/associate a person to a speech (e.g., [11]). There are relatively few studies that have performed VAD based on video-based cues only (called visual-VAD in this paper). In fact, VAD with solely visual cues can be very desirable when the audio is not available due to technical or privacy related reasons. There can also be cases that the task of distinguishing voices robustly becomes very challenging such as in social gatherings, where much background noise is present. In such conditions, an effective visual-VAD can compensate audio speaker diarization.

The majority of the studies on visual-VAD have been performed based on lip motion detection, e.g., [4,12,16,18]. Facial expressions [20], hand movement [4,9,14], head activity [9], and visual focus of attention (VFOA) [14] are other cues that have been utilized. On the other hand, visual activity cues extracted from whole body (without specifically focusing on a certain body part such as hands or head) [7,10] can result in very effective VAD. For instance, whole upper body activity cues outperformed lip motion cues in [4].

There are diverse way to detect/represent the visual activity of a person to perform visual-VAD. For example, in [14], a combination of motion vectors, DCT (discrete cosine transform) coefficients and residual coding bit-rate were used. In [10], motion history images (MHI) were utilized. Optical flow has been another popular method to represent the visual activity as applied in [7]. Recently, in [4,5], improved trajectory features that comprise of a concatenation of Histogram of Oriented Gradients (HOG), Histogram of Flow (HoF) and Motion Boundary Histogram (MBH) features were used. These examples all resulted in hand-crafted visual activity features. On the other hand, deep learning models, such as Convolutional Neural Networks (CNN) have demonstrated state-of-the-art results for many research problems, including activity recognition and localization (e.g., [2,8]), which are highly related to visual activity detection and representation. Therefore, there is no reason not to exploit the effectiveness of CNNs to visual-VAD. However, the way visual activity is initially represented (called visual activity primitives, from now on in this paper) to be fed to CNNs for training, can be critical to perform an effective VAD. In detail, some primitives can result in better detection performance on average as compared to others, or can perform more consistent VAD performance so that the detector can work equally well for any speaker.

In this study, we compare the most popular visual activity primitives by modeling them with CNN for video-based VAD, which has never been addressed before. This comparative analysis is performed not only quantitatively but also qualitatively allowing us to better show why some primitives are performing better than others. Another contribution of this work is presenting improved performances as compared to the state-of-the-art (SOA) visual-VAD methods. The results obtained are also more stable such that the detection performances are equally good for all persons. The way we perform VAD is data-driven, does not use either labels or features belonging to the test data, thus, supports person-invariant training, i.e., it is not requiring model re-training for each new person. This is advantageous as compared to SOA presenting person-specific visual-VAD methods with hand-crafted visual activity features.

The rest of this paper is organized as follows. In Sect. 2, existing video-based VAD approaches are reviewed and the main differences between our work and theirs are highlighted. In Sect. 3, the details of the visual activity primitives and the way CNN fine-tuning is applied are described. The experimental setup is illustrated in Sect. 4 with a brief description of the dataset used. Subsequently, in Sect. 5, we compare the quantitative visual-VAD results of different visual activity primitives with the results of SOA, while qualitative comparisons are also performed among visual activity primitives. Finally, conclusive remarks and future work are sketched in Sect. 6.

2   Related Work

VAD solely based on video-based cues can be categorized in terms of the body parts investigated such as: face-based approaches that includes lip motion, head activity, face gestures, visual focus of attention (VFOA) etc., body-based methods, which contain hand gestures, full body motion, upper body motion, etc., or composition of these two categories.

As an earlier work on video-based VAD, in [18] the results of face detection, skin color, skin texture and mouth motion sensors have been combined and a Bayes Net model has been applied. In [16], facial movements corresponds to mouth, head and entire face have been extracted by Spatiotemporal Gabor filters, while mouth region gave the best VAD results. Haider et al. [12] analyzed the performance of head movement vs. head and lip movements together, and lip movement vs. lip and head movements together for speaker-dependent, speaker-independent or hybrid human-machine multiparty interactive dialogue settings. The results in that study [12] showed that head movement contributes to VAD significantly such that it outperforms lips movement except speaker-independent setting, and in overall, the fusion of head and lips movements perform the best. As seen, lip motion-based VAD is popular e.g.; [12,16,18] and effective. However, existing techniques are limited as detecting lip motion is not always possible. For instance, when speaker presents a profile view to the camera or the camera resolution is low, or the speaker is far away from the camera or the speaker's lips is occluded by her hands, facial features detectors fail to detect the lips.

Hung et al. [14] analyzed the correlation between gaze and hand activities and speaking status given the assumptions that; the speaker is the one who moves most, and group's gaze (detected in terms of VFOA) is more likely to be on the speaker than on others. In that study [14], the visual activity of hands were detected by Discrete Cosine Transform (DCT) coefficients and residual coding bit-rate, while VFOA was determined by a Bayesian approach. The output features were tested with supervised and unsupervised learning in small group meeting datasets, and the results approved the assumptions regarding VFOA and hand motion. By using the same small group meeting dataset with [14], Gebre et al. [10] proposed using motion history images (MHI) as a likelihood measure of speaking activity, which resulted in promising performance as compared to [14], although only one type of cue was used. Detecting VFOA, head motion, body activity, lip motion and face is relatively less challenging in the meeting datasets [10,14]. For instance, the detection of VFOA is drastically robust when there are individual cameras capturing each person specifically at close distance and in the meeting datasets [10,14], the cameras are always static, there are more than one cameras capturing participants from their frontal view, and the places of the cameras are known by the participants.

On the other hand, Cristani et al. [7] performed visual-VAD for surveillance scenarios where the camera is located in a more distant place as compared to the meeting or human-machine interactive dialogue environments. In that method [7], a local video descriptor, which extracts the optical flow of human body, and encodes optical flow energy and complexity using an entropy-like measure was applied. Although, the results presented in [7] were successful, it is important to highlight that, the dataset they used has a top-view that already diminishes the possibility of occlusions and also the frames that the region of interests overlap (i.e., inter-person occlusions) were discarded from their analyses.

Directional audio information was used to label improved trajectory features extracted from upper body tracks of people as speaking or not-speaking in [4]. These labels were used for the training of an SVM to perform visual-VAD. Improved trajectories obtained for each 15 consecutive frames, pooled by a fisher vector representation were represented by the spatio-temporal features i.e.; the mean pixel location of the trajectory, and Histogram of Gradients (HoG), Histogram of Flow (HoF) and Motion Boundary Histogram (MBH). Chakravarty et al. [5] extended that scheme [4] to an online learning setting, starting from a generic VAD, which gradually adapts itself to a specific person. One drawback of that study [5] is, performing person-specific VAD, which requires training data for each new person. Additionally, even though, [5] performed person-specific

VAD, the results were still fluctuated, such that VAD was performed well for some persons, while for others highly insufficient results were obtained.

More recently, deep learning-based feature extraction has become common for visual-VAD as well. For instance, in [20], face features have been extracted from AlexNet, then Long Short-Term Memory (LSTM) has been used to model the temporal dependencies between face features over time, which was used to perform VAD in real-time multiparty interactions. That study is different than ours as focusing on face features and also limited due to requiring tightly cropped face images.

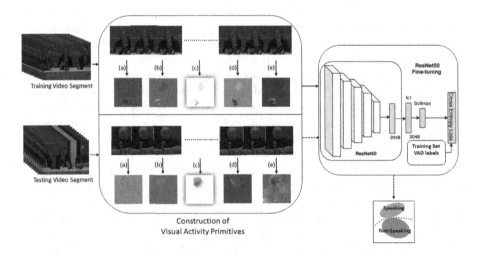

Fig. 1. The overall illustration of the methodology. See text for details.

3   Methodology

The methodology applied to compare visual activity primitives is illustrated in Fig. 1. During training, for each consecutive 10 RGB video frames, visual activity primitives: *(a)* optical flow image (OFI) as proposed in [3], *(b)* OFI as presented in [23], *(c)* dynamic image (DI) as proposed in [2], *(d)* the combination of OFI [3] with DI and *(e)* the combination of OFI [23] with DI are obtained. For each type of image, a ResNet50 model is fine-tuned with the VAD labels (speaking or not-speaking). Given a test video, the same type of primitive whichever ResNet50 model is fine-tuned with, is obtained and, softmax is used to perform classification (end-to-end). Alternatively, the fine-tuned ResNet50 model is used to extract features, which are given to a Support Vector Machine (SVM) trained with the same training data ResNet50 is fine-tuned. The predicted label corresponds to the test video frames, those the test optical flow images or dynamic images (or the combinations of both) are constructed from.

3.1   Visual Activity Primitives

A video segment having 10 frames is given as an example in Fig. 2 with the five visual activity primitives obtained from it. This 10 frames are equal to: one RGB dynamic image (DI), three optical flow images (OFI) obtained as in [3], three OFI obtained as in [23] and optical flow based dynamic images i.e.; one DI image for each optical flow method. These primitives are described as follows.

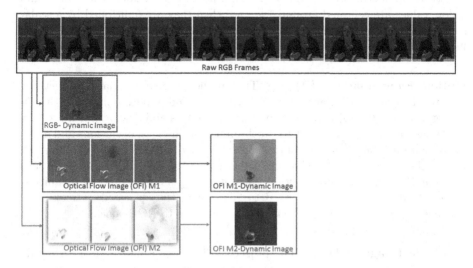

Fig. 2. Visual activity primitives: (1) RGB-dynamic image, (2) optical flow image M1; refers to [3], (3) optical flow image M2; refers to [23], (4) dynamic image obtained from optical flow image M1 and (5) dynamic image obtained from optical flow image M2. This example shows a video segment composed of 10 frames while the person is speaking.

Optical Flow Image (OFI) [3]: The main objective of the optical flow methods is to calculate a flow field by estimating the motion of pixels between two images. In this study, for all optical flow methods, this is performed for every F_i and F_{i+3} frames, such that F_{i+1} and F_{i+2} are discarded from the calculation. In other words, for every 30 frames (equals to 1 second for the dataset used), we obtain 10 OFIs. We discard the frames F_{i+1} and F_{i+2} to be able to better represent the motion because the image differencing applied to the consecutive frames showed that, the motion between two successive frames are very small, i.e. not creating informative flow images.

Brox et al. [3] presents a variational approach that applies a coarse-to-fine warping strategy to combine three assumptions: the gradient constancy, the grey-value constancy and the spatio-temporal smoothness constraint of the optical flow estimation. The gradient constancy deals with the aperture problem while the grey value constancy assumption makes the method robust against grey value changes. The spatio-temporal smoothness constraint allows to estimate the displacement of a pixel only locally by taking the interaction between neighbouring pixels into account. Given these, there are three parameters to be set: the weight between the grey value and the gradient constancy assumption, the smoothness parameter and the Gaussian convolution parameter to pre-process the input images. In our experiments smoothness parameter is 80, weight is 5 and Gaussian parameter is 0.9, which are empirically found. Once the optical flow is computed as described, we obtain the flow RGB images such that the first two channels are obtained from x and y flow values, respectively. The x and y flow values are centered around 128 and, then they are multiplied by a scalar such that they fall between 0–255. The third channel is created with the flow magnitude.

Optical Flow Image (OFI) [23]: This method is also a variational method, uses total variation regularization with L1-norm and applies point-wise thresholding strategy. Its objective is to preserve the edges and discontinuities in flow field while being robust against to the illumination changes, occlusions and noise. For visualization purpose, the optical flow field in x and y directions are normalized in the range of $[-1, 1]$, which is further converted into HSV color space such that hue (H) indicates the direction, saturation (S) is represented by magnitude of flow field and value (V) is fixed to 255. Then, the optical flow images are obtained by converting them from HSV color space to RGB space.

Dynamic Image (DI) [2]: The objective of dynamic image [2] is to obtain a compact representation of a video sequence summarizing the appearance and dynamics of it. DI discards the static pixels such as background pixels and focuses on the object in an action. Construction of a DI contains rank-pooling that encodes the temporal evolution of the frames. The resulting DI can be used to fine-tune any CNN model. Herein, DIs are obtained from RBG data (i.e., raw video frames) or from OFIs extracted as described above.

3.2 ResNet50 Fine-Tuning

Training a CNN from scratch might not be effective if the size of the data is limited. In this case, an alternative way is to fine-tune a pre-trained CNN model. Given the better performance of ResNet50 as compared to many other architectures [13], all the analysis regarding visual activity primitives are applied by fine-tuning ResNet50 (pre-trained on ImageNet dataset). During fine-tuning, a fully-connected layer having 2048 neurons is added after the final convolution layer. Its weights are randomly initialized and are updated during training. The weights of convolution layers are not updated. This model is trained with an end-to-end manner while cross entropy loss function, Adam optimizer, and $10e^{-5}$ learning rate are applied for 20 epochs.

The training data (more details are given in Sect. 4) is highly imbalanced such that there are a lot more not-speaking segments than speaking segments, which can mislead the classification task and result in poor performance. To overcome this, the training data in each batch (in total 128 samples) is balanced such that equal amount of randomly selected speaking and not-speaking samples (64 samples for each) are used. Furthermore, data augmentation is also applied such that some randomly selected training images are horizontally flipped and/or a 64×64 randomly selected patch is replaced with the mean value of the images, which can be observed as a dropout in input layer.

3.3 Classifier Learning and Inference

The ResNet50 fine-tuning of all visual activity primitives are applied with Softmax, which are used to classify the test data as speaking or not-speaking as well. Additionally, we apply a linear SVM for the best performing visual activity primitives to perform more fair comparisons with SOA [5]. The SVM kernel parameter C is taken as 10^k while $k = \{-4, -3, -2, -1, 0, 1, 2, 3, 4\}$.

Table 1. F1-scores (%). AVG and STD stand for average and standard deviation of F1-scores of all speakers, respectively. W, OFI, DI mean window size, optical flow image and dynamic image, respectively. The best results are emphasized in bold-face.

Method	Bell	Bollinger	Lieberman	Long	Sick	AVG	STD	Details
[5]	82.90	65.80	73.60	86.90	81.80	78.20	8.45	$W = 10$, SVM
[5]	90.30	69.00	82.40	96.00	89.30	85.40	10.36	$W = 100$, SVM
[6]	**93.70**	83.40	86.80	**97.70**	86.10	**89.54**	5.94	$W = 10$
OFI [3]	84.01	69.25	68.8	53.31	68.19	68.71	9.71	Softmax
OFI [23]	85.63	81.73	80.12	69.36	70.83	77.53	6.35	Softmax
RGB-DI	86.07	**93.30**	**91.88**	73.62	86.34	**86.24**	6.94	Softmax
RGB-DI	86.34	**93.78**	**92.34**	76.09	86.25	**86.96**	6.24	SVM
OFI [3]-DI	84.08	72.27	80.57	60.01	68.89	73.164	8.56	Softmax
OFI [23]-DI	**89.97**	86.56	85.15	82.46	85.43	**85.91**	**2.44**	Softmax
OFI [23]-DI	89.16	88.82	85.82	81.39	85.97	**86.23**	**2.79**	SVM

4   Experimental Setup

The visual activity primitives are compared using publicly available dataset, called Columbia [5], which contains a 87 minutes-long video (frame rate: 30 frames per second) of a panel discussion. The field of the view of the camera changes to focus on smaller groups of panelist at a time. Following SOA, we only focus on the parts of the video where there is more than one person in the frame and discard any person in the margins of the video. This results in 5 speakers (Bell, Bollinger, Lieberman, Long, Sick) out of 7, while 2–3 speakers are visible per frame. In order to compare our results with SOA [5], we use the VAD labels (speaking/not-speaking) belonging to these 5 persons for each video frame. As per the performed analyses, the whole upper body motion of each speaker is used (in other words, the entire body parts that are visible). Finally, leave-one-person-out cross validation with F1-score as the evaluation metric is used still for comparative purposes [5].

5   Results

The best SOA results [5,6] and the best result of each visual activity primitive with Softmax are given in Table 1. For the best performing visual activity primitives, their results with SVM are also given. As seen, the average performance of the visual activity primitives: RGB-DI, and OFI [23]-DI are the best out of all primitives and they also perform better than visual modality based SOA [5] method, no matter Softmax or SVM is used. Among all the SOA based on multi-modality, the method in [6] performed best as it uses audio and lip based visual information. The lip based visual information is not always reliable if the subject is more expressive through body motion. As shown in Table 1 the performance of RGB-DI for Bollinger and Lieberman is quite high as compared to multi-modality based SOA method [6], where in case Long (subject), it is the opposite. The performance of SOA [5] is highly dependent on the choice of window size (W) of temporal continuity algorithm that is based on the heuristics that if a person is speaking it is more likely that she will continue speaking for a while rather than stop speaking. Using temporal continuity largely corrected the mis-classification results, but it is not clear how the window size of the temporal continuity should be selected to obtain accurate VAD results. Given that we create dynamic images for each 10 consecutive frames, it can be fairer to compare the performances with SOA [5] while W is equal to 10. In this case, all visual activity primitives except OFI [3] and OFI [3]-DI, perform better than SOA [5].

Better average visual-VAD performance is definitely very important but having low VAD standard deviation (STD) of all speakers while still performing well on average, is also significant. In detail, the performance of SOA [5] has fluctuations such that it performs well for some persons (e.g., Long: 86.90%), while performs highly worse for some others (e.g., Bollinger: 65.89%). This can be observed from the high STD values, 8.45% and 10.36% as well. In other words, this means that SOA [5] is not able to overcome domain-shift problem such that the distributions of training data and the test data are different from each other, which results in poorer VAD performance for some speakers. Domain-shift problem is highly possible for visual-VAD given that the way people moves while speaking varies a lot from person to person, resulting in dissimilar visual activity representations, as also mentioned in the psychology literature. On the other hand, the performance of any visual activity primitives is more consistent showing the superiority of $fc1$ features of ResNet50 as compared to the features of SOA. Especially, OFI [23]-DI is able to detect speaking and not-speaking video segments equally well for every speaker.

5.1   Qualitative Analysis

Given 4 video segments, each composed of 10 video frames, two of them having the ground-truth label (GT) "speaking" and other two having GT "not-speaking", we visualize the class activation maps in Fig. 3 using the approach in [19] for the ResNet50 fine-tuned for VAD using visual activity primitives separately. Grad-CAM [19] is used to localize class-discriminative regions while they are overlaid with the intermediate raw RBG frame of the corresponding video segment in Fig. 3.

For the video segments having GT=speaking, it is expected that head and hand motions are detected as the body of the person is more stable. Out of all, OFI [3] (M1) is weaker to detect these motions, while RGB-DI and OFI [23] (M2)-DI localize the hands and head motions the best. For video segments having GT = not-speaking, in the first one, the person is slightly raising her hands up, whereas in the second one, the person is drinking water. RGB-DI and especially OFI M2-DI are still good at detecting the motions and more importantly, they are able to differentiate these types of motions from the motions during speech, i.e., they classify the frames correctly. However, OFI-M1 localizes other parts of the image such as background or the area close to person's shoulder, where the motion is very subtle to allow the correct classification of these frames. These results are in line with the quantitative results, showing that RGB-DI and OFI [23] (M2)-DI are better to localize the motion correlated with speech.

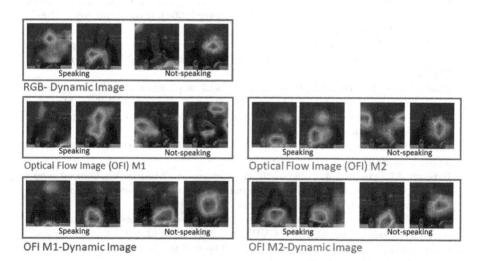

Fig. 3. The visualization of the class-discriminative regions overlaid with the intermediate raw RGB frame of the video segments when ResNet50 trained with visual activity primitives separately is used. Red regions in the heat map correspond to the high scores for the ground-truth class. M1 refers to [3] and M2 refers to [23]. (Color figure online)

6   Conclusions

We have addressed video-based voice activity detection (VAD) task with cues from whole body motion with a data-driven person-invariant setting. A detailed analysis was realized to compare the visual activity primitives representing the body motion, which are fed into CNNs to learn an effective VAD model. Some visual activity primitives resulted in better detection on average, while performing equally well for all speakers. Our detection results are also better on average and more consistent than the current literature.

As future work, a novel, effective way of combining these visual activity primitives will be investigated to perform visual-VAD in more complex scenarios such as in crowd or multiparty egocentric video streams, after construction of new benchmark datasets.

References

1. Beyan, C., Capozzi, F., Becchio, C., Murino, V.: Prediction of the leadership style of an emergent leader using audio and visual nonverbal features. IEEE Trans. Multimedia **20**(2), 441–456 (2018)
2. Bilen, H., Fernando, B., Gavves, E., Vedaldi, A., Gould, S.: Dynamic image networks for action recognition. In: IEEE CVPR (2016)
3. Brox, T., Bruhn, A., Papenberg, N., Weickert, J.: High accuracy optical flow estimation based on a theory for warping. In: Pajdla, T., Matas, J. (eds.) ECCV 2004. LNCS, vol. 3024, pp. 25–36. Springer, Heidelberg (2004). https://doi.org/10.1007/978-3-540-24673-2_3
4. Chakravarty, P., Mirzaei, S., Tuytelaars, T., hamme, H.V.: Who's speaking?: audio-supervised classification of active speakers in video. In: ACM ICMI, pp. 87–90 (2015)
5. Chakravarty, P., Tuytelaars, T.: Cross-modal supervision for learning active speaker detection in video. In: Leibe, B., Matas, J., Sebe, N., Welling, M. (eds.) ECCV 2016. LNCS, vol. 9909, pp. 285–301. Springer, Cham (2016). https://doi.org/10.1007/978-3-319-46454-1_18
6. Chung, J.S., Zisserman, A.: Learning to lip read words by watching videos. CVIU **173**, 76–85 (2018)
7. Cristani, M., Pesarin, A., Vinciarelli, A., Crocco, M., Murino, V.: Look at who's talking: voice activity detection by automated gesture analysis. In: International Joint Conference on Ambient Intelligence, pp. 72–80 (2011)
8. Donahue, J., et al.: Long-term recurrent convolutional networks for visual recognition and description. In: IEEE CVPR, pp. 2625–2634 (2015)
9. Gebre, B.G., Wittenburg, P., Heskes, T.: The gesturer is the speaker. In: IEEE ICASSP, pp. 3751–3755 (2013)
10. Gebre, B.G., Wittenburg, P., Heskes, T., Drude, S.: Motion history images for online speaker/signer diarization. In: IEEE ICASSP, pp. 1537–1541 (2014)
11. Gebru, I.D., Ba, S., Li, X., Horaud, R.: Audio-visual speaker diarization based on spatiotemporal bayesian fusion. IEEE Trans. PAMI **40**(5), 1086–1099 (2018)
12. Haider, F., Campbell, N., Luz, S.: Active speaker detection in human machine multiparty dialogue using visual prosody information. In: IEEE GlobalSIP, pp. 1207–1211 (2016)

13. He, K., Zhang, X., Ren, S., Sun, J.: Deep residual learning for image recognition. In: IEEE CVPR, pp. 770–778 (2016)
14. Hung, H., Ba, S.O.: Speech/non-speech detection in meetings from automatically extracted low resolution visual features. In: IEEE ICASSP (2010)
15. Jayagopi, D.B., Hung, H., Yeo, C., Gatica-Perez, D.: Modeling dominance in group conversations using nonverbal activity cues. IEEE Trans. Audio, Speech Lang. Process. **17**(3), 501–513 (2009)
16. Joosten, B., Postma, E., Krahmer, E.: Voice activity detection based on facial movement. J. Multimodal User Interfaces **9**(3), 183–193 (2015)
17. Lepri, B., Subramanian, R., Kalimeri, K., Staiano, J., Pianesi, F., Sebe, N.: Employing social gaze and speaking activity for automatic determination of the extraversion trait. In: ACM ICMI-MLMI (2013)
18. Rehg, J.M., Murphy, K.P., Fieguth, P.W.: Vision-based speaker detection using bayesian networks. In: IEEE CVPR, vol. 2, pp. 110–116 (1999)
19. Selvaraju, R.R., Cogswell, M., Das, A., Vedantam, R., Parikh, D., Batra, D.: Grad-CAM: visual explanations from deep networks via gradient-based localization. In: IEEE ICCV, October 2017
20. Stefanov, K., Beskow, J., Salvi, G.: Vision-based active speaker detection in multi-party interaction. In: International Workshop Grounding Language Understanding, pp. 47–51 (2017)
21. Tranter, S.E., Reynolds, D.A.: An overview of automatic speaker diarization systems. IEEE Trans. Audio, Speech Lang. Process. **14**(5), 1557–1565 (2006)
22. Vajaria, H., Sarkar, S., Kasturi, R.: Exploring co-occurence between speech and body movement for audio-guided video localization. IEEE Trans. CSVT **18**(11), 1608–1617 (2008)
23. Zach, C., Pock, T., Bischof, H.: A duality based approach for realtime tv-l1 optical flow. In: DAGM Conference on Pattern Recognition, pp. 214–223 (2007)

Vehicle Trajectories from Unlabeled Data Through Iterative Plane Registration

Federico Becattini[✉][iD], Lorenzo Seidenari[iD], Lorenzo Berlincioni[iD], Leonardo Galteri[iD], and Alberto Del Bimbo[iD]

Media Integration and Communication Center (MICC), University of Florence, Florence, Italy
{federico.becattini,lorenzo.seidenari,lorenzo.berlincioni, leonardo.galteri,alberto.delbimbo}@unifi.it

Abstract. One of the most complex aspects of autonomous driving concerns understanding the surrounding environment. In particular, the interest falls on detecting which agents are populating it and how they are moving. The capacity to predict how these may act in the near future would allow an autonomous vehicle to safely plan its trajectory, minimizing the risks for itself and others. In this work we propose an automatic trajectory annotation method exploiting an Iterative Plane Registration algorithm based on homographies and semantic segmentations. The output of our technique is a set of holistic trajectories (past-present-future) paired with a single image context, useful to train a predictive model.

Keywords: Autonomous driving · Trajectory prediction

1 Introduction

Autonomous driving the past years has been one of the fields in which machine learning and artificial intelligence were applied the most. Even though significant steps forward have been made [2], the problem is yet far to be solved. The complexity stems from the many facets of different nature that need to be taken into account: in addition to the actual movement of the car itself, a thorough understanding of the surrounding scene needs to be obtained, both for what concerns static components such as road layout and other moving agents [3]. To allow an effective planning of a safe route towards its destination, the autonomous car needs to recognize other agents and model their dynamics to the point of predicting their future behavior.

Predicting agents' future trajectories is a problem that can benefit from a complete understanding of the scene. The surrounding layout acts indeed as a physical constraint that outlines the possible routes that the vehicle can undertake. Without relying on maps or geolocalization sensors though, scene comprehension based only on computer vision systems can turn out to be extremely complex due to occlusion, background clutter and scene variability. Scene parsing

E. Ricci et al. (Eds.): ICIAP 2019, LNCS 11751, pp. 60–70, 2019.
https://doi.org/10.1007/978-3-030-30642-7_6

and semantic segmentation methods [6] can aid with this problem by providing a semantic category for each observed pixel.

On the other hand, modeling object dynamics from an autonomous car perspective is a hard task by itself. Since the observer is constantly moving, the first obstacle one has to deal with is separating the two observed motions: the real motion of agents and the apparent motion caused by the moving camera. The common approach in generating datasets to train autonomous vehicles involves the use of costly laser based range finders in order to obtain precise environment measurements and the integration of GPS sensors in order to refer such coordinates into the real world [11]. Currently dash cameras can be deployed at a very low cost on vehicles, indeed a simple video search for *Dash Camera* on a video repository such as Youtube yields hundred of thousands distinct results. Interestingly, mining videos from the web allows to obtain data on dangerous situations such as accidents which are not ethically reproducible in a controlled dataset.

In this paper we move the first steps towards a method that will allow to generate trajectory datasets from real-world scenarios without the need of an instrumented vehicle and hours of driving. We propose an automatic pipeline finalized to the generation of holistic trajectories composed by past-present-future positions of all other agents. We obtain trajectories for each frame in a video sequence, starting only from an RGB stream, without relying on complex sensors such as LIDARs or external sources like maps. Our pipeline is composed by several modules aimed at tracking both agents and the ground plane on which they are moving. By combining semantic segmentations and local descriptors we estimate a transformation to map the ground plane from one frame to another, enabling the projection of object positions through time, onto a desired frame (Fig. 1). We refer to this process as *Iterative Plane Registration (IPR)*.

The paper is organized as follows. In Sect. 2 we frame our method into an appropriate literature review. Section 3 is dedicated to our proposed technique,

Fig. 1. Holistic trajectories shown on the reference frame. Past: full squares. Present: full circle. Future: empty squares.

providing an outline of the Iterative Plane Registration algorithm. In Sect. 4 we show the obtained results and we draw conclusions in Sect. 5.

2   Related Work

Recently several works targeted trajectory prediction [1,15,21]. The majority of this line of research targets non motorized vehicles and pedestrian trajectories [1,21]. For proper path planning of autonomous vehicles a full understanding of every moving agent behavior is necessary.

Collecting data for autonomous driving is a complex, slow and expensive procedure. Most autonomous driving datasets [7,11,14,18,25] are collected with cars equipped with several dedicated sensors: dash cameras provide footage, stereo rigs are used to obtain depth, laser scanners (LIDARs) generate cloud points, Inertial Measurement Units (IMU) log how the vehicle is moving and position is pinned down with GPS. As an example KITTI [11], provides all the above sources at 10 Hz.

The lack of trajectory information at a large scale is currently a limitation of many commonly used datasets, such as Cityscapes [7]. Only a few datasets nowadays contain trajectory information. KITTI [11] has a small fraction of the dataset annotated for object tracking; Berkeley Deep Drive (BDD) [25] provides instance level segmentations with consistent IDs across frames and nuScenes [5] has trajectory informations for the short video snippets that compose the dataset. None of these datasets offers a satisfactory number of trajectories to train a prediction model. The ApolloScape dataset [14] has been recently extended with approximately 80k trajectories for a new trajectory prediction task [18]. Trajectories are obtained combining LIDAR and IMU readings and are represented in a world reference system, which is the most common setting for this task [15,22]. Similarly, other common datasets dedicated only to pedestrian trajectories [20,21] are in a top view reference system. This way of representing data is easy to process and evaluate, yet is hard to obtain due to the need of a laser scanner and loosens the correlation between pixels and vehicle dynamics. Nonetheless, these datasets have a high cost. They require the instrumentation of a car with cameras, inertial sensors, gps and even more expensive sensors such as LIDARs. Moreover, it must be taken into account the human effort in driving the instrumented vehicle and in the annotation phase if no automatic object labeling and tracking is used.

Differently from previous approaches, we avoid these problems by collecting full trajectories directly in the frame reference, pairing past and future paths to what the car has in front, mimicking what humans see when driving. Furthermore we do not require any specific equipment and we work solely with RGB frames. This aspect also thins the acquisition process since any dash cam recorded video (even scraped from the web, e.g. YouTube) can be used to generate trajectories, instead of relying on heavily equipped fleets.

Simultaneous Localization and Mapping (SLAM) [4] is a basic tool for any autonomous driving platform, providing ego-motion estimation, 3D reconstruction and self-localisation in a single optimization framework. Recently deep learning based frameworks [23,24] have been used to improve classical feature based SLAM algorithms [19]; the idea is either to provide single view depth estimation or directly computing frame-to-frame local feature correspondences.

Our proposed method shares some common traits with SLAM. Both approaches have a module dedicated to inferring the motion of the ego-vehicle: IPR by tracking the 2D ground plane and SLAM by tracking the whole 3D environment. Despite this similarity, the goal of the two methods is very different since we want to retain exactly what SLAM discards, i.e. model the dynamics of other vehicles rather than reconstructing ego-motion and the static environment. Indeed SLAM could serve as a ground motion estimator in our pipeline. Nonetheless SLAM algorithms require internal calibration parameters, while our approach is suitable for any RGB sequence.

3 Iterative Plane Registration

Iterative Plane Registration (IPR) is an procedure to track the ground plane in a video and obtain a series of homographies that can transform points across different frames. We refer to IPR as a meta-algorithm since it outlines a generic algorithmic procedure based on different computer vision modules, without relying on any specific model or architecture. The modules composing the Iterative Plane Registration meta-algorithm are shown in Fig. 2 and are the following: object detector, multiple target tracker, semantic segmentation model, local keypoint detector and descriptor and homography estimator.

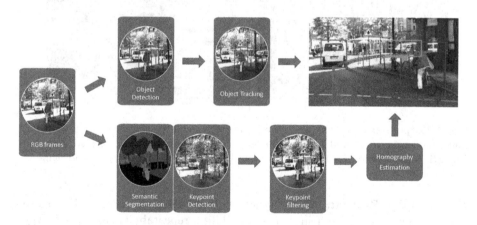

Fig. 2. Iterative Plane Registration pipeline. Objects are detected and tracked. The ground plane is tracked with an homography estimated through keypoints detected in the image and filtered with the semantic segmentation. Chains of homographies are estimated to warp the position of the objects across frames.

The advantage of defining IPR as a meta-algorithm is that, thanks to its highly modular nature, it can be easily updated by replacing its building blocks keeping up with future state of the art advancements.

Object Detection and Tracking. Agents have to be localized in each frame and tracked across the whole video. To this end, we use Mask-RCNN [13] as object detector and the bounding box association algorithm proposed in [8] as multiple target tracker. The method matches bounding boxes in consecutive frames according to their intersection over union and thus generates spatio-temporal tubes enclosing the objects. To ensure an accurate matching, bounding box future positions are predicted using dense optical flow [9] to compensate object and ego motion. To be able to detect relevant objects in an urban scene, we use a Mask-RCNN model pretrained on MS-COCO [16] and we track only objects which are relevant to our task, i.e. objects labeled by the detector as *car, person, bicycle, motorbike, truck* or *train*.

Semantic Segmentation Based Keypoint Detection. In order to estimate reliable transformations to map the ground plane from a frame to another, we extract local keypoints from the scene and filter them using the output of a semantic segmentation method. As keypoints we use SIFT [17], masking the input image with the semantic segmentation provided by DeepLab v3+ [6]. Since we want to obtain keypoints belonging to the ground plane, we retain only the ones centered in pixels labeled as *road* or *sidewalk*, independently of the scale of the detected keypoint.

Fig. 3. Keypoint matching between two frames. When all the keypoints are used (left), correspondences are found all over the scene. When keypoints are filtered with the semantic segmentation (right) matches are reliably found only on the ground plane.

Homography Estimation. In the following experiments we use SIFT since they are the best trade-off in terms of stability, repeatability and speed. Any other local feature could be employed in principle. SIFT keypoints and their associated descriptors are used to estimate homographies between frames. This is done using Random Sample Consensus (RANSAC) [10] between the two set of matching keypoints L_{t_i} and $L_{t_{i+1}}$, belonging to frames at time t_i and t_{i+1}. RANSAC finds the transformation $\mathbf{H}_{t_i}$ that maps keypoints $k_{t_i}^j \in L_{t_i}$ in their correspondent ones $k_{ti+1}^j \in L_{t+1}$ in the next frame, rejecting outlier correspondences. The semantic segmentation filter over all the keypoints in the scene is necessary since we only want to model the planar homography for the pixels belonging to the actual road. By doing so we are working unders the assumption that the ground can be locally approximated by a planar surface. Without relying on the semantic segmentation we cannot establish the correct correspondences between keypoints, yielding to an incorrect homography. Figure 3 shows an example of matched keypoints between two frames, with and without the segmentation mask. It can be seen that without segmenting the scene, it is likely to establish correspondences between other planar surfaces, such as buildings, which are often rich in texture and therefore keypoints.

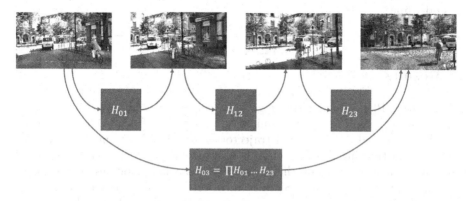

Fig. 4. Chained homographies to warp points lying on the ground plane across frames.

Trajectory Projection. To generate holistic trajectories of other agents in a given frame F_{t_i}, we project their positions in other frames F_{t_j} using a chain of homographies from t_j to t_i:

$$H = \prod H_{t_k} \quad \forall t_k \in [t_j, t_i]. \tag{1}$$

This procedure is also depicted in Fig. 4.

To map points forward in time we use the homographies estimated between pairs of consecutive frames, while to map points backward in time we use inverse homographies. Since each homography can only transform points belonging to the ground plane we cannot warp bounding boxes. We therefore project only the lower edge middle point of a bounding box, which is guaranteed to lie on the ground plane. An example of generated trajectories is depicted in Fig. 1.

Combining chains of homographies may lead to incorrect results due to numerical instability. To determine whether an homography is valid or not, we check the determinant of the transformation matrix [12]: $\det(\mathbf{H}) > 0$. If an homography is not valid, we interrupt the chain of homographies and we stop projecting the trajectories, marking the remaining portion as invalid.

Algorithm 1. Iterative Plane Registration

Input: RGB video sequence $F_{t_i}, t_i \in [t_0, t_{end}]$
Output: Homography set

1: Initial timestep t_0.
2: **while** $t_i < t_{end}$ **do**
3:     Apply semantic segmentation algorithm (e.g. DeepLab [6]) to frame F_{t_i}, obtaining a pixel-wise labeling $S_{t_i}^c, c \in \{\texttt{'road'}, \texttt{'car'}, \texttt{'sidewalk'} \ldots\}$.
4:     Extract local keypoints L_{t_i} (e.g. SIFT [17]) from F_{t_i}.
5:     Discard keypoints not laying on the ground plane based on the semantic segmentation: $L'_{t_i} = \{k \in L_{t_i} \text{ s.t. } S_{t_i}[k_x, k_y] \in \{\texttt{'road'}, \texttt{'sidewalk'}\}\}$
6:     Estimate homography to map the ground between frames $F_{t_{i-1}}$ and F_{t_i}: $\mathbf{H}_{t_{i-1}t_i} = \texttt{RANSAC}(L'_{t_{i-1}}, L'_{t_i})$
7:     $t_i = t_{i+1}$;
8: **end while**
9: **return** $\{\mathbf{H}_{t_i}\}$

---

4 Results

The Iterative Plane Registration algorithm can be used on any driving video taken from a dashcam since it requires no annotation. To provide an evaluation of the method, we generated trajectories for all LIDAR annotated videos in the KITTI tracking training set [11]. To evaluate how accurately we register the ground plane, we turn off the detection and tracking modules and consider annotated trajectories instead. Since each trajectory is annotated as a collection of 3D bounding boxes, we warp across frames the center of their lower face. Once the holistic trajectories are obtained, we project them in the LIDAR metric coordinate system using a frame to world homography. Whereas projecting points from LIDAR to frame can be done by changing coordinate system and using the camera projection matrix P, the opposite is not as1 straightforward since P is not invertible. To this end we estimate an homography between the pair of points belonging to the ground plane in the two reference systems. Differently from what happens in the IPR pipeline, we do not need to detect and match keypoints to estimate the homography since there is a direct correspondence between frame pixels and LIDAR points. We only need to filter the points by taking only the ones belonging to the ground plane, which can be done with the semantic segmentation of the scene [6]. The frame to world transformation allows us to project the estimated trajectories in the LIDAR metric reference system and to compare them with the ground truth, obtaining an error in meters (Fig. 5).

Figure 6 (left) shows the distribution of samples, i.e. individual points, as a function of the temporal offset from the current frame and the $\mathcal{L}_2$ distance from the ground truth. Most of the samples have a negligible error since almost half of the points lie in a 5 m radius from the target. Increasing the temporal offset, points estimates become less precise as an effect of error propagation when combining long chains of homographies (Algorithm 1). Furthermore some

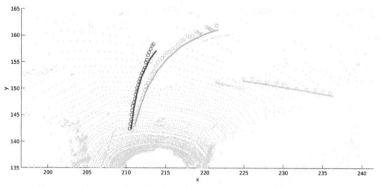

Fig. 5. Generated trajectories in the frame reference system (top) and comparison with ground truth in the LIDAR metric reference system (bottom).

samples exhibit high errors, which are mainly caused by instabilities in warping points far away from the camera, as shown in Fig. 6 (right). On the other hand, it has to be noted that the most relevant signal is in the first seconds ahead. We consider the most useful time span for training a prediction algorithm to be 12 s in the future. Therefore we report in Fig. 7 the distribution of errors for all points in an 12 s horizon.

We also analyze the error in function of distance from the sensor. As can be seen in Fig. 6, below 50 m of distance errors are mostly below 5 m. This distance can be regarded as a common visibility horizon in urban scenarios, with junctions, curved road and occlusions due to traffic. Consider that the KITTI LIDAR sensor reach is 120 m but we can, in certain cases obtain farther distances by ground plane registration.

Another interesting evaluation concerns the number of trajectories we are able to obtain. To this end we ran the Iterative Plane Registration algorithm on the whole KITTI tracking dataset (both train and test). We generate trajectories up to 12 s (120 frames at 10 FPS), both in the past and in the future. According to the determinant criterion explained in Sect. 3, parts of tracks generated by invalid homographies are discarded.

In Fig. 8 we show the number of obtained trajectories, as a function of past and future length. Both valid and invalid trajectories are shown. Interestingly enough, invalid homographies concern mostly past trajectories. This is due to

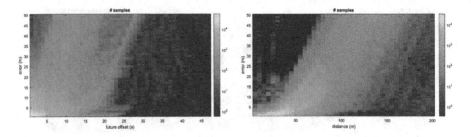

Fig. 6. Distribution of errors over samples (individual points) as a function of future offset (left) and distance (right).

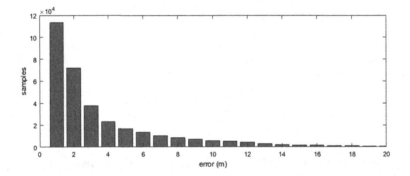

Fig. 7. Error distribution for points up to 12 s in the future.

the fact that from a car perspective the ground plane is observed from the car ahead, therefore the estimated homographies will be less precise in the portion of the plane behind the observer, which is often where the other agents lie in past time-steps.

Despite this, we are able to generate a surprisingly high number of trajectories, both in past and future directions. On the KITTI tracking dataset we obtain approximately 55K and 73K samples for the training and test set respectively, with an average of 6.7 trajectories per image. Note that the whole KITTI tracking dataset only contains 896 training trajectories. The different nature of our trajectories allows us to obtain a much higher number of samples both for training and for testing. This high number of trajectories stems from the fact that we are generating a new holistic trajectory from each frame in which the agent is observed. Whereas these trajectories are correlated since they represent the same agent, the resulting series of points is quite different due to camera motion and context variability. Overall, this acts as a form of data augmentation over existing trajectories, multiplying the occurrences of a trajectory for each frame in which the object is present.

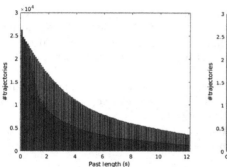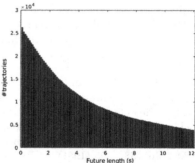

Fig. 8. Number of obtainable trajectories on the KITTI dataset (*train*) as a function of past and future number of frames. Both valid (blue) and invalid (red) trajectories are shown. (Color figure online)

5 Conclusions

In this paper we presented the Iterative Plane Registration meta-algorithm, a procedure for collecting holistic trajectories of agents in urban scenarios without requiring any prior annotation. The generated trajectories are composed by past, present, and future positions, all projected into a single frame context. Thanks to Iterative Plane Registration we are able to obtain an extremely high number of trajectories which can be used to train predictive models for autonomous driving vehicles.

Acknowledgements. This work has been developed within a collaboration with IMRA Europe. We gratefully acknowledge the support of NVIDIA Corporation with the donation of the Titan Xp GPU used for this research.

References

1. Alahi, A., Goel, K., Ramanathan, V., Robicquet, A., Fei-Fei, L., Savarese, S.: Social LSTM: human trajectory prediction in crowded spaces. In: Proceedings of CVPR, pp. 961–971 (2016)
2. Badue, C., et al.: Self-driving cars: a survey. arXiv preprint arXiv:1901.04407 (2019)
3. Berlincioni, L., Becattini, F., Galteri, L., Seidenari, L., Del Bimbo, A.: Road layout understanding by generative adversarial inpainting. arXiv preprint arXiv:1805.11746 (2018)
4. Bresson, G., Alsayed, Z., Yu, L., Glaser, S.: Simultaneous localization and mapping: a survey of current trends in autonomous driving. IEEE Trans. Intell. Veh. **20**, 1 (2017)
5. Caesar, H., et al.: nuScenes: a multimodal dataset for autonomous driving. arXiv preprint arXiv:1903.11027 (2019)
6. Chen, L.C., Papandreou, G., Schroff, F., Adam, H.: Rethinking atrous convolution for semantic image segmentation. arXiv preprint arXiv:1706.05587 (2017)

7. Cordts, M., et al.: The cityscapes dataset. In: Proceedings of CVPRW (2015)

8. Cuffaro, G., Becattini, F., Baecchi, C., Seidenari, L., Del Bimbo, A.: Segmentation free object discovery in video. In: Hua, G., Jégou, H. (eds.) ECCV 2016. LNCS, vol. 9915, pp. 25–31. Springer, Cham (2016). https://doi.org/10.1007/978-3-319-49409-8_4

9. Farnebäck, G.: Two-frame motion estimation based on polynomial expansion. In: Bigun, J., Gustavsson, T. (eds.) SCIA 2003. LNCS, vol. 2749, pp. 363–370. Springer, Heidelberg (2003). https://doi.org/10.1007/3-540-45103-X_50

10. Fischler, M.A., Bolles, R.C.: Random sample consensus: a paradigm for model fitting with applications to image analysis and automated cartography. Commun. ACM **24**(6), 381–395 (1981)

11. Geiger, A., Lenz, P., Urtasun, R.: Are we ready for autonomous driving? The KITTI vision benchmark suite. In: Proceedings of CVPR (2012)

12. Hartley, R., Zisserman, A.: Multiple View Geometry in Computer Vision. Cambridge University Press, Cambridge (2003)

13. He, K., Gkioxari, G., Dollár, P., Girshick, R.: Mask R-CNN. In: Proceedings of ICCV (2017)

14. Huang, X., et al.: The ApolloScape dataset for autonomous driving. In: Proceedings of CVPRW, pp. 954–960 (2018)

15. Lee, N., Choi, W., Vernaza, P., Choy, C.B., Torr, P.H., Chandraker, M.: Desire: distant future prediction in dynamic scenes with interacting agents. In: Proceedings of CVPR (2017)

16. Lin, T.-Y., et al.: Microsoft COCO: common objects in context. In: Fleet, D., Pajdla, T., Schiele, B., Tuytelaars, T. (eds.) ECCV 2014. LNCS, vol. 8693, pp. 740–755. Springer, Cham (2014). https://doi.org/10.1007/978-3-319-10602-1_48

17. Lowe, D.G.: Distinctive image features from scale-invariant keypoints. Int. J. Comput. Vision **60**(2), 91–110 (2004)

18. Ma, Y., Zhu, X., Zhang, S., Yang, R., Wang, W., Manocha, D.: TrafficPredict: trajectory prediction for heterogeneous traffic-agents. arXiv preprint arXiv:1811.02146 (2018)

19. Mur-Artal, R., Tardós, J.D.: ORB-SLAM2: An open-source SLAM system for monocular, stereo, and RGB-D cameras. IEEE Trans. Rob. **33**(5), 1255–1262 (2017)

20. Pellegrini, S., Ess, A., Schindler, K., Van Gool, L.: You'll never walk alone: modeling social behavior for multi-target tracking. In: Proceedings of ICCV (2009)

21. Robicquet, A., Sadeghian, A., Alahi, A., Savarese, S.: Learning social etiquette: human trajectory understanding in crowded scenes. In: Leibe, B., Matas, J., Sebe, N., Welling, M. (eds.) ECCV 2016. LNCS, vol. 9912, pp. 549–565. Springer, Cham (2016). https://doi.org/10.1007/978-3-319-46484-8_33

22. Srikanth, S., Ansari, J.A., Sharma, S., et al.: Infer: intermediate representations for future prediction. arXiv preprint arXiv:1903.10641 (2019)

23. Tang, J., Folkesson, J., Jensfelt, P.: Geometric correspondence network for camera motion estimation. IEEE Rob. Autom. Lett. **3**(2), 1010–1017 (2018)

24. Tateno, K., Tombari, F., Laina, I., Navab, N.: CNN-SLAM: real-time dense monocular SLAM with learned depth prediction. In: Proceedings of CVPR (2017)

25. Yu, F., et al.: BDD100K: a diverse driving video database with scalable annotation tooling. arXiv preprint arXiv:1805.04687 (2018)

Particle Filtering for Tracking in 360 Degrees Videos Using Virtual PTZ Cameras

Vito Monteleone$^{(\boxtimes)}$, Liliana Lo Presti, and Marco La Cascia

Dip. di Ingegneria (DI), Universita' degli Studi di Palermo, Palermo, Italy
vito.monteleone@unipa.it

Abstract. 360 degrees cameras are devices able to record spherical images of the environment. Such images can be used to generate views of the scene by projecting the spherical surface onto planes tangent to the sphere. Each of these views can be considered as the output of a virtual PTZ (vPTZ) camera with specific pan, tilt and zoom parameters.

This paper proposes to formulate the visual tracking problem as the one of selecting, at each time, the vPTZ camera to foveate on the target from the unlimited set of simultaneously generated vPTZ camera views. Assuming that the selected vPTZ camera is a stochastic variable, the paper proposes to model the posterior distribution of the underlying stochastic process by means of a set of particles each representing a vPTZ camera view.

Experiments on a publicly available dataset show that the proposed tracking strategy is viable and achieves state-of-the-art performance.

Keywords: Particle Filter · 360 degrees camera · vPTZ · Tracking

1 Introduction

Tracking with PTZ cameras is a challenging research topic in computer vision. Tracking algorithms for PTZ cameras are meant to work online and need to be fast enough to predict in time how to control the camera to keep the target at the center of the camera FOV. Such algorithms are difficult to evaluate and compare due to the unreproducibility of the environmental conditions (lights, shadows, pedestrian/object movements, servomotor control, etc.) they cope with. To solve this problem, recent papers [1–4] have proposed to simulate PTZ cameras (i.e., virtual PTZ cameras) from particular videos to allow not only the comparison of tracking algorithms for PTZ cameras, but also the development of new ones.

In particular, in [1], we proposed a framework to simulate virtual PTZ (vPTZ) cameras from pre-recorded 360° videos. A 360° video is a sequence of spherical images of the environment to monitor. Each spherical image is obtained by stitching together images acquired simultaneously from different viewpoints by several optical sensors on-board of the 360° camera. In general, such spherical

© Springer Nature Switzerland AG 2019
E. Ricci et al. (Eds.): ICIAP 2019, LNCS 11751, pp. 71–81, 2019.
https://doi.org/10.1007/978-3-030-30642-7_7

images are stored as equirectangular images whose pixel coordinates represent latitude and longitude of the corresponding point on the sphere surface (see Fig. 1). A geometrical transformation allows mapping the spherical surface onto a tangent plane. By varying this tangent plane, it is possible to generate different projections of the spherical surface [1]. Given a 360° video, we are then able to simulate an unlimited number of simultaneous vPTZ camera views. In this paper, we take advantage of this fact to formulate a new tracking algorithm for 360° videos.

Rather than formulating the tracking problem as the one of controlling a single vPTZ camera, as in [1], in this paper we assume that the vPTZ camera to foveate on the target at a time instant is a random variable, and we approximate the posterior distribution of the underlying stochastic process by means of a discrete set of vPTZ camera views. To model the posterior distribution over vPTZ camera views we adopt the particle filter framework in which each particle is a vPTZ camera with specific pan, tilt and zoom parameters (see Fig. 2).

For each frame of the 360° video, our tracking algorithm involves three main phases: prediction, updating and re-sampling. In the prediction step, our algorithm samples vPTZ camera views; in the update phase, our algorithm measures the likelihood that each generated vPTZ camera view can track the target, and updates the posterior distribution accordingly. The re-sampling procedure is applied to avoid particle degeneration. The vPTZ camera view to track the target is found as expected value of the posterior distribution.

The idea of using particle filter with vPTZ cameras is, at the best of our knowledge, new and not yet covered in other works. For the sake of clarity, we note here that our proposed application of the particle filter to model the posterior distribution of vPTZ camera views differs from the application of the same technique to model the posterior distribution of the target's location on the equirectangular image. Indeed, in our framework, a particle does not directly represent a patch of the equirectangular image. Instead, it represents the projection of the spherical surface onto a tangent plane accounting, in this way, for the sphericity of the 360° image. Furthermore, we focus on the problem of tracking a single target and, hence, we do not apply any data association technique as generally required in multi-target tracking framework.

To validate our pedestrian tracker, we used the publicly available dataset of spherical videos in [5]. Our experiments show that our technique is viable and achieves state-of-the-art performance.

The plan of the paper is as follows. Section 2 discusses related work; Sect. 3 explains the mathematical formulation of the particle filter. Section 4 presents our vPTZ camera filter for tracking in 360° videos; Sect. 5 presents experimental results and, finally, Sect. 6 discusses conclusions and future work.

2   Related Work

Visual tracking is a relevant topic in computer vision and in fields such as surveillance, robotics and human machine interface. Tracking is a difficult task due to background clutter, camera motion and object occlusions. State-of-the-art visual object tracking was based for a long time on Gaussian state-space models among which the best known is the Kalman filter [11]. This filter was developed under very restrictive hypotheses such as the assumption that the state vector probability density function is Gaussian. In a linear system with Gaussian noise, the Kalman filter is optimal; however, tracking objects usually involves the modeling of non-linear Gaussian systems. To adapt the filter to the case of non-Gaussian measurement noise, Extended or Unscented Kalman Filter [12–14] are used.

These methods soon proved to be inefficient to non-static scenes, in which non-linearity and multi-modality are likely to be significant. Sequential Monte Carlo techniques for filtering time series [7] and their specific use in visual tracking [15] have quickly become famous to manage these problems in a natural way, by providing more robustness than that offered by the Kalman filters. Sequential Monte Carlo, known also as Particle Filter, is one of the most popular among the Monte Carlo methods, and combines the Monte Carlo technique with Bayesian inference. The method implements a recursive Bayesian filter by Monte Carlo sampling. This idea was formally developed by Gordon et al. in [8], and gave birth to many Particle Filter variants [9,10].

For its intrinsic capability to adapt to changes and to track multiple hypotheses, particle filter was soon used for visual tracking by Isard and Blake in [15,16]. These works have shown that the particle filter framework provides a robust tracking framework, which led the visual tracking problem to be reviewed as an inference problem under the Bayesian framework. In this approach, given the state-space and observation models, the posterior probability density of the target state is recursively estimated by the use of the prior probability and the available observations [17–19]. The framework estimates probabilities of predicted states based on the observed data, by sampling from a well-know probability density function.

Fig. 1. An equirectangular image of the Cathedral in Palermo, Sicily

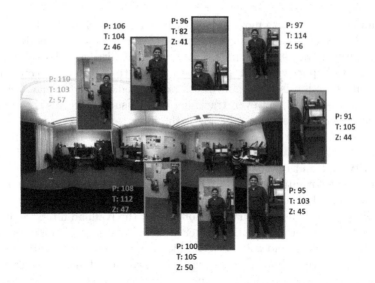

Fig. 2. The image shows an equirectangular image and a set of views acquired by different vPTZ cameras with the reported parameters.

In this paper, we propose to adopt the particle filter framework to track pedestrians in 360° videos. In contrast to other particle filter based visual tracking approaches, in which the particle state includes the target's location on the image, in this paper the particle state includes the parameters of a vPTZ camera and, as such, each particle models a vPTZ camera.

Tracking with a PTZ camera has been largely studied in computer vision [2–5,14,20,23]. These algorithms aim to control the camera in such a way that the target always appears at the center of the camera view.

The recent introduction of 360 degrees cameras gives the opportunity to acquire spherical images of the environment that can be used to simulate different PTZ camera views. Tracking a point on the spherical surface is not so different from controlling a PTZ camera: latitude and longitude of a point on the sphere actually correspond to the tilt and pan parameters of a vPTZ camera. The zoom permits to control the extension of the spherical surface to project onto the image (tangent) plane. The possibility of simulating PTZ cameras from equirectangular or cylindrical images acquired by 360° cameras has already been studied in [1–4,14,23].

In [3], a simulated virtual world with animated pedestrians was used for tracking purposes. Whilst the idea was novel, the simulated environment was based on unrealistic assumptions (e.g lighting conditions was not modeled in the artificial scenario). In [2,23], frameworks to simulate an unlimited number of PTZ cameras from 360° videos were proposed, enabling reproducibility of tracking results under fixed experimental conditions.

The work in [1] describes a pedestrian tracking-by-detection algorithm for $360°$ videos that aims at estimating the pan, tilt and zoom parameters required to control the virtual camera in such a way that the target is always at the center of the virtual camera view; a dynamic memory was also used to store the appearance models of the best past target detections to allow the update of the target's appearance.

In this work, we instead adopt the particle filter framework to model the posterior distribution over the vPTZ camera to use to track the target.

3   Mathematical Background

3.1   Sequential State Estimation Problem

Given a series of observations from time 1 to t, the sequential state estimation problem concerns the estimation of the current optimal state based on the observations up to time t, which in other words means estimating the posterior probability density of the state itself.

Given the state x_t and x_{t-1} at time t and $t-1$ respectively, and the stochastic noise d_{t-1}, we define the transition state function f_t as:

$$x_t = f_t(x_{t-1}, d_{t-1}). \tag{1}$$

The presence of the random variable d_{t-1} induces a conditional probability density function over the state x_t.

Let us define y_t as the observation at time t and v_t as the stochastic noise with which we observe the state. We define the dependency between y_t, x_t, v_t by means of the function g_t:

$$y_t = g_t(x_t, v_t). \tag{2}$$

Since v_t is a random variable, it induces a probability density function, known as likelihood, that is indicated as $p(y_t|x_t)$.

The states are hidden in the sense that they are not observable and all we can know about the system is through its observations at each time instant.

To solve the sequential state estimation problem we decided to adopt the algorithm of the particle filter that implements a Bayesian filter and estimates the states of the system on the basis of an indirect observation of the same.

3.2   Particle Filter

In its most generic sense, tracking is the problem of estimating a hidden state sequence $X_t = \{x_i\}_{i=1}^t$, from a sequence of noisy and possibly nonlinear observations $Y_t = \{y_i\}_{i=1}^t$ from time 1 to t. We assume the state sequence X_t follows a first order Markov chain, that is, at each time step, the state x_t only depends on the state at the previous time step x_{t-1} rather than on the entire state history X_t; we further assume that the observations Y_{t-1} are conditionally independent up the state at time t.

Particle filter implements a recursive Bayesian state estimator to solve the above mentioned problem by using a discrete sample set of weighted particles to recursively approximate the posterior distribution of the estimated state. We define the state x_t of an object with a set of variables k_i, that is $x_t = \{k_1, ..., k_n\}$, called *state vector*, to describe a dynamic system at a given instant t. As t varies, the *state vector* describes a trajectory in the state-space that is called the trajectory of the system.

In visual tracking applications, the state can represent the position of the target at a specific time t. The observation is often an appearance descriptor of the target.

The particle filter main steps are: prediction and update.

- Prediction: the algorithm uses the previous state to predict the current state;
- Update: the algorithm uses the current observation to correct the state estimate.

Assuming that the initial state distribution $P(x_0)$ is known, under the first order Markov chain assumption, the goal of particle filter is to estimate the posterior state distribution $p(x_t|y_{1:t-1})$.

Given all observations up to time $t - 1$, $\{y_1, ..., y_{t-1}\}$, the prediction phase uses the $p(x_t|x_{t-1})$ to predict the posterior state distribution $p(x_t|y_{1:t-1})$ by the recursive equation:

$$p(x_t|y_{1:t-1}) = \int_{x_{t-1}} p(x_t|x_{t-1})p(x_{t-1}|y_{1:t-1})dx_{t-1} \tag{3}$$

where $p(x_{t-1}|y_{1:t-1})$ represents the posterior distribution of x_{t-1} given all observations up to $t - 1$, and $p(x_t|x_{t-1})$ is the state transition probability.

At time t, the observation y_t becomes available and the state x_t can be updated by using the Bayesian Filter formula:

$$p(x_t|y_{1:t}) = \frac{p(y_t|x_t)p(x_t|y_{1:t-1})}{p(y_t|y_{1:t-1})} \tag{4}$$

where $p(y_t|x_t)$ is known as *observation likelihood*. In the above equation, it is in general difficult to evaluate the *normalization factor* $p(y_t|y_{1:t-1})$ in closed form. For this reason, we consider $p(x_t|y_{1:t}) \propto p(y_t|x_t)p(x_t|y_{1:t-1})$.

To overcome the complexity of such estimations, in particle filtering, the posterior density is approximated by a discrete set of particles $\{\tilde{x}_t^i\}_{i=1}^N$ each with a weight w_t^i. Since it is difficult to sample from the posterior distribution, particles $\tilde{x}_t^i$ are drawn from a proposal distribution $Q(x_t|x_{1:t-1}, y_{1:t})$.

At each time, when a new observation becomes available, the posterior distribution is updated by modifying the particle weights as follows:

$$w_t^i = w_{t-1}^i \cdot \frac{p(y_t|\tilde{x}_t^i)p(\tilde{x}_t^i|\tilde{x}_{t-1}^i)}{Q(\tilde{x}_t^i|x_{1:t-1}, y_{1:t})}. \tag{5}$$

Weights are then normalized to sum 1. To avoid particle degeneration, particles are resampled based on their importance weights.

4   vPTZ Camera Filtering for Tracking

In this section we present our novel tracker for 360° video. Our framework is based on the particle filter algorithm and the possibility to generate a number of N vPTZ cameras from a single 360° video.

In our approach, we define x_t as the vPTZ camera that can best track the target at time t; we also define y_t as the corresponding observation at time t, for example the target appearance descriptor extracted from the view of the vPTZ camera x_t.

We model x_t as a random variable and adopt particle filter to formulate the underlying stochastic process. We approximate the posterior distribution over the vPTZ cameras x_t by means of a set of particles $\{\tilde{x}_t^i\}_{i=1}^N$. Each particle $\tilde{x}_t^i$ is drawn from a proposal Gaussian distribution and represents a different vPTZ camera characterized by its own pan, tilt and zoom parameters. Some of these cameras will be directed towards non-interesting areas for the tracking purpose while others will be directed towards the target.

Each vPTZ camera $\tilde{x}_t^i$ is a particle weighted by w_t^i. The weights of the particles are updated as described in Eq. 5 and normalized to sum 1.

The vPTZ camera x_{t+1} to track the target is computed as:

$$x_{t+1} = \sum_{i=1}^N w_t^i \cdot \tilde{x}_t^i. \tag{6}$$

The above described steps are iterated frame-by-frame to keep the target at the center of the vPTZ camera FOV. To prevent the vPTZ cameras degenerate, multinomial resampling is used.

4.1   State Model

We describe the state of a vPTZ camera with five parameters: α, β, γ, which represent the pan, tilt, zoom angles, and the velocities of pan and tilt, that are $\dot{\alpha}$ and $\dot{\beta}$. We assume the zoom angle varies with zero velocity because its variations are in general smoothed. In particular, the state x_t is described as:

$$x_t = [\alpha, \ \beta, \ \gamma, \ \dot{\alpha}, \ \dot{\beta}]$$

We also assume that our system propagates particles according to a first order motion model specified by Eq. 7 where δt is a constant value:

$$x_t = A x_{t-1} + d_{t-1}, \text{ with } A = \begin{bmatrix} 1 & 0 & 0 & \delta t & 0 \\ 0 & 1 & 0 & 0 & \delta t \\ 0 & 0 & 1 & 0 & 0 \\ 0 & 0 & 0 & 1 & 0 \\ 0 & 0 & 0 & 0 & 1 \end{bmatrix} \tag{7}$$

4.2   Observation Model

The first target detection, extracted at specified *pan, tilt, zoom*, is used to initialize the appearance model y_1 of the tracker.

Inspired by the work of [21], to obtain more discriminative histograms, the image is divided into upper and lower parts and two different histograms are extracted from them. Our appearance model relies on these histograms computed on the Hue and Saturation channels of the image.

The observation likelihood $p(y_t|x_t)$ is modeled by a Gaussian distribution (centered in 0 and of variance σ_a^2) over the Bhattacharyya distance [22] of the appearance models y_t and y_1.

The Bhattacharyya distance is defined as:

$$d(H_1, H_2) = \sqrt[2]{1 - \frac{1}{\sqrt[2]{\overline{H_1}\,\overline{H_2}}N^2} \sum_I \sqrt[2]{H_1(I)H_2(I)}} \qquad (8)$$

where H_1 and H_2 are the histograms used to represent the appearance models y_1 and y_t respectively, N is the number of bins in each histogram, $\overline{H}$ indicates the mean value of the bin counts. This equation returns a value between 0 and 1, where 0 indicates that the two histograms are exactly the same.

When an occlusion arises (for example, the target is occluded by another pedestrian), the likelihood of the particles decreases and, consequently, particles begin to die (i.e., particles have low or uniform weights). To account for such particle impoverishment, a resampling procedure is used to refresh the set of particles [6]. We stress here that, since our tracking approach focuses only on a single target and no pedestrian detector is used during tracking, our algorithm does not require any data association procedure.

5   Experiments

We tested our framework on the publicly available dataset [23]. The video sequences were captured in two indoor environments and six randomly moving individuals are annotated. The length of each sequenc varies from a few seconds to one/two minutes. These video sequences are affected by common tracking perturbation factors, such as: Motion Blur (MB), Scale Change (SC), Out-of-Plane Rotation (OPR), Fast Motion (FM), Cluttered Background (CB), Illumination Variation (IV), Low Resolution (LR), Occlusion (OCC), presence of Distractors (DIS) and Articulated Objects (AO).

The video sequences are affected by serious illumination artifacts. Moreover there are numerous occlusions arising while people are moving around the camera alone or in groups. As baseline method, the work in [23] suggests to use CamShift, and we used the one implemented in the OpenCV Library. We also compare against the tracking-by-detection (TbD) method proposed in [1].

Each pedestrian tracker was initialized by the first bounding box of the target provided with the ground-truth. To initialize the tracker automatically, a pedestrian detector can be used on the vPTZ camera views obtained by setting the zoom angle to $90°$, the tilt angle to $0°$, and by varying the pan angle in $[-180, -90, 0, 90]$.

Table 1. Experimental Results: MAE stands for Mean Absolute Error, α, β, γ indicate pan, tilt and zoom respectively, TF stands for Track Fragmentation

Method	$MAE(\alpha)$	$MAE(\beta)$	$MAE(\gamma)$	TF
Pf vPTZ [ours]	3.14°	2.79°	9.85°	59.84%
CamShift [23]	3.86°	4.68°	36.11°	64.43%
TbyD [1]	2.43°	3.43°	15.26°	70.44%

Targets have been tracked over all the video frames. An automatic procedure that ends the tracker when the target is not detected for a prefixed number of consecutive frames can be introduced.

While the results in [23] consider all annotated objects in the dataset, we only focused on the full-body annotated pedestrians. In [23], the zoom angle is set to 90°. Our algorithm aims at estimating the best zoom angle to closely track the target. Furthermore, in [23], Center Location Error (CLE) and Target to Center Error (TCE) are expressed in pixels. These metrics are not general enough since these measurements depends on the image resolution of the projected views and on the zoom factor. For all the above reasons, we decided to not adopt the metrics suggested in [23], and to measure the average absolute differences in degrees between the estimated pan, tilt and zoom angles and the corresponding angles derived from the annotations.

In Table 1, we report the values of mean absolute error (MAE) in degrees for the estimated pan (α), tilt (β) and zoom (γ) angles. Furthermore, we report the Track Fragmentation (TF) error that measures the percentage of invalid detections in the tracks. A detection is considered valid if it falls within the FOV angle derived from the annotated target bounding-box. We note that our definition of Track Fragmentation is more restrictive than the one used in [23]. Indeed, in [23], a detection is invalid when it is outside the camera FOV, which was set to 90° and, hence, was much larger than the one we derive from the target bounding box.

By indicating with a * the ground-truth values at time t, TF is defined as:

$$TF_t = \begin{cases} 1 & \text{if } |\alpha_t - \alpha_t^*| \leq \frac{\gamma_t^*}{4} \text{ \& } |\beta_t - \beta_t^*| \leq \frac{\gamma_t^*}{2} \\ 0 & \text{otherwise.} \end{cases} \tag{9}$$

As shown in Table 1, our method outperforms both the CamShift algorithm and the work in [1] in terms of MAE and TF and, in particular, it seems to be able to handle better the zoom factor estimation. All methods show high values of TF, whilst the proposed method achieves the lowest one. We note here that all methods perform tracking in the HSV color space by employing color histograms. Overall, the results suggest that by adopting stronger appearance descriptors the performance of the method could improve.

6 Conclusions

In this paper we proposed a new framework to track a pedestrian in a 360° video by using particle filter and generating virtual PTZ cameras. At the best of our knowledge, there are no works using the particle filter framework to model the posterior distribution of vPTZ cameras.

In the proposed framework, the posterior distribution is approximated by a discrete set of particles. Each particle represents a vPTZ camera with specific values of pan, tilt and zoom. Such cameras are weighted and used, frame-by-frame, to estimate the vPTZ camera to track the target.

Experimental results on a publicly available dataset show that the proposed method outperforms state-of-the-art works on tracking in 360° videos.

In future work, we will focus on improving the observation likelihood model and, in general, the appearance model used to describe the target in order to make it adaptive. We will also study the possibility to use offline trained deep learning models to establish matches between the target and the candidate targets. We will investigate the possibility to extends our tracking approach to multiple targets. For example, a tracker could be initialized for each target and information about the estimated targets' locations on the sphere could be shared among trackers in order to disambiguate among them.

References

1. Monteleone, V., Lo Presti, L., La Cascia, M.: Pedestrian tracking in 360 video by vPTZ cameras. In: 2018 IEEE 4th International Forum on Research and Technology for Society and Industry (RTSI), IEEE (2018)
2. Greco, L., La Cascia, M.: 360° tracking using a virtual PTZ camera. In: Battiato, S., Gallo, G., Schettini, R., Stanco, F. (eds.) ICIAP 2017. LNCS, vol. 10484, pp. 62–72. Springer, Cham (2017). https://doi.org/10.1007/978-3-319-68560-1_6
3. Qureshi, F.Z., Terzopoulos, D.: Proactive PTZ camera control. In: Bhanu, B., Ravishankar, C., Roy-Chowdhury, A., Aghajan, H., Terzopoulos, D. (eds.) Distributed Video Sensor Networks, pp. 273–287. Springer, London (2011). https://doi.org/10.1007/978-0-85729-127-1_19
4. Salvagnini, P., Cristani, M., Del Bue, A., Murino, V.: An experimental framework for evaluating PTZ tracking algorithms. In: Crowley, J.L., Draper, B.A., Thonnat, M. (eds.) International Conference on Computer Vision Systems, pp. 81–90. Springer, Heidelberg (2011). https://doi.org/10.1007/978-3-642-23968-7_9
5. Chang, F., Zhang, G., Wang, X., Chen, Z.: PTZ camera target tracking in large complex scenes. In: 2010 8th World Congress on Intelligent Control and Automation (WCICA), pp. 2914–2918, IEEE, July 2010
6. Hol, J.D., Schon, T.B., Gustafsson, F.: On resampling algorithms for particle filters. In: 2006 IEEE Nonlinear Statistical Signal Processing Workshop, IEEE (2006)
7. Doucet, A., Godsill, S., Andrieu, C.: On sequential Monte Carlo sampling methods for Bayesian filtering. Stat. Comput. 10(3), 197–208 (2000)
8. Gordon, N.J., Salmond, D.J., Smith, A.F.M.: Novel approach to nonlinear/non-Gaussian Bayesian state estimation. In: IEE Proceedings F (Radar and Signal Processing), IET Digital Library, 140 (2) (1993)

9. Kitagawa, G.: Monte Carlo filter and smoother for non-Gaussian nonlinear state space models. J. Comput. Graph. Stat. **5**(1), 1–25 (1996)
10. Arulampalam, M.S., et al.: A tutorial on particle filters for online nonlinear non-Gaussian Bayesian tracking. IEEE Trans. Signal Process. **50**(2), 174–188 (2002)
11. Kalman, R.E.: A new approach to linear filtering and prediction problems. J. Basic Eng. **82**(1), 35–45 (1960)
12. Ljung, L.: Asymptotic behavior of the extended Kalman filter as a parameter estimator for linear systems. IEEE Trans. Autom. Control **24**(1), 36–50 (1979)
13. Evensen, G.: The ensemble Kalman filter: theoretical formulation and practical implementation. Ocean Dyn. **53**(4), 343–367 (2003)
14. Wan, E.A., Van Der Merwe, R.: The unscented Kalman filter for nonlinear estimation. In: Proceedings of the IEEE 2000 Adaptive Systems for Signal Processing, Communications, and Control Symposium (Cat. No. 00EX373), IEEE (2000)
15. Isard, M., Blake, A.: Condensation-conditional density propagation for visual tracking. Int. J. Comput. Vis. **29**(1), 5–28 (1998)
16. Isard, M., Blake, A.: Contour tracking by stochastic propagation of conditional density. In: Buxton, B., Cipolla, R. (eds.) ECCV 1996. LNCS, vol. 1064, pp. 343–356. Springer, Heidelberg (1996). https://doi.org/10.1007/BFb0015549
17. MacCormick, J., Blake, A.: A probabilistic exclusion principle for tracking multiple objects. Int. J. Comput. Vis. **39**(1), 57–71 (2000)
18. Beymer, D., et al.: A real-time computer vision system for measuring traffic parameters. In: Proceedings of IEEE Computer Society Conference on Computer Vision and Pattern Recognition, IEEE (1997)
19. Greiffenhagen, M., et al.: Statistical modeling and performance characterization of a real-time dual camera surveillance system. In: Proceedings IEEE Conference on Computer Vision and Pattern Recognition, CVPR 2000 (Cat. No. PR00662), IEEE, vol. 2 (2000)
20. Micheloni, C., Rinner, B., Foresti, G.L.: Video analysis in pan-tilt-zoom camera networks. IEEE Signal Process. Mag. **27**(5), 78–90 (2010)
21. Geng, Y., et al.: A person re-identification algorithm by exploiting region-based feature salience. J. Vis. Commun. Image Represent. **29**, 89–102 (2015)
22. Bhattacharyya, A.: On a measure of divergence between two statistical populations defined by their probability distributions. Bull. Calcutta Math. Soc. **35**, 99–109 (1943)
23. Chen, G., St-Charles, P.L., Bouachir, W., Joeisseint, T., Bilodeau, G.A., Bergevin, R.: Reproducible evaluation of Pan-Tilt-Zoom tracking (extended version of the 2015 ICIP paper) (2015)

Dynamic Texture Classification Using Deterministic Partially Self-avoiding Walks on Networks

Lucas C. Ribas[1,2]([✉]) [iD] and Odemir M. Bruno[2]

[1] Institute of Mathematics and Computer Science, University of São Paulo - USP,
Avenida Trabalhador são-carlense, 400, São Carlos, SP 13566-590, Brazil
lucasribas@usp.br
[2] São Carlos Institute of Physics, University of São Paulo - USP, PO Box 369,
São Carlos, SP 13560-970, Brazil
bruno@ifsc.usp.br

Abstract. This paper presents a new approach to dynamic texture classification based on deterministic partially self-avoiding (DPS) walks on complex networks (or graphs). In this approach, for each pixel is assigned a vertex and two vertices are connected according to a given distance. In order to analyze appearance and motion, we propose two graph modeling: a spatial graph and a temporal graph. The DPS walks are agents that can obtain rich characteristics of the environment in which they were performed. Thus, the DPS walks are performed in the two modeled graphs (spatial and temporal) and the feature vector is obtained by calculating the statistical measures from the trajectories of the DPS walks. The results in two well-known databases have demonstrated the effectiveness of the proposed approach using a small feature vector. The proposed approach also improved the performance when compared to the previous DPS walks based method and the graph-based method.

Keywords: Dynamic texture · Deterministic walks · Network sciences

1 Introduction

Dynamic textures can be defined as a sequence of images (or video) that exhibit certain stationary in time [6]. Examples of dynamic textures in the real world include sea waves, smoke, swaying trees, moving flag, fire, a crowd of people, among others. The approaches for dynamic texture representation are applied in different problems such as traffic condition recognition [9], human activity recognition [14], surveillance [29], among others.

In the literature, many approaches have been proposed based on different strategies to analyze the spatial and temporal characteristics of the dynamic textures. These approaches can be separated into five categories: motion-based methods [17], model-based methods [11,13,18], filter-based methods [7],

© Springer Nature Switzerland AG 2019
E. Ricci et al. (Eds.): ICIAP 2019, LNCS 11751, pp. 82–93, 2019.
https://doi.org/10.1007/978-3-030-30642-7_8

statistical-based methods [24,29] and, agent-based methods [9,10]. The agent-based methods use the deterministic partially self-avoiding (DPS) walks to describe the dynamic textures. These methods achieved promising results in classification, clustering, and segmentation of dynamic textures.

In this paper, we propose a new method for dynamic textures analysis and classification based on deterministic partially self-avoiding walks on complex networks. The DPS walks was introduced initially to investigate the effects of simple walks in random media [15]. After that, the DPS walks methodology was applied for texture and dynamic texture analysis [3,9,10]. Basically, a DPS walk can be understood as an agent who visits points (e.g. pixels, vertices) distributed in a map (e.g. image, video, graph) based on the neighborhood, a rule of movement and memory. Starting from a given point, the next step follows the rule: go to the nearest point on the neighborhood that has not been visited in the last μ steps (memory) [15]. Statistical features of the trajectories of the DPS walks are used to study the map.

In the proposed approach, we model the dynamic texture in two graphs (i.e. networks): spatial graph and temporal graph. The spatial graph models the appearance characteristics, while the temporal graph contains the motion properties of the dynamic texture. In this way, we apply the DPS walks on these two graphs and use statistical characteristics of the trajectories to represent the appearance and motion of the dynamic texture in a feature vector. The proposed approach is different of the previous works [9–11] because it combines graph modeling and DPS walks characteristics, while in [9,10] only the DPS walks is applied in the videos and in [11] only the complex network theory is used to modeling and characterization. In Sect. 2 our proposed method to dynamic texture analysis is detailed. The experimental setup is described in Sect. 3. In Sect. 4 the experimental results are presented and discussed. Finally, the paper is concluded in Sect. 5.

2   Proposed Approach

2.1   Network Modeling

The network sciences (also called complex network) field uses the formalism of graph theory with the incorporation of statistical mechanics and complex systems. It has attracted increased attention because of its ability to represent and study a wide range of systems and data. In computer vision, the networks have been used to model and analyze images and video analysis [2,21–23]. In this paper, we use the graph to represent the dynamic texture video. In dynamic texture analysis, it is important to obtain appearance and motion features in order to accurately represent the video. To achieve this, in the proposed approach, we model the dynamic texture video in two graphs (networks): the spatial graph $G_S = (V_S, E_S)$ that characterizes the appearance properties and the temporal graph $G_T = (V_T, E_T)$ that contains the motion properties.

In the two graphs, each pixel $i = (x_i, y_i, t_i)$ is mapped into a vertex $i \in V$, where x_i and y_i are the spatial coordinates and t_i the temporal coordinate of the pixel i. The main difference between the two graphs is the definition of the set of edges. In the spatial graph, the set E_S is defined by the connection of all vertices whose the Euclidean distance is smaller or equal than a given radius $\sqrt{2}$ and the time coordinates t_i and t_j are equal,

$$e_{ij} \in E_S \iff \sqrt{(x_i - x_j)^2 + (y_i - y_j)^2} \leq \sqrt{2} \text{ and } t_i = t_j \qquad (1)$$

On the other hand, in the temporal graph, the set of edges is defined by connecting the vertices whose the Euclidean distance is smaller or equal than $\sqrt{3}$ and the time coordinates are different,

$$e_{ij} \in E_T \iff \sqrt{(x_i - x_j)^2 + (y_i - y_j)^2 + (t_i - t_j)^2} \leq \sqrt{3} \text{ and } t_i \neq t_j \qquad (2)$$

Figure 1 illustrates three frames modeled as a graph. The frames are represented by the spheres in blue, green and red. For each edge e_{ij} connecting two vertices i and j, a weight $w(e_{ij})$ is defined by the difference of intensities between the two pixels that represent the vertices:

$$w(e_{ij}) = \frac{|I(i) - I(j)|}{255}, \qquad (3)$$

where $I(i) \in [0, 255]$ is the gray intensity of a pixel i.

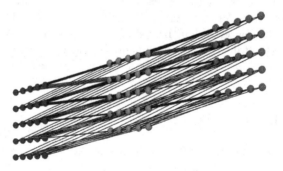

Fig. 1. Three frames modeled as a temporal graph. The edges connecting only vertices of different frames. (Color figure online)

2.2   DPS Walks on Networks

The deterministic partially self-avoiding (DPS) walk is an agent, which was initially used to study regular and random media [15]. This deterministic walk produces a set of trajectories that are used to characterize the environment in which they were performed. The DPS walk was applied with success for feature extraction in different classification tasks, such as in texture analysis [3], dynamic texture classification [9,10], shape analysis [20] and complex network classification [12].

In the proposed approach, the DPS walks are used for feature extraction of the graphs that model the dynamic texture videos. In this way, the DPS walks are performed on the vertices. The DPS walk is an agent that walks on the vertices of the graph based on a deterministic rule r. The agent starts the walk from a pre-defined vertex i and the movement to the next vertex j is given by: go to the vertex j in the neighborhood $\eta(i)$ (vertices connected to the vertex i) which minimizes the edge weight $w(e_{ij})$ and that has not been visited in the previous μ steps (i.e. that is not in memory $j \notin M_\mu$). Here, we will call this rule of movement as $r = min$. We also consider another rule of movement that moves the agent in the direction of the maximum edge weight $w(e_{ij})$ ($r = max$). The two rules of movement are used because each one produces different trajectories and, consequently, obtain different characteristics of the graph. The walk will end when the agent to find a set of vertices in which it cannot escape, called attractor.

The memory M_μ of size μ is the last μ vertices visited by the agent and that cannot be visited. This memory is updated in each step of the agent to save the last μ vertices visited. The trajectory of the agent can be divided into two parts: an initial part of size τ called transient, and, a final part named attractor, which is composed of vertices that form a cycle of period $\rho \geq \mu+1$ where the agent gets stuck. In the cases in which the agent cannot find an attractor, the trajectory is represented only by the transient part. For each vertex of the graph, a DPS walk is started with a given memory size μ and a rule of movement r. Therefore, for a graph with N vertices, we have N different trajectories. In order to measure this set of trajectories, the transient time and attractor period joint distribution $S_{\mu,r}(\tau, \rho)$ is considered. In this distribution, the frequency of trajectories with transient τ and attractor ρ is stored in each position [3],

$$S_{\mu,r}(\tau, \rho) = \frac{1}{N} \sum_{i \in V} \begin{cases} 1, & \text{if } \tau_i = \tau \text{ and } \rho_i = \rho \\ 0, & \text{otherwise} \end{cases}, \tag{4}$$

where μ is the memory size and r the rule of movement used.

2.3   Proposed Signature

The joint distribution contains relevant information about the trajectories of the DPS walks performed in a given graph. Thus, previous works [3] have used features obtained from this joint distribution for characterization. In this way, the best results were obtained using the histogram $h^t_{\mu,r}(l)$, which calculates the number of trajectories with size $l = \tau + \rho$ in a joint distribution computed with memory size μ and rule of movement r,

$$h_{\mu,r}(l) = \sum_{b=0}^{l-1} S^k_{\mu,r}(b, l - b). \tag{5}$$

In order to characterize the dynamic texture videos, the DPS walks are performed in the two graphs: G_S and G_T. Thus, for each graph a histogram $h_{\mu,r}(l)$ can be obtained. Several previous works have shown that the most discriminative information of the histogram $h_{\mu,r}(l)$ are concentrated on its first elements [3,9]. In this work, we use the n first descriptors of the histogram $h_{\mu,r}(l)$, with the first position defined as $(\mu + 1)$, since there is no attractor smaller than $(\mu + 1)$. Thus, given a memory size μ and a rule of movement r, a feature vector ν_u^Θ is obtained:

$$\nu_{\mu,r}^\Theta = [h_{\mu,r}^\Theta(\mu + 1), h_{\mu,r}^\Theta(\mu + 2), ..., h_{\mu,r}^\Theta(\mu + n)] \tag{6}$$

where Θ is the type of graph: spatial S or temporal T.

The size of the memory directly influences the complexity of the trajectories and, consequently, in the information extracted by the method. For example, DPS walks with low memory values perform better local analysis [10]. In this sense, histograms obtained with different memory sizes are used for a more robust characterization of the different patterns present in the graphs (i.e. dynamic texture videos), according to:

$$\vartheta_r^\Theta = [\nu_{\mu_1,r}^\Theta, \nu_{\mu_2,r}^\Theta, ..., \nu_{\mu_m,r}^\Theta]. \tag{7}$$

To characterize patterns of appearance and movement of dynamic textures, a feature vector that consists of the concatenation of the spatial and temporal descriptors is considered. Thus, this feature vector is composed of the characteristics extracted from the spatial ϑ_r^S and temporal ϑ_r^T graphs using different memory values, as described:

$$\lambda_r = [\vartheta_r^S, \vartheta_r^T]. \tag{8}$$

The feature vector obtained above refers to a single rule of movement. Although this vector may be able to properly characterize dynamic textures, another possibility is to combine the two rules of movement. The rule of movement is another parameter that influences the trajectory of the agent. In this sense, it is considered a final feature vector that consists of the concatenation of vectors obtained with the two rules of movement $r = min$ and $r = max$, as follows:

$$\lambda = [\lambda_{min}, \lambda_{max}] \tag{9}$$

2.4   Computational Complexity

Basically, the proposed approach models a dynamic texture with $N = w \times h \times T$ pixels in two graphs. For modeling, each pixel is mapped into a vertex, which is linked with 8 and 18 neighbors for the spatial and temporal graphs, respectively. As the number of neighbors is a multiplicative constant and much smaller than the number of pixels in the video, it can be disregarded. Thus, the computational complexity of the modeling is given then by $O(N)$ for each type of graph. Next, a DPS walk is started from each pixel, producing a trajectory of size $l = \tau + \rho$, where τ is the transient time and ρ is the attractor period. For cases where an attractor is not found, we finish the walk after M steps. In this work, we define $M = 20$ because we use only the first elements of the joint distribution for characterization. Therefore, the computational complexity to compute the features from each graph (temporal and spatial) is given by the number of pixels and the size of the trajectories, $O(N \times (\tau + 2\rho))$. We have 2ρ because it is necessary to go through twice the same cycle of pixels to identify an attractor.

3 Experimental Setup

To classify the feature vectors, we adopted the 1-Nearest Neighbor (1NN) classifier and a specific scheme for each database to separate the training and test set. The Dyntex++ [8] database is a compiled version of the Dyntex database [16]. The samples are preprocessed in order to eliminate static or dynamic non-representative backgrounds, zoom, and textures without movement. The database has 3600 samples divided into 36 classes (e.g. boiling water, river water, colony of ants and smoke). In the experiments, a 10-fold cross-validation scheme with 10 trials was used [11]. The accuracy is reported as the average performance of all experimental trials.

The UCLA [4] database is composed of 200 dynamic texture videos separated into 50 classes with 4 samples per class (named UCLA-50 version). Each sample has $48 \times 48 \times 75$ pixels. This database also has two variations of the original database proposed in [19]. On the UCLA-9 version, the samples are reorganized into 9 classes: boiling water (8 samples), fire (8), flower (12), fountains (20), plants (108), sea (12), smoke (4), water (12) and waterfall (16). In the UCLA-8 version, the plant class is eliminated due to the large number of samples. The experimental setup adopted in these databases is similar to [19]. For the UCLA-50 is used a $4-$fold cross-validation scheme with 10 repetitions. On the other versions, it is used for the testing set, half of the sequences (randomly selected from each class), and the remaining half is used for training. For these databases, the correct classification rate (CCR) or accuracy is reported as the average performance of all experimental trials.

4 Results and Discussion

First, we investigate the effects of the parameters of our proposed approach in the task of dynamic texture classification. The parameters analyzed were: (i) memory sizes μ and (ii) rules of movement r. In the experiments, it was used the first $n = 3$ elements of the histogram $h^{\ominus}_{\mu,r}(l)$ for the UCLA databases and the first $n = 5$ positions for the Dyntex++ database. These values were defined based on the idea that the main information are in the first elements and from the experimental tests.

Figure 2 shows the results of our proposed method on the two databases for different combinations of memory sizes and rules of movement. On both databases, the rule of movement $r = max$ obtained higher accuracies than the rule of movement $r = min$. The rule of movement $r = max$ is related to heterogeneous regions of the video (i.e. graph), that is, the agent walks on regions where the difference of the gray level between the pixels (i.e. high edge weight) is higher. On the other hand, in the rule $r = min$, the agent walks on homogeneous regions, that is, where the edge weight is smaller. This indicates that heterogeneous regions have more discriminative information of the dynamic texture. However, the best results are obtained when both rules of movement are combined.

Concerning the memory sizes, we note that low memory sizes provide inferior accuracies. Thus, as we increase the memory sizes, the accuracy also is increased. However, when using a combination of memory size higher than $[0, 1, 2, 3]$, the accuracy obtained starts to stabilize, suggesting that the proposed descriptors have reached their limits in terms of discrimination ability. Such behavior is expected: the larger the memory sizes μ, the harder find an attractor. From the results, we set up as default parameters of the proposed method $\mu = [0, 1, 2, 3, 4, 5, 6, 7, 8]$ and $r = [min, max]$. On both databases, the highest accuracy was using this configuration (94.5% and 96.0% for the Dyntex++ and UCLA-50, respectively). These results are interesting because they indicate that the method is not strongly parameter dependent.

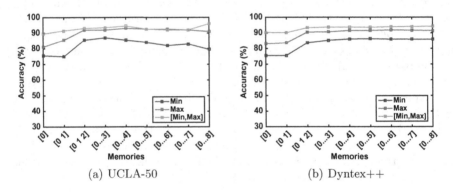

(a) UCLA-50   (b) Dyntex++

Fig. 2. Accuracies using different combination of memory sizes and rules of movement.

In order to improve the analysis of our proposed approach, we performed a comparison experiment using literature methods of dynamic textures. To achieve this, we considered the accuracy, standard deviation and number of features of the methods, when described in the original papers. In all comparison, we use the same experimental setup described in Sect. 3.

Table 1 presents the classification results of the proposed method and others on UCLA-50 database. Note that the proposed method obtained the best accuracy when compared to the others. Concerning the complex network based methods, the proposed method improves the accuracy compared to the CNDT [11] method by 1.0%. This method uses traditional complex networks measures while our method uses the DPS walk for complex network characterization. Thus, the results suggest that the DPS walk is more effective to describe the graph and, consequently, the dynamic texture.

Table 1. Comparison of the classification results of the proposed method and others on UCLA-50 database.

Methods	Number of features	Accuracy (%)
KDT-MD [5]	-	89.50
DFS [27]	-	89.50
3D-OTF [28]	290	87.10
CVLBP [24]	-	93.00
RI-VLBP [30]	16384	77.50 ($\pm$ 8.98)
LBP-TOP [29]	768	95.00 ($\pm$ 4.44)
DPSW-TOP [9]	75	95.00 ($\pm$ 4.78)
CNDT [11]	420	95.00 ($\pm$ 5.19)
Proposed method	180	96.00 ($\pm$ 3.16)

Table 2 summarizes the results on the UCLA-9 database. On this database, our approach yields the second best result (96.80%). This result is slightly inferior to the one obtained by CVLBP method (96.90%). On the other hand, on the UCLA-8 database, the proposed method achieved the best accuracy, as can be seen in Table 3. Here, the proposed method gives an accuracy of 96.59% against 95.65% of the CVLBP method. The proposed method also outperformed the method DPSW-TOP, which is a DPS walk based method. This method applies the DPS walk on three orthogonal planes to analyze the appearance and motion properties of the dynamic textures. In this way, the results indicate that our approach based on DPS walk applied on the graph is more effective for dynamic texture characterization.

Table 4 presents the results on the Dyntex++ database for different methods. The proposed method shows an improvement of 10.74% and 3.21% compared to the CNDT and DPSW-TOP methods, respectively. However, on this database, the proposed method obtained a performance lower than the RI-VLBP and LBP-TOP methods. Nevertheless, it is important to emphasize that the feature vector size of these methods is significantly higher than the feature vector of our method. Therefore, our method is still competitive due to the small feature vector, for example, the RI-VLBP extracts a long feature vector of dimension 16384, whereas our method produces only 180 characteristics.

Besides these compared methods, called hand-craft methods, we also compare our proposed signature with a method based on learned features. This method proposed in [1] uses a convolutional neural network (GoogleNet) to learn the characteristics of the dynamic textures in three orthogonal planes and obtain a signature. On the UCLA-50, UCLA-9 and UCLA-8 databases, the CNN-based

Table 2. Classification results for all methods on the UCLA-9 database.

Methods	Number of features	Accuracy (%)
3D-OTF [28]	290	96.32
CVLBP [24]	-	96.90
High level feature [25]	-	92.60
Chaotic vector [26]	300	85.10
RI-VLBP [30]	16384	96.30
LBP-TOP [29]	768	96.00
DPSW-TOP [9]	75	96.33 ($\pm$2.46)
CNDT [11]	336	95.61 ($\pm$2.72)
Proposed method	180	96.80 ($\pm$2.36)

Table 3. Comparison results on the UCLA-8 database.

Methods	Number of features	Accuracy (%)
3D-OTF [28]	290	95.80
CVLBP [24]	-	95.65
High level feature [25]	-	85.65
Chaotic vector [26]	300	85.00
RI-VLBP [30]	16384	91.96
LBP-TOP [29]	768	93.67
DPSW-TOP [9]	75	93.41 ($\pm$6.01)
CNDT [11]	336	94.32 ($\pm$4.18)
Proposed method	180	96.59 ($\pm$7.12)

Table 4. Comparison results for different dynamic texture methods on the Dyntex++ database.

Methods	Number of features	Accuracy (%)
RI-VLBP [30]	16384	96.14 ($\pm$0.77)
LBP-TOP [29]	768	97.72 ($\pm$0.43)
DPSW-TOP [9]	75	91.39 ($\pm$1.29)
CNDT [11]	336	83.86 ($\pm$1.40)
Proposed method	180	94.60 ($\pm$ 1.20)

method obtained 99.50%, 98.35% and 99.02% of accuracy, respectively. These results are higher than the obtained by our method. However, it is important to highlight that even with inferior results, our method is still competitive due to its computational simplicity.

5   Conclusion

This paper presents a new method for characterization and classification of dynamic textures using deterministic partially self-avoiding walks on complex networks. In this method, we have shown a graph modeling from dynamic texture videos, which allows us to analyze appearance (spatial graph) and motion (temporal graph) properties. Thus, the DPS walks are performed on these two graphs and the statistical information of its trajectories are used to compose a feature vector. Experimental results obtained on the UCLA and Dyntex++ databases showed that our method is very competitive when compared to other methods. Our method also outperformed the other previous DPSW-based and complex network based methods. In addition, the proposed approach is competitive in terms of dimensionality, producing feature vectors significantly smaller than other literature methods. In this way, the tradeoff between performance and feature vector size demonstrates the great potential of the proposed method for dynamic texture classification.

Acknowledgments. Lucas C. Ribas gratefully acknowledges the financial support grant #2016/23763-8 and #2019/03277-0, São Paulo Research Foundation (FAPESP). Odemir M. Bruno thanks the financial support of CNPq (Grant #307797/2014-7) and FAPESP (Grant #14/08026-1).

References

1. Andrearczyk, V., Whelan, P.F.: Convolutional neural network on three orthogonal planes for dynamic texture classification. Pattern Recogn. **76**, 36–49 (2018)
2. Backes, A.R., Casanova, D., Bruno, O.M.: Texture analysis and classification: a complex network-based approach. Inf. Sci. **219**, 168–180 (2013)
3. Backes, A.R., Gonçalves, W.N., Martinez, A.S., Bruno, O.M.: Texture analysis and classification using deterministic tourist walk. Pattern Recogn. **43**(3), 685–694 (2010)
4. Chan, A.B., Vasconcelos, N.: Probabilistics for the classification of auto-regressive visual processes. In: IEEE Computer Society Conference on Computer Vision and Pattern Recognition, CVPR 2005, vol. 1, pp. 846–851. IEEE (2005)
5. Chan, A.B., Vasconcelos, N.: Classifying video with kernel dynamic textures. In: CVPR, pp. 1–6 (2007)
6. Doretto, G., Jones, E., Soatto, S.: Spatially homogeneous dynamic textures. In: Pajdla, T., Matas, J. (eds.) ECCV 2004. LNCS, vol. 3022, pp. 591–602. Springer, Heidelberg (2004). https://doi.org/10.1007/978-3-540-24671-8_47
7. Dubois, S., Péteri, R., Ménard, M.: A comparison of wavelet based spatio-temporal decomposition methods for dynamic texture recognition. In: Araujo, H., Mendonça, A.M., Pinho, A.J., Torres, M.I. (eds.) IbPRIA 2009. LNCS, vol. 5524, pp. 314–321. Springer, Heidelberg (2009). https://doi.org/10.1007/978-3-642-02172-5_41
8. Ghanem, B., Ahuja, N.: Maximum margin distance learning for dynamic texture recognition. In: Daniilidis, K., Maragos, P., Paragios, N. (eds.) ECCV 2010. LNCS, vol. 6312, pp. 223–236. Springer, Heidelberg (2010). https://doi.org/10.1007/978-3-642-15552-9_17

9. Gonçalves, W.N., Bruno, O.M.: Dynamic texture analysis and segmentation using deterministic partially self-avoiding walks. Expert Syst. Appl. **40**(11), 4283–4300 (2013)
10. Gonçalves, W.N., Bruno, O.M.: Dynamic texture segmentation based on deterministic partially self-avoiding walks. Comput. Vis. Image Underst. **117**(9), 1163–1174 (2013)
11. Gonçalves, W.N., Machado, B.B., Bruno, O.M.: A complex network approach for dynamic texture recognition. Neurocomputing **153**, 211–220 (2015)
12. Gonçalves, W.N., Martinez, A.S., Bruno, O.M.: Complex network classification using partially self-avoiding deterministic walks. Chaos: Interdisc. J. Nonlinear Sci. **22**(3), 033139 (2012)
13. Junior, J.J.d.M.S., Ribas, L.C., Bruno, O.M.: Randomized neural network based signature for dynamic texture classification. Expert Systems with Applications (2019)
14. Kellokumpu, V., Zhao, G., Pietikäinen, M.: Human activity recognition using a dynamic texture based method. In: BMVC, vol. 1, p. 2 (2008)
15. Lima, G.F., Martinez, A.S., Kinouchi, O.: Deterministic walks in random media. Phys. Rev. Lett. **87**, 010603 (2001)
16. Péteri, R., Fazekas, S., Huiskes, M.J.: Dyntex: a comprehensive database of dynamic textures. Pattern Recogn. Lett. **31**(12), 1627–1632 (2010)
17. Polana, R., Nelson, R.: Temporal texture and activity recognition. In: Shah, M., Jain, R. (eds.) Motion-Based Recognition, pp. 87–124. Springer, Dordrecht (1997). https://doi.org/10.1007/978-94-015-8935-2_5
18. Qiao, Y., Weng, L.: Hidden markov model based dynamic texture classification. IEEE Sig. Process. Lett. **22**(4), 509–512 (2015)
19. Ravichandran, A., Chaudhry, R., Vidal, R.: View-invariant dynamic texture recognition using a bag of dynamical systems. In: 2009 IEEE Conference on Computer Vision and Pattern Recognition, pp. 1651–1657, June 2009
20. Ribas, L.C., Bruno, O.M.: Deterministic partially self-avoiding walks on networks for natural shapes classification (2019)
21. Ribas, L.C., Gonçalves, W.N., Bruno, O.M.: Dynamic texture analysis with diffusion in networks. Digit. Signal Proc. **92**, 109–126 (2019)
22. Ribas, L.C., de Sá Junior, J.J.M., Scabini, L.F.S., Bruno, O.M.: Fusion of complex networks and randomized neural networks for texture analysis. CoRR abs/1806.09170 (2018). http://arxiv.org/abs/1806.09170
23. Ribas, L.C., Neiva, M.B., Bruno, O.M.: Distance transform network for shape analysis. Inf. Sci. **470**, 28–42 (2019)
24. Tiwari, D., Tyagi, V.: Dynamic texture recognition based on completed volume local binary pattern. Multidimension. Syst. Signal Process. **27**(2), 563–575 (2016)
25. Wang, Y., Hu, S.: Exploiting high level feature for dynamic textures recognition. Neurocomputing **154**, 217–224 (2015)
26. Wang, Y., Hu, S.: Chaotic features for dynamic textures recognition. Soft. Comput. **20**(5), 1977–1989 (2016)
27. Xu, Y., Quan, Y., Ling, H., Ji, H.: Dynamic texture classification using dynamic fractal analysis. In: 2011 International Conference on Computer Vision, pp. 1219–1226, November 2011
28. Xu, Y., Huang, S., Ji, H., Fermüller, C.: Scale-space texture description on sift-like textons. Comput. Vis. Image Underst. **116**(9), 999–1013 (2012)

29. Zhao, G., Pietikainen, M.: Dynamic texture recognition using local binary patterns with an application to facial expressions. IEEE Trans. Pattern Anal. Mach. Intell. **29**(6), 915–928 (2007)
30. Zhao, G., Pietikäinen, M.: Dynamic texture recognition using volume local binary patterns. In: Vidal, R., Heyden, A., Ma, Y. (eds.) WDV 2005-2006. LNCS, vol. 4358, pp. 165–177. Springer, Heidelberg (2007). https://doi.org/10.1007/978-3-540-70932-9_13

Open Set Recognition for Unique Person Counting via Virtual Gates

Francesco Turchini, Matteo Bruni, Claudio Baecchi$^{(\boxtimes)}$, Tiberio Uricchio, and Alberto Del Bimbo

University of Florence, Florence, Italy
{francesco.turchini,matteo.bruni,claudio.baecchi,
tiberio.uricchio,alberto.delbimbo}@unifi.it
https://www.micc.unifi.it

Abstract. Retail shops or restaurants are interested in real-time profiling analysis of customer visit patterns, which could enable efficient management and target marketing. They need to know not only how many people entered but also if they are visiting for the first time and keep track of their exact number. As a result, in this paper we define the new variant of *unique counting* for videos, that is counting new persons who have not already been counted in the past. To this end, we propose a complete real-time system which is able to perform detection, tracking and unique counting in the wild with user drawn gates. A fine-tuned network on persons body is used to extract descriptors which are more privacy-oriented. Experiments of the system on the challenging DukeMTMC dataset show that our method is able to effectively count people in real time and discern between the persons which do multiple passages through the gates.

Keywords: Counting · Multitracking · Reidentification

1 Introduction

In recent times there is a great interest in computer vision for monitoring all types of environments. Many goals are impacted by new technological advances in video analysis, e.g., security, resource management, urban planning, or advertising. Of these technologies, counting people passing through a place is a fundamental problem. It is an essential building block for crowd analysis that is useful for several different applications, including crowd monitoring [14], scene understanding [19], surveillance [15] and customer analysis [4]. In particular, retail shops or restaurants are interested in real-time profiling analysis of customer visit patterns, which could enable efficient management and target marketing. They need to know not only how many people entered but also if they are visiting for the first time and keep track of their exact number.

F. Turchini and M. Bruni—Equal contribution.

© Springer Nature Switzerland AG 2019
E. Ricci et al. (Eds.): ICIAP 2019, LNCS 11751, pp. 94–105, 2019.
https://doi.org/10.1007/978-3-030-30642-7_9

As a result, in this paper we define the new variant of *unique counting* for videos i.e. counting new persons who have not already been counted in the past. At a high level, it requires to detect persons, remember and match previously observed individuals. The main challenge is the open-world setting: for each person detected the system must be able to tell if he is in the set of already known persons or if he is a new person, which is a very hard task and requires a memory based algorithm [10]. The task is different than person re-identification, which is usually performed on images and require only to match query to gallery persons. It is also different than multi-target tracking where it is required to track all people across the scene but does not address counting passages through an area or virtual line.

Fig. 1. The unique counting task. The task is to count the number of unique people who cross the virtual gate, drawn in blue. In this example, person #2 crosses the gate twice but he is only counted once. (Color figure online)

In the literature, people counting can refer to multiple different settings [14], from counting the number of instances in a single image to counting how many persons crossed a virtual gate or an area. Similarly to [9,15], in this paper we address counting by defining virtual gates. These are imaginary lines where the actual counting is made (see Fig. 1) and can be drawn freely by the user over the frame. Hence, we perform counting in the realistic setting commonly referred as "in the wild", i.e. realistic footage, including conditions contaminated by blur, non-uniform lighting, and non frontal pose. Moreover, multiple gates can be defined per single cameras, allowing monitoring of multiple entrances.

The contributions of this work are three-fold: *i.* we propose the task of unique counting which is a variation of counting task; *ii.* we propose a complete real-time system which is able to perform detection, tracking and unique counting in the wild with user drawn gates, and *iii.* we report experiments on the challenging DukeMTMC dataset [12] showing that our method is able to effectively count people in real time and discern between the few persons which do multiple passages through the gates.

The paper is organized as follows. Section 2 reports the most related work; Sect. 3 describes our method in detail, including the various parts of our pipeline;

Sect. 4 reports experiments on our adaptation of DukeMTMC to the task of unique counting and finally in Sect. 5 our conclusions are reported.

2 Related Work

The problem of unique people counting is mainly related to the topics of people counting and open world person re-identification.

2.1 People Counting

Vision-based people counting systems have become more popular in recent years, which allow counting in different scenarios [13,14]. Two different research directions are pursued: spatial people counting and temporal people counting.

Spatial People Counting. Works in this direction aim at counting the exact number of people who are present in a given image or video frame. The main difficulty of this task is related to detecting persons, taking careful attention to occlusions of people and their different appearance when in a crowd.

Detection based methods typically employ object detection methods specialized to detect people [5]. They train classifiers using features such as Haar wavelets, histogram oriented gradients [5] and more recently with convolutional neural network based methods [14]. To increase robustness to occlusions, Li et al [8] propose to use head and shoulder detectors, which are more distinct than full body. Xu et al. [17] add a tracker to reject false pedestrian detections. However, head and shoulder detectors make re-identification more difficult since they usually cover few pixels and the face can be in the opposite direction than the camera.

Temporal People Counting. These works are applied to videos and aim at counting the number of people who enter the recorded area, pass through a virtual line or a forced passage.

For areas where people flow can be forced, several researchers proposed to use overhead mounted depth cameras. They can accurately count people flowing through an entrance [4]. Nonetheless, they need proper installation and cannot be employed in other environments. For open areas where people can freely move, tracking of people is usually performed exploiting the entire body [20] or the face [21]. Since counting is often employed along waypoints or streets, a popular solution is using a virtual gate where only detection passing thorough are recorded [9,15]. For instance, Liu et al. [9] use segmentation to partition groups of people into individuals and individually track their movement crossing the gate. They track people in trajectories by formulating pedestrian hypotheses that are filtered and combined into accurate counting events. In [15], a surveillance system based on recent object detector YOLO [11] exploits an intersection over union tracker to count people who cross a gate.

This work is related to temporal people counting and is based on the use of a virtual gate. However, differently from all these works, we address the task of unique person counting which require re-identification of people who pass through the gate. We use the pedestrian appearance in a free context where a user can freely draw the counting gate. Previous work that perform re-identification uses only overhead mounted camera or face information which is limited to high resolution cameras and may not be privacy compliant.

2.2 Open World Person Re-identification

The proposed method needs to discriminate between already known and unknown persons as in the open-world setting [1]. The majority of person re-identification methods focus on closed world scenarios using discriminative view-invariant features or learning matching distance metrics [16]. Only recent work considers open-set person re-identification [7], first in small scale with basic features and distance learning [23], then with deep learning features in an end-to-end manner [18]. Nonetheless, scaling to large scale is still an open issue where only very recent work tries to address it, for instance, with hashing [25].

Differently from these methods, our approach do not need to explicitly maintain the full appearance of a person. We are only interested in the appearance at the gate proximity, which permits to reduce the uncertainty of the open-world setting and allows scaling with few resources.

3 Unique Counting System

Given a video stream, the proposed system aims to count the number of unique individuals crossing one or more *gates*. A gate is an imaginary line drawn by a user where the system has to count people, usually used to delimit a part of the scene from another.

Differently from the task of counting [14], unique person counting requires the re-identification of persons in open-world setting [10]. The system, beside detecting when a person crosses a gate, needs also to detect if an instance has already crossed a gate in the past to avoid counting it multiple times. It starts with no knowledge of the persons that will cross the gates, so it has to memorize a discriminative representation of each new person as it sees them.

For person re-identification one approach is to extract face features since they are strongly discriminative [21]. However, their use limit where the system can be applied due to technical requirements and privacy. Face detections should be at least of a minimum size to be discriminative, forcing to employ cameras with high resolutions, mounted to observe people facing the camera. Hence people cannot be recognized in both directions. Moreover, being a sensitive information, the acquisition of faces without explicit consent can raise privacy concerns. For these reasons, we propose to exploit body related features. Body features are not as discriminative as face features but they can be extracted in every pose and hardly poses any privacy concern.

The proposed system is composed of four submodules, shown in Fig. 2: *i.* a person detector to identify pedestrians in the frame; *ii.* a tracker to track the trajectory of each pedestrian and detect gate crossings; *iii.* a module to extract body features, and *iv.* a re-identification module that allows to recognize previously observed people. In the following sections we will explain in details each module.

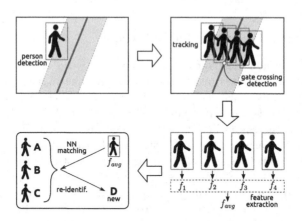

Fig. 2. Pipeline of the proposed system. Given a frame, persons are detected in the scene and tracked when they come near a gate. Upon gate crossing, features of the person in the red area near a gate are extracted and used to perform open-world re-identification. (Color figure online)

3.1   Person Detector

The person detector module is responsible of detecting pedestrian in the scene. We test two different state of the art methods which allow to process videos in real-time, with different settings. The first method we employ is a YOLO v3 network [11] which is a single-stage object detector that process an image in a single pass and generates a set of boxes with an associated probability. The method exploits a fully convolutional architecture where the last layer uses 1×1 filters to output a fixed amount of windows with different confidence. We used a network trained on the 80 classes in COCO dataset with a TensorRT implementation but detections are only taken for the class of *person*.

For this module, we also test the recent OpenPose detector [3] which is the first real-time multi-person system to jointly detect human body and its parts from single images. OpenPose exploits a sequential architecture composed of convolutional networks that directly operate on belief maps from previous stages. Part locations are increasingly refined without the need for explicit graphical model-style inference. This method emits 25 keypoints that encode the pose of each person detected, from which we derive a bounding box. More specifically, we first split these keypoints to identify head, upper body and lower body separately. Then we ensure that the three blocks that define the human body satisfy human body proportions (i.e. body height should be about $7 \times$ head height and body width should be about $2 \times$ head height). If we miss at most two of the three boxes due to keypoint absence or to low keypoint score, we can derive them by exploiting body proportions and the measures of the available ones. Finally, we take the box that tightly encompasses the three main human body parts obtained in this way. This makes our detections more robust, especially in borderline situations like cases where there are persons overlapping or partial occlusions.

3.2 Tracking and Gate Crossing Detection

Tracking detections allows the system to track movement of pedestrians and understand when they are crossing virtual gates. Each person is represented using a bounding box with its location. The detected boxes are joined together into tracks using a tracking by detection strategy, grouping bounding boxes in consecutive frames by looking at their Intersection over Union (IoU) and the optical flow estimation.

We only evaluate tracks around the gates, so that we can reduce the risk of incurring in tracking errors. We monitor the distance of the middle point of the bottom segment of the bounding box (ideally the point between the feet) from the gate line. Only when distance of the box is less than K pixels (that we empirically set to 100) from the gate, it is tracked.

The tracker continuously monitors all pedestrians in the tracks. At each frame a set of new detections is produced and we update the tracker state by associating each track to every detection, if possible. For unassociated detections we start new tracks. We employ a greedy association approach. At each frame we get a set of detections D_t; given the set of tracks T_{t-1} detected at the previous frame, we compute an association matrix $\mathbf{A}$ based on IoU, such that $\mathbf{A}_{ij} = \frac{d_i \cap t_j}{d_i \cup t_j}$. Then we apply the function *track* described in Algorithm 1.

FUNCTION track $(\mathcal{D}_t, \mathcal{T}_{t-1})$
Data: $\mathcal{T}_{t-1} : \{t_1 \ldots t_n\}, \mathcal{D}_t : \{d_1 \ldots d_m\}, \mathbf{A}_{ij} = \frac{d_i \cap t_j}{d_i \cup t_j}$
Result: $\mathcal{T}_t$
while $\max_{ij} \mathbf{A}_{ij} > \tau$ **do**
    if not $\mathbf{K}_{ij} \wedge \mathbf{A}_{ij} > \tau$ **then**
        $\langle \hat{i}, \hat{j} \rangle \leftarrow \arg\max_{ij} \mathbf{A}_{ij}$;
        $t_{\hat{i}} \leftarrow d_{\hat{j}}$ $\mathbf{K}_{\hat{i}:} \leftarrow$ TRUE;
        $\mathbf{K}_{:\hat{j}} \leftarrow$ TRUE;
    end
end
/* Tracks not used for γ frames are removed. */
$\mathcal{T}_t \leftarrow \mathcal{T}_{t-1} \setminus \{t_i | l_i > \gamma\}$;
/* Unassigned detections initialize new tracks. */
$\mathcal{T}_t \leftarrow \mathcal{T}_{t-1} \cup \{d | \mathbf{K}_{ij} =$ TRUE$\}$

Algorithm 1. Data association algorithm. We associate tracks and unassociated detection if $\mathtt{IoU} > \tau$ and remove a track if it is "dead" for ω frames. Matrix $\mathbf{A}$ keeps track of associations and vector l counts the amount of frames a track i is not associated with any detection.

The procedure generates the paths, i.e. a sequence of points followed by people on the scene. Gate crossing detection is performed by testing segment intersection between the sequences of points from each track and a given line of the gate. We address it as a segment intersection problem of 2nd degree, also known as the orientation test which robustness has been studied in [2]. Given two line segments $A = (s_1, e_1)$ and $B = (s_2, e_2)$, we can test if they intersect by checking the orientations of the ordered triplets formed by the four points (s_1, e_1, s_2, e_2). There is intersection between A and B if (s_1, e_1, s_2) and (s_1, e_1, e_2) have different orientations and similarly (s_2, e_2, s_1) and (s_2, e_2, e_1) have different orientations. If points are collinear, we handle this case by fitting a line through A and B and checking that the angle is around 0 or 180°. By looking at the orientations of the triplets we can also understand in which direction the intersection occurred.

In case of multiple gates per camera, by tracking a person that is moving across the scene we can re-identify the tracks who crosses multiple gates. In that case, the system can directly ignore the following intersections, without further advancing with the pipeline.

3.3 Body Feature Extractor

The body feature extractor module receives from the tracker those tracks that cross a gate and extract a characteristic representation of each person. We fine-tuned and tested two ResNet50 [6] networks pre-trained on the ImageNet dataset as body feature extractors. To this end, we chose two datasets which are popular for the task of person re-identification and that contain challenging visual conditions of people. The first net, named *ResNet50-Market*, is fine-tuned on the Market1501 dataset [22], while the other, *ResNet50-Duke* on the DukeMTMC-reID dataset [24]. For ResNet50-Market, we use the full training set of the Market1501 dataset which has 6 cameras and contains 32,668 annotated bounding boxes of 1,501 identities. For ResNet50-Duke, we use the full training set of the DukeMTMC-reID dataset, which is a subset of the DukeMTMC dataset, where 1,404 identities are selected and for whom 36,411 bounding boxes are extracted, sampling the videos every 120 frames. The resulting fine-tuned networks are evaluated on the respective validation sets, obtaining a mAP of 79.1% and a Rank-1 of 91.8% and a mAP of 59.4% and a Rank-1 of 77.2% respectively. In both cases the results, specifically the Rank-1 figures, show that the fine-tuned networks exhibit good re-identification capabilities.

For both network, each bounding box of a person is resized to the fixed size of 128×256 pixels as network input. The body feature is obtained by taking as output the penultimate layer feature maps of dimension 2048 normalization.

Given a track K that cross a gate, the module extracts the bounding box of the person and a feature f_i for each one of the $M = 90$ (empirically set) frames before and after the crossing, using one of the fine-tuned networks. As a result we obtain a set of feature per person crossing $F = \{f_{-45}, \ldots, f_{45}\}$. We obtain the final feature P_K by applying average pooling to the set following L2 normalization.

3.4 Re-identification

This module is responsible to keep track of the known identities and increment the counter of each gate when a new person is crossing. To this end, the module maintain a set of features $\mathcal{M}$ for each gate where new person features are stored upon crossing. To detect if a person was saw in the past we implement a simple distance strategy. Given a feature P_K, we compute its cosine distance $< P_K, M_i >$ from all features M_i in $\mathcal{M}$. When $M_i > \eta$, with η cross-validated on the training set, we consider the person as new. In that case the module increments the counter of the gate and adds P_K to $\mathcal{M}$. The number of known identities corresponds to the count of unique persons that have crossed each gate and is the final output of the system.

4 Experiments

In this section we report our experiments of the whole system and its components. We first describe the dataset used and the experimental settings. Then we report the experiments of our system on the unique counting task.

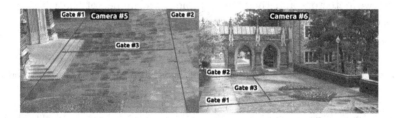

Fig. 3. Gates location. We drawn 3 gates per camera to count the flow of people along the principal directions. Note that the system allow a user to freely drawn them as many as needed.

4.1 Dataset and Ground Truth

We used the challenging DukeMTMC dataset [12]. The dataset is comprised of 8 static camera recordings of the Duke University campus. Each recording consists of roughly 85 min of 1080p 60 fps video footage with more than 2,000,000 manually annotated frames for multi-target tracking, 7,000 single camera trajectories and more than 2,000 identities. Identities have been manually annotated with the respective bounding box and unique ID. They follow unconstrained paths, moving between different cameras.

4.2   Experimental Setup

From the 8 cameras of the DukeMTMC dataset we selected 2 cameras for testing the system, specifically number 5 and 6 as they feature the most number
of identities exiting from the scene and later returning. We used the train_val
sequence as ground truth annotations are available for this one, while they are
not provided for test sequences. We cross-validated the cosine-distance threshold
η and the M frame length on camera 4.

For each scene we place 3 gates which cover all the main directions a person
can go. Images of the gates for each scene are shown in Fig. 3.

Naturally the dataset does not come with unique counting ground truth,
but we can generate it starting from its multi-target annotations. To this end,
identity annotations are used to identify which gate is crossed and by how many
persons. Counting is made when a person crosses one of the gates. Subsequent
crossing of the same or any other gate in the scene is ignored. We use the resulting
number as ground-truth for our method.

4.3   Results

For assessing the performance of the system, we first test the proposed tracker
with the two detectors and then we test the performance of the whole system
comprised also of feature extraction and re-identification.

Table 1. Counting results using the baseline approach.

	Cam. 5	Cam. 6
YL + Tracker	785	1187
OP + Tracker	644	1070
GT + Tracker	459	728
GT Unique	431	725

Table 2. Counting results using the full
system. R50 represents the ResNet50 network.

	Cam. 5	Cam. 6
YL + Tracker + R50-Market	561	778
OP + Tracker + R50-Market	533	762
GT + Tracker + R50-Market	501	741
YL + Tracker + R50-Duke	438	752
OP + Tracker + R50-Duke	434	748
GT + Tracker + R50-Duke	432	730
GT Unique	431	725

Detector + Tracker. For the first experiment, we test the tracker only in
absence of feature extractor and re-identification modules. The detector and
tracker can perform unique counting in presence of more than one gate by checking if a track intersects multiple gates. We use this method as baseline, named
YL + Tracker when using the YOLO detector and OP + Tracker when using
OpenPose. For reference, we also measure the tracker performance only by using
the ground truth boxes as detector. We name this combination GT + Tracker.

We report the resulting persons counted by the baseline in Table 1 and compare the methods to the ground truth person counting (GT Unique). We observe

that GT + Tracker and GT Unique are very narrow in gap. We note that both cameras exhibit the same observations. Given a perfect detector, our tracking method is able to obtain a very good result with only the 6.4 % of error, confirming that the tracker can effectively discern when the same person cross multiple gates. Looking at YL + Tracker and OP + Tracker we observe that the error is higher, while the latter has a slightly more correct result. This suggest that detector and tracking alone are not sufficient to perform the hard task of unique counting due to missing detections and tracker not able to completely recover from such issues. OpenPose result in more coherent detections as expected. Our tracker may miss some identities due to occlusions or persons abandoning the scene and re-entering later. This leads to double-counting, as re-entering persons would be considered new identities. At the same time, overlapping between tracks may lead to identity swap and thus to erroneous counting.

Full System. In this experiment we test the complete system, that is the four modules including feature extraction and re-identification, with the two fine-tuned networks (ResNet50-Market and ResNet50-Duke). The full system run at about ~12.2 FPS. We report in Table 2 the persons counted by the whole system in the various combinations. We can see that although having achieved a lower Rank-1 for re-identification, fine-tuning on the same domain dataset yields better results. In fact, between the various combinations, we observe that the best combination is OP + Tracker + ResNet50-Duke, resulting in a near perfect result. Comparing Tables 1 and 2, we note that by adding the last two modules, the system is able to recognize more passed people and outputs a counter more near the ground truth. This confirm that our re-identification approach is able to reduce the false counting by re-identify the track of same persons.

5   Conclusions

In this paper we proposed a system to perform the variant of unique counting, that is counting the unique persons which crosses a user drawn gate. The system is able to detect persons, track them when they are near a gate and crosses it. We perform open-world re-identification on the body feature, by exploiting fine-tuned features that we trained on Market and DukeMTMC-reid datasets. Experiments on the challenging DukeMTMC dataset showed that our system is able to effectively count people passing through the gates in real time and recognize already passed people.

Acknowledgments. This research was partially supported by NVIDIA Corporation with the donation of Titan X Pascal GPUs and Leonardo Finmeccanica SpA, Italy.

References

1. Bendale, A., Boult, T.: Towards open world recognition. In: Proceedings of the IEEE Conference CVPR, pp. 1893–1902 (2015)

2. Boissonnat, J., Preparata, F.: Robust plane sweep for intersecting segments. SIAM J. Comput. **29**(5), 1401–1421 (2000)
3. Cao, Z., Hidalgo, G., Simon, T., Wei, S.E., Sheikh, Y.: OpenPose: realtime multi-person 2D pose estimation using Part Affinity Fields. arXiv preprint arXiv:1812.08008 (2018)
4. Cho, S.I., Kang, S.J.: Real-time people counting system for customer movement analysis. IEEE Access **6**, 55264–55272 (2018)
5. Dollar, P., Wojek, C., Schiele, B., Perona, P.: Pedestrian detection: an evaluation of the state of the art. IEEE Trans. Pattern Anal. Mach. Intell. **34**(4), 743–761 (2012)
6. He, K., Zhang, X., Ren, S., Sun, J.: Deep residual learning for image recognition. In: Proceedings of the IEEE Conference on Computer Vision and Pattern Recognition, pp. 770–778 (2016)
7. Leng, Q., Ye, M., Tian, Q.: A survey of open-world person re-identification. IEEE Trans. Circuits Syst. Video Technol. (2019). https://doi.org/10.1109/TCSVT.2019.2898940
8. Li, M., Zhang, Z., Huang, K., Tan, T.: Estimating the number of people in crowded scenes by mid based foreground segmentation and head-shoulder detection. In: 2008 19th International Conference on Pattern Recognition, pp. 1–4. IEEE (2008)
9. Liu, X., Tu, P.H., Rittscher, J., Perera, A., Krahnstoever, N.: Detecting and counting people in surveillance applications. In: IEEE Conference on Advanced Video and Signal Based Surveillance, pp. 306–311. IEEE (2005)
10. Pernici, F., Bartoli, F., Bruni, M., Del Bimbo, A.: Memory based online learning of deep representations from video streams. In: Proceedings of the IEEE Conference on Computer Vision and Pattern Recognition, pp. 2324–2334 (2018)
11. Redmon, J., Farhadi, A.: Yolov3: An incremental improvement. arXiv preprint arXiv:1804.02767 (2018)
12. Ristani, E., Solera, F., Zou, R., Cucchiara, R., Tomasi, C.: Performance measures and a data set for multi-target, multi-camera tracking. In: Hua, G., Jégou, H. (eds.) ECCV 2016. LNCS, vol. 9914, pp. 17–35. Springer, Cham (2016). https://doi.org/10.1007/978-3-319-48881-3_2
13. Saleh, S.A.M., Suandi, S.A., Ibrahim, H.: Recent survey on crowd density estimation and counting for visual surveillance. Eng. Appl. Artif. Intell. **41**, 103–114 (2015)
14. Sindagi, V.A., Patel, V.M.: A survey of recent advances in CNN-based single image crowd counting and density estimation. Pattern Recogn. Lett. **107**, 3–16 (2018)
15. Turchini, F., Seidenari, L., Uricchio, T., Del Bimbo, A.: Deep learning based surveillance system for open critical areas. Inventions **3**(4), 69 (2018)
16. Wang, K., Wang, H., Liu, M., Xing, X., Han, T.: Survey on person re-identification based on deep learning. CAAI Trans. Intell. Technol. **3**(4), 219–227 (2018)
17. Xu, H., Lv, P., Meng, L.: A people counting system based on head-shoulder detection and tracking in surveillance video. In: 2010 International Conference On Computer Design and Applications, vol. 1, p. V1–394. IEEE (2010)
18. Xu, Y., Ma, B., Huang, R., Lin, L.: Person search in a scene by jointly modeling people commonness and person uniqueness. In: Proceedings of the 22nd ACM International Conference on Multimedia, pp. 937–940. ACM (2014)
19. Zhang, C., Li, H., Wang, X., Yang, X.: Cross-scene crowd counting via deep convolutional neural networks. In: Proceedings of the IEEE Conference on Computer Vision and Pattern Recognition, pp. 833–841 (2015)

20. Zhang, E., Chen, F.: A fast and robust people counting method in video surveillance. In: 2007 International Conference on Computational Intelligence and Security (CIS 2007), pp. 339–343. IEEE (2007)
21. Zhao, X., Delleandrea, E., Chen, L.: A people counting system based on face detection and tracking in a video. In: 2009 Sixth IEEE International Conference on Advanced Video and Signal Based Surveillance, pp. 67–72. IEEE (2009)
22. Zheng, L., Shen, L., Tian, L., Wang, S., Wang, J., Tian, Q.: Scalable person re-identification: a benchmark. In: Proceedings of the IEEE International Conference on Computer Vision (2015)
23. Zheng, W.S., Gong, S., Xiang, T.: Person re-identification by probabilistic relative distance comparison. In: CVPR 2011, pp. 649–656. IEEE (2011)
24. Zheng, Z., Zheng, L., Yang, Y.: Unlabeled samples generated by GAN improve the person re-identification baseline in vitro. In: Proceedings of the IEEE International Conference on Computer Vision (2017)
25. Zhu, X., Wu, B., Huang, D., Zheng, W.S.: Fast open-world person re-identification. IEEE Trans. Image Process. **27**(5), 2286–2300 (2018)

A Low-Cost Computer Vision System for Real-Time Tennis Analysis

S. Messelodi[1]([✉]), C. M. Modena[1], V. Ropele[2], S. Marcon[2], and M. Sgrò[2]

[1] FBK-irst, Via Sommarive 18, 38123 Trento, Italy
{messelod,modena}@fbk.eu
[2] Eyes VisiON srl, Via alla Cascata, 56C, 38123 Trento, Italy
{valerio.ropele,stefano.marcon,mario.sgro}@eyeson.tennis

Abstract. This paper describes a low-cost vision-based system for real-time tennis game analysis. The system elaborates videos captured by four synchronized and calibrated cameras installed at the sides of the court in order to accurately localize ball and players, and track them in real-time. From this low-level data mid-level events, like shots, bounces, ball in net, and high-level events, like stroke type and line calling, are detected. All this data is made available to the players both on-court during the play or through a web device at the end of the session. Currently, system prototypes are undergoing a field test in three locations in Italy. In addition to positive comments of users, robustness and reliability of the system have been demonstrated with specific evaluation tests. Detection rate of shots is 99.7% while miss detection rate is less than 0.8%. Reliability of the stroke classification is 97.1% and of *in/out* evaluation is 99.5%. On average reaction time for line calling is 152 ms.

Keywords: Tennis analysis · Real-time image processing · Line calling

1 Introduction

Sport is a physical activity aiming to improve skills through personal challenges and competitions and, at the same time, to provide recreation and enjoyment to participants. Competitive sport represents a source of entertainment for an ever increasing number of spectators around the world, especially thanks to the wide diffusion of television and digital media, making it an important business.

The topic of content-based analysis of broadcast sport material, including tennis, has received, and continues to receive, great attention and efforts from the computer vision research community. In particular, techniques have been proposed for automatic annotation of multimedia archives for information retrieval [19,21] and for video enhancement [16] using augmented reality methods to improve the engagement of spectators.

This work has been partially funded by Provincia Autonoma di Trento (Italy) under L.P. 6/99. Authors would like to thank the staff involved in the system development.

E. Ricci et al. (Eds.): ICIAP 2019, LNCS 11751, pp. 106–116, 2019.
https://doi.org/10.1007/978-3-030-30642-7_10

We propose a low-cost solution based on computer vision to extract in real-time low-level information from a tennis game on-court. Specifically, our system is able to detect and track the 3D position of ball and players. This data is then used by a higher level module to extract analytics than can be offered to the players both on the field and through a web application. Currently the system provides (i) classified detection of shots (forehand, backhand, serve) along with information about space/time localization, velocity and spin, (ii) detection of ball bounces with the estimation of the court contact region supporting the line calling functionality. The solution has been included in a novel system, called EYES ON[1] with the main purpose to allow players to experience the game in a novel and appealing modality, by checking their personal performance, their progress over time, and to get help in the evaluation of controversial in/out cases.

The paper is organized as follows: Sect. 2 provides a brief overview of the state of the art of products or systems devoted to the tennis world. Section 3 presents the main features and the general architecture of EYES ON. Section 4 provides a description of the computer vision sub-system, its modules and the low-level data they provide. Section 5 describes the analytics that are computed from data collected by the vision sub-system, and their visualization through a user interface. Experiments and system performance are provided in Sect. 6, while Sect. 7 concludes the paper with planned future upgrades.

2   Related Work

In the last two decades products devoted to tennis analysis with dedicated cameras in the court have been proposed. For example, LucentVision [15,16], Hawk-Eye [14], and Foxtenn are professional monitoring tennis systems. LucentVision, a system for enhanced tennis broadcasts using real-time game statistics and virtual replays, was launched in 1998 with the ATP Tour and has been used in broadcasts of international tennis tournaments. Hawk-Eye [1,14] ball tracking system is the most advanced tool used in official tennis matches since 2002, and still in use today. It is known for its electronic line calling functionality. Hawk-Eye uses up to ten high resolution cameras placed on the stadium roof, capturing images at 50/60 frame per second (fps) [12,20]. Foxtenn, proposed by Foxtennis Begreen, includes the line calling functionality and recently it received the official approval from the International Tennis Federation (ITF) [11] for its usage in competitions. The system uses up to 8 cameras at 120/2500 fps synchronized with a high-speed laser scanner system. Because of their cost and the complex installation and calibration procedure, they are targeted to the professional circuit. Recently, some monitoring products addressed to players appeared on the market, but aiming only at specific practice or training task, e.g. monitoring the hits of balls being shot from a ball machine [22], supporting coaches for player performance analysis [4,18], detecting where a ball has landed on the court to support the line calling function [9], with a camera mounted on a net-post.

---

[1] https://www.eyeson.tennis.

A few systems for monitoring tennis game have been proposed in the literature. A comprehensive system is TennisSense [3], an instrumented platform for indoor courts, devoted to player performance analysis and health monitoring. The project focuses on multi-modal sensors integration, including a computer vision system and wearable electronic sensing devices. Among the systems based solely on vision we cite the video indexing system outlined in [17] and the platform described in [18]. In both cases they suffer the limitation to operate only for indoor court and, most important, not in real-time.

To the best of our knowledge SmartCourt [10], offered by PlaySight Interactive, is the only system on the market that provides a complete monitoring of tennis game and that can be compared to EYES ON, at least in terms of functionalities. It is equipped with four high-definition cameras working at 50 fps, one or more web cameras, and a graphical interactive interface located in a kiosk structure next to the court. Cameras must be positioned at the top of poles placed at the four corners of the court. It employs image processing algorithms to extract information about strokes, ball trajectory, speed of shots, as well as player movements. Purpose of the web cameras is to support video recording for instant replay on the kiosk from different angles.

3   Outline of the System

The design and implementation of the proposed computer vision system took into account a list of requirements of the whole project: (i) extraction of useful information, part of which immediately available to the players, (ii) accuracy of detection in order to enable the line calling functionality, (iii) applicability in a wide range of different conditions, (iv) ease of installation and configuration, and (v) low-cost. The global architecture of EYES ON is schematized in Fig. 1. The core resides in Vision System whose task is to process video streams provided by cameras observing the court for a twofold purpose: (i) extract low-level data related to 3D position of ball and players with a sufficient temporal resolution to generate accurate trajectories, and (ii) detect relevant events - like ball bounce, ball in net, ball hit by racket - along with their localization in space and time. This data, as soon as it is available, is sent to a Supervisor module which controls the whole system by managing (i) the interaction with the user and (ii) the communication with a local database and the Cloud. The Supervisor includes a video analitycs module for the processing of low-level data coming from the Vision System to extract high-level meaningful information for the users, e.g. stroke classification or in/out decision. The interaction between Supervisor and user, through the on-court GUI, allows players to register and to select the desired game modality: match, warm-up, or drills. According to the selected mode the Supervisor properly configures the analitycs module. Computed analytics are stored in a local database and, upon request, are shown to the players through the GUI. At the end of each session the extracted data is sent to the Cloud and stored in a permanent database that can be remotely accessed to get personalized performance analysis, trends, or comparison with players community. The hardware configuration of the system includes a processing unit hosted in a cabinet on one side of the net along with a touch screen display, and four cameras that, in a common set-up, are mounted on two supports located next to the net-posts. The two halves of the court are monitored independently by pairs of cameras. They are synchronized and cable-connected to the processing unit. A position close to the net, besides simplifying the installation, helps in minimizing ball occlusions due to the body of players. But, as a matter of fact, cameras do not necessarily have to be mounted on such supports, and they can be installed on possibly existing structures provided they offer a comparable view of the scene. Other cameras may be optionally installed in the court with the aim to observe and record tennis action from different points of view.

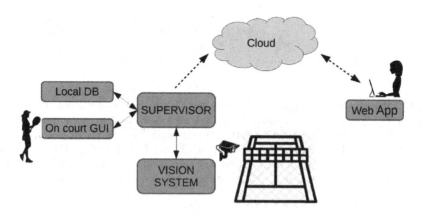

Fig. 1. EYES ON's software architecture. Through the On-court GUI players can register and select the game mode; Supervisor activates the Vision System and, accordingly to game mode, computes and stores analytics on local and cloud DBs. Results are accessible immediately through On-court GUI or via Web App at the end of the session.

4   Vision System

To meet system requirements we designed and implemented computer vision modules characterized by: (i) low complexity in order to run in real-time, (ii) adaptability to a wide range of illumination conditions, (iii) flexibility with respect to moderate variations of camera position, (iv) ability to detect and track accurately small and fast moving objects (e.g. 180 km/h). The Vision System is organized as a set of different specialized software modules which are coordinated at run time by a Vision Manager (VM), which is also in charge of communicating with the Supervisor. The software architecture is diagrammed in Fig. 2. Software modules run on different threads whose execution is orchestrated by VM. VM keeps track of the global state of the monitoring system including information like: a ball is currently tracked or both the players are in the court. In the following we describe different functionalities provided by the Vision System along with the role played by the modules in Fig. 2.

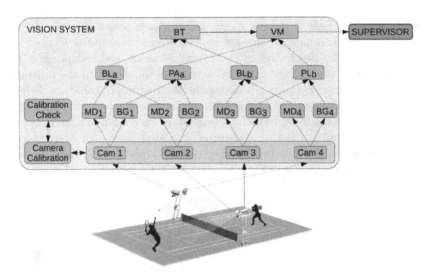

Fig. 2. Software architecture of the multi-thread Computer Vision system. The Vision Manager (VM) communicates with Supervisor and orchestrates the activity of the analysis modules: Motion Detection (MD), Background Analysis (BG), Ball Localization (BL), Player Localization and tracking (PL), and Ball Tracking (BT). Analysis modules use camera parameters produced and checked by two special modules. Each camera manager (Cam) acts as interface between a camera and the processing modules.

Configuration. The vision modules behaviour depends on the value of a set of parameters that have to be defined at installation time. The most relevant regard court and cameras: A COURT MODEL stores the position court elements (baselines, service lines, lateral lines, ...) with respect to a real-world coordinate system having origin in the centre of the court, X axis along the middle court line, Y axis along the net line and Z axis oriented upwards. The model includes also information about the court surface (clay, hard, grass, carpet). CAMERA CALIBRATION is a critical but essential step for 3D object localization from 2D images. Intrinsic camera parameters are estimated once and for all in laboratory by acquiring images of specific graphical patterns. Extrinsic parameters are estimated by an automatic module that works on images acquired at installation time after fixing cameras on their supports with a proper field of view. The auto-calibration module localizes the court lines intersections and put them in correspondence with the real-world positions stored in the COURT MODEL to calculate camera coordinates and orientation with respect to the reference system. An auxiliary module, called CALIBRATION CHECK, has been implemented for the periodical verification of camera poses. The alignment of expected court lines, according to calibration, and real ones is computed and if misalignment overcomes a given threshold a re-calibration step is automatically executed.

Image Analysis for Object Detection. Image acquisition and delivery to processing modules is managed by the *Cam* modules (see Fig. 2): each camera acquires color images 1920×1200 at 50 fps, or 1920×1024 at 60 fps. Images are stored in circular buffers and provided upon request to the analysis modules. Two approaches are adopted to detect foreground objects from single images: background subtraction and motion detection (or frame difference). Four background updating modules (BG), running in parallel, get frames from camera managers and process them to create and maintain four images that store the appearance of the scene without foreground objects, e.g. players. To compute the so called foreground the current frame is compared to the background image. The background reference image is periodically updated (typically 3/5 times per second) in order to model scene changes, which otherwise would lead to the detection of false objects. Our method for background generation and updating is based on [13]. Motion Detector (MD) is another low-level processing module that gets frames from Cam and puts them in a short circular buffer. These are processed to identify pixels corresponding to moving objects in an image and to produce a motion map. It is analyzed to detect regions compatible with a moving ball using two methods: (i) after thresholding, extraction of connected components and morphological filtering, (ii) detection of peaked moving regions having a circular or elliptical shape. For each frame, the motion detector output is a set of candidate ball regions. The module is applied to the entire frame or to selected sub-regions according to the global state of the ball detection system stored in the Vision Manager.

3D Ball Localization and Tracking. This task is in charge to Ball Localization (BL) and Ball Tracking BT modules. BL is based on the analysis of the 2D candidate ball regions produced by two MD modules looking at the same half court. The type of analysis depends on the state of the tracking system, in particular we distinguish two states: (a) the system is searching for a moving ball (*search*), (b) the system is currently tracking a ball (*track*). In the first case both BL modules run in parallel looking for a moving ball in their respective half court. A BL collects candidate regions from a short sequence of consecutive frames and, through triangulation, provides a cloud of ball candidates in the 3D space. By means of graph analysis, 3D candidates collected through time are filtered to build a 'tracklet' consistent with the physical model of a flying ball [8]. When a BL detects a 3D ball the state of the system switches to *track* and the expected trajectory of the ball is estimated according to the motion model. If the system is in state *track*, the computation of the current ball location depends on the distance of candidate regions to their predicted position according to the expected trajectory. The system estimates the new ball position along with a confidence factor. In case of high confidence the new position is used to update the expected trajectory. A low confidence means a detection failure which is notified to BT for a proper management of the condition. BT monitors the output of the BL modules and, as soon as it is not consistent with the predicted trajectory, it performs a detailed analysis in order to identify the reason, that typically is included in the following list: ball went out the field of view, ball bounced, ball went in the net, ball touched the net chord, ball hit by a player. If the module recognizes one of these conditions it deals with it in a specific way, otherwise it labels the track as lost and the state is set again to *search*.

The management of the bounce event is particularly critical to support the *line calling* functionality. As described in [7], the ball cannot be assimilated to a material point with non-zero mass, but as a moving elastic sphere, that rolls and slides, and its contact with the ground is not a point but an area. For this, we use a bouncing model [2,5,6], and describe the impact region as an ellipsis. Accurate detection of the ball during the impact with a racket is a critical task, mainly because of fast movements and possible ball occlusions. For this reasons we infer the time and space coordinates of the impact point by analysing in-coming and out-going branches of the ball trajectory. BT returns to VM the ball coordinates at each time and the occurrences of mid-level events, like bounce, ball in net, impact with racket, net chord, along with the spatio-temporal coordinates they happened.

Player Detection and Tracking. Player Localization module *PL*, one for each half-court, aims to estimate player position and movement (Fig. 3). It computes two foreground maps from the output of BG modules related to the same half court. The module exploits a correspondence map that associates foreground pixels to lists of possible player locations in the real-world. This map is pre-computed in an off-line configuration phase by virtually placing a player model on a grid of locations on the court, projecting it on the image plane, and collecting the coordinates of changed pixels. The correspondence map permits to compute, at run-time, a discretized probability map of player location, in real-world coordinates, by accumulating the contribution of every foreground pixel. The probability maps are multiplied to combine information coming from the two points of view. To take into account spatio-temporal continuity, a prior probability map is considered that enforce the player location to be in a neigh-bourhood of the previous one. At the beginning, the prior map favours positions close to the baseline. The entropy of the probability map is used to determine if a player is in the court: high entropy values mean low probability of a person to be in the scene. PL modules run typically at 5–10 Hz and return to the Vision Manager information about presence and position of players in each half court.

Fig. 3. Player localization: probability maps that explain foreground regions in two correspondent views (second and third maps) and an updated prior map of player location (first map) are used to estimates a posterior distribution (fourth map). The most probable location is reported in the 2D top view.

5   Analytics and Their Visualization

The Supervisor includes a module to process data produced by Vision System to compute video analytics, i.e. meaningful information about the observed activity useful for players to asses their skills and measure their progress. Knowledge about 3D trajectories of ball and players in real-time enables the extraction of useful data, like classification of the stroke type, building of bounce and serve maps, computation of shot speed, analysis of relative position of ball, player and racket during an impact. At an even higher level, it is also possible to obtain information about the sequence of individual strokes and to provide a description of player strategies. In the following we describe the most relevant implemented analytics.

Stroke Classification. In general, the stroke type depends on ball and player absolute and relative positions, e.g. serve, forehand, backhand, smash, but in order to provide a more detailed classification other data have to be considered: ball spin (top-spin, slice), ball direction (cross, long-line), opponent position (passing, lob), ball bounce before (volley) or after (drop-shot) the hit. At present, the system implements the classification of serve, forehand and backhand.

Line Calling. This analytic computes the possible intersection of the *legal region* with the ellipse provided by the Computer Vision along with the bounce event, to establish if the ball has fallen in or not. The *legal region* is differently defined by the tennis rule depending on the fact that the stroke originating the bounce is a serve, or not. In the first case it depends on the server player position (cross-court service box), while in all the other cases it is the opposite half court. The analytic considers therefore the playing situation: type of stroke and, if necessary, player position.

Other information are computed and made available to the players, like landing point map, player occupancy and movements maps, traveled distance, as well as statistics on speed/spin of the ball by type of stroke. Results of analytics are almost instantaneously accessible to players, through the on-court GUI. Data is visualized on the dashboard in a traditional tabular form as well as by means of geolocalized maps which enable the player to interpret spatio-temporal data at a glance. Figure 4 reports some examples. Video of the whole match or selected video clips are uploaded to a web server at the end of the game session and then accessible from any web device and shareable on social media.

Fig. 4. Analytics examples. From left to right: real-time visualization during a match (shot classification, speed, spin); reconstruction of the landing point; statistics and map about a serve drill.

6 System Performance

EYES ON is currently installed in three tennis clubs and has almost completed the test phase (Fig. 5): Circolo Tennis (CT) Trento (Italy) - clay court covered with an air dome system during autumn and winter; Circolo Tennis Arco (Trento, Italy) - hard court inside a sport building; Centro di Preparazione Olimpica (CPO) of Tirrenia (Pisa, Italy) - belongs to the Italian Tennis Federation which has decided to evaluate EYES ON as a tool to support training of young top players. The various installations allowed players with different needs to test the system and provide their qualitative feedback. To assess the system quantitatively, we collected and examined data contained in a total of 1 h 23' 35" of game (match and drills), corresponding to 250.750 frames per camera, in sequences acquired from different court scenarios. In the considered videos 1069 shots are present, defining as shot the event in which a flying ball has an impact with a racket. The system has correctly detected 1061 shots (Precision 99.3%) and generated 3 false detection (Recall 99.7%). Table 1 reports performance about stroke classification by type (*Forehand, Backhand, Serve*) and by destination (*IN, OUT, Fault*). In the tables each row represents the instances of a true class, while the columns represent the classification provided by the system. In both cases data refers to the set of 1061 shots correctly detected. The system exhibits a reliability rate greater than 97% to declare the correct type of stroke and a reliability of 99.5% relatively to the shot destination.

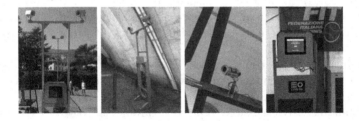

Fig. 5. System installed at CT Trento court without and with covering. Camera on the timber joists at CT Arco, and cabinet at CPO Tirrenia.

Running Time. We evaluate system performance in terms of processing time through various working sessions, with different lighting conditions and game modes. Table 2-Left reports mean elaboration time for the most time consuming tasks, i.e. 3D ball localization and player localization. On average, half of the time is dedicated to the first task, while player localization, which is computed in parallel at a lower frame rate, requires only 75 ms every second. Therefore, the processing power can be dedicated to the other software components of the system for about 50% of the time, on average.

System Reactivity. We have estimated the *reaction time* of the system, that is the time needed by the system to signal an event (hit or bounce) after it happened.

Table 1. Left: Confusion table related to the classification of the three basic stroke types. Right: Confusion table related to the classification of shot as *IN, OUT, Fault*. GT columns report the ground-truth number of events.

	GT	*Fore*	*Back*	*Serve*	Reliability(%)		GT	*IN*	*OUT*	*Fault*	Rel(%)
Forehand	590	571	19	0	96.8	*IN*	855	852	3	0	99.7
Backhand	310	12	298	0	96.1	*OUT*	104	1	103	0	99.0
Serve	161	0	0	161	100.00	*Fault*	102	1	0	101	99.0
total	1061				97.1	total	1061				99.5

It is a sum of a small constant time, intrinsic in low-level image processing, plus the time to reliably detect the ball trajectory after the event and, finally, the time to compute the shot parameters. As reported in Table 2-Right complete information about the shot preceding the event is available after about 300 ms the event occurred. In the case spin calculation is not required, e.g. for in/out estimation, the average reaction time results to be 152 ms.

Table 2. Left: Average processing time for the main computer vision tasks: 3D ball localization and player localization. Right: Statistics on system reactivity (in milliseconds). We reported the average delay times (μ) in detecting a shot or a bounce, with and without computation of motion parameters (MP), and the standard deviation σ.

task	time (ms)	freq (Hz)	ms per sec		event	samples	with MP	w/o MP	σ
ball	10	50	500		*racket*	447	319	220	124
player	15	5	75		*bounce*	291	307	152	84

7 Conclusion

We have described a real-time vision-based system that offers to tennis players a new training and matching style. The system collects data and provide analysis usable by players, managers, coaches to improve game performance, highlighting weaknesses or strengths. The system is low-cost, flexible, easy to install, user friendly and reliable. Positive feedback has been collected from players who tested the system in three pilot installations. System reliability has been assessed in tests on real games. According to market needs, in the future we would like to extend the functionality of the system and improve its accuracy in order to submit the product to the ITF evaluation for obtaining the approval for automated line calling systems. Furthermore, research work continues to extend the system to analysis of other sports by taking advantage of the flexibility of the implemented modules.

References

1. Baodong, Y.: Hawkeye technology using Tennis match. Comput. Model. New Technol. **18**(12C), 400–402 (2014)

2. Brody, H.: Bounce of a tennis ball. J. Sci. Med. Sport **6**(1), 113–119 (2003)
3. Conaire, C.O., Kelly, P., Connaghan, D., O'Connor, N.: TennisSense: a platform for extracting semantic information from multi-camera tennis data. In: International Conference on Digital Signal Processing, Santorini, Greece (2009)
4. Connaghan, D., Moran, K., O'Connor, N.E.: An automatic visual analysis system for tennis. Proc. Inst. Mech. Eng. Part P J. Sports Eng. Technol. **227**(4), 273–288 (2013)
5. Cross, R.: The bounce of a ball. Am. J. Phys. **67**(3), 222–227 (1999)
6. Cross, R.: Measurements of the horizontal coefficient of restitution for a superball and a tennis ball. Am. J. Phys. **70**(5), 482–489 (2002)
7. Cross, R.: The footprint of a tennis ball. Sports Eng. **17**(4), 239–247 (2014)
8. Cross, R., Lindsey, C.: Measurements of drag and lift on tennis balls in flight. Sports Eng. **17**, 89–96 (2014)
9. In/Out: The Portable Ready-to-Use Line Call Device (2019). https://inout.tennis
10. ITF: Player Analysis Technology. PlaySight SmartCourt. Approval report PAT-13-003, Int. Tennis Federation, February 2014
11. ITF: Player Analysis Technology. FOXTENN. Approval report PAT-16-014, Int. Tennis Federation, May 2017
12. ITF: Player Analysis Technology. Hawk-Eye. Approval report PAT-18-001, Int. Tennis Federation, July 2018
13. Messelodi, S., Modena, C.M., Segata, N., Zanin, M.: A Kalman filter based background updating algorithm robust to sharp illumination changes. In: Roli, F., Vitulano, S. (eds.) ICIAP 2005. LNCS, vol. 3617, pp. 163–170. Springer, Heidelberg (2005). https://doi.org/10.1007/11553595_20
14. Owens, N., Harris, C., Stennett, C.: Hawk-eye tennis system. In: International Conference on Visual Information Engineering, Surrey, UK, pp. 182–185 (2003)
15. Pingali, G., Jean, Y., Opalach, A., Carlbom, I.: LucentVision: converting real world events into multimedia experiences. In: IEEE International Conference on Multimedia and Expo, Singapore (2000)
16. Pingali, G., Opalach, A., Jean, Y., Carlbom, I.: Instantly indexed multimedia databases of real world events. IEEE Trans. Multimed. **4**, 269–282 (2002)
17. Poliakov, A., Marruad, D., Reithler, L., Chatain, C.: Physics based 3D ball tracking for tennis videos. In: International Workshop of Content Based Multimedia Indexing, Grenoble, France (2010)
18. Renó, V., et al.: A technology platform for automatic high-level tennis game analysis. Comput. Vis. Image Underst. **159**, 164–175 (2017)
19. Teachabarikiti, K., Chalidabhongse, T., Thammano, A.: Players tracking and ball detection for an automatic tennis video annotation. In: International Conference on Control, Automation, Robotics and Vision, Singapore (2010)
20. Thomas, G., Gade, R., Moeslund, T., Carr, P., Hilton, A.: Computer vision for sports: current applications and research topics. Comput. Vis. Image Underst. **159**, 3–18 (2017)
21. Yan, F., et al.: Automatic annotation of tennis games: an integration of audio, vision, and learning. Image Vis. Comput. **32**, 896–903 (2014)
22. Yoo, W., Jones, Z., Atsbaha, H., Wingfield, D.: Painless tennis ball tracking system. In: IEEE Computer Software and Applications Conference, Tokyo, Japan (2018)

Virtual Crowds: An LSTM-Based Framework for Crowd Simulation

Niccoló Bisagno, Nicola Garau, Andrea Montagner, and Nicola Conci[✉]

DISI - University of Trento, Trento, Italy
{niccolo.bisagno,nicola.garau,andrea.montagner,nicola.conci}@unitn.it

Abstract. Social modeling of pedestrian dynamics is a key element to understand the behavior of crowded scenes. Existing crowd models like the Social Force Model and the Reciprocal Velocity Obstacle, traditionally rely on empirically-defined functions to characterize the dynamics of a crowd. On the other hand, frameworks based on deep learning, like the Social LSTM and the Social GAN, have proven their ability to predict pedestrians trajectories without requiring a predefined mathematical model. In this paper we propose a new paradigm for crowd simulation based on a pool of LSTM networks. Each pedestrian is able to move independently and interact with the surrounding environment, given a starting point and a destination goal.

Keywords: Crowd modeling · Crowd simulation · LSTM · Behavior analysis

1 Introduction

Although a considerable amount of research has been carried out in the domain of behavior understanding and crowd motion analysis, there is still lack of a unified framework for validation. This is due to the fragmentation and heterogeneity of datasets used for testing and benchmarking, which often suffer from scarcity of training and testing data. Furthermore, quality of videos, size of datasets, duration of sequences, content, density of the crowd, and quality of the annotation, are only a few of the multiple factors that make it difficult to critically evaluate the performance of machine vision algorithms. To address this problem, one of the possibilities is to rely on simulators, which, although they might not resemble the scenes as natural as the real videos, they provide a considerable number of advantages, as automatic data annotation, and full control of camera parameters. The integration of simulators in the processing pipeline has been little investigated in the existing literature, and has initially been ruled by purely agent-based models [5], thus conducting the analysis on the agents ground-truth position.

The use of simulators in computer vision is not new per se, in particular for object tracking and camera control [16], and, in computer vision, we have recently observed an increasing interest in the generation of virtual videos instead

© Springer Nature Switzerland AG 2019
E. Ricci et al. (Eds.): ICIAP 2019, LNCS 11751, pp. 117–127, 2019.
https://doi.org/10.1007/978-3-030-30642-7_11

of virtual agents behaviors. The substantial difference between the two consists of carrying out the analysis with standard computer vision techniques, using the videos generated by the simulator for testing purposes. This allows taking into account potentially all the challenges of a real video, including the presence of occlusions, obstacles, changes in the illumination conditions, similarity of objects in the appearance model, etc.

In pedestrian dynamics, researchers have focused in the past on the study of trajectories and social interactions between agents. The Social Force Model (SFM) [10], the Reciprocal Velocity Obstacle model [20], and the continuum crowds model [19] are among the best existing empirical models for crowd simulation derived from observation of the real world.

Recently, deep learning has been applied to prediction and forecasting of agents in a video. Recurrent Neural Networks (RNNs), and in particular Long-Short Term Memory (LSTM) networks, have successfully been adopted to predict the scene evolution over time [1]. This kind of networks has shown the ability to learn the relation between spatially distributed data and its evolution. LSTMs has also proven to be capable of generating video sequences complying with predefined patterns [7]. Starting form the work in [1], we extend the use of LSTM networks from path prediction to simulation of crowded video sequences. The proposed method is implemented via a recurrent deep neural network based on LSTM cells. Each agent in the simulation is driven by its own LSTM network, which is aware of the hidden state of neighbouring agents. We train the LSTM on our synthetic dataset, showing how the network is effectively able to learn and replicate the simulated motion model. This demonstrates that gathering person-specific datasets of real subjects would open to the opportunity to learn person-specific behaviors, allowing for the inclusion of personal inclinations in the virtual crowd model for a more realistic simulation.

To prove the feasibility of our approach in simulating end-to-end trajectories, we validate our model using a synthetic dataset where agents move according to the SFM [10], demonstrating how the proposed framework can effectively learn the typical features of the SFM and reproduce them on different agents. The compliance of the predicted paths against the SFM is measured using the spatial distribution metric introduced in [9].

2   Related Work

The so-called Social Force Model relies on Newtonian forces to model the interaction between pedestrians and to guide each agent towards its goal. Similarly, in robotics, the Reciprocal velocity Obstacle (RVO) [20] is widely used to model the collision avoidance behavior between agents.

In the work by Treuille et al. [19], the crowd is modeled as a fluid, where agents are influenced by their goal, position, their preferred speed and a discomfort factor. However, the models mentioned above require the estimation or computation of parameters, in order to replicate the interaction among agents. The literature has tackled this issue relying on common optimization methods, like the Gradient-based Newton method [17] and Genetic Algorithms [15]. All these methods are able to describe crowd behaviors assuming the availability of a strong prior for the model. While they are good in describing the movements of the whole crowd, they often fail in correctly representing the agent's personality, which is a key feature to enrich the model and make the simulation closer to the behavior of real subjects. Data-driven approaches have recently been employed to capture and model interactions among people in a crowd. Patil et al. [14] use vector fields, either learned or manually sketched, to guide the crowd flow in the environment. Goal-dependent velocity fields have also been used to guide the simulation at a global level [3]. Lerner et al. [12] guide the agents using learned trajectories, choosing the one that best matches the situation that the agent is facing. Empirically-defined models can only tweak the behavior of different agents by varying parameters such as personal distances and preferred velocities; data-driven simulations allow instead learning and simulating common social rules, such as the behavior at a roundabout, but local descriptors for each agent personality cannot be handled directly. Cognitive models have been employed to allow agents performing high-levels tasks such as path planning [6]. Various approaches have been employed to vary the pedestrian behavior in the same situation, such as the OCEAN model [5] and the general adaptation syndrome [2]. These models focus on local shaping of the motion, based on personality traits, rather than long-term tasks.

As far as path prediction and activity forecasting is concerned, the literature reports a good amount of relevant works. The Social Force Model has shown good results in predicting pedestrian trajectories in the environment. Pellegrini et al. have proposed the Linear Trajectory Avoidance model [15], which predicts the short term path of a pedestrian. Interactive Gaussian processes have shown the ability to effectively improve the capability of a robot to predict pedestrian trajectories and navigate a crowded environment [18]. More recently, Recurrent Neural Networks, in particular LSTMs, have proven good capabilities in describing spatially distributed data, also providing a temporal link in sequences. LSTMs have been applied to crowd trajectory prediction by Alahi et al. [1]. However, as mentioned above, one important issue in crowd simulation is the lack of a recognized evaluation metric to assess the quality of a simulation. If the simulation refers to an existing, real-life scenario, it can be evaluated using common tools, by measuring global features, such as density and distribution of the elements in the scene. Density-based [13] and entropy-based metrics [8] are often used to compare real and synthetic data.

In [9], Helbing et al. present a metric based on the density distribution between two sets of trajectories. As detailed later, we will adopt this metric to evaluate the performances of our simulator in a quantitative manner.

3   The Proposed Model

Empirically-defined parametric functions are generally good in reproducing the global motion properties of the crowd, but they tend to fail when capturing the complexity that leads each human to react differently when facing the presence of other subjects or obstacles.

In the domain of path prediction, LSTM networks [11] have shown good capabilities in predicting the behavior of pedestrians, if properly trained. In particular, the Social LSTM model [1] is able to capture the status of the neighborhood around each agent (number and position of other agents), which is then used to refine the trajectory prediction. In our work, we propose a model able to perform a simulation of a crowded scene by learning the motion properties of the agents from a set of training video sequences. Each agent in the simulation is provided with an autonomous network, based on LSTM cells. Each pedestrian tries to reach its target destination given a starting point, a goal and the status of his neighborhood.

Depending on the set of trajectories used to train the specific network, each LSTM network can react in a different way to the same scenario. For example, if an LSTM network is trained with a set of trajectories belonging to a specific person, it will then be able to learn that model, thus replicating the subject reactions (personality traits) to specific situations occurring in the simulation. The possibility of reproducing different personality traits makes it possible to simulate semantically rich realistic situations, which do not rely on purely deterministic models. To the best of our knowledge, such paradigm has not been explored in the state-of-the-art and no dataset in this form has been made available to the research community.

3.1   Virtual Crowds

Extending the LSTM paradigm to crowd simulation, each agent's movements are controlled by an LSTM network, able to guide it through the environment.

Agents (pedestrians in our scenario) moving in the crowd are influenced by their goal, their personality, and the state of their neighborhood. All necessary details are provided in the next paragraphs.

Goal Modeling. At the beginning of the simulation each agent/pedestrian ped_i, whose position is defined as (x_t^i, y_t^i), is initialized at a starting position (x_0^i, y_0^i). The goal of the i-th pedestrian ped_i is defined as

$$g^i = (x_g^i, y_g^i) \tag{1}$$

where x_g^i and y_g^i are coordinates defined in meters in the simulator.

The chain structure of a cell of the neural network is shown in Fig. 1. At each time step, the inputs of the LSTM cell representing a pedestrian are (i) the previous position (x_{t-1}^i, y_{t-1}^i), (ii) the goal g^i, and (iii) the Social pooling tensor H_t^i. The output of the LSTM cell is the agent position (x_t^i, y_t^i).

When the Euclidean distance between the current position (x_t^i, y_t^i) and the goal g^i is less then one meter, the simulation of that pedestrian is terminated.

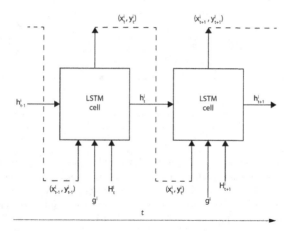

Fig. 1. The figure represents the chain structure of the LSTM network between two consecutive time steps, t and $t+1$. At each time step, the inputs of the LSTM cell representing a pedestrian are the previous position (x_{t-1}^i, y_{t-1}^i), the goal g^i and the Social pooling tensor H_t^i. The output of the LSTM cell is the current position (x_t^i, y_t^i).

Neighborhood Modeling. The state of the neighborhood of each pedestrian is represented by a "Social" hidden-state tensor, as proposed by [1]. The Social pooling layer allows pedestrians to share their hidden states, thus enabling each network to predict the next position, reasoning about its hidden state and the neighborhood state.

The pedestrian ped^j at time t in the scene is represented by the hidden-state h_t^j of a LSTM network. We choose the hidden-state dimension D and the neighborhood size N_0. The neighborhood of the agent ped^i is handled by a "Social" pooling layer. This layer has the aim of pooling information received from the LSTM cells of its neighbors while preserving also their spatial mapping. This spatial mapping is preserved through a grid pooling as explained in Eq. 3. The pooled information is used to build a tensor, called "Social" hidden-state tensor H_t^i, with dimensions $N_0 \times N_0 \times D$:

$$H_t^i(m, n, :) = \sum_{j \in N_i} 1_{mn}[x_t^j - x_t^i, y_t^j - y_t^i]h_{t-1}^j \qquad (2)$$

where h_{t-1}^j represents the hidden-state of the LSTM of ped^j ($\forall j \neq i$) at $t-1$, N^i represents the set of neighbors of pedestrian ped^i and $1_{mn}[x, y]$ is an indicator function defined as:

$$1_{mn}[x, y] = \begin{cases} 0 & \text{if } [x, y] \notin \text{cell mn} \\ 1 & \text{if } [x, y] \in \text{cell mn} \end{cases} \qquad (3)$$

A graphical representation of the pooling operation is shown in Fig. 2.

Once computed, the Social hidden-state tensor is embedded into a vector a_t^i. The output coordinates are embedded in the vector e_t^i. The resulting recurrence is then defined by the following equations:

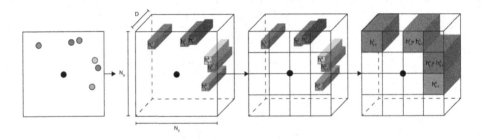

Fig. 2. Representation of the Social pooling layer. The black dot represents the pedestrian of interest ped_i. Other pedestrians ped_j ($\forall j \neq i$) are shown in different color codes. The state of the neighborhood of ped_i is described by $N_0 \times N_0$ cells, which pooling together spatially-close neighbors preserves the spatial information. This will later be used to construct the hidden-state tensor H_t^i.

$$r_t^i = \Phi(x_t^i, y_t^i; W_r) \tag{4}$$

$$e_t^i = \Phi(a_t^i, H_t^i; g^i, W_e) \tag{5}$$

$$h_t^i = LSTM(h_{t-1}^i, e_t^i; W_l) \tag{6}$$

where Φ is an embedding function with ReLU activation; W_r and W_e represent the embedding weights, and W_l represents the LSTM weights.

The next position (x_{t+1}^i, y_{t+1}^i) in the simulation depends on the hidden-state at the previous time-step h_t^i. Inspired by [7], and as performed in [1], we predict the following parameters, which characterize a bivariate Gaussian distribution: the mean $\mu_{t+1}^i = (\mu_x, \mu_y)_{t+1}^i$, the standard deviation $\sigma_{t+1}^i = (\sigma_x, \sigma_y)_{t+1}^i$ and the correlation coefficient ρ_{t+1}^i. We use a $5 \times D$ weight matrix W_p to estimate the parameters. Thus, the coordinates at the next time-step $t+1$ are computed as:

$$(x_{t+1}^i, y_{t+1}^i) \sim N(\mu_t^i, \sigma_t^i, \rho_t^i) \tag{7}$$

In order to estimate the parameters of the LSTM model, the negative log-Likelihood loss L^i for agent ped^i is minimized for the current time instant t:

$$[\mu_t^i, \sigma_t^i, \rho_t^i] = W_p h_{t-1}^i \tag{8}$$

$$L^i(W_e, W_l, W_p) = - \sum_{t=T_{cur}+1}^{T_{step}} log\Big(\mathbb{P}(x_t^i, y_t^i \mid \mu_t^i, \sigma_t^i, \rho_t^i)\Big) \tag{9}$$

Our model is trained minimizing the log-Likelihood loss for all the trajectories belonging to the dataset.

Personality. As far as the personality and decision making is concerned, the motion of the pedestrian in the crowd has been modeled in existing simulators by empirically varying parameters, such as pedestrian velocities and personal distances. Although this could actually increase the diversity of the agents' motion, it is still not sufficient for a realistic modeling of the personality traits, which in general lead to non-deterministic and non-linear motion models. Providing a "personal" set of trajectories to each agent in the scene would allow for a much more complex and diverse simulation.

Let us consider two pedestrians in the real world, where one exhibits an *aggressive* behavior, while the other exhibits a shy behavior [2]. Let us assume that we are able to collect a significant set of trajectories for each of the two pedestrians. During simulation we associate ped_i as the aggressive subject, and ped_j as the shy one. In this way, if we introduce both of them in the same simulated scenario, such that the social pooling tensor is $H_t^i(m, n, :) = H_t^j(m, n, :)$, and goals are $g^i = g^j$, the two pedestrians will take different decisions, depending on the specific features.

3.2 Implementation Details

To achieve our results, we have used the following configuration. The embedding dimension for the spatial coordinates is set to 64. The spatial pooling size, which corresponds to an area of $4 \times 4\,m^2$, is set to 32. The pooling operation is performed using a sum pooling window of size 8×8 with no overlaps. The hidden state dimension is 128. The learning rate parameter is set to 0.003 and RMS-prop [4] is used as the optimizer. The model is trained on a single GPU using a PyTorch[1] implementation.

At the input of the LSTM, each trajectory consists of a set of coordinates (X_{real}, Y_{real}) in meters, which needs to be normalized. Each pair (x_{real}, y_{real}) in the set is normalized between $[-1, 1]$ using the following conversion:

$$(x_{norm}, y_{norm}) = \left(2 * \frac{x_{real} - min(X_{real})}{Norm} - 1, 2 * \frac{y_{real} - min(Y_{real})}{Norm} - 1\right) \quad (10)$$

where $Norm$ represents the maximum range (in meters) of the biggest scene. This normalization is in line with the experiments conducted in previous works in this area [11].

4 Results

Dataset. To test our approach, we created a dataset composed of 5 fully annotated scenes, which visually match other known real datasets, namely the ETH [15] and UCY dataset [12], used in the experiments in [1]. An example is shown in Fig. 3. The choice of using real datasets as reference is to confront the agents' motion to scenes known to the community, rather than reproducing all the very fine details in terms of appearance, which is in this work not relevant.

The average density of pedestrians per frame is 10. The five different scenes include 204, 177, 194, 210, and 174 trajectories, respectively. The videos have been recorded at a rate of 15 fps. The preferred velocity in the Social Forces model is set to 4.7 km/h, which corresponds to the average speed of a walking pedestrian.

---

[1] http://pytorch.org.

(a) Real dataset   (b) Synthetic dataset

Fig. 3. A comparison of two frames of the real and synthetic datasets. The scene of interest is the so-called Hotel scene of the ETH dataset [15].

Experiments. To demonstrate the learning capabilities of the proposed framework, we rely on the simulated sequences based on SFM. Each LSTM network is trained for 100 epochs. Both training and test are conducted according to the leave-one-out strategy. This corresponds to training on 4 sets of trajectories and simulate a scene, which is similar to the fifth one. The prediction is updated at steps of 0.4 s. In other words, the agent will re-consider its next displacement according to its surroundings after 6 frames.

For each agent, the simulation starts in the time instant it appears in the scene. Each pedestrian is assigned a goal, namely the last known position in the scene. Our model computes the trajectories for each pedestrian and returns the set of positions for all of them at each time step, for a complete and exhaustive representation of the scene content.

4.1 Validation

To evaluate the simulation of the model with the dataset trajectories, we compare the density distribution $\rho_{i,j}$. The density of the distribution is computed using the equation suggested by Helbing et al. [9], as shown in Eq. 11, where n represents the total number of points of all trajectories; $d(i, j, k)$ is the Euclidean distance between the $k - th$ point along a trajectory and the (i, j) point of the grid; and R is a scaling factor:

Table 1. For each video sequence, the table reports the number of points available in the simulated video, and the number of grid cells in the horizontal (i) and vertical (j) dimensions.

	n	i	j
ETH Univ	356	4	25
ETH Hotel	383	4	18
UCY Zara1	455	25	14
UCY Zara2	654	25	15
UCY Univ	3006	30	18

Table 2. Simulation of the five different video scenes that mimic real datasets, as used in our experiments. The left column reports an overview of the scene, while the central and right columns report an example of the original video density and a sample of the one simulated using our framework. The value of ρ is color-coded: warmer colors represent higher densities, while colder colors represent lower values. Numerical values are reported on the right column at the right of each plot.

Name	Scene	Original Density	Simulated Density
ETH Hotel			
ETH Univ			
UCY Univ			
UCY Zara1			
UCY Zara2			

$$\rho_{i,j} = \frac{1}{2\pi R^2} \sum_{k=1}^{n} exp\Big(- \frac{d(i,j,k)^2}{R^2} \Big) \tag{11}$$

The accumulation points (i,j) are displaced in a grid that covers the whole image with a distance of 1 m between them. The real dimensions of each scene, grid size (i,j), and the number of total points n are shown in Table 1. Scaling factor is equal to 10. The plot of the density distribution of a set of trajectories for each dataset is shown in Table 2.

5   Conclusions

We have presented a framework for crowd simulation. The model assigns a neural network to each agent in the simulation. The pedestrians are connected by a social-pooling layer, which allows them to be aware of the status of their neighborhood. Compared to empirically-defined functions used in the literature to model crowds, the proposed solution allows simulating a more complex and enriched variety of behaviors. Training the network with different datasets allows in fact to reproduce the behavior of agents with different personalities. As stated at the beginning, the proposed method does not have the goal of improving the state of the art, but proposing a novel approach based on a simulator. Due to this reason, there is no comparison with the any state of the art method for trajectories, since, to the best of our knowledge, there are no other simulators in literature which we can compare to. In future works we plan to incorporate an Ego-Vision framework such that each pedestrian navigates the environment according to the information gathered from a first-person perspective. This would also allow us to better extract personality traits, since the first person view contains many more fine-grained details about the person wearing the camera.

References

1. Alahi, A., Goel, K., Ramanathan, V., Robicquet, A., Fei-Fei, L., Savarese, S.: Social LSTM: human trajectory prediction in crowded spaces. In: Conference on Computer Vision and Pattern Recognition (CVPR), pp. 961–971. IEEE (2016)
2. Bera, A., Randhavane, T., Manocha, D.: Aggressive, tense, or shy? identifying personality traits from crowd videos. In: International Joint Conference on Artificial Intelligence (IJCAI), pp. 112–118 (2017)
3. Bisagno, N., Conci, N., Zhang, B.: Data-driven crowd simulation. In: Advanced Video and Signal Based Surveillance (AVSS), pp. 1–6. IEEE (2017)
4. Dauphin, Y., de Vries, H., Bengio, Y.: Equilibrated adaptive learning rates for non-convex optimization. In: Advances in Neural Information Processing Systems (NIPS), pp. 1504–1512 (2015)
5. Durupinar, F., Allbeck, J., Pelechano, N., Badler, N.: Creating crowd variation with the ocean personality model. In: International Conference on Autonomous Agents and Multiagent Systems (AAMAS), vol. 3, pp. 1217–1220 (2008)
6. Godoy, J., Karamouzas, I., Guy, S.J., Gini, M.L.: Moving in a crowd: safe and efficient navigation among heterogeneous agents. In: International Joint Conference on Artificial Intelligence (IJCAI), pp. 294–300 (2016)

7. Graves, A.: Generating sequences with recurrent neural networks. arXiv preprint arXiv:1308.0850 (2013)
8. Guy, S.J., Van Den Berg, J., Liu, W., Lau, R., Lin, M.C., Manocha, D.: A statistical similarity measure for aggregate crowd dynamics. Trans. Graph. (TOG) 31(6), 190 (2012)
9. Helbing, D., Johansson, A., Al-Abideen, H.Z.: Dynamics of crowd disasters: an empirical study. Phys. Rev. E. APS 75(4), 046109 (2007)
10. Helbing, D., Molnar, P.: Social force model for pedestrian dynamics. Phys. Rev. E. APS 51(5), 4282 (1995)
11. Hochreiter, S., Schmidhuber, J.: Long short-term memory. Neural Comput. 9(8), 1735–1780 (1997)
12. Lerner, A., Chrysanthou, Y., Lischinski, D.: Crowds by example. Comput. Graph. Forum 26(3), 655–664 (2007)
13. Lerner, A., Chrysanthou, Y., Shamir, A., Cohen-Or, D.: Data driven evaluation of crowds. In: Egges, A., Geraerts, R., Overmars, M. (eds.) MIG 2009. LNCS, vol. 5884, pp. 75–83. Springer, Heidelberg (2009). https://doi.org/10.1007/978-3-642-10347-6_7
14. Patil, S., Van Den Berg, J., Curtis, S., Lin, M.C., Manocha, D.: Directing crowd simulations using navigation fields. Trans. Vis. Comput. Graph. 17(2), 244–254 (2011)
15. Pellegrini, S., Ess, A., Schindler, K., Van Gool, L.: You'll never walk alone: modeling social behavior for multi-target tracking. In: International Conference on Computer Vision (ICCV), pp. 261–268. IEEE (2009)
16. Qureshi, F.Z., Terzopoulos, D.: Surveillance camera scheduling: a virtual vision approach. Multimed. Syst. 12(3), 269–283 (2006)
17. Scovanner, P., Tappen, M.F.: Learning pedestrian dynamics from the real world. In: International Conference on Computer Vision (ICCV), pp. 381–388. IEEE (2009)
18. Trautman, P., Ma, J., Murray, R.M., Krause, A.: Robot navigation in dense human crowds: the case for cooperation. In: International Conference on Robotics and Automation (ICRA), pp. 2153–2160. IEEE (2013)
19. Treuille, A., Cooper, S., Popović, Z.: Continuum crowds. Trans. Graph. (TOG) 25(3), 1160–1168 (2006)
20. Van Den Berg, J., Guy, S.J., Lin, M., Manocha, D.: Reciprocal n-body collision avoidance. In: Pradalier, C., Siegwart, R., Hirzinger, G. (eds.) Robotics Research, pp. 3–19. Springer, Heidelberg (2011). https://doi.org/10.1007/978-3-642-19457-3_1

Worldly Eyes on Video: Learnt vs. Reactive Deployment of Attention to Dynamic Stimuli

Vittorio Cuculo$^{(\boxtimes)}$ ⓘ, Alessandro D'Amelio ⓘ, Giuliano Grossi ⓘ,
and Raffaella Lanzarotti ⓘ

PHuSe Lab - Dipartimento di Informatica, University of Milan,
via Celoria 18, 20133 Milan, Italy
{vittorio.cuculo,alessandro.damelio}@unimi.it,
{grossi,lanzarotti}@di.unimi.it
http://phuselab.di.unimi.it

Abstract. Computational visual attention is a hot topic in computer vision. However, most efforts are devoted to model saliency, whilst the actual eye guidance problem, which brings into play the sequence of gaze shifts characterising overt attention, is overlooked. Further, in those cases where the generation of gaze behaviour is considered, stimuli of interest are by and large static (still images) rather than dynamic ones (videos). Under such circumstances, the work described in this note has a twofold aim: (i) addressing the problem of estimating and generating visual scan paths, that is the sequences of gaze shifts over videos; (ii) investigating the effectiveness in scan path generation offered by features dynamically learned on the base of human observers attention dynamics as opposed to bottom-up derived features. To such end a probabilistic model is proposed. By using a publicly available dataset, our approach is compared against a model of scan path simulation that does not rely on a learning step.

Keywords: Visual attention · Scan path · HMM ·
Bag of visual words · Video gaze prediction

1 Introduction

Real world contains a huge amount of visual information. Indeed, our brain is very skillful in selecting the relevant one so that visual attention is guided to scene regions and events in real time. The same competence would be desirable for machine vision systems, so that relevant information could be gathered and treated with the highest priority.

To such end the fundamental problem concerning what factors guide attention within scenes can be articulated in two related questions: (i) *where* do we look within the scene and (ii) *how* we visit regions where attention will be allocated.

© Springer Nature Switzerland AG 2019
E. Ricci et al. (Eds.): ICIAP 2019, LNCS 11751, pp. 128–138, 2019.
https://doi.org/10.1007/978-3-030-30642-7_12

The latter issue, which involves the actual mechanism of shifting the gaze from one location of the scene to another (i.e., producing a scan path), is seldom taken into account in computational models of visual attention. By overviewing the field [4,5,7,8,18], computational modelling of attention has been mainly concerned with the *where* issue.

As to the latter, at the most general level, approaches span an horizon defined by two theoretical frameworks [15]. On the one side, image guidance theories posit that attention basically is a reaction to the image properties of the stimulus confronting the viewer. The most prominent approach of this type is based on visual salience: resources are allocated to visually salient regions in the scene, relying on a saliency map computed from basic image features such as luminance contrast, colour and edge orientation and motion [5,7,8].

On the other side cognitive guidance theories suggest that attention is directed to scene regions that are semantically informative. Visual resources are deployed to scene's meaningful regions based on experience with general scene concepts and the specific scene instance currently in view. A remarkable early example of cognitive guidance modelling was provided by Chernyak and Stark [9]; more recent works are described in [12,15,20–22].

In this note, we present a preliminary attempt at balancing image and cognitive guidance of gaze on dynamic stimuli. The main contribution of the work presented here lies in the following:

- modelling the gaze evolution taking into account three peculiar component: perceptual, cognitive, and motor.
- exploiting the actual behaviour of eye-tracked observers to learn dynamically which semantically meaningful regions are gazed, and adopt this knowledge to generate new scan paths on unseen videos with the same semantic content.
- bridging the gap between perceptual features, such as low-level spatial and temporal features, and the cognitive elements captured through semantic components gathered inter-videos.

The remainder of the paper is organized as follows. Sect. 2 introduces the probabilistic model, Sect. 3 gives the implementative details. Experiments are reported in Sect. 4, and Sect. 5 is left to conclusions.

2 Proposed Model

Visual attention deployment in time can be considered as the allocation of visual resources on regions of the viewed scene. In overt attention the signature of such process can be represented by gaze dynamics. Consider such dynamics as described by the stochastic process $\{G_t, t > 0\}$ and let the time series $g_1, g_2, \cdots, g_T$ be a realisation of the process. In the following with some abuse of notation we will use lower case g for both the realisation and the time-varying random variable G; also we adopt the compact notation $g_{1:T} = \{g_1, g_2, \cdots, g_T\}$.

Under Markov assumption the joint probability $p(g_{1:T})$ can be written:

$$p(g_{1:T}) = p(g_1) p(g_2|g_1) \cdots p(g_T|g_{1:T-1}) = p(g_1) \prod_{t=2}^{T} p(g_t|g_{t-1}). \qquad (1)$$

Gaze evolution $g_t \to g_{t+1}$ can be conceived as the consequence of the evolution of an *ensemble* of time-varying random variables accounting for the fundamental aspects of attention deployment: (1) the gaze-dependent perception of the external world, (2) the internal cognition state-space (the mind's eye), (3) the motor behaviour grounding actual gaze dynamics. More precisely, to characterize this dynamic random process, let us define the following random variables.

1. **Perceptual component**
   Low level features: f_t^{spatial} and f_t^{temporal} collect low-level features accounting for both *spatial* and *temporal* domains, respectively.
   Semantic components w_t: starting from the spatial features f_t^{spatial}, the semantic components w_t are derived to describe semantic concepts/objects [13] within the scene independently from their spatial positions.
   Temporal features y_t: starting from f_t^{temporal}, they are responsible for capturing where the movements within a scene drive the attention of an observer independently from either the semantic or the task.

2. **Cognitive component**
   Semantic concepts z_t: since an observer progressively allocate the attention to the most relevant parts of the scene depending on either implicit or explicit tasks, z_t captures high-level semantic contents, such as {Person, Car, Street}. Due to the difficulties to make explicit this cognitive components, they lie in a latent space of categories.
   Duration s_t: this is conceived as a *"switch"* variable controlling the duration of permanence in the latent state z_t, i.e., it approximately regulates gaze dwell time.

3. **Motor component**
   Scan path u_t: this variable denotes the actual spatial point of gaze, accounting for the *how* problem of overt attention deployment. It is important to note that the prior $p(u_{t+1}|u_t)$ is useful to incorporate oculomotor biases [16,19]. For instance it has been shown that saccade amplitudes are likely to follow heavy-tailed laws [1–3,6].

To sum up, the time-varying gaze shift random variable $g_t = \{u_t, z_t, s_t, w_t, y_t\}^1$ has conditional distribution

$$p(g_{t+1}|g_t) = p(u_{t+1}, z_{t+1}, s_{t+1}, w_{t+1}, y_{t+1} \mid u_t, z_t, s_t, w_t, y_t). \qquad (2)$$

---

[1] Naturally, it holds that $p\left(w_t|f_t^{\text{spatial}}\right)$ and $p\left(y_t|f_t^{\text{temporal}}\right)$. For sake of simplicity we omit to recall these dependencies.

Thanks to suitable conditional independence assumptions, Eq. (2) can be simplified as follows:

$$p\left(g_{t+1}\mid g_t\right)=p\left(y_{t+1}\mid y_t\right) \tag{3}$$
$$p\left(w_{t+1}\mid z_{t+1}\right)$$
$$p\left(z_{t+1}\mid z_t,s_{t+1}\right)$$
$$p\left(s_{t+1}\mid s_t,z_t\right)$$
$$p\left(u_{t+1}\mid u_t,w_{t+1},y_{t+1}\right).$$

In other words, in our model of human vision dynamics, gaze brings together low level perceptual components acting as saliency maps, with latent cognitive components playing a central role in task-driven attention [10,25], together with the prior knowledge of the oculomotor behaviour. The PGM in Fig. 1 represents graphically this idea, highlighting the above conditional probability.

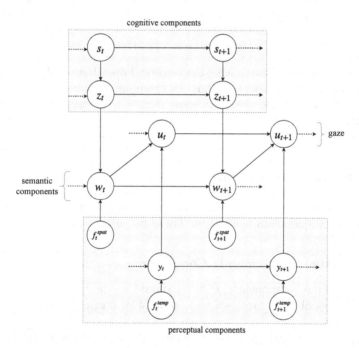

Fig. 1. Probabilistic graphical model including conditional independence assumptions established in Eq. (3).

After model learning, gaze shift simulation is obtained by the following generative/sampling process having distribution as in Eq. (3):

Concerning the transition probability $z_t \rightarrow z_{t+1}$ between (discrete) semantic concepts of the scene conditioned on state duration s_{t+1}, we have

$$\hat{z}_{t+1} \sim p\left(z_{t+1}\mid z_t,s_{t+1}\right). \tag{4}$$

This should be implemented via latent dynamical models, such as HMM [11] or recurrent neural networks (see Sect. 3.2), in which the generation of semantic elements depend on the sampling

$$\hat{w}_{t+1} \sim p\left(w_{t+1} \mid z_{t+1}\right).$$ (5)

In particular, the set of semantic elements assumed by w_t is determined from low level spatial features f_t^{spatial} adopting either clustering, learning sparse dictionaries [14] or other ensemble techniques as discussed in Sect. 3.1.

From the side of temporal features we simply have

$$\hat{y}_{t+1} \sim p\left(y_{t+1} \mid y_t\right),$$ (6)

where y_t is derived from low level temporal features f_t^{temporal} such as optical flow or temporal saliency maps (Sect. 3.1).

The state duration distribution is conditioned on its previous state and on the semantic concept gazed at time t

$$\hat{s}_{t+1} \sim p\left(s_{t+1} \mid s_t, z_t\right).$$ (7)

This can be modelled by computing the empirical distribution of fixations duration on training data and, at test time, by sampling from it.

Finally, we can draw the next gaze shift $g_t \rightarrow g_{t+1}$ by sampling the distribution

$$\hat{u}_{t+1} \sim p\left(u_{t+1} \mid u_t, y_{t+1}, w_{t+1}\right).$$ (8)

3   Model Implementation

In order to derive the gaze shift generation according to the model outlined in Sect. 2, several implementative choices should be put in place.

3.1   Perceptual and Semantic Components

Spatial perceptual components ($f^{spatial}$) should be discriminative and able to consistently describe the local semantic content of image portions (cells), even between videos.

This goal is achieved by resorting to convolutional neural networks (CNN) as feature extractors: given a pool of videos with coherent semantic content (e.g. dialogue between people), we characterize each frame applying the pretrained AlexNet CNN[2], and extracting the activation produced by the deepest convolutional layer (conv5). More specifically, each frame is scanned by the CNN using overlapping windows[3], in order to discard the activation coefficient produced with padding, and keeping only the central activation coefficients. This way, each frame v_t of a video $v \in RGB$, s.t. $|v| = (h \times w \times T)$ is mapped in a $(n \times m)$

---

[2] https://it.mathworks.com/help/deeplearning/ref/alexnet.html.

[3] Window is 227-by-227 pixel size, according to the AlexNet input.

grid $y_t^{spatial}$, where each cell is characterized by a 256-dimensional feature vector. Here, $n = h/f$ and $m = w/f$; f being the decimation factor, responsible for the spatial resolution of the scan path generation process.

A succinct vocabulary $\mathcal{W} = \{w_1, \ldots, w_M\}$, corresponding to the semantic components, is derived applying the k-means algorithm to the $f^{spatial}$ features.

Quantizing $y_t^{spatial}$ according to $\mathcal{W}$ gives rise to the desired semantic content w_t (Fig. 2).

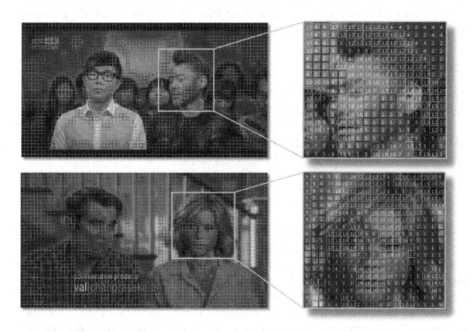

Fig. 2. Examples of w_t characterizations, obtained quantizing two frames of two different videos, while referring to the same dictionary $\mathcal{W}$. Notice in the zooms that cells are clustered according to a coherent semantic.

Analogously, y_t is obtained by averaging over the $(n \times m)$ cells the dense $f_t^{temporal}$ computed as the video optical flow.

3.2 Latent Cognitive Components

Our approach relies on a supervised method in which the cognitive components lie in a latent space and provide a substantial contribute to estimate gaze shifts. We instantiate the cognitive components in the shape of the hidden space z_t of an HMM whose emissions w_t are a finite set of "gazed" visual words, i.e., the semantics providing visible clues of the scene. This allows to accomplish the generation steps described in Eq. (4) for the hidden state, and in Eq. (5) for the visual cues.

Naturally, also in case of indirect task-driven attention, the training phase requires that videos in training and test share a common content (e.g., people or faces, animals, cars), in order to learn visual attention patterns guided by semantics. To such end, the training process requires a collection of saccadic scan paths samples eye-tracked from several observers while viewing the set of videos.

The generation phase uses ancestral sampling directly from the HMM trained on gazed visual words. This gives rise to a frame-based prediction of a new word w_t for each frame t directly sampling from learnt conditional distribution $p(w_t|z_t)$.

3.3 Motor Component

As proposed in [6] the saccade amplitude distribution is well described by heavy tailed distributions. As a consequence, the motor component can be modeled as a Levy flight or a Markovian process with the shifts following a α-stable distribution. Following this rationale, the shift prior probability $p(u_{t+1}|u_t)$ is modelled as a Cauchy 2D distribution ($\alpha = 1$, [1,6]).

4 Simulation

In the following we present results so far achieved by a preliminary simulation of the model outlined in Sect. 2. In particular we compare with the baseline method described in [3],[4] which only relies on reactive guidance with respect to the stimulus, while accounting for oculomotor biases (long-tailed distribution of gaze shift amplitudes) much like as we do. It is worth noting that few models are available to compare with that, going beyond classic saliency models, account for the actual generation of gaze shifts; by and large, further available models limit to static stimuli processing [1,17,23].

4.1 Dataset

The adopted dataset is the one presented in [24]. It includes fixations of 39 subjects, recorded with an eye tracker at 60 Hz, viewing 65 videos gathered from YouTube and Youku. The database is specialized for multiple-face videos, which contain various numbers of faces varying from 1 to 27. The duration of each video was cut down to be around 20 s and the subjects were asked to free-view videos displayed at random order.

---

[4] Matlab source code available at http://boccignone.di.unimi.it/Ecological_Sampling. html.

4.2   Experimental Setup

In this preliminary test series, we used several randomly chosen video pairs, one for training e one for test. Both are taken into account for the dictionary construction $\mathcal{W}$, while only the scan paths of the first video are employed to train the HMM via gazed visual words.

The simulation process is concerned with both the baseline and the proposed approach providing the generation of 50 scan paths for each test video. The whole model has mainly three parameters that affect the performance, namely the grid granularity f, the number of visual words, i.e. number of cluster for the K-means algorithm (M) and the number of hidden states of the HMM (N). These values have been chosen experimentally: optimal values in terms of both quantitative evaluation (section below) and computational cost have been found with $f = 17$, $M = 20$ and $N = 4$. A qualitative assessment of the proposed model can be carried out via the comparison of the fixation density maps.

Ground Truth	Baseline	Proposed

Fig. 3. Visualization of different fixation density maps from human data, baseline method and our proposed approach. The density maps refers to the same frames of three different considered videos in the dataset.

In Fig. 3 we show three examples, extracted from as many videos, of fixation density maps obtained by aggregating all the fixations (either artificial or human) performed in the corresponding frames. At a glance it can be noted that the baseline approach is more attracted by locations that include movements or, more generally, low-level features, despite their semantic value. Differently, the proposed approach seeks the locations that include relevant features in terms of their visual word representation.

4.3   Results

The proposed model is validated quantitatively by comparing the ground truth and generated distributions of observer's fixations. In particular, for each video frame, a fixation density map is computed by aggregating spatially the fixations of all the available observers, either real or artificial, yielding at each time t, the result exemplified in Fig. 3. The proposed model is then compared to the baseline by computing the Kullback-Leibler Divergence (KLD) between the real and generated density maps. In Fig. 4 the empirical distribution of KL values for both proposed and baseline models is depicted. As can be observed, the proposed model produces on average much lower KLD values if compared to the baseline with a remarkable difference in terms of uncertainty of the distributions.

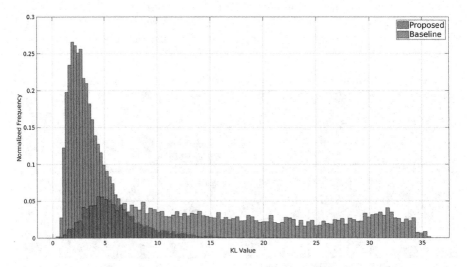

Fig. 4. Histogram plot of the distribution of Kullback-Leibler Divergence values between density maps of real and generated scan paths, using the proposed and baseline methods

5   Conclusions

In this work we propose a model for estimating human scan paths by modeling visual attention over videos. We find that to be effective the generation process should leverage on three primary factors: low-level saliency features, semantic objects identified through cognitive guidance, and oculomotor eye movements. In our model the main role is played by a supervised method focusing on gazed semantic objects that attract the attention during either free or task oriented viewing. This allows to conclude that the ability to reproduce gaze shifts is mainly yielded by a prior distribution on hidden states describing the semantic content of the scenes. Future work will investigate the applicability of our method to other datasets with different semantic contents. Furthermore, other techniques could be adopted to implement the different parts of model. For example clustering could be substituted by learning sparse dictionaries, and HMM by recurrent neural networks. An investigation in these directions should allow us to optimize the implementation in term of both efficiency and efficacy.

References

1. Boccignone, G., Ferraro, M.: Modelling gaze shift as a constrained random walk. Physica A **331**(1–2), 207–218 (2004)
2. Boccignone, G., Ferraro, M.: Gaze shift behavior on video as composite information foraging. Signal Process. Image Commun. **28**(8), 949–966 (2013)
3. Boccignone, G., Ferraro, M.: Ecological sampling of gaze shifts. IEEE Trans. Cybern. **44**(2), 266–279 (2014)
4. Boccignone, G., Cuculo, V., D'Amelio, A., Grossi, G., Lanzarotti, R.: Give ear to my face: modelling multimodal attention to social interactions. In: Leal-Taixé, L., Roth, S. (eds.) ECCV 2018. LNCS, vol. 11130, pp. 331–345. Springer, Cham (2019). https://doi.org/10.1007/978-3-030-11012-3_27
5. Borji, A., Itti, L.: State-of-the-art in visual attention modeling. IEEE Trans. Pattern Anal. Mach. Intell. **35**(1), 185–207 (2013)
6. Brockmann, D., Geisel, T.: The ecology of gaze shifts. Neurocomputing **32**(1), 643–650 (2000)
7. Bruce, N.D., Wloka, C., Frosst, N., Rahman, S., Tsotsos, J.K.: On computational modeling of visual saliency: examining what's right, and what's left. Vision Res. **116**, 95–112 (2015)
8. Bylinskii, Z., DeGennaro, E., Rajalingham, R., Ruda, H., Zhang, J., Tsotsos, J.: Towards the quantitative evaluation of visual attention models. Vision. Res. **116**, 258–268 (2015)
9. Chernyak, D.A., Stark, L.W.: Top-down guided eye movements. IEEE Trans. Syst. Man Cybern. B **31**, 514–522 (2001)
10. Clavelli, A., Karatzas, D., Lladós, J., Ferraro, M., Boccignone, G.: Towards modelling an attention-based text localization process. In: Sanches, J.M., Micó, L., Cardoso, J.S. (eds.) IbPRIA 2013. LNCS, vol. 7887, pp. 296–303. Springer, Heidelberg (2013). https://doi.org/10.1007/978-3-642-38628-2_35
11. Coen-Cagli, R., Coraggio, P., Napoletano, P., Boccignone, G.: What the draughtsman's hand tells the draughtsman's eye: a sensorimotor account of drawing. Int. J. Pattern Recognit Artif Intell. **22**(05), 1015–1029 (2008)
12. Cuculo, V., D'Amelio, A., Lanzarotti, R., Boccignone, G.: Personality gaze patterns unveiled via automatic relevance determination. In: Mazzara, M., Ober, I., Salaün, G. (eds.) STAF 2018. LNCS, vol. 11176, pp. 171–184. Springer, Cham (2018). https://doi.org/10.1007/978-3-030-04771-9_14
13. Fei-Fei, L., Perona, P.: A Bayesian hierarchical model for learning natural scene categories. In: IEEE Computer Society Conference on Computer Vision and Pattern Recognition (CVPR 2005), vol. 2, pp. 524–531. IEEE (2005)
14. Grossi, G., Lanzarotti, R., Lin, J.: Orthogonal procrustes analysis for dictionary learning in sparse linear representation. PLoS ONE **12**(1), 1–16 (2017). https://doi.org/10.1371/journal.pone.0169663
15. Henderson, J.M., Hayes, T.R., Rehrig, G., Ferreira, F.: Meaning guides attention during real-world scene description. Sci. Rep. **8**, 10 (2018)

16. Le Meur, O., Coutrot, A.: Introducing context-dependent and spatially-variant viewing biases in saccadic models. Vision Res. **121**, 72–84 (2016)
17. Le Meur, O., Liu, Z.: Saccadic model of eye movements for free-viewing condition. Vision Res. **116**, 152–164 (2015)
18. Tatler, B., Hayhoe, M., Land, M., Ballard, D.: Eye guidance in natural vision: reinterpreting salience. J. Vision **11**(5), 5 (2011)
19. Tatler, B., Vincent, B.: The prominence of behavioural biases in eye guidance. Vis. Cogn. **17**(6–7), 1029–1054 (2009)
20. Torralba, A.: Contextual priming for object detection. Int. J. Comput. Vis. **53**, 153–167 (2003)
21. Torralba, A.: Modeling global scene factors in attention. JOSA A **20**(7), 1407–1418 (2003)
22. Torralba, A., Oliva, A., Castelhano, M., Henderson, J.: Contextual guidance of eye movements and attention in real-world scenes: the role of global features in object search. Psychol. Rev. **113**(4), 766 (2006)
23. Xia, C., Han, J., Qi, F., Shi, G.: Predicting human saccadic scanpaths based on iterative representation learning. IEEE Trans. Image Process., 1 (2019)
24. Xu, M., Liu, Y., Hu, R., He, F.: Find who to look at: turning from action to saliency. IEEE Trans. Image Process. **27**(9), 4529–4544 (2018)
25. Yang, S.C.H., Wolpert, D.M., Lengyel, M.: Theoretical perspectives on active sensing. Curr. Opin. Behav. Sci. **11**, 100–108 (2016)

Pattern Recognition and Machine Learning

Relation, Transition and Comparison Between the Adaptive Nearest Neighbor Rule and the Hypersphere Classifier

Mauricio Orozco-Alzate[1(✉)], Sisto Baldo[2], and Manuele Bicego[2]

[1] Departamento de Informática y Computación, Universidad Nacional de Colombia - Sede Manizales, km 7 vía al Magdalena, Manizales 170003, Colombia
morozcoa@unal.edu.co
[2] Dipartimento di Informatica, Università degli Studi di Verona, Strada Le Grazie, 15, Verona 37134, Italy
{sisto.baldo,manuele.bicego}@univr.it

Abstract. The Adaptive Nearest Neighbor (ANN) rule and the Hypersphere Classifier (HC) are two very simple and relatively new variants of the classical nearest neighbor (1NN) rule. Even if they share a similar formulation—they correct the query-to-prototype distance by taking into account the distance of the prototype to the nearest one from other classes—their relation has never been investigated. The main goal of this paper is studying this relation and providing an exhaustive performance comparison of both methods, highlighting occasions when their performances differ as well as identifying cases in which their application is advisable or leads to poorer results. Moreover, we propose a smooth transition between the two classifiers by studying the use of several convex combinations of their penalized distances. Experiments show that a combination is particularly helpful when both ANN and HC are worse than 1NN.

Keywords: Adaptive Nearest Neighbor · Convex combination · Comparison · Hypersphere Classifier · Relation · Transition

1 Introduction

The nearest neighbor rule (1NN) [1,2] represents a well known and widely applied classifier, which assigns an unknown object (query or test object) to the class of the object of the training set (prototype) whose distance to the testing object is minimum (i.e. the nearest neighbor). Over the years, numerous variants for improving this rule have been proposed. Some of them consist in either reducing the size of the set of prototypes [3] or generating new ones [4]; others focus on proposing novel dissimilarity measures and making them well-behaved in high dimensional spaces [5] or adaptive to particular local distributions. Two relatively recent and very similar approaches belong to the latter category, which have been independently proposed, namely the *Hypersphere Classifier* (HC) [6]

© Springer Nature Switzerland AG 2019
E. Ricci et al. (Eds.): ICIAP 2019, LNCS 11751, pp. 141–151, 2019.
https://doi.org/10.1007/978-3-030-30642-7_13

and the *Adaptive Nearest Neighbor rule* (ANN) [7]. Apparently, authors of HC—the most recently proposed method—were not aware of ANN since they do not refer to it in spite of the clear relationship between the two methods.

HC and ANN are both based on the rationale of penalizing the distance between the query point $\mathbf{x}$ and a prototype $\mathbf{x}_i$ by using the concept of a hypersphere, centered at $\mathbf{x}_i$, whose radius is defined by the distance to the prototype's nearest prototype which belongs to a different class. This radius measures how "inside" a class a given prototype is – a large radius indicates that the other classes are far away from it, thus it can be trusted more. Given this radius, both HC and ANN correct the distance of the testing point to the prototype: HC subtracts it from $\|\mathbf{x} - \mathbf{x}_i\|$ while ANN divides $\|\mathbf{x} - \mathbf{x}_i\|$ by the radius. In both cases, prototypes well inside their class have more importance (their distance to the testing object is decreased). Despite the idea behind the two approaches is very similar, a relation between them has not been analyzed yet, this representing the first goal of this manuscript. Actually, an empirical comparison of these methods would serve not just to judge whether there are significant performance differences between the two methods but also to better understand the overall effect of the corresponding penalizations.

The second goal of this paper originates from the fact that another way of improving the behavior of the (dis)similarity measures for classification is by combining them, such that the resulting measure outperforms the individual ones. In this paper we investigated a simple combination of the two penalized distances, in order to show if it is possible to improve even more the accuracies. One of the simplest possibilities is to use a convex linear combination. According to [8], such a combination of two distance functions is particularly useful when combining an overestimate and an underestimate of the Euclidean distance, provided that both are either suitable for non-Euclidean topological spaces or cheaper to be computed than the Euclidean distance itself, by, for instance, avoiding the computation of costly square root operations. Kernels—i.e. similarity functions—have also been interpolated by convex combinations. Gönen and Alpaydın [9], referring to [10], point out that the convex combination—or, more in general, a weighted average—is beneficial if both kernels exhibit similar classification performances but their class assignments rely sometimes on different support vectors.

Summarizing, the main contributions of this paper are the following: (i) first, we highlight the affinity and discuss the relation between HC and ANN; (ii) we compare their behaviors in terms of accuracy; (iii) we propose a modified convex combination of them in order to give further insights on the transition from one to the other. The remaining part of the paper is organized as follows. HC and ANN are explained in more detail in Sect. 2. Afterwards, in Sect. 3, their relation is analyzed and four linear transitions between HC and ANN by convex combinations are proposed. Experimental results and their discussions are given in Sect. 4. Finally, our concluding remarks are provided in Sect. 5.

2 Methods

In this section we introduce the two variants of 1NN, namely the Hypersphere Classifier and the Adaptive Nearest Neighbor Rule. Then, we study their relation in terms of a logarithmic scaling and, afterwards, present a simple model for the transition between the two.

2.1 The Hypersphere Classifier

This classifier was originally proposed [6] as an incremental method, usable to reduce the number of prototypes. Clearly it can also be used without memory restrictions and, therefore, without forgetting prototypes. In this study, we do not make use of the incremental property of HC. Let us present the approach starting from [6], coming later to the formulation with the radius. In [6] authors define as ρ_i the region of influence of $\mathbf{x}_i$; given that, the distance from $\mathbf{x}$ to $\mathbf{x}_i$ is computed as follows:

$$d_{HC}(\mathbf{x}, \mathbf{x}_i) = ||\mathbf{x} - \mathbf{x}_i|| - g\rho_i, \tag{1}$$

The region of influence ρ_i is defined as $1/2$ of the radius of the hypersphere associated to $\mathbf{x}_i$, namely the hypershpere having as center $\mathbf{x}_i$ and as radius (r_i) the distance to the nearest prototype of $\mathbf{x}_i$ belonging to a different class. The radius r_i can be formally defined as:

$$r_i = \min_{\mathbf{x}_j \in OT(\mathbf{x}_i)} d(\mathbf{x}_i, \mathbf{x}_j) \tag{2}$$

with

$$OT(\mathbf{x}_i) = \{\mathbf{x}_k \text{ such that } label(\mathbf{x}_k) \neq label(\mathbf{x}_i)\} \tag{3}$$

In Eq. (1), g is a free parameter. Even though ρ_i is defined as half of the radius of the hypersphere in order to avoid overlapping between hyperspheres from different classes, in [6] it is shown that the best value for g is 2 which, in words, means that the best configuration is considering the region of influence as the whole volume of the hypersphere in spite of the overlapping, i.e. $r_i = 2\rho_i$. For the sake of simplification, here we only consider that recommended configuration and use Eq. (2) to rewrite Eq. (1) as:

$$d_{HC}(\mathbf{x}, \mathbf{x}_i) = ||\mathbf{x} - \mathbf{x}_i|| - r_i. \tag{4}$$

Notice that Eq. (4) produces negative distances when a query point is inside the hypersphere associated to $\mathbf{x}_i$; this is not a practical problem with the nearest neighbor rule, which simply takes the minimum of the distances to all prototypes (no matter this value is negative).

2.2   The Adaptive Nearest Neighbor Rule

Similarly to HC, this classifier [7] weights distances of a testing point to a prototype according to the size of the hypersphere associated to that prototype—the hypersphere is defined as in the HC method. Similarly to HC, the effect is to promote prototypes well inside their class: distances to points having small hyperspheres are enlarged while distances to points having large hyperspheres are diminished. This effect is simply obtained by dividing the distances by the radius, as follows:

$$d_{ANN}(\mathbf{x}, \mathbf{x}_i) = \frac{||\mathbf{x} - \mathbf{x}_i||}{r_i}. \tag{5}$$

Notice that Eq. (5) does not generate negative values but has a much stronger penalization than the one of Eq. (4). However, the distance might diverge if $r_i \to 0$. In order to avoid the uncontrolled increase of d_{ANN}, in [7] it is proposed to add an arbitrarily small ϵ to the radius. In general, the numerical problem is unlikely to occur for real-world data satisfying the compactness hypothesis [11].

3   Relation and Transition Between HC and ANN

Relation. It has been shown in some recent works [12,13] that scaling the distance with a convex non linear transformation can be beneficial for distance-based classifiers. One example of such non linear scaling is to raise the distance to a power less than one. Another possibility, which has been investigated for the feature space but not for distances [14], is to use the logarithm, which has the same convex monotonic behavior of the power transformation (for feature spaces, the power transformation corresponds to the well known Box-Cox transform [15,16]).

Clearly, in distance-based classifiers, such monotonic transformation has no effect if the classifier only relies on rankings (such as the K-Nearest Neighbor methods). However, if the classifier uses more complex mechanisms, this non linear scaling can drastically change the results – see [12,13] for an analysis in the dissimilarity-based representation.

Suppose now that we apply the non linear scaling logarithm to our input distance $d(\mathbf{x}, \mathbf{x}_i) = ||\mathbf{x} - \mathbf{x}_i||$, getting a novel distance $\tilde{d}(\mathbf{x}, \mathbf{x}_i)$:

$$\tilde{d}(\mathbf{x}, \mathbf{x}_i) = \log d(\mathbf{x}, \mathbf{x}_i) \tag{6}$$

Consider again the notation that was introduced in Eq. (3). Now the HC rule redefines the distance with $\tilde{d}_{HC}(\mathbf{x}, \mathbf{x}_i)$:

$$\tilde{d}_{HC}(\mathbf{x}, \mathbf{x}_i) = \tilde{d}(\mathbf{x}, \mathbf{x}_i) - \tilde{r}_i, \qquad \text{where} \quad \tilde{r}_i = \min_{\mathbf{x}_j \in OT(\mathbf{x}_i)} \tilde{d}(\mathbf{x}_i, \mathbf{x}_j) \tag{7}$$

This radius can be expressed in terms of original distances, as follows:

$$\tilde{r}_i = \log \left(\min_{\mathbf{x}_j \in OT(\mathbf{x}_i)} e^{\tilde{d}(\mathbf{x}_i, \mathbf{x}_j)} \right)$$

$$= \log \left(\min_{\mathbf{x}_j \in OT(\mathbf{x}_i)} e^{\log d(\mathbf{x}_i, \mathbf{x}_j)} \right)$$

$$= \log \left(\min_{\mathbf{x}_j \in OT(\mathbf{x}_i)} d(\mathbf{x}_i, \mathbf{x}_j) \right)$$

$$= \log r_i \tag{8}$$

Where the first step is possible since the exponential does not change the argument of the minimum of the distance. Now,

$$\tilde{d}_{HC}(\mathbf{x}, \mathbf{x}_i) = \tilde{d}(\mathbf{x}, \mathbf{x}_i) - \tilde{r}_i$$

$$= \log d(\mathbf{x}, \mathbf{x}_i) - \log r_i$$

$$= \log \frac{d(\mathbf{x}, \mathbf{x}_i)}{r_i}$$

$$= \log d_{ANN}(\mathbf{x}, \mathbf{x}_i) \tag{9}$$

Therefore, the application of the HC correction to the logarithm of the original distances is equivalent to the application of the logarithm to the ANN correction computed on the original distances.

Transition. The above-mentioned affinity of HC and ANN motivated us to propose a link between the two classifiers. Let us call $s = \|\mathbf{x} - \mathbf{x}_i\|$ and $t = r_i$. Given that, the two distances d_{ANN} and d_{HC} can be rewritten as s/t and $s - t$, respectively. In order to combine d_{ANN} and d_{HC}, we propose four variants of their convex combination:

$$d_\lambda(s, t) = (1 - \lambda)\frac{s}{t} + \lambda(s - t) \tag{10}$$

$$d_\lambda(s, t) = \frac{(1 - \lambda)s}{(t + \lambda)} + \lambda(s - t) \tag{11}$$

$$d_\lambda(s, t) = \frac{(1 - \lambda)s}{(t + \lambda^2)} + \lambda(s - t) \tag{12}$$

$$d_\lambda(s, t) = \frac{(1 - \lambda)s}{(t + \sqrt{\lambda})} + \lambda(s - t) \tag{13}$$

Equation (10) corresponds to the canonical convex combination of s and t, where $\lambda \in [0, 1]$ controls the transition from ANN to HC. In order to cope with a possible singularity, Eq. (11) might be preferred instead, as well as other variants that damp faster or slower the singularity, e.g. Eqs. (12) and (13). Please note that also in these variants $\lambda \in [0, 1]$ controls the transition from ANN to HC (for $\lambda = 0$ we have the d_{ANN} distance, whereas for $\lambda = 1$ we have the d_{HC} one).

4   Experimental Results and Discussion

For the sake of reproducible research and fair comparison, we consider the union of the two collections of data sets that were used for the experiments in the original papers of HC and ANN. In [6], results were computed for the following data sets: WDBC, Ecoli, German credit data, Glass, Haberman, Heart, Ionosphere, Iris, Pima, Sonar, Tic-Tac-Toe, Vehicles, Wine and Yeast. In [7], experiments were performed for WDBC, Ionosphere, Pima, Liver and Sonar. Besides, with the aim of considering a wider range of data conditions, we included additional data sets to the collection; namely: Arrhytmia, WPBC, Soybean1, Soybean2, Malaysia, x80, Imox, Chromo and Spirals. The main properties of the collection of 24 data sets are summarized in Table 1.

Table 1. Main properties of the considered data sets

Dataset	# feat	# obj	# class	Dataset	# feat	# obj	# class
German-credit	20	1000	2	Wine	13	178	3
Pima	8	768	2	Sonar	60	208	2
WDBC	30	569	2	Soybean1	35	266	15
Tic-Tac-Toe	9	958	2	Chromo	8	1143	24
Yeast	8	1484	10	Vehicles	18	846	4
Ecoli	7	336	8	Malaysia	8	291	20
Arrhythmia	278	420	12	Imox	8	192	4
Heart	13	297	2	x80	8	45	3
Haberman	3	306	2	Soybean2	35	136	4
Ionosphere	34	351	2	Iris	4	150	3
Liver	6	345	2	Glass	9	214	6
WPBC	32	194	2	Spirals	2	194	2

4.1   First Experiment: Classifier Comparison

All the results reported in Table 2 were computed for repeated train and test with 50 repetitions. In each repetition, data sets were split into two random equal-sized parts, one used for training and the other for testing. Classification accuracies are computed as the number of correctly classified elements in the testing set. In the second, third and fourth columns of Table 2 we reported such accuracies, together with the standard errors. In order to have a statistically robust pairwise comparison between the three methods, we performed a two-tailed t-test, at the 5% of significance, to compare the 50 repetitions of each pair of methods (namely 1NN vs. ANN, 1NN vs. HC and ANN vs. HC). This permits to judge whether the observed differences are statistically significant or not [17]. The null hypothesis was that the performances of the two examined techniques are equivalent: when it is rejected, a statistically significant difference is found. Results of the t-tests are reported in the last three columns of Table 2. In case of rejection of the null hyphothesis, a slanted arrow points to the best

Table 2. Accuracies and t-tests

Dataset	Accuracies			t-tests		
	1NN	ANN	HC	1NN vs. ANN	1NN vs. HC	ANN vs. HC
◇ German-credit	68.59 ± 0.29	70.92 ± 0.29	71.27 ± 0.29	Reject ↗	Reject ↗	Reject ↗
◇ Pima	69.03 ± 0.33	71.91 ± 0.32	72.19 ± 0.32	Reject ↗	Reject ↗	Reject ↗
◇ WDBC	95.27 ± 0.18	96.01 ± 0.16	96.23 ± 0.16	Reject ↗	Reject ↗	Reject ↗
◇ Tic-Tac-Toe	79.07 ± 0.26	80.79 ± 0.25	82.51 ± 0.25	Reject ↗	Reject ↗	Reject ↗
◇ Yeast	50.81 ± 0.26	52.87 ± 0.26	53.54 ± 0.26	Reject ↗	Reject ↗	Reject ↗
◇ Ecoli	79.42 ± 0.44	81.95 ± 0.42	82.71 ± 0.41	Reject ↗	Reject ↗	Reject ↗
□ Arrhythmia	56.42 ± 0.48	55.8 ± 0.48	58.07 ± 0.48	Accept	Reject ↗	Reject ↗
▲ Heart 2	76.48 ± 0.49	78.28 ± 0.48	78.59 ± 0.48	Reject ↗	Reject ↗	Accept
▲ Haberman	66.3 ± 0.54	68.39 ± 0.53	68.24 ± 0.53	Reject ↗	Reject ↗	Accept
▲ Ionosphere	85.27 ± 0.38	92.92 ± 0.27	92.82 ± 0.28	Reject ↗	Reject ↗	Accept
▲ Liver	60.35 ± 0.53	62.08 ± 0.52	62.15 ± 0.52	Reject ↗	Reject ↗	Accept
▲ WPBC	66.25 ± 0.68	71.11 ± 0.65	70.99 ± 0.65	Reject ↗	Reject ↗	Accept
▲ Wine	94.47 ± 0.34	95.37 ± 0.31	95.28 ± 0.32	Reject ↗	Reject ↗	Accept
◆ Sonar	82.96 ± 0.52	83.77 ± 0.51	83.75 ± 0.51	Accept	Accept	Accept
◆ Soybean1	84.24 ± 0.45	83.32 ± 0.46	83.41 ± 0.46	Accept	Accept	Accept
◆ Chromo	54.32 ± 0.29	54.06 ± 0.29	53.95 ± 0.29	Accept	Accept	Accept
△ Vehicles	68.56 ± 0.32	67.93 ± 0.32	68.0 ± 0.32	↘ Reject	↘ Reject	Accept
△ Malaysia	66.07 ± 0.55	64.96 ± 0.56	64.64 ± 0.56	↘ Reject	↘ Reject	Accept
△ Imox	91.77 ± 0.4	90.81 ± 0.42	90.67 ± 0.42	↘ Reject	↘ Reject	Accept
■ x80	90.17 ± 0.88	87.48 ± 0.98	87.83 ± 0.96	↘ Reject	Accept	Accept
■ Soybean2	83.68 ± 0.63	82.5 ± 0.65	82.62 ± 0.65	↘ Reject	Accept	Accept
▽ Iris	93.79 ± 0.39	94.32 ± 0.38	93.76 ± 0.39	Reject ↗	Accept	↘ Reject
▼ Glass	66.62 ± 0.64	64.99 ± 0.65	66.07 ± 0.65	↘ Reject	Accept	Reject ↗
★ Spirals	72.95 ± 0.64	68.76 ± 0.67	68.02 ± 0.67	↘ Reject	↘ Reject	↘ Reject

classifier. To better clarify this notation, for example, in the "1NN vs. ANN" column, "German-credit" row, the arrow following the "Reject" indicates that the ANN rule was statistically significantly better than the 1NN rule on the German-credit dataset.

By looking at the table, different observations can be derived. According to the performances, a number of groups of data sets can be identified. The first group (denoted with ◇) corresponds to six data sets for which HC is better than ANN and both, in turn, are better than 1NN. A slightly different behavior is exhibited by Arrhytmia (denoted with □) for which there is no statistical difference between 1NN and ANN. Another large group (denoted by ▲) is composed by data sets for which there is no difference between ANN and HC but both are better than 1NN. Subsequently, we find a group of three data sets (◆) for which there is no statistical difference between the three classifiers.

Continuing with the descending reading of the table, there is a group of three data sets (△) for which 1NN is better than both ANN and HC while there is no difference between the latter. A slightly different behavior is shown by x80 and Soybean2 (denoted with ■), for which—in contrast to the previous case—HC is equivalent to 1NN. The last group (▽, ▼ and ★) contains three data sets whose results are special: Iris is the only case in which ANN is better than both 1NN and HC; for Glass, HC is better than ANN, even though the former is not significantly different than 1NN while the latter is worse than 1NN. Finally, results for the Spirals data set show an artificial case—deliberately included by us for illustration purposes, see Fig. 1—in which 1NN is significantly better in accuracy (by 4.19% and 4.93%, respectively) than ANN and HC. Notice that the spheres defined for Spirals would occupy the space between the spiral arms and their corresponding radii are the half of the width of the inter-arm corridors. Penalizations by the radius, that are so beneficial in other cases, appear to be counterproductive for this data set due to its particular configuration.

In general we can see that in many cases the correction of both HC and ANN is beneficial with respect to 1NN, but there are some other cases where this correction is not useful at all. Concerning the two techniques, the HC method seems to be slightly superior to the ANN variant. We tried to derive a relation between such classification accuracies and data set properties (in terms of dimensionality, number of classes and so on): however, it was not possible to derive many regularities, apart from the facts that (i) the

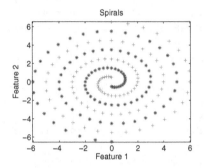

Fig. 1. Scatter plot of Spirals data set

behavior for Arrhythmia—the highest-dimensional data set—is special; (ii) the large group of datasets for which there is no difference between ANN and HC but both are better than 1NN is homogeneous with respect to the number of classes (five two-class problems and a three-class one) and (iii) two of the three data sets with more classes (Soybean1 and Chromo) do not exhibit any profit from the use of ANN and HC.

4.2   Second Experiment: Transition Between ANN and HC

In this second experiment we tested if and how much helpful is to employ a smooth transition between ANN and HC. Actually, the penalizations of the distances implemented by these two rules have different nature, due to the two different mathematical operations involved (subtraction vs. division). Therefore, it seems reasonable to try to employ a combination of the two, as explained in Sect. 3. To test this aspect we repeated the classification experiments on the 24 datasets of before, by using the convex combinations of the two modified distances (in all the variants proposed in Sect. 3). The parameter λ has been varied from 0 (ANN rule) to 1 (HC rule) with step 0.1.

The results showed that when the HC and the ANN rules were both outperforming the 1NN rule (namely in the first fourteen data sets, from German-credit until Sonar), there are no improvements by their convex combinations, with a smooth transition between the accuracies of the two methods.

More interesting are the situations where ANN, HC or both are worse than 1NN. Such situations are shown in Fig. 2, where accuracies are shown when varying λ. In all plots, the red line represents the 1NN result, whereas the four variants defined by Eqs. (10), (11), (12) and (13) are represented by the blue, cyan, black and magenta lines, respectively.

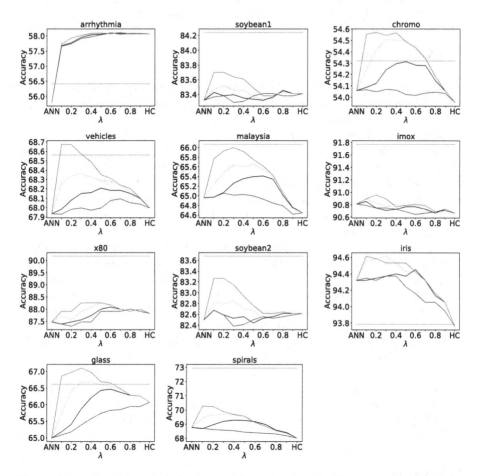

Fig. 2. (Best viewed in color) Analysis of the transition. Red line represents the 1NN result, whereas the four variants defined by Eqs. (10), (11), (12) and (13) are represented by the blue, cyan, black and magenta lines, respectively. (Color figure online)

For these data sets, it is interesting to observe that the convex combinations improve over both ANN and HC, except in the Arrhytmia case. Equation 13 is consistently the best for all these cases. Notice, in addition, that in four out of eleven occasions—for Chromo, Vehicle, Iris and Glass—at least one of the convex combinations outperforms 1NN for either some values of λ or all its range (cf. Iris). This represents a valuable result, since it supports the idea that the combination can be really useful when ANN and HC both fail. Concerning the parameter λ, we observed that in general the best value lies in the interval $[0.1, 0.3]$.

A ranking of the variants of the convex combinations, according to their effects, is clearly observed in some of the subfigures; see, for instance, results for `Chromo`, `Vehicles`, and `Malaysia`. In such cases, the sequence of the variants, starting from the best one, is: Eqs. (13), (11), (12) and (10).

5   Conclusion

In this paper we presented an empirical comparison and analysis of two related techniques, namely the Adaptive Nearest Neighbor Rule and the Hypersphere Classifier. Both approaches improve 1NN by correcting the distance query-prototype with information related to the distance of the prototype to the other classes, the difference consists in the way such correction is implemented. The relation between them is that the application of the HC correction to the logarithm of the original distances is equivalent to the application of the logarithm to the ANN correction computed on the original distances. We also performed a thorough experimental comparison between the two methods, also investigating how to integrate them via convex combinations.

Results lead us to conclude that HC, overall, should be preferred over ANN. However, since ANN does not yield negative distances, it might be considered as a processing step to apply, afterwards, alternative decision rules that are not necessarily based on the smallest dissimilarity values. We also showed that the convex combination of the two approaches is useful when both methods are worse than the original 1-Nearest Neighbor. In these cases, in general, $0.1 \leq \lambda \leq 0.3$ seems to be a convenient interval to select the parameter for the convex combination. Its proper tuning, however, is a matter for further study.

Acknowledgements. Part of this work was done while the first author was visiting the Computer Science Department at Università degli Studi di Verona, Italy, during his Sabbatical Year 2017–2018 granted by Universidad Nacional de Colombia - Sede Manizales.

References

1. Duda, R.O., Hart, P.E., Stork, D.G.: Pattern Classification, 2nd edn. Wiley, New York (2001)
2. Fukunaga, K.: Introduction to Statistical Pattern Recognition. Academic Press, Boston (1990)
3. Pekalska, E., Duin, R.P.W., Paclík, P.: Prototype selection for dissimilarity-based classifiers. Pattern Recogn. **39**(2), 189–208 (2006). Part Special Issue: Complexity Reduction
4. Triguero, I., Derrac, J., García, S., Herrera, F.: A taxonomy and experimental study on prototype generation for nearest neighbor classification. IEEE Trans. Syst. Man Cybern. Part C (Appl. Rev.) **42**(1), 86–100 (2012)

5. Pal, A.K., Mondal, P.K., Ghosh, A.K.: High dimensional nearest neighbor classification based on mean absolute differences of inter-point distances. Pattern Recogn. Lett. **74**, 1–8 (2016)

6. Lopes, N., Ribeiro, B.: Incremental hypersphere classifier (IHC). Machine Learning for Adaptive Many-Core Machines - A Practical Approach. SBD, vol. 7, pp. 107–123. Springer, Cham (2015). https://doi.org/10.1007/978-3-319-06938-8_6

7. Wang, J., Neskovic, P., Cooper, L.N.: Improving nearest neighbor rule with a simple adaptive distance measure. Pattern Recogn. Lett. **28**(2), 207–213 (2007)

8. Mukherjee, J.: Linear combination of norms in improving approximation of Euclidean norm. Pattern Recogn. Lett. **34**(12), 1348–1355 (2013)

9. Gönen, M., Alpaydın, E.: Multiple kernel learning algorithms. J. Mach. Learn. Res. **12**, 2211–2268 (2011)

10. Joachims, T., Cristianini, N., Shawe-Taylor, J.: Composite kernels for hypertext categorisation. In: Brodley, C.E., Danyluk, A.P. (eds.) Proceedings of the Eighteenth International Conference on Machine Learning (ICML 2001), Williamstown, MA, USA, pp. 250–257. Morgan Kaufmann, June 2001

11. Duin, R.P.W.: Compactness and complexity of pattern recognition problems. In: Perneel, C. (ed.) Proceedings of the International Symposium on Pattern Recognition "In Memoriam Pierre Devijver", Brussels, Belgium, Royal Military Academy, pp. 124–128, February 1999

12. Orozco-Alzate, M., Duin, R.P.W., Bicego, M.: Unsupervised parameter estimation of non linear scaling for improved classification in the dissimilarity space. In: Robles-Kelly, A., Loog, M., Biggio, B., Escolano, F., Wilson, R. (eds.) S+SSPR 2016. LNCS, vol. 10029, pp. 74–83. Springer, Cham (2016). https://doi.org/10.1007/978-3-319-49055-7_7

13. Duin, R.P.W., Bicego, M., Orozco-Alzate, M., Kim, S.-W., Loog, M.: Metric learning in dissimilarity space for improved nearest neighbor performance. In: Fränti, P., Brown, G., Loog, M., Escolano, F., Pelillo, M. (eds.) S+SSPR 2014. LNCS, vol. 8621, pp. 183–192. Springer, Heidelberg (2014). https://doi.org/10.1007/978-3-662-44415-3_19

14. Bicego, M., Baldo, S.: Properties of the Box-Cox transformation for pattern classification. Neurocomputing **218**, 390–400 (2016)

15. Sakia, R.M.: The Box-Cox transformation technique: a review. J. Roy. Stat. Soc. Ser. D (The Statistician) **41**(2), 169–178 (1992)

16. Box, G.E.P., Cox, D.R.: An analysis of transformations. J. Roy. Stat. Soc.: Ser. B (Methodol.) **26**(2), 211–243 (1964)

17. Bramer, M.: 15: comparing classifiers. In: Principles of Data Mining. Undergraduate Topics in Computer Science, 2nd edn, pp. 221–236. Springer, London (2013). https://doi.org/10.1007/978-1-4471-7307-6_15

A Novel Anomaly Score for Isolation Forests

Antonella Mensi[✉] and Manuele Bicego

Department of Computer Science, University of Verona, Verona, Italy
{antonella.mensi,manuele.bicego}@univr.it

Abstract. Isolation Forests represent a recent variant of Random Forests, specifically designed for one-class classification problems. In the original version, this method builds a set of extremely randomized trees to describe the set of points, subsequently measuring the "anomaly" of a testing point by looking at how much deep it arrives in each tree. Even if few extensions have been recently proposed – mainly aimed at improving the training stage – in most cases the anomaly score is still kept in its original formulation, which does not completely exploit all the information contained in the trained forest. This paper is focused on improving this aspect, and proposes a new approach for the computation of the anomaly score, which exploits the different information linked to the different nodes of the trees of the forest. We investigate three different variants of the novel anomaly score, evaluating them with twelve UCI benchmark datasets, with encouraging results.

Keywords: One-class classification · Random Forests ·
Outlier Detection · Isolation Forests

1 Introduction

Random Forests [5] represent a widely used tool for classification and regression, based on creating an ensemble of randomized decision trees [4], where each tree is built on a random subsample of the data and of the features. Randomness is crucial to get diverse trees, reducing the risk of overfitting and the computational complexity. The obtained ensemble method is more robust and performs better than a single tree [5,18]; actually it has been shown that these tools perform very well in many different fields such as computer vision [3], bioinformatics [6], remote sensing [23] and others, reaching performances which are comparable with other state-of-the-art techniques such as Support Vector Machines and Neural Networks [12].

Even if Random Forests have been mainly used for classification and regression, there also exist some random forest-based approaches for alternative learning paradigms, such as clustering [1,21,26,27,30], survival analysis [16], ranking problems [7], multi-label classification [17] and one-class classification [8,14,15,20,26]. In this paper we focus on this latter class, i.e. one-class classification [22], a learning problem in which only objects from one class are available

E. Ricci et al. (Eds.): ICIAP 2019, LNCS 11751, pp. 152–163, 2019.
https://doi.org/10.1007/978-3-030-30642-7_14

(the target, or positive, class), and where the aim is to identify whether new objects belong to that class or not [22,29]. The objects that do not belong to the positive class are also known as outliers or anomalies.

Even if the exploitation of Random Forests in the one-class classification field has not been studied as extensively as for classification and regression, some interesting approaches have been proposed, which can be subdivided mainly into two classes. The first class includes all those methods, such as [8,26], that solve the one-classification task by creating a synthetic negative class (the outliers), so that a classic classification random forest can be trained. The outlier generating process is often based on assuming a well-defined distribution: one possibility is to sample outliers uniformly on the domain space or to locate them in sparse, isolated regions that contain few inliers [26]. The main advantage of this class of approaches is that standard classification forests can be used without any modification. At the same time these methods can arise some issues: the most important is that the choice of the sampling technique is crucial. For example in a high-dimensional space if we assume outliers to be uniformly distributed, we have to generate a very big number of points to populate the space, and this is often not feasible. In addition, given a specific problem, the chosen distribution may not truly reflect how the outliers would distribute.

The second class of approaches are those based on Isolation Forests, a particular kind of Random Forests introduced by Liu and colleagues in [19,20]. Within these tools, the goal is not to discriminate objects of different classes but rather to isolate instances, that is to separate one object from the remaining ones. To do that, Isolation Forests partition the data through random and recursive splits along feature axes: a point is isolated when the leaf containing that point is created. Outliers, which are very different in terms of feature values and number, are likely to be separated earlier in the tree building process than inliers. Therefore, to quantitatively measure how much an object is isolated, the authors of [19,20] propose a scoring function, called *anomaly score*, which is inversely proportional to the length of the path in a tree that the object traverses to reach its leaf, averaged along all trees. As said before, the defined score will be higher for outliers since they are likely to be separated closer to the root. Isolation Forests present many advantages: they can work with only positive instances –and therefore no outliers need to be artificially generated– and they are computationally efficient thanks to the random split mechanism.

Even if Isolation Forests have been shown to be very effective for one-class classification–e.g authors of [11] empirically demonstrated that they are the best existing method to solve one-class classification tasks–, streaming data [13] and clustering [1], their full potential has not yet been completely exploited, especially for what concerns the testing phase. In almost all works dealing with Isolation Forests (see for example [9,11,28] or the extension proposed by [14]) the anomaly score is still kept in its original formulation of [19,20], which does not completely exploit all the information contained in the trained forest[1]. More

---

[1] For the sake of completeness, please note that a new scoring function has been proposed in [15]. This measure, however, is specifically designed for streaming data.

in detail, the scoring function is based on the length of the path traversed by an object (the shorter the path, the more isolated the point). Even if being very reasonable, this measure does not consider the information carried by each node, i.e. it does not consider that not all nodes are equally important in the path –for example a node with few points, e.g. a leaf, is usually more descriptive of the feature space than a bigger node, such as the root. In this paper we overcome this drawback, and propose an extension of the anomaly score: the novel score, which we called *path-weighted anomaly score*, is based on the estimation of a *weighted path length*, which exploits and takes into account the importance of the different nodes of the trees. We designed three different variants of the score, which consider different ways of measuring the "importance" of a node in a path. It is important to note that node weights are computed on training data and therefore, to not increase the testing procedure complexity, we compute them while building the tree, i.e. during the training phase.

The proposed schemes have been evaluated on 12 UCI benchmark datasets for one-class classification [10]. We investigated different parametrizations and configurations, comparing the proposed approach with the standard counterpart: the obtained results are very promising. The rest of the paper is organized as follows: in Sect. 2 we explain in detail the Isolation Forests, while in Sect. 3 we thoroughly define the proposed methodology. Section 4 is dedicated to the experimental part and the related results. Finally, Sect. 5 contains some conclusions.

2   Isolation Forests

Isolation Forests are variants of Random Forests introduced by Liu in [19,20]. The basic idea behind these methods is that one-class classification can be solved via *isolation*, that is by separating one object from the rest of the data, without focusing on discriminating objects of different classes.

To encode the concept of isolation the authors in [19,20] propose a new tree structure, called *ITree*. The ITree is based on the *Extra-Trees* proposed in [13]. These tools introduce different levels of randomness in the tree construction: for example, instead of evaluating at each node every possible split on a subset of features (as in standard decision trees), Extra Trees select a random split for each feature in the subset. The ITree exploits the extreme version of the Extra-Trees, called *totally randomized trees*, in which every split is completely random (at every node, a random feature is extracted, and a random threshold in the feature domain is chosen). Clearly, ITrees can be built using data coming from only one class. Very recently, some authors [14,15] investigated alternative approaches to build Isolation Forests: in particular in [14] they develop a function able to evaluate every possible split in a one-class context, while in [15] they design a new criteria which chooses the feature to split on randomly but proportionally to the feature relevance.

To recover the isolation capability of an object, an anomaly score is defined on the basis of the length of the path that the object traverses from the root to its leaf. This measures the number of partitions needed to separate it from the rest [20]: if an object is found closer to the root, i.e. its path is short, it means that it is easier to separate it, and thus to isolate it from the rest, with respect to objects that end up in deeper leaves. More in detail the anomaly score of an object x with respect to an Isolation Forest $\mathcal{F}$ is the following –in the paper we consider the dependence of the score on $\mathcal{F}$ implicit in order not to make the notation too heavy–:

$$s(x, N) = 2^{-\frac{E(h(x))}{c(N)}} \tag{1}$$

where N is the number of samples used to train each tree of the forest, $E(h(x))$ is the average path length across all trees (see below) and $c(N)$ is a normalization factor, needed to compare trees built on sets of different sizes. To estimate $c(N)$, which can be seen as the average path length, we can use the estimation of the average path length of unsuccessful searches in Binary Search Trees [19, 20], which is defined in the following way according to [24]

$$c(N) = \begin{cases} 2H(N-1) - 2(N-1)/N & \text{if } N > 2 \\ 1 & \text{if } N = 2 \\ 0 & \text{otherwise} \end{cases} \tag{2}$$

where H(i) stands for the harmonic number. The term $E(h(x))$ in formula (1) is computed as:

$$E(h(x)) = \frac{\sum_{t \in \mathcal{F}} h_t(x) + \sum_{t \in \mathcal{F}} c(|l_t(x)|)}{|\mathcal{F}|}. \tag{3}$$

where t is a tree, $c(|l_t(x)|)$ is a normalization factor needed when t is not fully grown (which estimates the average depth of the tree which can be built from $l_t(x)$) and $h_t(x) = |\mathcal{P}_t(x)|$ with $\mathcal{P}_t(x)$ being the path of x, i.e. the set of nodes visited by x from the root to the leaf containing x. From formula (1) it can be inferred that the score of an object x is proportional to the inverse of its average path length in the forest: if x ends up in leaves that are very deep in the trees, its score will be quite low (close to 0), if instead its path ends very early the score will be high (close to 1).

The anomaly score defined in (1) represents a reasonable way to characterize outliers, and thus to solve the one-class classification problem: actually outliers are usually very heterogeneous and low in number with respect to inliers, and they do not follow a predefined distribution. When building an Isolation Forest, they will be more likely separated from the rest of the data very quickly, i.e. after few partitions. In other words, outliers will be likely to traverse a shorter path with respect to inliers, producing an higher anomaly score (usually ≥ 0.5 as stated in [20]).

3   Proposed Methodology

In this section we describe the proposed approach. The starting observation is that the anomaly score considers each node visited in a path to have the same importance. In this sense, the path length $h_t(x)$ of a x in a tree t can be written as

$$h_t(x) = \sum_{k \in \mathcal{P}_t(x)} 1. \tag{4}$$

The main idea behind the proposed approach is to define a novel anomaly score where nodes in the path are given a weight, which corresponds to specific information that can be retrieved in the forest. The novel scoring function is called *path-weighted anomaly score* and is based on re-defining $h_t(x)$ as follows.

Given a tree t and the path $\mathcal{P}_t(x)$ of an object x, $h_t(x)$ is defined as:

$$h_t(x) = \sum_{k \in \mathcal{P}_t(x)} w_{tk} \tag{5}$$

where w_{tk} represents the weight the node k has in the tree t. Clearly, when considering $w_{tk} = 1 \; \forall t, k$, we have the original anomaly score. The weights w_{tk} can be defined in several ways, here we investigated three different versions, presented in the following.

3.1 Variant 1 – Neighborhood

The first variant is based on the concept of neighborhood defined in [30]: considering a node k and an object x in that node, the neighborhood of x is defined as the set of all the other objects that would pass from k. More in general, we can define the neighborhood N_{tk} of a node k of a tree t as the set of the objects of the dataset that would pass by k in their path from the root to the leaves of the tree t. Clearly the neighborhood of the root is the whole dataset, whereas the neighborhood of a leaf contains only few points. To define the weight, we observe that a node which has a very small and restrictive neighborhood is more important than a larger one, since it is more specific for the object under analysis. In particular, in an Isolation Forest a small neighborhood occurs when we are very deep in the tree (since the number of objects decreases from the root to the leaves) or we are high in the tree and there is an outlier that has been isolated after few partitions (i.e. we have leaves at small depths).

We thus want to give more weight to nodes with a smaller neighborhood, which leads to the following definition of w_{tk}^N. Given a tree t and a node k in t, its weight w_{tk}^N is:

$$w_{tk}^N = \frac{1}{|N_{tk}|} \tag{6}$$

where N_{tk} is the neighborhood of the node k, i.e. the set of points passing by that node in the path from the root to their leaves.

3.2 Variant 2 – Proxy

The second variant starts from [14], an extension of Isolation Forests which improves the training stage: instead of a random train, trees are built by optimizing a predefined function. In particular, while building a tree, the authors of [14] find a split by minimizing the so-called proxy function, a function which indicates the loss of information obtained when doing a particular split. In the classification setting, this function is typically defined using the class labels (an example is the Gini impurity): however, in the case of Isolation Forests, labels are not available and thus such function must be defined in an alternative way.

The definition given by [14] is based on the following intuition: the best split is the one which best separates instances, i.e. where one of the two children contains the maximum number of objects in a minimum volume and the other child the minimum number of instances in a maximum volume. In principle, the former child should characterize the inliers, whereas the latter should characterize the outliers. In practice, the proxy is an adaptation of the Gini impurity for the one-class context, and for its definition we need: a volume measure, the number of inliers and an estimation of the number of outliers. Aside from the number of inliers, which is known, we define the other two elements as follows:

(i) The volume of a node k is computed via the Lebesgue measure $Leb(k)$. In the proxy, the ratio $\lambda_k = \frac{Leb(k)}{Leb(parent(k))}$ between the volume of a node k and its parent is measured to retrieve the best split.
(ii) In [14] the distribution of outliers within the node k to be split is assumed to be constant with respect to node k. Therefore the number of outliers n'_k is defined as $n'_k = n_k\gamma$ where n_k is the number of inliers and γ some constant.

Leaving aside further mathematical processing steps (for all the details, please see [14]), the one-class proxy is defined as:

$$proxy(k) = \frac{n_{k_L}\gamma n_k \lambda_L}{n_{k_L} + \gamma n_k \lambda_L} + \frac{n_{k_R}\gamma n_k \lambda_R}{n_{k_R} + \gamma n_k \lambda_R} \tag{7}$$

where k_L and k_R are respectively the left and right child of k and $\gamma = 1$.

From our perspective, the one-class proxy can be used to measure the goodness of a split at a node k (the lower the proxy the better the split): actually, a high proxy means that the split does not separate well the data the node contains, i.e. the node is not very important in the isolation process. On the contrary a low proxy means that the node is split in a good way, i.e. some objects will likely to be isolated after it. Following this reasoning, we can define a new weight w^P_{tk}, given a tree t and a node k in t, as:

$$w^P_{tk} = \frac{1}{proxy_t(k)} \tag{8}$$

where $proxy_t(k)$ is the proxy computed at node k.

3.3 Variant 3 – Proxy-Neighborhood

The third variant we propose combines the two previous versions, taking into account both the neighborhood and the proxy of a node.

Given a tree t and a node k in t, its weight w_{tk}^{PN} is:

$$w_{tk}^{PN} = \frac{1}{proxy_t(k)|N_{tk}|} \qquad (9)$$

where $proxy_t(k)$ and N_{tk} are respectively the proxy and the neighborhood of the node k.

4   Experimental Evaluation

The evaluation is based on 12 datasets from the UCI-ML repository [10] which are benchmarks for one-class classification [14] (they were preprocessed following the specifications in [14]). Table 1 presents an overview of the datasets. We can see that the datasets cover a large range of situations: they differ in size (the smallest one has 351 samples while the biggest 567498), in the number of features (from 3 up to 164) and in the outlier percentage (from 0.03% up to 45.8%).

Isolation Forests were trained with standard parameters, as defined in [19,20], which are: number of objects $N = 256$ sampled without replacement, size of the forest $T = 100$, number of features available per tree $F = All$ and maximum depth $D = log(N)$. In addition we also performed the experiments using $D = N - 1$ to understand whether more descriptive trees produce better results.

Following [14], we adopted a Novelty Detection framework [25], i.e. only inliers are used in the training phase[2]. For each experiment the dataset has been split equally, i.e. 50% of the samples, in training and testing set. Each experiment has been repeated 30 times. Finally, as often done in many one-class classification problems [14,19,20] as accuracy measure we adopted the area under the ROC curve (AUC).

Table 1. Overview of the 12 UCI datasets used for the experimental evaluation.

Datasets	Nr. of objects	Nr. of features	Outlier %
Adult	48842	6	16.10%
Annthyroid	7200	6	7.42%
Arrhythmia	452	164	45.80%
ForestCover	286048	10	0.96%
Http	567498	3	0.39%
Ionosphere	351	32	35.90%
Pendigits	10992	16	10.41%
Pima	768	8	34.90%
Shuttle	49097	9	7.15%
Smtp	95156	3	0.03%
Spambase	4601	57	39.40%
Wilt	4839	5	5.39%

[2] An alternative framework to adopt would be Outlier Detection [2] which uses both outliers and inliers in the training stage.

The first analysis compares the novel anomaly score with the standard unweighted version. In Table 2 we present the results obtained when using standard parametrization with depth $log(N)$ and $N-1$. The last row is the average across all the datasets. The best result is highlighted in bold. To assess the statistical significance we computed the standard errors of the mean, which are comprised in the range $4*10^{-9}$ and $8*10^{-5}$. As a first general observation, if we look at the average across the datasets, we can see that the newly defined scores outperform the standard anomaly score. More in detail, except for two datasets, Spambase and Adult, the best score is always obtained with a path-weighted variant; for Shuttle instead, it seems there is no difference in using the standard or the novel score. On the other hand, in some cases, such as for Wilt, the improvement is quite relevant (0.718 versus 0.535). Table 2 also shows that varying the depth parameter is advantageous for our proposal, while for the anomaly score the performances vary only slightly.

Table 2. Results for the standard parametrization setting. Anomaly stands for the standard definition of the anomaly score, Variant 1 for the neighborhood-based variant, Variant 2 for the proxy-based one and Variant 3 for the variant based on both the neighborhood and the proxy.

Dataset	Anomaly		Variant 1		Variant 2		Variant 3	
	$N-1$	$log(N)$	$N-1$	$log(N)$	$N-1$	$log(N)$	$N-1$	$log(N)$
Adult	**0.631**	0.630	0.625	0.629	0.627	0.630	0.610	0.629
Annthyroid	0.915	0.912	**0.939**	0.903	0.934	0.908	0.915	0.904
Arrhythmia	0.770	0.759	**0.773**	0.753	**0.773**	0.756	0.750	0.752
ForestCover	0.845	0.852	**0.869**	0.827	0.860	0.838	0.815	0.829
Http	0.994	0.993	**0.997**	0.994	**0.997**	0.996	**0.997**	0.992
Ionosphere	0.905	0.898	0.945	0.881	**0.959**	0.901	0.946	0.880
Pendigits	0.840	0.798	**0.928**	0.805	0.927	0.834	0.913	0.803
Pima	0.732	0.729	0.694	**0.734**	0.712	**0.734**	0.677	0.733
Shuttle	0.996	0.996	0.996	0.995	0.995	0.996	0.987	0.995
Smtp	0.902	0.913	0.908	0.920	0.918	**0.927**	0.890	0.915
Spambase	0.825	**0.832**	0.798	0.827	0.824	0.829	0.755	0.828
Wilt	0.535	0.483	0.704	0.476	0.691	0.484	**0.718**	0.477
Average	0.824	0.816	0.848	0.812	**0.851**	0.819	0.831	0.811

As second experiment, we performed an analysis to study how the performances change when varying the size of the forest, i.e. $T \in \{50, 100, 200, 500\}$: results are presented in Table 3. For each T we report the best anomaly score (A) and the best path-weighted anomaly score (PW). We also indicate the variant reaching the best result. In bold we highlight the best result for each T. To assess the statistical significance we computed the standard errors of the

Table 3. Results for different Ts. A stands for anomaly score, PW for path-weighted score. We report the best weighted variant between parenthesis.

Dataset	$T=50$			$T=100$			$T=200$			$T=500$		
	A	PW		A	PW		A	PW		A	PW	
Adult	**0.629**	0.628	(V2)	**0.631**	0.630	(V2)	**0.632**	0.631	(V2)	0.631	0.631	(V2)
Annthyroid	0.912	**0.929**	(V1)	0.915	**0.939**	(V1)	0.917	**0.943**	(V1)	0.918	**0.946**	(V1)
Arrhythmia	**0.764**	0.760	(V2)	0.770	**0.773**	(V2)	0.772	**0.778**	(V1)	0.775	**0.784**	(V1)
ForestCover	0.845	**0.849**	(V1)	0.852	**0.869**	(V1)	0.856	**0.885**	(V1)	0.861	**0.896**	(V1)
Http	0.992	**0.996**	(V2)	0.994	**0.997**	(V2)	0.994	**0.998**	(V2)	0.994	**0.998**	(V3)
Ionosphere	0.900	**0.951**	(V2)	0.905	**0.959**	(V2)	0.906	**0.961**	(V2)	0.907	**0.962**	(V2)
Pendigits	0.834	**0.913**	(V2)	0.840	**0.928**	(V1)	0.842	**0.939**	(V3)	0.844	**0.953**	(V3)
Pima	0.727	**0.730**	(V2)	0.732	**0.734**	(V2)	0.734	**0.736**	(V2)	0.735	**0.737**	(V2)
Shuttle	**0.996**	0.994	(V2)	0.996	0.996	(V1)	0.997	0.997	(V1)	0.997	0.997	(V1)
Smtp	0.911	**0.923**	(V2)	0.913	**0.927**	(V2)	0.913	**0.927**	(V2)	0.913	**0.927**	(V2)
Spambase	**0.827**	0.824	(V2)	**0.832**	0.829	(V2)	**0.837**	0.834	(V2)	**0.840**	0.837	(V2)
Wilt	0.534	**0.687**	(V1)	0.535	**0.718**	(V3)	0.537	**0.753**	(V3)	0.535	**0.779**	(V3)
Average	0.823	**0.849**		0.826	**0.858**		0.828	**0.865**		0.829	**0.871**	

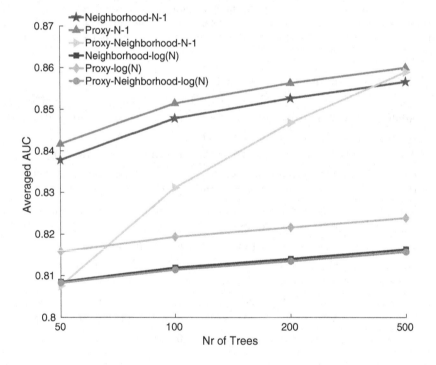

Fig. 1. Datasets average-standard parametrization

mean, which are comprised in the range $2*10^{-9}$ and $9*10^{-5}$. As in Table 2, the last row presents the average across all the datasets. We can observe that the proposed method works well and the performances increase as T, the size of the forest, does. This is not true for the standard anomaly score, which improvement reaches a plateau when $T = 100$. Indeed if we look at the results for $T = 50$ the best score for 4 datasets is reached with the standard score, but if we observe the results for $T = 500$ there is only one dataset which prefers the unweighted anomaly score. This analysis also shows that in 27/48 cases the variant based on the one-class proxy, Variant 2 is the best one. On the contrary, Variant 3 rarely achieves the best results. We can also observe that for more than half datasets the best variant does not change when varying the number of trees.

The last analysis aims at a deeper understanding of the three versions of the path-weighted anomaly score. We analysed how the performance of the different variants, averaged across all the datasets, varies when varying the size of the forest. The results are depicted in Fig. 1: we can observe that among the three variants, if we fix the depth to either $log(N)$ or $N-1$, the best variant is in both cases the one based on the proxy, confirming the results of Table 3. It makes sense since the proxy measures the goodness of a node in terms of split, and thus how well it isolates the data. Another observation we can make is that in general, using fully grown trees, i.e. depth $N - 1$, increases the performances no matter which variant we consider.

5   Conclusions

This paper proposes an improvement of the classical anomaly score of Isolation Forests by exploiting node-related information. The proposed approach is very robust and compares well to the state of the art; in particular it achieves the best performances when working with large forests and with completely grown trees. Nevertheless we could make some further improvements, such as developing an automated method that given a dataset chooses a priori the best variant. In the future we would like to investigate novel ways to define the importance of a node and to design new methodologies to isolate points, i.e. modify the training phase.

References

1. Bicego, M.: K-random forests: a k-means style algorithm for random forest clustering. In: International Joint Conference on Neural Networks (2019, accepted)
2. Bishop, C.M.: Novelty detection and neural network validation. IEE Proc. Vis. Image Signal Process. **141**(4), 217–222 (1994)
3. Bosch, A., Zisserman, A., Munoz, X.: Image classification using random forests and ferns. In: IEEE International Conference on Computer Vision, pp. 1–8 (2007)
4. Breiman, L., Friedman, J., Stone, C., Olshen, R.: Classification and Regression Trees. Taylor & Francis, The Wadsworth and Brooks-Cole Statistics-Probability Series (1984)
5. Breiman, L.: Random forests. Mach. Learn. **45**(1), 5–32 (2001)
6. Chen, X., Ishwaran, H.: Random forests for genomic data analysis. Genomics **99**(6), 323–329 (2012)
7. Clémençon, S., Depecker, M., Vayatis, N.: Ranking forests. J. Mach. Learn. Res. **14**, 39–73 (2013)

8. Désir, C., Bernard, S., Petitjean, C., Heutte, L.: One class random forests. Pattern Recogn. **46**, 3490–3506 (2013)
9. Ding, Z., Fei, M.: An anomaly detection approach based on isolation forest algorithm for streaming data using sliding window. IFAC Proc. Volumes **46**(20), 12–17 (2013)
10. Dua, D., Graff, C.: UCI machine learning repository (2017). http://archive.ics.uci.edu/ml
11. Emmott, A.F., Das, S., Dietterich, T., Fern, A., Wong, W.K.: Systematic construction of anomaly detection benchmarks from real data. In: Proceedings of the ACM SIGKDD Workshop on Outlier Detection and Description, pp. 16–21 (2013)
12. Fernández-Delgado, M., Cernadas, E., Barro, S., Amorim, D.: Do we need hundreds of classifiers to solve real world classification problems? J. Mach. Learn. Res. **15**(1), 3133–3181 (2014)
13. Geurts, P., Ernst, D., Wehenkel, L.: Extremely randomized trees. Mach. Learn. **63**(1), 3–42 (2006)
14. Goix, N., Drougard, N., Brault, R., Chiapino, M.: One class splitting criteria for random forests. In: ACML, pp. 1–16 (2017)
15. Guha, S., Mishra, N., Roy, G., Schrijvers, O.: Robust random cut forest based anomaly detection on streams. In: ICML (2016)
16. Ishwaran, H., Kogalur, U.B., Blackstone, E.H., Lauer, M.S., et al.: Random survival forests. Ann. Appl. Stat. **2**(3), 841–860 (2008)
17. Joly, A., Geurts, P., Wehenkel, L.: Random forests with random projections of the output space for high dimensional multi-label classification. In: Calders, T., Esposito, F., Hüllermeier, E., Meo, R. (eds.) ECML PKDD 2014. LNCS (LNAI), vol. 8724, pp. 607–622. Springer, Heidelberg (2014). https://doi.org/10.1007/978-3-662-44848-9_39
18. Kittler, J.: Combining classifiers: a theoretical framework. Pattern Anal. Appl. **1**(1), 18–27 (1998)
19. Liu, F.T., Ting, K.M., Zhou, Z.H.: Isolation forest. In: IEEE International Conference on Data Mining, IEEE Computer Society, pp. 413–422 (2008)
20. Liu, F.T., Ting, K.M., Zhou, Z.H.: Isolation-based anomaly detection. ACM Trans. Knowl. Discov. Data **6**(1), 3:1–3:39 (2012)
21. Moosmann, F., Triggs, B., Jurie, F.: Fast discriminative visual codebooks using randomized clustering forests. In: Advances in Neural Information Processing Systems, pp. 985–992 (2007)
22. Moya, M.M., Koch, M.W., Hostetler, L.D.: One-class classifier networks for target recognition applications. NASA STI/Recon Technical Report N **93** (1993)
23. Pal, M.: Random forest classifier for remote sensing classification. Int. J. Remote Sens. **26**(1), 217–222 (2005)
24. Preiss, B.R.: Data Structures and Algorithms. Wiley (1999)
25. Ritter, G., Gallegos, M.T.: Outliers in statistical pattern recognition and an application to automatic chromosome classification. Pattern Recogn. Lett. **18**(6), 525–539 (1997)
26. Shi, T., Horvath, S.: Unsupervised learning with random forest predictors. J. Comput. Graph. Stat. **15**, 118–138 (2005)
27. Shotton, J., Johnson, M., Cipolla, R.: Semantic texton forests for image categorization and segmentation. In: IEEE Conference on Computer Vision and Pattern Recognition, pp. 1–8 (2008)
28. Susto, G.A., Beghi, A., McLoone, S.: Anomaly detection through on-line isolation forest: an application to plasma etching. In: Annual SEMI Advanced Semiconductor Manufacturing Conference (2017)

29. Tax, D.: One-class classification; concept-learning in the absence of counter-examples. Ph.D. thesis, Delft University of Technology (2001)
30. Zhu, X., Loy, C.C., Gong, S.: Constructing robust affinity graphs for spectral clustering. In: IEEE Conference on Computer Vision and Pattern Recognition, pp. 1450–1457 (2014)

Adaptive Hybrid Representation for Graph-Based Semi-supervised Classification

F. Dornaika[1,2]([✉]) [iD] and A. Bosaghzadeh[3]

[1] University of the Basque Country UPV/EHU, San Sebastian, Spain
`fadi.dornaika@ehu.es`
[2] IKERBASQUE, Basque Foundation for Science, Bilbao, Spain
[3] Shahid Rajaee Teacher Training University, Tehran, Iran

Abstract. Building an informative graph over a collection of images or signals is one of the most important tasks in semi-supervised learning (SSL). Local Hybrid Coding (LHC) was recently proposed as an alternative to the sparse coding scheme that is used in Sparse Representation Classifier (SRC). The LHC blends sparsity and bases-locality criteria in a unified optimization problem. This paper introduces a data-driven graph construction method that exploits and extends the LHC scheme. We propose a new coding scheme coined Adaptive Local Hybrid Coding (ALHC). The main contributions are as follows. First, the proposed coding scheme automatically selects the local and non-local bases of LHC using data similarities calculated by Locality-constrained Linear code. Second, the estimated similarities are used in the regularization of the final solution. Third, the proposed ALHC scheme is used in order to construct graphs over image datasets. For SSL tasks adopting label propagation, we show that the proposed graph outperforms many state-of-the art graphs on three public face datasets.

Keywords: Graph construction · Sparse coding · Local hybrid code · Label propagation

1 Introduction

Semi-supervised learning is one of the most important fields in machine learning. It is mainly used in the cases where there are a huge amount of labeled samples, but very few labeled ones.

It can be an interesting solution specially in the cases where acquiring unlabeled data is easy and cheap but obtaining labeled data is difficult which is the case in many real world problems such as: (i) image classification, (ii) webpage classification, (iii) speech recognition, (iv) person emotion recognition in videos [1], and (v) protein sequence classification.

Graph-based semi-supervised learning which adopts an affinity graph to represent the relation between the samples has gain a lot of attention in the last

© Springer Nature Switzerland AG 2019
E. Ricci et al. (Eds.): ICIAP 2019, LNCS 11751, pp. 164–174, 2019.
https://doi.org/10.1007/978-3-030-30642-7_15

decade (e.g., [4,6]). Indeed, graph-based algorithms are widely used nowadays in a variety of machine learning tasks such as: (i) semi-supervised learning for label propagation and regression [7], (ii) feature selection, (iii) graph-based embedding [8], and (iv) spectral clustering [14]. Over the past decade, several graph construction techniques have been proposed. In this paper, we propose a new technique to construct a graph based on the Local Hybrid Coding [18]. Considering both the bases-locality and sparsity constraints in a unified framework, LHC obtains the advantages of both types of coding. Dense coding with ℓ_2 regularization can better represent the geometric structure of data manifold which can increase the accuracy of classification due to better discrimination power [15]. At the same time, the ℓ_1-sparsity guarantees the correct representation of input data in case very few samples are available [12,17].

The main differences between our approach and the LHC scheme of [18] are as follows. Firstly, in our work, we construct a data-driven graph using data self-representativeness whereas in [18], the authors propose a variant of the Sparse Representation Classifier that uses the hybrid coding instead of the sparse coding. Hence, in our work the adopted dictionary is obtained from the data whereas in [18] they use a pre-trained database. Secondly, in our work the similarity between the samples are derived from the coefficients that are obtained from a coding scheme namely, Locality-constrained Linear Coding (LLC) while in [18] the selection of local and non-local bases is based on Euclidean distance.

Thirdly, we adopt a biased weight for the coefficients of the local bases.

The remainder of this paper is organized as follows. Section 2 provides a brief review of graph construction and reviews the Local Hybrid Coding scheme. Our proposed method is introduced in Sect. 3. In Sect. 4, we present some experimental results obtained with three benchmark face image datasets. Section 5 concludes the paper. In this paper, capital bold letters denote matrices and small bold letters denote vectors.

2   Related Work

This section describes some existing methods for graph construction. Then, it will present a review of the recent Local Hybrid Coding scheme. k-nearest neighbor and ε-neighborhoods are two traditional graph construction methods. Let the original data set be denoted by $\mathbf{X} = [\mathbf{x}_1, \mathbf{x}_2, \ldots, \mathbf{x}_n] \in \mathbb{R}^{d \times n}$.

Locally Linear Embedding (LLE) focuses on preserving the local structure of data [11]. LLE formulates the manifold learning problem as a neighborhood-preserving embedding, which learns the global structure by exploiting the local linear reconstructions. It estimates the reconstruction coefficients by minimizing the reconstruction error of the set of all local neighborhoods in the dataset. It turned out that the linear coding used by LLE can be used for computing the graph weight matrix. Thus, LLE graph can be obtained by applying two stages: adjacency matrix computation followed by the linear reconstruction of samples from their neighbors. The adjacency matrix can be computed using the KNN or ϵ-Neighborhood method. In [5], the authors utilize LLC for graph construction. They propose a graph construction method that is based on a variant of LLC.

On the other hand, sparsity representation based graph is parameter-free. [10] and [19] proposed sparsity representation based graph construction methods in which every sample is represented as a sparse linear combination of the rest of input samples and the coefficients are considered as weights.

$$\min \|\mathbf{w}_i\|_1, \, s.t. \, \mathbf{x}_i = \mathbf{X}\,\mathbf{w}_i, \tag{1}$$

where $\mathbf{w}_i = [w_{i1}, \ldots, w_{i,i-1}, 0, w_{i,i+1}, \ldots, w_{in}]^T$ is an n-dimensional vector with the i-th element being zero (implying that the $\mathbf{x}_i$ is removed from $\mathbf{X}$), $\|.\|_1$ is the ℓ_1 norm of a vector or matrix, and the elements $w_{ij}, j \neq i$ denote the contribution of $\mathbf{x}_j$ in the reconstruction of $\mathbf{x}_i$.

After the weight vector $\mathbf{w}_i$ for each $\mathbf{x}_i$, $i = 1, 2, \ldots, n$ is obtained, the affinity matrix $\mathbf{W} = (w_{ij})_{n \times n}$ is obtained as:

$$\mathbf{W} = [\mathbf{w}_1, \mathbf{w}_2, \ldots, \mathbf{w}_n]^T, \tag{2}$$

where $\mathbf{w}_i$ is the optimal solution of Eq. (1) problem: A robust version of the sparse graph can be obtained by solving the following problem:

$$\min \|\mathbf{w}_i\|_1 + \|\mathbf{e}\|_1, \, s.t. \, \mathbf{x}_i = \mathbf{X}\,\mathbf{w}_i + \mathbf{e}. \tag{3}$$

In this article, we call the graph that is constructed by the weights obtained from Eq. (1) as standard sparse graph (ℓ_1-s) and the graph obtained by solving the Eq. 3 as robust sparse graph (ℓ_1-r).

2.1   Review of Local Hybrid Coding

The authors in [18] propose a Local Hybrid Coding scheme to encode image descriptors by taking into account the bases-locality and ℓ_1-sparsity. Hence their proposed method retains the advantages of Least Square coding scheme and ℓ_1-sparsity.

Let $\mathbf{B} = [\mathbf{b}_1, \mathbf{b}_2, \ldots, \mathbf{b}_n] \in \mathbb{R}^{d \times n}$ denote a pre-trained dictionary which contains n samples each with dimensionality of d. Let $\mathbf{x} \in \mathbb{R}^d$ denote a test sample. The objective is to project this sample onto the bases of $\mathbf{B}$ via computing a code vector $\mathbf{c}$ such that $\mathbf{x} \approx \mathbf{B}\mathbf{c}$. LHC ensembles the ℓ_1-sparsity and bases-locality criteria into a unified optimization problem. The coding of sample $\mathbf{x}$ with respect to the dictionary $\mathbf{B}$ can be obtained by applying two steps.

In the first step, based on the distance between the sample $\mathbf{x}$ and the atoms of the dictionary, the pre-trained dictionary is divided into two disjoint sets of $\mathbf{B}^{(l)}$ that contain the k-nearest-neighbor (KNN) atoms (k_l) and $\mathbf{B}^{(s)}$ that contains the non-k-nearest-neighbor (k_s) atoms. The $\mathbf{B}^{(l)}$ which contains the local samples are used for local coding and $\mathbf{B}^{(s)}$ that contains non-local samples are used for sparse coding.

In the second step, based on the local codes $\mathbf{c}^{(l)}$ that are obtained from the local bases $\mathbf{B}^{(l)}$ and the sparse codes $\mathbf{c}^{(s)}$ that are obtained from the $\mathbf{B}^{(s)}$ basis, a hybrid code will be constructed by:

$$\min_{\mathbf{c}} \|\mathbf{x} - [\mathbf{B}^{(l)}, \mathbf{B}^{(s)}] [\mathbf{c}^{(l)T}, \mathbf{c}^{(s)T}]^T\|_2^2 + \gamma \, \|\mathbf{c}^{(l)}\|_2^2 + \lambda \, \|\mathbf{c}^{(s)}\|_1 \tag{4}$$

where $\mathbf{c} = [\mathbf{c}^{(l)T}, \mathbf{c}^{(s)T}]^T$ is the hybrid code formed from two parts, local code $\mathbf{c}^{(l)}$ and sparse code $\mathbf{c}^{(s)}$. $||.||_1$ and $||.||_2$ denote the ℓ_1-norm and ℓ_2-norm of a vector, respectively. Criterion 4 has three terms: the first term is the residual error of the sample reconstruction, the second term is the ℓ_2 norm of local basis coefficients and the third term is the ℓ_1 norm of the non-local bases coefficients.

Although the dictionary $\mathbf{B}$ is partitioned into two disjoint subsets, their coefficients $\mathbf{c}^{(l)}$ and $\mathbf{c}^{(s)}$ are coupled, thus the convex optimization problem (4) is solved in an alternating optimization procedure. The two sets of unknown coefficients are then iteratively obtained by alternating regularized ℓ_2 coding and ℓ_1 coding over the local bases and the non-local bases, respectively. Note that when the sparse code $\mathbf{c}^{(s)}$ is constant, the minimization problem in Eq. (4) reduces to a regularized Least Square problem that can be solved using a closed-form solution. Let $\mathbf{x}^{(l)} = \mathbf{x} - \mathbf{B}^{(s)}\mathbf{c}^{(s)}$. The optimal $\mathbf{c}^{(l)}$ is then given by $\mathbf{c}^{(l)} \leftarrow (\mathbf{B}^{(l)T}\mathbf{B}^{(l)} + \gamma \mathbf{I})^{-1}\mathbf{B}^{(l)T}\mathbf{x}^{(l)}$. When the local part $\mathbf{c}^{(l)}$ is constant, then the minimization problem in Eq. (4) reduces to a ℓ_1 regularized sparse coding problem that can be efficiently solved by the feature-sign search method [9].

Algorithm 1 describes the procedure of the proposed method. The *FeatureSign*() function is the algorithm described in [9] which computes the sparse code of a given sample w.r.t. a given dictionary. It should be noted that in each iteration only the local code (i.e. $\mathbf{c}^{(l)}$) and sparse code (i.e. $\mathbf{c}^{(s)}$) change. According to [18], convergence can be obtained in five iterations.

Input: Dictionary matrix $\mathbf{B} \in \mathbb{R}^{d \times n}$, sample $\mathbf{x}$, γ, λ, k_l, and k_s.
Output: LHC Code vector $\mathbf{c}$

$\mathbf{c}^{(s)} \leftarrow \mathbf{0}$;
Sort the vectors of $\mathbf{B}$ in ascending order of their distances to $\mathbf{x}$ and obtain
 basis vectors into the matrix $\mathbf{B}$;
Split $\mathbf{B}$ into KNN bases $\mathbf{B}^{(l)}$ (k_l bases) and non-KNN bases $\mathbf{B}^{(s)}$ (k_s bases) ;
repeat
     $\mathbf{x}^{(l)} \leftarrow \mathbf{x} - \mathbf{B}^{(s)}\mathbf{c}^{(s)}$;
     $\mathbf{c}^{(l)} \leftarrow (\mathbf{B}^{(l)T}\mathbf{B}^{(l)} + \gamma \mathbf{I})^{-1}\mathbf{B}^{(l)T}\mathbf{x}^{(l)}$;
     $\mathbf{x}^{(s)} \leftarrow \mathbf{x} - \mathbf{B}^{(l)}\mathbf{c}^{(l)}$;
     $\mathbf{c}^{(s)} \leftarrow FeatureSign(\mathbf{B}^{(s)}, \mathbf{x}^{(s)})$;
until *Convergence*;
$\mathbf{c} = [\mathbf{c}^{(l)T}, \mathbf{c}^{(s)T}]^T$

Algorithm 1: Local Hybrid Coding.

---

3   Proposed Approach: Adaptive LHC (ALHC) Graph

In this paper, we propose an adaptive graph construction method that is based on data self-representativeness and adopted a modified version of the LHC method. The proposed method is different from LHC is several aspects. First, in our work, we construct a data-driven graph using data self-representativeness whereas in [18], the authors target a coding scheme that can replace the sparse coding stage in the Sparse Representation Classifier. Hence, the dictionary in the proposed method is constructed from the data themselves, compared to a pre-trained dictionary in [18]. Second, while [18] determined the similarity between the samples (and the selection of local and non-local bases) adopting Euclidean distance, in this article we use the similarity coefficients obtained by a Locality-constrained Linear Code (LLC) method. Third, our proposed scheme is able to adaptively select the local and non-local bases without any user-defined parameter. Fourth, our coding introduces weights for the local bases coefficients.

To construct the graph, for every sample, we estimate its code with respect to the rest of the samples in the database. Let $\mathbf{X}_i \in \mathbb{R}^{d \times (n-1)}$ denote the data matrix associated with the set $S_i = \{\mathbf{x}_1, \mathbf{x}_2 \ldots, \mathbf{x}_{i-1}, \mathbf{x}_{i+1}, \ldots, \mathbf{x}_n\}$. The whole process has two steps. In the first step, based on the similarity between a sample (i.e. $\mathbf{x}_i$) and the rest of the samples (i.e. S_i), the local and non-local bases are selected. In the second step, we obtain a hybrid code from the local and non-local sets. We proceed as follows.

First Step. We first estimate the coding of the sample $\mathbf{x}_i$ with respect to the data matrix $\mathbf{X}_i$ using LLC. Let $\mathbf{a} \in \mathbb{R}^{n-1}$ denote this code. This vector is given by minimizing the LLC criterion:

$$\mathbf{a} = \arg\min_{\mathbf{a}} (\|\mathbf{x}_i - \mathbf{X}_i\,\mathbf{a}\|_2^2 + \sigma \sum_{j=1}^{n-1} p_j\, a_j^2) = \arg\min_{\mathbf{a}} \left(\|\mathbf{x}_i - \mathbf{X}_i\,\mathbf{a}\|_2^2 + \sigma \,\|\mathbf{P}^{1/2}\,\mathbf{a}\|^2 \right) \tag{5}$$

where $\mathbf{P}$ is a diagonal matrix with elements $P_{jj} = p_j$. Any formula which forms a distance criterion between the sample $\mathbf{x}_i$ and the sample $\mathbf{x}_j$ can be used to calculate p_j. In our work, we use the following formula:

$$p_j = 1 - \exp(-\|\mathbf{x}_i - \mathbf{x}_j\|^2) \tag{6}$$

By using simple linear algebra calculations, the solution to (5) has a closed-form solution:

$$\mathbf{a} = \left(\mathbf{X}_i^T \mathbf{X}_i + \sigma\, \mathbf{P} \right)^{-1} \mathbf{X}_i^T \mathbf{x}_i \tag{7}$$

Since the score $|a_j|$ encodes the similarity between the sample $\mathbf{x}_i$ and the sample $\mathbf{x}_j \in S_i = \{\mathbf{x}_1, \mathbf{x}_2 \ldots, \mathbf{x}_{i-1}, \mathbf{x}_{i+1}, \ldots, \mathbf{x}_n\}$, it is expected to be much better than the classic Euclidean distance $\|\mathbf{x}_i - \mathbf{x}_j\|^2$. Thus, $|a_j|$ can be a good measure of locality between samples $\mathbf{x}_i$ and $\mathbf{x}_j$.

We use the $|a_j|, j = 1, ..., n-1$ to split the data matrix $\mathbf{X}_i$ (equivalently the set S_i) into two disjoint sets of local $\mathbf{X}_i^{(l)}$ and non-local $\mathbf{X}_i^{(s)}$ bases.

The scores $|a_j|$ are sorted in a descending order (i.e. decreasing the similarity) and correspondingly the samples in the set S_i are sorted into the set $\hat{S}_i$.

An adaptive threshold can be the result of applying any statistical function on the coefficients as:

$$t(\mathbf{x}_i) = f(|a_1|, \ldots, |a_{n-1}|), \tag{8}$$

where $f(|a_1|, \ldots, |a_{n-1}|)$ is a statistical function that returns a scalar that depends on the set of $|a_j|$. One possible choice for this function can be the average of the obtained coefficients:

$$t(\mathbf{x}_i) = \frac{1}{n-1} \sum_{j=1}^{n-1} |a_j|. \tag{9}$$

Based the estimated threshold $t(\mathbf{x}_i)$, we can generate from the original set $S_i = \{\mathbf{x}_1, \mathbf{x}_2 \ldots, \mathbf{x}_{i-1}, \mathbf{x}_{i+1}, \ldots, \mathbf{x}_n\}$ the local set $S_i^{(l)}$ and the non-local set $S_i^{(s)}$. The local set $S_i^{(l)} = \{\mathbf{x}_j\}$ is determined by selecting the samples who coding coefficient satisfies $|a_j| > t(\mathbf{x}_i)$.

The non-local set is given by $S_i^{(s)} = S_i - S_i^{(l)}$. It should be noticed that the cardinality of both $S_i^{(l)}$ and $S_i^{(s)}$ depends on the current sample $\mathbf{x}_i$. However, in the case of LHC the cardinality of both local and non-local bases is fixed a priori for the whole dataset. Furthermore, the samples in $S_i^{(s)}$ are ordered according to their scores $|a_j|$. Let k_l denote the size of the local bases (i.e., the size of $S_i^{(l)}$), and k_s the size of the non-local bases (the size of $S_i^{(s)}$).

Second step. In this step, we estimate the hybrid code $\mathbf{c}_i$ for every sample $\mathbf{x}_i$ using a modified LHC scheme.

For the sake of clarity, the subscript i is omitted in Eqs. (10) and (12). The hybrid code is obtained by:

$$\min_{\mathbf{c}} \|\mathbf{x} - [\mathbf{X}^{(l)}, \ \mathbf{X}^{(s)}][\mathbf{c}^{(l)T}, \ \mathbf{c}^{(s)T}]^T\|_2^2 + \gamma \|\mathbf{D}\,\mathbf{c}^{(l)}\|_2^2 + \lambda \|\mathbf{c}^{(s)}\|_1 \tag{10}$$

where $\mathbf{D} \in \mathbb{R}^{k_l \times k_l}$ is a diagonal matrix containing the weights D_{jj} associated with each jth component of the local code $\mathbf{c}_i^{(l)}$. In our work, we use the following expression for D_{jj}:

$$D_{jj} = 1/|a_j|, j = 1, ..., k_l \tag{11}$$

The solution to the above minimization can be obtained by Algorithm 1 where the solution for the local part is now given by:

$$\mathbf{c}^{(l)} = (\mathbf{B}^{(l)T}\mathbf{B}^{(l)} + \gamma\,\mathbf{D})^{-1}\mathbf{B}^{(l)T}\mathbf{x}^{(l)} \tag{12}$$

The ALHC is summarized in Fig. 1. We stress the fact that in the proposed method the size of local and non-local basis is sample dependent.

3.1   Kernel Variant of ALHC

The motivation behind using kernel representation relies on the fact that a linear model for data self-representation cannot be the best model. Therefore, by adopting non-linear models for data self-representation, it is expected that the estimated coding coefficients could better quantify the dependency and relation among samples and hence, better graph coefficients can be derived. Let $\Phi : \mathbf{X} \to \Phi(\mathbf{X})$ be a non-linear mapping that projects original data samples onto a space of high dimension. Following the Kernel theory, it is not necessary to know the explicit function Φ since what is really needed is the dot product among the projected samples. In this new space, the data samples are represented by the

---

Adaptive LHC graph

Input: Data matrix $\mathbf{X} = [\mathbf{x}_1, \ldots, \mathbf{x}_n] \in \mathbb{R}^{d \times n}$, parameters σ, γ and λ.
Output: Affinity matrix $\mathbf{W}$ (constructed graph)

For each sample $\mathbf{x}_i$, $i = 1, \ldots, n$:
- Form the coding dictionary $\mathbf{X}_i$ from $S_i = \{\mathbf{x}_1, \mathbf{x}_2 \ldots, \mathbf{x}_{i-1}, \mathbf{x}_{i+1}, \ldots, \mathbf{x}_n\}$
- Compute the diagonal matrix $\mathbf{P}$ such that $P(j, j) = 1 - exp(-\||\mathbf{x}_i - \mathbf{x}_j\||^2)$, $j = 1, \ldots, n - 1$.
- Estimate the coding vector $\mathbf{a}$ using Eq. (7)
- Calculate the adaptive threshold $t(\mathbf{x}_i)$ using Eq. (9)
- Form the set $S_i^{(l)}$ by selecting the samples of S_i whose $|a_j| > t(\mathbf{x}_i)$
- Set the set $S_i^{(s)}$ to $S_i - S_i^{(l)}$
- Form the local bases $\mathbf{X}_i^{(l)}$ and non-local bases $\mathbf{X}_i^{(l)}$ from $S_i^{(l)}$ and $S_i^{(s)}$, respectively
- Form the diagonal $k_l \times k_l$ matrix $\mathbf{D}$ using Eq. (11)
- Estimate the hybrid code vector $\mathbf{c}_i$ using Algorithm 1 (Eq. (10)) in which the identity matrix is replaced by $\mathbf{D}$
- The ith row of $\mathbf{W}$ is given by $\mathbf{W}_{i*} = |\mathbf{c}_i|^T$

Fig. 1. The proposed ALHC graph.

matrix $\Phi = [\phi(\mathbf{x}_1), \phi(\mathbf{x}_2), \ldots, \phi(\mathbf{x}_n)]$. Let $K_{ij} = \phi^T(\mathbf{x}_i)\,\phi(\mathbf{x}_j)$ be the dot product of the projection of two samples $\mathbf{x}_i$ and $\mathbf{x}_j$. This dot product quantifies a similarity measure between samples $\mathbf{x}_i$ and $\mathbf{x}_j$. The kernel matrix $K(.,.)$ can be built using Gaussian, polynomial, or any other function that satisfies Mecer's conditions. It is easy to show that the matrix $\mathbf{K}$ will be given by $\Phi^T \Phi$. By adopting the mapped data, Φ, the kernel variant of the proposed method can be obtained by replacing the data with their non-linear projections. Thus, the code vector associated with each sample will be estimated by minimizing the following:

$$\min_{\mathbf{c}} \|\phi(\mathbf{x}) - [\Phi(\mathbf{X}^{(l)}), \ \Phi(\mathbf{X}^{(s)})][\mathbf{c}^{(l)T}, \ \mathbf{c}^{(s)T}]^T\|_2^2 + \gamma \ \|\mathbf{c}^{(l)}\|_2^2 + \lambda \ \|\mathbf{c}^{(s)}\|_1 \quad (13)$$

4   Performance Evaluation: Graph-Based Label Propagation for Image Classification

The graph-construction method is assessed by the performance of the post-graph construction task. The latter is given by label propagation over the graph. In the experiments, we will use the Gaussian Fields and Harmonic Functions (GFHF) method [21] since it is non-parametric.

We used the following three public face datasets:

1. **Extended Yale - part B[1]:** It contains images of 38 human subjects. Each subject has about 60 images. The images are resized to 32×32 pixels.

---

[1] http://cvc.yale.edu/projects/yalefacesB/yalefacesB.html.

Table 1. Recognition performance (Mean recognition accuracy %) on the Extended Yale, PF01 and FERET datasets over ten different random splits.

Ext. Yale Method \ Lab.	q = 9	q = 14	q = 20
KNN	80.55	82.06	83.25
GoLPP [20]	35.85	48.62	59.65
LNP [13]	93.45	94.23	95.05
$\ell_1 - s$ [3]	82.15	86.59	89.98
$\ell_1 - r$ [19]	93.19	95.01	96.35
$\ell_1 - c$ [2]	80.15	84.44	87.76
LLC [5]	88.57	92.34	95.37
LHC [18]	87.56	89.72	92.45
SRLS [16]	91.44	93.80	95.22
ALHC	**94.79**	**96.06**	**97.15**

PF01 Method \ Lab.	q = 5	q = 8	q = 12
KNN	44.38	49.44	52.17
GoLPP [20]	42.81	61.32	73.91
LNP [13]	64.07	72.61	74.47
$\ell_1 - s$ [3]	53.81	59.33	62.39
$\ell_1 - r$ [19]	72.06	79.53	84.00
$\ell_1 - c$ [2]	53.80	60.65	64.50
LLC [5]	72.87	79.57	83.25
LHC [18]	66.85	75.14	80.39
SRLS [16]	71.55	76.61	78.17
ALHC	**74.07**	**80.92**	**85.53**

FERET Method \ Labeled	q = 2	q = 3	q = 4
KNN	31.33	38.96	49.70
GoLPP [20]	12.05	17.31	25.00
LNP [13]	56.20	70.24	77.95
$\ell_1 - s$ [3]	55.93	66.59	74.78
$\ell_1 - r$ [19]	55.05	69.13	81.27
$\ell_1 - c$ [2]	51.18	61.01	72.50
LLC [5]	57.06	71.09	80.25
LHC [18]	56.81	70.59	82.00
SRLS [16]	57.36	68.62	73.55
ALHC	**61.65**	**74.72**	**83.93**

2. **PF01**[2]: It contains the true-color face images of 103 people, 53 men and 50 women, representing 17 different images (1 normal face, 4 illumination variations, 8 pose variations, 4 expression variations) per person.
3. **FERET**[3]: In our experiments, we use a subset of FERET. This subset consists of 1400 images for 200 different person (7 images per person).

4.1 Method Comparison

For quantitative evaluation of the proposed method, we compare the performance of the classification of the graph obtained from the proposed method with the ones obtained from several state of the art graph construction techniques. We divide the database into two sets of labeled and unlabeled, and then construct the graph using the union of both sets.

---

[2] https://sites.google.com/site/postechimlab2012/databases/face-database-2001.
[3] http://www.itl.nist.gov/iad/humanid/feret.

For every database, we randomly select q samples in each class as labeled samples and leave the rest as unlabeled samples.

The adopted graph construction methods are: KNN graph, LNP graph [13], GoLPP graph [20], standard ℓ_1 Graph (ℓ_1-s), Robust ℓ_1 Graph (ℓ_1-r), constrained ℓ_1 graph (ℓ_1-c) [2], LHC graph, SRLS [16], and our proposed construction method ALHC. In each database, q labeled samples are selected and the label of the rest of the nodes (samples) are estimated using (GFHF) [21] method adopting the constructed graph of every graph construction technique. The process is repeated ten times for ten different combinations of labeled/unlabeled samples and the average classification accuracy is reported. The above process is repeated for three different q values, corresponding to three numbers of labeled samples.

KNN and LNP methods have the neighborhood size parameter k. The standard and robust ℓ_1 graphs have λ (ℓ_1-sparsity). The constrained sparse graph has α and β. The LHC method has γ (local regularization), λ (ℓ_1-sparsity), k_l and k_s. The LLC method has σ. The proposed ALHC method has σ, γ (local regularization), and λ (ℓ_1-sparsity). In our experiments, k is chosen from 5 to 60 with a step of 5 for kNN and LNP graph construction methods. σ is set to one. The ℓ_1-sparsity parameter λ used in ℓ_1-s and ℓ_1-r is fixed to 0.1. For LHC and ALHC, this parameter is chosen from $\{0.01, 0.02, 0.03, 0.04, 0.05, 0.06, 0.1, 0.15, 0.2\}$. The parameter γ is tuned from $\{0.03, 1\}$. k_l is chosen from $\{10, 20, 30, 40, 50, 100\}$ and k_s is chosen from $\{50, 100, 150, 200, 250, 300\}$. We used the regularization parameters of the ℓ_1-c and SRLS graphs as the ones suggested in [2] and [16].

For every graph construction method, several values for the parameter are used. We then report the best recognition accuracy of each method from the best parameter configuration. Table 1 illustrates the average classification rate in % of label propagation using different graph construction methods for Extended Yale, PF01, and FERET datasets.

We can observe that the proposed ALHC method outperformed other graph construction techniques and obtained the highest accuracy in all databases and different number of labeled samples. It demonstrates that the graph constructed by the proposed method is very informative. Moreover, we can see that the performance of the graph obtained by the proposed method is better than that of standard and constrained ℓ_1 graphs and outperforms the three types of sparse graphs.

4.2 Sensitivity to Parameters

In this section, we evaluate the sensitivity of the proposed method with respect to the variation of its parameters, namely σ, γ, and λ. The goal is to study the performance of the proposed method when these parameters vary. The first parameter is a simple regularization parameter in Locality-constrained coding–the phase in which similarities are computed. The last two parameters are two regularization parameters that are used in the hybrid coding scheme where γ penalizes a weighted ℓ_2 norm and λ penalizes the ℓ_1 norm. Figure 2 (left) illustrates the variation of the recognition rates as a function of σ for the PF01

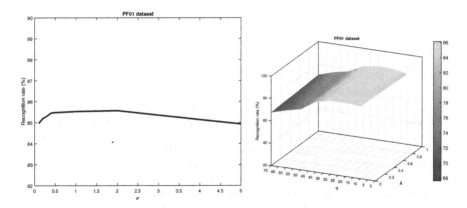

Fig. 2. Performance variation (recognition rate) as a function of the regularization parameter σ (Left) and of the two regularization parameters γ and λ (Right).

dataset. In this experiment, we use 12 labeled samples per class and fixed the other two parameters.

Figure 2 (right) illustrates the variation of the recognition rates as a function of γ and λ for the PF01 dataset. In this experiment, the parameter σ was kept fixed to one since this value seems to be a near optimal value. From the above observations, we can conclude that it is easy to define a near optimal domain for all parameters.

5   Conclusion

In this paper, we have proposed a new graph construction method that is based on data self-representativeness. The main contribution of this paper is the adaptive selection of local and non-local bases for the Local Hybrid Coding. The proposed method simultaneously takes into account the locality and sparsity in the graph construction. Thus, the adaptively constructed graph can be very informative.

Experimental results obtained on image databases, demonstrate that in the task of graph-based label propagation, the graph constructed by the proposed method can give better results compared to many state-of-the art graph construction techniques. Currently, we are quantifying the improvement of results trough the use of the kernel variant.

References

1. Araujo, R., Kamel, M.S.: Audio-visual emotion analysis using semi-supervised temporal clustering with constraint propagation. In: Campilho, A., Kamel, M. (eds.) ICIAR 2014. LNCS, vol. 8815, pp. 3–11. Springer, Cham (2014). https://doi.org/10.1007/978-3-319-11755-3_1

2. Chen, S.B., Ding, C.H., Luo, B.: Similarity learning of manifold data. IEEE Trans. Cybern. **99**, 1–13 (2014)
3. Cheng, B., Yang, J., Yan, S., Fu, Y., Huang, T.S.: Learning with L1-graph for image analysis. IEEE Trans. Image Process. **19**(4), 858–866 (2010)
4. Dornaika, F., Bosaghzadeh, A.: Adaptive graph construction using data self-representativeness for pattern classification. Inf. Sci. **325**, 118–139 (2015)
5. Dornaika, F., Bosaghzadeh, A., Raducanu, B.: Efficient graph construction for label propagation based multi-observation face recognition. In: Salah, A.A., Hung, H., Aran, O., Gunes, H. (eds.) HBU 2013. LNCS, vol. 8212, pp. 124–135. Springer, Cham (2013). https://doi.org/10.1007/978-3-319-02714-2_11
6. Dornaika, F., Weng, L., Jin, Z.: Structured sparse graphs using manifold constraints for visual data analysis. Neurocomputing **315**, 107–114 (2018)
7. Gong, C., Tao, D., Liu, W., Liu, L., Yang, J.: Label propagation via teaching-to-learn and learning-to-teach. IEEE Trans. Neural Netw. Learn. Syst. **28**(6), 1452–1465 (2016)
8. Gong, C., Tao, D., Yang, J., Fu, K.: Signed Laplacian embedding for supervised dimension reduction. In: Proceedings of the Twenty-Eighth AAAI Conference on Artificial Intelligence (2014)
9. Lee, H., Battle, A., Raina, R., Ng, A.: Efficient sparse coding algorithms. In: Advances in Neural Information Processing System (2006)
10. Qiao, L., Chen, S., Tan, X.: Sparsity preserving projections with applications to face recognition. Pattern Recogn. **43**(1), 331–341 (2010)
11. Roweis, S., Saul, L.: Nonlinear dimensionality reduction by locally linear embedding. Science **290**(5500), 2323–2326 (2000)
12. Sprechmann, P., Bronstein, A.M., Sapiro, G.: Learning efficient sparse and low rank models. IEEE Trans. Pattern Anal. Mach. Intell. **37**(9), 1821–1833 (2015)
13. Wang, F., Zhang, C.: Label propagation through linear neighborhoods. IEEE Trans. Knowl. Data Eng. **20**(1), 55–67 (2008)
14. Wang, X., Qian, B., Davidson, I.: On constrained spectral clustering and its applications. Data Min. Knowl. Disc. **28**(1), 1–30 (2014)
15. Waqas, J., Yi, Z., Zhang, L.: Collaborative neighbor representation based classification using l2-minimization approach. Pattern Recogn. Lett. **34**(2), 201–208 (2013)
16. Weng, L., Dornaika, F., Jin, Z.: Graph construction based on data self-representativeness and Laplacian smoothness. Neurocomputing **207**, 476–487 (2016)
17. Wright, J., Yang, A., Ganesh, A., Sastry, S., Ma, Y.: Robust face recognition via sparse representation. IEEE Trans. Pattern Anal. Mach. Intell. **31**(2), 210–227 (2009)
18. Xiang, W., Wang, J., Long, M.: Local hybrid coding for image classification. In: IEEE International Conference on Pattern Recognition (2014)
19. Yan, S., Wang, H.: Semi-supervised learning by sparse representation. In: SIAM International Conference on Data Mining, pp. 792–801. SIAM (2009)
20. Zhang, L., Qiao, L., Chen, S.: Graph-optimized locality preserving projections. Pattern Recogn. **43**, 1993–2002 (2010)
21. Zhu, X., Ghahramani, Z., Lafferty, J., et al.: Semi-supervised learning using Gaussian fields and harmonic functions. ICML **3**, 912–919 (2003)

Active Two Phase Collaborative Representation Classifier for Image Categorization

F. Dornaika[1,2(✉)] 🆔, Y. El Traboulsi[1], and Y. Ruicheck[3]

[1] University of the Basque Country UPV/EHU, San Sebastian, Spain
fadi.dornaika@ehu.es
[2] IKERBASQUE Foundation, Bilbao, Spain
[3] Laboratoire CIAD, University of Bourgogne Franche-Comte,
UTBM, 90010 Belfort, France

Abstract. In recent times, the Sparse Representation Classifier (SRC), the Collaborative Representation Classifier (CRC), and the Two Phase Test Sample Sparse Representation (TPTSSR) classifier were proposed as classification tools that exploit sparse representation. Inspired by active learning techniques, this paper proposes an active Collaborative Representation Classifier that can be exploited by these supervised frameworks. The introduced Active Two Phase Collaborative Representation Classifier (ATPCRC) begins by estimating the label of the available unlabeled samples. At testing stage, based on the TPTSSR framework any test sample will have two representations that are calculated separately by using two different dictionaries. The first dictionary is composed of all samples having original labels. The second dictionary contains the whole dataset samples (original and predicted labels). The two kinds of class-wise reconstruction error are then fused in order to infer the label of the test sample. The proposal is validated on four public image datasets. The results shoe that the introduced ATPCRC can outperform the classic TPTSSR as well as several state-of-the-art approaches that use label and unlabeled data samples.

Keywords: Two Phase Collaborative Representation Classifier ·
Semi-supervised learning · Image classification

1 Introduction

Image categorization was a hot topic in the computer vision and patter recognition community. Researchers brought many progresses to this domain by deploying semi-supervised learning (SSL) paradigms [2,7,8,15].

Unlike unsupervised and supervised learning, SSL exploits both labeled and unlabeled data samples in estimating the models. However, SSL may face some difficulties especially in cases where the labels are very scarce. Therefore, one interesting approach is to increase the size of the labeled data by invoking active

© Springer Nature Switzerland AG 2019
E. Ricci et al. (Eds.): ICIAP 2019, LNCS 11751, pp. 175–184, 2019.
https://doi.org/10.1007/978-3-030-30642-7_16

learning paradigms (e.g., [1,11,18]). One main goal of active learning is to generate more labeled samples by simply predicting the labels of unlabeled samples, and exploit them to build new models and classifiers. The main problems that these paradigms solve are: (i) identifying the most relevant unlabeled samples that the system should predict their label first, (ii) preserving confident predictions. Usually, the proposed solutions rely on the concept of confidence in prediction and classification. For instance, if the confidence of a label prediction is not enough for a specific data sample (i.e., the predicted label has a high uncertainty), then the corresponding sample will not be exploited by the final model. At most, it will be used as an unlabeled sample since its estimated label is uncertain. In addition to the uncertainty and confidence concepts, some methods proposed other criteria. In order to avoid having many labeled samples in the same cluster, Nguyen et al. [21] exploit the diversity concept by deploying a pre-clustering method. In [6], the authors proposed an active cluster based sampling method. However, since this approach employs a hierarchical clustering of unlabeled samples, the final performance can be impacted by the performance of clustering process itself. In [17], the authors introduced an active probabilistic variant of the K-NN classifier that can be used for multi-class problems. In [14], the authors proposed an approach that is based on informativeness and representativeness of unlabeled samples. Besides active learning paradigms, sparse representation has brought significant advances to the pattern recognition field [5]. This is due to its capacity to acquire, represent and compress knowledge of the domain, and thus to reconstruct the data with minimal loss [26]. The Sparse Representation based Classifier (SRC) [27] can be thought as a generalization of the Nearest Neighbor classifier (NN) and the Nearest Feature Subspace (NFS) [16]. Unlike the NN and NFS classifiers, SRC can be more robust in the presence of deviations and occlusions [25]. Despite the fact that SRC has good performance, it has a high computational cost since it is based on the ℓ_1 minimization in the coding process. Therefore, SRC cannot practical for real-world problems requiring a fast decision and classification. Thus, many researchers exploited data locality [9]. For instance, the work of [19] limited the sparse coding dictionary to the nearest neighbors only. Xu et al. [28] proposed a Two Phase Test Sample Sparse Representation (TPTSSR) approach in which the regularization is given by the ℓ_2 norm. This method has two phases. In the first phase, the testing sample is represented as a linear combination of all training samples. The first M samples that provide its best representation are then chosen to be the atoms of a new compact dictionary. In the second phase, the testing sample is coded using the new dictionary of M samples. The label of the test sample is made upon this representation. The Collaborative Representation Classifier (CRC) is the classifier that uses the first phase of the TPTSSR classifier. This paper is organized as follows: Sect. 2 presents our Active Two Phase Collaborative Representation classifier (ATPCRC). The experimental results and methods comparison are presented in Sect. 3. Section 4 concludes the paper. In the paper, capital bold letters denote matrices and bold letters denote vectors.

2   Active Two Phase Collaborative Representation Classifier

Proposed Method. In this section, we propose the Active Two Phase Collaborative Representation Classifier (ATPCRC). While our proposed ATPCRC makes the TPTSSR classifier active, it is also able to make any collaborative representation-based classifier (e.g., CRC and SRC) active. Our proposed ATPCRC aims to construct a classifier that exploits both labeled and unlabeled samples. Let $\mathbf{x}_1, \mathbf{x}_2, \ldots, \mathbf{x}_L$ denote the labeled data samples and $\mathbf{x}_{L+1}, \mathbf{x}_{L+2}, \ldots, \mathbf{x}_N$ denote the unlabeled data samples. The matrix of labeled samples is denoted by $\mathbf{X}_l = [\mathbf{x}_1, \mathbf{x}_2, \ldots, \mathbf{x}_L] \in \mathbb{R}^{D \times L}$ and the matrix of unlabeled samples is denoted by $\mathbf{X}_u = [\mathbf{x}_{L+1}, \mathbf{x}_{L+2}, \ldots, \mathbf{x}_N] \in \mathbb{R}^{D \times U}$ where L and $U = N - L$ are the numbers of labeled and unlabeled samples, respectively. The training data are defined by the matrix $\mathbf{X} = [\mathbf{x}_1, \mathbf{x}_2, \ldots, \mathbf{x}_N] \in \mathbb{R}^{D \times N}$.

Using active learning strategies, we first estimate the labels of all unlabeled samples, $\mathbf{X}_u$. We then use both the original labeled data and the predicted ones, $\mathbf{X}$, to build a new classifier. We recall that the TPTSSR is a lazy classifier in the sense that all of its computation stages run at the testing step. In order to predicting the label of the unlabeled samples any classifier can be invoked. In our work, we employ the TPTSSR classifier in which the original set of labeled samples are used. Once this stage is achieved, every sample in the training data matrix $\mathbf{X}$ has either an original label or a predicted one. In order to classifying a testing sample by the proposed ATPCRC, we proceed as follows. Two coding schemes are carried out independently, each has two phases of coding like in TPTSSR. The first coding scheme uses the labeled data $\mathbf{X}_l$. The second coding scheme uses the whole training data matrix $\mathbf{X}$. To infer the class of any testing sample, a fusion of the class-wise reconstruction error is exploited. Let M_l and M denote the parameters of the two coding processes. We proceed as follows.

First Phase. In the first phase, the testing sample $\mathbf{y} \in \mathbb{R}^D$ will have two representation or codes: the first code vector is computed from a linear combination of the labeled samples $\mathbf{X}_l$ and the second code results from a linear combination of the whole training data $\mathbf{X}$. These two codes of $\mathbf{y}$ are given by:

$$\mathbf{y} = a_1^l \mathbf{x}_1 + a_2^l \mathbf{x}_2 + \ldots + a_L^l \mathbf{x}_L \tag{1}$$

$$\mathbf{y} = a_1 \mathbf{x}_1 + a_2 \mathbf{x}_2 + \ldots + a_L \mathbf{x}_L + \ldots + a_N \mathbf{x}_N \tag{2}$$

Equations (1) and (2) can be rewritten in matrix form as follows:

$$\mathbf{y} = \mathbf{X}_l \, \mathbf{a}^l \quad \text{and} \quad \mathbf{y} = \mathbf{X} \, \mathbf{a}$$

where $\mathbf{a}^l = [a_1^l, a_2^l, \ldots, a_L^l]^T$ and $\mathbf{a} = [a_1, a_2, \ldots, a_N]^T$. The unknown code vectors $\mathbf{a}^l$ and $\mathbf{a}$ are recovered using ℓ_2 regularization. These two vectors are solutions to the following optimization problems, respectively:

$$\mathbf{a}^{l\star} = arg \min_{\mathbf{a}^l} \|\mathbf{y} - \mathbf{X}_l \, \mathbf{a}^l\|^2 + \lambda_l \, \|\mathbf{a}^l\|^2$$

$$\mathbf{a}^{\star} = arg \min_{\mathbf{a}} \|\mathbf{y} - \mathbf{X} \, \mathbf{a}\|^2 + \lambda \, \|\mathbf{a}\|^2$$

where λ_l and λ are two regularization parameters. The solutions for $\mathbf{a}^l$ and $\mathbf{a}$ are provided by:

$$\mathbf{a}^{l\star} = (\mathbf{X}_l^T \, \mathbf{X}_l + \lambda_l \, \mathbf{I}_l)^{-1} \mathbf{X}_l^T \mathbf{y}$$
$$\mathbf{a}^{\star} = (\mathbf{X}^T \, \mathbf{X} + \lambda \, \mathbf{I})^{-1} \mathbf{X}^T \mathbf{y} \tag{3}$$

where $\mathbf{I}$ and $\mathbf{I}_l$ are identity matrices with an appropriate size. From Eqs. (1) and (2), one can see that each data sample, $\mathbf{x}_i$, has its own contribution in the reconstruction of the test sample $\mathbf{y}$. Thus, from Eq. (1) the contribution of $\mathbf{x}_i$ is $a_i^l \mathbf{x}_i$. From (2), the contribution is $a_i \mathbf{x}_i$. Therefore, $\mathbf{x}_i$ has a large contribution in Eq. (1) if $\|\mathbf{y} - a_i^l \, \mathbf{x}_i\|^2$ is small, and it has a large contribution in Eq. (2) if $\|\mathbf{y} - a_i \, \mathbf{x}_i\|^2$ is small. Thus, the M_l samples ($1 \leq M_l \leq L$) that have the largest M_l contributions when approximating $\mathbf{y}$ in Eq. (1) and the M samples ($1 \leq M \leq N$) that have the largest M contributions when approximating $\mathbf{y}$ in Eq. (2) are chosen to be handed over to the second phase of coding. The two subsets of selected samples are denoted by $\{\widetilde{\mathbf{x}}_1^l, \widetilde{\mathbf{x}}_2^l, \ldots, \widetilde{\mathbf{x}}_{M_l}^l\}$, and $\{\widetilde{\mathbf{x}}_1, \widetilde{\mathbf{x}}_2, \ldots, \widetilde{\mathbf{x}}_M\}$. In matrix form, these two dictionaries are given by $\widetilde{\mathbf{X}}_l = [\widetilde{\mathbf{x}}_1^l, \widetilde{\mathbf{x}}_2^l, \ldots, \widetilde{\mathbf{x}}_{M_l}^l]$ and $\widetilde{\mathbf{X}} = [\widetilde{\mathbf{x}}_1, \widetilde{\mathbf{x}}_2, \ldots, \widetilde{\mathbf{x}}_M]$.

Second Phase. In the second phase, the testing sample $\mathbf{y}$ is represented by two code vectors: the first one is a linear combination of the remaining M_l labeled samples and the second one is a linear combination of the remaining M training samples. This can be written as:

$$\mathbf{y} = \widetilde{\mathbf{X}}_l \, \mathbf{b}^l \quad \text{and} \quad \mathbf{y} = \widetilde{\mathbf{X}} \, \mathbf{b}$$

where $\mathbf{b}^l$ and $\mathbf{b}$ denote the second phase vectors. Similarly to (1) and (2), the unknown vectors $\mathbf{b}^l$ and $\mathbf{b}$ are provided by:

$$\mathbf{b}^{l\star} = (\widetilde{\mathbf{X}}_l^T \, \widetilde{\mathbf{X}}_l + \gamma_l \, \mathbf{I}_l)^{-1} \widetilde{\mathbf{X}}_l^T \, \mathbf{y}$$
$$\mathbf{b}^{\star} = (\widetilde{\mathbf{X}}^T \, \widetilde{\mathbf{X}} + \gamma \, \mathbf{I})^{-1} \widetilde{\mathbf{X}}^T \, \mathbf{y} \tag{4}$$

where γ and γ_l are two regularization parameters.

Suppose we have t_l data samples, from the M_l labeled samples, belonging to the cth class: $(\widetilde{\mathbf{x}}_1^l)^c, (\widetilde{\mathbf{x}}_2^l)^c, \ldots, (\widetilde{\mathbf{x}}_{t_l}^l)^c$, and their corresponding coefficients are $(b_1^l)^c, (b_2^l)^c, \ldots, (b_{t_l}^l)^c$. Suppose that, from the M training samples, there are t data samples belonging to the cth class (or predicted to be in this class): $(\widetilde{\mathbf{x}}_1)^c, (\widetilde{\mathbf{x}}_2)^c, \ldots, (\widetilde{\mathbf{x}}_t)^c$ and their corresponding coefficients are $(b_1)^c, (b_2)^c, \ldots, (b_t)^c$. We can define the reconstruction error associated to class c, $Dev(c)$ by:

$$\eta \left\| \mathbf{y} - \sum_{j=1}^{t_l} \widetilde{\mathbf{x}}_j^c \, (b_j^l)^c \right\|^2 + (1 - \eta) \left\| \mathbf{y} - \sum_{j=1}^{t} \widetilde{\mathbf{x}}_j^c \, (b_j)^c \right\|^2 \tag{5}$$

where η is a balance parameter ($0 \leq \eta \leq 1$). The above proposed residual is a way of fusing the collaborative contribution of the selected samples of the cth class, in representing the testing sample $\mathbf{y}$ by both $\mathbf{X}_l$ and $\mathbf{X}$. A large contribution corresponds to small residual. Therefore, the label of $\mathbf{y}$ is estimated by:

$$l(\mathbf{y}) = arg \min_c Dev(c) \qquad 1 \leq c \leq C$$

where C is the number of classes and $l(\mathbf{y})$ is the predicted class label of the testing sample $\mathbf{y}$. This, is the output of the ATPCRC. By using this merging rule, we are able to down-weigh the residual associated with the samples in $\mathbf{X}$ since their labels are not all correct. The introduced class-wise reconstruction errors avoid the use of an ad-hoc sample-based confidence measure. Based on Eq. (5), we can observe that if η is set to 1, we get the classic TPTSSR. If η is set to zero, we get a trivial active variant of TPTSSR. In the sequel, we will show that the proposed ATPCRC can outperform both the classic TPTSSR and the trivial active variant of TPTSSR.

The Algorithm. The introduces ATPCRC has the following inputs: the labeled data matrix $\mathbf{X}_l = [\mathbf{x}_1, \mathbf{x}_2, \ldots, \mathbf{x}_L] \in \mathbb{R}^{D \times L}$, the training data matrix $\mathbf{X} = [\mathbf{x}_1, \mathbf{x}_2, \ldots, \mathbf{x}_N] \in \mathbb{R}^{D \times N}$ (it has both labeled and unlabeled samples), the testing sample $\mathbf{y} \in \mathbb{R}^D$ and the parameters M and M_l.

1. Estimate the labels of the samples $\mathbf{x}_{L+1}, \mathbf{x}_{L+2}, \ldots, \mathbf{x}_N$ using the TPTSSR classifier and the training data $\mathbf{X}_l$. M is the TPTSSR parameter.
2. Calculate the code vectors $\mathbf{a}^\star$ and $\mathbf{a}^{l\star}$ using Eq. (3).
3. Compute the vector $\mathbf{e} = (e_1, e_2, \ldots, e_N)^T$ where $e_i = \|\mathbf{y} - a_i \mathbf{x}_i\|^2$. Sort $\mathbf{e}$ and choose the samples that corresponding to the smallest M elements of $\mathbf{e}$. These selected samples are denoted $\widetilde{\mathbf{x}}_1, \widetilde{\mathbf{x}}_2, \ldots, \widetilde{\mathbf{x}}_M$. Finally, form the matrix $\widetilde{\mathbf{X}} = [\widetilde{\mathbf{x}}_1, \widetilde{\mathbf{x}}_2, \ldots, \widetilde{\mathbf{x}}_M]$.
4. Similarly form the matrix $\widetilde{\mathbf{X}^l} = [\widetilde{\mathbf{x}}_1^l, \widetilde{\mathbf{x}}_2^l, \ldots, \widetilde{\mathbf{x}}_{M_l}^l]$ using $e_i^l = \|\mathbf{y} - a_i^l \mathbf{x}_i\|^2$ instead of $e_i = \|\mathbf{y} - a_i \mathbf{x}_i\|^2$ and M_l instead of M.
5. Compute the code vectors $\mathbf{b}^\star$ and $\mathbf{b}^{l\star}$ using Eq. (4).
6. For every class c $(1 \leq c \leq C)$ calculate the global residual defined in Eq. (5).
7. The label of $\mathbf{y}$ is the class that corresponds to the smallest residual error.

3 Performance Study

In this section, we compare the performance of the proposed ATPCRC with that of twelve methods: Nearest Neighbor classifier (NN), Support Vector Machines (SVM) adopting a polynomial kernel, Sparse Representation based Classifier (SRC) [27], Two Phase Test Sample Representation Classifier (TPTSSR) [28], Semi-supervised Discriminant Embedding (SDE) [13], Semi-supervised Discriminant Analysis (SDA) [4], Transductive Component Analysis (TCA) [20], Sparsity Preserving Discriminant Analysis (SPDA) [23], Laplacian Regularized Least Squares (LapRLS) [3], Flexible Manifold Embedding (FME) [22], Kernel Flexible Manifold Embedding (KFME) [12], and Semi-supervised Exponential Discriminant Embedding (ESDE) [10]. The SVM, NN, SRC, and TPTSSR classifiers are supervised methods while the other competing approaches are exploiting both unlabeled and labeled samples.

Experimental Setup. The experiments are run on four public image datasets. These four datasets belong to several categories: one object database (COIL20), one handwritten digits database (USPS), and two face datasets (Extended Yale and Honda).

COIL20[1]: The Columbia Object Image Library (COIL20) The COIL20 image database has 1440 images. There are 20 objects and each object provides 72 images which are taken at pose intervals of five degrees. In our experiments, we use a subset having 18 images for each object (one image for every $20°$ of rotation).

Extended Yale[2]: There are 1774 images depicting 28 persons. Each person has 59–64 frontal images.

Honda: We use 1138 face images retrieved from the public Honda Video DataBase (HVDB). These images correspond to 22 persons.

USPS Handwritten Digits[3]: This dataset consists of 11000 images of handwritten digits from "0" to "9" (1100 images per digit). We utilize the tenth of this database.

Each dataset is randomly split into labeled, unlabeled and testing samples. In the conducted experiments, we adopt three different partitions of the data. These partitions are illustrated in Table 1. The labeled and unlabeled parts are used in the methods that use bot labeled and unlabeled data. The test part is used to evaluate the performance.

For each partition, the splitting process is repeated ten times. As a preprocessing step, all datasets used PCA in order to reduce the dimensions. We used a PCA that preserves 98% of the variability.

Table 1. Data partitions for the used image datasets.

Partition	Training samples		Testing samples
	Labeled samples	Unlabeled samples	
Partition 1	15%	35%	50%
Partition 2	25%	25%	50%
Partition 3	35%	15%	50%

Method Comparison. Table 2 depicts the recognition performance of the proposed ATPCRC and that of 12 competing methods. In this table, we report the recognition rate average as well as its standard deviation over the ten random splits.

---

[1] http://www.cs.columbia.edu/CAVE/software/softlib/coil-20.php.
[2] http://vision.ucsd.edu/~leekc/ExtYaleDatabase/ExtYaleB.html.
[3] http://www.cs.nyu.edu/~roweis/data.html.

For the FME, KFME, SDE, SDA, SPDA, LapRLS and TCA methods, all parameters are tuned using the set $\{10^{-9}, 10^{-6}, 10^{-3}, 1, 10^{+3}, 10^{+6}, 10^{+9}\}$. For the ATPCRC method, M and M_l parameters are chosen in $\{30, 60, 90, ..., N\}$. The regularization parameters of the proposed ATPCRC method (i.e., λ, λ_l, γ and γ_l) are set to 0.01. η is set to 0.8. This value for η was empirically found to be a good choice for all datasets.

For the projection methods (SDE, SDA, SPDA, TCA, and ESDE), the classification was performed using the nearest neighbor (NN) classifier. The reported results correspond to the best parameters configuration over ten splits. Bold numbers correspond to the best recognition rates. Several observations can be made from Table 2. The main ones are as follows. (1) The performance of the introduced active classifier (ATPCRC) can be batter than that of many other competing methods. (2) The outperformance of the proposed ATPCRC method is significant for the Honda and Extended Yale datasets which have face images with a high variability.

Table 3 compares our proposed ATPCRC with the trivial active TPTSSR. The trivial active TPTSSR is obtained by setting the η parameter of ATPCRC to zero. For the trivial active TPTSSR, the entire set of data samples $\mathbf{X}$ is used: those with ground-truth labels and those with predicted ones. From this table, we can see that the ATPCRC is superior to the trivial active TPTSSR in most of the cases. Thus, the use of weighted class-wise reconstruction residuals (i.e., Eq. (5)) was crucial for reaching a good performance.

Statistical Significance. In the section we conduct a statistical analysis of the results. To this end, we use the well known paired sample t-test [24]. We adopt a confidence level of 95% (i.e., the statistical significance threshold p is set to 0.05). Table 2 shows the outcome of all paired sample t-tests. For a given competing approach, an underlined rate indicates that there is no significant statistical difference between the proposed ATPCRC and this competing approach. Among the 144 paired tests, the proposed ATPCRC was significantly better in 134 configurations representing 93.08% of the tested pairs.

Computational Time. We measure the computational time needed by the TPTSSR, SRC, and the proposed ATPCRC method. We fix the number of labeled images to 50% of the whole data and the remaining images are used as test images. Table 4 depicts the CPU time in seconds associated with classification of the whole test images. The experiments have been run using MATLAB on a 128 GB RAM intel core I7-6900k 8 cores 3.6 GHz CPU computer. As it can be seen, the proposed ATPCRC approach is much faster than the SRC method.

4 Conclusion

In this paper, we introduced an active Two Phase Collaborative Representation Classifier. Indeed, transforming the original TPTSSR (or any collaborative representation classifier) to an active classifier is a challenging task. The proposed fused class-wise reconstruction residual avoided adopting an ad-hoc

Table 2. Average and standard deviation over ten random splits of the correct classification rate (%) using several methods.

Ext. Yale

Method	Partition 1	Partition 2	Partition 3
NN	66.4 ± 5.6	75.2 ± 5.3	79.3 ± 3.2
SVM	75.2 ± 11.1	87.7 ± 5.8	92.2 ± 2.2
SRC [27]	_86.1_ ± 4.5	91.3 ± 3.4	93.5 ± 2.1
TPTSSR [28]	84.5 ± 5.4	91.2 ± 3.4	93.2 ± 2.0
SDE [13]	81.3 ± 6.5	86.5 ± 4.1	88.5 ± 3.2
SDA [4]	79.5 ± 9.9	88.0 ± 5.8	91.4 ± 3.3
TCA [20]	_84.7_ ± 8.4	91.7 ± 3.0	_93.7_ ± 2.1
SPDA [23]	78.3 ± 9.8	87.8 ± 6.0	91.3 ± 3.4
LapRLS [3]	76.1 ± 8.9	80.9 ± 6.0	82.1 ± 5.3
FME [22]	73.2 ± 5.8	77.1 ± 5.6	79.6 ± 4.6
KFME [12]	80.4 ± 8.7	90.3 ± 5.2	_94.0_ ± 3.5
ESDE [10]	78.6 ± 10.1	85.4 ± 7.8	89.2 ± 5.8
ATPCRC	**88.2 ± 3.8**	**93.0 ± 2.7**	**94.4 ± 1.9**

Honda

Method	Partition 1	Partition 2	Partition 3
NN	56.9 ± 2.6	67.5 ± 3.0	73.7 ± 2.4
SVM	31.1 ± 4.4	35.9 ± 3.2	38.4 ± 3.4
SRC [27]	57.6 ± 3.0	69.2 ± 2.3	73.1 ± 2.0
TPTSSR [28]	61.0 ± 2.2	72.5 ± 2.9	_78.6_ ± 2.9
SDE [13]	55.7 ± 2.7	66.3 ± 2.9	72.7 ± 2.5
SDA [4]	56.7 ± 3.1	67.8 ± 3.0	74.7 ± 3.8
TCA [20]	49.7 ± 2.4	61.9 ± 3.4	69.4 ± 2.6
SPDA [23]	50.6 ± 2.4	67.2 ± 2.9	74.6 ± 3.6
LapRLS [3]	42.9 ± 2.8	45.4 ± 2.6	53.4 ± 1.5
FME [22]	51.4 ± 3.4	57.0 ± 2.3	59.6 ± 1.6
KFME [12]	56.9 ± 3.1	66.0 ± 3.0	69.9 ± 2.0
ESDE [10]	57.9 ± 2.9	68.3 ± 3.5	74.4 ± 3.0
ATPCRC	**62.2 ± 2.4**	**73.3 ± 2.7**	**78.9 ± 2.1**

USPS

Method	Partition 1	Partition 2	Partition 3
NN	_78.4_ ± 1.6	83.1 ± 2.3	85.1 ± 1.8
SVM	66.1 ± 5.3	74.9 ± 4.1	81.1 ± 3.5
SRC	74.2 ± 1.9	82.0 ± 1.5	85.1 ± 1.5
TPTSSR	_80.0_ ± 1.7	85.0 ± 1.8	85.9 ± 1.6
SDE	75.1 ± 1.7	82.7 ± 2.4	85.4 ± 1.2
SDA	77.3 ± 1.9	83.4 ± 1.0	85.4 ± 0.8
TCA	66.9 ± 2.2	74.0 ± 1.5	77.8 ± 1.5
SPDA	55.6 ± 2.8	76.9 ± 2.7	83.5 ± 1.5
LapRLS	74.0 ± 1.8	75.3 ± 4.6	76.5 ± 4.3
FME	73.7 ± 1.8	76.5 ± 1.7	77.6 ± 1.6
KFME	80.5 ± 1.7	84.7 ± 1.3	87.4 ± 1.8
ESDE	_78.5_ ± 1.6	83.1 ± 2.3	85.1 ± 1.8
ATPCRC	**81.1 ± 2.0**	**86.2 ± 1.2**	**88.4 ± 1.6**

COIL20

Method	Partition 1	Partition 2	Partition 3
NN	73.5 ± 6.1	81.5 ± 5.4	83.6 ± 3.7
SVM	69.6 ± 6.8	80.8 ± 4.4	84.8 ± 4.5
SRC	73.9 ± 6.0	81.6 ± 4.2	83.4 ± 3.4
TPTSSR	60.2 ± 6.6	_83.7_ ± 4.4	86.7 ± 3.4
SDE	72.2 ± 6.6	80.7 ± 4.7	83.2 ± 3.4
SDA	66.8 ± 6.5	77.1 ± 3.6	80.1 ± 3.2
TCA	68.0 ± 4.4	66.8 ± 4.1	69.6 ± 3.9
SPDA	34.8 ± 3.2	56.2 ± 3.5	67.1 ± 5.3
LapRLS	_76.0_ ± 5.4	81.2 ± 4.2	83.9 ± 3.7
FME	68.9 ± 5.7	74.7 ± 3.9	77.1 ± 3.2
KFME	72.0 ± 5.3	78.7 ± 6.0	80.7 ± 4.6
ESDE	73.6 ± 6.1	81.5 ± 5.4	83.6 ± 3.7
ATPCRC	**76.8 ± 6.2**	**84.8 ± 4.1**	**87.3 ± 3.7**

Table 3. Average recognition rate and standard deviation in % of a simple active TPTSSR and the proposed ATPCRC classifier.

Ext. Yale

Method	Partition 1	Partition 2	Partition 3
TPTSSR (active)	84.1 ± 5.4	87.7 ± 2.6	89.4 ± 2.1
ATPCRC	**88.2 ± 3.8**	**93.0 ± 2.7**	**94.4 ± 1.9**

Honda

Method	Partition 1	Partition 2	Partition 3
TPTSSR (active)	61.2 ± 3.3	72.5 ± 2.4	78.4 ± 2.1
ATPCRC	**62.2 ± 2.4**	**73.3 ± 2.7**	**78.9 ± 2.1**

USPS

Method	Partition 1	Partition 2	Partition 3
TPTSSR (active)	**81.7 ± 2.5**	85.7 ± 1.8	88.1 ± 1.7
ATPCRC	81.1 ± 2.0	**86.2 ± 1.2**	**88.4 ± 1.6**

COIL20

Method	Partition 1	Partition 2	Partition 3
TPTSSR (active)	74.9 ± 5.3	82.2 ± 2.4	84.8 ± 2.2
ATPCRC	**76.8 ± 6.2**	**84.8 ± 4.1**	**87.3 ± 3.7**

Table 4. CPU time (in seconds) of the SRC, TPTSSR and ATPCRC classifiers when 50% of the dataset are labeled images and the remaining 50% are test images.

	ATPCRC	TPTSSR	SRC
Ext. Yale	19.59	9.22	60.33
USPS	5.09	2.55	28.11
Honda	5.68	2.75	29.96
COIL20	0.45	0.20	5.13

sample-based confidence measure. Experiments conducted on four public images datasets show the outperformance of the proposed method over 12 classification methods. These experiments demonstrate that active learning can lead to a performance which is significantly better than that provided by the passive classifiers TPTSSR and SRC.

References

1. Al Rahhal, M.M., Bazi, Y., AlHichri, H., Alajlan, N., Melgani, F., Yager, R.R.: Deep learning approach for active classification of electrocardiogram signals. Inf. Sci. **345**, 340–354 (2016)
2. Ashfaq, R.A.R., Wang, X.Z., Huang, J.Z., Abbas, H., He, Y.L.: Fuzziness based semi-supervised learning approach for intrusion detection system. Inf. Sci. **378**, 484–497 (2017)
3. Belkin, M., Niyogi, P., Sindhwani, V.: Manifold regularization: a geometric framework for learning from labeled and unlabeled examples. J. Mach. Learn. Res. **7**, 2399–2434 (2006)
4. Cai, D., He, X., Han, J.: Semi-supervised discriminant analysis. In: IEEE International Conference on Computer Vision, pp. 1–7 (2007)
5. Chang, X., Ma, Z., Lin, M., Yang, Y., Hauptmann, A.: Feature interaction augmented sparse learning for fast kinect motion detection. IEEE Trans. Image Process. **26**, 3911–3920 (2017)
6. Dasgupta, S., Hsu, D.: Hierarchical sampling for active learning. In: Proceedings of the 25th International Conference on Machine Learning, pp. 208–215. ACM (2008)
7. Dornaika, F., El Traboulsi, Y.: Learning flexible graph-based semi-supervised embedding. IEEE Trans. Cybern. **46**(1), 206–218 (2016)
8. Dornaika, F., El Traboulsi, Y.: Matrix exponential based semi-supervised discriminant embedding for image classification. Pattern Recogn. **61**, 92–103 (2017)
9. Dornaika, F., El Traboulsi, Y., Assoum, A.: Adaptive two phase sparse representation classifier for face recognition. In: Blanc-Talon, J., Kasinski, A., Philips, W., Popescu, D., Scheunders, P. (eds.) ACIVS 2013. LNCS, vol. 8192, pp. 182–191. Springer, Cham (2013). https://doi.org/10.1007/978-3-319-02895-8_17
10. Dornaika, F., Traboulsi, Y.E.: Matrix exponential based semi-supervised discriminant embedding. Pattern Recogn. **61**, 92–103 (2017)
11. Drugman, T., Pylkkönen, J., Kneser, R.: Active and semi-supervised learning in ASR: benefits on the acoustic and language models. In: INTERSPEECH, pp. 2318–2322 (2016)
12. El Traboulsi, Y., Dornaika, F., Assoum, A.: Kernel flexible manifold embedding for pattern classification. Neurocomputing **167**, 517–527 (2015)

13. Huang, H., Liu, J., Pan, Y.: Semi-supervised marginal fisher analysis for hyperspectral image classification. ISPRS Ann. Photogramm. Remote Sens. Spat. Inf. Sci. **3**, 377–382 (2012)
14. Huang, S.J., Jin, R., Zhou, Z.H.: Active learning by querying informative and representative examples. In: Advances in Neural Information Processing Systems, pp. 892–900 (2010)
15. Iwayemi, A., Zhou, C.: SARAA: semi-supervised learning for automated residential appliance annotation. IEEE Trans. Smart Grid **8**(2), 779–786 (2017)
16. Jafarpour, S., Xu, W., Hassibi, B., Calderbank, R.: Efficient and robust compressed sensing using optimized expander graphs. IEEE Trans. Inf. Theory **55**(9), 4299–4308 (2009)
17. Jain, P., Kapoor, A.: Active learning for large multi-class problems. In: IEEE Conference on Computer Vision and Pattern Recognition, CVPR 2009, pp. 762–769. IEEE (2009)
18. Joshi, A.J., Porikli, F., Papanikolopoulos, N.: Multi-class active learning for image classification. In: IEEE Conference on Computer Vision and Pattern Recognition, CVPR 2009, pp. 2372–2379. IEEE (2009)
19. Li, C.G., Guo, J., Zhang, H.G.: Local sparse representation based classification. In: 2010 20th International Conference on Pattern Recognition (ICPR 2010), pp. 649–652. IEEE (2010)
20. Liu, W., Tao, D., Liu, J.: Transductive component analysis. In: Eighth IEEE International Conference on Data Mining, ICDM 2008, pp. 433–442. IEEE (2008)
21. Nguyen, H.T., Smeulders, A.: Active learning using pre-clustering. In: Proceedings of the Twenty-First International Conference on Machine Learning, p. 79. ACM (2004)
22. Nie, F., Xu, D., Tsang, I.W.H., Zhang, C.: Flexible manifold embedding: a framework for semi-supervised and unsupervised dimension reduction. IEEE Trans. Image Process. **19**(7), 1921–1932 (2010)
23. Qiao, L., Chen, S., Tan, X.: Sparsity preserving discriminant analysis for single training image face recognition. Pattern Recogn. Lett. **31**(5), 422–429 (2010)
24. http://www.statisticssolutions.com/manova-analysis-paired-sample-ttest/
25. Wang, J., Lu, C., Wang, M., Li, P., Yan, S., Hu, X.: Robust face recognition via adaptive sparse representation. IEEE Trans. Cybern. **44**(12), 2368–2378 (2014)
26. Wright, J., Ma, Y., Mairal, J., Sapiro, G., Huang, T.S., Yan, S.: Sparse representation for computer vision and pattern recognition. Proc. IEEE **98**(6), 1031–1044 (2010)
27. Wright, J., Yang, A.Y., Ganesh, A., Sastry, S.S., Ma, Y.: Robust face recognition via sparse representation. IEEE Trans. Pattern Anal. Mach. Intell. **31**(2), 210–227 (2009)
28. Xu, Y., Zhang, D., Yang, J., Yang, J.Y.: A two-phase test sample sparse representation method for use with face recognition. IEEE Trans. Circ. Syst. Video Technol. **21**(9), 1255–1262 (2011)

Gesture Recognition by Leap Motion Controller and LSTM Networks for CAD-oriented Interfaces

Lisa Mazzini$^{(\boxtimes)}$ (iD), Annalisa Franco (iD), and Davide Maltoni (iD)

Department of Computer Science and Engineering, University of Bologna,
Via dell'Universitá 50, 47521 Cesena, Italy
{lisa.mazzini,annalisa.franco,davide.maltoni}@unibo.it

Abstract. This paper presents a gesture recognition approach for CAD interfaces where the Leap Motion Controller is used for its high precision in modelling user hands. A simple, compact and effective hand representation is proposed to encode trajectory and pose across time. Recognition is based on Recurrent Neural Networks, particularly suited for processing data sequences. An effective data augmentation technique is also described to increase the size of the training set. Experiments conducted on a novel dataset of gesture performed by 30 volunteers show the effectiveness of the proposed technique; the dataset will be made available to the community for future studies.

Keywords: Gesture recognition · Leap Motion Controller ·
LSTM networks · Computer-Aided Design

1 Introduction

Gestures are one of the most common and natural ways people use to communicate; humans move arms, hands, fingers or even the whole body to transmit information or interact with the environment. In recent years, the development of Human-Computer Interaction systems received great attention from the research community with the aim of developing natural and unobtrusive interfaces, and making users able to interact with the system without any hand-held device. Gesture recognition systems can be profitably used in a variety of applications [4]; among others, sign language translation, daily assistance to elders or disabled people, security application and gaming are probably the most relevant.

This work focuses on the development of a gesture recognition system for CAD interfaces. Although the realisation of a complete 3D model requires fine user movements quite difficult to realise outside the sophisticated traditional CAD interfaces, more intuitive and natural interactions can be useful for initial prototyping or successive interaction with existing models. The widespread diffusion of low-cost RGB-D sensors (e.g. Kinect) and their ability to track users' movements greatly fostered research in this field. The approach proposed in this

© Springer Nature Switzerland AG 2019
E. Ricci et al. (Eds.): ICIAP 2019, LNCS 11751, pp. 185–195, 2019.
https://doi.org/10.1007/978-3-030-30642-7_17

paper is based on the use of the Leap Motion Controller (LMC) [13,17], which provides interesting functionalities for detecting and tracking user's hands; being it designed to work at short distance, hands information is provided with a noticeably higher level of precision with respect to previous devices operating at larger distances and tracking the whole human body.

The proposed gesture recognition approach is based on a novel, compact but effective hand representation coupled with Long-Short Term Memory networks (LSTM), which represent a natural choice for their ability of managing sequences of inputs over time. When dealing with networks, the level of accuracy reachable is often influenced by the availability of training data; while, for its nature, gesture recognition is in general considered a small-scale problem, the set of data for network training can be incremented by artificially generated data. One further contribution of this paper is the definition of data augmentation techniques able to produce additional data for training while keeping unaltered the semantic of gestures. Finally, a new dataset of gestures will be made available to the research community to allow for future comparisons.

The paper is organised as follow: Sect. 2 presents the state of the art, with particular reference to gesture recognition for CAD applications, Sect. 3 describes the proposed approach, the experiments are described in Sect. 4 and Sect. 5 draws some conclusions.

2   Related Works

The recent literature on human gesture recognition is huge and a comprehensive review goes beyond the scope of this work; interested readers can refer to [3,4,15] for recent surveys on 3D hand gesture recognition. Several solutions for natural CAD interfaces have been proposed in the literature. Many works propose contact-based solutions where the user interacts with the system by means of ad-hoc input devices. In [10] different techniques for sketch-based modeling are described, where the users interact with CAD applications by means of sketches; in [19] a Virtual Reality based system is described, where an electronic data glove is suggested as input device. Several vision-based techniques have also been proposed as an alternative to contact-based solutions, with the aim of providing to the user a more natural interface. No direct interactions with input devices are requested in this case; gesture interpretation is based on data streams acquired by cameras of different nature (e.g. RGB or depth). One of the most interesting sensors in this context is Microsoft Kinect [12,18], a low-cost device able to capture in parallel RGB and Depth data streams; its success is largely related to the skeleton representation provided by the SDK which allows to easily track subjects and analyze their behaviour. The use of Kinect for gesture recognition in CAD applications is proposed in some works [7,8,16]; however it is worth noting that the fine hand gestures needed to precisely interact with the system are difficult to capture with Kinect due to its simplified skeleton model where hands are simply identified by a single joint (in the palm) and no information about fingers is provided. Leap Motion Controller works at smaller distances with respect to Kinect and offers a much more detailed hand representation, where each finger is represented by several joints. In [2] LMC multiple applications in Human-Computer Interaction are described, ranging from the medical field to human-robot interaction, from games and gamification to sign language recognition. A CAD interface based on LMC is described in [14] where a proof of concept system able to recognize a set of gestures is described; the details of the recognition approach are not given and the dataset used for testing is not available, thus making impossible a comparison with our proposal. A relevant work for our study is [1] where the use of LMC coupled with recurrent neural networks is discussed for sign language and semaphoric gesture recognition. The authors adopt a complex hand model and a deep network to deal with gestures of different nature with interesting results; we will show in our experiments that, for the specific CAD context, also a simplified representation and a relatively small network allow to reach fully satisfactory results.

3   Proposed Approach

This paper proposes a novel approach for gesture recognition based on the use of Leap Motion Controller. The Leap Motion Controller is a device designed to detect and track user hands, usually placed on the user physical desktop in front of the computer, or mounted on a headset for virtual reality. The device has two monochromatic IR cameras and three infrared LEDs. The IR light emitted from the LEDs is reflected by the user hands and then read by the cameras. Thanks to these tools, the device is able to perceive user hands inside a hemispherical area until a distance of 1 m, with a precision of 0,7 mm and a frame rate up to 200 fps. The information acquired by the sensor is then used to create an internal representation of the two hands, easily accessible thanks to the provided SDK.

3.1   Hand Representation

The hand skeleton information extracted by the LMC consists of a set of attributes, providing geometric data about the user palm, fingers and arm, but also high-level information like acquisition confidence and grabbing or pinching strength. Among the different data provided, the geometric ones are more relevant to our model. Our objective is to define a representation capturing the gesture evolution represented by hand pose, without including any information related to hand shape which is user-specific and not meaningful for gesture recognition. For this reason we neglect most of the data related to the hand position in space (except palm position, used as a reference to evaluate hand translation in time), and we mainly rely on the directions characterizing hand and fingerprints. In particular we exploited for our representation (see Fig. 1a):

- *arm*: described by its direction $\mathbf{d_a}$;
- *palm*: described by its 3D position $\mathbf{p}$ and its direction $\mathbf{d_p}$;

– *fingers*: each finger is a complex object, consisting of a list of bones representing the single phalanges. We consider the direction of each bone $\mathbf{d_{b_{f,p}}}$, with f being the finger index ($f = 1, .., 5$) and p the phalanx index ($p = 1, .., 3$).

Starting from the hand information provided by LMC, we defined a set of numerical features able to encode the hand pose as well as its movement in space across time. The use of angle values, instead of joint positions, allows to achieve a good level of invariance with respect to users' specific hand characteristics. In this work only gestures involving a single hand are considered, but the proposed model can be easily extended to a more general case where the user exploits both hands.

Using the above described raw data, different types of features are extracted for each frame i:

– the translation $\mathbf{\Delta p}(i)$ of the palm position with respect to frame $i - 1$:

$$\mathbf{\Delta p}(i) = \mathbf{p}(i) - \mathbf{p}(i - 1)$$

– the angle $\omega(i)$ between the palm direction and the arm direction, computed as:

$$\omega(i) = arccos(\frac{\mathbf{d_p}(i) \cdot \mathbf{d_a}(i)}{|\mathbf{d_p}(i)| \cdot |\mathbf{d_a}(i)|})$$

– a set of angles $\alpha_{f,p}(i)$, with $f = 1, .., 5$ and $p = 1, .., 3$, representing for each finger the angle between the palm direction and each finger phalanx:

$$\alpha_{f,p}(i) = arccos(\frac{\mathbf{d_p}(i) \cdot \mathbf{d_{b_{f,p}}}(i)}{|\mathbf{d_p}(i)| \cdot |\mathbf{d_{b_{f,p}}}(i)|})$$

Please note that for the thumb finger, only the $\alpha_{f,p}$ angles referred to two phalanges can be computed (i.e. for $f = 1$, $p = 1, 2$).

The angles $\alpha_{f,p}$ are computed to capture the finger extension or closure; ω angle can detect the wrist movement during the gesture. Each angle is measured in the plane formed by the two directions involved. In order to keep track of the hand spatial movement, we decided to consider only the variation of the palm center coordinates; by considering only point variation and not its absolute coordinates, the resulting features are invariant from the initial hand position. Each frame of the video sequence is therefore represented by a 18-dimensional vector obtained by the ordered concatenation of the above described values (3 values for translation on the three axis, 1 ω angle, and 14 $\alpha_{f,p}$ values). The sequence length is fixed to 60 frames per gesture.

3.2   Network Structure

Our approach exploits Recurrent Neural Network to recognize gestures; in particular we evaluated two variants: Long Short-Term Memory [9] and Gated Recurrent Unit [5]. All RNNs have internal state vectors than can store past events

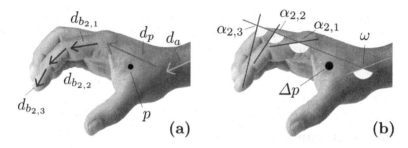

Fig. 1. Hand model: the palm direction (red) intersects the different phalanges directions (blue) and the arm direction (green), forming the angles used to model the hand pose (for instance, the features are represented for each phalanx $i = 1, .., 3$ for $f = 2$). The palm position (black dot) is used to keep track of the hand movement. (Color figure online)

and process current data based on the past, but in particular LSTM and GRU are able to handle longer-term dependencies characterising longer sequences of data. The results obtained using LSTM or GRU are often comparable in terms of accuracy [6]. We chose a *many-to-one* network model; in fact the network processes all the sequence elements before returning the predicted class. We chose a fixed length of 60 frames the sake of simplicity, because it has proved to be a sufficient time span for every gesture (about 2–3 s per gesture). The model can be easily adapted to different frame lengths or even variable lengths among samples. For our problem, we sized the network as shown in Fig. 2: the input layer has 18 neurons, corresponding to the size of feature vectors; it is then connected to two hidden layers, each one composed by 200 LSTM neurons. The final layer

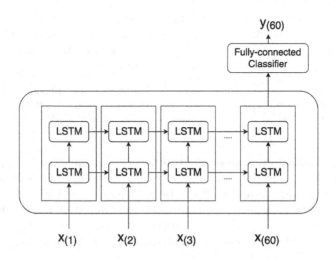

Fig. 2. Network structure unrolled through time.

is a fully-connected layer, which takes as input the last output of the second hidden layer; this layer works as a classifier and it will return the probability of each class for the current gesture. As optimizing algorithm to minimize the loss function during the training phase, we chose Adam Optimizer because it provides in several contexts better performance than other optimizers [11]. The learning rate is fixed to 0.0005.

3.3   Data Augmentation

In order to increase the data available for network training, a data augmentation technique is proposed; in particular, some transformations to the original data are applied to produce new gestures which reproduce the main gesture characteristics without introducing "unnatural" movements or hand poses.

Please note that the same random transformations are applied to the whole gesture since applying independent variations to the single frames would produce a noisy, non-smooth pattern.

Trajectory Rotation and Scaling. The first transformation applies to hand trajectory, described by the palm position $\mathbf{p}_i$ across time. An affine transform is applied to produce trajectory rotation and scaling; trajectory translation would be totally ineffective, since the trajectory is finally encoded in terms of pose variations ($\mathbf{\Delta p}_i$ features) to achieve independence from the absolute coordinates. The affine transform given in Eq. (1) produces:

- a trajectory rotation of θ_x, θ_y and θ_z degrees on the X, Y and Z axis, respectively;
- a trajectory scaling of s_x, s_y, s_z on the three axis.

The transformation parameters are randomly generated within the ranges given in Table 1. The rotation on the X axis is quite small, because higher values would affect excessively the gesture nature; larger variations on the Y and Z axes can be applied. Moreover a uniform scaling is applied.

$$\begin{bmatrix} p'_x \\ p'_y \\ p'_z \end{bmatrix} = \begin{bmatrix} 1 & 0 & 0 \\ 0 & cos(\theta_x) & -sin(\theta_x) \\ 0 & sin(\theta_x) & cos(\theta_x) \end{bmatrix} \begin{bmatrix} cos(\theta_y) & 0 & sin(\theta_y) \\ 0 & 1 & 0 \\ -sin(\theta_y) & 0 & cos(\theta_y) \end{bmatrix} \begin{bmatrix} cos(\theta_z) & -sin(\theta_z) & 0 \\ sin(\theta_z) & cos(\theta_z) & 0 \\ 0 & 0 & 1 \end{bmatrix} \begin{bmatrix} s_x & 0 & 0 \\ 0 & s_y & 0 \\ 0 & 0 & s_z \end{bmatrix} \begin{bmatrix} p_x \\ p_y \\ p_z \end{bmatrix} \quad (1)$$

Hand Pose Variation. The second transformation applies to hand pose, represented by the $\alpha_{f,p}$ angles. Each angle is slightly modified to generate a new pose that is still natural and realistic. In particular, to emulate effectively the natural movement of fingers, the amplitude of the variation applied is directly proportional to the phalanx distance from the palm (see v_1, v_2 and v_3 in Table 1). In fact, the farther the phalanx is from the palm, the wider is the angle resultant from the variation applied.

For this reason, the transformation factor chosen for the fingers is slightly modified from phalanx to phalanx. Let $\alpha'_{f,p}$ be the generated angle from the original $\alpha_{f,p}$, it can be computed as:

$$\alpha'_{f,p} = v_p \cdot \alpha_{f,p}$$

Variations can be applied in both directions evenly (extending all the fingers or making them more closed).

Table 1. Transformations applied in data augmentation for trajectory rotation and scaling and for hand pose modification.

Variation	Range	Variation	Range
θ_x	$\pm(5° - 10°)$	v_1	$[0.95, 0.99] \cup [1.01, 1.05]$
θ_y, θ_z	$\pm(10° - 15°)$	v_2	$[0.945, 0.989] \cup [1.011, 1.055]$
s_x, s_y, s_z	$[0.85, 0.9] \cup [1.1, 1.15]$	v_3	$[0.94, 0.988] \cup [1.012, 1.06]$

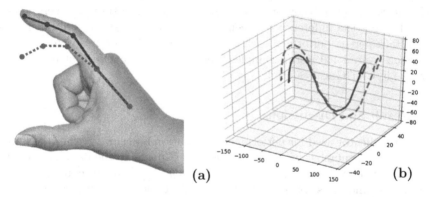

(a)   (b)

Fig. 3. Examples of data augmentation: (a) hand pose variation (example on a single finger) and (b) gesture trajectory scaling. Solid blue lines represent the original data, orange dotted lines the derived one. (Color figure online)

4   Experiments

4.1   Dataset

To the best of our knowledge no public benchmarks including raw data acquired by LMC are available. The authors of [1] share their dataset but only in terms of extracted features; the raw data needed to derive our representation are not available thus making impossible the evaluation. We decided therefore to collect a new dataset including gestures that can be applied in a hypothetical CAD software. In particular, starting from the interface described in [14], we defined 8 gesture:

- *Translation*: using only index finger, the user draws a straight trajectory.
- *Rotation*: extending both index and middle finger, the user rotates the hand of 180°, facing the palm upwards.
- *Extrusion*: extending thumb, index and middle finger, the user draws a straight or undulating trajectory.
- *Left swipe*: using only index finger, the user moves the hand quickly from right to left.
- *Right swipe*: using only index finger, the user moves the hand quickly from left to right.
- *Close*: using only index finger, the user moves down the hand quickly.
- *Scale enlargement*: starting with thumb, index and middle finger tips close together, the user moves them apart.
- *Scale reduction*: starting with thumb, index and middle finger far apart, the user moves them close together.

Each of the 30 volunteers used his/her dominant hand to perform the gesture, so there are also left-handed samples; a small training about the gestures is provided by letting them to watch a short video (available at https://youtu.be/ZWPTjusyaoo). Then, they proceeded to perform the gestures, at their chosen speed (keeping the difference between standard speed gestures and quick gestures). Each person performed each gesture twice, so 16 gestures were obtained per person, overall 480 gesture samples. The dataset is available at http://biolab.csr.unibo.it/CADGestures.html.

4.2   Result and Discussion

The main indicator used for performance evaluation is accuracy, which is simply computed as the number of correct predictions C made by the network over the total number of examined instances N: $accuracy = \frac{C}{N}$. Furthermore, to extract more precise and class-specific information about the recognition accuracy, we also analyzed the confusion matrix where the rows refer to the real gesture class and the columns to the predicted one. All tests have been performed on a PC with Linux OS, on a GeForce GTX1070 GPU with 8 GB of dedicated memory and 16 GB RAM. We implemented the LSTM and GRU networks using Tensorflow, while Scikit-learn was used test SVM.

The dataset is partitioned in training set and test set in proportion 80–20, so we have 384 gestures for network training, and 96 for testing purpose. This basic training set is referred to as TS_{Base}. Moreover, to evaluate the effectiveness of data augmentation, we derived two additional training set, TS_{A1} and TS_{A2}, obtained generating respectively 1 or 2 gestures for each original gesture in TS_{Base}; the resulting cardinality is then $|TS_{A1}| = 768$ and $|TS_{A2}| = 1152$.

We tested two versions of the proposed network, i.e. built with LSTM and GRU cells; moreover, as a term of comparison, we also evaluated the proposed hand model coupled with a SVM classifier. Since SVMs are not able to process data sequences, we concatenated in a single vector all the sequence feature vectors (overall 1080 features).

The results obtained with the base and augmented training sets are summerized in Table 2 and Fig. 3. Both LSTM and GRU reach 100% accuracy on the training set, but the first one better generalizes its knowledge on the test set, thus producing overall better results. SVMs are not designed to evaluate the sequential nature of the input, which is significant in this particular problem and this may be the reason of their lower accuracy.

In general, even if a good testing accuracy is reached with TS_{Base}, the results clearly show that data augmentation is important and significantly impacts performance for all the tested classifiers (+6% accuracy for LSTM). We can then deduce that the proposed data augmentation allows to produce new instances maintaining the nature and the spontaneity of the gesture performed.

Table 2. Results obtained using different algorithms and training sets.

Algorithm	Training set	Acc. on test set
LSTM network	TS_{Base}	87,3%
	TS_{A1}	91,6%
	TS_{A2}	93,7%
GRU network	TS_{Base}	84,3%
	TS_{A1}	87,5%
	TS_{A2}	88,5%
SVM	TS_{Base}	70,8%
	TS_{A1}	75,0%
	TS_{A2}	71,8%

An analysis of the confusion matrices in Fig. 3 shows that the most difficult gesture to recognize is Extrusion, probably due to its similarity with the Rotation gesture pose (the only difference is the extension of the thumb), even if Extrusion requires a well defined trajectory in the space, whilst Rotation is almost static. This is comprehensible if we consider that in the proposed model, only one feature value is related to trajectory and the pose information has a much higher influence on the final decision.

Even though a direct comparison with [1] is not possible since different gesture datasets are used, we can observe that our compact representation, coupled with proper data augmentation techniques, allows to reach an overall accuracy of 93,7%, comparable to that of more complex systems, like the one proposed in [1] where the reached accuracy is 96,4% (Fig. 4).

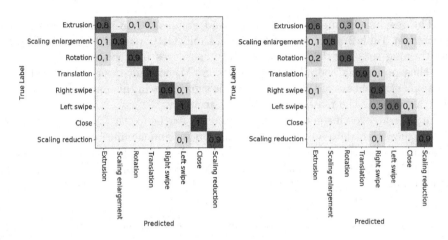

Fig. 4. Confusion matrix of the LSTM network (on the left) and the GRU network (on the right).

5   Conclusions

In this paper a new approach to gesture recognition has been proposed, based on LSTM recurrent networks and Leap Motion Controller. The results obtained are overall quite satisfactory; the fine representation of user hands allows to discriminate precise gestures with a good accuracy. Moreover, the data augmentation technique proposed to increase the set of data for network training allowed to achieve a further performance improvement. An analysis of the main causes of errors suggests some possible future works; in particular, the extracted features are mainly related to hand pose, while hand trajectory contributes to a little extent to the whole representation. Improving this aspect would allow to better discriminate gestures characterized by a similar hand posture by different trajectories across space.

References

1. Avola, D., Bernardi, M., Cinque, L., Foresti, G.L., Massaroni, C.: Exploiting recurrent neural networks and leap motion controller for the recognition of sign language and semaphoric hand gestures. IEEE Trans. Multimedia **21**(1), 234–245 (2019). https://doi.org/10.1109/TMM.2018.2856094
2. Bachmann, D., Weichert, F., Rinkenauer, G.: Review of three-dimensional human-computer interaction with focus on the leap motion controller. **18**(7), 2194 (2018). https://doi.org/10.3390/s18072194
3. Chaudhary, A., Raheja, J.L., Das, K., Raheja, S.: A survey on hand gesture recognition in context of soft computing. In: Meghanathan, N., Kaushik, B.K., Nagamalai, D. (eds.) CCSIT 2011. CCIS, vol. 133, pp. 46–55. Springer, Heidelberg (2011). https://doi.org/10.1007/978-3-642-17881-8_5

4. Cheng, H., Yang, L., Liu, Z.: Survey on 3D hand gesture recognition. IEEE Trans. Circuits Syst. Video Technol. **26**(9), 1659–1673 (2016). https://doi.org/10.1109/TCSVT.2015.2469551

5. Cho, K., et al.: Learning phrase representations using RNN encoder-decoder for statistical machine translation. arXiv preprint arXiv:1406.1078 (2014)

6. Chung, J., Gulcehre, C., Cho, K., Bengio, Y.: Empirical evaluation of gated recurrent neural networks on sequence modeling. arXiv preprint arXiv:1412.3555 (2014)

7. Cohen, M.W., Frid, A., Malin, M., Ladijenski, V.: Generating 3D cad art from human gestures using kinect depth sensor. Comput.-Aided Des. Appl. **12**(5), 608–616 (2015). https://doi.org/10.1080/16864360.2015.1014740

8. Dave, D., Chowriappa, A., Kesavadas, T.: Gesture interface for 3D cad modeling using kinect. Comput.-Aided Des. Appl. **10**(4), 663–669 (2013). https://doi.org/10.3722/cadaps.2013.663-669. https://www.tandfonline.com/doi/abs/10.3722/cadaps.2013.663-669

9. Hochreiter, S., Schmidhuber, J.: Long short-term memory. Neural Comput. **9**(8), 1735–1780 (1997)

10. Kazmi, I.K., You, L., Zhang, J.J.: A survey of sketch based modeling systems. In: 2014 11th International Conference on Computer Graphics, Imaging and Visualization, pp. 27–36, August 2014. https://doi.org/10.1109/CGiV.2014.27

11. Kingma, D.P., Ba, J.: Adam: a method for stochastic optimization. arXiv preprint arXiv:1412.6980 (2014)

12. Microsoft: Kinect for windows. https://developer.microsoft.com/en-us/windows/kinect

13. Leap Motion: Leap motion controller. https://developer.leapmotion.com/get-started/

14. Pareek, S., Sharma, V.: Development of cad interface using leap motion (2014)

15. Shabnam, S.: Real time hand gesture recognition system: a review (2015)

16. Shiratuddin, M.F., Wong, K.W.: Non-contact multi-hand gestures interaction techniques for architectural design in a virtual environment. In: ICIMU 2011: Proceedings of the 5th International Conference on Information Technology Multimedia, pp. 1–6, November 2011. https://doi.org/10.1109/ICIMU.2011.6122761

17. Weichert, F., Bachmann, D., Rudak, B., Fisseler, D.: Analysis of the accuracy and robustness of the leap motion controller. Sensors **13**(5), 6380–6393 (2013)

18. Zhang, Z.: Microsoft kinect sensor and its effect. IEEE Multimedia **19**(2), 4–10 (2012)

19. Zheng, J.M., Chan, K.W., Gibson, I.: A VR-based CAD system. In: Mo, J.P.T., Nemes, L. (eds.) Global Engineering, Manufacturing and Enterprise Networks. ITIFIP, vol. 63, pp. 264–274. Springer, Boston, MA (2001). https://doi.org/10.1007/978-0-387-35412-5_31

A Decision Tree for Automatic Diagnosis of Parkinson's Disease from Offline Drawing Samples: Experiments and Findings

Antonio Parziale[(✉)] [iD], Antonio Della Cioppa[iD], Rosa Senatore[iD],
and Angelo Marcelli[iD]

Natural Computation Lab, DIEM, University of Salerno, Fisciano (SA), Italy
{anparziale,adellacioppa,rsenatore,amarcelli}@unisa.it

Abstract. We address the problem of designing a machine learning tool for the automatic diagnosis of Parkinson's disease that is capable of providing an explanation of its behavior in terms that are easy to understand by clinicians. For this purpose, we consider as machine learning tool the decision tree, because it provides the decision criteria in terms of both the features which are actually useful for the purpose among the available ones and how their values are used to reach the final decision, thus favouring its acceptance by clinicians. On the other side, we consider the random forest and the support vector machine, which are among the top performing machine learning tool that have been proposed in the literature, but whose decision criteria are hidden into their internal structures. We have evaluated the effectiveness of different approaches on a public dataset, and the results show that the system based on the decision tree achieves comparable or better results that state-of-the-art solutions, being the only one able to provide a plain description of the decision criteria it adopts in terms of the observed features and their values.

Keywords: E-health · Trusted Artificial Intelligence ·
Parkinson's disease · Machine learning

1 Introduction

Parkinson's disease (PD) is a neurodegenerative disorder that affects dopaminergic neurons in the Basal Ganglia, whose death causes several motor and cognitive symptoms. PD patients show impaired ability in controlling movements and disruption in the execution of everyday skills, due to postural instability, onset of tremors, stiffness and bradykinesia [8–10,15]. In the last decades, the analysis of handwriting and/or drawing movements has brought many insights for uncovering the processes occurring during both physiological and pathological conditions [2,16,17], and for providing a non-invasive method for evaluating the

© Springer Nature Switzerland AG 2019
E. Ricci et al. (Eds.): ICIAP 2019, LNCS 11751, pp. 196–206, 2019.
https://doi.org/10.1007/978-3-030-30642-7_18

stage of the disease [14]. A comprehensive survey of the literature on handwriting to support neurodegenerative diseases, including PD, may be found in [4]. As the authors pointed out, the large majority of studies aimed at investigating the handwritten production for the purpose of inferring which are the features that best characterize the production of PD patients with respect to healthy subjects. A variety of tests have been proposed, requiring the subject to write simple letters patterns, geometric figures, words, sentence and so on, but it has been recently shown that the most suitable ones are those requiring the drawing of geometric shapes such as spirals and meanders, with or without a reference pattern printed on the paper [20].

Following these suggestions, Pereira and his collaborators have collected the NewHandPD data set, which include both off-line images and on-line signals of the traces produced by the subjects while drawing 4 samples of spirals and 4 samples of meanders by writing on paper with a digitizing pen. A variety of top performing machine learning algorithms, such as Convolutional Neural Networks (CNN), Support Vector Machine (SVM), Optimal Path Finder (OPF), Random Forest (RF) and Restricted Boltzmann Machines (RBM) have been evaluated, showing that when on-line data are used, the ImageNet architecture could achieve a global accuracy of 87.14% in its best configuration, while the top performance on off-line data were achieved by the SVM, with a global accuracy of 66.72% on the meander drawings [11, 12].

In this framework, the aim of the work reported here is twofold: improving the performance on off-line data and providing an explicit representation of the criteria developed by the system for discriminating between PD patients and healthy subjects. Improving the performance obtained with static features is a goal worth to be pursued for two main reasons: (1) it would allow to analyze old writings or drawings produced by the subject (available only on paper given the age of insurgence of the diseases) for reconstructing the patient's medical history or to date the onset of the disease; (2) it would avoid that some subjects, especially elderly ones, feeling uncomfortable writing on a graphic tablet, may change their usual handwriting/drawing, thus introducing in their production unnatural characteristics that can lead to errors in assessment. Developing systems capable of explaining the decision procedure they have learned and adopted is currently a topic of investigation in the framework of so called explainable artificial intelligence (xAI) [1, 6]. In particular, in medical applications, adopting a decision procedure that can be described in a way that resembles the one routinely followed by clinicians when considering the results of tests, will favour their acceptance as supporting tool for early diagnosis.

To address both the issues, we propose to adopt a decision tree as the machine learning tool to perform the discrimination between handwritten samples produced by PD patients and healthy subjects. This choice is motivated by the structure of the tree that can be naturally "translated" into a chain of if-then decision rules, thus resembling very closely the diagnostic procedure. Other approaches such as fuzzy rule based systems have been also proposed, but they need specialized tools for automatically generating the decision rules [19]. The performance of the decision tree are then compared with those achieved by a Support Vector Machine, that in the previous studies mentioned above has provided the best performance, and with those exhibited by a Random Forest, as it exploits the same basic idea of decision tree, but whose decision criteria are much more complex and much less explicable than those of the decision tree. In the remaining of the paper, Sect. 2 briefly summarizes the main features of the three machine learning tools we have compared, and the data set we have used during the experimental work. Section 3 describes the experiments we have designed and performed for the automatic learning of the decision trees and reports the results obtained in terms of patient classification, as to show to which extent the proposed tool can be used by clinicians in their daily practice. Eventually, in the conclusion, we summarize the work that has been done, discuss the experimental results and outline our future investigations.

2   Machine Learning Tools and Dataset

We briefly summarize in the following the machine learning tools we have compared and the dataset used for performance evaluation.

2.1   C4.5

C4.5 is a statistical classifier introduced by Quinlan [13] and used in data mining for inducing classification rules in the form of decision trees, which can be employed to generate a decision from a set of training data. At each node of the tree, C4.5 chooses the feature that most effectively splits the set of samples into subsets that best differentiate the instances contained in the training data. The splitting criterion is the normalized information gain (difference in entropy). The attribute with the highest normalized information gain is chosen to take the decision. Once C4.5 creates a tree node whose value is the chosen attribute, it creates child links from this node where each link represents a unique value for the chosen attribute and uses the child link values to further subdivide the instances into subsets.

2.2   Random Forest

A random forest [7] is a meta estimator that aggregates a number of decision tree classifiers, i.e., the forest, on various sub-samples of the dataset and use averaging to enhance the predictive accuracy while mitigating the over-fitting. In general, the more trees in the forest the more robust the forest looks like. In random forest algorithm, instead of using information gain for calculating the root node, the process of finding the root node and splitting the feature nodes will happen randomly.

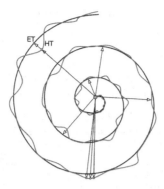

Fig. 1. The feature extraction process for a spiral. The blue line is the template trace ET, while the red line is the handwritten trace HT. The arrows indicate the radii for both ET and HT, the white circles indicate the intersection of a radius with the ET and the HT traces and the red circle represents the center of the ET. In order to compute all the features, the radius is shifted by using a predefined spanning angle. (Color figure online)

2.3 Support Vector Machines

The objective of the support vector machine [3] algorithm is to find a hyper-plane in an n-dimensional space (n is the number of features) that distinctly classifies the data points. To separate the two classes of data points, there are many possible hyper-planes that could be chosen. The objective is to find an hyper-plane that has the maximum margin, i.e., the maximum distance among data points of both classes. Maximizing the margin distance provides some reinforcement so that future data points can be classified with more confidence. Support vectors are data points that are closer to the hyper-plane and influence the position and orientation of the hyper-plane. Deleting the support vectors will change the position of the hyper-plane. Using these support vectors, we maximize the margin of the classifier.

2.4 The Dataset

NewHandPD dataset contains handwritten data collected from graphical tests performed by 31 PD patients and 35 healthy subjects. Each subject produced 4 samples of spirals and meanders, and from each sample 9 features, reported in Table 1, were extracted. As a result, the dataset is composed of 264 spirals and 264 meanders drawn by the participants following a printed template on paper with a pen. As a consequence, we have two unbalanced datasets, i.e., spirals and meanders, each of which is composed of 124 samples belonging to PD patients and 140 belonging to healthy subjects. Figure 1 shows, together on one sample, the two main geometric entities, namely the distance between the centre of the template and the template/written trace (ET/HT radius), from which all the features are computed.

Table 1. Features description of the dataset used. HT: handwritten trace, ET: exam template

Feature	Description
x_0	RMS of the difference between HT and ET radius
x_1	Maximum difference between HT and ET radius
x_2	Minimum difference between HT and ET radius
x_3	Standard Deviation of the difference between HT and ET radius
x_4	Mean Relative Tremor
x_5	Maximum HT radius
x_6	Minimum HT radius
x_7	Standard Deviation of HT radius
x_8	Number of times the difference between HT and ET radius changes sign

3 Experiments

To evaluate the performance of the proposed approach in providing explainable yet effective solutions, we performed a patient classification experiment, as described below.

3.1 Patient Classification

We divided the dataset into a Training set and a Test set made of 70% and 30% of the original dataset, respectively, in such a way as to maintain the relative occurrence of patients and healthy subjects. In particular, the Training set was made of 25 healthy subjects and 22 PD patients while the Test set was composed by 10 healthy subjects and 9 PD patients. The minimum and the maximum of each feature were computed on the Training set and a min-max normalization was applied to the whole dataset in order to scale all the features in the range $[0, 1]$.

The health condition of an individual was evaluated by classifying each of his/her handwritten samples and by applying a majority vote: an individual was classified as healthy or patient if the majority of his/her samples were assigned to the "healthy" or to the "patient" class, respectively. A decision about the health condition was rejected when the same number of samples were assigned to both the classes. The experimentation was performed with the aim of understanding: (1) which is the most performing classification schema among the ones described in Sect. 2, (2) if both meanders and spirals are necessary for evaluating the healthy condition, (3) how many samples are required for reaching the best performance. Therefore, we evaluated the health condition of individuals by classifying only the meanders, only the spirals and both meanders and spirals and by varying the number of samples per subject used during the training and the classification phases. In particular, samples were progressively included in

Table 2. Classifiers' parameters.

Classifier	Parameters
Decision Tree	Pruning confidence: 0.25, Minimum number of instances per leaf: 2
Random Forest	Bag size: 100, Number of iterations: 100, Maximum depth of the tree: unlimited
SVM	Kernel: radial basis, Gamma: 0.11, Cost: 1

the datasets following the order in which the subjects traced them. It follows that each experimental configuration differs from the others in the classifier and the type and number of samples belonging to the Training set and the Test set.

The implementation of the classifiers are those provided by Weka [18] as well as their parameter values and have not been fine-tuned to provide a baseline comparison among the selected classifiers. The parameter values are the same for all the experiments presented in this paper and are reported in Table 2.

The effectiveness of the classifiers was evaluated in term of *Accuracy*, *Reject*, *False Negative Rate* (FNR), which measures the percentage of healthy people who are identified as PD patients, and *False Positive Rate* (FPR), which measures the percentage of PD patients who are identified as healthy.

For each experimental configuration, a 6-fold cross validation was performed during the training phase and the classifier obtaining the best performance on the validation set, i.e. the one with the smallest values of FNR and FPR and with the greatest value of Accuracy, was selected for classifying individuals in the Test set.

All the experiments were repeated 15 times by shuffling the individuals between Training and Test set. Results obtained on the Test set when it was made up of only meanders, only spirals and both the patterns are reported in Tables 3, 4 and 5, respectively.

As it is evident from the results, all the classifiers exhibit the worst performance on the dataset containing both meanders and spirals, while the best performance is achieved on the meander dataset. Moreover, if we take into account the performance as a function of the number of samples per subject, it is possible to infer that the top performing scenario is represented by the one with the first 3 samples traced by each subject. Finally, by taking into account all the scenarios together, RF results the most performing classifier. In order to evaluate whether the performance in terms of accuracy by RF is significantly different from that provided by other methods, a statistical analysis, based on a non-parametric statistical test [5], is carried out. Following the results reported in the Tables 3, 4 and 5, the analysis has been performed considering the performance achieved by the classifiers on the datasets with only meanders and only spirals.

Table 3. Results obtained on Meanders. The first column reports the number of meanders for each subject.

# of samples	Accuracy (%)		Error (%)		Reject (%)		FNR (%)		FPR (%)	
	Mean	St.Dev.	Mean	St.Dev.	Mean	St.Dev.	Mean	St.Dev.	Mean	St.Dev.
Decision Tree										
1	72.98	12.29	27.02	12.29	0.00	0.00	32.00	16.41	21.48	20.48
2	69.82	9.31	4.21	3.94	25.96	9.11	6.00	8.00	2.22	4.44
3	85.97	9.15	14.03	9.15	0.00	0.00	24.67	15.43	2.22	4.44
4	72.63	8.42	11.58	5.83	15.79	6.37	22.00	11.08	0.00	0.00
Random Forest										
1	76.84	6.60	23.16	6.60	0.00	0.00	26.67	11.35	19.26	13.12
2	70.88	6.34	5.96	6.34	23.16	5.70	8.67	11.47	2.96	4.91
3	85.96	8.08	14.04	8.08	0.00	0.00	20.00	14.61	7.41	9.66
4	72.98	9.96	8.77	5.32	18.25	7.66	16.00	10.20	0.74	2.77
SVM										
1	75.79	9.76	24.21	9.76	0.00	0.00	40.67	19.48	5.93	6.87
2	62.45	7.16	15.09	8.57	22.46	9.11	28.67	16.28	0.00	0.00
3	72.98	8.78	27.02	8.78	0.00	0.00	51.33	16.68	0.00	0.00
4	58.95	5.83	18.95	8.11	22.11	8.20	35.33	15.43	0.74	2.77

Table 4. Results obtained on Spirals. The first column reports the number of spirals for each subject.

# of samples	Accuracy (%)		Error (%)		Reject (%)		FNR (%)		FPR (%)	
	Mean	St.Dev.	Mean	St.Dev.	Mean	St.Dev.	Mean	St.Dev.	Mean	St.Dev.
Decision Tree										
1	64.21	10.73	35.79	10.73	0.00	0.00	36.00	13.06	35.55	18.68
2	51.23	10.43	10.53	5.44	38.25	10.61	14.00	10.20	6.67	8.89
3	77.54	5.25	22.46	5.25	0.00	0.00	27.33	13.40	17.04	17.15
4	60.00	7.88	16.14	6.78	23.86	9.96	22.67	13.89	8.89	10.10
Random Forest										
1	65.61	9.58	34.39	9.58	0.00	0.00	37.33	16.52	31.11	19.12
2	57.19	8.78	5.61	4.89	37.19	8.26	4.67	6.18	6.67	10.58
3	84.91	4.65	15.09	4.65	0.00	0.00	12.67	9.29	17.78	12.03
4	68.77	10.61	7.72	3.78	23.51	8.78	6.67	7.89	8.89	9.25
SVM										
1	61.40	8.74	38.60	8.74	0.00	0.00	39.33	25.94	37.78	29.20
2	53.33	7.89	12.63	7.88	34.04	6.04	21.33	16.68	2.96	6.37
3	68.77	9.51	31.23	9.51	0.00	0.00	55.33	21.25	4.44	8.89
4	61.40	8.74	16.49	8.78	22.11	9.06	28.67	16.68	2.96	11.09

3.2 Statistical Analysis

The statistical analysis has been performed through the Friedman Aligned Ranks test, configured with multiple comparison methods. The null hypothesis H0 for the test states equality of medians between the different algorithms. The goal

Table 5. Results obtained on Spirals (S) and Meanders (M). The first column reports the number of samples, equally divided between spirals and meanders, for each subject.

# of samples	Accuracy (%)		Error (%)		Reject (%)		FNR (%)		FPR (%)	
	Mean	St.Dev.	Mean	St.Dev.	Mean	St.Dev.	Mean	St.Dev.	Mean	St.Dev.
Decision Tree										
2 (1S+1M)	51.23	13.52	15.79	11.04	32.98	14.44	24.00	21.54	6.67	12.03
4 (2S+2M)	67.72	9.39	9.12	6.22	23.16	5.70	13.33	11.35	4.44	7.91
6 (3S+3M)	75.44	9.15	10.53	6.37	14.04	7.36	15.33	14.54	5.18	6.87
8 (4S+4M)	73.68	7.19	15.44	5.91	10.88	8.48	24.67	13.60	5.18	7.98
Random Forest										
2 (1S+1M)	56.49	9.51	9.47	4.79	34.03	10.50	14.00	10.20	4.44	6.79
4 (2S+2M)	77.54	8.48	5.61	6.22	16.84	7.24	8.67	10.24	2.22	4.44
6 (3S+3M)	82.45	8.74	6.67	4.89	10.88	7.05	8.67	8.06	4.44	5.44
8 (4S+4M)	81.75	6.89	8.77	5.66	9.47	6.14	14.00	10.20	2.96	4.91
SVM										
2 (1S+1M)	58.60	9.19	21.05	9.61	20.35	7.66	38.67	19.96	1.48	3.78
4 (2S+2M)	65.96	8.57	18.24	9.39	15.79	5.77	34.67	17.84	0.00	0.00
6 (3S+3M)	69.82	8.03	20.70	7.05	9.47	6.43	39.33	13.40	0.00	0.00
8 (4S+4M)	62.46	6.04	19.65	6.51	17.90	6.32	36.67	13.00	0.74	2.77

Table 6. The ranking of the classification methods according to the Friedman Aligned Ranks test.

	Rank
Random Forest	6.000
Decision Tree	12.625
SVM	18.875

of the test is to either confirm this hypothesis or reject it, at a given level of confidence α. As it is typically done in scientific literature, we have used here $\alpha = 0.05$.

Table 6 reports the ranking of the methods and highlights that RF is the best-performing method followed by DT and SVM. The statistic for Friedman Aligned Ranks with control method is 9.46, distributed according to a chi-square distribution with 2 degrees of freedom, while the p-value is 0.00881. This value is lower than the chosen level of confidence 0.05, which suggests the existence of statistically significant differences among the algorithms considered. Given that H0 is rejected, meaning that the statistical equivalence among all the algorithms does not hold true, we can proceed with the post-hoc procedures to investigate where these differences between the algorithms exist. When using these procedures, a new null hypothesis H0' is used, which states the statistical equivalence for couples of algorithms, rather than for the whole set of algorithms as it was for H0.

Table 7 reports the adjusted p-values for the post-hoc procedures for Friedman Aligned Ranks test, when RF is used as control method. In the table the generic (i, j) adjusted p-value represents the smallest level of significance that results in the rejection of H0' between algorithm i and the control method, i.e., the lowest value for which the algorithm i and the control method are not statistically equivalent, for the j-th post-hoc procedure. The lower the adjusted p-value, the more likely the statistical equivalence can be rejected. A very important feature of such a table is that it is not tied to a pre-set level of significance α. Rather, depending on the value of α we choose, the post-hoc procedures will either accept or reject H0'. Considered that $\alpha = 0.05$, the table says that the statistical equivalence between RF and SVM can be statistically rejected for all the post-hoc procedures apart Hochberg, while there is a statistical equivalence between DT and RF. A general conclusion coming from the statistical analysis is that DT and RF perform better than SVM.

Table 7. Adjusted p-values for the post-hoc procedures for Friedman Aligned Ranks test (RF is the control method).

Algorithm	Statistic	Adjusted p-value				
		Bonferroni-Dunn	Holm	Finner	Hochberg	Li
SVM	3.642	0.00054	0.00054	0.00054	0.06095	0.00029
Decision Tree	1.874	0.12191	0.06095	0.06095	0.06095	0.06095

4   Conclusions

We have presented an approach for the automatic diagnosis of Parkinson's disease that aims at developing a system that is capable of providing an explanation of its behavior in terms that are easy to understand by the clinicians, thus favouring their acceptance/reject of the machine diagnostic suggestions.

In this frameworks, we have chosen as machine learning tool the Decision Tree, as it provides a description of the decision process in terms of if-then rules applied to the feature values, a decision process clinicians are very familiar with, and explicitly establishes a ranking of the features relevance. To illustrate this point, the best performing decision tree obtained by C4.5 on the meander dataset is reported below (Algorithm 1). It shows that the Mean Relative Tremor (x_4) results the most relevant feature, followed by the Maximum HT radius (x_5), the Minimum difference between the HT and ET radius (x_2) and, eventually, the Minimum HT radius (x_6). Those findings are in accordance with the literature, according to which tremor and deviation from a desired trajectory (either coded into the subject motor plan or provided as task) are among the most distinctive features of PD patients handwritten production. Even more important, it shows how the selected features are combined to reach the final decision. In contrast, for the other classifiers considered in this study, the SVM is unable to provide an explanation of its decision, while the RF provides a global ranking of the

Algorithm 1. Best performing model obtained by C4.5 on the Meander dataset.

```
if (x₄ > 0.1729) then
    output = "control"
else
    if (x₄ > 0.0905) then
        if (x₂ > 0.3016) then
            output = "control"
        else if (x₆ > 0.0381) then
            output = "control"
        else
            output = "patient"
        end if
    else if (x₅ > 0.2849) then
        output = "patient"
    else
        output = "control"
    end if
end if
```

features relevance, but not a description of the way they are intertwined in the decision making process.

Eventually, the experimental results show that the performance of the Decision Tree is comparable to that of the RF and better than the SVM one. As in a previous study comparing SVM with OPF and NB [12] SVM was the top performing classifier, we conclude that the DT proposed here achieves state-of-the-art performance on off-line data, while being the only one capable of describing its decision process in terms that can be simply and naturally understood by clinicians.

The experimental results also suggest that care should be paid in collecting the data to ensure that the task is neither too difficult nor too easy to carry on, so to avoid that fatigue/boredom may introduce misleading data that can negatively affect the performance.

In our future work we will investigate if and to which extent our method can be used to monitor the progress of the disease, as well as to trace back its onset.

Acknowledgment. The work reported in this paper was partially funded by the "Bando PRIN 2015 - Progetto HAND" under Grant H96J16000820001 from the Italian Ministero dell'Istruzione, dell'Università e della Ricerca.

References

1. Adadi, A., Berrada, M.: Peeking inside the black-box: a survey on explainable artificial intelligence (xAI). IEEE Access **6**, 52138–52160 (2018)
2. Broderick, M.P., Van Gemmert, A.W.A., Shill, H.A., Stelmach, G.: Hypometria and bradykinesia during drawing movements in individuals with Parkinson's disease. Exp. Brain Res. **197**(3), 223–233 (2009)

3. Cortes, C., Vapnik, V.: Support-vector networks. Mach. Learn. **20**(3), 273–297 (1995)
4. De Stefano, C., Fontanella, F., Impedovo, D., Pirlo, G., Scotto di Freca, A.: Handwriting analysis to support neurodegenerative diseases diagnosis: a review. Pattern Recogn. Lett. **121**, 37–45 (2019)
5. Derrac, J., García, S., Molina, D., Herrera, F.: A practical tutorial on the use of nonparametric statistical tests as a methodology for comparing evolutionary and swarm intelligence algorithms. Swarm Evol. Comput. **1**(1), 18 (2011)
6. Doran, D., Schulz, S., Besold, T.R.: What does explainable AI really mean? A new conceptualization of perspectives. arXiv preprint arXiv:1710.00794 (2017)
7. Ho, T.K.: Random decision forests. In: Proceedings of the Third International Conference on Document Analysis and Recognition, ICDAR 1995, vol. 1, pp. 278. IEEE Computer Society, Washington, DC (1995)
8. Hurrel, J., Flowers, K.A., Sheridan, M.R.: Programming and execution of movement in Parkinson's disease. Brain **110**(5), 1247–1271 (1987)
9. Jankovic, J.: Parkinson's disease: clinical features and diagnosis. J. Neurol. Neurosurg. Psychiatry **79**(4), 368–376 (2008). https://doi.org/10.1136/jnnp.2007.131045
10. Marsden, C.: Slowness of movement in Parkinson's disease. Mov. Disord. **4**(1 S), S26–S37 (1989)
11. Pereira, C.R., Passos, L.A., Lopes, R.R., Weber, S.A.T., Hook, C., Papa, J.P.: Parkinson's disease identification using Restricted Boltzmann Machines. In: Felsberg, M., Heyden, A., Krüger, N. (eds.) CAIP 2017. LNCS, vol. 10425, pp. 70–80. Springer, Cham (2017). https://doi.org/10.1007/978-3-319-64698-5_7
12. Pereira, C.R., et al.: A new computer vision-based approach to aid the diagnosis of Parkinson's disease. Comput. Methods Programs Biomed. **136**, 79–88 (2016)
13. Quinlan, J.R.: C4.5: Programs for Machine Learning. Morgan Kaufmann Publishers Inc., San Francisco (1993)
14. Senatore, R., Marcelli, A.: A paradigm for emulating the early learning stage of handwriting: performance comparison between healthy controls and Parkinson's disease patients in drawing loop shapes. Hum. Mov. Sci. (2018). https://doi.org/10.1016/J.HUMOV.2018.04.007
15. Stelmach, G.E., Teasdale, N., Phillips, J., Worringham, C.J.: Force production characteristics in Parkinson's disease. Exp. Brain Res. **76**(1), 165–172 (1989)
16. Tucha, O., et al.: Kinematic analysis of dopaminergic effects on skilled handwriting movements in Parkinson's disease. J. Neural Transm. **113**(5), 609–623 (2006)
17. Van Gemmert, A.W.A., Adler, C.H., Stelmach, G.E.: Parkinson's disease patients undershoot target size in handwriting and similar tasks. J. Neurol. Neurosurg. Psychiatry **74**(11), 1502–1508 (2003)
18. Witten, I.H., Frank, E., Hall, M.A., Pal, C.J.: Data Mining: Practical Machine Learning Tools and Techniques. Morgan Kaufmann, Burlington (2016)
19. Yao, J.F.F., Yao, J.S.: Fuzzy decision making for medical diagnosis based on fuzzy number and compositional rule of inference. Fuzzy Sets Syst. **120**(2), 351–366 (2001). https://doi.org/10.1016/S0165-0114(99)00071-8
20. Zham, P., Arjunan, S.P., Raghav, S., Kumar, D.K.: Efficacy of guided spiral drawing in the classification of Parkinson's disease. IEEE J. Biomed. Health Inform. **22**(5), 1648–1652 (2018)

Contrastive Explanations to Classification Systems Using Sparse Dictionaries

A. Apicella, F. Isgrò[✉], R. Prevete, and G. Tamburrini

Dipartimento di Ingegneria Elettrica e delle Teconologie dell'Informazione,
Università degli Studi di Napoli Federico II, Naples, Italy
{andrea.apicella,francesco.isgro}@unina.it

Abstract. Providing algorithmic explanations for the decisions of machine learning systems to end users, data protection officers, and other stakeholders in the design, production, commercialisation and use of machine learning systems pipeline is an important and challenging research problem. Much work in this area focuses on image classification, where the required explanations can be given in terms of images, therefore making explanations relatively easy to communicate to end-users. For a classification problem, a contrastive explanation tries to understand why the classifier has not answered a particular class, say B, instead of the returned class A. Sparse dictionaries have been recently used to identify local image properties as main ingredients for a system producing humanly understandable explanations for the decisions of a classifier developed based on machine learning methods. In this paper, we show how the system mentioned above can be extended to produce contrastive explanations.

Keywords: XAI · Explainable artificial intelligence ·
Machine learning · Sparse coding · Contrastive explanations

1 Introduction

Machine Learning (ML) techniques make possible to develop systems that learn from observations. Many ML techniques (e.g., Support Vector Machines (SVM) and Deep Neural Networks (DNN)) give rise to systems the behaviour of which is often hard to interpret [18]. A crucial ML interpretability issue concerns the generation of explanations for an ML system behaviour that are understandable to a human being. In general, this issue is addressed as a scientific and technological problem by so-called explainable artificial intelligence (XAI) [1,9,20,23]. Providing XAI solutions to the ML explainability problem is important for many AI and computer science research areas: to improve intelligent systems design,

The research presented in this paper was partially supported by the national project Perception, Performativity and Cognitive Sciences (PRIN Bando 2015, cod. 2015TM24JS_009).

© Springer Nature Switzerland AG 2019
E. Ricci et al. (Eds.): ICIAP 2019, LNCS 11751, pp. 207–218, 2019.
https://doi.org/10.1007/978-3-030-30642-7_19

testing and revision processes, to make the rationale of automatic decisions more transparent to end users and systems managers, thereby leading to better forms of HCI and HRI involving learning systems, to improve interactions between learning agents in Distributed AI, and so on. Providing a solution to the ML explainability problem is also important from an ethical and legal viewpoint. ML systems are being increasingly used to make or to support decisions that have an impact on the life of persons, including career development, court decisions, medical diagnosis, insurance risk profiles and loan decisions.

Various senses of interpretability and explainability for learning systems have been identified and analysed [9], and various approaches to overcoming their opaqueness are now being pursued [11,27]. For example, in [24] a series of techniques for the interpretation of DNN are discussed, and in [20] a wide variety of motivations underlying interpretability needs are examined, thereby refining the notion of interpretability in ML systems. In the context of this multifaceted interpretability problem [34,35], we focus on the issue of what it is to explain the behaviour of ML perceptual classification systems for which only I/O relationships are accessible, i.e., the learning system is seen as a black-box. In literature, this type of approach is known as *model agnostic* [31].

Various model agnostic approaches have been proposed to give *global* explanations by exhibiting a class prototype to which the input data can be associated [11,24,27,34]. These explanations are given in response to requests usually expressed as why-questions: "Why was input x associated to class C?". Specific why-questions which may arise in connection with actual learning systems are: "Why was this loan application rejected?" and "Why was this image classified as a fox?". However, prototypes often make rather poor explanations available. For instance, if an image x is classified as "fox", the explanation provided by means of a fox-prototype is nothing more than a "because it looks like this" explanation: one would not be put in the position to understand what features (parts) of the prototype are associated to what characteristics (parts) of x. In order to go beyond this level of understanding, instead of merely giving the user a global explanation, one might attempt to provide a *local* explanation, which highlights salient parts of the input [31]. Furthermore, [13,23] highlight that an human explanation of an event is often given in *contrastive* terms, that is, instead of trying to answer to the question "why this outcome?", a possible answer to the question "why this outcome and not another one?" is given. This result can be reached considering, during the generation of the explanation, an event that did not occur instead of the event that really happened, for example searching for an explanation on the reasons behind an classifier returns "dog" as answer to a given input image and not "cat". So, in contrastive explanation approaches, a different hypothetical outcome, which [19] calls the "foil", is always used to build the explanation.

In this paper, we exploit a model agnostic framework that returns local explanations of classifications [2,29] in order to obtain an explanation in contrastive terms. This framework, which is based on *dictionaries* of local and humanly interpretable elements of the input, can be functionally described as a three entities model, composed of an *Oracle* (an ML system, e.g. a classifier), an *Interrogator* raising explanations requests about the Oracle's responses, and a *Mediator* helping the Interrogator to understand the answer given by the Oracle. In this framework, local explanations are provided by a module (the Mediator) which is different from the classifier itself. The Mediator plays the crucial explanatory role, by advancing hypotheses on what humanly interpretable elements are likely to have influenced the Oracle output, building explanations both in classical terms ("why P?") and in contrastive terms ("why P and not Q?"). More specifically, elements are computed which represent humanly interpretable features of the input data, with the constraint that both prototypes and input can be reconstructed as linear combinations of these elements. Thus, one can establish meaningful associations between key features of the prototype and key features of the input. To this end, we exploit the representational power of sparse dictionaries learned from the data, where atoms of the dictionary selectively play the role of humanly interpretable elements, insofar as they afford a local representation of the data. Indeed, these techniques provide data representations that are often found to be accessible to human interpretation [22]. The dictionaries are obtained by a Non-negative Matrix Factorisation (NMF) method [4,14,17], and the explanations are determined using an Activation-Maximisation (AM) [11,34] based technique.

The paper is organised as follows: Sect. 2 briefly reviews related approaches, in Sect. 3 we present the overall architecture; experiments and results are discussed in Sect. 4, while Sect. 5 is devoted to concluding remarks and future developments.

2   Related Work

In recent years, various attempts have been made to interpret and explain the output of a classification system. Initial attempts concerned SVM classifiers (see for example [28]) or rule-based systems [6,8].

In the neural network context, recent surveys on explainable AI are proposed in [1,12,30,40]. A significant attempt to explain in terms of images what a computational neural unit computes is found in [11] using the *Activation Maximisation* method. AM-like approaches applied to CNN were proposed in [21,34]. Additional attempts to give interpretability to CNNs were proposed in [37] and [10], where Deconvolutional Network (already presented by [38] as a way to do unsupervised learning) and *up-convolutional network* are proposed, while [26,27] uses an image generator network (similar to GANs) as priors for AM algorithm to produce synthetic preferred images. In these approaches, explanations are given in terms of prototypes or approximate input reconstructions. However, one does not take into account the issue whether the given explanations are in some manner interpretable by humans. Moreover, the proposed approaches seem to be model-specific for CNN, differently from our model which is to be considered as model-agnostic, and consequently applicable in principle to any classifier. From another point of view, [36] studies the influence on the output of hardly perceptible perturbation on the input, empirically showing that it is possible to arbitrarily change the network's prediction even when the input is left apparently unchanged. Although this type of noise is extremely unlikely to occur in realistic situations, the fact that such noise is imperceptible to an observer opens interesting questions about the semantics of network components. However, approaches of this kind are quite distant from our present concerns, insofar as they focus on entities that are hardly meaningful to humans. Important works are also made into [3,5,25] where Pixel-Wise Decomposition, Layer-Wise Relevance propagation ad Deep Taylor Decomposition are presented. [33] builds explanations as difference in output from a "reference" output in terms of the difference of the input from a "reference" input.

[41] presents a work based on *prediction difference analysis* [32] where a features relevance vector is built which estimates how much each feature is "important" for the classifier to return the predicted class. In [31] , the model-agnostic explainer LIME is proposed, which takes into account the model behaviour in the proximity of the instance being predicted. The LIME framework is more similar to our approach than the other approaches mentioned in this section, and many other approaches found in the literature. The LIME framework differs from our own mainly in its use of super-pixels instead of a learned dictionary constrained in order to have a compact representation.

In [39] a XAI methods based on the contrastive explanations is proposed. However, this method relies on Deep Neural Network (specifically a CNN), making this approach model-specific, differently from our proposed model which is model-agnostic, that is independent by the chosen model to explain.

3   Proposed Approach

Given an oracle Ω, an input x and an Ω's answer $\hat{c}$ (regardless of whether it is correct or not), we want to give an explanation of the answer provided by the model Ω that is humanly interpretable. As we want to obtain humanly interpretable elements which, combined together, can provide an acceptable explanation for the choice made by Ω, we search for an explanation having the following qualitative properties:

1. the explanation must be expressed in terms of a *dictionary* V whose elements (atoms) are easily understandable by an interrogator;
2. the elements of the dictionary V have to represent "local properties" of the input x;
3. the explanation must be composed by few dictionary elements.

We claim that considering as elements atoms of a sparse coding from a sparse dictionary, and using sparse coding methods together with an AM-like algorithm we obtain explanations satisfying the properties described above. Furthermore, since the proposed method gives explanations in terms of relevant components (atoms) which contributed to the classifier decision, we take advantage of this property to generate discriminative explanations comparing the explanation produced for the real classifier outcome with the explanation produced for a contrast class given the same input. We think that, showing explanations generated for different classes can help in understanding the reason behind the "preference" given by an Oracle to an answer instead of another one.

3.1 Sparse Dictionary Learning

The first step of the proposed approach consists in finding a "good" dictionary V that can represent data in terms of humanly interpretable atoms.

Let us assume that we have a set $D = \{(x^{(1)}, c^{(1)}), (x^{(2)}, c^{(2)}), \ldots, (x^{(n)}, c^{(n)})\}$ where each $x^{(i)} \in \mathbb{R}^d$ is a column vector representing a data point, and $c^{(i)} \in C$ its class. We can learn a Dictionary $V \in \mathbb{R}^{d \times k}$ of k atoms across multiple classes and an encoding $H \in \mathbb{R}^{k \times n}$ s.t. $X = VH + \epsilon$ where $X = (x^{(1)}|x^{(2)}|\ldots|x^{(n)})$ and ϵ is the error introduced by the coding. Every column $x^{(i)}$ in X can be expressed as $x^{(i)} = Vh_i$ with h_i i–th column of H. The dictionary forms the basis of our explanation framework for an ML system.

We selected as dictionary learning algorithm an NMF scheme [17] with the additional sparseness constraint proposed by [14]; this choice is motivated by the fact that it respects our requirements described above, giving a "local" representation of data, and *non-negativity*, that ensures only additive operations in data representations, giving a better human understanding with respect to other techniques. The sparsity level can be set using two parameters γ_1 and γ_2 which control the sparsity on the dictionary and the encoding, respectively.

3.2 Explanation Maximisation

Unlike traditional dictionary-based coding approaches, our main goal is not to get an "accurate" representation of the input data, but to get a representation that helps humans to understand the decision taken by a trained model. To this aim, we modify the AM algorithm so that, instead of looking for the input that just maximises the answer of the model, it searches for the dictionary-based encoding h that maximises the answer and, at the same time, is sparse enough but without being "too far" from the original input x. More formally, indicating with $\Pr(\hat{c}|x)$ the probability given by a learned model that input x belongs to class $\hat{c} \in C$, V the chosen dictionary, $S(\cdot)$ a sparsity measure, the objective function that we optimise is

$$\max_{h \geq 0} \log \Pr\left(\hat{c}|Vh\right) - \lambda_1 \|Vh - x\|_2 + \lambda_2 S(h) \tag{1}$$

where λ_1, λ_2 are hyper-parameters regulating the input reconstruction and the encoding sparsity level, respectively. The first regularisation term leads the algorithm to choose dictionary atoms that, with an appropriate encoding, form a good representation of the input, while the second regularisation term ensures a certain sparsity degree, i.e., that only few atoms are used. The $h \geq 0$ constraint ensures that one has a purely additive encoding. Thus, each h_i, $\forall i.1 \leq i \leq d$,

---

Algorithm 1: Explanation Maximization procedure

Input: data point $x \in \mathbb{R}^d$, the output class $\hat{c}$,learned model Γ, a dictionary
$\quad\quad V \in \mathbb{R}^{d \times k}$, λ_1, λ_2
Output: the encoding $h \in \mathbb{R}^d$

1   $h \sim U^d(0,1)$;
2   **while** $\neg$ *converge* **do**
3      $r \leftarrow Vh$;
4      $h \leftarrow \arg\max_{h} \Pr\left(\hat{c}|r; \Gamma\right) - \lambda_1 ||r - x||_2$;
5      $h \leftarrow \mathrm{proj}(h, \lambda_2)$; $\triangleright$ proj$(\cdot, \cdot)$ is given by [14]
6   **end**
7   **return** h ;

---

measures the "importance" of the i-th atom. Equation 1 is solved by using a standard gradient ascent technique, together with a projection operator given by [14] that ensures both sparsity and non-negativity. The complete procedure is reported in Algorithm 1.

3.3 Contrastive Explanation Maximisation

The aim of this we paper is to obtain a contrastive explanation approach exploiting the EM procedure described in Sect. 3.2. We remember that, instead of answering to the question "why the classifier returns the class P?", contrastive explanations wants to answer to the question "why the Oracle returns the class P and not the class Q?". The described EM procedure generates a possible explanation searching for a good subset of atoms which pushes the classifier toward the predicted class and, at the same time, is similar enough to the input under investigation. We can easily use the same procedure to push the classifier towards a contrastive class, so searching for a good set of atoms which is again near enough to the input but that gives a different outcome if fed to the classifier. An answer to the question "why the Oracle returns the class P and not the class Q?" can be given inspecting the difference between atoms in the generated explanations. For example, in a dataset of letters, if I have an image of an "e" and a classifier gives the correct class, I expect that the explanation of "why is it an "e"? " differs from the explanation of, for example, "why should it be a "c"?" by the use of some atom representing a centre line which characterises the "e" letter respect to the "c" letter. In other words, we search for two (or more) good enconding h_{c^*} and $h_{\bar{c}}$ such that

$$
\begin{aligned}
h_{c^*} &= \arg\max_{h \geq 0} \log \Pr\left(c^*|Vh\right) - \lambda_1 ||Vh - x||_2 + \lambda_2 S(h) \\
h_{\bar{c}} &= \arg\max_{h \geq 0} \log \Pr\left(\bar{c}|Vh\right) - \lambda_1 ||Vh - x||_2 + \lambda_2 S(h)
\end{aligned}
\tag{2}
$$

with $c^*, \bar{c} \in C, c^*$ classifier outcome for the input x and $\bar{c} \neq c^*$.

Algorithm 2: Contrastive Explanation Maximization procedure

Input: data point $x \in \mathbb{R}^d$, the number of antagonist classes q, the Oracle Ω, a dictionary $V \in \mathbb{R}^{d \times k}$

Output: the encoding $h \in \mathbb{R}^d$

1 $p \leftarrow$ getClassProbabilities (x, Ω);
2 $(c_1, c_2, \ldots, c_{q+1}) \leftarrow$ getBestClasses$(p, q + 1)$;
3 $h_{expl} \leftarrow$ EMExplanationBuilder(x, c_1, Ω, V);
4 **for** $i = 2$ **to** $q + 1$ **do**
5 | $h_{anta}^{(i)} \leftarrow$ EMExplanationBuilder(x, c_i, Ω, V);
6 **end**
7 **return** $h_{expl}, h_{anta}^{(2)}, \ldots, h_{anta}^{(q+1)}$

---

4   Experimental Assessment

To test our framework, we chose as Oracle a convolutional neural network architecture, LeNet-5 [16], generally used for digit recognition as MNIST. We have trained the network from scratch using two different datasets: MNIST [16], and a subset of the e-MNIST dataset [7] composed of the first 10 lowercase letters. The model is learned using the Adam algorithm [15].

NMF with sparseness constraints [14] is used to determine the dictionaries. We set the number of atoms to 200, relying on PCA analysis which showed that the first 100 principal components explain more than 95% of the data variance. We construct different dictionaries with different sparsity values in the range $\gamma_1, \gamma_2 \in [0.6, 0.8]$ [14], then we choose the dictionaries having the best trade-off between sparsity level and reconstruction error. The dictionaries are determined by looking for a good trade-off between reconstruction error and sparsity level.

The atoms forming our explanations are selected by taking those with larger encoding values (i.e., those that are more "important" in the representation).

In Fig. 1 we show the proposed explanation from different inputs. The explanations are expressed in terms of two different set of atoms which in Sect. 3.3 we computed using h_{c*} and $h_{\bar{c}}$: the first one is the set of atoms which mostly contribute (in terms of weights) to the outcome of the Oracle, the second one the set of atoms which mostly contribute to a given constrastive outcome. For clarity, we chose the first five.

We can see that the atoms selected by h_{c*} provide elements which can be considered discriminative for the selected outcome, for example in Fig. 1a (red) EM selects many components which represent a diagonal line, showing that it is probably one of the main feature selected by the classifier to make its choice. In the second column (blue) we chose a contrast class (a "3") and we ask to the algorithm to make an explanation. We can see that the selected components which are mostly different and varied, showing that the given image, to be classified as a "3", should have also other characteristics, as the central horizontal line.

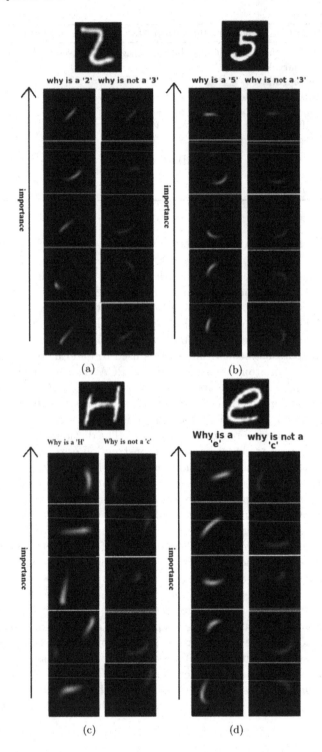

Fig. 1. Examples of direct and contrastive explanations. See discussion in Sect. 4 for more details (Color figure online)

Similar considerations can be made for the example shown in Fig. 1b, where the choice of a "five" can be motivated by the presence of the showed components (red), while in the blue column, we can notice the total absence of component on the left side, suggesting that the absence of a "left side" on the input image can be an explanation of why the given input has not been classified as a "3". in other terms, the input, to be classified as a "3", should have the visual components on the right side not relevant in terms of weights. In Fig. 1c the given input is correctly classified by the presence of the red component with high weights. The presence of the central line can be considered as the main discriminative feature between the outcome "H" and "c" (which is absent in the blue column). Similar considerations can be made for the input in Fig. 1d.

5 Conclusions

We proposed a model-agnostic framework to explain the answers given by classification systems. To achieve this objective, we started by defining a general explanation framework based on three entities: an Oracle (providing the answers to explain), an Interrogator (posing explanation requests) and a Mediator (helping Interrogator to interpret the Oracle's decisions). We propose a Mediator using known and established techniques of sparse dictionary learning, together with Interpretability ML techniques, to give a humanly interpretable explanation of a classification system outcomes. The proposed mediator can give explanation both in traditional and contrastive terms, since "why not?" questions are particularly relevant, from an ethical and legal viewpoint, to address user complaints about purported misclassifications and corresponding user requests to be classified otherwise. We tried our proposed approach by using an NMF-based scheme as sparse dictionary learning technique. However, we expect that any other technique that meets the requirements outlined in Sect. 3 may be successfully used to instantiate the proposed framework. The results of the experiments that we carried out are encouraging, insofar as the explanations provided seem to be qualitatively significant. Nevertheless, more experiments are necessary to probe the general interest of our approach to explanation. We plan to perform both a quantitative assessment, to evaluate explanations by techniques such as those proposed in [24], and a subjective quality assessment to test how do humans perceive and interpret explanations of this kind.

The proposed approach does not take so far into account factors such as the internal structure of the dictionary used. Accordingly, the present work can be extended by considering, for example, whether there are atoms that are sufficiently "similar" to each other or whether the presence in the dictionary of atoms which can be expressed as combinations of other atoms may affect the explanations that are arrived at.

References

1. Adadi, A., Berrada, M.: Peeking inside the black-box: a survey on explainable artificial intelligence (xai). IEEE Access **6**, 52138–52160 (2018)
2. Apicella, A., Isgrò, F., Prevete, R., Sorrentino, A., Tamburrini, G.: Explaining classification systems using sparse dictionaries. In: Proceedings of the European Symposium on Artificial Neural Networks, Computational Intelligence and Machine Learning, Special Session on Societal Issues in Machine Learning: When Learning from Data is Not Enough (2019)
3. Bach, S., Binder, A., Montavon, G., Klauschen, F., Müller, K.R., Samek, W.: On pixel-wise explanations for non-linear classifier decisions by layer-wise relevance propagation. PloS One **10**(7), e0130140 (2015)
4. Bao, C., Ji, H., Quan, Y., Shen, Z.: Dictionary learning for sparse coding: algorithms and convergence analysis. IEEE Trans. Pattern Anal. Mach. Intell. **38**(7), 1356–1369 (2016)
5. Binder, A., Montavon, G., Lapuschkin, S., Müller, K.-R., Samek, W.: Layer-wise relevance propagation for neural networks with local renormalization layers. In: Villa, A.E.P., Masulli, P., Pons Rivero, A.J. (eds.) ICANN 2016. LNCS, vol. 9887, pp. 63–71. Springer, Cham (2016). https://doi.org/10.1007/978-3-319-44781-0_8
6. Caruana, R., Lou, Y., et al.: Intelligible models for healthcare: predicting pneumonia risk and hospital 30-day readmission. In: ACM SIGKDD International Conference on Knowledge Discovery and Data Mining, pp. 1721–1730. ACM (2015)
7. Cohen, G., Afshar, S., Tapson, J., van Schaik, A.: EMNIST: an extension of MNIST to handwritten letters. arXiv e-prints arXiv:1702.05373 February 2017
8. Cooper, G.F., Aliferis, C.F., et al.: An evaluation of machine-learning methods for predicting pneumonia mortality. Artif. Intell. Med. **9**(2), 107–138 (1997)
9. Doran, D., Schulz, S., Besold, T.R.: What does explainable ai really mean? A new conceptualization of perspectives. arXiv preprint arXiv:1710.00794 (2017)
10. Dosovitskiy, A., Brox, T.: Inverting visual representations with convolutional networks. In: IEEE Conference on Computer Vision and Pattern Recognition, pp. 4829–4837 (2016)
11. Erhan, D., Bengio, Y., Courville, A., Vincent, P.: Visualizing higher-layer features of a deep network. University of Montreal 1341(3), p. 1 (2009)
12. Guidotti, R., Monreale, A., Ruggieri, S., Turini, F., Giannotti, F., Pedreschi, D.: A survey of methods for explaining black box models. ACM Comput. Surv. (CSUR) **51**(5), 93 (2018)
13. Hilton, D.J.: Conversational processes and causal explanation. Psychol. Bull. **107**(1), 65 (1990)
14. Hoyer, P.O.: Non-negative matrix factorization with sparseness constraints. J. Mach. Learn. Res. **5**(Nov), 1457–1469 (2004)
15. Kingma, D., Ba, J.: Adam: a method for stochastic optimization. In: International Conference on Learning Representations, December 2014
16. Lecun, Y., Bottou, L., Bengio, Y., Haffner, P.: Gradient-based learning applied to document recognition. Proc. IEEE **86**(11), 2278–2324 (1998)
17. Lee, D.D., Seung, H.S.: Algorithms for non-negative matrix factorization. In: Advances in neural information processing systems, pp. 556–562 (2001)
18. Letham, B., Rudin, C., McCormick, T.H., Madigan, D., et al.: Interpretable classifiers using rules and bayesian analysis: Building a better stroke prediction model. Ann. Appl. Stat. **9**(3), 1350–1371 (2015)
19. Lipton, P.: Contrastive explanation. Roy. Inst. Philos. Suppl. **27**, 247–266 (1990)

20. Lipton, Z.C.: The mythos of model interpretability. Queue **16**(3), 30:31–30:57 (2018)
21. Mahendran, A., Vedaldi, A.: Understanding deep image representations by inverting them. In: CVPR, pp. 5188–5196 (2015)
22. Mensch, A., Mairal, J., Thirion, B., Varoquaux, G.: Dictionary learning for massive matrix factorization. In: International Conference on Machine Learning, pp. 1737–1746 (2016)
23. Miller, T.: Explanation in artificial intelligence: insights from the social sciences. Artif. Intell. **267**, 1–38 (2018)
24. Montavon, G., Samek, W., Müller, K.: Methods for interpreting and understanding deep neural networks. Digital Signal Process. **73**, 1–15 (2018)
25. Montavon, G., Lapuschkin, S., Binder, A., Samek, W., Müller, K.R.: Explaining nonlinear classification decisions with deep taylor decomposition. Pattern Recogn. **65**, 211–222 (2017)
26. Nguyen, A., Clune, J., Bengio, Y., Dosovitskiy, A., Yosinski, J.: Plug & play generative networks: Conditional iterative generation of images in latent space. In: Proceedings of the IEEE Conference on Computer Vision and Pattern Recognition, pp. 4467–4477 (2017)
27. Nguyen, A., Dosovitskiy, A., Yosinski, J., Brox, T., Clune, J.: Synthesizing the preferred inputs for neurons in neural networks via deep generator networks. In: Advances in Neural Information Processing Systems, pp. 3387–3395 (2016)
28. Núñez, H., Angulo, C., Català, A.: Rule extraction from support vector machines. In: Esann, pp. 107–112 (2002)
29. Prevete, R., Apicella, A., Isgrò, F., Tamburrini, G.: Explaining the behavior of learning classification systems: a black-box approach. In: Proceedings of the 15th Conference of the Italian Association for Cognitive Sciences (2018)
30. Qin, Z., Yu, F., Liu, C., Chen, X.: How convolutional neural network see the world-a survey of convolutional neural network visualization methods. arXiv preprint arXiv:1804.11191 (2018)
31. Ribeiro, M.T., Singh, S., Guestrin, C.: Why should i trust you? Explaining the predictions of any classifier. In: ACM SIGKDD International Conference on Knowledge Discovery and Data Mining, pp. 1135–1144. ACM (2016)
32. Robnik-Šikonja, M., Kononenko, I.: Explaining classifications for individual instances. IEEE Trans. Knowl. Data Eng. **20**(5), 589–600 (2008)
33. Shrikumar, A., Greenside, P., Kundaje, A.: Learning important features through propagating activation differences. In: Proceedings of the 34th International Conference on Machine Learning-Volume 70, pp. 3145–3153. JMLR. org (2017)
34. Simonyan, K., Vedaldi, A., Zisserman, A.: Deep inside convolutional networks: visualising image classification models and saliency maps. arXiv preprint arXiv:1312.6034 (2013)
35. Sturm, I., Lapuschkin, S., Samek, W., Müller, K.: Interpretable deep neural networks for single-trial eeg classification. J. Neurosci. Methods **274**, 141–145 (2016)
36. Szegedy, C., Zaremba, W., et al.: Intriguing properties of neural networks. arXiv preprint arXiv:1312.6199 (2013)
37. Zeiler, M.D., Fergus, R.: Visualizing and understanding convolutional networks. In: Fleet, D., Pajdla, T., Schiele, B., Tuytelaars, T. (eds.) ECCV 2014. LNCS, vol. 8689, pp. 818–833. Springer, Cham (2014). https://doi.org/10.1007/978-3-319-10590-1_53
38. Zeiler, M.D., Taylor, G.W., Fergus, R.: Adaptive deconvolutional networks for mid and high level feature learning. In: ICCV, pp. 2018–2025 (2011)

39. Zhang, J., Bargal, S.A., et al.: Top-down neural attention by excitation backprop. Int. J. Comput. Vision **126**, 1084–1102 (2017)
40. Zhang, Q., Zhu, S.: Visual interpretability for deep learning: a survey. Front. Inf. Technol. Electron. Eng. **19**(1), 27–39 (2018)
41. Zintgraf, L.M., Cohen, T.S., Adel, T., Welling, M.: Visualizing deep neural network decisions: Prediction difference analysis. arXiv preprint arXiv:1702.04595 (2017)

Regularized Evolutionary Algorithm for Dynamic Neural Topology Search

Cristiano Saltori[1(✉)], Subhankar Roy[1,2], Nicu Sebe[1], and Giovanni Iacca[1]

[1] Department of Information Engineering and Computer Science,
University of Trento, Trento, Italy
`cristiano.saltori@studenti.unitn.it`,
{`subhankar.roy,niculae.sebe,giovanni.iacca`}`@unitn.it`
[2] Fondazione Bruno Kessler (FBK), Trento, Italy

Abstract. Designing neural networks for object recognition requires considerable architecture engineering. As a remedy, *neuro-evolutionary* network architecture search, which automatically searches for optimal network architectures using evolutionary algorithms, has recently become very popular. Although very effective, evolutionary algorithms rely heavily on having a large population of individuals (i.e., network architectures) and are therefore memory expensive. In this work, we propose a Regularized Evolutionary Algorithm with low memory footprint to evolve a dynamic image classifier. In details, we introduce novel custom operators that regularize the evolutionary process of a micro-population of 10 individuals. We conduct experiments on three different digits datasets (MNIST, USPS, SVHN) and show that our evolutionary method obtains competitive results with the current state-of-the-art.

Keywords: Deep Learning · Neural Architecture Search · Regularized Evolution · Evolutionary algorithms

1 Introduction

Deep Learning has made a remarkable progress in a multitude of computer vision tasks, such as object recognition [1,2], object detection [3], semantic segmentation [4], etc. The success of deep neural networks (DNNs) has been attributed to the ability to learn hierarchical features from massive amounts of data in an end-to-end fashion. Despite the breakthroughs of manually designed networks, such as Residual Networks [5] and Inception Net [6], these networks suffer from two major drawbacks: (i) the skeleton of the architectures is not tailored for a dataset at hand; and (ii) it requires expert knowledge to design high-performance architectures. To circumvent the cumbersome network architecture design process, there has been lately an increased interest in automatic design through *Neural Architecture Search* [7] (NAS). The objective of NAS is to find an optimal network architecture for a given task in a data-driven way. In spite of being

© Springer Nature Switzerland AG 2019
E. Ricci et al. (Eds.): ICIAP 2019, LNCS 11751, pp. 219–230, 2019.
https://doi.org/10.1007/978-3-030-30642-7_20

in its nascent stages, NAS has consistently outperformed hand-engineered network architectures on some common tasks such as object recognition [8], object detection [8] and semantic segmentation [9].

Among NAS methods, *neuro-evolutionary* algorithms [13,14,21,24] have recently resurfaced that use bio-inspired evolutionary principles for finding optimized neural architectures. A promising work in this direction was conducted by Real *et al.* [13], who proposed an *aging*-based evolutionary algorithm and demonstrated that favouring younger individuals (i.e., network architectures) against the best individuals in a population is beneficial in terms of convergence to better network architectures.

The performance of neuro-evolutionary methods is, however, heavily dependent on the population size (i.e, the number of individuals in the current population) and as a result on the availability of computational resources. For instance, Real *et al.* [13] used a population of 100 individuals evaluated in parallel on 450 GPUs. In this work, we propose an improved evolutionary algorithm, named *Regularized Evolutionary Algorithm*, to accomplish NAS in limited computational settings. Specifically, our method is based on the regularized algorithm by Real *et al.* [13] with various modifications that can be summarized as follows: (i) an evolving cell with a variable number of hidden nodes where each node (see Fig. 1b) can be thought of as a pairwise combination of common operations (such as convolution, pooling, etc); (ii) a custom *crossover* operation that allows recombination between two parent individuals in a population, to accelerate the evolutionary search; (iii) a custom *mutation* mechanism, to generate new architectures by randomly modifying their hidden states, operations and number of hidden nodes inside a cell; and iv) a *stagnation avoidance* mechanism to avoid premature convergence. More details on the algorithm can be found in the Supplementary Material available at https://arxiv.org/abs/1905.06252. Noticeable is the implicit regularization performed by the stagnation avoidance and the mutation of B, as shown in details in Sect. 3.2.

As we show in our experiments conducted on three different *digits* datasets, the proposed modifications improve on the exploratory capability of the evolutionary algorithm when very limited memory and computational resources are at disposal during training. In our experiments, we used a micro-population of 10 individuals evaluated on a single GPU, obtaining competitive results when compared with much larger computational setups such as those used in [13].

2   Background

The recent successes of NAS algorithms [8,10–14,16,17] have opened new doors in the field of Deep Learning by outperforming traditional DNNs [1,5] that are manually designed. Mostly, the NAS algorithms differ in the way they explore the search space of the neural architectures. The search strategy can be broadly divided into three different categories. The first category of methods [11,12] use Bayesian optimization techniques to search for optimal network architectures and have led to some early successes before reinforcement learning (RL) based methods [8,10,17] became mainstream, which is the second predominant category. In RL based methods the agent's action can be considered as the generation of a neural architecture within a given search space, whereas the agent's reward is the performance of the trained architecture on the validation set. Zoph *et al.* [10] used a recurrent neural network to sample a set of operations for the network architecture. In another work, the best performing network, dubbed as NASNet [8], is searched by using Proximal Policy Optimization.

The final category of NAS algorithms leverage evolutionary algorithms for finding the optimal network architectures. Surprisingly, the first work on using genetic algorithm for searching network architectures [18] dates back several decades ago. Since then, there have been several works [19,20] which use evolutionary algorithm both to search network architectures and to optimize the weights of the proposed networks. However, in practice Stochastic Gradient Descent (SGD) based optimization of network weights works better than evolution based optimization. Therefore, a series of methods [13,14,21] have been proposed which restrict the usage of evolutionary algorithm just to guide architecture search, while using SGD for network weight optimization. The evolution based NAS methods differ in the way the sampling of parents are done, the update policy of the population, and how the offspring are generated. For instance, in [13] parents are selected according to a tournament selection [15], while in [22] this is accomplished through a multi-objective Pareto selection. The variations in the population update can be noticed in [13,21] where the former removes the worst individual and the latter removes the oldest individual from a population, respectively. Similar to [21], but differently from [13], in this work we propose a $\mu + \lambda$ methodology to remove the worst individuals from the population, where μ and λ is the population size and number of offspring, respectively. With our approach, the best individual is preserved in the population (elitism). Furthermore, as opposed to [13,21] who only considered mutation as the sole offspring generation process, here we additionally consider a crossover operator whose purpose is to accelerate the evolutionary process by recombining "building blocks" obtained by the parents undergoing crossover.

Finally, the choice of population size plays a very crucial role in the exploration of the search space of network architectures. For instance, the availability of mammoth computing power (450 GPUs) allowed [13] to use a population size $P = 100$, as opposed to our experiments which use a micro-population of size $P = 10$. Thus, we compensate the lack of computational resources with various modifications to the evolution process, so to allow an efficient exploration of the search space with a very limited computational budget.

3   Method

In this section we present our method by first introducing the search space, and then describing in detail the proposed Regularized Evolutionary Algorithm.

3.1 Search Space

We consider the NASNet search space, introduced in [8], comprised of image classifiers that have a fixed structure (see Fig. 1a), each one composed of repeated motifs called *cells*, similar to Inception-like modules in [6]. Each architecture is composed of two building-block cells called *normal cell* and *reduction cell*. By design, all the normal and reduction cells should have the same architecture, but the internal structure of a normal cell could vary from the reduction cell (see Sect. 4.3). Another fundamental difference between the two is that the reduction cell is followed by an average pooling operation with a 2×2 kernel and stride of 2, whereas the normal cells preserve the size.

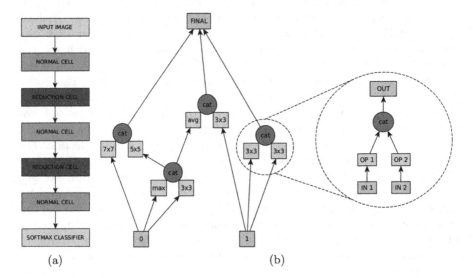

Fig. 1. (a) The full outer architecture used during the search phase; (b) Example of an evolved cell's internal structure and the depiction of a hidden node's structure.

As seen from Fig. 1b and borrowing the taxonomy from [8], each cell is composed of two input states (designated as "0" and "1"), an output state (designated as "final") and a variable number of B hidden nodes. Excluding the input and output states, each *intermediate* hidden node is constructed by a pairwise combination of two independent operations (or *op*) on two inputs, followed by the concatenation of their corresponding outputs. We refer to each hidden node's output as hidden states.

In total, each cell has a maximum of $B + 3$ states. Ops consist of commonly used convnet operations, essentially only a subset of [8], defined as: identity layer; 3×3 convolution; 5×5 convolution; 7×7 convolution; 3×3 max pooling; 3×3 average pooling. For example, in Fig. 1b, the *zoomed-in* hidden node is constructed by two unique 3×3 convolution operations on the input state "1", followed by concatenation of resulting feature maps to yield another hidden state.

It is worth noting that in [8,13] B is fixed for both the normal and reduction cell, while in our method we treat B as a parameter which is also optimized during the evolution, thus allowing different B (where $B \in [B_{min}, B_{max}]$) for normal and reduction cells. In details, the input state is composed of a 1×1 convolutional layer with stride 1, to preserve the number of input channels, while the output state is composed of a concatenation of the activations coming from the previous unused hidden states. The inputs to each intermediate hidden node can come from any of the previous states, including duplicates, while the output from a hidden node can be connected to any of the following states. Finally, the hidden states that are not connected with any (unused) op are concatenated in the output hidden state.

Given a normal and a reduction cell, the architecture is built by alternating these motifs as in [13], with the major difference that we avoid the use of skip-connections and thus reduce the number of repetitions, in order to obtain a simpler and faster training procedure. As in [13], we keep the same number of feature maps inside each cell fixed, while this number is multiplied by a factor K after each reduction cell. A sample overall architecture structure is reported in Fig. 1a. The final goal of the NAS process is to find optimal architectures for normal and reduction cells. Once their architectures have been chosen by the algorithm, there are two hyper-parameters that need to be determined: the number of normal cells (N) and the number of output features or filters (D).

3.2 Regularized Evolutionary Algorithm

The proposed Regularized Evolutionary Algorithm, see Algorithm 1, is based on a micro-population of $P = 10$ individuals (i.e., network architectures). Each individual represents a solution in the NASNet space, which as said is further composed of normal and reduction cells. During evolution the population is evolved in order to maximize the classification accuracy on a hold out validation set. In the following, we describe in details each step of the proposed algorithm.

Population Initialization. In this initial step P individuals with random cells are initialized and evaluated. Since we use a small value of P, the population is strongly affected by badly initialized solutions. To solve this problem we initialize all individuals with B hidden nodes (with B randomly selected in the range $[B_{min}, B_{max}/2]$), in order to allow the algorithm to optimize and gradually increase B during the evolution.

Offspring Generation. At each generation F offspring (i.e., new network architectures) are generated and inserted into the population. More specifically, for each i-th offspring to generate, $1 \leq i \leq F$, a sample of S individuals is selected randomly from the population P. From these S individuals, two are selected as parents for the i-th offspring: the best individual in the sample, P_1 (this is equivalent to a tournament selection), and another individual P_2, which is instead randomly selected from the sample. P_1 and P_2 are then used to generate the offspring through crossover and mutation.

Crossover. The crossover operation aims at merging two parent individuals, thus enabling inheritance through generations. Let us assume that P_1 and P_2 have B_1 and B_2 hidden nodes, respectively. The offspring cell, derived from P_1 and P_2, will have $B_{temp} = max(B_1, B_2)$ intermediate hidden nodes. The hidden nodes of the parent cells are then merged through sequential random selection with probability τ_{cross}, as follows. For the sake of generality we assume $B_1 \neq B_2$. The first $min(B_1, B_2)$ intermediate hidden nodes H_j^{off} in the offspring network, $1 \leq j \leq min(B_1, B_2)$, are set as:

$$H_j^{off} = \begin{cases} H_j^{P_1} & \text{if } p \leq \tau_{cross} \\ H_j^{P_2} & \text{otherwise} \end{cases}$$

where p is a uniform random number drawn in $[0, 1)$ and τ_{cross} is the crossover probability threshold. This threshold plays an important role in the exploration/exploitation balance in the algorithm, allowing to inherit the hidden nodes either from P_1 if $p \leq \tau_{cross}$ (more exploitation), or from P_2 if $p > \tau_{cross}$ (more exploration). In our experiments, we set $\tau_{cross} = 0.6$ to have a higher probability of inheriting the hidden nodes from the best individual in the sample (P_1), rather than from a random individual P_2. The remaining intermediate hidden nodes H_j^{off}, $min(B_1, B_2) < j \leq B_{temp}$, are then derived directly from the corresponding j-th node in the parent which has higher B. The edges of each hidden node in the offspring are inherited from the parent without modifications.

Mutation. The mutation operation is a key ingredient in the evolution process, as it allows the search to explore new areas of the search space but also refine the search around the current solutions. Apart from the *op mutation* and *hidden state mutation* introduced in [13], here we additionally introduce a specific mutation for tuning the number of hidden nodes B. The first step is the op mutation which requires a random choice to be made in order to select either the normal cell or the reduction cell C. Once selected, the mutation operation will select one of the B pairwise combinations (or hidden nodes) at random. From the chosen pairwise combination, one of the two ops is replaced, with a probability τ_{m-op}, by another op allowed in the search space. Following op mutation, hidden state mutation is performed which, akin to op mutation, also oversees random choice of cells, one of the B pairwise combinations and one of the two elements in a combination. However, hidden state mutation differs from op mutation in that it replaces (with probability τ_{m-edge}) the incoming hidden state or cell input, which corresponds to the chosen element, with another one that is inside C, instead of the op itself. It is important to notice that the new input is chosen from the previous hidden nodes or cell inputs to ensure the feed-forward nature of a cell. Finally, to encourage further exploration a third mutation allows to increment the parameter B of C by 1, with probability τ_b, such that a new node with index $B + 1$ is introduced with random weights, if $B < B_{max}$. It is to be noted that all unused states are concatenated at the end of the cell. Finally, the offspring individual is evaluated and added to the population.

Survivor Selection. The survivor selection is conducted at the end of each generation. It is crucial since it permits the removal of the worst solutions from the population and facilitates the convergence of the evolutionary search. In this phase, the selection and removal of the worst individuals is conducted according to a $\mu + \lambda$ selection scheme, where based on the symbols we have used so far $\mu = P$ is the population size and $\lambda = F$ is the number of generated offspring. Therefore, at each step F worst individuals are removed from the set of $P + F$ individuals, so that the parent population for the next generations has a fixed size of P individuals. It should be noted that, compared to other survivor selection schemes, this scheme is implicitly elitist (i.e., it always preserves the best individuals found so far) and also allows inter-generational competition between parents and offspring.

Stagnation Avoidance. To avoid premature convergence of the population to a local minimum we propose two stagnation avoidance mechanisms: *soft* and *hard* stagnation avoidance. When stagnation occurs (i.e., the best accuracy does not improve for more than A_{stag} generations, as detected in the method StagnationDetected() in Algorithm 1), the mutation probabilities τ_{m-op} and τ_{m-edge} are increased to $\tau_{m-op-avoid}$ and $\tau_{m-edge-avoid}$, respectively, where $\tau_{m-op-avoid}$ and $\tau_{m-edge-avoid}$ denote increased mutation probabilities (such that $\tau_{m-op-avoid} > \tau_{m-op}$ and $\tau_{m-edge-avoid} > \tau_{m-edge}$). The choice to increase τ_{m-op} and τ_{m-edge} is due to the fact that higher mutation probabilities, in general, allow a higher exploration of the search space. On the other hand, τ_b is not increased because the addition of more hidden nodes (which would likely follow from a higher mutation probability) would increase the complexity of the cell and does not alleviate stagnation. Finally, the hard stagnation avoidance is a brute force remedy to stagnation. Specifically, if soft stagnation avoidance fails, $P - 1$ worst solutions are replaced by $P - 1$ individuals with random cells, while retaining the best solution found so far.

4   Experiments Results

In this section we describe the datasets and report the experimental setup used in the evolutionary algorithm and network training. Finally, we report our experimental evaluation on the considered datasets.

4.1   Datasets

We conducted all our experiments on the well-known MNIST, USPS and SVHN datasets, all consisting of digits ranging from 0 to 9. MNIST and USPS are taken from U.S. Envelopes and consist of grayscale handwritten digits. The SVHN is a real-world dataset of coloured digits taken from Google Street View.

4.2   Experimental Setup

As mentioned in Sect. 2, our proposed method belongs to the category of neuro-evolutionary methods where the optimal network is searched by an evolutionary

---

Algorithm 1. Regularized Evolutionary Algorithm

$population \leftarrow \emptyset$, $softTried \leftarrow$ False, $g \leftarrow 1$
while $|population| < P$ **do**   ▷ Initialize population
   $individual.arch \leftarrow$ RandomArchitecture()
   $individual.accuracy \leftarrow$ TrainAndEval($individual.arch$)
   add $individual$ to $population$

while $g \leq G$ **do**   ▷ Evolve for G generations
   while $|population| < P + F$ **do**   ▷ Generate F offspring
      $sample \leftarrow \emptyset$ ▷ Parent candidates
      while $|sample| < S$ **do**
         $candidate \leftarrow$ randomly sampled $individual$ from $population$
         add $candidate$ to $sample$
      $P_1 \leftarrow$ highest accuracy individual in $sample$ ▷ Tournament selection
      $P_2 \leftarrow$ randomly selected individual in $sample$
      $offspring.arch \leftarrow$ Crossover(P_1, P_2)
      $offspring.arch \leftarrow$ Mutation($offspring.arch$)
      $offspring.accuracy \leftarrow$ TrainAndEval($offspring.arch$)
      add $offspring$ to $population$
   remove F worst individuals from $population$ ▷ $\mu + \lambda$ selection
   if StagnationDetected() **then**   ▷ Prevent Stagnation
      if $softTried$ **then**   ▷ Hard Stagnation Avoidance
         remove $P - 1$ worst individuals from $population$
         add $P - 1$ random individuals to $population$
      else   ▷ Soft Stagnation Avoidance
         $\tau_{m-op} \leftarrow \tau_{m-op-avoid}$, $\tau_{m-edge} \leftarrow \tau_{m-edge-avoid}$
         $softTried \leftarrow$ True
  $g \leftarrow g + 1$

---

algorithm while the weights of the networks are trained with gradient descent algorithm. Hence, we separately provide details about the chosen experimental setup for the evolutionary algorithm and the network architecture and training. For the experiments we used a Linux workstation equipped with a CPU Intel(R) Core(TM) i9-7940X and a TITAN Xp GPU. The lack of massive computation resource has led us to the following choice of parameters.

Evolutionary Algorithm. The experiments were conducted with $P = 10$, $F = 10$, $B_{min} = 2$, $B_{max} = 6$ and ran for $G = 200$ generations. A sample size $S = 2$ has been used to have a low selection pressure. For the crossover operation, $\tau_{cross} = 0.6$ was used to allow a higher probability of exploitation of the best solutions in the populations. Instead, in the mutation phase, the probabilities τ_{m-op}, τ_{m-edge} and τ_b were set to 0.4, 0.4 and 0.2, respectively, to allow both a moderate exploration of the search space without significantly increasing the complexity of the cells. Finally, the stagnation check has been enabled after 50 generations and the evolution is considered to be stagnating if the same best result (in terms of accuracy) is provided for at least $A_{stag} = 40$ generations. In that case, $\tau_{m-op-avoid}$ and $\tau_{m-edge-avoid}$ were both set to 0.6.

Network Architecture. The network architectures which conform to the over-all structure in Fig. 1a were trained during the experiments. Due to limited memory, the initial channels D in the normal cell was set to 24 and then subsequently multiplied by a factor $K = 2$ after each reduction cell, with a total of 3 normal cells and 2 reduction cells. During the search phase, each individual has been trained for 15 epochs with mini-batches of size 64 using an Adam optimizer having an initial learning rate of 1e-4 with exponential decay. Dropout layer with drop probability of 0.2 has been used in the final softmax classifier. To further reduce the computations, our cells take duplicated output states H_{prev} from the previous cell instead of H_{prev} and H_{prev-1}, thereby eliminating skip connections between cells unlike [8,13]. At the end of the search phase, when the final best individual has been retrieved by the evolutionary algorithm, a training has been performed with that best individual for 100 epochs with the same previous parameters but with an initial learning rate of 1e-3. Batch normalization layers were also inserted after each convolutional layer. Standard cross-entropy loss was used for training the networks.

4.3 Results

Since the exploration in the NASNet search space is time consuming and also memory intensive, the best cells were searched only using the MNIST dataset due to its small size and reduced complexity. This has led to the evolution of a best normal cell and a best reduction cell, which collectively form the best network, dubbed as *EvoA*. The second best network is called *EvoB*.

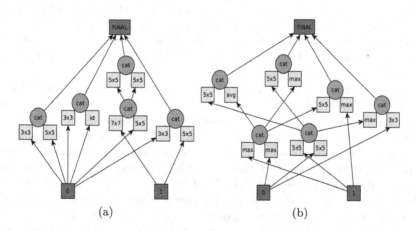

(a)   (b)

Fig. 2. Architecture of the best cells of EvoA found using MNIST: (a) Normal cell; (b) Reduction cell. The inputs "0" and "1" are the output states from the previous cells. The output "FINAL" is the concatenation operation resulting from the remaining hidden nodes inside the cell. The blocks in cyan represent a pairwise combination of operations and their concatenation. Note that the colour corresponds to Fig. 1b. (Color figure online)

To show the benefit of having variable B hidden nodes in a cell, we considered the following baselines: (i) EvoA, our best network with variable B; and (ii) EvoB, our second best network also with variable B; (iii) Model-A with $B = 3$; and (iv) Model-B with $B = 4$. As seen from Table 1, EvoA, the network found by our proposed method, outperforms all baselines which consider fixed B. This highlights the advantage of keeping B variable.

Table 1. Ablation study comparing the classification accuracy of our best evolved networks EvoA and EvoB with networks having fixed B hidden nodes inside cells.

Model	EvoA	EvoB	Model-A	Model-B
Hidden States	Variable	Variable	3	4
Final Accuracy	**99.59**	99.55	99.47	99.49

Table 2. Digits test set results for EvoA and EvoB when compared with baselines.

Model	MNIST		SVHN	
	# Parameters	Accuracy (%)	# Parameters	Accuracy (%)
ResNet18 [5]	11.18M	99.56	11.18M	92.00
DeepSwarm [23]	0.34M	99.53	0.34M	**93.15**
EvoB (ours)	0.21M	99.55	0.37M	91.56
EvoA (Ours)	0.22M	**99.59**	0.39M	91.80

In Fig. 2 the architectures of EvoA's internal cells, both normal and reduction, are presented. As it can be observed, normal cells in EvoA have $B = 5$ hidden nodes whereas the reduction cell has $B = 6$. While the input states "0" and "1" are duplicates of each other, unlike [8,13], we still observed good performance without using skip connections.

We have compared our method with the following baselines: (i) ResNet18 [5] and (ii) DeepSwarm [23], a NAS algorithm based on Ant Colony Optimization. Due to the lack of availability of code from our closest competitor [13], we re-implemented their aging-based evolution but the solutions never converged due to the small size of our population, caused by limited memory and GPU availability. This resonates the fact that [13] is feasible only when large compute resources are available. As seen from Table 2, EvoA outperforms all baselines on MNIST, with the lowest number of tunable parameters. Importantly, for the SVHN experiments we used an augmented architecture (with $N = 4$, $D = 32$ and each normal cell repeated thrice), composed of already evolved cells obtained from the search phase with MNIST. The network, despite not being evolved with SVHN, produced competitive results (slightly worse than ResNet18 and DeepSwarm).

Transfer Learning. We also investigated the transferability of the trained networks on unseen target data. In details, we trained EvoA and EvoB on MNIST and used the trained weights to classify USPS test images. As seen from Table 3, our EvoA and EvoB networks outperform all the baselines. Notably, while Deep-Swarm outperforms both EvoA and EvoB on SVHN (as seen in Table 2), it performs significantly worse when used for transfer learning. On the other hand, our networks achieve near target test accuracy on unseen data.

Table 3. Classification accuracy on USPS with networks trained only on MNIST.

Model	ResNet18 [5]	DeepSwarm [23]	EvoB (Ours)	EvoA (Ours)
Accuracy (%)	89.08	61.56	**96.72**	96.40

5   Conclusions

In this work we have addressed Neural Architecture Search through a Regularized Evolutionary Algorithm. The proposed algorithm is especially useful when limited memory and limited computational resources are at disposal. Our main contributions can be summarized as follows: (i) an evolving cell topology with variable number of hidden nodes; (ii) ad hoc crossover and mutation operators for improved exploration; and (iii) a novel stagnation avoidance for better convergence. We have conducted experiments on three different digits datasets and obtained competitive results. As a future work, we plan to scale our method to larger populations of individuals (parallelized on multiple GPUs) and test it on more complex datasets, also including videos.

Acknowledgments. We gratefully acknowledge the support of NVIDIA Corporation with the donation of the TITAN Xp GPU used for this research.

References

1. Krizhevsky, A., Sutskever, I., Hinton, G.E.: ImageNet classification with deep convolutional neural networks. In: NIPS (2012)
2. Roy, S., Siarohin, A., Sangineto, E., Bulò, S.R., Sebe, N., Ricci, E.: Unsupervised domain adaptation using feature-whitening and consensus loss. In: CVPR (2019)
3. Ren, S., He, K., Girshick, R., Sun, J.: Faster R-CNN: towards real-time object detection with region proposal networks. In: NIPS (2015)
4. He, K., Gkioxari, G., Dollr, P., Girshick, R.: Mask R-CNN. In: CVPR (2017)
5. He, K., Zhang, X., Ren, S., Sun, J.: Deep residual learning for image recognition. In: CVPR (2016)
6. Szegedy, C., Vanhoucke, V., Ioffe, S., Shlens, J., Wojna, Z.: Rethinking the inception architecture for computer vision. In: CVPR (2016)
7. Elsken, T., Metzen, J.H., Hutter, F.: Neural architecture search: a survey. JMLR (2019)
8. Zoph, B., Vasudevan, V., Shlens, J., Le, Q.V.: Learning transferable architectures for scalable image recognition. In: CVPR (2018)
9. Chen, L.C., et al.: Searching for efficient multi-scale architectures for dense image prediction. In: NIPS (2018)

10. Zoph, B., Le, Q.V.: Neural architecture search with reinforcement learning. In: ICLR (2017)
11. Bergstra, J., Yamins, D., Cox, D.D.: Making a science of model search: hyperparameter optimization in hundreds of dimensions for vision architectures. In: ICML (2013)
12. Domhan, T., Springenberg, J.T., Hutter, F.: Speeding up automatic hyperparameter optimization of deep neural networks by extrapolation of learning curves. In: AAAI (2015)
13. Real, E., Aggarwal, A., Huang, Y., Le, Q.V.: Regularized evolution for image classifier architecture search. In: AAAI (2019)
14. Stanley, K.O., Clune, J., Lehman, J., Miikkulainen, R.: Designing neural networks through neuroevolution. Nature Mach. Intell. (2019)
15. Goldberg, D.E., Deb, K.: A comparative analysis of selection schemes used in genetic algorithms. In: FOGA (1991)
16. Zhong, Z., Yan, J., Wu, W., Shao, J., Liu, C.L.: Practical block-wise neural network architecture generation. In: CVPR (2018)
17. Baker, B., Gupta, O., Naik, N., Raskar, R.: Designing neural network architectures using reinforcement learning. In: ICLR (2017)
18. Miller, G.F., Todd, P.M., Hegde, S.U.: Designing Neural Networks using Genetic Algorithms. In: ICGA (1989)
19. Angeline, P.J., Saunders, G.M., Pollack, J.B.: An evolutionary algorithm that constructs recurrent neural networks. IEEE Trans. Neural Netw. 5, 54–65 (1994)
20. Stanley, K.O., Miikkulainen, R.: Evolving neural networks through augmenting topologies. Evol. Comput. 10, 99–127 (2002)
21. Real, E., et al.: Large-scale evolution of image classifiers. In: ICML (2017)
22. Elsken, T., Metzen, J.H., Hutter, F.: Efficient multi-objective neural architecture search via lamarckian evolution. In: ICLR (2018)
23. Edvinas, B., Wei, P.: DeepSwarm: optimising convolutional neural networks using swarm intelligence. arXiv preprint arXiv:1905.07350 (2019)
24. Yaman, A., Mocanu, D.C., Iacca, G., Fletcher, G., Pechenizkiy, M.: Limited evaluation cooperative co-evolutionary differential evolution for large-scale neuroevolution. In: GECCO (2018)

Deep Learning

Manual Annotations on Depth Maps
for Human Pose Estimation

Andrea D'Eusanio, Stefano Pini, Guido Borghi$^{(\boxtimes)}$, Roberto Vezzani,
and Rita Cucchiara

Department of Engineering "Enzo Ferrari",
University of Modena and Reggio Emilia, Modena, Italy
{andrea.deusanio,s.pini,guido.borghi,roberto.vezzani,
rita.cucchiara}@unimore.it

Abstract. Few works tackle the *Human Pose Estimation* on depth maps. Moreover, these methods usually rely on automatically annotated datasets, and these annotations are often imprecise and unreliable, limiting the achievable accuracy using this data as ground truth. For this reason, in this paper we propose an annotation refinement tool of human poses, by means of body joints, and a novel set of fine joint annotations for the *Watch-n-Patch* dataset, which has been collected with the proposed tool. Furthermore, we present a fully-convolutional architecture that performs the body pose estimation directly on depth maps. The extensive evaluation shows that the proposed architecture outperforms the competitors in different training scenarios and is able to run in real-time.

Keywords: Human Pose Estimation · Depth maps · Body joints

1 Introduction

In recent years, the task of estimating the human pose has been widely explored in the computer vision community. Many deep learning-based algorithms that tackles the 2D human pose estimation have been proposed [5,19,22] along with a comprehensive set of annotated datasets, collected both in real world [1,8,11] or in simulations [7,17]. However, the majority of these works and data collections are based on standard intensity images (*i.e.* RGB and gray-level data) while datasets and algorithms based only on depth maps, *i.e.* images in which the value of each pixel represents the distance between the acquisition device and that point in the scene, have been less explored, even though this kind of data contains fine 3D information and it can be used in particular settings, like the automotive one [4,18], since depth maps are usually acquired through IR.

A milestone in the human pose estimation on depth maps is the work of Shotton *et al.* [15], based on the *Random Forest* algorithm, that has been implemented in both commercial versions of the *Microsoft Kinect SDK*. This real time

© Springer Nature Switzerland AG 2019
E. Ricci et al. (Eds.): ICIAP 2019, LNCS 11751, pp. 233–244, 2019.
https://doi.org/10.1007/978-3-030-30642-7_21

algorithm has been widely used to automatically produce body joints annotations in depth-based public datasets. However, these annotations have limited accuracy: in [15], the authors report a mean average precision of 0.655 on synthetic data with full rotations.

For these reasons, in this paper we present *Watch-R-Patch*, a novel refined set of annotations of the well-known *Watch-n-Patch* dataset [20], which contains annotations provided by Shotton *et al.* 's method [15].

Original wrong, imprecise, or missing body joints have been manually corrected for 20 training sequences and 20 testing sequences, equally split between the different scenarios of the dataset, *i.e. office* and *kitchen.*

Furthermore, we present a deep learning-based architecture, inspired by [5], that performs the human pose estimation on depth images only. The model is trained combining the original *Watch-n-Patch* dataset with the manually-refined annotations, obtaining remarkable results. Similar to [15], the proposed system achieves real time performance and can run at more than 180 fps.

2 Related Work

The majority of the literature regarding the Human Pose Estimation task is focused on intensity images [6,13,22]. In [19] a sequential architecture is proposed in order to learn implicit spatial models. Dense predictions, that corresponds to the final human body joints, are increasingly refined through different stage into the network model. The evolution of this method [5] introduces the concept of *Part Affinity Fields* that allows learning the links between the body parts of each subject present in the image.

Only a limited part of works is based on depth maps, *i.e.* images that provide information regarding the distance of the objects in the scene from the camera, One plausible limitation of depth-based methods is the lack of rich depth-based datasets which have been specifically collected for the human pose estimation task and contains manual body joint annotations. Indeed, available datasets are often small, both in terms of number of annotated frames and in terms of subjects. limiting their usability for the training of deep neural networks. In 2011, a method to quickly predict the positions of body joints from a single depth image was proposed in [15]. An object recognition approach is adopted, in order to shift the human pose estimation task in a per-pixel classification problem. The method is based on the random forest algorithm and on a wide annotated dataset, which has not been publicly released. A viewpoint invariant model for the human pose estimation was recently proposed in [9], in which a discriminant model embeds local regions into a particular feature space. This work is based on the *Invariant-Top View Dataset*, a dataset with frontal and top-view recordings of the subjects.

Recently, approaches performing the head detection directly on depth maps were proposed in [2,3]. In [3], a shallow deep neural network is exploited to classify depth patches as head or non-head in order to obtain an estimation of the head centre joint. The *Watch-n-Patch* dataset [20,21] has been collected for the unsupervised learning of relations and actions task. Its body joints annotation are obtained applying an off-the-shelf method [15], therefore they are not particularly accurate, in particular when subjects stand in a non-frontal position.

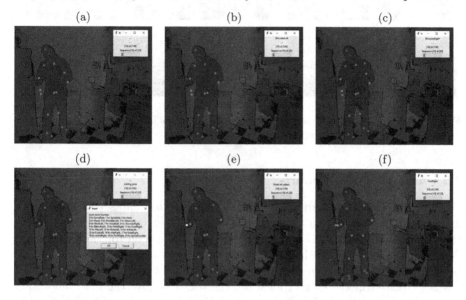

Fig. 1. Annotation tool overview. The tool initially shows the original joint locations (a). Then, each joint can be selected to view its name (b) or to move it in the correct location (c). Missing joints can be added in the right position (d) (e). Finally, the annotations (f) can be saved and the next sequence frame is shown.

3 Dataset

In this section, we firstly report an overview of the *Watch-n-Patch* dataset [20]. Then, we present the procedure we used to improve the original joint annotations and the statistics of the manually refined annotations which are referred as *Watch-R(efined)-Patch*. The dataset will be publicly available[1].

3.1 *Watch-n-Patch* Dataset

Watch-n-Patch [20] is a challenging RGB-D dataset acquired with the second version of the *Microsoft Kinect* sensor: differently from the first one, it is a *Time-of-Flight* depth device. The dataset contains recordings of 7 people performing 21 different kinds of actions. Each recording contains a single subject performing multiple actions in one room chosen between 8 offices and 5 kitchens.

The dataset contains 458 videos, corresponding to about 230 min and 78k frames. The authors provide both RGB and depth frames (with a spatial resolution of 1920 × 1080 and 512 × 424, respectively) and human body skeletons (composed of 25 body joints) estimated and tracked with the method proposed in [15].

---

[1] *Watch-R-Patch*: http://imagelab.ing.unimore.it/depthbodypose.

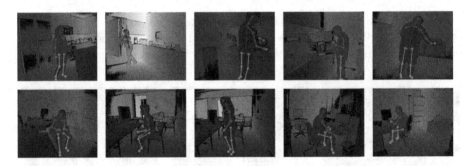

Fig. 2. *Watch-R-Patch* dataset overview. Kitchen and office sequences are shown in the first and second row, respectively.

3.2 Annotation Procedure

We collect refined annotations for the *Watch-n-Patch* dataset using a quick and easy-to-use annotation tool. In particular, we develop a system that shows the original body joints (*i.e.* the *Watch-n-Patch* joints) on top of the acquired depth image. The user is then able to move the incorrect joints in the proper positions using the mouse in a drag-and-drop fashion. Once every incorrect joint has been placed in the correct location, the user can save the new annotation and move to the next frame. It is worth noting that, in this way, the user has only to move the joints in the wrong position while already-correct joints do not have to be moved or inserted. Therefore, original correct joints are preserved, while improving wrongly-predicted joints. We have ignored finger joints (tip and thumb) since original annotations are not reliable and these joints are often occluded. An overview of the developed annotation tool is shown in Fig. 1. The annotation tool is publicly released[2].

3.3 Statistics

We manually annotate body joints in 20 sequences from the original training set and 20 sequences from the original testing set. Sequences are equally split between office and kitchen sequences. To speed up the annotation procedure and increase the scene variability, we decided to fine-annotate a frame every 3 frames in the original sequences. In some test sequences, every frame has been fine-annotated. The overall number of annotated frames is 3329, 1135 in the training set, 766 in the validation one, and 1428 in the testing one. We also propose an official validation set for the refined annotations, composed of a subset of the testing set, in order to standardize the validation and testing procedures.

For additional statistics regarding the annotated sequences and the proposed train, validation, and test splits, please refer to Table 1. A qualitative overview of the dataset is reported in Fig. 2.

---

[2] Annotation tool: https://github.com/aimagelab/human-pose-annotation-tool.

Table 1. Statistics of the *Watch-R-Patch* dataset.

Split	Sequences		Frames	Annotated	Modified	mAP
	Kitchen	Office		frames	joints (%)	
Train	data_02-28-33	data_01-50-09	3385	1135	0.757	0.574
	data_03-22-44	data_03-28-59				
	data_03-38-20	data_04-02-43				
	data_03-42-37	data_04-31-13				
	data_03-46-49	data_04-41-55				
	data_03-50-38	data_04-47-41				
	data_04-07-17	data_04-56-00				
	data_04-17-37	data_05-31-10				
	data_04-31-11	data_05-34-47				
	data_04-34-13	data_12-03-57				
Val	data_01-52-55	data_02-32-08	995	766	0.643	0.600
	data_03-53-06	data_02-50-20				
	data_04-52-02	data_03-25-32				
Test	data_02-10-35	data_03-04-16	2213	1428	0.555	0.610
	data_03-45-21	data_03-05-15				
	data_04-13-06	data_03-21-23				
	data_04-27-09	data_03-35-07				
	data_04-51-42	data_03-58-25				
	data_05-04-12	data_04-30-36				
	data_12-07-43	data_11-11-59				
Overall	–	–	6593	3329	0.644	0.595

4 Proposed Method

In the development of the human pose estimation architecture, we focus on both the performance (in terms of *mean Average Precision* (mAP)) and the speed (in terms of *frames per second* (fps)).

To guarantee high performance, we decided to develop a deep neural network derived from [5] while, to guarantee high fps, even on cheap hardware, we do not include the *Part Affinity Fields* section (for details about PAF, see [5]).

4.1 Network Architecture

An overview of the proposed architecture is shown in Fig. 3.

The first part of the architecture is composed of a VGG-like feature extraction block which comprises the first 10 layers of VGG-19 [16] and two layers that gradually reduce the number of feature maps to the desired value. In contrast to [5], we do not use ImageNet pre-trained weights and we train these layers

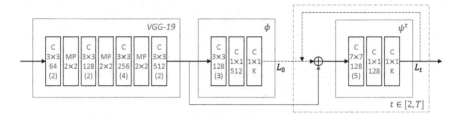

Fig. 3. Proposed architecture overview. Each block contains its type (C: convolution, MP: max pool), the kernel size, the number of feature maps, and the number of repetitions (if higher than 1). In our experiments, $K = 21$ and $T = 6$.

from scratch in conjunction with the rest of the architecture since the input is represented by depth maps in place of RGB images.

The feature extraction module is followed by a convolutional block that produces an initial coarse prediction of human body joints analyzing the image features extracted by the previous block only. The output of this part can be expressed as:

$$\mathbf{P}^1 = \phi(\mathbf{F}, \theta^1) \tag{1}$$

where $\mathbf{F}$ are the feature maps computed by the feature extraction module and ϕ is a parametric function that represents the first convolutional block of the architecture with parameters θ^1. Here, $\mathbf{P}^1 \in \mathbb{R}^{k \times w \times h}$.

Then, a multi-stage architecture is employed. A common convolutional block is sequentially repeated $T - 1$ times in order to gradually refine the body joint prediction. At each stage, this block analyzes the concatenation of the features extracted by the feature extraction module and the output of the previous stage, refining the earlier prediction. The output at each step can be represented with

$$\mathbf{P}^t = \psi^t(\mathbf{F} \oplus \mathbf{P}^{t-1}, \theta^t) \quad \forall t \in [2, T] \tag{2}$$

where $\mathbf{F}$ are the feature maps computed by the feature extraction module, $\mathbf{P}^{t-1}$ is the prediction of the previous block, $\oplus$ is the concatenation operation, and ψ^t is a parametric function that represents the repeated convolutional block of the architecture with parameters θ^t. As in the previous case, $\mathbf{P}^t \in \mathbb{R}^{k \times w \times h}$.

The model is implemented in the popular framework *Pytorch* [14]. Further details regarding the network architecture are reported in Fig. 3.

4.2   Training Procedure

The architecture is trained in an end-to-end manner applying the following objective function

$$L^t = \sum_{k=1}^{K} \alpha_k \cdot \sum_{\mathbf{p}} \|\mathbf{P}_k^t(\mathbf{p}) - \mathbf{H}_k(\mathbf{p})\|_2^2, \tag{3}$$

where K is the number of considered body joints, α_k is a binary mask with $\alpha_k = 0$ if the annotation of joint k is missing, t is the current stage, and $\mathbf{p} \in \mathbb{R}^2$ is the spatial location.

Here, $\mathbf{P}_k^t(\mathbf{p})$ represents the prediction at location $\mathbf{p}$ for joint k while $\mathbf{H}_k \in \mathbb{R}^{w \times h}$ is the ground-truth heatmap for joint k, defined as

$$\mathbf{H}_k(\mathbf{p}) = e^{-||\mathbf{p}-\mathbf{x}_k||_2^2 \cdot \sigma^{-2}} \tag{4}$$

where $\mathbf{p} \in \mathbb{R}^2$ is the location in the heatmap, $\mathbf{x}_k \in \mathbb{R}^2$ is the location of joint k, and σ is a parameter to control the Gaussian spread. We set $\sigma = 7$.

Therefore, the overall objective function can be expressed as $L = \sum_{t=1}^{T} L^t$ where T is the number of stages. In our experiments, $T = 6$.

As outlined in [5], applying the supervision at every stage of the network mitigates the *vanishing gradient* problem and, in conjunction with the sequential refining of the body joint prediction, leads to a faster and more effective training of the whole architecture.

The network is trained in two steps. In the first stage, the original body joint annotations of *Watch-n-Patch* are employed to train the whole architecture from scratch. It is worth noting that the *Watch-n-Patch* body joints are inferred by the *Kinect SDK* which makes use of a random forest-based algorithm [15].

In the second stage, the network is finetuned using the training set of the presented dataset. During this phase, we test different procedures. In the first tested procedure, the whole architecture is fine-tuned, in the second one the feature extraction block is frozen and not updated, while in the last procedure all the blocks but the last one are frozen and not updated.

During both training and finetuning, we apply data augmentation techniques and dropout regularization to improve the generalization capabilities of the model. In particular, we apply random horizontal flip, crop (extracting a portion of 488×400 from the original image with size 512×424), resize (to the crop dimension), and rotation (degrees in $[-4°, +4°]$). Dropout is applied between the first convolutional block and each repeated block.

In our experiments, we employ the *Adam* optimizer [10] with $\alpha = 0.9$, $\beta = 0.999$, and weight decay set to $1 \cdot 10^{-4}$. During the training phase, we use a learning rate of $1 \cdot 10^{-4}$ while, during the finetuning step, we use a learning rate of $1 \cdot 10^{-4}$ and apply the dropout regularization with dropout probability of 0.5.

5 Experimental Results

5.1 Evaluation Procedure

We adopt an evaluation procedure following what proposed for the COCO Keypoints Challenge on the COCO website [12].

In details, we employ the *mean Average Precision* (mAP) to assess the quality of the human pose estimations compared to the ground-truth positions. The mAP is defined as the mean of 10 Average Precision calculated with different *Object Keypoint Similarity* (OKS) thresholds:

Table 2. Comparison of the mAP reached by different methods computed on the *Watch-R-Patch* dataset. See Sect. 4 for further details.

	Shotton *et al.* [15]	Ours$_{orig}$	*Ours$_{last}$*	Ours$_{blk}$	**Ours**
AP$^{OKS=0.50}$	0.669	0.845	0.834	0.894	**0.901**
AP$^{OKS=0.75}$	0.618	0.763	0.758	0.837	**0.839**
mAP	0.610	0.729	0.726	0.792	**0.797**

$$\text{mAP} = \frac{1}{10} \sum_{i=1}^{10} \text{AP}^{OKS=0.45+0.05i} \tag{5}$$

The OKS is defined as

$$\text{OKS} = \frac{\sum_i^K [\delta(v_i > 0) \cdot \exp \frac{-d_i^2}{2s^2 k_i^2}]}{\sum_i^K [\delta(v_i > 0)]} \tag{6}$$

where d_i is the Euclidean distance between the ground-truth and the predicted location of the keypoint i, s is the area containing all the keypoints, and k_i is defined as $k_i = 2\sigma_i$. Finally, v_i is a visibility flag: $v_i = 0$ means that keypoint i is not labeled while $v_i = 1$ means that keypoint i is labeled.

The values of $\boldsymbol{\sigma}$ depend on the dimension of each joint of the human body. In particular, we use the following values: $\sigma_i = 0.107$ for the spine, the neck, the head, and the hip joints; $\sigma_i = 0.089$ for the ankle and the foot joints; $\sigma_i = 0.087$ for the knee joints; $\sigma_i = 0.079$ for the shoulder joints; $\sigma_i = 0.072$ for the elbow joints; $\sigma_i = 0.062$ for the wrist and the hand joints.

5.2 Results

Following the evaluation procedure described in Sect. 5.1, we perform extensive experimental evaluations in order to assess the quality of the proposed dataset and method. Results are reported in Table 2.

Firstly, we have assessed the accuracy obtained by our architecture after a training step employing the original *Watch-n-Patch* dataset. This experiment corresponds to Ours$_{orig}$ in Table 2. As expected, when trained on the Kinect annotations, our model is capable of learning to predict human body joints accordingly to the Shotton *et al.* 's method [15], reaching a remarkable mAP of 0.777 on the *Watch-n-Patch* testing set.

We also test the performance of the network employing our annotations as the ground-truth. In this case, our method reach a mAP of 0.729, outperforming the Shotton *et al.* 's method with an absolute margin of 0.119. It is worth noting that our method has been trained on the Kinect annotations only, but the overall performance on the manually-annotated sequences is considerably higher than the one of [15]. We argue that the proposed architecture has better generalization capabilities than the method proposed in [15], even if it has been trained on the

G.T.   Shotton *et al.* [15]   **Ours**

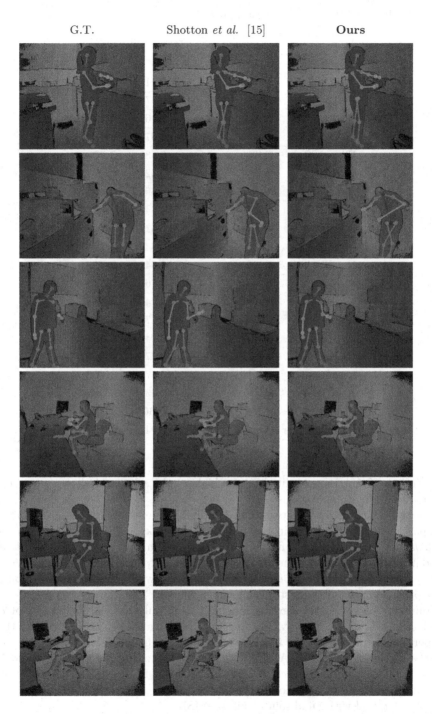

Fig. 4. Qualitative results obtained on the *Watch-R-Patch* dataset.

Table 3. mAP of each body joint present in the *Watch-R-Patch* dataset.

Joint	Shotton *et al.* [15]	Ours$_{orig}$	**Ours**
SpineBase	0.832	0.841	**0.905**
SpineMid	0.931	0.911	**0.935**
Neck	**0.981**	0.975	0.978
Head	**0.971**	0.961	0.962
ShoulderLeft	0.663	0.673	**0.819**
ElbowLeft	0.490	0.635	**0.772**
WristLeft	0.456	0.625	**0.677**
HandLeft	0.406	0.599	**0.680**
ShoulderRight	0.538	0.547	**0.782**
ElbowRight	0.454	0.618	**0.748**
WristRight	0.435	0.642	**0.727**
HandRight	0.412	0.641	**0.712**
HipLeft	0.646	0.766	**0.824**
KneeLeft	0.494	0.743	**0.788**
AnkleLeft	0.543	0.771	**0.800**
FootLeft	0.497	0.743	**0.801**
HipRight	0.696	0.778	**0.860**
KneeRight	0.493	0.670	**0.763**
AnkleRight	0.508	0.630	**0.648**
FootRight	0.388	**0.605**	0.605
SpineShoulder	**0.969**	0.942	0.955

predictions of [15], therefore it obtains a higher mAP when tested on scenes with actual body joint annotations.

Then, we report the results obtained applying different finetuning procedures. In particular, we firstly train the proposed network on the original *Watch-n-Patch* annotations then we finetune the model with the proposed annotations updating different parts of the architecture. In the experiment Ours$_{last}$, we freeze the parameters of all but the last repeated block, which means updating only the parameters θ^6 of the last convolutional block ψ^6. In Ours$_{blk}$, we freeze the parameters of the feature extraction block, *i.e.* only the parameters θ^t of ϕ and ψ^t are updated. Finally, we finetune updating the whole network in the experiment Ours. As shown in Table 2, finetuning the whole architecture leads to the highest $AP^{OKS=0.50}$, $AP^{OKS=0.75}$, and mAP scores. The proposed model, trained on the original *Watch-n-Patch* dataset and finetuned on the presented annotations, reaches a remarkable mAP of 0.797, outperforming the Shotton *et al.* 's method with an absolute gain of 0.187.

Finally, we report per-joint mAP scores in Table 3. As it can be observed, the proposed method outperforms the competitor and the baseline in nearly every joint prediction, confirming the capabilities and the quality of the model and the employed training procedure. Qualitative results are reported in (Fig. 4).

The model is able to run in real-time (5.37 ms, 186 fps) on a workstation equipped with an *Intel Core* i7-6850K and a GPU *Nvidia 1080 Ti*.

6 Conclusions

In this paper we have investigated the human pose estimation on depth maps. We have proposed a simple annotation refinement tool and a novel set of fine joint annotations for a representative subset of the *Watch-n-Patch* dataset, which we have published free-of-charge. We have presented a deep learning-based architecture that performs the human pose estimation by means of body joints, reaching state-of-the-art results on the challenging fine annotations of the *Watch-R-Patch* dataset. As future work, we plan to publicly release the annotation tool and to complete the annotation of the *Watch-n-Patch* dataset.

References

1. Andriluka, M., Pishchulin, L., Gehler, P., Schiele, B.: 2D human pose estimation: new benchmark and state of the art analysis. In: CVPR (2014)
2. Ballotta, D., Borghi, G., Vezzani, R., Cucchiara, R.: Fully convolutional network for head detection with depth images. In: 2018 24th International Conference on Pattern Recognition (ICPR), IEEE, pp. 752–757 (2018)
3. Ballotta, D., Borghi, G., Vezzani, R., Cucchiara, R.: Head detection with depth images in the wild. In: VISAPP (2018)
4. Borghi, G., Fabbri, M., Vezzani, R., Cucchiara, R., et al.: Face-from-depth for head pose estimation on depth images. IEEE Trans. Pattern Anal. Mach. Intell. (2018). https://doi.org/10.1109/TPAMI.2018.2885472, https://ieeexplore.ieee.org/document/8567956
5. Cao, Z., Simon, T., Wei, S.E., Sheikh, Y.: Realtime multi-person 2D pose estimation using part affinity fields. In: CVPR (2017)
6. Carreira, J., Agrawal, P., Fragkiadaki, K., Malik, J.: Human pose estimation with iterative error feedback. In: CVPR (2016)
7. Chen, W., et al.: Synthesizing training images for boosting human 3D pose estimation. In: International Conference on 3D Vision (3DV) (2016)
8. Güler, R.A., Neverova, N., Kokkinos, I.: Densepose: dense human pose estimation in the wild. In: CVPR (2018)
9. Haque, A., Peng, B., Luo, Z., Alahi, A., Yeung, S., Fei-Fei, L.: Towards viewpoint invariant 3D human pose estimation. In: Leibe, B., Matas, J., Sebe, N., Welling, M. (eds.) ECCV 2016. LNCS, vol. 9905, pp. 160–177. Springer, Cham (2016). https://doi.org/10.1007/978-3-319-46448-0_10
10. Kingma, D.P., Ba, J.: Adam: a method for stochastic optimization. arXiv preprint arXiv:1412.6980 (2014)
11. Lin, T.Y., et al.: Microsoft COCO: common objects in context. In: Fleet, D., Pajdla, T., Schiele, B., Tuytelaars, T. (eds.) ECCV 2014. LNCS, vol. 8693, pp. 740–755. Springer, Cham (2014). https://doi.org/10.1007/978-3-319-10602-1_48

12. COCO - Keypoint Evaluation. http://cocodataset.org/#keypoints-eval
13. Newell, A., Yang, K., Deng, J.: Stacked hourglass networks for human pose esti-mation. In: Leibe, B., Matas, J., Sebe, N., Welling, M. (eds.) ECCV 2016. LNCS, vol. 9912, pp. 483–499. Springer, Cham (2016). https://doi.org/10.1007/978-3-319-46484-8_29
14. Paszke, A., et al.: Automatic differentiation in PyTorch. In: NIPS Autodiff Work-shop (2017)
15. Shotton, J., et al.: Real-time human pose recognition in parts from single depth images. In: CVPR (2011)
16. Simonyan, K., Zisserman, A.: Very deep convolutional networks for large-scale image recognition. arXiv preprint arXiv:1409.1556 (2014)
17. Varol, G., et al.: Learning from synthetic humans. In: CVPR (2017)
18. Venturelli, M., Borghi, G., Vezzani, R., Cucchiara, R.: Deep head pose estimation from depth data for in-car automotive applications. In: International Workshop on Understanding Human Activities through 3D Sensors, pp. 74–85 (2016)
19. Wei, S.E., Ramakrishna, V., Kanade, T., Sheikh, Y.: Convolutional pose machines. In: CVPR (2016)
20. Wu, C., Zhang, J., Savarese, S., Saxena, A.: Watch-n-Patch: unsupervised under-standing of actions and relations. In: CVPR (2015)
21. Wu, C., Zhang, J., Sener, O., Selman, B., Savarese, S., Saxena, A.: Watch-n-Patch: unsupervised learning of actions and relations. IEEE Trans. Pattern Anal. Mach. Intell. **40**(2), 467–481 (2018)
22. Xiao, B., Wu, H., Wei, Y.: Simple baselines for human pose estimation and tracking. In: ECCV (2018)

Low-Complexity Scene Understanding Network

Livia Iordache[1]([✉]), Vlad Paunescu[1], Wonjun Kang[2], Joonhyung Kwon[2],
Andrei Leica[1], and ByeongMoon Jeon[2]

[1] Arnia Software, Bucharest, Romania
`livia.iordache@arnia.ro`
[2] Advanced Camera Laboratory, LG Electronics, Seoul, Korea

Abstract. Multi-task networks often rely on complex architectures in order to perceive and understand the driving scene. Computationally intensive networks achieve state of the art results at the cost of real-time inference on embedded devices. Our proposed unified solution obtains competitive results on multiple tasks, while targeting an embedded platform. We build upon our previous work of performing low-complexity object detection and bottom point prediction and add semantic and instance segmentation tasks while maintaining 19 FPS on the NVIDIA Jetson TX2 embedded platform. We find that sharing layers between task sub-networks is essential for achieving real-time inference. Due to the task similarity and correlation between object detection, bottom point prediction, semantic segmentation and instance segmentation we find that the individual task performance is not greatly impacted by the reduced computational capacity resulted from sharing layers amongst the task sub-networks.

Keywords: Low-complexity · Multi-task · Embedded

1 Introduction

Scene perception and understanding refers to multiple detection tasks regarding the driving scene such as object detection, free space detection, lane detection, traffic sign detection, semantic and instance segmentation. Dedicated, high complexity networks are employed for each of these tasks in order to achieve state of the art results. Recently, multi-task networks have been proposed to jointly predict multiple tasks in place of individual, specialized networks [16]. Using a single multi-task network reduces the computational burden and has the potential to achieve better performance than individual networks if the learned tasks are complementary [10].

In this paper we target an embedded architecture for use in autonomous driving systems – the NVIDIA Jetson TX2. Existing multi-task networks often rely on complex architectures that are unsuitable for embedded platforms due to their time and memory constraints. To achieve real-time inference on embedded

© Springer Nature Switzerland AG 2019
E. Ricci et al. (Eds.): ICIAP 2019, LNCS 11751, pp. 245–256, 2019.
https://doi.org/10.1007/978-3-030-30642-7_22

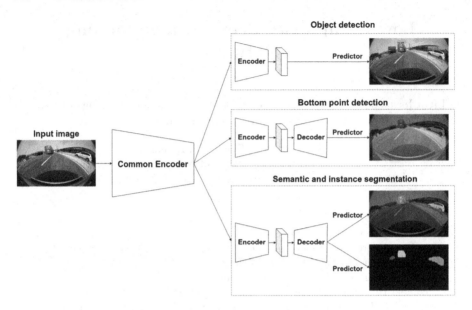

Fig. 1. Unified scene understanding network.

platforms, unified models of lower complexity are used. Our proposed architecture is a unified, low-complexity model that jointly performs in real-time 4 tasks – object detection, bottom point prediction, semantic segmentation and instance segmentation – achieving 19 FPS on the NVIDIA Jetson TX2 embedded platform. The chosen tasks construct the free drivable area around the car and identify the surrounding objects.

We leverage the object detection and bottom point prediction low-complexity network from our previous work [3] and add semantic and instance segmentation tasks to the unified network. The network is built so that the additional tasks do not add significant overhead to the inference time. The unified network reuses features by having a common encoder backbone which subsequently splits into individual task branches. Each branch further refines the features and predicts the branch task. The unified network is shown in Fig. 1.

To maximize the amount of information that we can infer from a scene, we construct a wide-angle dataset that contains images captured with a fisheye camera with 190° FOV. The wide FOV allows the camera to capture more information from the surrounding area of the car. The dataset is discussed in detail in Sect. 4.

In summary, our contributions in this paper are:

– We build on top of previous work and propose a low-complexity unified architecture that performs scene perception by jointly predicting 4 tasks: 5-class object detection, free space prediction through bottom point detection, semantic segmentation and instance segmentation.

- A unified network designed to share the computational burden and reuse the layers can achieve real-time inference on an embedded platform even when predicting 4 complex tasks.
- Our low-complexity unified network can achieve 19 FPS on the NVIDIA Jetson TX2 embedded platform.

2   Related Work

2.1   Object Detection

Object detection architectures can be divided into high-complexity, two-stage approaches and low-complexity, single-shot approaches. The two-stage methods first propose class-agnostic bounding boxes which are fed to the second stage where they are refined and assigned class probabilities. Among the two-stage approaches we mention state of the art PANet [13] that builds upon the Mask R-CNN [8] architecture by adding a top-down and bottom-up feature pyramid network (FPN) [12]. Two-stage architectures are computationally expensive and cannot be deployed on embedded devices. For platforms with limited resources, single-shot architectures are introduced in order to reduce both memory and resource requirements. SSD [14] is a single-shot architecture that predicts object bounding boxes with their associated class at multiple scales. Single-shot multi-scale architectures achieve better results than single-shot single-scale architectures by decorrelating the prediction of different object scales.

2.2   Free Space Detection

Free space detection delimits the free drivable area. The task can be formulated in terms of semantic segmentation, where the road class is predicted. The task can also be formulated as object bottom point prediction in which the objects include curb, sidewalk, and any obstacles so that the free space is defined as a space beneath those objects. The bottom point prediction refers to predicting the maximal height for each pixel along the image width, at which point an obstacle exists [2,3].

2.3   Semantic and Instance Segmentation

Semantic segmentation predicts a dense, per-pixel class association. Deeplabv3 [4] achieves state of the art segmentation results on the Cityscapes [6] dataset by using an FCN [15] to extract image features that are subsequently passed through an Atrous Spatial Pyramid Pooling (ASPP) module that applies parallel atrous convolutions with different rates in order to exploit the multi-scale contextual information. The image resolution is recovered from the downscaled feature map through bilinear upsampling. In Deeplabv3+ [5] the direct upsampling operation is replaced by a decoder module in which the resolution is gradually recovered. In order to obtain a sharper segmentation, the information from an earlier layer in the encoder is added to the decoder features. In our proposed model, we use a simplified version of the Deeplabv3+ decoder, in order to maintain a fast inference time.

Instance segmentation predicts a per-pixel instance association for each object instance in a scene. This task can be predicted alongside either semantic segmentation, since they are both per-pixel tasks, or alongside object detection, in an attempt to better separate object instances and better fit the enclosing bounding boxes. Mask R-CNN and PANet achieve state of the art results on the COCO dataset for the object detection and instance segmentation tasks. The instance segmentation prediction task is simplified using these architectures on account of the two-stage approach. For each predicted bounding box, a reduced-resolution mask is predicted per class. For two-stage approaches, the masks are computed on the ROIs, and thus the task is simplified since we can only have one instance in each ROI. In contrast, for single-stage methods, where we do not have ROIs, the network is required to predict the instance segmentation mask on the entire image. This task is arguably harder since the number of instances in an image is not known beforehand, and a convolutional network is unable to count. To bypass the counting problem, the task is often reformulated in two ways. One formulation is to predict per-pixel vectors that point towards the instance center [10]. The network predicts per-pixel vectors (2 dimensions) and extracts the final instances in the post-processing step using the OPTICS clustering algorithm [1]. Another formulation transforms the instance segmentation task into a semantic segmentation task, in which instances are colored [11]. The segmentation network assigns a constant number of labels – colors – to an unknown number of instances. The ground truth is assigned at training time and can be viewed as being part of the network loss.

2.4   Multi-task Networks

Task specific networks are employed in order to achieve state of the art results without resource limitations. Multi-task networks reuse features among multiple tasks so as to reduce the computational burden. Additionally, if the tasks learned are similar and the training procedure is adequate, multi-task networks can achieve better results than their independent counterparts [10].

Existing multi-task networks commonly predict a combination of object detection, semantic or instance segmentation and depth prediction. MultiNet [16] is a multi-task network that predicts vehicle object detection, road segmentation and street classification. In [10] the multi-task network predicts semantic segmentation, instance segmentation and depth prediction. We find that existing networks do not provide a complete view of the car's surroundings and the available drivable area. To this end, our proposed model predicts 5-class object detection (*car, bus, truck, pedestrian* and **-cycle*), bottom point prediction, semantic segmentation and instance segmentation.

3   Low-Complexity Unified Scene Understanding Network

Our proposed scene understanding model jointly predicts 4 tasks – object detection, bottom point prediction, semantic segmentation and instance segmentation, using a lightweight architecture suitable for embedded devices. We build on our previous work of low-complexity object detection and bottom point prediction and augment our unified network with semantic and instance segmentation tasks. Multi-task networks share the same architecture design: a common encoder where the features are reused by the tasks followed by individual encoder and decoder layers for each individual task. Branching out at later layers in the encoder allows the sub-networks to share the computation and reuse features, while branching out at earlier layers allows the networks to specialize.

In order to reduce the inference time, we share not only the common encoder between all tasks but for the segmentation tasks (semantic and instance) we also share the task-specific encoders and decoders, leaving only the predictors to be task specific. This architecture modification provides a significant gain in inference time at a small accuracy cost for the segmentation tasks. The common encoder used is MobileNetV1 [9] until the Conv5 layer. Through experiments, we have found that splitting at the Conv5 layer offered the best trade-off in terms of accuracy and inference time. Each task keeps an independent copy of the remaining encoder layers (Conv5-Conv11), except the segmentation tasks which share the entire encoder as well as the decoder. The task predictors are independent. In Fig. 1 we show our proposed unified model with its task specific predictions. We illustrate the object detection predictions with bounding boxes colored according to the predicted class. We use the same colors to overlay the semantic segmentation predictions with the input image. For bottom point visualization we color the free space area delimited by the predicted bottom points. For instance segmentation we show the final extracted object instances.

3.1   Object Detection

In order to achieve competitive results while maintaining a fast inference time, we adopt SSD as our object detection architecture, viewed independently in Fig. 2. We predict objects at 6 scales, starting from Conv11 at 1/16 downscaled resolution for the first scale. We add the remaining 5 layers on top of the encoder.

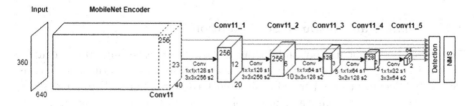

Fig. 2. Object detection network deploying SSD with MobileNetV1.

3.2   Bottom Point Prediction

We perform free space detection through predicting the obstacle bottom point for each pixel in the image width. The network can be viewed as a standard classification network on height (H) classes, where for each pixel in the image width we predict the height index of the obstacle bottom. The union of the bottom points for all the width columns would build either the curb or the free drivable area. In Fig. 3 the column-wise bottom point predictions are illustrated. Since the bottom point network predicts the height index at each column in the image width, the encoded features need to be decoded to the required image resolution. The network's final layer is the softmax classification layer that predicts the bottom height index for each column in the image width. After passing the image through the encoder, we recover the image resolution from the features through the depth-to-space operation as illustrated in Fig. 4. The depth-to-space operation reuses the channels in the feature maps to reconstruct the height and width of the image.

Fig. 3. Bottom point. Left: column-wise bottom prediction (red dot), Right: free space detection (red line). (Color figure online)

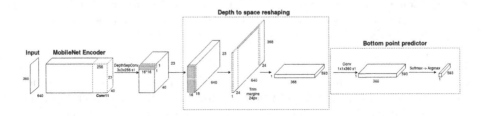

Fig. 4. Bottom point detection network deploying MobileNetV1.

3.3   Semantic and Instance Segmentation

The semantic segmentation and instance segmentation sub-networks can be viewed in Fig. 5. The segmentation sub-networks share the entire encoder, as well as the decoder to further reduce inference time. Similar to Deeplabv3+, we decode the features by bilinearly upsampling them from 1/16 to 1/8 downscaled resolution. In order to recover object boundaries we concatenate the features from a lower layer at the same resolution and apply a depthwise separable convolution in order to refine the features. The resulting features from the slim decoder are then passed to the semantic segmentation predictor. The resulting segmentation mask is further bilinearly upsampled to the input image resolution in order to compute the loss. The predictors for the semantic and instance segmentation are independent.

Following the vectors-to-center paradigm [10], we formulate our instance prediction task as predicting a per-pixel 2-D displacement vector, in which for each pixel in an instance we predict a 2-D vector pointing to the instance center of mass to which the pixel belongs. Adding the pixel coordinates to the predicted vector yield the instance center coordinates. For each instance I with its instance center of mass $C(x_{center}, y_{center})$, adding the instance pixel coordinates (x_i, y_i) to the predicted displacement vectors (dx_i, dy_i) yields C. These vectors can be visualized similar to an optical flow, where the color represents the vector orientation and the color opacity represents the vector magnitude. In Fig. 6, instance segmentation ground truths and predictions are illustrated.

On top of the shared decoded features we add a final instance segmentation predictor. The loss is computed on the input image resolution, using the bilinearly upsampled predictions. The instance segmentation predictions need to be post-processed in order to extract the object instances. We follow the same procedure as [10] and apply the OPTICS clustering algorithm. Figure 6 illustrates an example of extracted instances.

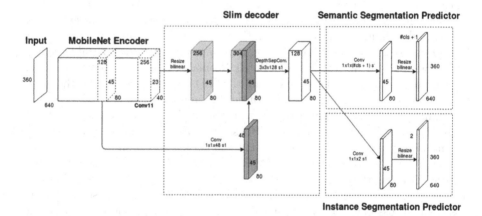

Fig. 5. Semantic and instance segmentation network deploying MobileNetV1 encoder and a slim decoder.

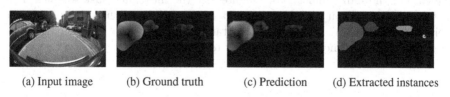

(a) Input image   (b) Ground truth   (c) Prediction   (d) Extracted instances

Fig. 6. Instance segmentation task.

4 Implementation

AVM Camera System. In order to maximize the available information in the input, we use an Around View Monitoring (AVM) system to construct our dataset. We use the same dataset as described in our previous work [3]. An AVM system represents a 4-camera setup with which a top-view, 360° view of a car's surroundings can be constructed. The 4 cameras are positioned around the car (front, rear and sides). Each camera is an HD fisheye camera with 190° FOV. We shall further refer to this dataset as the AVM dataset. The dataset is manually annotated for object detection and bottom point prediction. We use a high-complexity instance segmentation network in order to extract ground truth for the semantic and instance segmentation tasks. We use a pre-trained Mask R-CNN [8] model and only train the object detection sub-network on the AVM dataset, keeping the instance segmentation sub-network freezed. We find that the predicted masks are high quality and can be used as ground truth to train a low-complexity segmentation network. The dataset statistics can be found in Table 1.

Network Details. Our unified network receives as input a single RGB, front-facing AVM image of size 640 × 360. We resize our AVM 720p high resolution images to 640 × 360 in order to reduce inference time. We use MobileNetV1 encoder with depth multiplier 0.5 as the network backbone. All layers in the shared and individual encoders are initialized with pre-trained weights on the COCO dataset. Unless otherwise specified, we use depthwise separable convolutions with ReLU activations and Batch Normalization. The object detection branch predicts objects at 6 scales using the SSD architecture. We set the minimum bounding box scale to be 0.06 with the maximum 0.95 for our AVM dataset. The minimum value is specific to our dataset, being the smallest scale of an object in the dataset. We use the standard SSD settings for the remaining parameters. The network predicts the box localization and class association between the box and the 5 classes present in the AVM dataset (*car, bus, truck, pedestrian* and **-cycle*). We use the standard SSD losses. For bottom point classification and semantic segmentation we use the cross-entropy loss. The instance segmentation loss is an L1 loss between the predicted displacement vector and the labels. The segmentation losses are computed on the input resolution, between the ground truth and the bilinearly upsampled predictors. The total loss is computed as the sum of the individual losses, weighted by the individual task weights. The instance segmentation task has a weight of $\lambda = 0.1$ with the others having a weight of $\lambda = 1$. The instance segmentation task is learned the slowest and should be allowed time to achieve better results.

Table 1. Dataset statistics: number of objects in class.

Split	Class				
	car	bus	truck	pedestrian	*-cycle
Train	5948	669	858	1130	320
Test	1132	271	414	121	50

Table 2. Unified architecture ablation experiments.

Architecture	Car AP	Bus AP	Truck AP	Pedestrian AP	*-cycle AP	mAP	Bottom MAE	SEM[1] mIOU	IS[2] MAE	TX2 inference time (ms)
Unified independent decoders	0.71	0.68	0.39	0.32	0.45	0.51	3.31	0.63	0.57	107.33
Unified shared decoder	0.71	0.7	0.36	0.26	0.54	0.51	3.09	0.63	0.60	79.3
Unified shared decoder (slim)	0.72	0.71	0.33	0.26	0.49	0.5	3.15	0.62	0.65	51.46

[1] SEM: Semantic segmentation
[2] IS: Instance segmentation

5 Experiments

Metrics. For the object detection task we use the Pascal VOC mean average precision (mAP) metric at 0.5 intersection over union (IOU). For bottom prediction and instance segmentation we use the mean absolute error (MAE) and for semantic segmentation we use the mean IOU (mIOU).

AVM Experiments. The AVM training dataset consists of front-facing fisheye RGB images. The network is trained for 100 000 iterations with a batch size of 8, using the ADAM optimizer with an initial learning rate of 7e-4. The learning rate is decayed every 15 000 iterations with a 0.5 decay factor. The network is initialized with COCO weights. We use random cropping, horizontal flipping and color distortion (brightness, contrast, hue, saturation) in order to augment our data. We have experimented with the complexity of our unified architecture and the trade-off between accuracy and inference time. To this end we report results for independent decoders for the semantic and instance segmentation branches, a shared decoder and a final slim shared decoder in Table 2. When the decoders are independent between the two tasks, the specialized encoder features from Conv5 to Conv11 are also independent. The non-slim variant of the decoder follows the Deeplabv3+ architecture. By sharing the decoder between the semantic segmentation and instance segmentation we can gain significant speed-up at no significant cost to the model performance. The semantic segmentation branch seems largely unaffected by the shared decoder, while the instance segmentation accuracy seems to be impacted by this. We report instance segmentation MAE in terms of the predicted displacement vectors, without taking into account the OPTICS post-processed instances. The object detection and bottom prediction

Table 3. Component inference time.

Component					TX2 inference time (ms)	TX2 FPS
Shared encoder (Conv0-Conv5)	OD	Bottom	Semantic segmentation	Instance segmentation		
✓					18.44	54
✓	✓				31.8	31
✓	✓	✓			40.38	25
✓	✓	✓	✓		50.92	20
✓	✓	✓	✓	✓	51.46	19

Fig. 7. Bottom point prediction on the KITTI dataset.

tasks achieve similar results between the three variants. We choose the third, slim variant as our subsequent unified model, that is able to achieve competitive results for 4 tasks – object detection, bottom point prediction, semantic segmentation and instance segmentation – in 19 FPS on the NVIDIA Jetson TX2 embedded platform.

For timing the inference we do not include OPTICS post-processing overhead. We test the inference time of the models using TensorFlow 1.7 on the NVIDIA Jetson TX2 embedded platform, with the 3.3 JetPack with CUDA 9.0 and cuDNN 7.0. We perform component ablation tests in Table 3 in order to quantify each component's impact on the model inference time. A majority of the total inference time is spent in the shared network encoder (18 ms), with each component adding additional inference time. In our proposed model we prioritized our object detection and bottom tasks and chose to limit the inference time through the semantic and instance segmentation branches. The segmentation branches add only 11 ms inference time on top of the remaining architecture, providing relevant information at a small overhead.

KITTI Experiments. We perform additional experiments on the KITTI [7] open dataset. We use a padded resolution of 1242 × 376 in order to jointly train on all tasks. We train the object detection, semantic and instance segmentation tasks only on the evaluated classes in KITTI. The bottom prediction ground truths are extracted from the road segmentation ground truths, by finding the top point in the segmentation contour for each column in the image width. The network is

Table 4. Unified architecture trained on the KITTI dataset.

Car AP	Pedestrian AP	Cyclist AP	mAP	Bottom MAE	SEM[1]mIOU	IS[2]MAE
0.86	0.5	0.51	0.62	4.25	0.45	2.43

[1]SEM: Semantic segmentation
[2]IS: Instance segmentation

Table 5. KITTI object detection test set evaluation.

Class	Easy	Moderate	Hard
Car	69.65%	61.26%	55.57%
Pedestrian	38.44%	31.66%	29.58%
Cyclist	34.27%	25.80%	23.71%

trained for 40 000 iterations with a batch size of 8, using the ADAM optimizer with an initial learning rate of 1e-3, decayed every 10 000 iterations with a 0.5 decay factor. The network is initialized with Cityscapes weights. We use centered random cropping, horizontal flipping and color distortion in order to augment our data. We first report the KITTI results using the AVM evaluation metrics described previously. We randomly split the train set into a train and validation set with an 80/20 split. In Table 4 we report the results on the validation set. The object detection task was trained on approximately 6 000 images and obtains competitive results. The semantic and instance segmentation tasks perform poorly due in part to the small dataset with many classes, and in part due to the low-complexity segmentation branches. The bottom task is able to achieve good performance despite the small training dataset. The bottom results can be visualized in Fig. 7. The MAE for the bottom task is dependent on the image resolution, and as such the KITTI bottom MAE cannot be directly compared to the AVM bottom MAE performance. For comparison purposes we present the KITTI test set evaluations for object detection in Table 5. The results are competitive with respect to the network inference time. The low-complexity segmentation network requires sufficient data in order to learn a valuable representation, as such the results for the semantic and instance segmentation tasks on the KITTI dataset are bad. When the dataset is sufficiently large as in the AVM dataset, the tasks learn a useful representation. We do not report the bottom point results due to the task incompatibility with the road segmentation evaluation.

6   Conclusions

In this paper we have proposed a low-complexity unified architecture that jointly predicts in real-time 4 complex tasks –5-class object detection, bottom point detection, semantic segmentation and instance segmentation– achieving 19 FPS on the NVIDIA Jetson TX2 embedded platform. The flexibility and modularity of our model allows for future improvements to each individual task, as well as the possibility of adding additional tasks.

References

1. Ankerst, M., Breunig, M.M., Kriegel, H.P., Sander, J.: Optics: ordering points to identify the clustering structure. In: ACM SIGMOD Record, vol. 28, pp. 49–60 (1999)
2. Badino, H., Franke, U., Pfeiffer, D.: The stixel world - a compact medium level representation of the 3D-world. In: Denzler, J., Notni, G., Süße, H. (eds.) DAGM 2009. LNCS, vol. 5748, pp. 51–60. Springer, Heidelberg (2009). https://doi.org/10.1007/978-3-642-03798-6_6
3. Baek, J.Y., et al.: Scene understanding networks for autonomous driving based on around view monitoring system. In: 2018 IEEE/CVF Conference on Computer Vision and Pattern Recognition (CVPR), pp. 1013–1020. IEEE (2018)
4. Chen, L., Papandreou, G., Schroff, F., Adam, H.: Rethinking atrous convolution for semantic image segmentation. CoRR abs/1706.05587 (2017). http://arxiv.org/abs/1706.05587
5. Chen, L.C., Zhu, Y., Papandreou, G., Schroff, F., Adam, H.: Encoder-decoder with atrous separable convolution for semantic image segmentation. arXiv preprint arXiv:1802.02611 (2018)
6. Cordts, M., et al.: The cityscapes dataset for semantic urban scene understanding. In: Proceedings of the IEEE Conference on Computer Vision and Pattern Recognition, pp. 3213–3223 (2016)
7. Geiger, A., Lenz, P., Urtasun, R.: Are we ready for autonomous driving? The KITTI vision benchmark suite. In: Conference on Computer Vision and Pattern Recognition (CVPR) (2012)
8. He, K., Gkioxari, G., Dollár, P., Girshick, R.: Mask R-CNN. In: 2017 IEEE International Conference on Computer Vision (ICCV), pp. 2980–2988. IEEE (2017)
9. Howard, A.G., et al.: Mobilenets: efficient convolutional neural networks for mobile vision applications. arXiv preprint arXiv:1704.04861 (2017)
10. Kendall, A., Gal, Y., Cipolla, R.: Multi-task learning using uncertainty to weigh losses for scene geometry and semantics. arXiv preprint arXiv:1705.07115 (2017)
11. Kulikov, V., Yurchenko, V., Lempitsky, V.: Instance segmentation by deep coloring. arXiv preprint arXiv:1807.10007 (2018)
12. Lin, T.Y., Dollár, P., Girshick, R., He, K., Hariharan, B., Belongie, S.: Feature pyramid networks for object detection. In: Proceedings of the IEEE Conference on Computer Vision and Pattern Recognition, pp. 2117–2125 (2017)
13. Liu, S., Qi, L., Qin, H., Shi, J., Jia, J.: Path aggregation network for instance segmentation. In: Proceedings of the IEEE Conference on Computer Vision and Pattern Recognition, pp. 8759–8768 (2018)
14. Liu, W., et al.: SSD: single shot multibox detector. In: Leibe, B., Matas, J., Sebe, N., Welling, M. (eds.) ECCV 2016. LNCS, vol. 9905, pp. 21–37. Springer, Cham (2016). https://doi.org/10.1007/978-3-319-46448-0_2
15. Long, J., Shelhamer, E., Darrell, T.: Fully convolutional networks for semantic segmentation. In: Proceedings of the IEEE Conference on Computer Vision and Pattern Recognition, pp. 3431–3440 (2015)
16. Teichmann, M., Weber, M., Zoellner, M., Cipolla, R., Urtasun, R.: Multinet: real-time joint semantic reasoning for autonomous driving. In: 2018 IEEE Intelligent Vehicles Symposium (IV), pp. 1013–1020. IEEE (2018)

Image Anomaly Detection with Capsule Networks and Imbalanced Datasets

Claudio Piciarelli[(✉)] [iD], Pankaj Mishra [iD], and Gian Luca Foresti [iD]

University of Udine, via delle Scienze 206, 33100 Udine, Italy
{claudio.piciarelli,gianluca.foresti}@uniud.it,
mishra.pankaj@spes.uniud.it

Abstract. Image anomaly detection consists in finding images with anomalous, unusual patterns with respect to a set of normal data. Anomaly detection can be applied to several fields and has numerous practical applications, e.g. in industrial inspection, medical imaging, security enforcement, etc. However, anomaly detection techniques often still rely on traditional approaches such as one-class Support Vector Machines, while the topic has not been fully developed yet in the context of modern deep learning approaches. In this paper we propose an image anomaly detection system based on capsule networks under the assumption that anomalous data are available for training but their amount is scarce.

Keywords: Anomaly detection · Deep learning · Capsule networks · Imbalanced datasets

1 Introduction

Anomaly detection has always been a challenging problem in the field of machine learning. It consists in identifying anomalies within datasets, where an anomaly is anything that significantly differs from the majority of the data. Anomaly detection is thus achieved by building a model of "normality" and then comparing any subsequent data with that model.

The topic has many potential application fields, such as identification of defective product parts in industrial vision applications [13], fault-prevention in industrial sensing systems [8], detection of anomalous network activity in intrusion detection systems [1], medical image analysis for tumor detection [3], traffic analysis [17], structural integrity check in hazardous or inaccessible environments [16] and many more.

Many classical machine learning techniques have been adopted to identify anomalies in data [7], such as Bayesian networks, rule-based systems, clustering algorithms, statistical analysis, etc. One of the most popular approaches relies on

This work is partially supported by beanTech s.r.l. and by the Italian Ministry of Defense project 171/2016 RA^{2}M.

© Springer Nature Switzerland AG 2019
E. Ricci et al. (Eds.): ICIAP 2019, LNCS 11751, pp. 257–267, 2019.
https://doi.org/10.1007/978-3-030-30642-7_23

Support Vector Machines and in particular on their one-class variant, in which the standard SVM technique is used to split the feature space in two parts, one with high-density data (the normal class) and the other with outliers. Despite this huge interest of the research community on anomaly detection, the topic has not been fully developed in the context of modern deep learning. In this field (which we will call from now on *deep anomaly detection*), relatively few works have been published, mostly relying on reconstruction-based or generative-based approaches. The aim of this paper is to investigate the use of deep learning techniques for image anomaly detection: the task is to search for those images that are visually different from a reference group. In particular, we will focus on a recent evolution of deep learning techniques, the so-called capsule networks [19], to check if they could fit image anomaly detection tasks.

Anomaly detection techniques can be roughly classified in three main groups depending on the availability of data and labels: fully-supervised, semi-supervised and unsupervised [7]. In the *fully-supervised* case, it is assumed that both normal and anomalous data are available for training, and the problem reduces to a standard classification task. In this case, the main difference between anomaly detection and other classification problems is the imbalanced nature of the dataset: anomalies may be available for training, but their amount is by definition much smaller than normal data. In the *semi-supervised* case only normal data is labeled and available for training, and the goal is to classify new data as either normal or anomalous—this is why this approach is often called "novelty detection". Finally, the *unsupervised* case (also called "outlier detection") is similar to a clustering problem: no labels are given for the training set, which could potentially contain both normal and anomalous data, and the goal is to identify the normal cluster while leaving out the outliers. In this paper we will focus on the fully-supervised approach, and a capsule network will be used as regular classifier on imbalanced data.

The paper is organized as follows: in Sect. 2 we give an overview of the most recent works in the field of deep anomaly detection. Section 3 describes our capsule-based architecture and how it has been adapted to the task of anomaly detection. Finally, in Sect. 4 we provide experimental results on several datasets to show the effectiveness of the proposed method.

2   Related Works

As mentioned in Sect. 1, anomaly detection has been widely studied in the field of classical machine learning. Chandola et al. [7] give an excellent survey on the topic, highlighting the different types of anomalies, application fields, and possible non-deep approaches. From a deep learning point of view, the topic has been less extensively covered. Kiran et al. published a survey on this topic, but it is exclusively focused on anomaly detection in videos [14].

The fully-supervised approach is generally addressed with generic techniques for handling imbalanced data, such as undersampling the dominant class or oversampling the smaller class either by data duplication or by synthetic generation of new data. In both cases the idea is to use a pre-processing step to make the dataset balanced before applying any classification algorithm [4]. A recent work proposes to use extra datasets as a source of anomalies to improve the detection of the normal class by means of a process called outlier exposure [10].

Regarding semi-supervised or unsupervised approaches, early works adopted techniques such as Deep Belief Networks [21] for medical diagnosis on EEG waveforms or Restricted Boltzmann Machines [12] for network traffic analysis. More recently, hybrid approaches have been proposed in which deep architectures are used together with ideas from classical machine learning: for example Ruff et al. [18] propose the Deep Support Vector Data Description method, in which a deep neural network is trained under the same constraints adopted by one-class Support Vector Machines. However, the majority of the proposed works currently rely either on deep autoencoders or generative models.

Autoencoders are neural networks in which the differences between the output and the input are minimized: the ideal autoencoder thus is an identity function. However, autoencoders are implemented as a concatenation of an encoder and a decoder with an intermediate bottleneck, a low-dimension layer in which the original data are compressed. If the decoder part can reconstruct the original input, then the latent representation in the bottleneck captures all the relevant features of the original data. Despite autoencoders have been initially developed for dimensionality reduction tasks, they can be adapted to anomaly detection problems: if an autoencoder is trained on the normal class, it will learn how to represent its main features in its latent space. When an anomalous input is fed in the network, it is assumed it cannot be properly represented in the latent space, and thus the decoder reconstruction will be poor [5, 6, 23].

The other main approach is based on generative models, and in particular on generative adversarial networks (GAN). GAN are based on two competing networks: a generator, trying to create new data similar to the training ones, and a discriminator, trying to discern original data from the generated ones. The competition between the two networks leads the generator to learn how to create novel data which are similar to the training ones. This way, if trained on normal data, the generator learns a "normality model" much like autoencoders do. If the generator is inverted, a comparison on the latent representations of normal and anomalous data can be used to detect anomalies [2, 11, 20].

3   System Description

In this work we address the anomaly detection problem as a fully-supervised classification with highly imbalanced datasets. The model we adopted is a capsule network, in particular we rely on the CapsNet architecture proposed by Hinton in [19]. The rationale behind this choice is that capsule networks proved to be excellent classifiers thanks to their equivariance and spatial coherence properties, thus we want to investigate if anomaly detection problems could benefit from this architecture.

The original network has been developed to recognize MNIST digits and consists of two main parts: an encoder, converting an input image into 10 vectors

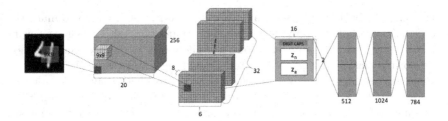

Fig. 1. The CapsNet architecture adopted in this work.

of instantiation parameters (digit caps), and a decoder, which reconstructs the original input. The network is trained in order to maximize the vector length of the correct digit caps and to minimize the decoder reconstruction loss. Although the decoder is not strictly necessary, it is used to force the digit caps to learn meaningful instantiation parameters describing visual properties of the digits. The main components of the network are:

- **Convolution:** It is a traditional convolutional layer. The aim is to extract basic features from the image. The network uses 256 kernels of size 9×9 with ReLU output.
- **PrimaryCaps:** This layer is similar to the convolution layer, and it outputs 1152 feature vectors in $\mathbb{R}^8$. These vectors are fed to a squash function, which preserves their orientation and normalizes the length in the range $[0, 1]$.
- **Routing by Agreement:** Routing by agreement is somewhat similar to max pooling. It decides what information to send to the next level. In this method each capsule tries to predict the next layer's activations based on its length and orientation.
- **DigitCaps:** After routing by agreement, 10 digit caps are obtained. These squashed vectors in $\mathbb{R}^{16}$ represent the instantiation parameters of each digit class. The vector length is proportional to the probability of the input belonging to a specific class, while its orientation represents the "pose", this is the specific instance of a digit among the many possible appearances for the same digit.
- **Reconstruction:** The reconstruction part takes the longest digit caps vector and uses three fully connected layers to reconstruct the input image.

In our implementation, we adopt the CapsNet architecture to perform fully-supervised anomaly detection, and thus we reduced the number of digit caps to 2: one representing the normal class, and the other representing the anomaly class, as shown in Fig. 1. However, in Sect. 4 we will show that this basic network has extremely poor performances when the dataset is highly imbalanced. In order to deal with the class imbalance, we adopted two anomaly measures: reconstruction loss and vector length difference.

Reconstruction loss r_l is a MSE loss computed on the difference between original and reconstructed image. We force the decoder network to be trained only on normal data and using the output of the normal digit caps. This way, the network will be able to reconstruct correctly only normal data, and it will behave poorly on anomalous data. This is the same technique adopted by nearly all the autoencoder-based methods described in Sect. 2.

Vector length difference uses the length of digit caps vectors as a measure of anomaly. Let z_n and z_a the two output vectors for normal and anomaly classes. Recall that, in CapsNet, these vector lengths are forced to assume values in the range $[0, 1]$, where higher values denote a better detection confidence. Using the standard CapsNet approach, an image is classified as anomaly if $\|z_a\| > \|z_n\|$, but this approach does not give good results on imbalanced datasets. With imbalanced datasets we noticed that the system behaves as expected on the dominant class ($\|z_n\| \approx 1, \|z_a\| \approx 0$), while on anomalous data the difference between the two vectors lengths is typically smaller. For example, $\|z_n\| = 0.8, \|z_a\| = 0.6$ is a strong hint that the sample is anomalous, even though it would be classified as normal from a standard CapsNet. We thus propose to use $\|z_a\| - \|z_n\|$ as anomaly score.

The final anomaly score AS is a combination of the two measures:

$$AS = \|z_a\| - \|z_n\| + r_l \tag{1}$$

with $\|z_a\|, \|z_n\|, r_l \in [0, 1]$. The ROC curve in Fig. 2 shows that the combination of the two anomaly measures leads to better results than using only one of the two. Once computed the anomaly score on the training data, it is fed into a logistic regressor to find the optimal threshold separating normal from anomalous data. The threshold can later be used to classify new data based on their anomaly score (see Fig. 3).

4   Results

Following a popular approach in deep anomaly detection works, the proposed method has been evaluated on the MNIST dataset [15]. We also considered two similar datasets, namely Fashion-MNIST [22] and Kuzushiji-MNIST [9]. Each dataset has 10 classes, respectively representing digits, clothing and ancient Japanese characters. Training has been performed by iterating the following schema over all classes:

1. Choose a class as the normal class
2. The training dataset contains all the training images of the chosen class plus some training images randomly picked from the other classes. The amount of training anomalies is either 10% or 1%
3. Train the network and compute the anomaly score threshold
4. Test the system on the whole test dataset

Note that the test dataset is not imbalanced, this avoids biased accuracy results. Table 1 shows the training hyperparameters.

MNIST Dataset: For the MNIST dataset the network is trained on $28 \times 28 \times 1$ MNIST digit images. The images have been standardized with mean 0.1307 and

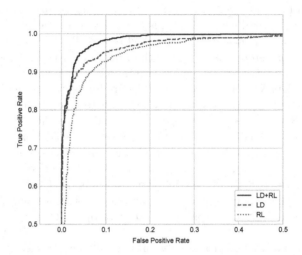

Fig. 2. ROC curve for three anomaly detection measures: vector length difference, reconstruction loss, and vector length difference + reconstruction loss.

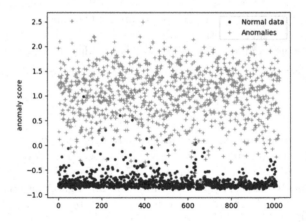

Fig. 3. Anomaly scores on test data, training done with 10% anomalies. Logistic regression threshold: −0.09.

Table 1. Training hyperparameters

Adam learning rate	0.001
% of anomalies in training data	1%–10%
Batch size	32
Epochs	10

std. deviation 0.3081. Table 2 shows the achieved results with a standard Cap-sNet and with the proposed approach, in the cases of 10% and 1% of anomalies in the training set. As it can be seen, the standard CapsNet approach fails when the dataset is extremely imbalanced: when anomalies are 1% of the training dataset, the standard CapsNet has an average accuracy of 51.44%, which is very close to a random guess. On the other hand, the proposed system keeps a high accuracy even with imbalanced training data (accuracy is on average 98.84% and 96.46% for the 10% and 1% anomaly cases respectively). Figure 4 shows the reconstructed images for both normal and anomalous data. The figure confirms that reconstruction is poor on anomalies, thus motivating the use of reconstruction error in the anomaly score definition.

Table 2. Accuracy % on MNIST dataset for standard CapsNet and the proposed method. The amount of anomalies in the training data is 10% (top rows) or 1% (bottom rows).

	0	1	2	3	4	5	6	7	8	9	avg
Standard, 10% an.	97.46	98.78	97.02	92.87	96.36	93.42	96.87	96.83	95.50	92.13	95.72
Proposed, 10% an.	**99.50**	**99.27**	**99.22**	**99.21**	**99.10**	**98.33**	**98.74**	**98.05**	**99.00**	**97.93**	**98.84**
Standard, 1% an.	48.90	73.58	50.00	49.66	48.95	46.56	48.34	50.00	48.75	49.63	51.44
Proposed, 1% an.	**99.20**	**98.24**	**98.19**	**95.48**	**94.37**	**95.46**	**98.34**	**97.07**	**97.85**	**90.41**	**96.46**

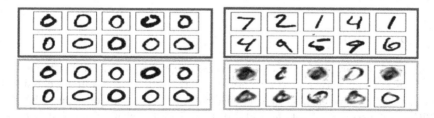

Fig. 4. Top rows: normal (left) and anomalous (right) samples from the MNIST test set. Bottom rows: the reconstructed images.

Fashion MNIST Dataset: Fashion MNIST dataset is composed of images from an online clothing store. it contains 60,000 examples as a training set and 10,000 examples as a test set organized in 10 classes (see Table 3). The images are 28 × 28 grayscale images and have been standardized as in the MNIST case. Results are shown in Table 4 and reconstructions are shown in Fig. 5. The dataset is more challenging, but the results confirm that the proposed method outperforms standard CapsNet when the number of training anomalies is small.

Table 3. Fashion MNIST label encoding

Label	0	1	2	3	4	5	6	7	8	9
Desc	T-shirt/top	Trouser	Pullover	Dress	Coat	Sandal	Shirt	Sneaker	Bag	Ankle boot

Table 4. Accuracy % on fashion MNIST dataset.

	0	1	2	3	4	5	6	7	8	9	avg
Standard, 10% an.	88.14	96.89	85.08	92.19	85.77	96.15	76.93	95.11	94.96	97.18	90.84
Proposed, 10% an.	**93.28**	**98.07**	**87.50**	**95.01**	**91.50**	**98.07**	**84.44**	**96.64**	**97.73**	**97.83**	**94.01**
Standard, 1% an.	49.41	49.41	49.41	49.41	49.41	49.41	49.41	49.46	49.41	49.41	49.41
Proposed, 1% an.	**87.45**	**95.31**	5 **84.98**	**90.86**	**87.70**	**94.27**	**77.32**	**93.33**	**92.14**	**96.15**	**89.95**

Kuzushiji-MNIST(K-MNIST): It is a dataset of 28×28 grayscale images of ancient Japanese handwritten characters. The dataset contains 60,000 images for training and 10,000 images for testing. Images have been standardized before processing. It is a challenging dataset, as it can be seen in Fig. 6, where the 10 rows corresponding to each class can be seen. The accuracy for K-MNIST dataset can be seen in Table 5 and reconstruction examples are in Fig. 7. The results obtained on other datasets are confirmed: the proposed method outperforms standard capsule network classification, especially in the 1% training anomaly case.

5   Conclusions

In this work we proposed a fully-supervised deep anomaly detection technique based on capsule networks. The network is trained as in a binary classification problem, where each sample is either normal or anomalous, but with the additional constraint of imbalanced datasets. To deal with data imbalance, we

Fig. 5. Top row: normal (left) and anomalous (right) samples from the Fashion MNIST test set. Bottom row: the reconstructed images.

Fig. 6. 10 classes of Kuzushiji-MNIST, with the first column showing each character's modern hiragana counterpart.

Table 5. Accuracy % on K-MNIST dataset.

	0	1	2	3	4	5	6	7	8	9	avg
Standard, 10% an.	91.55	80.58	72.88	87.40	49.41	87.10	83.05	93.23	81.92	81.97	80.91
Proposed, 10% an.	**96.54**	**93.92**	**88.69**	**96.25**	**88.19**	**93.43**	**93.08**	**93.48**	**95.85**	**95.01**	**93.44**
Standard, 1% an.	49.95	49.95	49.95	49.95	49.95	49.95	49.95	49.95	49.95	49.95	49.95
Proposed, 1% an.	**92.31**	**86.11**	**79.17**	**93.06**	**83.27**	**90.81**	**86.56**	**76.37**	**87.91**	**90.71**	**86.63**

proposed a novel anomaly score based on output vectors length difference and reconstruction error. Experimental results are very promising, since the network has state-of-the-art performance even with highly imbalanced datasets where the standard network fails.

To the best of our knowledge, this is the first use of capsule networks for anomaly detection tasks. We believe that the ability of capsule networks to create equivariant models can boost anomaly detection in the same way it has proven to boost standard classification problems.

Fig. 7. Top row: normal (left) and anomalous (right) samples from the K-MNIST test set. Bottom row: the reconstructed images.

The proposed method currently outperforms or it is comparable to other deep learning anomaly detection techniques as the ones discussed in Sect. 2, however a direct comparison would be unfair since most of those methods use semi-supervised or unsupervised techniques. Fully-supervised anomaly detection is a very relevant topic with many practical applications in which anomalous data are available, but of course semi-supervised or unsupervised approaches are more challenging and can deal with those problems where anomalous data are not available or not labeled. For this reason, as a future work we plan to investigate the use of capsule networks in this direction.

References

1. Ahmed, M., Mahmood, A.N., Hu, J.: A survey of network anomaly detection techniques. J. Netw. Comput. Appl. **60**, 19–31 (2016)
2. Akcay, S., Atapour-Abarghouei, A., Breckon, T.: Ganomaly: semi-supervised anomaly detection via adversarial training. In: Proceedings Asian Conference on Computer Vision. Springer (2018, to appear)
3. Antonie, M.L., Zaïane, O.R., Coman, A.: Application of data mining techniques for medical image classification. In: Proceedings of the Second International Conference on Multimedia Data Mining, MDMKDD 2001, pp. 94–101. Springer-Verlag, Heidelberg (2001)
4. Buda, M., Maki, A., Mazurowski, M.A.: A systematic study of the class imbalance problem in convolutional neural networks. Neural Netw. **106**, 249–259 (2018)
5. Chalapathy, R., Menon, A.K., Chawla, S.: Robust, deep and inductive anomaly detection. In: Ceci, M., Hollmén, J., Todorovski, L., Vens, C., Džeroski, S. (eds.) ECML PKDD 2017. LNCS (LNAI), vol. 10534, pp. 36–51. Springer, Cham (2017). https://doi.org/10.1007/978-3-319-71249-9_3
6. Chalapathy, R., Toth, E., Chawla, S.: Group anomaly detection using deep generative models. In: Berlingerio, M., Bonchi, F., Gärtner, T., Hurley, N., Ifrim, G. (eds.) ECML PKDD 2018. LNCS (LNAI), vol. 11051, pp. 173–189. Springer, Cham (2019). https://doi.org/10.1007/978-3-030-10925-7_11
7. Chandola, V., Banerjee, A., Kumar, V.: Anomaly detection: a survey. ACM Comput. Surv. **41**(3), 15:1–15:58 (2009)
8. Chen, P., Yang, S., McCann, J.A.: Distributed real-time anomaly detection in networked industrial sensing systems. IEEE Trans. Industr. Electron. **62**(6), 3832–3842 (2015)
9. Clanuwat, T., Bober-Irizar, M., Kitamoto, A., Lamb, A., Yamamoto, K., Ha, D.: Deep learning for classical Japanese literature. arXiv preprint arXiv:1812.01718 (2018)
10. Hendrycks, D., Mazeika, M., Dietterich, T.: Deep anomaly detection with outlier exposure. In: International Conference on Learning Representations (2019)
11. Deecke, L., Vandermeulen, R., Ruff, L., Mandt, S., Kloft, M.: Image anomaly detection with generative adversarial networks. In: Berlingerio, M., Bonchi, F., Gärtner, T., Hurley, N., Ifrim, G. (eds.) ECML PKDD 2018. LNCS (LNAI), vol. 11051, pp. 3–17. Springer, Cham (2019). https://doi.org/10.1007/978-3-030-10925-7_1
12. Fiore, U., Palmieri, F., Castiglione, A., De Santis, A.: Network anomaly detection with the restricted boltzmann machine. Neurocomputing **122**, 13–23 (2013)
13. Huang, S.H., Pan, Y.C.: Automated visual inspection in the semiconductor industry: a survey. Comput. Ind. **66**, 1–10 (2015)

14. Kiran, B.R., Thomas, D.M., Parakkal, R.: An overview of deep learning based methods for unsupervised and semi-supervised anomaly detection in videos. J. Imaging **4**(2), 36 (2018)
15. LeCun, Y., Bottou, L., Bengio, Y., Haffner, P., et al.: Gradient-based learning applied to document recognition. Proc. IEEE **86**(11), 2278–2324 (1998)
16. Piciarelli, C., Avola, D., Pannone, D., Foresti, G.L.: A vision-based system for internal pipeline inspection. IEEE Trans. Industr. Inf. (2018). https://doi.org/10.1109/TII.2018.2873237. early access
17. Piciarelli, C., Micheloni, C., Foresti, G.L.: Trajectory-based anomalous event detection. IEEE Trans. Circuits Syst. Video Technol. **18**(11), 1544–1554 (2008)
18. Ruff, L., et al.: Deep one-class classification. In: Dy, J., Krause, A. (eds.) Proceedings of the 35th International Conference on Machine Learning, Proceedings of Machine Learning Research, Stockholm, Sweden, PMLR, vol. 80, pp. 4393–4402. Stockholmsmässan (2018)
19. Sabour, S., Frosst, N., Hinton, G.E.: Dynamic routing between capsules. In: Advances in Neural Information Processing Systems, pp. 3856–3866 (2017)
20. Schlegl, T., Seeböck, P., Waldstein, S.M., Schmidt-Erfurth, U., Langs, G.: Unsupervised anomaly detection with generative adversarial networks to guide marker discovery. In: Niethammer, M., et al. (eds.) IPMI 2017. LNCS, vol. 10265, pp. 146–157. Springer, Cham (2017). https://doi.org/10.1007/978-3-319-59050-9_12
21. Wulsin, D., Blanco, J., Mani, R., Litt, B.: Semi-supervised anomaly detection for EEG waveforms using deep belief nets. In: 2010 Ninth International Conference on Machine Learning and Applications, pp. 436–441 (2010)
22. Xiao, H., Rasul, K., Vollgraf, R.: Fashion-mnist: a novel image dataset for benchmarking machine learning algorithms. arXiv preprint arXiv:1708.07747 (2017)
23. Zhou, C., Paffenroth, R.C.: Anomaly detection with robust deep autoencoders. In: Proceedings of the 23rd ACM SIGKDD International Conference on Knowledge Discovery and Data Mining, KDD 2017, pp. 665–674. ACM, New York, NY, USA (2017)

Improving Facial Emotion Recognition Systems with Crucial Feature Extractors

Ram Krishna Pandey$^{(\boxtimes)}$, Souvik Karmakar, A. G. Ramakrishnan, and N. Saha

Department of Electrical Engineering, Indian Institute of Science, Bangalore, India
{ramp,souvikk,agr}@iisc.ac.in, snabagata@nitw.ac.in

Abstract. In this work, we have proposed enhancements that improve the performance of state-of-the-art facial emotion recognition (FER) systems. We believe that the changes in the positions of the fiducial points and the intensities capture the crucial information regarding the emotion of a face image. We propose the inputting of the *gradient* and the *Laplacian* of the input image together with the original into a convolutional neural network (CNN). *These modifications help the network learn additional information from the gradient and Laplacian of the images. However, as shown by our results, the CNN in the existing state-of-the-art models is not able to extract this information from the raw images.* In addition, we employ spatial transformer network to add robustness to the system against rotation and scaling. We have performed a number of experiments on two well known datasets, namely KDEF and FERplus. Our approach enhances the already high performance of the state-of-the-art FER systems by 3 to 5%.

In another contribution, we have proposed an efficient architecture that performs better than the state-of-the-art system on FERplus dataset, with the number of parameters reduced by a factor of about 24. Here also, the fusion of gradient or Laplacian image with the original image improves the recognition performance of the proposed model.

Keywords: Laplacian · Gradient · Convolutional neural network · Facial emotion recognition

1 Introduction

Machine recognition of human emotions is an important and challenging artificial intelligence problem. Human emotions can be recognized from voice [1], body language, facial expression and electroencephalography [2]. However, facial expression forms a simpler and more powerful way of recognizing emotions. Excluding neutral, there are seven types of human emotions that are recognized universally: anger, disgust, fear, happiness, sadness, surprise and contempt. In certain situations, humans are known to simultaneously express more than one emotion. Developing systems for facial emotion recognition (FER) has application

© Springer Nature Switzerland AG 2019
E. Ricci et al. (Eds.): ICIAP 2019, LNCS 11751, pp. 268–279, 2019.
https://doi.org/10.1007/978-3-030-30642-7_24

in areas such as clinical practice, human-computer interaction, behavioural science, virtual reality, augmented reality, entertainment and advanced driver assistant systems. Traditional techniques for FER mainly consist of four successive steps: (i) pre-processing (ii) face and landmark detection (iii) feature extraction and (iv) emotion classification. These approaches heavily depend on the algorithms used for face detection, landmark detection, the handcrafted features and the classifiers used. Recent developments in deep learning reduce the burden of handcrafting the features. Deep learning approaches perform well for all the above-mentioned tasks by learning an end-to-end mapping from the input data to the output classes. Out of all the learning based techniques, convolutional neural network (CNN) based techniques are preferred.

There is a tendency in researchers to design deep neural networks (DNN's) as end to end systems, where every kind of processing is accomplished by the network, including the feature extraction, by learning from the data. Some opine that there is no need for any hard-coded feature extraction in any machine learning system. However, the deep neural networks have been designed to simulate the biological neural network in the brain. It is well known that there are many hard-coded feature extractors in the human brain, and even animal sensory systems, in addition to the natural neural network, that also learns from data (exposure and experience). One might argue that it is possible for the visual neural pathway or cortex to extract the gray image from the colour image obtained by the cones in the retina. However, nature has chosen to have many more rods than cones to directly obtain the gray images also in parallel. Further, the work of Hubel and Wiezel [3] showed the existence of orientation selective cells in the lateral geniculate nucleus and visual cortex of kitten. Also, different regions of the basilar membrane in the cochlea respond to different frequencies [4] in both man and animals and this processing is akin to sub-band decomposition of the input audio signal. Thus, there are many examples of hard-coded feature extraction in the brain, which enhance the classification potential of the biological neural network; our work reported here, is inspired from this aspect of nature's processing.

2   Related Work

Darwin and Phillip suggested that human and animal facial emotions are evolutionary [5]. Motivated by Darwin's work, Ekman et al. [6,7] found that the seven expressions, namely happiness, anger, fear, surprise, disgust, sadness and contempt remain the same across different cultures. Facial action coding system (FACS) is proposed in [8] to investigate the facial expressions and the corresponding emotions described by the activity of the atomic action units (cluster of facial muscles). Facial expression can be analyzed by mapping facial action units for each part of the face (eyes, nose, mouth corners) into codes.

2.1   Traditional Approaches

Features are desired that possess maximal inter-class and minimal intra-class variabilities for each of the expressions. Traditional systems for facial emotion recognition depend mainly on what and how the features are extracted from the facial expression. The features extracted can be categorized into (i) geometric features, (ii) appearance based features or (iii) their combination. In the work reported by Myunghoon et al. [9], facial features are extracted by active shape model, whereas Ghimire and Lee [10] extract geometric features from the sequences of facial expression images and multi-class Ada-boost and SVM classifiers are used for classification. Global face region or regions containing different facial information are used to extract appearance-based features. Gabor wavelets, Haar features, local binary pattern [11] or its variants such as [12] are used to extract appearance-based features. Ghimire et al. [13] proposed a single frame classification of emotion using geometric as well as appearance based features and SVM classifier. In [14], features are extracted using pyramid histogram of orientation gradients. Here, the facial edge contours are constructed using Canny edge detector. Histograms are calculated by dividing the edge maps into different pyramid resolution levels. The histogram vectors are concatenated to generate the final feature to be used for classification using SVM or AdaBoost classifier.

2.2   Deep Learning Based Approaches

The above techniques in the literature depend heavily on handcrafted features. However, deep learning algorithms have shown promising results in the recent years. CNN based models have shown significant performance gain in various computer vision and image processing tasks, such as image segmentation, denoising, super-resolution, object recognition, face recognition, scene understanding and facial emotion recognition. Unlike the traditional techniques, deep learning based techniques learn ("end-to-end") to extract features from the data. For FER, the network generally uses four different kinds of layers, namely convolution, max-pool, dense layer and soft-max. Batch normalization with skip connection is also used to ease the training process. The features extracted have information about local spatial relation as well as global information. The max-pool layer makes the model robust to small geometrical distortion. The dense and soft-max layers help in assigning the class score.

Breuer and Kimmel [15] demonstrate the capability of the CNN network trained on various FER datasets by visualizing the feature maps of the trained model, and their corresponding FACS action unit. Motivated by Xception architecture proposed in [16], Arriaga et al. [17] proposed mini-Xception. Jung et al. [18] proposed two different deep network models for recognising facial expressions. The first network extracts temporal appearance features, whereas the second extracts temporal geometric features and these networks are combined and fine tuned in the best possible way to obtain better accuracy from the model. Motivated by these two techniques, we have trained and obtained multiple models, the details of which are explained in Sect. 5.

For the task of FER, the current state of the art model [24] proposed a miniature version of VGG net, called VGG13. The network has 8.75 million parameters. The dataset used is the FERplus dataset [24], which has 8 classes, adding neutral to the existing seven classes. The reported test accuracy is ≈84%. In 2014, Levi et al. [19] obtained improved performance of emotion recognition using CNN. They convert images to local binary patterns (LBP). These patterns are mapped to a 3D metric space and used as input to the existing CNN architectures, thus addressing the problem of appearance variation due to illumination. They trained the existing VGG network [20], on CASIA Webface dataset [33], and then used transfer learning to train the static facial expressions in the wild (SFEW), to address the problem of the small size of SFEW dataset [34].

Ouellet [21] used a CNN based architecture for realtime detection of emotions. The author uses transfer learning to train the Cohn-Kanade [22] dataset on AlexNet. The author used the model to capture the emotions of gamers, while they are playing games.

3   Datasets Used for the Study

We have used the KDEF [23] and FERplus [24,25] datasets for our experiments. The FERplus dataset contains nearly 35000 images divided into 8 classes, including contempt. The FERplus dataset improves upon the FER dataset by crowdsourcing the tagging operation. Ten taggers were asked to choose one emotion per image, which resulted in a distribution of emotions for each image. The training set contains around 28000 images. The remaining are divided equally into validation and test sets. The original image size is 48 × 48 pixels. Figure 1 shows some sample face images from the FERplus dataset, with multiple emotion labels for each image. KDEF dataset contains a total of 4900 images (divided into the 7 classes of neutral, anger, disgust, fear, happiness, sadness, and surprise), with equal number of male and female expressions. Figure 2(a), (b) and (c) show, respectively, a sample input image from KDEF dataset, its derivative image obtained by the Sobel operator (gradient) and its second derivative obtained by the Laplacian operator.

Fig. 1. Face image samples from FERplus dataset, with multiple emotion labels for each image [24]

Fig. 2. (a) A sample input image from the KDEF dataset [23]. (b) Its derivative image obtained by the Sobel operator (Gradient). (c) Its second derivative obtained by the Laplacian operator. Zoom to see the details in the Laplacian image.

4   The Proposed Models and Our Contributions

Rather than proposing a totally new architecture, which performs marginally better than the state-of-the-art model, one approach could be to work on good existing models and propose enhancements to significantly improve their performance. Another approach could be to come out with a computationally efficient model that performs as good as the state of the art models. We propose that the performance of a classifier for facial emotion recognition can be improved by making it robust to transformations such as scaling and rotation. The fiducial points of a face change predictably, depending upon the specific emotion and these changes are the important features for emotion recognition. Such changes in the image landmark points and their intensities can be effectively captured by the gradient and Laplacian of an image. Thus, in our first approach, we have significantly improved the emotion recognition performance of two state-of-the-art architectures by adding the following enhancements [35].

Spatial Transformer Layer (STL): CNN is a very powerful model, invariant to some transformations like in-plane rotation and scaling. To obtain such invariance, CNN requires a huge amount of training data. To achieve such invariance in a computationally efficient manner, spatial transformer network [26] is used as the input layer, called here as the spatial transformer layer. This allows spatial manipulation of the data within the network. This differentiable module, when combined with the CNN, infuses invariance to rotation, scaling, and translation, with less training data than that needed by the normal CNN.

Sobel and Laplacian Operators: The gradient captures information such as the direction of the maximum change and the Laplacian identifies regions of rapid changes in the intensity. Thus, by adding the gradient and Laplacian images as additional inputs, we can largely obviate the need for extracting the fiducial or the landmark points. The gradient and Laplacian of an image $f(x,y)$, denoted by $\Delta f(x,y)$ and $\Delta^2 f(x,y)$, can be approximated by applying Sobel [27] and Laplacian [28] operators on an image. We have taken the input images from the dataset and applied Sobel and Laplacian operators on them to obtain their first and second derivatives, respectively. They detect the intensity discontinuities as contours. These images are fed as inputs, in series or parallel with the original image, into the state of art models for FER.

Global Average Pooling and DepthSep Layers: The real time convolutional neural network (RTNN) architecture selected by us [17] uses global average pooling (GAP) [29]. The GAP layer has multiple advantages over the dense layer: (i) it reduces over-fitting to a large extent; (ii) huge reduction in the number of parameters compared to dense layer; (iii) the spatial average of feature maps is fed directly to the soft-max layer. The latter enforces better correspondence between the feature maps and the categories.

The RTNN model also employs depthwise separable convolution (DepSep) layers [16]. The advantage of using depthwise separable convolution layer is that it greatly reduces the number of parameters compared to the convolution layer. At a particular layer, let the total number of filters be N, the depth of the feature maps be D, and the size of the filter (spatial extent) used be S_e. In such a case, the total number of parameters in normal convolution is $S_e \times S_e \times D \times N$. DepSep is a two-step process: (i) filters of size $S_e \times S_e \times 1$ are applied to each feature; therefore, the total number parameters at this step is $S_e \times S_e \times D$; (ii) then, N filters of size $1 \times 1 \times D$ are applied. So, the number of parameters required at this step are $D \times N$. Combining steps (i) and (ii), the total number of parameters in DepSep layer are $S_e \times S_e \times D + D \times N$. Hence, the reduction in the number of parameters compared to normal convolution at each layer, where convolution is replaced by DepSep convolution, is: $\frac{S_e \times S_e \times D + D \times N}{S_e \times S_e \times D \times N} = (1/N) + (1/S_e^2)$

Our Contributions: In this work, our main contributions are:

- By adding the spatial transformer layer as the input processing block, we have introduced robustness to scaling, rotation and translation.
- By adding the gradient and/or Laplacian image(s) as additional inputs to the system, we have improved the recognition accuracies of three different FER architectures by a good margin (see Tables 1, 2 and 4).
- We have trained multiple models to validate the performance gain obtained due to the addition of gradient and Laplacian, on KDEF [23] and FER-Plus [24] datasets.
- We have proposed an efficient architecture (refer Table 3) that performs better than the state-of-the-art system on FERplus dataset (refer Table 4), while reducing the number of parameters by a factor of 24.
- Our proposed architecture (reported in Table 3) has model size of around 9.7 MB compared to the original VGG-13 [24], which has the model size of 107.4 MB. Thus, our model can be run on a mobile phone more efficiently.

5   Experiments and Results

Three sets of different experiments have been carried out.

Experiment 1: In the first set of experiments, the *Real-time neural network (RTNN)* model, with all the modifications proposed by us, has been tested on

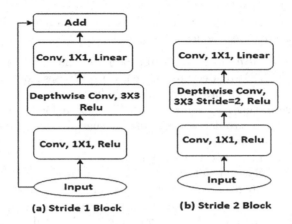

(a) Stride 1 Block   **(b) Stride 2 Block**

Fig. 3. Inverted bottleneck module used in MobileNetV2 [31].

Table 1. FER results of RTNN and its various modifications proposed by us (parallel networks) on the KDEF dataset (4900 images with 7 classes).

Architecture details	Accuracy %
Orig. RTNN by Arriaga et al. [17]	**83.16**
STL + RTNN	84.08
RTNN + Lap. RTNN	84.39
STL with RTNN + Grad RTNN	85.10
STL with RTNN + Lap RTNN	85.51
STL with Orig., Grad and Lap. RTNN	**88.16**

the KDEF dataset. RTNN is the model proposed by Arriaga et al. [17], trained on the KDEF dataset and validated. Table 1 reports the results of the experiments conducted. *STL + RTNN* is the RTNN model trained with the addition of STL at the input. *RTNN + Lap. RTNN* is the architecture, where the input image and its Laplacian are fed in parallel. The outputs of these parallel networks are combined and passed to a soft-max layer for classification. *STL with RTNN + Grad RTNN* is the case when the input image and its gradient are first fed to a STL, followed by the parallel subnetworks. The parallel networks extract more useful features in the beginning layer, which are combined to obtain better accuracy. *STL with RTNN + Lap. RTNN* is the architecture, where the model is trained in parallel with the input image and its Laplacian. *STL with Orig., Grad & Lap. RTNN* is the case, where the model is trained in parallel with the original, the gradient, and the Laplacian images. These input streams are first fed independently to a STL, before being fed to the subnetworks in parallel.

Experiment 2: We have reimplemented the VGG13 network, used in [24], in Tensorflow. We use the majority voting technique, as described in [24], for labelling each image. The only modification we have made to the original model is the use of Adam optimizer [30] instead of momentum optimizer. Table 2 compares the results of the original network with those after our enhancements. In our setup, we get an average accuracy of 83.56% instead of 83.85% as reported in the original paper. Next we propose two experimental setups. First, we modify the input by taking the Laplacian of the original image and channel wise concatenating it with the original image. The resultant image is a 2 channel 64*64 input. In this setup, without modifying the learning rate, we get an average accuracy improvement of close to 3% on an average, compared to our VGG13 implementation. In the second setup, we use Sobel operator instead of Laplacian, and get gradients in x and y directions. The resultant gradients are again concatenated to the original image channelwise to get 3 channel input. This setup again gives an improvement of close to 3%.

Table 2. FER accuracies on FERPlus dataset and the number of parameters (in millions) of our models vs. VGG13 [24]. Each type of model has been trained 4 times and its maximum, minimum and average accuracies are reported. Training set: 28000 images; validation and test sets: 3500 images each; number of classes: 8.

Models	Avg	Min	Max	Parameters
VGG13 (reported)	83.85	83.15	84.89	8.75
VGG13 (our implementation)	83.56	82.99	84.08	8.75
VGG13 + Laplacian (input concatenated)	86.22	85.94	86.56	8.75
VGG13 + Sobel (input concatenated)	86.42	86.08	86.55	8.75

Experiment 3: We propose our own architecture (details listed in Table 3, having (1/24)-th the number of parameters compared to all the architectures reported in Table 2), developed using inverted bottleneck module (refer Fig. 3) reported in [31]. Even in this model, fusion of the Laplacian or the gradient image to the input image (by concatenation) enhances the recognition performance by 2.3 and 2.5 %, respectively. The results with this proposed model and its feature-fusion enhancements are listed in Table 4. The *base+Sobel* model performs better than the original VGG13 model listed in Table 2 by 0.62%.

6 Conclusion

We have shown that feeding the gradient and/or Laplacian of the image, in addition to the input image, improves the performance of any FER system. We have performed many experiments on KDEF and FERplus datasets and enhanced the recognition accuracies of state-of-the-art techniques [17,24]. We believe that our proposed approach will largely impact the community working on similar area. The advantages of our proposal are many folds: (i) improves the recognition accuracy of any classifier (ii) the dataset size increases by two or three times (depending on the Laplacian or/and gradient used together with the

Table 3. Details of the architecture proposed by us, with *inverted bottleneck* 3 as the core module. c, s and t denote the number of output channels from each layer, stride and expansion factor used in the bottleneck module, respectively.

Layer	Parameters	Input ($H \times W \times C$)	c	s	t
conv2d 3×3	64	$64 \times 64 \times 1$	64	2	–
bottleneck	6720	$64 \times 64 \times 32$	32	1	1
bottleneck	12480	$32 \times 32 \times 32$	24	2	6
bottleneck	8208	$16 \times 16 \times 24$	24	1	6
bottleneck	9360	$16 \times 16 \times 24$	32	2	6
bottleneck	14016	$8 \times 8 \times 32$	32	1	6
bottleneck	14016	$8 \times 8 \times 32$	32	1	6
bottleneck	20160	$8 \times 8 \times 32$	64	1	6
bottleneck	52608	$8 \times 8 \times 64$	64	1	6
bottleneck	52608	$8 \times 8 \times 64$	64	1	6
bottleneck	52608	$8 \times 8 \times 64$	64	1	6
bottleneck	77184	$8 \times 8 \times 64$	128	1	6
conv2d 1×1	40960	$8 \times 8 \times 128$	320	1	–
avg_pool	0	$8 \times 8 \times 320$	320	–	–
conv2d 1×1	2048	$1 \times 1 \times 320$	8	1	–
Total	363616	–	–	–	–

input), which is desirable in most deep learning tasks; (iii) the variability in the input image space increases (iv) DepSep, inverted bottleneck module and GAP layers help in reducing the computational complexity of the model. The proposed enhancements result in absolute performance improvements, as listed in Tables 1, 2 and 4, over those of the original models. Researchers working on similar areas can use our proposed features to add performance gain to any existing DNN based classifier, thus obviating the need for designing a new classifier to achieve similar performance gain. We have also proposed an efficient architecture that performs better than the state of the art algorithm proposed in [24] with (1/24)-th the number of parameters. Thus, if there is any need for designing any new

Table 4. FER performance of our models, with less complexity than VGG13, on FERPlus [24] dataset. Models are trained 4 times with the same hyper-parameter settings and their average, maximum and minimum accuracies are reported.

Models	Avg	Min	Max	Parameters
Base model (given in Table 3)	81.95	81.79	82.15	0.36 million
Base + Laplacian (input concatenated)	84.26	83.84	84.87	0.36 million
Base + Sobel (input concatenated)	84.47	84.21	84.69	0.36 million

classifier, it can be made computationally efficient to a good extent with our proposed approaches.

One might argue that the gradient and Laplacian of the input image can very well be computed by the CNN. However, there are strong evidences for the need for appropriate representations in accomplishing certain vision and motor control tasks [32]. It is also clear from the results that at least the networks proposed by Arriaga et al. [17] and VGG13 [24] are not able to compute these derived images internally. On the other hand, pre-computing these features and feeding them to the same network in parallel or in series, is clearly able to improve the performance of the network. Thus, our experiments show that there is a clear case for optimally combining appropriate feature extractors with learning neural networks, to obtain better performance for specific pattern recognition tasks.

References

1. El Ayadi, M., Kamel, M.S., Karray, F.: Survey on speech emotion recognition: features, classification schemes, and databases. Pattern Recogn. **44**(3), 572–587 (2011)
2. Davidson, R.J., Ekman, P., Saron, C.D., Senulis, J.A., Friesen, W.V.: Approach-withdrawal and cerebral asymmetry: emotional expression and brain physiology: I. J. Pers. Soc. Psychol. **58**(2), 330 (1990)
3. Hubel, D.H., Wiesel, T.N.: Receptive fields, binocular interaction and functional architecture in the cat's visual cortex. J. Physiol. **160**(1), 106–154 (1982)
4. Greenwood, D.D.: A cochlear frequencyposition function for several species-29 years later. J. Acoust. Soc. Am. **87**(6), 2592–2605 (1990)
5. Darwin, C., Prodger, P.: The Expression of the Emotions in Man and Animals. Oxford University Press, Oxford (1998)
6. Ekman, P., Friesen, W.V.: Nonverbal leakage and clues to deception. Psychiatry **32**(1), 88–106 (1969)
7. Ekman, P., Dacher, K.: Universal facial expressions of emotion. Calif. Ment. Health Res. Digest **8**(4), 151–158 (1970)
8. Friesen, E., Ekman, P.: Facial Action Coding System: A Technique for the Measurement of Facial Movement. Consulting Psychologists Press, Palo Alto (1978)
9. Suk, M., Prabhakaran, B.: Real-time mobile facial expression recognition system-a case study. In: Proceedings IEEE Conference on Computer Vision and Pattern Recognition Workshops (2014)
10. Ghimire, D., Lee, J.: Geometric feature-based facial expression recognition in image sequences using multi-class adaboost and support vector machines. Sensors **13**(6), 7714–7734 (2013)
11. Happy, S.L., George, A., Routray, A.: A real time facial expression classification system using local binary patterns. In: 4th International Conference on Intelligent Human Computer Interaction (IHCI), pp. 1–5. IEEE (2012)
12. Zhao, G., Pietikainen, M.: Dynamic texture recognition using local binary patterns with an application to facial expressions. IEEE Trans. Pattern Anal. Mach. Intell. **29**(6), 915–928 (2007)
13. Ghimire, D., Jeong, S., Lee, J., Park, S.H.: Facial expression recognition based on local region specific features and support vector machines. Multimed. Tools Appl. **76**(6), 7803–7821 (2017)

14. Bai, Y., Guo, L., Jin, L., Huang, Q.: A novel feature extraction method using pyramid histogram of orientation gradients for smile recognition. In: International Conference on Image processing (ICIP) (2009)
15. Breuer, R., Kimmel, R.: A deep learning perspective on the origin of facial expressions. arXiv preprint arXiv:1705.01842 (2017)
16. Chollet, F.: Xception: deep learning with separable convolutions. arXiv Preprint arXiv1610 2357 (2016)
17. Arriaga, O., Valdenegro-Toro, M., Ploger, P.: Real-time convolutional neural networks for emotion and gender classification. arXiv preprint arXiv:1710.07557 (2017)
18. Jung, H., Lee, S., Yim, J., Park, S., Kim, J.: Joint fine-tuning in deep neural networks for facial expression recognition. In: Proceedings IEEE International Conference on Computer Vision (2015)
19. Levi, G., Hassner, T.: Emotion recognition in the wild via convolutional neural networks and mapped binary patterns. In: Proceedings ACM International Conference on Multimodal Interaction (ICMI), November 2015
20. Simonyan, K., Zisserman, A.: Very deep convolutional networks for large-scale image recognition. arXiv preprint arXiv:1409.1556 (2014)
21. Ouellet, S.: Real-time emotion recognition for gaming using deep convolutional network features. arXiv preprint arXiv:1408.3750 (2014)
22. Lucey, P., Cohn, J.F., Kanade, T., Saragih, J., Ambadar, Z., Matthews, I.: The extended cohn-kanade dataset (CK+): a complete dataset for action unit and emotion-specified expression. In: IEEE Computer Society Conference on Computer Vision and Pattern Recognition, Workshops, San Francisco, CA (2010)
23. Lundqvist, D., Flykt, A., Öhman, A.: The Karolinska directed emotional faces (KDEF). CD ROM from Department of Clinical Neuroscience, Psychology section, Karolinska Institutet, pp. 91–630 (1998)
24. Barsoum, E., Zhang, C., Ferrer, C.C., Zhang, Z.: Training deep networks for facial expression recognition with crowd-sourced label distribution. In: Proceedings of the 18th ACM International Conference on Multimodal Interaction. ACM (2016)
25. https://github.com/Microsoft/FERPlus/
26. Jaderberg, M., Simonyan, K., Zisserman, A.: Spatial transformer networks. In: Advances in Neural Information Processing Systems (2015)
27. Sobel, I., Feldman, G.: A 3×3 isotropic gradient operator for image processing. A talk at the Stanford Artificial Project in 271–272 (1968)
28. Haralick, R.M., Shapiro, L.G.: Computer and Robot Vision. Addison-Wesley, Boston (1992)
29. Lin, M., Chen, Q., Yan, S.: Network in network. arXiv preprint arXiv:1312.4400 (2013)
30. Kingma, D.P., Ba, L.J.: Adam: a method for stochastic optimization. In: International Conference on Learning Representations (ICLR) (2015)
31. Sandler, M., Howard, A., Zhu, M., Zhmoginov, A., Chen, L.C.: Mobilenetv 2: inverted residuals and linear bottlenecks. In: IEEE/CVF Conference on Computer Vision and Pattern Recognition (2018)
32. Schomaker, L.: Anticipation in cybernetic systems: a case against mindless anti-representationalism. In: International Conference on Systems, Man and Cybernetics, vol. 2. IEEE (2004)
33. Yi, D., Lei, Z., Liao, S., Li, S.Z.: Learning face representation from scratch. arXiv preprint arXiv:1411.7923 (2014)

34. Dhall, A., Ramana Murthy, O.V., Goecke, R., Joshi, J., Gedeon, T.: Video and image based emotion recognition challenges in the wild: EmotiW 2015. In: Proceedings International Conference on Multimodal Interaction, pp. 423–426. ACM (2015)
35. Krishna Pandey, R., Karmakar, S., Ramakrishnan, A.G., Saha, N.: Improving facial emotion recognition systems using gradient and Laplacian images. arXiv preprint arXiv:1902.05411 (2019)

MetalGAN: A Cluster-Based Adaptive Training for Few-Shot Adversarial Colorization

Tomaso Fontanini[✉][iD], Eleonora Iotti[iD], and Andrea Prati[iD]

IMP Lab, Department of Engineering and Architecture,
University of Parma, Parma, Italy
tomaso.fontanini@studenti.unipr.it,
{eleonora.iotti,andrea.prati}@unipr.it

Fig. 1. Example images generated using MetalGAN for 100-epochs, and 100-meta-iterations. From left to right: gray scale image, ground truth, output of the network. The example images belong to two different clusters.

Abstract. In recent years, the majority of works on deep-learning-based image colorization have focused on how to make a good use of the enormous datasets currently available. What about when the data at disposal are scarce? The main objective of this work is to prove that a network can be trained and can provide excellent colorization results even without a large quantity of data. The adopted approach is a mixed one, which uses an adversarial method for the actual colorization, and a meta-learning technique to enhance the generator model. Also, a clusterization *a-priori* of the training dataset ensures a task-oriented division useful for meta-learning, and at the same time reduces the per-step number of images. This paper describes in detail the method and its main motivations, and a discussion of results and future developments is provided.

Keywords: Automatic image colorization ·
Conditional Generative Adversarial Networks · Meta-learning ·
Clusterization method

© Springer Nature Switzerland AG 2019
E. Ricci et al. (Eds.): ICIAP 2019, LNCS 11751, pp. 280–291, 2019.
https://doi.org/10.1007/978-3-030-30642-7_25

1   Introduction

The *automatic image colorization* task is an image processing problem that is fundamental and extensively studied in the field of computer vision. The task consists in creating an algorithm that takes as input a gray-scale image and outputs a colorized version of the same image. The challenging part is to colorize it in a plausible and well-looking way. Many systems were developed over the years, exploiting a wide variety of image processing techniques, but recently, the image colorization problem, as many other problems in computer vision, was approached with deep-learning methods. Colorization is a *generative* problem from a machine learning perspective. Generative techniques, such as *Generative Adversarial Networks (GANs)* [7], are then suitable to approach such a task. In particular, *conditional GANs (cGANs)* models seem especially appropriate to this purpose, since their structure allows the network to learn a mapping from an image x and (only if needed) a random noise vector z to an output generated image y. On the contrary, standard GANs only learn the mapping from the noise z to y.

As many deep-learning techniques, the training of a GAN or a cGAN needs a large amount of images. Large datasets usually grant a great diversity among images, allowing the network to better generalize its results. Nevertheless, having a huge number of images is often not feasible in real-world applications, or simply it requires too much storage space for an average system, and high training computational times. Hence, porting the current deep-learning colorization technologies to a more accessible level and achieving a better understanding of the colorization training process are eased by using a smaller dataset.

For these reasons, one of the aims of this work is to achieve good performances in the colorization task using a little number of images compared to standard datasets. In *few-shot learning*, a branch of the deep-learning field, the goal is to learn from a small number of inputs, or from one single input in the ideal case (*one-shot learning*): the network is subject to a low quantity of examples, and it has to be capable to infer something when posed face-to-face to a new example. This problem underpins a high generalization capability of the network, which is a very difficult task and an open challenging problem in deep networks research.

Recently, some novel interesting ideas highlight a possible path to reach a better generalization ability of the network. These ideas are based on the concept of learning to learn, i.e., adding a meta-layer of learning information above the usual learning process of the network. The generalization is achieved by introducing the concept of *tasks distribution* instead of a single task, and the concept of *episodes* instead of instances. A tasks' distribution is the family of those different tasks on which the model has to be adapted to. Each task in the distribution has its own training and test sets, and its own loss function. A meta-training set is composed of training and test images samples, called episodes, belonging to different tasks. During training, these episodes are used to update the initial parameters (weights and bias) of the network, in the direction of the sampled task. Results of meta-learning methods investigated in literature are encouraging and obtain good performances on some few-shot datasets. For this reason and since the goal of this work is to colorize images with a few number of examples, a meta-learning algorithm to tune the network parameters on many different tasks was employed. The chosen algorithm is Reptile [15], and it was combined with an adversarial colorization network composed by a Generator G and a Discriminator D. In other words, the proposed method approaches the colorization problem as a meta-learning one. Intuitively, Reptile works by randomly selecting tasks, then it trains a fast network on each task, and finally it updates the weights of a slow network.

In this proposal, tasks are defined as clusters of the initial dataset. In fact, a typical initial dataset is an unlabeled dataset that contains a wide variety of images, usually photographs. In this setting, for example, a task could be to color all seaside landscape, and another could be to color all cats photos. Those tasks refer to the same problem and use the same dataset, but they are very different at a practical level. A very large amount of images could overwhelm the problem, showing as much seasides and cats as the network needs in order to differentiate between them. The troubles start when only a small dataset is available. As a matter of fact, such a dataset could not have the suitable number of images for making the network learning how to perform both the two example colorizations decently. The idea is to treat different classes of images as different tasks. For dividing tasks, features were extracted from the dataset using a standard approach—e.g., a Convolutional Neural Network (CNN)—and the images were clusterized through K-means. Each cluster is thus considered as a single task. During training, Reptile tunes the network G on the specific task corresponding to an input query image and therefore it adapts the network to a specific colorization class.

The problems and main questions that emerge in approaching a few-shot colorization are various. First of all, how the clusterization should be made in order to generate a coherent and meaningful distribution of tasks? Does a task specialization really improve the colorization or the act of automatically coloring a photo is independent from the subject of the photo itself? Second, how the meta-learning algorithm should be combined with cGAN training, also to prevent overfitting the generator on few images? And last, since the purpose of the work is not to propose a solution to the colorization problem in general, but to propose a method that substantially reduce the amount of images involved in training without—or with minor—losses in state-of-the-art results, how to evaluate the actual performance of the network compared to other approaches? In particular, what are the factors that should be taken in account to state an enhancement, not in the proper colorization, but in few-shot colorization? In the light of these considerations, the contributions of this work are summarized as follows:

- A new architecture that combines meta-learning techniques and cGAN called *MetalGAN* is proposed, specifying in detail how the generator and the discriminator parameters are updated;
- A clusterization and a novel algorithm are described and their ability to tackle image-to-image translation problems is highlighted;
- An empirical demonstration that a very good colorization can be achieved even with a small dataset at disposal during training is provided by showing visual results;

– A precise comparison between two modalities (i.e. our algorithm and only cGAN training) is performed at experimental time, using the same network model and hyper-parameters.

2 Related Work

Image Retrieval: Since we need the clusterization to be as accurate as possible we reserved a particular attention to the recent image retrieval techniques that focus on obtaining optimal descriptors. Recently, deep learning allowed to greatly improve the feature extraction phase of image retrieval. Some of the most interesting papers on the subject are [2,6,19,20,33] and, in particular, MAC descriptors [27], that we ended up using.

Conditional GANs: When a GAN generator is not only conditioned with a random noise vector, but also with more complex information like text [21], labels [13], and especially images, the model to use is a *conditional* GANs (*cGANs*). cGANs allow a better control over the output of the network and thus are very suitable in a lot of image generation tasks. In particular, cGANs conditioned on images were used both in a paired [9] and unpaired [35] way, to produce complex texture [32], to colorize sketches [25] or images [3] and more recently to produce outstanding image synthesis results [16,30]. In this work, the output must be conditioned by the input gray-scale image, in order to train the network at only generating the colors of the image but not shapes, or the image itself.

Meta-Learning: The most relevant meta-learning studies for this work are the Model-Agnostic Meta-Learning (MAML) [5] algorithm and Reptile [15] ones. In particular, we incorporate the Reptile algorithm inside the training phase, allowing the parameters of the generator to be updated in the same fashion as Reptile works. A similar work using MAML is MetaGAN [34], where a generator is used to enhance classification models in order to discriminate between real and fake data, providing generated samples for a task. The main purpose of Meta-GAN is not to improve a generative network, but to perform a better few-shot classification, using generated images to sharpen the decision boundary of the problem. On the contrary, in our approach, the generator is fed with task-related images, and the meta-learner is used to enhance the generator itself, instead of a few-shot classifier. Both MAML and Reptile are based on hyper-parameterized gradient descent, and they learn how to initialize network parameters. Other types of meta-learners work differently. For example, there are many algorithms that learn how to parameterize the optimizer of the network [8,18], or in other cases the optimizer itself is a network [1,12,31]. Moreover, one of the most general approach is to use a recurrent neural network trained on the episodes of a set of tasks [4,14,26,29]. The most interesting result of these meta-learners is the achievement of high performance on small datasets [10,22,28], or datasets used for few-shot learning (e.g., Omniglot) [11].

Fig. 2. Some of the results of the clusterization. It is evident how all the images have lots of features in common.

3 Algorithm

This section goes in detail within the algorithm we propose. Therefore, each subsection focuses on a different aspect of the method. Then, the complete architecture is explained.

3.1 Clusterization of the Dataset

In order to exploit Reptile for image colorization we need to treat our image dataset as it would be composed by a series of separate tasks. For this reason we extract features from each image in the dataset using *activation_43* layer of Resnet50. Then, we calculate MAC descriptors by applying max pooling and L2 normalization on the features. Having these MAC descriptors set F, we first apply Principal Component Analysis (PCA) to reduce features dimension from 2048 to 512 and then apply K-means. K-means produces k clusters, and therefore it divides the dataset in k tasks.

Hence, we expect to find, in each of these clusters, images which are similar to each other, accordingly to their features. For example, a cluster could contain images with grass, another one images with pets and so on and so forth. A visual proof of this assumption is showed in Fig. 2.

3.2 cGAN

As generator architecture, we choose the U-net [23] which is one of the most common for this type of task and we built the discriminator following the classic DCGAN architecture [17], i.e., having each modules composed by Convolutions, Batch Normalization and ReLU layers. Lab is the color space used in this work, because is the one that best approximate human vision and therefore the generator takes as input a grayscale image x_i (the L channel) and outputs the ab channels. Then, we concatenate input and outputs and obtain the final results.

We use L1 loss to model the low-frequencies of our output images and adversarial loss to model the high-frequencies in a similar way of the pix2pix architecture proposed by Isola *et al.* [9].

Therefore, our objective function became:

$$\mathcal{L} = \mathbf{w_{adv}}\mathcal{L}_{adv} + \mathbf{w_{L1}}\mathcal{L}_{L1} \qquad (1)$$

where $\mathbf{w_{adv}}$ and $\mathbf{w_{L1}}$ are weights assigned to the different losses, because we want L1 loss to be more effective than adversarial loss during training.

3.3 Meta-learning

As previously briefly mentioned, we approached the generator training with a Reptile meta-learner. This means that, once a task had been chosen, for a fixed number of meta-iterations, the task is sampled and the gradient of the generator loss function (1) is evaluated to perform a SGD step of optimization. Fixed the initial generator parameters as θ_G, the inner-loop training defines a sequence $\left(\tilde{\theta}_G^{(j)}\right)_{j=0}^{N_{meta-iter}}$, where $\tilde{\theta}_G^{(0)} = \theta_G$. Hence it updates the $\tilde{\theta}_G^{(j)}$ parameters in the direction of the task. Once the inner-loop is completed, the parameter are re-aligned with the Reptile rule:

$$\theta_G \leftarrow \theta_G + \lambda_{ML}\left(\tilde{\theta}_G^{(N_{meta-iter})} - \theta_G\right) \qquad (2)$$

where λ_{ML} is the stepsize hyperparameter of Reptile.

3.4 Complete Architecture of the System

The *MetalGAN* training process is detailed in Algorithm 1. The algorithm is parameterized by the number of epochs N_{epochs}, the number of meta-iterations

---

Algorithm 1. MetalGAN algorithm

1: **for** *epoch* **in** $0 \ldots N_{epochs}$ **do**
2: **for** q_i **in** Q **do**
3:   $K(q_i) \leftarrow$ retrieve_clusters(q_i)
4:   $\tau(q_i) \leftarrow$ get_task_from_cluster($K(q_i)$)
5:   **for** j **in** $0 \ldots N_{meta-iter}$ **do**
6:    sample $\langle input, target \rangle$ from task $\tau(q_i)$
7:    $\varepsilon_{GAN} \leftarrow \nabla_{\theta_D}\mathcal{L}_{adv}(D(G(input)), label\_real)$
8:    $\varepsilon_{L1} \leftarrow \nabla_{\theta_G}\mathcal{L}_{L1}(D(G(input)), target)$
9:    $\varepsilon_G \leftarrow \mathbf{w_{adv}}\varepsilon_{GAN} + \mathbf{w_{L1}}\varepsilon_{L1}$ ▷ calculates loss gradient
10:    $\tilde{\theta}_G^{(j)} \leftarrow \tilde{\theta}_G^{(j-1)} - \lambda_G\varepsilon_G$ ▷ updates inner-loop generator parameters
11:   **end for**
12:   $\theta_G \leftarrow \theta_G + \lambda_{ML}\left(\tilde{\theta}_G^{(N_{meta-iter})} - \theta_G\right)$ ▷ updates generator parameters
13:   **for all** $\langle input, target \rangle$ **in** $\tau(q_i)$ **do**
14:    $\varepsilon_{D_{real}} \leftarrow \nabla_{\theta_D}\mathcal{L}_{adv}(D(target), label\_real)$
15:    $\varepsilon_{D_{fake}} \leftarrow \nabla_{\theta_D}\mathcal{L}_{L1}(D(G(input)), label\_fake)$
16:    $\varepsilon_D \leftarrow \varepsilon_{D_{real}} + \varepsilon_{D_{fake}}$ ▷ calculates discriminator loss gradients
17:    $\theta_D \leftarrow \theta_D - \lambda_D\varepsilon_D$ ▷ update discriminator parameters
18:   **end for**
19: **end for**
20: **end for**

$N_{\text{meta}-\text{iter}}$, the generator and discriminator learning rates λ_G and λ_D, the Reptile stepsize parameter λ_{ML}, and the loss weights $\mathbf{w_{adv}}$ and $\mathbf{w_{L1}}$. During training, we randomly select a query set $Q = \{q_0, \ldots, q_z\}$. Each query q_i corresponds to a single cluster $K(q_i)$. It is worth noting that two queries could point to the same cluster. Having this set, we are able to pick z different images at each epoch by sampling the task $\tau(q_i)$ and to update the generator G as showed in Fig. 3.

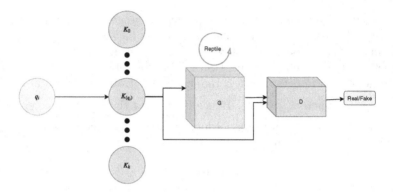

Fig. 3. The MetalGAN architecture: the query q_i points to a cluster $K(q_i)$ that is used as a task to train the generator G with reptile.

The generator is updated by evaluating gradients of its loss functions (adversarial loss $\mathcal{L}_{\text{adv}}$ and L1 loss $\mathcal{L}_{\text{L1}}$), and by adding them to obtain the error ε_G. Then, the network parameters obtained in the inner-loop $\tilde{\theta}_G^{N_{\text{meta}-\text{iter}}}$ are used to update the outer-loop generator parameters θ_G. In the last step, all images of the task $\tau(q_i)$ are used to train the discriminator, calculating the gradients of the discriminator adversarial and L1 losses, and adding them to obtain the discriminator error ε_D. The discriminator parameters θ_D are updated consequently.

4   Experimental Results

For our experiments we choose a slightly modified version of Mini-Imagenet [18]. Since our goal is not classification, we create our training and test set using only images from the 64 classes contained in the training section of Mini-Imagenet. The total number of images in the dataset is 38392. We define two sets of experiments: the first one consists in training the cGAN without the use of Reptile and the second one introduces Reptile and the features clusterization. For both of them we set $\mathbf{w_{adv}} = 1$ and $\mathbf{w_{L1}} = 10^2$. Learning rates of both the generator and the discriminator were set to $\lambda_G = \lambda_D = 10^{-4}$. For K-means clusterization, the parameter k was set to 64 in order to have clusters as much disjoint as possible. For Reptile, we use 100 *meta-iter*, and a stepsize $\lambda_{ML} = 10^{-3}$. The 10% of the dataset images are used as query images. The number of epochs was set to 200. All tests have been executed on a GPU Nvidia 1080 Ti.

Fig. 4. Results obtained using the cGAN only. Each group of three images is composed of the input of the network (grayscale image), the ground truth, and the output of the network.

4.1 cGAN Results

In Fig. 4 are reported some results produced after the training of the cGAN without the clusterization and without Reptile, i.e., with a standard adversarial algorithm. The training data at disposal are very scarce ($\sim$38 k images compared to 1.3 M of the whole Imagenet dataset) and, for this reason, the network is not able to produce compelling results. In particular, the network often fails to understand the difference between foreground and background objects and therefore it applies the colors without following edges and borders. In general, for the cGAN is very difficult to propagate the color correctly and is more common the tendency to apply uneven patches of color. Finally, due to the scarcity of data, the network cannot generalize in an acceptable way and hence the colors in the outputs are not sharp, but, on the contrary, the produced results are very blurry and often colors are applied almost randomly.

4.2 MetalGAN Results

Results of MetalGAN are showed in Fig. 5. It is immediately evident how Reptile improves the results of the cGAN. In particular, colors are sharper and more bright. The reason is that Reptile tunes the generator on each cluster and therefore allows the network to focus more on the more predominant colors present in each task and, as a consequence, even with few examples the produced results are compelling and plausible. For example, in a task with lots of images containing grass or plants there will be an abundance of different shades of green and thus the network will learn very quickly to reproduce similar colors over the test set. On the contrary, an image that is very different from the majority of images in the rest of its task could be colorized poorly. This problem, however, is not very frequent since the difference has to be very large in order to produce nasty results.

Other examples can be found at implab.ce.unipr.it/?page_id=1011.

4.3 Quantitative Evaluation

In order to evaluate the quality of the generated samples, we used the Inception Score [24], because it is a very good metric to simulate human judgement. We calculated the Inception Score of generated images using both cGAN and MetalGAN (see Table 1). The score also measures the diversity of the generated images, so a high score is better than a lower one. The MetalGAN approach significantly improves standard cGAN score.

Fig. 5. Results of MetalGAN. Each of three images consists of the grayscale input given to the network, the ground truth, and the output of the network. The four represented images belong to different clusters.

Table 1. The Inception Scores are computed on generated images from the Mini-ImageNet dataset, mean and standard deviation are reported for both cGAN and MetalGAN results.

Dataset	Mean	Std
cGAN	3.20	0.83
MetalGAN	9.16	1.12

5 Conclusions

In normal adversarial generative settings, having few images at disposal during training produces a complete failure in the colorization. In this paper, we proposed a novel architecture which mix adversarial training with meta-learning techniques, called MetalGAN. As shown by experimental results, even with few images the network trained with MetalGAN was able to produce a well-looking colorization. The clusterization of the dataset and the use of clusters as tasks help at directing the colorization to the most probable suitable colors for the image, and meta-learning allows to train the network on few examples. As future developments, we plan to include the discriminator in the meta-learning training phase, and to test the method on other small datasets in order to prove the generalization capability of the proposed MetalGAN architecture.

References

1. Andrychowicz, M., et al.: Learning to learn by gradient descent by gradient descent. In: Advances in Neural Information Processing Systems, pp. 3981–3989 (2016)
2. Babenko, A., Slesarev, A., Chigorin, A., Lempitsky, V.: Neural codes for image retrieval. In: Fleet, D., Pajdla, T., Schiele, B., Tuytelaars, T. (eds.) ECCV 2014. LNCS, vol. 8689, pp. 584–599. Springer, Cham (2014). https://doi.org/10.1007/978-3-319-10590-1_38
3. Cao, Y., Zhou, Z., Zhang, W., Yu, Y.: Unsupervised diverse colorization via generative adversarial networks. In: Ceci, M., Hollmén, J., Todorovski, L., Vens, C., Džeroski, S. (eds.) ECML PKDD 2017. LNCS (LNAI), vol. 10534, pp. 151–166. Springer, Cham (2017). https://doi.org/10.1007/978-3-319-71249-9_10
4. Duan, Y., Schulman, J., Chen, X., Bartlett, P.L., Sutskever, I., Abbeel, P.: RL^2: fast reinforcement learning via slow reinforcement learning. arXiv preprint arXiv:1611.02779 (2016)
5. Finn, C., Abbeel, P., Levine, S.: Model-agnostic meta-learning for fast adaptation of deep networks. In: Proceedings of the 34th International Conference on Machine Learning-Volume 70, pp. 1126–1135 (2017). JMLR.org
6. Gong, Y., Wang, L., Guo, R., Lazebnik, S.: Multi-scale orderless pooling of deep convolutional activation features. In: Fleet, D., Pajdla, T., Schiele, B., Tuytelaars, T. (eds.) ECCV 2014. LNCS, vol. 8695, pp. 392–407. Springer, Cham (2014). https://doi.org/10.1007/978-3-319-10584-0_26
7. Goodfellow, I., et al.: Generative adversarial nets. In: Advances in Neural Information Processing Systems, pp. 2672–2680 (2014)
8. Hochreiter, S., Younger, A.S., Conwell, P.R.: Learning to learn using gradient descent. In: Dorffner, G., Bischof, H., Hornik, K. (eds.) ICANN 2001. LNCS, vol. 2130, pp. 87–94. Springer, Heidelberg (2001). https://doi.org/10.1007/3-540-44668-0_13
9. Isola, P., Zhu, J.Y., Zhou, T., Efros, A.A.: Image-to-image translation with conditional adversarial networks. In: Proceedings of the IEEE Conference on Computer Vision and Pattern Recognition, pp. 1125–1134 (2017)
10. Yelamarthi, S.K., Reddy, S.K., Mishra, A., Mittal, A.: A zero-shot framework for sketch based image retrieval. In: Ferrari, V., Hebert, M., Sminchisescu, C., Weiss, Y. (eds.) ECCV 2018. LNCS, vol. 11208, pp. 316–333. Springer, Cham (2018). https://doi.org/10.1007/978-3-030-01225-0_19
11. Lake, B.M., Salakhutdinov, R., Tenenbaum, J.B.: Human-level concept learning through probabilistic program induction. Science **350**(6266), 1332–1338 (2015)
12. Li, K., Malik, J.: Learning to optimize neural nets. arXiv preprint arXiv:1703.00441 (2017)
13. Mirza, M., Osindero, S.: Conditional generative adversarial nets. arXiv preprint arXiv:1411.1784 (2014)
14. Mishra, N., Rohaninejad, M., Chen, X., Abbeel, P.: A simple neural attentive meta-learner. arXiv preprint arXiv:1707.03141 (2017)
15. Nichol, A., Achiam, J., Schulman, J.: On first-order meta-learning algorithms. CoRR, abs/1803.02999 (2018)
16. Park, T., Liu, M.Y., Wang, T.C., Zhu, J.Y.: Semantic image synthesis with spatially-adaptive normalization. arXiv preprint arXiv:1903.07291 (2019)
17. Radford, A., Metz, L., Chintala, S.: Unsupervised representation learning with deep convolutional generative adversarial networks. arXiv preprint arXiv:1511.06434 (2015)

18. Ravi, S., Larochelle, H.: Optimization as a model for few-shot learning (2016)
19. Razavian, A.S., Sullivan, J., Carlsson, S., Maki, A.: Visual instance retrieval with deep convolutional networks. ITE Trans. Media Technol. Appl. **4**(3), 251–258 (2016)
20. Reddy Mopuri, K., Venkatesh Babu, R.: Object level deep feature pooling for compact image representation. In: Proceedings of the IEEE Conference on Computer Vision and Pattern Recognition Workshops, pp. 62–70 (2015)
21. Reed, S., Akata, Z., Yan, X., Logeswaran, L., Schiele, B., Lee, H.: Generative adversarial text to image synthesis. arXiv preprint arXiv:1605.05396 (2016)
22. Rezende, D.J., Mohamed, S., Danihelka, I., Gregor, K., Wierstra, D.: One-shot generalization in deep generative models. In: Proceedings of the 33rd International Conference on International Conference on Machine Learning - Volume 48, ICML 2016, pp. 1521–1529 (2016). JMLR.org, http://dl.acm.org/citation.cfm?id=3045390.3045551
23. Ronneberger, O., Fischer, P., Brox, T.: U-Net: convolutional networks for biomedical image segmentation. In: Navab, N., Hornegger, J., Wells, W.M., Frangi, A.F. (eds.) MICCAI 2015. LNCS, vol. 9351, pp. 234–241. Springer, Cham (2015). https://doi.org/10.1007/978-3-319-24574-4_28
24. Salimans, T., Goodfellow, I., Zaremba, W., Cheung, V., Radford, A., Chen, X.: Improved techniques for training gans. In: Advances in Neural Information Processing Systems, pp. 2234–2242 (2016)
25. Sangkloy, P., Lu, J., Fang, C., Yu, F., Hays, J.: Scribbler: controlling deep image synthesis with sketch and color. In: Proceedings of the IEEE Conference on Computer Vision and Pattern Recognition, pp. 5400–5409 (2017)
26. Santoro, A., Bartunov, S., Botvinick, M., Wierstra, D., Lillicrap, T.: Meta-learning with memory-augmented neural networks. In: International Conference on Machine Learning, pp. 1842–1850 (2016)
27. Tolias, G., Sicre, R., Jégou, H.: Particular object retrieval with integral max-pooling of CNN activations. arXiv preprint arXiv:1511.05879 (2015)
28. Vinyals, O., Blundell, C., Lillicrap, T., Wierstra, D., et al.: Matching networks for one shot learning. In: Advances in Neural Information Processing Systems, pp. 3630–3638 (2016)
29. Wang, J.X., et al.: Learning to reinforcement learn. arXiv preprint arXiv:1611.05763 (2016)
30. Wang, T.C., Liu, M.Y., Zhu, J.Y., Tao, A., Kautz, J., Catanzaro, B.: High-resolution image synthesis and semantic manipulation with conditional GANs. In: Proceedings of the IEEE Conference on Computer Vision and Pattern Recognition, pp. 8798–8807 (2018)
31. Wichrowska, O., et al.: Learned optimizers that scale and generalize. In: Proceedings of the 34th International Conference on Machine Learning-Volume 70, pp. 3751–3760 (2017). JMLR.org
32. Xian, W., et al.: Texturegan: controlling deep image synthesis with texture patches. In: Proceedings of the IEEE Conference on Computer Vision and Pattern Recognition, pp. 8456–8465 (2018)
33. Yue-Hei Ng, J., Yang, F., Davis, L.S.: Exploiting local features from deep networks for image retrieval. In: Proceedings of the IEEE Conference on Computer Vision and Pattern Recognition Workshops, pp. 53–61 (2015)

34. Zhang, R., Che, T., Ghahramani, Z., Bengio, Y., Song, Y.: Metagan: an adversarial approach to few-shot learning. In: Advances in Neural Information Processing Systems, pp. 2365–2374 (2018)
35. Zhu, J.Y., Park, T., Isola, P., Efros, A.A.: Unpaired image-to-image translation using cycle-consistent adversarial networks. In: Proceedings of the IEEE International Conference on Computer Vision, pp. 2223–2232 (2017)

Towards Multi-source Adaptive Semantic Segmentation

Paolo Russo[1,2]([✉]) [iD], Tatiana Tommasi[3] [iD], and Barbara Caputo[1,3] [iD]

[1] Istituto Italiano di Tecnologia, Genoa, Italy
`paolo.russo@uniroma1.it`
[2] Sapienza Università di Roma, Rome, Italy
[3] Politecnico di Torino, Turin, Italy
{`tatiana.tommasi,barbara.caputo`}`@polito.it`

Abstract. When applying powerful deep learning approaches on real world tasks like pixel level annotation of urban scenes it becomes clear that even those strong learners may fail dramatically and are still not ready for deployment in the wild. For semantic segmentation, one of the main practical challenges consists in finding large annotated collection to feed the data hungry networks. Synthetic images in combination with adaptive learning models have shown to help with this issue, but in general, different synthetic sources are analyzed separately, not leveraging on the potential growth in data amount and sample variability that could result from their combination. With our work we investigate for the first time the multi-source adaptive semantic segmentation setting, proposing some best practice rule for the data and model integration. Moreover we show how to extend an existing semantic segmentation approach to deal with multiple sources obtaining promising results.

Keywords: Semantic segmentation · Domain adaptation

1 Introduction

Semantic segmentation has recently become one of the most prominent task in computer vision. Indeed the ability to assign a label to each pixel of an input image is crucial whenever a very detailed description of the observed scene is needed, as in fine-grained object categorization [25] and autonomous driving [21,24]. However, due to the complexity of manual labeling each image pixel, this task is plagued by the scarcity of large annotated datasets, which are instead essential to leverage the power of deep learning algorithms. Synthetic images appear a useful alternative, but they reduce only in part the described issue. In the case of urban scene scenarios for autonomous driving, computer games can be used to generate automatically images with their ground truth labels, but their level of realism is still low which induces the further need of domain adaptation methods. Thus, while solving the lack of data problem, other challenges come from the development of methods able to reduce the domain gap. Up today,

E. Ricci et al. (Eds.): ICIAP 2019, LNCS 11751, pp. 292–301, 2019.
https://doi.org/10.1007/978-3-030-30642-7_26

those two aspects of the same problem has always been tackled separately. On one side several research groups have focused on developing different simulators with an increasing set of visual details like urban layouts, buildings, vehicles and several weather conditions, with the aim of augmenting the realism of the produced images [4,18]. On the other side, many recent works focus on integrating techniques to align the domains either at feature, pixel or output label space level, even considering combination of those levels with different adversarial losses [2,7,21]. Each of the proposed synthetic domains is generally used to train a model and test it on real images, but the different synthetic sources are always kept separated even if this choice limits again the amount and variance of annotated samples usable as source. The domain adaptation literature for object classification has shown that integrating multiple sources helps generalization [5,6,26]. With our work we import this strategy for the first time in the semantic segmentation framework, studying how the positive trend can be maintained by practically merging the two solutions described above. The path to this goal is not trivial due to the practical differences in class statistics across domains, as well as in texture, resolution and aspect ratio for which we propose best practice rules. Moreover, we go over the simple source sample combination, exploiting a multi-level strategy that adapts each single source to the target while cooperating with the adaptation of the joint data source. Besides the standard synthetic to real direction, we extend our analysis to the case of a synthetic dataset used as target when the source combines real images and a different synthetic collection. This setting allows to better understand the difference across various synthetic sources and paves the way to the simultaneous exploitation of both the synthetic-to-real and real-to-synthetic adaptive directions [19].

2 Related Works

The deep learning revolution started within the context of object classification [9] but has rapidly extended to many other tasks. The first work to put semantic segmentation under the deep learning spotlight was [14] that showed how fully connected networks could be used to assign a label to each image pixel. Several following works have then extended the interest around this task proposing tailored architectures which involve multi-scale feature combinations [1,23] or integrate context information [13,27]. The main issue with deep semantic segmentation remains that of collecting a large amount of images with pixel-based expensive annotations. Some solutions in this sense have been proposed either developing methods able to deal with weak annotations [8,15], or leveraging on other domain images, as the synthetic ones produced by 3D renderings of urban scenes [4,17,18]. To avoid the drop in performance due to the synthetic to real shift, domain adaptation techniques have been integrated with approaches involving different network levels. The most widely used solution consists in adding a domain classifier used adversarially to minimize the gap among different feature spaces [2]. In [21], adversarial learning is used both on the segmentation output and on inner network features. A third family of methods applies adaptation directly at the pixel level with GAN-based style transfer techniques [7].

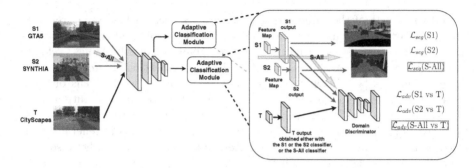

Fig. 1. Training Phase: our network has two *Adaptive Classification Modules* at different levels. In each module the source segmentation is predicted either with two separate source-specific branches or just using one overall *S-All* branch (we did not explicitly draw the *S-All* branch to avoid cluttering the image). The segmentation loss is computed based on the sources ground truth. Moreover a domain discriminator is used adversarially to reduce the domain shift comparing the target T either with each source-specific output, or with the output obtained by *S-All*.

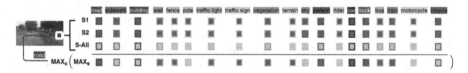

Fig. 2. Test Phase: each classifier produces a semantic segmentation output (*S1*: blue, *S2*: red, *S-All*: yellow). For every pixel we apply a max-pooling operator over the three outputs. Finally the class assigned to the pixel is the one with the highest score over the C classes ($C = 19$ when testing on Cityscapes). (Color figure online)

Other alternative strategies have focused on the introduction of critic networks to identify samples close to the classification boundary and exploit them to improve feature generalization [20], or defined a curriculum adaptation to focus first on easy and then on hard samples during the learning process [24], or even introduced tailored loss functions [28].

Our work is orthogonal to all those research efforts. Indeed up to our knowledge, none of the mentioned previous works have investigated the challenging case of multi-source adaptive semantic segmentation. We build over the multi-level approach presented in [21] and extend it to tackle two different sources and one target domain. Moreover, we investigate the effect of integrating a further pixel-level adaptive approach originally presented for unsupervised image style transfer [11] to further reduce the domain shift.

3   Method

An overall view of the proposed architecture can be seen in Fig. 1. Our domain adaptation method starts with a segmentation network **G** which takes the sources annotated images (I^s, Y^s) and the unlabeled target images (I^t) as input. The network ends with an *Adaptive Classification Module* that contain separate classification branches for each source as well as a domain discriminator **D**. Each source classification branch produces a segmentation softmax output $P^s = \mathbf{G}(I^s) \in \mathbb{R}^{H,W,C}$, where (H, W) are the height and width image dimensions and C is the number of categories. The used semantic segmentation loss is

$$\mathcal{L}^s_{seg}(I^s) = -\sum_{h,w} \sum_{c=1,ldots,C} Y^s_{h,w,c} \log(P^s_{h,w,c}), \tag{1}$$

where $s = 1, 2$ for the two sources.

The domain discriminator **D** takes as input the segmentation output of both the source and target data and is optimized through the binary loss

$$\mathcal{L}_d(P) = -\sum_{h,w} (1 - z) \log(\mathbf{D}(P)_{h,w,0}) + (z) \log(\mathbf{D}(P)_{h,w,1}), \tag{2}$$

with $z = 0$ if the sample is drawn from the target domain, and $z = 1$ for the sample from the source domains. Finally the adversarial loss whose gradients backpropagates on the segmentation network to maximize the confusion between P^s and P^t is

$$\mathcal{L}_{adv}(I^t) = -\sum_{h,w} \log(\mathbf{D}(P^t)_{h,w,1}). \tag{3}$$

To further improve the adaptation effect involving inner-features, another adaptive classification module is also applied to a lower network level. Thus the overall loss is

$$\mathcal{L}(I_s, I_t) = \sum_{k=feature,output} \left\{ \sum_{s=1,2} \lambda^s_{seg} \mathcal{L}^s_{seg}(I^s) + \lambda^s_{adv} \mathcal{L}^s_{adv}(I^t) \right\}_k \tag{4}$$

and the network is optimized on the basis of the following criterion

$$\max_{\mathbf{D}} \min_{\mathbf{G}} \mathcal{L}(I_s, I_t). \tag{5}$$

We also repeated the whole training considering a single source branch that sees all the images together regardless of the domain identity: we indicate it as *S-All*, with its own $\mathcal{L}^{S-All}_{seg}$ loss. From the predictions of each available source and from *S-All*, we finally need a single segmentation target output. For this purpose we apply a max-pooling operator that runs on the prediction logits $\hat{Y}$ and selects the highest score per class, then followed by a second max-pooling over the classes:

$$\text{Assigned Label}(h, w) = \max_{c=1...,C} \max_{s=\{1,2,S-All\}} (\hat{Y}^s_{h,w,c}). \tag{6}$$

As illustrated in Fig. 2. Note that by keeping only *S-All* we fall back to the single source original method in [21].

3.1   Adding Pixel-Level Adaptation

As explained above the proposed adaptation process is applied both at the output and at the feature level. Inspired by the extensive GAN-based literature on style-transfer, we integrated in our method also a pixel-level adaptation process, directly modifying the input images. Specifically we used the Unsupervised Image-to-Image Translation (UNIT, [11]) method. It assumes that a pair of corresponding images in two different domains can be mapped to the same latent code in a shared space. By using a Coupled GANs [12] and imposing weight sharing constraints on the mapping functions, the method is able to change the style of an image so that it looks like coming from a different domain. We applied UNIT to produce target-like copies of the source images. After this (totally unsupervised) pre-processing step, the proposed architecture is used on the new stylized sources.

4   Experiments

4.1   Datasets and Setup

We used three publicly available datasets in our experiments as detailed in the following.

Cityscapes [3] is a real-world, vehicle-egocentric image dataset collected in 50 cities in Germany and nearby countries. It provides a training set made of 2,993 images as well as 503 images for validation purpose, having 2048 × 1024 resolution. All the training, validation, and test images are accurately annotated with per pixel category labels by human experts. We followed the VisDA Semantic Segmentation challenge protocol, focusing on 19 labeled classes.

GTA5 [17] is composed by 24,966 images with resolution 1914 × 1052, synthesized from the homonym video game and set in Los Angeles. Ground truth and annotations are compatible with the Cityscapes dataset [3] that contains 19 categories. Depending on the role of the dataset in the experiments we used either all the available images (as source) or a 500 sample subset (as target).

Synthia [18] is made of 9400 images at 1280 × 760 resolution compatible with the Cityscapes dataset, but covering only 16 object categories. Even if the virtual city used to generate the synthetic images does not correspond to any of the real cities covered by Cityscapes, Synthia shows almost photo-realistic frames with different light conditions and weather, multiple season, and a great variety of dynamic objects. With the same approach of GTA5, we used the full dataset for training and the first 500 images while testing.

We ran each experiment by choosing two datasets as sources domains, and the third as target (unsupervised) domain. In previous works, the standard setting consists in evaluating the recognition performance only of the shared classes across domains, thus operating a subselection on Cityscapes when used against Synthia. We find it natural that different data collections may have only partially overlapping class sets and it should not be necessary to proceed every time to an ad-hoc class choice [22]. Thus, we decided to keep all the datasets with their own original categories. Furthermore we investigate the effect of the resolution on the final segmentation accuracy considering a high and a low resolution case. In the first, all the images keep their own original size, while in the second they are all downscaled by halving the native image dimensions. Finally we remark that the three analyzed domains present remarkable differences on mean values. Since the adversarial approaches are very sensitive to non-zero mean data, we have chosen to work by removing from each dataset its own calculated image mean.

4.2   Implementation Details

The main backbone of our segmentation network is the DeepLabv2 [1], which uses a ResNet-101 pretrained on ImageNet and COCO [10]. This architecture incorporates atrous convolution, which effectively enlarge the field of view of filters without increasing the number of parameters. Within the *Adaptive Classification Module* we have two separate network branches, one for each source, producing a 2D predictions followed by an interpolation function that rises the resolution to that of the original ground truth label (during training). At test time the same interpolation function was used to calculate accuracy using the target ground truth as reference. Following [21,29], the module contains also a discriminator that classify the images on the basis of their source or target domain label. The discriminators model is the same of DCGAN [16], with convolutional layers interspersed by Leaky Relu non-linearities. Note that although there are two adaptive classification modules in the network, the classification output produced by the inner module has shown to be less reliable than the ending one which is actually the only used at test time.

The network is trained with the Adam solver and learning rate 0.0001, while for the architecture hyperparameters we kept the same values of [21]. The number of iterations was set to 50k, but we observed convergence already after 20k iterations.

Table 1. Performance values on the chosen experiments expressed with mIoU. The proposed method outperform the no adaptation results as well as single branches and *S-All* method on all the experiments but the one with GTA5 as target at high resolution, where it lags behind *S-All* result due to the poor performance of S2 branch.

Res	Sources	Target	No adapt	S1	S2	S-All	Max merge
Orig.	GTA5, Synthia	Cityscapes	39.98	39.55	34.51	41.81	**42.76**
	Cityscapes, GTA5	Synthia	35.55	35.25	34.07	36.37	**37.52**
	Cityscapes, Synthia	GTA5	37.97	41.17	23.60	**40.57**	39.49
Redu.	GTA5, Synthia	Cityscapes	–	39.44	33.36	40.89	**41.32**
	Cityscapes, GTA5	Synthia	–	30.52	30.02	32.87	**33.11**
	Cityscapes, Synthia	GTA5	–	44.93	23.28	41.87	**42.78**

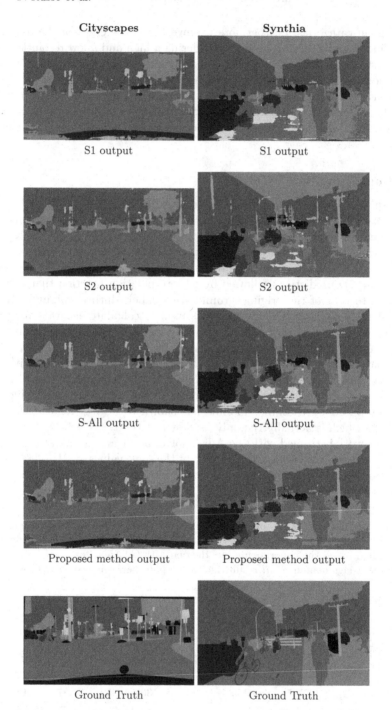

Fig. 3. Predicted labels in the case of Cityscapes and Synthia target datasets. The proposed method is able to better recognize some parts of the images like road pieces (dark violet) w.r.t. single branches or *S-All* approach. (Color figure online)

Table 2. Intersection over Union for each experiment category. The experiments are performed on full resolution. Some particular categories (road, terrain, cars) seems to better exploit the power of the proposed method w.r.t the *S-All* one, and they contribute to the final accuracy increase due to their frequent presence on the scene.

Setting	Road	Sidewalk	Building	Wall	Fence	Pole	Light	Sign	Vegetation	Terrain	Sky	Person	Rider	Car	Truck	Bus	Train	Motocycle	Bycycle
T: Cityscapes, *S-All*	85.0	36.3	79.9	21.5	18.0	29.5	25.5	19.3	81.4	23.5	78.0	57.6	23.9	75.4	35.0	40.7	2.6	31.7	29.9
T: Cityscapes, Max Merge	87.8	37.1	80.2	20.3	14.9	29.8	26.0	20.5	82.0	31.4	78.0	57.6	25.3	80.5	31.6	43.5	0.0	29.8	36.1
T: GTA5, Max Merge	82.4	29.4	56.5	41.6	6.7	31.1	26.4	19.3	64.4	7.4	88.1	42.8	50.3	74.2	36.8	31.4	0.0	32.5	29.3
T: Synthia, Max Merge	68.3	66.8	86.6	1.7	1.7	39.5	27.2	10.9	73.7	0.0	90.6	55.5	33.7	55.7	0.0	48.5	0.0	23.0	29.3

4.3 Results

The main experiment results are reported in Table 1. The values reported are the mean Intersection Over Union (mIoU) which is the standard accuracy measurement used on semantic segmentation tasks.

The proposed method is able to improve the *S-All* results on almost all the performed experiments, even while the single source branch prove to reach lower accuracy w.r.t. the *S-All* result, getting a boost ranging from 0.4% to 1.2%, while w.r.t. the results without any adaptation at all (No Adapt column) the difference of performance are from 1.5% to 2.7%. Looking more into detail, the most difficult setting is the one with GTA5 as target domain, as the Synthia source domain fails to properly reach an acceptable accuracy, and this worsen the final performance in the full resolution case. The input data resolution has an impact on final accuracy ranging from 1.44% in the case of Cityscapes as target, to 4.41% in the case of Synthia target, showing that in order to obtain the best possible accuracy is preferable to keep resolution as high as possible, while at the same time demonstrates that in some cases a lower resolution can dramatically speed up the training phase (around 3x faster in our case) while losing a small amount of accuracy (target Cityscapes experiment).

Looking at per-class IoU measurements in Table 2, we noticed how the overall increase of performance can be attributed to some specific classes IoU improvement; terrain, road, vegetation and car seem to be the classes which better take advantage of the proposed method. This effect can be noticed also in the produced images in Fig. 3, where some parts of the road are better reproduced in our method w.r.t *S-All* output.

A final additional experiment have been performed by applying UNIT method to the GTA5 and Synthia datasets in order to convert their style to the Cityscapes one, after which the proposed architecture have been trained regularly with two stylized GTA5 and Synthia datasets as sources and Cityscapes as target. The measured accuracy obtained by merging the two branches *S1* and *S2* is 44.5%, which is very promising result, taking also into account that it can be further improved by exploiting *S-All* branch too. The UNIT architecture and our method have been trained separately because of the huge amount of GPU memory required in order to train them jointly.

5 Conclusions

We have presented a study on multi-sources domain adaptation on semantic segmentation tasks. The study revealed how simply putting all the sources together is a sub-optimal approach, and we proposed a simple method to leverage on individual sources as well as *S-All* method. The experiment performed show promising results, with a small but steady improvement on the majority of settings. Further investigation is required in order to better understand the effect of some parameters like the chosen data resolution and the datasets means, and the possibility of applying a style transfer method like UNIT jointly with the domain adaptation method into a fully integrated architecture.

References

1. Chen, L.-C., Papandreou, G., Kokkinos, I., Murphy, K., Yuille, A.L.: DeepLab: semantic image segmentation with deep convolutional nets, atrous convolution, and fully connected CRFs. IEEE Tran. Pattern Anal. Mach. Intell. **40**(4), 834–848 (2018)
2. Chen, Y.-H., Chen, W.-Y., Chen, Y.-T., Tsai, B.-C., Frank Wang, Y.-C., Sun, M.: No more discrimination, cross city adaptation of road scene segmenters. In: ICCV (2017)
3. Cordts, M.: The cityscapes dataset for semantic urban scene understanding. In: Proceedings of the IEEE Conference on Computer Vision and Pattern Recognition, pp. 3213–3223 (2016)
4. Dosovitskiy, A., Ros, G., Codevilla, F., Lopez, A., Koltun, V.: CARLA: an open urban driving simulator. In: Conference on Robot Learning (CoRL) (2017)
5. Duan, L., Tsang, I.W., Dong, X., Chua, T.-S.: Domain adaptation from multiple sources via auxiliary classifiers (2009)
6. Duan, L., Dong, X., Tsang, I.W.: Domain adaptation from multiple sources: a domain-dependent regularization approach. IEEE Trans. Neural Netw. Learn. Syst. **23**(3), 504–518 (2012)
7. Hoffman, J., et al.: CyCADA: Cycle-consistent adversarial domain adaptation. In: ICML (2018)
8. Khoreva, A., Benenson, R., Hosang, J., Hein, M., Schiele, B.: Simple does it: weakly supervised instance and semantic segmentation. In CVPR (2017)
9. Krizhevsky, A., Sutskever, I., Hinton, G.E.: ImageNet classification with deep convolutional neural networks. In: Advances in Neural Information Processing Systems, pp. 1097–1105 (2012)
10. Lin, T.-Y., et al.: Microsoft COCO: common objects in context. In: Fleet, D., Pajdla, T., Schiele, B., Tuytelaars, T. (eds.) ECCV 2014. LNCS, vol. 8693, pp. 740–755. Springer, Cham (2014). https://doi.org/10.1007/978-3-319-10602-1_48
11. Liu, M.-Y., Breuel, T., Kautz, J.: Unsupervised image-to-image translation networks. In: Advances in Neural Information Processing Systems, pp. 700–708 (2017)
12. Liu, M.-Y., Tuzel, O.: Coupled generative adversarial networks. In: Advances in Neural Information Processing Systems, pp. 469–477 (2016)

13. Liu, W., Rabinovich, A., Berg, A.C.: ParseNet: looking wider to see better (2016)
14. Long, J., Shelhamer, E., Darrell, T.: Fully convolutional networks for semantic segmentation. In: Proceedings of the IEEE Conference on Computer Vision and Pattern Recognition, pp. 3431–3440 (2015)
15. Pathak, D., Krahenbuhl, P., Darrell, T.: Constrained convolutional neural networks for weakly supervised segmentation. In: ICCV (2015)
16. Radford, A., Metz, L., Chintala, S.: Unsupervised representation learning with deep convolutional generative adversarial networks. arXiv preprint arXiv:1511.06434 (2015)
17. Richter, S.R., Vineet, V., Roth, S., Koltun, V.: Playing for data: ground truth from computer games. In: Leibe, B., Matas, J., Sebe, N., Welling, M. (eds.) ECCV 2016. LNCS, vol. 9906, pp. 102–118. Springer, Cham (2016). https://doi.org/10.1007/978-3-319-46475-6_7
18. Ros, G., Sellart, L., Materzynska, J., Vazquez, D., Lopez, A.M.: The synthia dataset: a large collection of synthetic images for semantic segmentation of urban scenes. In: The IEEE Conference on Computer Vision and Pattern Recognition (CVPR), June 2016
19. Russo, P., Carlucci, F.M., Tommasi, T., Caputo, B.: From source to target and back: symmetric bi-directional adaptive GAN. In: Computer Vision and Pattern Recognition (CVPR) (2018)
20. Saito, K., Ushiku, Y., Harada, T., Saenko, K.: Adversarial dropout regularization. In: ICLR (2018)
21. Tsai, Y.-H., Hung, W.-C., Schulter, S., Sohn, K., Yang, M.-H., Chandraker, M.: Learning to adapt structured output space for semantic segmentation. In: IEEE Conference on Computer Vision and Pattern Recognition (CVPR) (2018)
22. Xu, R., Chen, Z., Zuo, W., Yan, J., Lin, L.: Deep cocktail network: multi-source unsupervised domain adaptation with category shift. In: Computer Vision and Pattern Recognition (CVPR) (2018)
23. Yu, F., Koltun, V.: Multi-scale context aggregation by dilated convolutions. In: ICLR (2016)
24. Zhang, Y., David, P., Gong, B.: Curriculum domain adaptation for semantic segmentation of urban scenes. In: Proceedings of the IEEE International Conference on Computer Vision, pp. 2020–2030 (2017)
25. Zhao, B., Feng, J., Xiao, W., Yan, S.: A survey on deep learning-based fine-grained object classification and semantic segmentation. Int. J. Autom. Comput. 14(2), 119–135 (2017)
26. Zhao, H., Zhang, S., Wu, G., Costeira, J.P., Moura, J.M.F., Gordon, G.J.: Multiple source domain adaptation with adversarial learning. In: Workshop of the International Conference on Learning Representations (ICLR-W) (2018)
27. Zhao, H., Shi, J., Qi, X., Wang, X., Jia, J.: Pyramid scene parsing network. In: CVPR (2017)
28. Zhu, X., Zhou, H., Yang, C., Shi, J., Lin, D.: Penalizing top performers: conservative loss for semantic segmentation adaptation. In: Ferrari, V., Hebert, M., Sminchisescu, C., Weiss, Y. (eds.) ECCV 2018. LNCS, vol. 11211, pp. 587–603. Springer, Cham (2018). https://doi.org/10.1007/978-3-030-01234-2_35
29. Zou, Y., Yu, Z., Vijaya Kumar, B.V.K., Wang, J.: Unsupervised domain adaptation for semantic segmentation via class-balanced self-training. In: Ferrari, V., Hebert, M., Sminchisescu, C., Weiss, Y. (eds.) ECCV 2018. LNCS, vol. 11207, pp. 297–313. Springer, Cham (2018). https://doi.org/10.1007/978-3-030-01219-9_18

Learning Pedestrian Detection
from Virtual Worlds

Giuseppe Amato, Luca Ciampi$^{(\boxtimes)}$, Fabrizio Falchi, Claudio Gennaro,
and Nicola Messina

Institute of Information Science and Technologies (ISTI), Italian National Research
Council (CNR), Via G. Moruzzi 1, 56124 Pisa, Italy
{giuseppe.amato,luca.ciampi,fabrizio.falchi,claudio.gennaro,
nicola.messina}@isti.cnr.it

Abstract. In this paper, we present a real-time pedestrian detection
system that has been trained using a virtual environment. This is a
very popular topic of research having endless practical applications and
recently, there was an increasing interest in deep learning architectures
for performing such a task. However, the availability of large labeled
datasets is a key point for an effective train of such algorithms. For this
reason, in this work, we introduced *ViPeD*, a new synthetically generated set of images extracted from a realistic 3D video game where
the labels can be automatically generated exploiting 2D pedestrian positions extracted from the graphics engine. We exploited this new synthetic
dataset fine-tuning a state-of-the-art computationally efficient Convolutional Neural Network (CNN). A preliminary experimental evaluation,
compared to the performance of other existing approaches trained on
real-world images, shows encouraging results.

1 Introduction

Pedestrian detection remains a very popular topic of research having endless
practical applications. An important application domain of this topic is certainly
video surveillance for public security, such as crime prevention, identification of
vandalism, etc. A real-time response in the case of an incident, however, requires
manual observation of the video stream, which is in most cases economically not
feasible.

We propose a real-time CNN-based solution that is able to localize pedestrian
instances in images captured by smart cameras. CNNs are a popular choice for
current objects detectors since they are able to automatically learn features characterizing the objects themselves; in the last years, these solutions outperformed
approaches relying instead on hand-crafted features.

The great challenge we must address using CNNs is the ability of these
algorithms to generalize to new scenarios having different characteristics, like
different perspectives, illuminations and object scales. This is a must when we
are dealing with smart devices that should be easily installed and deployed,
without the need for an early tuning phase. Therefore, the availability of large

E. Ricci et al. (Eds.): ICIAP 2019, LNCS 11751, pp. 302–312, 2019.
https://doi.org/10.1007/978-3-030-30642-7_27

labeled training datasets that cover as much as possible the differences between various scenarios is a key point for training state-of-the-art CNNs. Although there are some large annotated generic datasets, such as ImageNet [1] and MS COCO [2], annotating the images is a very time-consuming operation, since it requires great human effort, and it is error-prone. Furthermore, sometimes it is also problematic to create a training/testing dataset with specific characteristics.

A possible solution to this problem is to create a suitable dataset collecting images from *virtual* world environments that mimics as much as possible all the characteristics of our target real-world scenario. In this paper, we introduce a new dataset named *ViPeD* (*Virtual Pedestrian Dataset*), a large collection of images taken from the highly photo-realistic video game *GTA V - Grand Theft Auto V* developed by *Rockstar North*, that extends the *JTA (Joint Track Auto)* dataset presented in [3]. We demonstrate that we can improve performance and achieve competitive results compared to the state-of-the-art approaches in the pedestrian detection task.

In particular, we train a state-of-the-art object detector, YOLOv3 [4], over the newly introduced ViPeDdataset. Then, we test the trained detector on the MOT17 detection dataset (*MOT17Det*) [5], a real-world dataset suited for pedestrian detection, in order to measure the generalization capabilities of the proposed solution with respect to real-world scenarios.

To summarize, in this work we propose a real-time CNN-based system able to detect pedestrians for surveillance smart cameras. We train the algorithm using a new dataset collected using images from a realistic video game and we take advantage of the graphics engine for extracting the annotations without any human intervention. Finally, we evaluate the proposed method on a real-world dataset demonstrating his effectiveness and robustness to other scenarios.

2   Related Work

In this section, we review the most important works in object and pedestrian detection. We also analyze previous studies on using synthetic datasets as training sets. Pedestrian detection is highly related to object detection. It deals with recognizing the specific class of pedestrians, usually walking in urban environments. Approaches for tackling the pedestrian detection problem are usually subdivided into two main research areas. The first class of detectors is based on hand-crafted features, such as ICF (Integral Channel Features) [6–10]. Those methods can usually rely on higher computational efficiency, at the cost of lower accuracy. On the other hand, deep neural networks approaches have been explored. [11–14] proposed some modifications around the standard CNN network [15] in order to detect pedestrians, even accounting for different scales.

Many datasets are available for pedestrian detection. Caltech [16], MOT17Det [5], INRIA [17], and CityPersons [18] are among the most important ones. Since they were collected in different living scenarios, they are intrinsically very heterogeneous datasets. Some of them [16,17] were specifically collected for detecting pedestrians in self-driving contexts. Our interest, however, is mostly concentrated on video-surveillance tasks and, in this scenario, the recently introduced

MOT17Det dataset has proved to be enough challenging due to the high variability of the video subsets. State-of-the-art results on this dataset are reached by [13]. With the need for huge amounts of labeled data, generated datasets have recently gained great interest. [19,20] have studied the possibility of learning features from synthetic data, validating them on real scenarios. Unlike our work, however, they did not explore deep learning approaches. [21,22] focused their attention on the possibility to perform domain adaptation in order to map virtual features onto real ones. Authors in [3] created a dataset taking images from the highly photo-realistic video game *GTA V* and demonstrated that it is possible to reach excellent results on tasks such as people tracking and pose estimation when validating on real data.

To the best of our knowledge, [23] and [24] are the works closest to our setup. In particular, [23] also used *GTA V* as the virtual world but, unlike our method, they used Faster-RCNN [25] and they concentrated on vehicle detection.

Instead, [24] used a synthetically generated dataset to train a simple convolutional network to detect objects belonging to various classes in a video. The convolutional network dealt only with the classification, while the detection of objects relied on a background subtraction algorithm based on Gaussian mixture models (GMMs). The real-world performance was evaluated on two common pedestrian detection datasets, and one of these (MOTChallenge 2015 [26]) is an older version of the dataset we used to carry out our experimentation.

3   The ViPeD Dataset

In this section, we describe the datasets exploited in this work. First, we introduce *ViPeD-Virtual Pedestrian Dataset*, a new virtual collection used for training the network. Then we outline *MOT17Det* [5], a real dataset employed for the evaluation of our proposed solution. Finally, we illustrate *CityPersons* [18], a real-world dataset for pedestrian detection we used as baseline. In order to show the validity of *ViPeD*, we have compared our network trained with CityPersons against the same network trained with *ViPeD*.

3.1   ViPeD-Virtual Pedestrian Dataset

As mentioned above, CNNs need large annotated datasets during the training phase in order to learn models robust to different scenarios, and creating the annotations is a very time-consuming operation that requires a great human effort.

The main contribution of this paper is the creation of *ViPeD*, a huge collection of images taken from the highly photo-realistic video game *GTA V* developed by *Rockstar North*. This newly introduced dataset extends the *JTA (Joint Track Auto)* dataset presented in [3]. Since we are dealing with images collected from a *virtual* world, we can extract pedestrian bounding boxes for free and without the manual human effort, exploiting 2D pedestrian positions extracted from the video card. The dataset includes a total of about 500 K images, extracted from 512 full-HD videos (256 for training and 256 for testing) of different urban scenarios.

In the following, we report some details on the construction of the bounding boxes and on the data augmentation procedure that we used to extend the *JTA* dataset for the pedestrian detection task.

(A) Bounding Boxes: Since *JTA* is specifically designed for pedestrian pose estimation and tracking, the provided annotations are not directly suitable for the pedestrian detection task. In particular, the annotations included in *JTA* are related to the joints of the human skeletons present in the scene (Fig. 1a), while what we need for our task are the coordinates of the bounding boxes surrounding each pedestrian instance.

Bounding box estimation can be addressed using different approaches. The GTA graphic engine is not publicly available, so it is not easy to extract the detailed masks around each pedestrian instance; [23] overcame this issue by extracting semantic masks and separating the instances by exploiting depth information. Instead, our approach exploits the skeletons annotations already extracted by the *JTA* team in order to reconstruct the precise bounding boxes. This seems to be a more reliable solution than the depth separation approach, especially when instances are densely distributed, as in the case of crowded pedestrian scenarios.

The very basic setup consists of drawing the smallest bounding box that encloses all the skeleton joints. The main issue with this simple approach is that each bounding box perfectly contains the skeleton, but not the pedestrian mesh. Indeed, we can note that the mesh is always larger than the skeleton (Fig. 1b). We solved this problem by estimating a pad for the skeleton bounding box, exploiting another information produced by the GTA graphic engine and already present in *JTA*, i.e. the distance of all the pedestrians in the scene from the camera.

(a)   (b)

Fig. 1. (a) Pedestrians in the *JTA* dataset with their skeletons. (b) Examples of annotations in the ViPeDdataset; original bounding boxes are in yellow, while the sanitized ones are in light blue. (Color figure online)

In particular, the height of the ith mesh, denoted as h_m^i, can be estimated from the height of the ith skeleton h_s^i by means of the formula:

$$h_m^i = h_s^i + \frac{\alpha}{z^i} \tag{1}$$

where z^i is the distance of the ith pedestrian center of mass from the camera, and α is a parameter that depends on the camera projection matrix.

Given that z^i is already available for every pedestrian, we estimated the parameter α by manually annotating 30 random pedestrians, obtaining for them the correct value for h_m^i, and then performing linear regression. We visually checked that the α parameter estimation was correct even for all the other non-manually annotated pedestrians.

We then estimated the mesh width w_m^i. Unlike the height, the width is strongly linked to the specific pedestrian pose, so it is difficult to be estimated with only the camera distance information. We decided to estimate w_m^i directly from h_m^i, assuming no changes in the aspect ratio for the original and adjusted bounding boxes:

$$w_m^i = h_m^i \frac{w_s^i}{h_s^i} = h_m^i r^i \tag{2}$$

where r^i is the aspect ratio of the ith bounding box. Examples of final estimated bounding boxes are shown in Fig. 1b.

Finally, we performed a global analysis of these new annotations. As we can see in Fig. 2, in the dataset there are annotations of pedestrians farthest than 30–40 m from the camera. However, we evaluated that humans annotators tend to avoid annotating objects farthest than this amount. We performed this analysis by measuring the height of the smallest bounding boxes in the human-annotated MOT17Det dataset [5] and catching out in our dataset at what distance from the camera the bounding boxes assume this human-limit size. Therefore, in order to obtain annotations comparable to real-world human-annotated ones, we decided to prune all the pedestrian annotations furthest than 40 m from the camera.

From this point on, we will refer to the basic skeleton bounding boxes as *original* bounding boxes. Instead, we will refer to the bounding boxes processed by means of the previously described pipeline as *sanitized* (Fig. 1b).

(B) Data Augmentation: Synthetic datasets should contain scenarios as close as possible to real-world ones. Even though images grabbed from the *GTA* game were already very realistic, we noticed some missing details. In particular, images grabbed from the game are very sharp, edges are very pronounced and common lens effects are missing. In light of this, we prepared a more realistic version of the original images.

We used *GIMP* image manipulation software, used in batch mode, in order to modify every image of the original dataset, using a set of different filters: radial blur, Gaussian blur, bloom effect, exposure/contrast. Parameters for these effects are randomly sampled from a uniform distribution.

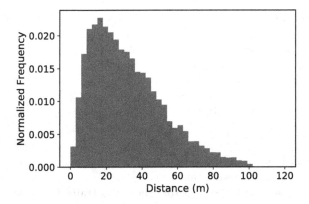

Fig. 2. Histogram of distances between pedestrians and cameras.

3.2 MOT17Det

We evaluate our solution using the recently introduced *MOT17Det* dataset [5], a collection of challenging images for pedestrian detection taken from 14 sequences with various crowded scenarios having different viewpoints, weather conditions, and camera motions. The annotations for all the sequences are generated by human annotators from scratch, following a specific protocol described in their paper. The training images are taken from sequences 2, 4, 5, 9, 10, 11 and 13 (for a total of 5,316 images), while test images are taken from the remaining sequences (for a total of 5,919 images). It should be noted that the authors released only the ground-truth annotations belonging to the training subset. The performance metrics concerning the test subset are instead available only submitting results to the *MOT17Det Challenge*[1].

3.3 CityPersons

In order to compare our solution trained using synthetic data against the same network trained with real images, we have also considered the *CityPersons* dataset [18], a recent collection of images of interest for the pedestrian detection community. It consists of a large and diverse set of stereo video sequences recorded in streets from different cities in Germany and neighboring countries. In particular, authors provide 5,000 images from 27 cities labeled with bounding boxes and divided across train/validation/test subsets.

4 Method

We use *YOLOv3* [4] as object detector architecture, exploiting the original Darknet [27] implementation. The architecture of YOLOv3 jointly performs a regression of the bounding box coordinates and classification for every proposed region.

---

[1] https://motchallenge.net/data/MOT17Det/.

Unlike other techniques, YOLOv3 performs these tasks in an optimized fully-convolutional pipeline that takes pixels as input and outputs both the bounding boxes and their respective proposed categories. It is particularly robust to scale variance since it performs the detections at three different scales, down-sampling the input image by factors 32, 16 and 8.

As a starting point, we considered a model of YOLO pre-trained on the COCO dataset [2], a large dataset composed of images describing complex every-day scenes of common objects in their natural context, categorized in 80 different categories. Since this network is a generic objects detector, we then specialized it to recognize and localize object instances belonging to a specific category - i.e. the pedestrian category in our case.

Our goal is to evaluate the detector when it is trained with synthetic data. For this reason, we need to partially retrain the architecture to include new information deriving from a different domain.

In this particular work, domain adaptation between virtual and real scenarios is simply carried out by fine-tuning the pre-trained YOLOv3 architecture. In particular, we first extract the weights of the first 81 layers of the pre-trained model, since these layers capture universal features (like curves and edges) that are also relevant to our new problem. Then, we fine-tune YOLO initialing the firsts 81 layers with the previously extracted weights, and the weights associated with the remaining layers at random. In this way, we get the network to focus on learning the dataset-specific features in the last layers. All the weights are left unfrozen, so they can be adjusted by the back-propagation algorithm. With this technique, we are forcing the architecture to adjust the learned features to match those from the destination dataset.

5   Experimental Evaluation

We evaluate our solution in two different cases: first, in order to test the generalization capabilities, we train the detector using only our new synthetic dataset; then, in order to obtain best results on the MOT17Det dataset and compare them with the state-of-the-art, we evaluate detections after fine-tuning the detector also on the MOT17Det dataset itself.

Since the authors did not release the ground-truth annotations belonging to the test subset, we submitted our results to the MOT17Det Challenge in order to obtain the performance metrics. In order to prevent overfitting during the training in the second scenario, we create a validation split from the training subset considering a randomly chosen sequence. For the first scenario, instead, we validate on the full training set of MOT17Det.

Following other object detectors benchmarks, we use Precision, Recall and Average Precision (AP) as the performance metrics. A key parameter in all these metrics is the intersection-over-union threshold (IoU), which determines if a bounding box is matched to an annotation or not, i.e. if it is a true positive or a false positive.

Precision and Recall are defined as:

$$Precision = \frac{TPs}{TPs + FPs} \qquad Recall = \frac{TPs}{TPs + FNs} \qquad (3)$$

where TPs are the True Positives, FPs the False Positives and FN the False Negatives. Average Precision is instead defined as the average of the maximum precisions at different recall values.

It is fairly common to observe detection algorithms compared under different thresholds, and there are often many variables and implementation details that differ between evaluation scripts which may affect results significantly. In this work, we consider only MOT17Det and COCO performance evaluators. We also use the standard IoU threshold value of 0.5.

Evaluation of the Generalization Capabilities. Considering the first scenario, we first obtained a baseline using the original detector, i.e. the detector trained using the real-world general-purpose COCO dataset. Then, we trained the detector using our synthetic dataset, performing an ablation study over the introduced extensions.

First, we considered the original images and the original bounding boxes. Then, in order to evaluate how much the bounding-box construction policy can affect the detection quality, we considered the sanitized bounding boxes. Third, we considered also augmented images. Finally, we train the detector using the real-world dataset CityPersons, specific for the pedestrian detection task. We employ this experiment as a baseline over our ViPeD trained network. Results are reported in Table 1.

Comparison with the State-of-the-art on MOT17Det. Concerning the second scenario, we obtained a baseline starting from the original detector trained with COCO and fine-tuning it with the training set of the MOT17Det dataset. Then, we considered our previous detector trained with ViPeD (the one with the sanitized bounding boxes and the augmented images) and we fine-tuned again the network with the training set of the MOT17Det dataset. Results are reported in Table 2, together with the ones obtained using the state-of-the-art approaches publicly released in the MOT17 Challenge (at the time of writing).

Table 1. Results of YOLOv3 detector on MOT17Det

Training Dataset	MOT AP	COCO AP	Precision	Recall
COCO (Baseline)	0.69	0.41	87.4	72.4
CityPersons	0.58	0.37	69.0	60.5
ViPeD: Orig. BBs - Orig. Imgs	0.58	0.37	68.6	64.8
ViPeD: Sanitized BBs - Orig. Imgs	0.63	0.40	**91.1**	69.2
ViPeD: Sanitized BBs - Aug. Imgs	**0.71**	**0.48**	89.3	**73.9**

Table 2. Results on MOT17Det: comparison with the state-of-the-art

Method	MOT AP	Precision	Recall
YOLOv3 on COCO + MOT	0.80	89.9	82.8
YTLAB [13]	**0.89**	86.2	91.3
KDNT [28]	0.89	78.7	**92.1**
ZIZOM [29]	0.81	88.0	83.3
SDP [12]	0.81	**92.6**	83.5
YOLOv3 on ViPeD + MOT	0.80	90.2	84.6

Discussion. Results in Table 1 show that we obtained best performances training the detector with ViPeD, using the sanitized bounding boxes and the augmented images, overtaking also the networks trained with COCO and with
CityPersons. Therefore, our solution is able to generalize the knowledge learned
from the virtual-world to a real-world dataset, and it is also able to perform better than the solutions trained using the real-world manual-annotated datasets.

Results in Table 2 demonstrate that our training procedure is able to reach
competitive performance even when compared to specialized pedestrian detection approaches.

6   Conclusions

In this work, we propose a real-time system able to detect pedestrian instances
in images. Our approach is based on a state-of-the-art fast detector, YOLOv3,
trained with a synthetic dataset named *ViPeD*, a huge collection of images rendered out from the highly photo-realistic video game *GTA V* developed by
Rockstar North.

The choice of training the network using synthetic data is motivated by
the fact that a huge amount of different examples are needed in order for the
algorithm to generalize well. This huge amount of data is typically manually
collected and annotated by humans, but this procedure usually takes a lot of
time and it is error-prone. We demonstrated that our solution is able to transfer
the knowledge learned from the synthetic data to the real-world, outperforming
the same approach trained instead on real-world manually-labeled datasets.

The YOLOv3 network is able to run on low-power devices, such as the
NVIDIA Jetson TX2 board, at 4 FPS. In this way, it could be deployed directly
on smart devices, such as smart security cameras or drones. Even if we trained
YOLOv3 detector on the specific task of pedestrian detection, we think that
the presented procedure could be applied at a larger scale even on other related
tasks, such as object segmentation or image classification.

Acknowledgments. This work was partially supported by the AI4EU project, funded by the EC (H2020 - Contract n. 825619). We gratefully acknowledge the support of NVIDIA Corporation with the donation of the Jetson TX2 board used for this research.

References

1. Deng, J., Dong, W., Socher, R., Li, L., Li, K., Fei-Fei, L.: Imagenet: a large-scale hierarchical image database. In: 2009 IEEE Conference on Computer Vision and Pattern Recognition, pp. 248–255 (2009)
2. Lin, T., et al.: Microsoft COCO: common objects in context. CoRR, vol. abs/1405.0312 (2014)
3. Fabbri, M., Lanzi, F., Calderara, S., Palazzi, A., Vezzani, R., Cucchiara, R.: Learning to detect and track visible and occluded body joints in a virtual world. In: European Conference on Computer Vision (ECCV) (2018)
4. Redmon, J., Farhadi, A.: Yolov3: an incremental improvement. CoRR, vol. abs/1804.02767 (2018)
5. Milan, A., Leal-Taixé, L., Reid, I.D., Roth, S., Schindler, K.: MOT16: a benchmark for multi-object tracking. CoRR, vol. abs/1603.00831 (2016)
6. Benenson, R., Omran, M., Hosang, J., Schiele, B.: Ten years of pedestrian detection, what have we learned? In: Agapito, L., Bronstein, M.M., Rother, C. (eds.) ECCV 2014. LNCS, vol. 8926, pp. 613–627. Springer, Cham (2015). https://doi.org/10.1007/978-3-319-16181-5_47
7. Zhang, S., Bauckhage, C., Cremers, A.B.: Informed haar-like features improve pedestrian detection. In: The IEEE Conference on Computer Vision and Pattern Recognition (CVPR), June 2014
8. Zhang, S., Benenson, R., Schiele, B.: Filtered channel features for pedestrian detection. In: 2015 IEEE Conference on Computer Vision and Pattern Recognition (CVPR), June 2015, pp. 1751–1760 (2015)
9. Zhang, S., Benenson, R., Omran, M., Hosang, J., Schiele, B.: How far are we from solving pedestrian detection? In: The IEEE Conference on Computer Vision and Pattern Recognition (CVPR), June 2016
10. Nam, W., Dollar, P., Han, J.H.: Local decorrelation for improved pedestrian detection. In: Advances in Neural Information Processing Systems, vol. 27, pp. 424–432. Curran Associates Inc, New York (2014)
11. Tian, Y., Luo, P., Wang, X., Tang, X.: Deep learning strong parts for pedestrian detection. In: 2015 IEEE International Conference on Computer Vision (ICCV), December 2015, pp. 1904–1912 (2015)
12. Yang, F., Choi, W., Lin, Y.: Exploit all the layers: fast and accurate CNN object detector with scale dependent pooling and cascaded rejection classifiers. In: 2016 IEEE CVPR, June 2016, pp. 2129–2137 (2016)
13. Cai, Z., Fan, Q., Feris, R.S., Vasconcelos, N.: A unified multi-scale deep convolutional neural network for fast object detection. In: Leibe, B., Matas, J., Sebe, N., Welling, M. (eds.) ECCV 2016. LNCS, vol. 9908, pp. 354–370. Springer, Cham (2016). https://doi.org/10.1007/978-3-319-46493-0_22
14. Sermanet, P., Kavukcuoglu, K., Chintala, S., Lecun, Y.: Pedestrian detection with unsupervised multi-stage feature learning. In: The IEEE Conference on Computer Vision and Pattern Recognition (CVPR), June 2013
15. Lecun, Y., Bottou, L., Bengio, Y., Haffner, P.: Gradient-based learning applied to document recognition. Proc. IEEE **86**(11), 2278–2324 (1998)

16. Dollar, P., Wojek, C., Schiele, B., Perona, P.: Pedestrian detection: an evaluation of the state of the art. IEEE Trans. Pattern Anal. Mach. Intell. **34**(4), 743–761 (2012)
17. Dalal, N., Triggs, B.: Histograms of oriented gradients for human detection. In: 2005 IEEE Computer Society Conference on Computer Vision and Pattern Recognition (CVPR 2005), vol. 1, June 2005, pp. 886–893 (2005)
18. Zhang, S., Benenson, R., Schiele, B.: Citypersons: a diverse dataset for pedestrian detection. CoRR, vol. abs/1702.05693 (2017)
19. Kaneva, B., Torralba, A., Freeman, W.T.: Evaluation of image features using a photorealistic virtual world. In: 2011 International Conference on Computer Vision, November 2011, pp. 2282–2289 (2011)
20. Marín, J., Vázquez, D., Gerónimo, D., López, A.M.: Learning appearance in virtual scenarios for pedestrian detection. In: 2010 IEEE Computer Society Conference on Computer Vision and Pattern Recognition, June 2010, pp. 137–144 (2010)
21. Vazquez, D., Lopez, A.M., Ponsa, D.: Unsupervised domain adaptation of virtual and real worlds for pedestrian detection. In: Proceedings of the 21st International Conference on Pattern Recognition (ICPR 2012), November 2012, pp. 3492–3495 (2012)
22. Vázquez, D., López, A.M., Marín, J., Ponsa, D., Gerónimo, D.: Virtual and real world adaptation for pedestrian detection. IEEE Trans. Pattern Anal. Mach. Intell. **36**(4), 797–809 (2014)
23. Johnson-Roberson, M., Barto, C., Mehta, R., Sridhar, S.N., Vasudevan, R.: Driving in the matrix: can virtual worlds replace human-generated annotations for real world tasks? CoRR, vol. abs/1610.01983 (2016)
24. Bochinski E., Eiselein, V., Sikora, T.: Training a convolutional neural network for multi-class object detection using solely virtual world data. In: 2016 13th IEEE International Conference on Advanced Video and Signal Based Surveillance (AVSS), pp. 278–285. IEEE (2016)
25. Ren, S., He, K., Girshick, R., Sun, J.: Faster R-CNN: towards real-time object detection with region proposal networks. In: Advances in Neural Information Processing Systems, vol. 28, pp. 91–99. Curran Associates Inc., New York (2015)
26. Leal-Taixé, L., Milan, A., Reid, I.D., Roth, S., Schindler, K.: Motchallenge 2015: towards a benchmark for multi-target tracking. CoRR, vol. abs/1504.01942 (2015)
27. Redmon, J.: Darknet: open source neural networks in c (2013)
28. Yu, F., Li, W., Li, Q., Liu, Y., Shi, X., Yan J.: POI: multiple object tracking with high performance detection and appearance feature. CoRR, vol. abs/1610.06136 (2016)
29. Lin, C., Lu, J., Wang, G., Zhou, J.: Graininess-aware deep feature learning for pedestrian detection. In: The European Conference on Computer Vision (ECCV), September 2018

Video Synthesis from Intensity and Event Frames

Stefano Pini, Guido Borghi$^{(\boxtimes)}$, Roberto Vezzani, and Rita Cucchiara

Department of Engineering "Enzo Ferrari",
University of Modena and Reggio Emilia, Modena, Italy
{s.pini,guido.borghi,roberto.vezzani,rita.cucchiara}@unimore.it

Abstract. Event cameras, neuromorphic devices that naturally respond to brightness changes, have multiple advantages with respect to traditional cameras. However, the difficulty of applying traditional computer vision algorithms on event data limits their usability. Therefore, in this paper we investigate the use of a deep learning-based architecture that combines an initial grayscale frame and a series of event data to estimate the following intensity frames. In particular, a fully-convolutional encoder-decoder network is employed and evaluated for the frame synthesis task on an automotive event-based dataset. Performance obtained with pixel-wise metrics confirms the quality of the images synthesized by the proposed architecture.

Keywords: Video synthesis · Event camera · Event frames ·
Automotive · Deep learning

1 Introduction

Event cameras are optical sensors that asynchronously output events in case of brightness variations at pixel level. The major advantages of this type of neuromorphic sensors are the low power consumption, the low data rate, the high temporal resolution, and the high dynamic range [8]. On the other hand, despite exhibiting a higher power consumption and often a lower dynamic range, traditional cameras are able to record local information, like textures, and the majority of the computer vision algorithms are designed to work on this kind of data. Indeed, being able to apply existing algorithms to the output of event cameras could help the adoption of event-based sensors.

In this paper, aiming to conjugate the advantages of traditional and event cameras, we investigate the use of a deep learning-based method to interpolate intensity frames acquired by a low-rate camera with the support of the intermediate event data. Specifically, we exploit a fully-convolutional encoder-decoder architecture to predict intensity frames, relying on an initial or a periodic set of key-frames and a series of event frames, *i.e.* frames that collect the information captured by event cameras in a certain time interval.

© Springer Nature Switzerland AG 2019
E. Ricci et al. (Eds.): ICIAP 2019, LNCS 11751, pp. 313–323, 2019.
https://doi.org/10.1007/978-3-030-30642-7_28

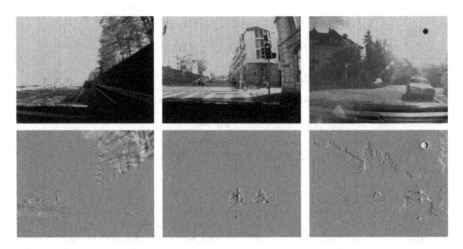

Fig. 1. Samples from the *DDD17* dataset. The first row contains the intensity grayscale images while the second one contains the event frames.

Focusing on the automotive scenario, we employ a novel event-based dataset called DDD17 [4] (see Fig. 1) and evaluate the feasibility of the proposed method with a wide set of pixel-level metrics. Quantitative and qualitative comparisons with a recent competitor [26] shows the superior quality of the images synthesized by the proposed model.

Summarizing, our contributions are twofold:

- We propose a fully-convolutional encoder-decoder architecture that combines traditional images and event data (as event frames) to interpolate consecutive intensity frames;
- We evaluate the effectiveness of the proposed approach on a public automotive dataset, assessing the ability to generate reasonable images and providing a fair comparison with a state-of-the-art approach.

2   Related Work

In the last years, event-based vision has increased its popularity in the computer vision community. Indeed, many novel algorithms have been proposed to deal with event-based data, produced by *Dynamic Vision Sensors* [11] (DVSs), like visual odometry [29], SLAM [17], optical flow estimation [8], and monocular [21] or stereo [1,28] depth estimation.

Event cameras have also been exploited for the ego-motion estimation [7,14], the real-time feature detection and tracking [15,20], and the robot control in predator/prey scenarios [16]. Furthermore, it has been shown that event data can be employed to solve many classification tasks, such as the classification of characters [19], gestures [13], and faces [10]. Recently, an optimization-based algorithm that simultaneously estimates the optical flow and the brightness intensity

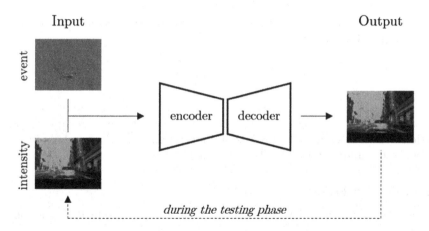

Fig. 2. Overview of the proposed method. The input of the encoder-decoder architecture is represented by the stack of an intensity and an event frame, while the output is the predicted intensity frame. During inference, the output at each step is used as the input intensity image in the following step.

was proposed in [3], while [18,23] presented a manifold regularization method that reconstructs intensity frames from event data.

Lately, Scheerlinck *et al.* [26] proposed a complementary filter that combines image frames and events to estimate the scene intensity. The filter asynchronously updates the intensity estimation whenever new events or intensity frames are received. If the grayscale frames are missing, the estimation can be produced using events only.

This method is recent (at the time of writing) and outperforms previous existing works. Thus, we selected it as a baseline reference to evaluate our approach (see Sect. 4).

3 Proposed Method

In this Section, we formally define the event frame concept. Then, we present the investigated task from both a mathematical and an implementation point of view.

3.1 Event Frames

Following the notation of [14], the j-th event e_j provided by an event camera can be expressed as:

$$e_j = (x_j, y_j, t_j, p_j) \tag{1}$$

where x_j, y_j, and t_j are the spatio-temporal coordinates of a brightness change and $p_j \in \{-1, +1\}$ is the polarity of the brightness change (*i.e.* positive or negative variation).

An event frame can be defined as the pixel-wise integration of the events occurred in a time interval $[t, t + \tau]$:

$$\Psi_\tau(t) = \sum_{e_j \in [t, t+\tau]} p_j \qquad (2)$$

where $e_j \in [t, t + \tau]$ means $\{e_j \,|\, t_j \in [t, t + \tau]\}$. In practice, an event frame can be formulated as a grayscale image that summarizes the events captured in a particular time interval. There is loss of information when the number of events exceeds the number of gray levels of the image.

3.2 Intensity Frame Estimation

We propose a method that corresponds to a learned parametric function F defined as:

$$F : \mathbb{R}^{2 \times w \times h} \to \mathbb{R}^{w \times h} \qquad (3)$$

that takes as input an intensity image $I_t \in \mathbb{R}^{w \times h}$ recorded at time t and an event frame $\Psi_\tau(t) \in \mathbb{R}^{w \times h}$ (which summarizes pixel-level brightness variations in the time interval $[t, t + \tau]$) in order to estimate the intensity image $\hat{I}(t + \tau) \in \mathbb{R}^{w \times h}$ at time $t + \tau$. w and h correspond to the width and the height of the event frames and the intensity images.

Formally, the synthesized image $\hat{I}(t + \tau)$ can be defined as:

$$\hat{I}(t + \tau) = F\left(I(t), \Psi_\tau(t), \theta\right) \qquad (4)$$

where θ corresponds to the parameters of the function F.

3.3 Architecture

In practice, the parametric function F corresponds to an encoder-decoder architecture that predicts the intensity frame $\hat{I}(t + \tau)$ from the concatenation of an intensity frame $I(t)$ and an event frame $\Psi_\tau(t)$, as represented in Fig. 2. In particular, the model is a fully-convolutional deep neural network with skip connections between layers i and $n - i$, with n corresponding to the total number of layers.

As in the *U-Net* architecture [24], the number of layers with skip connections is set to $n = 4$ with 128, 256, 512, 512 3×3 kernels in the encoder layers and with 256, 128, 64, 64 3×3 kernels in the decoder layers.

These skip-connected layers are preceded by two convolutional layers with 64 feature maps and followed by a convolutional layer with 1 feature map that projects the internal network representation to the final intensity estimation.

3.4 Training Procedure

The network is trained in a supervised manner using the *Mean Squared Error* (MSE) loss as objective function:

$$MSE = \frac{1}{N} \sum_{i=0}^{N} (y_i - \hat{y}_i)^2 \qquad (5)$$

Table 1. Pixel-wise metrics (lower is better) computed on the synthesized frames of *DDD17*.

Method	Norm ↓		Difference ↓		RMSE ↓		
	L_1	L_2	Abs	Sqr	Lin	Log	Scl
[26]	0.080	29.249	0.269	0.027	0.098	4.830	4.352
Ours	**0.027**	**8.916**	**0.179**	**0.007**	**0.040**	**4.048**	**3.571**

where y_i and $\hat{y}_i$ are respectively the i-th pixels of the ground truth and the generated image of the same size $N = w \cdot h$.

We optimize the network using the *Adam* optimizer [9] with learning rate $2 \cdot 10^{-4}$, $\beta_1 = 0.5$, $\beta_2 = 0.999$ and a mini-batch size of 8.

During the training phase, two consecutive frames (one as input, one as ground-truth of the output) and the intermediate event frame (as input) are employed. During the testing phase, instead, in order to obtain a sequence of synthesized frames, the model iteratively receives the previously generated image as intensity input or a new key-frame after λ iterations.

4 Experimental Evaluation

In this section, we firstly present the dataset that has been employed to train and evaluate the proposed method. In the following, we report the procedure that we have adopted to evaluate the quality of the estimated intensity frames. Finally, we present and analyze the experimental results.

4.1 DDD17: End-to-end DAVIS Driving Dataset

Recently, Binas *et al.* [4] presented *DDD17: End-to-end DAVIS Driving Dataset*, the first open dataset of annotated DAVIS driving recordings. The dataset contains more than 12 h of recordings captured with a *DAVIS* sensor [5] (some sample images are shown in Fig. 1). Each recording includes both event data and grayscale frames along with vehicle information (*e.g.* vehicle speed, throttle, brake, steering angle). Recordings are captured in cities and highways, in dry and wet weather conditions, during day, evening, and night.

However, the quality of the gray-level images is low, the spatial resolution is limited to 346×260 pixels, and the framerate is variable (it depends on the brightness of the scene).

In our experiments, similar to [14], we use only the recordings acquired during the day. In contrast to Maqueda *et al.* [14], however, we create the train, validation, and test sets using different recordings.

4.2   Metrics

Inspired by [6], we employed a variety of metrics to check the quality of the generated images, being aware that evaluating synthesized images is in general a difficult and still open problem [25].

Table 2. Starting from the left, we report the percentage of pixels under three different thresholds, the *Peak Signal-to-Noise Ratio* (PSNR), and the *Structural Similarity* (SSIM) indexes, computed on the synthesized frames of *DDD17*. Higher is better.

Method	Threshold ↑			Indexes ↑	
	1.25	1.25^2	1.25^3	PSNR	SSIM
[26]	0.671	0.781	0.827	20.542	0.702
Ours	**0.775**	**0.848**	**0.875**	**29.176**	**0.864**

In particular, we use distances (L_1 and L_2), differences (absolute and squared relative difference), the root mean squared error (in the linear, logarithmic, and scale-invariant version), and the percentage of pixels under a certain error threshold. Furthermore, with respect to [6], we introduce two additional metrics: the *Peak Signal-to-Noise Ratio* (PSNR) and the *Structural Similarity* index (SSIM) [27]. They are calculated to respectively evaluate the image noise level (in logarithmic scale) and the perceived image quality.

From a mathematical perspective, the PSNR is defined as:

$$\text{PSNR} = 10 \cdot \log_{10} \left(\frac{m \cdot |I|}{\sum_{y \in I} (y - \hat{y})^2} \right) \tag{6}$$

where I is the ground truth image, $\hat{I}$ is the synthesized image, and m is the maximum possible value of I and $\hat{I}$. $\hat{y} \in \hat{I}$ corresponds to the element of the generated image at the same location of $y \in I$. In our experiments $m = 1$.

The SSIM is defined as:

$$\text{SSIM}(p, q) = \frac{(2\mu_p \mu_q + c_1)(2\sigma_{pq} + c_2)}{(\mu_p^2 + \mu_q^2 + c_1)(\sigma_p^2 + \sigma_q^2 + c_2)} \tag{7}$$

Given two windows $p \in I$, $q \in \hat{I}$ of equal size 11×11, $\mu_{p,q}$, $\sigma_{p,q}$ are the mean and variance of p and q while σ_{pq} is the covariance of p, q.

c_1 and c_2 are defined as $c_1 = (0.01 \cdot L)^2$ and $c_2 = (0.03 \cdot L)^2$ where L is the dynamic range (*i.e.* the difference between the maximum and the minimum theoretical value) of I and $\hat{I}$. In our experiments $L = 1$.

4.3   Experimental Results

We analyze the quality of the intensity estimations produced by our approach and by the method presented in [26] employing the pixel-wise metrics reported in Sect. 4.2.

GT   Sheerlinck *et al.* [26]   **Ours**

Fig. 3. Samples of synthesized frames produced by our method (last column) and the one of Scheerlinck *et al.* [26] (second column), while the first column contains ground truth images. As shown, the proposed method produces less artefacts, in the form of black or white spots, maintaining a good level of details, and it is able to preserve the overall structure and appearance of the original scene.

In the experiments, we empirically set the number of consecutive synthesized frames (*i.e.* the sequence length) to $\lambda = 6$. It is worth noting that, within a sequence, the input intensity frame of the proposed method is the intensity estimation of the previous step except for the initial key-frame. We adapt the input images of *DDD17* to match the architecture requirements: the input data is resized to a spatial resolution of 256×192.

Quantitative results are reported in Tables 1 and 2. As it can be seen, the proposed method outperforms the competitor with a clear margin in every evaluation. In particular, PSNR and SSIM confirm the fidelity of the representation and the good level of perceived similarity between the generated and the ground truth images, respectively. Indeed, compared to the output of [26], frames synthesized by our method contain less artifacts and shadows and the overall structure of the scene is better preserved.

Visual examples, which are reported in Fig. 3, highlight the ability of the proposed network to correctly handle the input event frames.

Finally, we investigate the performance of a traditional vision-based detection algorithm tested on the generated images. We adopt the well-known object detection network Yolo-v3 [22], pre-trained on the *COCO* dataset [12], to investigate the ability of the proposed method to preserve the appearance of objects which are significant in the automotive context, like pedestrians, trucks, cars, and stop signals.

Since ground truth object annotations are not available in the dataset, we first run the object detector on the real images contained in *DDD17*, obtaining a sort of ground truth annotation. Then, we run Yolo-v3 on the generated images and compare these detections with the produced annotations.

Results are expressed in terms of *Intersection-over-Union* (IoU) [2], which is defined as follows:

$$IoU(A, B) = \frac{\text{Area of Overlap}}{\text{Area of Union}} = \frac{|A \cap B|}{|A \cup B| - |A \cap B|} \tag{8}$$

where A and B are the bounding boxes found in the original and the generated frames, respectively. A detection is valid if:

$$IoU(A, B) > \tau, \ \tau = 0.5 \tag{9}$$

A weighted object detection score is also employed: each class contributes to the final average according to its associated weight computed as the number of its occurrence on the total number present in the test sequences.

We obtained a mean Intersection-over-Union of 0.863 (the maximum reachable value is 1) with 61% of valid object detections. We believe that these results are remarkably promising because they show that the generated frames are semantically similar to the real ones. Therefore, the proposed method can be an effective way to apply traditional vision algorithms to the output of event cameras.

5   Conclusion

In this work, we have presented a deep learning-based method that performs intensity estimation given an initial or periodic collection of intensity key-frames and a group of events.

The model relies on a fully convolutional encoder-decoder architecture that learns to combine intensity and event frames to produce updated intensity estimations. The experimental evaluation shows that the proposed method can be effectively employed to the intensity estimation task and that it is a valid alternative to current state-of-the-art methods.

As future work, we plan to test the framework on additional datasets as well as to take into account the long-term temporal evolution of the scene.

References

1. Andreopoulos, A., Kashyap, H.J., Nayak, T.K., Amir, A., Flickner, M.D.: A low power, high throughput, fully event-based stereo system. In: IEEE International Conference on Computer Vision and Pattern Recognition, pp. 7532–7542 (2018)
2. Ballotta, D., Borghi, G., Vezzani, R., Cucchiara, R.: Fully convolutional network for head detection with depth images. In: 2018 24th International Conference on Pattern Recognition (ICPR), pp. 752–757. IEEE (2018)
3. Bardow, P., Davison, A.J., Leutenegger, S.: Simultaneous optical flow and intensity estimation from an event camera. In: IEEE International Conference on Computer Vision and Pattern Recognition, pp. 884–892 (2016)
4. Binas, J., Neil, D., Liu, S.C., Delbruck, T.: Ddd17: end-to-end davis driving dataset. In: Workshop on Machine Learning for Autonomous Vehicles (MLAV) in ICML 2017 (2017)
5. Brandli, C., Berner, R., Yang, M., Liu, S.C., Delbruck, T.: A 240 × 180 130 db 3 μs latency global shutter spatiotemporal vision sensor. IEEE J. Solid-State Circuits **49**(10), 2333–2341 (2014)
6. Eigen, D., Puhrsch, C., Fergus, R.: Depth map prediction from a single image using a multi-scale deep network. In: Neural Information Processing Systems (2014)
7. Gallego, G., Lund, J.E., Mueggler, E., Rebecq, H., Delbruck, T., Scaramuzza, D.: Event-based, 6-dof camera tracking from photometric depth maps. IEEE Trans. Pattern Anal. Mach. Intell. **40**(10), 2402–2412 (2018)
8. Gallego, G., Rebecq, H., Scaramuzza, D.: A unifying contrast maximization framework for event cameras, with applications to motion, depth, and optical flow estimation. In: IEEE International Conference on Computer Vision and Pattern Recognition, vol. 1 (2018)
9. Kingma, D.P., Ba, J.: Adam: A method for stochastic optimization. CoRR abs/1412.6980 (2014). http://arxiv.org/abs/1412.6980
10. Lagorce, X., Orchard, G., Galluppi, F., Shi, B.E., Benosman, R.B.: HOTS: a hierarchy of event-based time-surfaces for pattern recognition. IEEE Trans. Pattern Anal. Mach. Intell. **39**(7), 1346–1359 (2017)

11. Lichtsteiner, P., Posch, C., Delbruck, T.: A 128 × 128 120 db 30 mw asynchronous vision sensor that responds to relative intensity change. In: 2006 IEEE International Solid State Circuits Conference-Digest of Technical Papers. pp. 2060–2069. IEEE (2006)

12. Lin, T.-Y., et al.: Microsoft COCO: common objects in context. In: Fleet, D., Pajdla, T., Schiele, B., Tuytelaars, T. (eds.) ECCV 2014. LNCS, vol. 8693, pp. 740–755. Springer, Cham (2014). https://doi.org/10.1007/978-3-319-10602-1_48

13. Lungu, I.A., Corradi, F., Delbrück, T.: Live demonstration: convolutional neural network driven by dynamic vision sensor playing RoShamBo. In: IEEE International Symposium on Circuits and Systems (ISCAS), pp. 1–1. IEEE (2017)

14. Maqueda, A.I., Loquercio, A., Gallego, G., García, N., Scaramuzza, D.: Event-based vision meets deep learning on steering prediction for self-driving cars. In: IEEE International Conference on Computer Vision and Pattern Recognition, pp. 5419–5427 (2018)

15. Mitrokhin, A., Fermuller, C., Parameshwara, C., Aloimonos, Y.: Event-based moving object detection and tracking. arXiv preprint arXiv:1803.04523 (2018)

16. Moeys, D.P., et al.: Steering a predator robot using a mixed frame/event-driven convolutional neural network. In: 2016 Second International Conference on Event-based Control, Communication, and Signal Processing (EBCCSP), pp. 1–8. IEEE (2016)

17. Mueggler, E., Rebecq, H., Gallego, G., Delbruck, T., Scaramuzza, D.: The event-camera dataset and simulator: event-based data for pose estimation, visual odometry, and slam. Int. J. Robot. Res. **36**(2), 142–149 (2017)

18. Munda, G., Reinbacher, C., Pock, T.: Real-time intensity-image reconstruction for event cameras using manifold regularisation. Int. J. Comput. Vision **126**(12), 1381–1393 (2018)

19. Orchard, G., Meyer, C., Etienne-Cummings, R., Posch, C., Thakor, N., Benosman, R.: HFirst: a temporal approach to object recognition. IEEE Trans. Pattern Anal. Mach. Intell. **37**(10), 2028–2040 (2015)

20. Ramesh, B., Zhang, S., Lee, Z.W., Gao, Z., Orchard, G., Xiang, C.: Long-term object tracking with a moving event camera. In: British Machine Vision Conference (2018)

21. Rebecq, H., Gallego, G., Scaramuzza, D.: EMVS: event-based multi-view stereo. In: British Machine Vision Conference (2016)

22. Redmon, J., Farhadi, A.: YOLOv3: an incremental improvement. arXiv preprint arXiv:1804.02767 (2018)

23. Reinbacher, C., Graber, G., Pock, T.: Real-time intensity-image reconstruction for event cameras using manifold regularisation. In: British Machine Vision Conference (2016)

24. Ronneberger, O., Fischer, P., Brox, T.: U-Net: convolutional networks for biomedical image segmentation. In: Navab, N., Hornegger, J., Wells, W.M., Frangi, A.F. (eds.) MICCAI 2015. LNCS, vol. 9351, pp. 234–241. Springer, Cham (2015). https://doi.org/10.1007/978-3-319-24574-4_28

25. Salimans, T., Goodfellow, I., Zaremba, W., Cheung, V., Radford, A., Chen, X.: Improved techniques for training GANs. In: Neural Information Processing Systems, pp. 2234–2242 (2016)

26. Scheerlinck, C., Barnes, N., Mahony, R.: Continuous-time intensity estimation using event cameras. In: Asian Conference on Computer Vision (2018)

27. Wang, Z., Bovik, A.C., Sheikh, H.R., Simoncelli, E.P.: Image quality assessment: from error visibility to structural similarity. IEEE Trans. Image Process. **13**(4), 600–612 (2004)

28. Zhou, Y., Gallego, G., Rebecq, H., Kneip, L., Li, H., Scaramuzza, D.: Semi-dense 3D reconstruction with a stereo event camera. In: European Conference on Computer Vision (2018)
29. Zhu, A.Z., Atanasov, N., Daniilidis, K.: Event-based visual inertial odometry. In: IEEE International Conference on Computer Vision and Pattern Recognition, pp. 5816–5824 (2017)

Hebbian Learning Meets Deep Convolutional Neural Networks

Giuseppe Amato[1] , Fabio Carrara[1(✉)] , Fabrizio Falchi[1] ,
Claudio Gennaro[1] , and Gabriele Lagani[2]

[1] ISTI CNR, Pisa, Italy
{giuseppe.amato,fabio.carrara,fabrizio.falchi,
claudio.gennaro}@isti.cnr.it
[2] University of Pisa, Pisa, Italy
gabriele.lagani@gmail.com

Abstract. Neural networks are said to be biologically inspired since they mimic the behavior of real neurons. However, several processes in state-of-the-art neural networks, including Deep Convolutional Neural Networks (DCNN), are far from the ones found in animal brains. One relevant difference is the training process. In state-of-the-art artificial neural networks, the training process is based on backpropagation and Stochastic Gradient Descent (SGD) optimization. However, studies in neuroscience strongly suggest that this kind of processes does not occur in the biological brain. Rather, learning methods based on Spike-Timing-Dependent Plasticity (STDP) or the Hebbian learning rule seem to be more plausible, according to neuroscientists. In this paper, we investigate the use of the Hebbian learning rule when training Deep Neural Networks for image classification by proposing a novel weight update rule for shared kernels in DCNNs. We perform experiments using the CIFAR-10 dataset in which we employ Hebbian learning, along with SGD, to train parts of the model or whole networks for the task of image classification, and we discuss their performance thoroughly considering both effectiveness and efficiency aspects.

Keywords: Hebbian learning · Deep learning · Computer vision · Convolutional neural networks

1 Introduction

Backpropagation is the most common learning rule for artificial neural networks. Despite being initially developed for biologically inspired artificial networks, it is commonly known by neuroscience that this process is unlikely to be

This work was partially supported by "Automatic Data and documents Analysis to enhance human-based processes" (ADA), CUP CIPE D55F17000290009, and by the AI4EU project, funded by the EC (H2020 - Contract n. 825619). We gratefully acknowledge the support of NVIDIA Corporation with the donation of a Tesla K40 GPU used for this research.

E. Ricci et al. (Eds.): ICIAP 2019, LNCS 11751, pp. 324–334, 2019.
https://doi.org/10.1007/978-3-030-30642-7_29

implemented by nature. Seeking for more plausible models that mimic biological brains, researchers introduced several alternative learning rules for artificial networks.

In this work, we explore one of these alternative learning rules—*Hebbian learning*—in the context of modern deep neural networks for image classification. Specifically, the concept of Hebbian learning refers to a family of learning rules, inspired by biology, according to which the weight associated with a synapse increases proportionally to the values of the pre-synaptic and post-synaptic stimuli at a given instant of time [2,4].

Different variants of Hebbian rules can be found in the literature. In this work, we investigate two main Hebbian learning approaches, that is the *Winner-Takes-All* competition [3,12] and the *supervised Hebbian learning* solution. We apply these rule to train image classifiers that we extensively evaluate and compare with respect to standard models trained with Stochastic Gradient Descent (SGD). Moreover, we experiment with hybrid models in which we apply Hebbian and SGD updates to different parts of the network. Experiments on the CIFAR-10 dataset suggest that the Hebbian approach is adequate for training the lower and the higher layers of deep convolutional neural networks, while current results suggest that it has some limitations when used in the intermediate layers[1]. On the other hand, the Hebbian approach is much faster than Gradient Descent in terms of numbers of epochs required for training. Moreover, Hebbian update rules are inherently local and thus fully parallelizable in the backward/update phase, and we think that strategies to enhance the scalability of current models can benefit from this property. The main contributions of this work are:

- the use of Hebbian learning in DCNN, with a novel proposal for weight updates in shared kernels (Sect. 3.4);
- the definition of various hybrid deep neural networks, obtained combining SGD and Hebbian learning in the various network layers (Sect. 4);
- extensive experimentation and analysis of the results (Sect. 5).

The paper is organized as follows. Section 2 gives a brief overview of other works in this context. Section 3 introduces the Hebbian learning model. Section 4 discusses the deep network architecture that we defined and how we set the experiments to assess the performance of the approach. Section 5 discusses the experiments and the results. Section 6 concludes.

2   Related Works

Recently, several works investigated the Hebbian rule for training neural networks for image classification. In [15], the authors propose a deep *Convolutional Neural Network* (CNN) architecture consisting of three convolutional layers, followed by an SVM classifier. The convolutional layers are trained, without supervision, to extract relevant features from the inputs. This technique was applied

---

[1] For the implementation details about the experiments described in this document and the related source code, the reader is referred to [8,9].

on different image datasets, among which CIFAR-10 [6], on which the algorithm achieved above 75% accuracy with a three-layer network.

In [10], the authors obtain the Hebbian weight update rules by minimizing an appropriate loss function, defined as the *strain loss*. Intuitively, they aim at minimizing how the differences, between the similarity among input vectors and output vectors, get distorted when moving from the input space and the output space. Also in this case, the authors use CIFAR-10 to perform the experiments, achieving accuracy up to 80% with a single layer followed by an SVM classifier [1].

In the above approaches, the Hebbian rule application remains limited to relatively shallow networks. On the other hand, in our work, we explore the possibility of applying Hebbian learning rules to deeper network architectures and discuss the opportunities and limitations arisen in this context.

3   Hebbian Learning Model

The Hebbian plasticity rule can be expressed as

$$\Delta w = \eta\, y(x,\, w)\, x\,, \tag{1}$$

where x is the vector of input signals on the neuron synapses, w is the weight vector associated with the neuron, η is the learning rate coefficient, Δw is the weight update vector, and $y(x,\, w)$ is the post-synaptic activation of the neuron— a function of the input and the weights that is assumed to be non-negative (e.g. a dot product followed by a ReLU or sigmoid activation).

3.1   Weight Decay

Rule 1 only allows weights to grow, not to decrease. In order to prevent the weight vector from growing unbounded, Rule 1 is extended by introducing a *weight decay* (forgetting) term [2] $\gamma(x,\, w)$

$$\Delta w = \eta\, y(x,\, w)\, x - \gamma(x,\, w)\,. \tag{2}$$

When the weight decay term is $\gamma(x,\, w) = \eta\, y(x,\, w)\, w$ [4], we obtain

$$\Delta w = \eta\, y(x,\, w)\, (x - w)\,. \tag{3}$$

If we assume that $\eta\, y(x,\, w)$ is smaller than 1, the latter equation obtains the following physical interpretation: at each iteration, the weight vector is modified by taking a step towards the input, the size of the step being proportional to the similarity between the input and the weight vector, so that if a similar input is presented again in the future, the neuron will be more likely to produce a stronger response. If an input (or a cluster of similar inputs) is presented repeatedly to the neuron, the weight vector tends to converge towards it, eventually acting as a matching filter. In other words, the input is *memorized* in the synaptic weights. In this perspective, the neuron can be seen as an entity that, when stimulated with a frequent pattern, learns to recognize it.

3.2   Competitive Hebbian Learning: Winner Takes All

Equation 3 can be also used in the context of *competitive learning* [3,5,12,14]. When more than one neuron is involved in the learning process, it is possible to introduce some forms of lateral interaction in order to force different neurons to learn different patterns. A possible scheme of interaction is *Winner Takes All* (WTA) competition [3,12] which works as follows:

1. when input is presented to the network, the neurons start a competition;
2. the winner of the competition is the neuron whose weight vector is the clos-est to the input vector (according to some distance metric, e.g. angular dis-tance [3] or euclidean distance [4]), while all the other neurons get inhibited;
3. the neurons update their weights according to Eq. 3, where y is set to 0 for the inhibited neurons and to 1 for the winner neuron.

3.3   Supervised Hebbian Learning

Hebbian learning is inherently an unsupervised approach to neural network train-ing because each neuron updates its weight without relying on labels provided with the data. However, it is possible to use a simple trick to apply Hebbian rules in a supervised fashion: the *teacher neuron* technique [11,13] involves imposing a teacher signal on the output of the neurons that we want to train, thus replacing the output that they would naturally produce. By doing so and by applying a Hebbian learning rule, neurons adapt their weights in order to actually reproduce the desired output when the same input is provided.

Applying this technique to the output layer is straightforward, as the teacher signal coincides with the output target, but the choice of the teacher signal for supervised training of internal neurons is not trivial. Similarly to [15], we use the following technique to guide the neurons to develop a certain class-specificity in intermediate layers: we divide the kernels of a layer in as many groups as the number of classes and associate each group with a unique class; in addition, we also devote a set of kernels to be in common to all the classes; when an input of a given class is presented to the network, a high teacher signal $y = 1$ is provided to all the neurons sharing kernels that belong to the group corresponding to the given class, while the others receive a low teacher signal $y = 0$ (neurons sharing kernels associated with the set common to all the classes always receive a high teacher signal).

3.4   Hebbian Rule with Shared Kernels in DCNN

Eq. 3 allows computing Δw for each neuron in a given layer. Due to weight shar-ing in convolutional neural networks, different neurons in the same convolutional layer that shares the same kernel might be associated with different Δw's. In order to allow weight sharing in kernels of deep convolutional layers, we propose to perform an *aggregation* step in which the different Δw's, obtained at different spatial locations, are used to produce a global Δw_{agg} used for the update of the

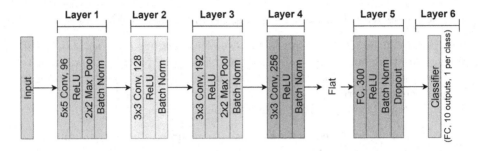

Fig. 1. Architecture of the Deep Convolutional Neural Network used in our experiments.

kernel. Δw_{agg} is computed as a weighted average of the Δw, where the weights are proportional to the coefficient that determines the step size (y when the basic Hebbian rule is used, 1 or 0 for winners and losers, respectively, when the WTA rule is used, and the teacher signal when supervised Hebbian learning is used).

4 Neural Network Architecture and Experiment Settings

To evaluate the Hebbian rule in deep learning, we designed a reference deep network architecture inspired to AlexNet [7]. The deep network structure, shown in Fig. 1, is composed of four convolutional layers followed by a fully connected layer (layer 5). Layer 6 is a linear classifier with one output per class. We performed several experiments in which we combined Hebbian learning with SGD learning in various ways, and we measured the classification performance obtained on the CIFAR-10 dataset [6]. In the first and second experiment, discussed in Sects. 5.1 and 5.2, we modified the architecture in Fig. 1 as shown in Fig. 2a. Specifically, we placed in turn Hebbian classifiers and SGD classifiers on top of feature extracted from various layers of, respectively, an SGD- and an Hebbian-trained network. In other words, the entire network was trained using a single approach (either Hebbian or SGD) and just the top layer (the classifier) was changed. In the third and fourth experiment, discussed in Sects. 5.3 and 5.4, we placed SGD-trained layers on top of Hebbian-trained layers, and vice-versa, at various level of the network, as shown in Fig. 2b. In the fifth experiment, discussed in Sect. 5.5, we put various Hebbian-trained layers in between SGD trained layers, as shown in Fig. 2c. In all the experiments, when lower layers were trained with the Hebbian rule, we also pre-processed images with ZCA-whitening [6], which provided us with better performance.

5 Experiments

As a baseline for the various experiments, we trained the defined network by applying the Stochastic Gradient Descent (SGD) algorithm to minimize the Cross-Entropy Loss. Training was executed using the following configuration:

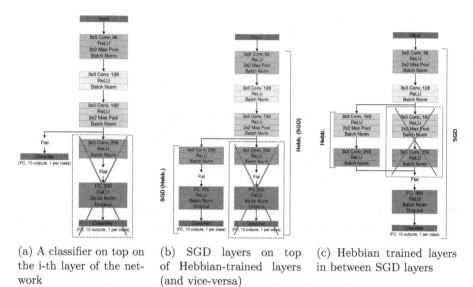

(a) A classifier on top on the i-th layer of the network

(b) SGD layers on top of Hebbian-trained layers (and vice-versa)

(c) Hebbian trained layers in between SGD layers

Fig. 2. Architecture modifications applied in our experiments.

SGD with Nesterov correction and momentum of 0.9, L2 penalty of 0.06, and a batch size of 64. The network was trained for 20 epochs on the first four of the five training batches of the CIFAR-10 dataset [6], corresponding to the first 40,000 samples, while the fifth batch, corresponding to the last 10,000 samples, was used for validation. Testing was performed on the CIFAR-10 test batch provided specifically for this purpose. Images were normalized to have zero mean and unit standard deviation. Early stopping was used so that, at the end of the 20 epochs, the network parameter configuration that we kept was the one achieving the highest accuracy. The learning rate was set to 10^{-3} for the first ten epochs, then halved every epoch for the next ten epochs. This baseline was used both for comparing with the performance obtained with Hebbian learning and to produce pre-trained SGD layers to be combined with Hebbian-trained layers. In the next sections, we discuss the results obtained by the various combinations of Hebbian-trained and SGD-trained layers, introduced in Sect. 4.

5.1 Hebbian vs. SGD Classifiers on SGD-Trained Layers

In this first experiment, we used the baseline trained network, discussed in Sect. 5, as a pre-processing module to extract features from an image, which were then fed to a classifier as shown in Fig. 2a. We compared both a classifier trained using SGD and the Hebbian rule.

To perform an exhaustive test, we measured the performance obtained by placing (and training) a classifier after every layer of the network. The SGD classifiers were trained with the same parameters used for the baseline, except that the L2 penalty is reduced to $5 \cdot 10^{-4}$. The Hebbian classifiers were trained

Table 1. Accuracy (%) of SGD- and Hebbian-trained classifiers built on top of various internal layers of an SGD- or Hebbian-trained network.

Classifier	Layer 1	Layer 2	Layer 3	Layer 4	Layer 5
	SGD	SGD	SGD	SGD	SGD
SGD	60.71	66.30	72.39	82.69	84.95
Hebbian	46.58	56.59	67.79	82.18	84.88
	Hebbian	Hebbian	Hebbian	Hebbian	Hebbian
SGD	63.92	63.81	58.28	52.99	41.78

with learning rate 0.1, the similarity between neuron inputs and weight vectors was measured in terms of angular distance (lower angular distance means higher similarity and vice-versa), and the activation function adopted was simply the scalar product between the input and the normalized weight vectors.

Table 1 (top two rows) reports the results of tested configurations. We can see that classifiers placed on top of higher layers and trained with the Hebbian rule achieve accuracy values practically overlapped to those of an SGD classifier. On the other hand, Hebbian classifiers placed on top of lower layers obtain a lower accuracy. However, it is worth mentioning that Hebbian classifiers can be trained in just a few epochs (usually one or two in our experiments), while classifiers trained with Gradient Descent need from five to ten epochs to converge.

5.2   SGD Classifiers on Hebbian-Trained Layers

Experiments discussed in this section are complementary to those discussed above. The entire deep network is trained with Hebbian approach, and the features extracted from the various layers are fed to an SGD classifier.

The goal is to evaluate the performance of the Hebbian approach for training the feature extraction layers of the network. To train the network, we set the learning rate of the Hebbian weight update rule to 0.1. The similarity between neuron inputs and weight vectors was measured in terms of angular distance (lower angular distance means higher similarity and vice-versa), and the activation function used for neurons of Hebbian hidden layers was the cosine similarity between input and weight vector, followed by the ReLU non-linearity. We used the WTA approach (Sect. 3.2) for updating the weight of the internal layers, we applied ZCA-whitening (see Sect. 4) to the input images. We imposed a teacher signal on the layers of the network trained with Hebbian approach, even if they are not classification layers, according to the logic discussed Sect. 3.3. In our experiments, we used 96 common kernels at layer 1, 8 kernels per class plus 16 common kernels at layer 2, 16 kernels per class plus 32 common kernels at layer 3, 24 kernels per class plus 16 common kernels at layer 4, and 28 kernels per class plus 20 common kernels at layer 5.

Table 1 (bottom row) reports the achieved results It can be observed that the accuracy slowly degrades with the number of layers. We conclude that training with the basic Hebbian rule has some disadvantages when the depth of the network increases, while it is still competitive when the layers are less than 4.

5.3 Hybrid: SGD Layers on Top of Hebbian Layers

In the previous experiments, the entire network was trained using a single approach and we changed just the classifier. Here, we created hybrid networks where the bottom layers were trained with the Hebbian rule and the top layers were trained with SGD. The goal of the following set of experiments is to assess the limits within which layers trained with the Hebbian algorithm can replace layers trained with SGD.

The architectures of these hybrid networks are as in Fig. 2b, where a layer was chosen as the *splitting point* between Hebbian trained layers and SGD trained ones. All the layers from the first to the fifth were used in different experiments as splitting points. The features extracted from the Hebbian-trained layers up to the splitting point were fed to the remaining network which was re-trained from scratch with SGD on the Hebbian feature maps provided as input. During this re-training process, the Hebbian-trained network was kept in evaluation mode and its parameters were left untouched. As before, also in this case, when training the Hebbian layers, we used the WTA approach, and the images were processed with ZCA-whitening.

Table 2 (second group) shows the accuracy on CIFAR-10 of a network composed of bottom layers trained with the Hebbian algorithm and top layers trained with Gradient Descent. In addition, the accuracy of the baseline fully trained with Gradient Descent and that of the same network fully trained with the Hebbian algorithm are also shown for comparisons (Table 2, first group). We also report the results of a network where the bottom layers are left completely untrained (randomly initialized), so that it is possible to assess whether Hebbian training gives a positive contribution w.r.t. pure randomness or it is completely destructive (Table 2, third group).

It can be observed that the first layer trained with the Hebbian algorithm can perfectly replace the corresponding Gradient Descent layer. There is a certain accuracy loss when also the second layer is switched to Hebbian learning, however it is still competitive. Accuracy heavily degrades when further layers are set to Hebbian learning. As expected, Hebbian training is better than untrained layers.

5.4 Hybrid: Hebbian Layers on Top of SGD Layers

The experiments presented in this section complement those discussed in Sect. 5.3: bottom layers are SGD-trained, while the top layers are Hebbian-trained. Table 2 (fourth group) shows the accuracy on CIFAR-10 of a network composed of bottom layers trained with Gradient Descent and top layers trained with the Hebbian algorithm. The table compares the accuracy of hybrid networks obtained by choosing layers 1, 2, ..., 5 to be the splitting point, i.e. all the layers on top of the first, second, ..., fifth (respectively) were trained with the Hebbian algorithm, while the rest of the network was kept in evaluation mode and its parameters were left untouched.

In this case, we can observe that the last layer trained with the Hebbian algorithm (i.e. the supervised Hebbian classifier) can perfectly replace the corresponding Gradient Descent layer. The fifth layer can also be replaced with a Hebbian layer with only a minimal accuracy decrease. We observe a slightly higher accuracy loss when also the fourth layer is replaced. Accuracy heavily degrades when further layers are replaced.

Table 2. Accuracy (%) on the CIFAR-10 test set of various configurations of learning rules. Columns 'L1–L5' and 'Classif' report the learning rule (G gradient descent, H Hebbian rule, R random init.) used to train respectively layers 1 to 5 and the final classifier.

Group	Description	L1	L2	L3	L4	L5	Classif	Accuracy
1	Full SGD	G	G	G	G	G	G	84.95
	Full Hebbian	H	H	H	H	H	H	28.59
2	1-bottom Hebbian	H	G	G	G	G	G	84.93
	2-bottom Hebbian	H	H	G	G	G	G	78.61
	3-bottom Hebbian	H	H	H	G	G	G	67.87
	4-bottom Hebbian	H	H	H	H	G	G	57.56
	5-bottom Hebbian	H	H	H	H	H	G	41.78
3	1-bottom Random	R	G	G	G	G	G	80.19
	2-bottom Random	R	R	G	G	G	G	71.87
	3-bottom Random	R	R	R	G	G	G	54.96
	4-bottom Random	R	R	R	R	G	G	45.56
	5-bottom Random	R	R	R	R	R	G	9.52
4	1-top Hebbian	G	G	G	G	G	H	84.88
	2-top Hebbian	G	G	G	G	H	H	83.16
	3-top Hebbian	G	G	G	H	H	H	71.18
	4-top Hebbian	G	G	H	H	H	H	50.43
	5-top Hebbian	G	H	H	H	H	H	32.95
5	Layer 1 Hebbian	G	H	G	G	G	G	80.36
	Layer 2 Hebbian	G	G	H	G	G	G	80.68
	Layer 3 Hebbian	G	G	G	H	G	G	80.92
	Layer 4 Hebbian	G	G	G	G	H	G	83.75
6	Layer 2-3 Hebbian	G	H	H	G	G	G	72.12
	Layer 3-4 Hebbian	G	G	H	H	G	G	74.98
	Layer 4-5 Hebbian	G	G	G	H	H	G	76.86
7	Layer 2-3-4 Hebbian	G	H	H	H	G	G	63.68
	Layer 3-4-5 Hebbian	G	G	H	H	H	G	62.43
8	Layer 2-3-4-5 Hebbian	G	H	H	H	H	G	47.24

5.5   Hybrid: Hebbian Layers Between SGD Layers

Finally, more complex configurations were also considered in which network layers were divided into three groups: bottom layers, middle layers, and top layers, as shown in Fig. 2c. The bottom layers were trained with SGD, the middle layers with the Hebbian algorithm and the top layers again with SGD.

Table 2 (fifth to eighth group) shows the accuracy on CIFAR-10 of these configurations. The table compares the accuracy of hybrid networks obtained by choosing various combinations of inner layers to be converted to Hebbian training. It can be observed that a minor accuracy loss occurs when a single inner layer is switched to a Hebbian equivalent. A slightly larger accuracy loss occurs when two layers are replaced. Specifically, lower layers are more susceptible than higher layers. Accuracy degrades more when further layers are replaced. However, the replacement of inner layers has more influence on the resulting accuracy than the replacement of outer layers.

6   Conclusion

We explored the use of the Hebbian rules for training a deep convolutional neural network for image classification. We extended the Hebbian weight update rule to convolutional layers, and we tested various combinations of Hebbian and SGD learning to investigate the advantages and disadvantages of mixing the two.

Experiments on CIFAR-10 showed that the Hebbian algorithm can be effectively used to train a few layers of a neural network, but the performance decreases when more layers are involved. In particular, the Hebbian algorithm is adequate for training the lower and the higher layers of a neural network, but not for the intermediate layers, which lead to the main performance drops when switched from Gradient Descent to its Hebbian equivalent.

On the other hand, the algorithm is advantageous with respect to Gradient Descent in terms of the number of epochs needed for training. In fact, a stack of Hebbian layers (for instance the top portion of a hybridly-trained network, or even a full Hebbian network), can be trained in fewer epochs (e.g. one or two on the architecture we used) than a network trained with SGD, which needs twenty epochs. Although the performance of deep full Hebbian networks is not yet comparable to the one of gradient-based models, according to our results, current Hebbian learning approaches could be efficiently and effectively adopted in scenarios like fine-tuning and transfer learning, where Hebbian layers on top of pre-trained SGD layers can be re-trained fast and effectively.

Moreover, the local nature of the Hebbian rule potentially provides huge speed-ups for large models with respect to backpropagation, thus encouraging further research to improve current approaches.

References

1. Bahroun, Y., Soltoggio, A.: Online representation learning with multi-layer hebbian networks for image classification tasks. arXiv preprint arXiv:1702.06456 (2017)

2. Gerstner, W., Kistler, W.M.: Spiking Neuron Models: Single Neurons, Populations, Plasticity. Cambridge University Press, Cambridge (2002)
3. Grossberg, S.: Adaptive pattern classification and universal recoding: i. parallel development and coding of neural feature detectors. Biol. Cybern. **23**(3), 121–134 (1976)
4. Haykin, S.: Neural Networks and Learning Machines, 3rd edn. Pearson, Upper Saddle River (2009)
5. Kohonen, T.: Self-organized formation of topologically correct feature maps. Biol. Cybern. **43**(1), 59–69 (1982)
6. Krizhevsky, A., Hinton, G.: Learning multiple layers of features from tiny images (2009)
7. Krizhevsky, A., Sutskever, I., Hinton, G.E.: Imagenet classification with deep convolutional neural networks. In: Advances in neural information processing systems (2012)
8. Lagani, G.: Hebbian learning algorithms for training convolutional neural networks. Master's thesis, School of Engineering, University of Pisa, Italy (2019)
9. Lagani, G.: Hebbian learning algorithms for training convolutional neural networks - project code (2019). https://github.com/GabrieleLagani/HebbianLearningThesis
10. Pehlevan, C., Hu, T., Chklovskii, D.B.: A hebbian/anti-hebbian neural network for linear subspace learning: a derivation from multidimensional scaling of streaming data. Neural comput. **27**(7), 1461–1495 (2015)
11. Ponulak, F.: Resume-new supervised learning method for spiking neural networks. Tech. rep. Institute of Control and Information Engineering, Poznan University of Technology (2005)
12. Rumelhart, D.E., Zipser, D.: Feature discovery by competitive learning. Cogn. Sci. **9**(1), 75–112 (1985)
13. Shrestha, A., Ahmed, K., Wang, Y., Qiu, Q.: Stable spike-timing dependent plasticity rule for multilayer unsupervised and supervised learning. pp. 1999–2006 (2017)
14. Von der Malsburg, C.: Self-organization of orientation sensitive cells in the striate cortex. Kybernetik **14**(2), 85–100 (1973)
15. Wadhwa, A., Madhow, U.: Learning sparse, distributed representations using the hebbian principle. arXiv preprint arXiv:1611.04228 (2016)

Classification of Skin Lesions by Combining Multilevel Learnings in a DenseNet Architecture

Pierluigi Carcagnì[✉], Marco Leo, Andrea Cuna, Pier Luigi Mazzeo, Paolo Spagnolo, Giuseppe Celeste, and Cosimo Distante

CNR-ISASI, Ecotekne Campus via Monteroni snc, 73100 Lecce, Italy
pierluigi.carcagni@cnr.it

Abstract. Automatic recognition and classification of skin diseases is an area of research that is gaining more and more attention. Unfortunately, most relevant works in the state of the art deal with a binary classification between malignant and non-malignant examples and this limits their use in real contexts where the classification of the specific pathology would be very useful. In this paper, a convolutional neural network (CNN) based on DenseNet architecture has been introduced and exploited for the automatic recognition of seven classes (Melanoma, Melanocytic nevus, Basal cell carcinoma, Actinic keratosis, Benign keratosis, Dermatofibroma, Vascular) of epidermal pathologies starting from dermoscopic images. Specialized network architecture and an innovative multilevel fine-tuning method that generates a set of specialized networks able to provide highly discriminative features have been designed. Finally, an SVM model is used for the final classification of the seven skin lesions. The experiments were carried out using an extended version of the HAM10000 dataset: starting from the publicly available images, geometric transformations such as rotations, flipping and affine were carried out in order to obtain a more balanced dataset.

Keywords: Deep Learning · Center loss · Skin lesion classification

1 Introduction

The development of systems based on image analysis for the automatic recognition and classification of skin diseases is an area of research that in recent years is gaining more and more attention. It is indeed a challenging multidisciplinary research area in which the application of modern machine learning techniques, with particular attention to those based on Deep Learning methodologies, have made automatic classification systems increasingly performing and attractive for real uses [13].

Automatic systems for the classification of skin lesions are very desired because, on the one hand, can drive the doctor's attention (allowing the screening of a larger number of patients in the same portion of time) and, on the

© Springer Nature Switzerland AG 2019
E. Ricci et al. (Eds.): ICIAP 2019, LNCS 11751, pp. 335–344, 2019.
https://doi.org/10.1007/978-3-030-30642-7_30

other hand, can even allow the development of domestic tools to identify persons most at risk. In the scientific literature, several computer vision based approaches making use of handcrafted features for skin lesions classification can be found [1,4,5,12]. Due to huge inter/intraclass variation and high visual similarity among different classes, the above-mentioned approaches were not able to get satisfying performance in terms of accuracy. In the last years, Deep Convolutional Neural Networks (DCNN) have increasingly being used in the computer vision field for tasks such as image recognition and classification, showing to exceed human performance. This surprising popularity of CNN pushed some researchers to investigate how they can impact on automatic skin lesion classification. Two relevant works exploiting CNN for skin lesion classification are those proposed in [3,6]. Unfortunately, the work in [6] only deals with the binary classification between malignant and non-malignant examples. The work in [3] proposes a unique model to classify multiple classes of skin lesions and to do that a huge amount of data was used in order to handle the large number of parameters in the model. Authors in [14] propose an approach that combines Deep Learning techniques with a low-level segmentation algorithm to distinguish malignant and benign skins lesions. The starting idea of [21] is not far from this, but here authors perform both the segmentation and the classification stages by means of very deep networks with the goal of obtaining more discriminative features for more accurate recognition. The typical degradation problem that occurs when a network goes deeper is overcome by utilizing residual learning technique [7]. In [18] an additional class, representing the visual patterns of regions outside the lesion to reduce their influence on the classification decision, is introduced. In [20] multiple imaging modalities together with patient metadata are provided to a deep neural network to improve the performance of automated diagnosis of five classes of skin cancer. The same five classes are the focus of the approach proposed in [11]. Recently, an interesting comparison between the performance of human experts and Convolutional Neural Networks for skin lesion detection has been proposed in [16].

In this paper, a convolutional neural network (CNN) based on DenseNet architecture [8] has been introduced and exploited for the automatic recognition of seven classes of epidermal pathologies starting from dermoscopic images. In particular, a network architecture more suited to the problem and an innovative multilevel fine-tuning method that generates a set of specialized networks able, also thanks to the linear combination of *soft-max* and *center-loss* [19], to provide highly discriminating features have been designed. To the best of our knowledge, the use of a model ensemble built by starting from one network architecture and generating from that a set of specialized networks through a multilevel fine-tuning method is the main contribution of the paper.

Starting from dermoscopic images, through each network new features are obtained. Features are then concatenated and supplied as input to an SVM model [15] for the final classification of seven skin lesions: Melanoma, Melanocytic nevus, Basal cell carcinoma, Actinic keratosis, Benign keratosis, Dermatofibroma, Vascular. The experiments were carried out using an extended version of the HAM10000 dataset [17]. In particular, starting from the publicly available images, geometric transformations such as rotations, flipping and affine were carried out in order to obtain a dataset that is as balanced as possible.

The rest of the paper is organized as follow. In Sect. 2 the proposed classification system is described whereas Sect. 3 reports the experimental results. Finally, Sect. 4 concludes the paper and give a glimpse of future works.

2 Methodology

The challenging problem of the classification of seven classes of skin lesions has been faced by a novel CNN architecture. The architecture was designed by taking as a starting point the one of the Densenet-121 presented in [8]. From the original implementation, the first two Transition Layers and the first two Dense Blocks were maintained whereas the number of layers in the third Dense Block was reduced. The initial internal parameters of the net were set up as provided after the pre-training on the IMAGENET dataset [2]. The third dense block was simplified by reducing the number of its layers and the whole architecture is reported in Table 1.

Table 1. The employed CNN architecture

Layers	Output size	Densenet-62
Convolution	112×112	7×7 conv, stride 2
Pooling	56×56	3×3 max pool, stride 2
Dense Block (1)	56×56	$\begin{bmatrix} 1 \times 1\,\text{conv} \\ 3 \times 3\,\text{conv} \end{bmatrix} \times 6$
Transition Layer (1)	56×56 28×28	1×1 conv 2×2 average pool, stride 2
Dense Block (2)	28×28	$\begin{bmatrix} 1 \times 1\,\text{conv} \\ 3 \times 3\,\text{conv} \end{bmatrix} \times 12$
Transition Layer (2)	28×28 14×14	1×1 conv 2×2 average pool, stride 2
Dense Block (3)	14×14	$\begin{bmatrix} 1 \times 1\,\text{conv} \\ 3 \times 3\,\text{conv} \end{bmatrix} \times 11$
Classification Layer	1×1	7×7 global average pool 7D fully-connected, softmax

The resulting CNN was then fine-tuned on the *HAM10000 Dataset* [17] that consist of 10,015 dermoscopic images regarding the considered classes of skin lesions: melanoma (MEL), melanocytic nevus (NV), basal cell carcinoma (BCC), actinic keratosis (AKIEC), benign keratosis (BKL), dermatofibroma (DF), vascular (VASC). Some representative samples in the aforementioned dataset are reported in Fig. 1.

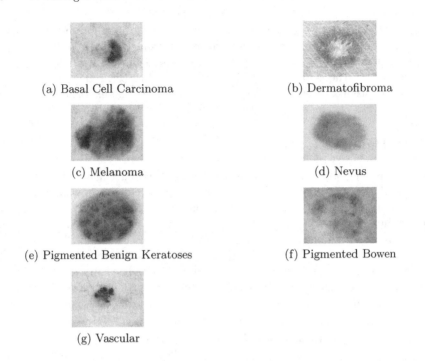

(a) Basal Cell Carcinoma

(b) Dermatofibroma

(c) Melanoma

(d) Nevus

(e) Pigmented Benign Keratoses

(f) Pigmented Bowen

(g) Vascular

Fig. 1. One representative example for each of the seven Skin Lesion Classes of the HAM10000 dataset.

Besides, in order to obtain a higher discriminative CNN model, in the learning phase the center-loss function based approach, proposed in [19], was exploited. In particular, in the course of CNN training, high discriminative features are learned considering jointly softmax and center loss functions balanced by means of a hyper parameter. The center loss function was defined by:

$$L_{center} = \frac{1}{2} \sum_{i=1}^{m} \|\mathbf{x}_i - \mathbf{c}_{y_i}\|_2^2 \qquad (1)$$

where the term $\mathbf{c}_i \in \Re^d$ denotes the y_ith class center of deep features $\mathbf{x}_i$.

Finally, the total loss function was defined as linear combination of soft-max L_s and center-loss L_c functions as following:

$$L = L_s + \gamma L_c \qquad (2)$$

where the term γ is a scalar used for balancing the two loss functions. Intra-class minimizations, during the learning phase, were controlled by means of L_c, inter-class maximizations by means of L_s.

3   Experimental Results

The CNN introduced in Sect. 2 was trained by employing a $k - fold$ approach with $k = 5$. The whole HAM10000 (Table 2) was partitioned into five splits: four

Table 2. HAM10000 Training Dataset. Number of images for each class.

MEL	NV	BCC	AKIEC	BKL	DF	VASC	Total
1113	6705	514	327	1099	115	142	10015

of them were used for training and the remaining one for test. The procedure was iterated in order to cover all the combinations of training and test splits. Given the complexity of the network and the number of parameters to be trained during the fine-tuning procedure, the samples of each training/test split were increased by means of geometric transformations. In particular, from each base image in a split additional images were obtained by rotation, flipping and affine transformations (see examples in Fig. 2) in order to obtain training/test sets having the representatives of each class as balanced as possible.

Each image in the balanced splits was then squared by centered cropping of amplitude equal to the shorter side of the starting image. The resulting patch was subsequently resized to a dimension of 224 × 224 pixels as requested by the input layer of the network.

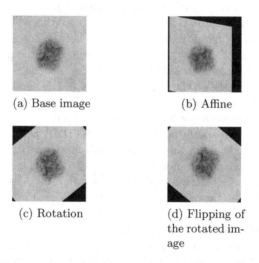

(a) Base image   (b) Affine

(c) Rotation   (d) Flipping of the rotated image

Fig. 2. Image transformations on a Melanoma sample

A multilevel fine-tuning, on the last Dense Block of the employed CNN architecture, was carried out using the training/test data splits provided by the $k - fold$ procedure. In each fine-tuning session, together with the last fully-connected layer, the last two, the last four, the last six, the last eight, the last ten and the last twelve convolution layers of the third Dense Block were modified respectively. To explain better this step, in the first session the last three convolution layers were fine-tuned whereas the parameters in the remaining layers of the network were not modified. In the second session, the last five convolution layers were fine-tuned and so on. This led to six different models, namely Mod.1, Mod.2, Mod.3, Mod.4, Mod.5, Mod.6 respectively. The classification scores, averaging the obtained $per fold$ results for each model, are in Tables 3 and 4 where Precision/Recall and F1-score are reported.

In Tables 3 and 4 it is evident that each model performs better on a particular class of skin lesions and this experimental evidence led to use an ensemble of nets instead of an end-to-end classifier. To this end, the probability outputs of each network were considered as features and chained in order to obtain a single feature vector in order to represent all the classes as a whole. Feature extraction was then performed on training data and the resulting feature vectors, after dimensional reduction by means of PCA, were used to train a seven class SVM classifier. The obtained SVM model was tested on the test data. The entire procedure was carried out using the $k - fold$ partitioned data and the averaged results related to Precision, Recall, F1-score and confusion matrix of the ensemble classifier are reported in Table 5 and Fig. 3 respectively.

In order to highlight the improvement in the performance of the proposed, the same validation procedure with $k - folded$ splitting of data and the same $center - loss$ approach was carried out by using the Densenet-121 CNN. In this case, the last two convolution layers of the last Dense Block were fine-tuned. Results, in terms of Precision, Recall and F1-Score, of this additional experiment are reported in Table 6. Despite the deeper layout of the net, Densenet-121 CNN showed a worse capacity, in terms of generalization, than the proposed approach to classify the 7 classes of skin lesions.

This can be attributed to the high complexity of the network in terms of the number of layers and to the low numerosity of the dataset used for which the strategy for data augmentation used was not sufficient.

Network training was performed using two NVIDIA GTX 1080Ti cards and the Caffe [9] framework. As optimizer, SGD was chosen with learning rate starting at 0.01, weight decay and momentum equal to 0.0001 and 0.9 respectively. The maximum number of iterations has been set at 75000, decreasing the learning rate by a factor of 10 at each step of 20000 iterations. Finally, the 0.008 value was used for the γ parameter in the Eq. 2. Regarding SVM classifier, an RBF kernel with $\lambda = 0.01$ and $C = 10$ were used.

Experimented outcomes are very encouraging. For all the classes the F1-score was greater than 0.8, except for Melanoma (0.72) and Keratosis (0.62). Since this is a relatively unexplored research field the fair comparison with leading approaches in the literature is not trivial. There is no published work exploiting the HAM10000 dataset indeed. Anyway, it is still possible to get a fair comparison in a quite simple way. In 2018 a dedicated challenge (ISIC 2018: Skin Lesion Analysis Towards Melanoma Detection[1]) was held rightly on the HAM10000 dataset. Task 3 in the challenge was devoted to the seven classes of skin diseases in the HAM10000 dataset. Task 3 was addressed by 141 research groups and, excluding solutions using external data for training, the best one was the ensem-

---

[1] https://challenge2018.isic-archive.com.

Table 3. Results obtained using the 6 fine tuned models (In each row, upper value refers to Precision score, lower value refers to Recall score)

	Mod. 1	Mod. 2	Mod. 3	Mod. 4	Mod. 5	Mod. 6
MEL	0.70	0.70	0.73	0.70	0.75	0.72
	0.56	0.52	0.54	0.60	0.55	0.68
NV	0.91	0.92	0.92	0.94	0.92	0.94
	0.95	0.97	0.97	0.95	0.97	0.96
BCC	0.84	0.83	0.81	0.87	0.83	0.80
	0.82	0.78	0.84	0.80	0.84	0.78
AKIEC	0.79	0.73	0.78	0.76	0.74	0.74
	0.69	0.60	0.56	0.59	0.53	0.53
BKL	0.74	0.76	0.77	0.74	0.78	0.78
	0.72	0.80	0.78	0.82	0.79	0.80
DF	0.80	1.00	0.90	0.75	0.90	0.82
	0.72	0.82	0.82	0.82	0.82	0.82
VASC	0.93	1.0	0.91	0.93	0.92	1.00
	0.93	0.79	0.71	0.93	0.86	1.00
Average	0.81	0.85	0.83	0.93	0.83	0.82
	0.77	0.75	0.75	0.80	0.77	0.80

Table 4. F1-Score results related to the 6 fine tuned models

	Mod. 1	Mod. 2	Mod. 3	Mod. 4	Mod. 5	Mod. 6
MEL	0.62	0.60	0.62	0.65	0.64	0.70
NV	0.93	0.94	0.95	0.94	0.94	0.95
BCC	0.83	0.81	0.83	0.84	0.83	0.80
AKIEC	0.73	0.66	0.65	0.67	0.62	0.62
BKL	0.73	0.78	0.78	0.77	0.79	0.80
DF	0.76	0.90	0.86	0.78	0.86	0.82
VASC	0.93	0.90	0.80	0.93	0.90	1.00
Average	0.79	0.79	0.78	0.80	0.79	0.81

ble of CNN described in [10]. Using PNASNet on 5-fold Validation Data authors in [10] reported a mean precision on 7 classes (namely MCA) of 82,6% ± 2.0 whereas the MCA score, as reported in Table 5 for the ensemble approach proposed in this paper, is 88%.

A final consideration should be made: the approach proposed in this paper is based on an ensemble of models generated by the same reduced network architecture. This leads to reduced models extracted by the same network architecture that can be exploited into embedded systems that are very desirable to quickly move towards portable devices for domestic diagnosis of skin lesions.

Table 5. Precision, Recall and F1-Score results for the proposed ensemble approach.

	Precision	Recall	F1-Score
MEL	0.77	0.68	0.72
NV	0.92	0.98	0.95
BCC	0.91	0.82	0.87
AKIEC	0.80	0.50	0.62
BKL	0.86	0.77	0.81
DF	1.00	0.82	0.90
VASC	0.92	0.86	0.89
Average	0.88	0.76	0.82

Table 6. Precision, Recall and F1-Score results for the original Densenet-121.

	Precision	Recall	F1-Score
MEL	0.60	0.03	0.05
NV	0.95	0.44	0.60
BCC	0.63	0.27	0.38
AKIEC	0.67	0.19	0.29
BKL	0.17	0.93	0.28
DF	0.22	0.18	0.20
VASC	0.21	0.50	0.30
Average	0.49	0.36	0.30

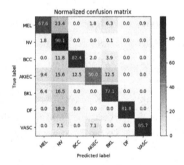

Fig. 3. Ensemble classifier Confusion Matrix

4   Conclusions and Future Work

In this work, a novel approach, based on deep CNNs, for classification of skin lesions has been introduced. It works by using a unique (and not very deep) network architecture from which six models have been generated (each one better performing for specific classes of skin lesions) and then used in an ensemble able to handle 7 different classes of output. Due to the particular configuration of the CNN, this approach could be exploited into embedded systems that are very desirable to quickly move towards portable devices for domestic diagnosis of skin lesions. Future works will deal with the challenging task of increasing the dataset adding annotated data that can bring to more robust learning of the network parameters. Besides, the possibility to take advantage of some pre-processing step on input images (e.g. colour constancy) will be investigated. Finally, also the use of a preliminary segmentation phase could be considered in order to obtain registered images into a common reference.

Acknowledgement. The Authors thank Arturo Argentieri for his contribution to the realization of the GPUs and software set-up used for the experiments.

References

1. Barata, C., Celebi, M.E., Marques, J.S.: Improving dermoscopy image classification using color constancy. IEEE J. Biomed. Health Inf. **19**(3), 1146–1152 (2015)
2. Deng, J., Dong, W., Socher, R., Li, L.J., Li, K., Fei-Fei, L.: ImageNet: a large-scale hierarchical image database. In: IEEE Conference on Computer Vision and Pattern Recognition, CVPR 2009, pp. 248–255. IEEE (2009)
3. Esteva, A., et al.: Dermatologist-level classification of skin cancer with deep neural networks. Nature **542**(7639), 115 (2017)
4. Garnavi, R., Aldeen, M., Bailey, J.: Computer-aided diagnosis of melanoma using border-and wavelet-based texture analysis. IEEE Trans. Inf Technol. Biomed. **16**(6), 1239–1252 (2012)
5. Glaister, J., Wong, A., Clausi, D.A.: Segmentation of skin lesions from digital images using joint statistical texture distinctiveness. IEEE Trans. Biomed. Eng. **61**(4), 1220–1230 (2014)
6. Haenssle, H., et al.: Man against machine: diagnostic performance of a deep learning convolutional neural network fordermoscopic melanoma recognition in comparison to 58 dermatologists. Ann. Oncol. (2018)
7. He, K., Zhang, X., Ren, S., Sun, J.: Deep residual learning for image recognition. In: Proceedings of the IEEE Conference on Computer Vision and Pattern Recognition, pp. 770–778 (2016)
8. Huang, G., Liu, Z., Van Der Maaten, L., Weinberger, K.Q.: Densely connected convolutional networks. In: CVPR, vol. 1, p. 3 (2017)
9. Jia, Y., et al.: Caffe: convolutional architecture for fast feature embedding. arXiv preprint arXiv:1408.5093 (2014)
10. Zhuangy, J., Liy, W.: Skin lesion analysis towards melanoma detection using deep neural network ensemble (2018)
11. Kawahara, J., BenTaieb, A., Hamarneh, G.: Deep features to classify skin lesions. In: 2016 IEEE 13th International Symposium on Biomedical Imaging (ISBI), pp. 1397–1400. IEEE (2016)
12. Kaya, S., et al.: Abrupt skin lesion border cutoff measurement for malignancy detection in dermoscopy images. BMC Bioinf. **17**, 367 (2016)
13. Leo, M., Furnari, A., Medioni, G.G., Trivedi, M., Farinella, G.M.: Deep learning for assistive computer vision. In: Leal-Taixé, L., Roth, S. (eds.) ECCV 2018. LNCS, vol. 11134, pp. 3–14. Springer, Cham (2019). https://doi.org/10.1007/978-3-030-11024-6_1

14. Premaladha, J., Ravichandran, K.: Novel approaches for diagnosing melanoma skin lesions through supervised and deep learning algorithms. J. Med. Syst. **40**(4), 96 (2016)
15. Suykens, J.A., Vandewalle, J.: Least squares support vector machine classifiers. Neural Process. Lett. **9**(3), 293–300 (1999)
16. Tschandl, P., et al.: Expert-level diagnosis of nonpigmented skin cancer by combined convolutional neural networks. JAMA Dermatol. **155**(1), 58–65 (2019)
17. Tschandl, P., Rosendahl, C., Kittler, H.: The ham10000 dataset: a large collection of multi-source dermatoscopic images of common pigmented skin lesions. arXiv preprint arXiv:1803.10417 (2018)
18. Vasconcelos, C.N., Vasconcelos, B.N.: Experiments using deep learning fordermoscopy image analysis. Pattern Recogn. Lett. (2017)
19. Wen, Y., Zhang, K., Li, Z., Qiao, Y.: A discriminative feature learning approach for deep face recognition. In: Leibe, B., Matas, J., Sebe, N., Welling, M. (eds.) ECCV 2016. LNCS, vol. 9911, pp. 499–515. Springer, Cham (2016). https://doi.org/10.1007/978-3-319-46478-7_31
20. Yap, J., Yolland, W., Tschandl, P.: Multimodal skin lesion classification using deep learning. Exp. Dermatol. **27**(11), 1261–1267 (2018)
21. Yu, L., Chen, H., Dou, Q., Qin, J., Heng, P.A.: Automated melanoma recognition in dermoscopy images via very deep residual networks. IEEE Trans. Med. Imaging **36**(4), 994–1004 (2017)

Take a Ramble into Solution Spaces for Classification Problems in Neural Networks

Enzo Tartaglione$^{(\boxtimes)}$ ⓘ and Marco Grangetto ⓘ

University of Torino, Turin, Italy
`enzo.tartaglione@unito.it`

Abstract. Solving a classification problem for a neural network means looking for a particular configuration of the internal parameters. This is commonly achieved by minimizing non-convex object functions. Hence, the same classification problem is likely to have several, different, equally valid solutions, depending on a number of factors like the initialization and the adopted optimizer.

In this work, we propose an algorithm which looks for a zero-error path joining two solutions to the same classification problem. We witness that finding such a path is typically not a trivial problem; however, our heuristics is able to succeed in such a task. This is a step forward to explain why simple training heuristics (like SGD) are able to train complex neural networks: we speculate they focus on particular solutions, which belong to a connected solution sub-space. We work in two different scenarios: a synthetic, unbiased and totally-uncorrelated (hard) training problem, and MNIST. We empirically show that the algorithmically-accessible solutions space is connected, and we have hints suggesting it is a convex sub-space.

Keywords: Neural networks · Solution space · Image classification

1 Introduction

One of the core problems in computer vision is image classification. Solving an image classification problem means being able to correctly recognize an image as being part of a class, which translates into the correct identification of key features. Image classification finds a number of direct applications, not restricted to tumor classification and detection [1], bio-metric identification [15,20,23], object classification [9] and even emotions [7]. This problem is typically complex to be solved, and a number of algorithms have been designed to tackle it [8,17,24]. However, the top-performance model is here represented by neural networks. In particular, the so-called convolutional neural networks (CNNs) are able to automatically take as input images, process them in order to extract the key features for the particular classification problem, and perform the classification itself. Applying very simple optimizing heuristics to minimize the loss

ⓒ Springer Nature Switzerland AG 2019
E. Ricci et al. (Eds.): ICIAP 2019, LNCS 11751, pp. 345–355, 2019.
https://doi.org/10.1007/978-3-030-30642-7_31

function, like SGD [4,27], slightly more complex optimizers like Nesterov [19] or Adam [14] moving to the sophisticated local entropy minimizer [2,6], it is nowadays possible to succeed in training extremely complex systems (deep networks) on huge datasets. Theoretically speaking, this is the "miracle" of deep learning, as the dimensionality of the problem is huge (indeed, these problems are typically over-parametrized, and the dimensionality can be efficiently reduced [25]). Furthermore, minimizing non-convex objective functions is typically supposed to make the trained architecture stuck into local minima. However, the empirical evidence shows that something else is happening under the hood: understanding it, in order to provide some warranty for all the possible applications of image classification, is critical.

In this work, we propose an heuristic approach which should help us to understand some basic properties of the found solutions in neural network models. Here, we aim to find a path joining two (or, in general, more) different solutions to the same classification problem. Early attempts to explore possible joining paths were performed using random walk-based techniques, but the complexity of the task, due to the typical high-dimensionality of the problem, made it extremely inefficient [13].

A recent work [12] suggests that solutions to the same problem are typically divided by a loss barrier, but a later work by Draxler et al. [10] shows the existence of low-loss joining paths between similar-performance solutions. Such a work, however, focuses on the loss function, which is a necessary but not sufficient condition to guarantee the performance on the training/test set. Our heuristics puts a hard constraint on it: we will never have a *performance* (evaluated as the number of samples correctly classified by the neural network model) below a fixed threshold. In the case we ask our model to correctly classify the whole training set, we will say we lie in the *solution region S* of the training model, also known as *version space*. This will be our focus along this work.

In the last few years, thanks to the ever-increasing computational capability of computers, bigger and bigger neural networks have been proposed, in order to solve always more complex problems. However, explaining why they succeed in solving complex classification tasks is nowadays a hot research topic [11,21,22]. Still, it is object of study why, using simple optimizers like SGD to minimize problems which are typically non-convex, is a sufficient condition to succeed in training deep models [5,16,18]. The aim of this work is to move a step in the direction of explaining such a phenomenon, analyzing some typical solutions to learning problems, and inspecting properties of them. In this way, we aim to give some hints on which type of solutions SGD finds, guessing whether there is some room for improvement or not.

The rest of this paper is organized as follows. In Sect. 2 we set-up the problem environment, aim and the algorithm is illustrated and justified. Next, in Sect. 3 we test our algorithm on MNIST and on training sets containing uncorrelated, randomly-generated patterns. The experiments show that our proposed method is able to always find joining paths in S between any found solution for the same problem. Furthermore, hints on some properties of S are deduced studying the joining path. Finally, Sect. 4 draws the conclusions and suggests further directions for future research.

2   The Proposed Algorithm

2.1   Preliminaries

In our setting, we have a *training set* Ξ_{tr} made of M pairs (ξ_i, σ_i), in which we identify the set of inputs ξ_i and their associated desired output σ_i. For the purpose of our work, we ask for some configuration W of the neural network such that the entire Ξ_{tr} problem is correctly solved. If such a condition is met, we say that the configuration W is a *solution* for the learning problem Ξ_{tr}. In other words, a weights configuration W_k is a solution when

$$y_i \,|\xi_i, W_k = \sigma_i \; \forall i \in \Xi_{tr} \tag{1}$$

If we define S as the subset of all the W configurations which solve the whole training problem Ξ_{tr}, we can say that $W_k \in S$. Let us imagine two solutions to the same problem Ξ_{tr}, W_a and W_b, are provided. We aim to find a path $\Omega_{ab} \subset S$ which joins W_a to W_b. At this point, we might face two different scenarios:

1. Ω_{ab} is simply a straight line. According to the work by Goodfellow et al., we could draw a straight line between W_a and W_b which might be parametrized, for example, as

$$l_{ab}(t) = (W_b - W_a)t + W_a \tag{2}$$

   with $t \in [0, 1]$. According to this scenario, this is a sufficient condition to join the two different solutions. However, as showed by the same work of Goodfellow et al., this is not typical [12].
2. Ω_{ab} is a "non-trivial" path as $l_{ab} \not\subset S$, and is not a-priori guaranteed to exist. This is the typical scenario, and the setting in which we are going to work. The work by Draxler et al. [10] shows that there exists a path Γ_{ab} having low loss value, however, in general, $\Gamma_{ab} \not\subset S$. Our heuristics not only works for the case $\Omega_{ab} \neq l_{ab}$, but it guarantees $\Omega_{ab} \subset S$ (Fig. 1).

2.2   Finding the Path

Our heuristics generates the path Ω_{ab} in a "Markov chain" fashion: we are going to use a "survey" network W_x, whose task is to modify its configuration (i.e. the value of its parameters) in order to move from W_a's configuration to W_b, never leaving S. Hence, at time $t = 0$ we initialize $W_x = W_a$, and we ask W_x to explore S such that, at some time t_f, $W_x = W_b$. The exploration algorithm is designed according to three, very simple, basic concepts:

- We will never leave S.
- As we start from W_a, we want to arrive to W_b using a survey network W_x, which draws Ω_{ab} in t_f steps.

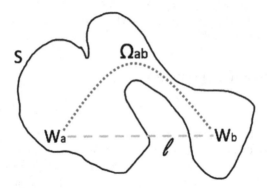

Fig. 1. Example of the "non trivial" scenario. Here, while l_{ab} goes out the solution region S, Ω_{ab} still remains inside it.

- At time t', W_x will just have knowledge of the training set, direction and distance towards the target W_b.

In order to reach W_b, we need to drive W_x at any time t to it. Towards this end, we use an elastic force:

$$\Delta W_x^t = \gamma(W_b - W_x^{t-1}) \tag{3}$$

where γ is an *elastic constant*, whose value is typically $\gamma \ll 1$.

If we just apply Eq. 3, in the non-trivial scenario, W_x will leave the solution region, as we will have $\Omega_{ab} \equiv l_{ab}$. Hence, what we need here is to change the trajectory for our Ω_{ab} in a "smart" way. It will be nice to stay away from the *frontier* of S. A local information we have, which might come handy in this context, is the gradient on the training set. If we perform a GD step, W_x should be naturally driven down the loss function and, supposedly, drives W_x away from the frontier of S.

Along with the elastic coupling and the GD step, we impose a norm constraint for W_x, acting as a regularizer, to be applied layer-by-layer, which bounds W_x's norm to:

$$n\left(W_x^l\right) = \|W_b^l\|_F - \frac{\|W_b^l\|_F - \|W_a^l\|_F}{\|W_b^l - W_a^l\|_F}\|W_b^l - W_x^l\|_F \tag{4}$$

where W_x^l indicates the l-th layer of W_x and $\|\cdot\|_F$ is the Frobenius norm. Essentially, we are imposing a linear constraint to the norm of W_x, which is function of the distance from W_b. Finally, as we have the hard constraint on remaining into S, we need to impose small steps for W_x

$$W_x^t = W_x^{t-1} + \delta W_x^t \tag{5}$$

where, typically,

$$\delta W_x^t \ll \nabla W_x^{t-1} \tag{6}$$

In this way, unless we find a local minimum very close to W_b and exactly on the same path followed by W_x (extremely unlikely as empirically observed, issue which can be anyway easily tackled with a proper tuning of γ), we avoid to get stuck in any local minimum.

To sum-up, in order to generate Ω_{ab}, after we have initialized W_x to W_a, we iteratively perform the following steps:

1. Apply an elastic coupling in the direction of W_b (Eq. 3), with the hard constraint of never leaving S (this is hard because we will simulate a "hitting a wall"-like fashion, i.e. we will discard all the steps which will put W_x outside S)
2. Perform N_{epochs} of gradient descent (GD) steps evaluated on Ξ_{tr}
3. Properly normalize W_x (Eq. 4)

The general algorithm is summarized in Algorithm 1.

Algorithm 1. Find joining path between W_a and W_b

1: **procedure** TRACK $\Omega(W_a, W_b, \Xi_{tr})$▷ Implicitly, W_x always normalized as in Eq. 4
2:     $W_x = W_a$
3:     $\Omega = W_x$
4:     **while** $W_x \neq W_b$ **do**
5:         **for** N_{epochs} **do**
6:             $W_x = W_x - \eta \nabla W_x$ ▷ ∇W_x computed on Ξ_{tr}
7:             **if** $W_x \notin S$ **then**
8:                 **return** $\emptyset$ ▷ η, γ not properly set
9:         $W_x\text{-tmp} = W_x - \gamma(W_b - W_x)$
10:        **if** $W_x\text{-tmp} \in S$ **then**
11:            $W_x = W_x\text{-tmp}$
12:        $\Omega = \text{append}(\Omega, W_x)$
13:    **return** Ω

2.3 Properties of the Path

Once we have obtained Ω_{ab}, we can perform an empirical investigation on it. There are some interesting observations we can perform on it:

– Is there any property related to the shape of S? As typical problems are extremely high-dimensional, it is very difficult to deduct some global property on S. However, we might have some hint on how S is shaped from two indicators:
  • If we are always able to find $\Omega_{ab} \subset S$, then we might suggest that all the algorithmically-accessible solutions in S, collected in $S_{algo} \subset S$, live in a connected subspace.
  • We can study the Hessian along Ω_{ab}. Even though this is not a fully-informative observation for S, we can deduce some properties, like the shape of the loss in S_{algo}.

- Verify how the loss function varies along Ω_{ab}: as our technique is strictly bounded to S and not necessarily to the minimization of the loss function, it may happen that some solutions to Ξ_{tr} have high loss.
- Check how the generalization error, defined as the error on the test set, varies along Ω_{ab}.

All of these aspects will be empirically investigated in Sect. 3.

3   Experiments

The proposed algorithm was tested under two very different settings and architectures. In both cases, a $\Omega_{ab} \subset S$ path has always been found.

3.1   Tree Committee Machine on Random Patterns

In our first experiments, we use a simple kind of neural network, the so-called Tree Committee Machine (TCM). It is a binary classifier, consisting in one-hidden neural network having N inputs and K neurons in the hidden layer. The connectivity of the hidden layer is here tree-like: each k-th neuron of the hidden layer is able to receive data from an exclusive $\frac{N}{K}$ subset of the input. In particular, for our setting, the general output of the TCM is defined as

$$\hat{y}_i = \tanh \left[\sum_{k=1}^{K} \text{htanh} \left(\sum_{j=1}^{\frac{N}{K}} W_{kj} \cdot \xi_{k\frac{N}{K}+j}^{\mu} \right) \right] \tag{7}$$

where htanh is the hard tanh.

The training set Ξ_{tr} is randomly generated: the input patterns $\xi_i \in \{-1; +1\}^{(N \times M)}$ and random desired outputs $\sigma \in \{-1, +1\}^{M}$.

All the experiments here shown are performed on TCMs having size $N = 300$ and $K = 3$ and the training sets consist in $M = 620$ samples. The training of the reference solutions to Ξ_{tr} has been performed using the standard GD technique, minimizing the binary cross-entropy loss function, with $\eta = 0.1$. The network has been initialized using a gaussian initializer. In this setting, $\gamma = 0.001$ and $N_{epochs} = 5$. The algorithm was tested on 10 different, randomly-generated datasets, and for each of them 3 different configurations $W_i \in S$ were obtained and attempted to be connected. The implementation of the neural network and of the algorithm is in Julia 0.5.2 [3].

Even though we are in the typical scenario for which the error on $l_{ab} > 0$, we are able to find a non-trivial path in S. For this network, it is also possible to compute the exact Hessian matrix. Surprisingly, the typical observed scenario here is that, along any found $\Omega \subset S$, all the non-zero eigenvalues of the Hessian matrix are strictly positive, the cardinality of non-zero eigenvalues is constant and the reference solutions represent local minima for the trace of the Hessian matrix. An example of this observed result is shown in Fig. 2. This result is obtained in a hard learning scenario, and may suggest us that, even though the learning problems are typically non-convex, GD-based techniques work because the algorithmically accessible S_{algo} region, is convex.

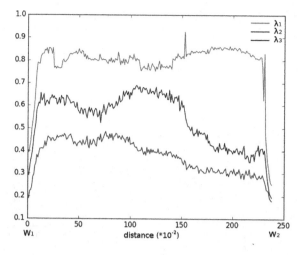

Fig. 2. Hessian eigenvalues along Ω_{ab} in TCM for random patterns. In this case, just three eigenvalues are non-zero and all positive. Along the path, the loss on the training set is proportional to the trace of the Hessian.

3.2 LeNet5 on MNIST

Experiments on LeNet5 solutions trained on the MNIST dataset have been performed. In particular, at first simulations on a reduced MNIST are shown (training is performed on the first 100 images: we are going to call it MNIST-100) and on the full MNIST dataset. The software used for the following simulations is PyTorch 1.1 with CUDA 10.

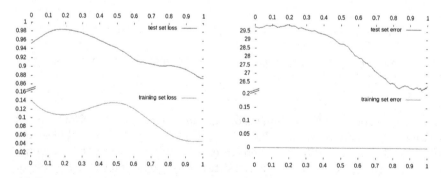

(a) Loss on training and test set in Ω_{ab} (b) Error [%] on training and test set in Ω_{ab}

Fig. 3. Example of Ω_{ab} for LeNet5 with MNIST-100. The x axis is a normalized distance between W_a and W_b.

For the MNIST-100 case, the networks have been trained using SGD with $\eta = 0.1$, and initialized with Xavier. The joining path heuristic used $\gamma = 0.001$ and

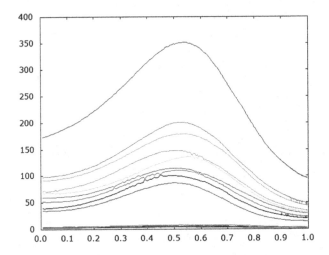

Fig. 4. Hessian eigenvalues along Ω_{ab} for LeNet5 trained on MNIST-100 (same experiment as Fig. 3). Here the top-20 Hessian eigenvalues are plotted.

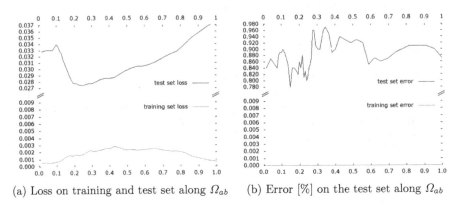

(a) Loss on training and test set along Ω_{ab} (b) Error [%] on the test set along Ω_{ab}

Fig. 5. Example of Ω_{ab} for LeNet5 with the entire training set. The x axis is a normalized distance between W_a and W_b.

$N_{epochs} = 5$. Despite the higher dimensionality and complexity of LeNet5, also in this case it has always been possible to find a Ω_{ab} path in S. A typical observed behavior is shown in Fig. 3. It is here interesting to observe that in general, moving through Ω, both the training and test loss are no longer monotonic or bi-tonic, but they show a more complex behavior (an example is in Fig. 3(a)). Furthermore, observing the test set error, it shows a similar behavior to the test set loss, but not locally exactly the same (Fig. 3(b)).

It can be here interesting to investigate the behavior of the eigenvalues of the Hessian along Ω_{ab} also in this scenario. Figure 4 is a plot for the top-20 eigenvalues. The Hessian eigenvalue computation has been performed here using the code by Gholami [26]. Interestingly, even for a more complex architecture like LeNet5, along the entire Ω_{ab} path, the top eigenvalues are all positive.

Besides the simulations on MNIST-100, we also attempted to find a joining path between two solutions for the entire MNIST dataset, still using LeNet5. In this case, $\gamma = 0.1$ and $N_{epochs} = 5$, while the training of the initial configuration is performed using SGD with $\eta = 0.1$ and initializing with Xavier. According to our findings, in this setting, a zero-error joining path, even for the whole MNIST problem, typically exists (Fig. 5). Interestingly, the best generalization performance (at about 0.2 in the normalized distance scale) is here found far from both the solutions found by SGD, and typically can not be found by vanilla-SGD, as there is a higher training loss value (even if it lies in the version space).

4   Conclusion

In this work, a heuristic approach to find a path Ω_{ab} joining two solutions W_a and W_b to the same training problem Ξ_{tr} is proposed. The main property of Ω_{ab} is that it entirely lies in the solution space S of the W's configurations which solve the training problem. In general, such an approach is not guaranteed to produce an Ω: if S is not connected and W_a and W_b belong to two different sub-spaces of S, by construction, Ω_{ab} can not exist. By our empirical observations, with a randomly-generated, uncorrelated, synthetic training set and with MNIST, the subspace $S_{algo} \subseteq S$ accessed by GD-based techniques seems to be connected. Furthermore, we have some hints indicating that S_{algo} might be convex and a further proof that SGD alone is not sufficient to guarantee the best generalization, neither for nowadays simple classification problems like MNIST.

The proposed technique potentially allows us to extend the investigation of S also to non-typical algorithmic solutions to the learning problem, along the drawn Ω paths. These findings open to new researches in the field of explainable neural networks. Future work involves the study of how the generalization error varies along Ω on more complex classification tasks and the design of an algorithm to boost it.

References

1. Al-Shaikhli, S.D.S., Yang, M.Y., Rosenhahn, B.: Brain tumor classification using sparse coding and dictionary learning. In: 2014 IEEE International Conference on Image Processing (ICIP), pp. 2774–2778. IEEE (2014)
2. Baldassi, C., Ingrosso, A., Lucibello, C., Saglietti, L., Zecchina, R.: Local entropy as a measure for sampling solutions in constraint satisfaction problems. J. Stat. Mech: Theory Exp. **2016**(2), 023301 (2016)
3. Bezanson, J., Karpinski, S., Shah, V.B., Edelman, A.: Julia: a fast dynamic language for technical computing. arXiv preprint arXiv:1209.5145 (2012)
4. Bottou, L.: Large-scale machine learning with stochastic gradient descent. In: Lechevallier, Y., Saporta, G. (eds.) Proceedings of COMPSTAT 2010, pp. 177–186. Springer, Heidelberg (2010). https://doi.org/10.1007/978-3-7908-2604-3_16

5. Brutzkus, A., Globerson, A., Malach, E., Shalev-Shwartz, S.: SGD learns over-parameterized networks that provably generalize on linearly separable data. arXiv preprint arXiv:1710.10174 (2017)
6. Chaudhari, P., et al.: Entropy-SGD: biasing gradient descent into wide valleys. arXiv preprint arXiv:1611.01838 (2016)
7. Chen, M., Zhang, L., Allebach, J.P.: Learning deep features for image emotion classification. In: 2015 IEEE International Conference on Image Processing (ICIP), pp. 4491–4495. IEEE (2015)
8. Chen, Y., Nasrabadi, N.M., Tran, T.D.: Hyperspectral image classification via kernel sparse representation. IEEE Trans. Geosci. Remote Sens. **51**(1), 217–231 (2013)
9. Doulamis, N., Doulamis, A.: Semi-supervised deep learning for object tracking and classification. In: 2014 IEEE International Conference on Image Processing (ICIP), pp. 848–852. IEEE (2014)
10. Draxler, F., Veschgini, K., Salmhofer, M., Hamprecht, F.A.: Essentially no barriers in neural network energy landscape. arXiv preprint arXiv:1803.00885 (2018)
11. Frosst, N., Hinton, G.: Distilling a neural network into a soft decision tree. arXiv preprint arXiv:1711.09784 (2017)
12. Goodfellow, I.J., Vinyals, O., Saxe, A.M.: Qualitatively characterizing neural network optimization problems. arXiv preprint arXiv:1412.6544 (2014)
13. Ishihara, A.K., Ben-Menahem, S.: Control on landscapes with local minima and flat regions: a simulated annealing and gain scheduling approach. In: 47th IEEE Conference on Decision and Control, CDC 2008, pp. 105–110. IEEE (2008)
14. Kingma, D.P., Ba, J.: Adam: a method for stochastic optimization. arXiv preprint arXiv:1412.6980 (2014)
15. Klimanee, C., Nguyen, D.T.: Classification of fingerprints using singular points and their principal axes. In: 2004 International Conference on Image Processing, ICIP 2004, vol. 2, pp. 849–852. IEEE (2004)
16. Li, H., Xu, Z., Taylor, G., Studer, C., Goldstein, T.: Visualizing the loss landscape of neural nets. In: Advances in Neural Information Processing Systems, pp. 6389–6399 (2018)
17. Li, J., Najmi, A., Gray, R.M.: Image classification by a two-dimensional hidden markov model. IEEE Trans. Signal Process. **48**(2), 517–533 (2000)
18. Li, Y., Liang, Y.: Learning overparameterized neural networks via stochastic gradient descent on structured data. In: Advances in Neural Information Processing Systems, pp. 8157–8166 (2018)
19. Nesterov, Y., Polyak, B.T.: Cubic regularization of newton method and its global performance. Math. Program. **108**(1), 177–205 (2006)
20. Rattani, A., Derakhshani, R., Saripalle, S.K., Gottemukkula, V.: ICIP 2016 competition on mobile ocular biometric recognition. In: 2016 IEEE International Conference on Image Processing (ICIP), pp. 320–324. IEEE (2016)
21. Sabour, S., Frosst, N., Hinton, G.E.: Dynamic routing between capsules. In: Advances in Neural Information Processing Systems, pp. 3856–3866 (2017)
22. Samek, W., Wiegand, T., Müller, K.R.: Explainable artificial intelligence: understanding, visualizing and interpreting deep learning models. arXiv preprint arXiv:1708.08296 (2017)
23. Soleymani, S., Torfi, A., Dawson, J., Nasrabadi, N.M.: Generalized bilinear deep convolutional neural networks for multimodal biometric identification. In: 2018 25th IEEE International Conference on Image Processing (ICIP), pp. 763–767. IEEE (2018)

24. Tarabalka, Y., Benediktsson, J.A., Chanussot, J.: Spectral-spatial classification of hyperspectral imagery based on partitional clustering techniques. IEEE Trans. Geosci. Remote Sens. **47**(8), 2973–2987 (2009)
25. Tartaglione, E., Lepsøy, S., Fiandrotti, A., Francini, G.: Learning sparse neural networks via sensitivity-driven regularization. In: Advances in Neural Information Processing Systems, pp. 3878–3888 (2018)
26. Yao, Z., Gholami, A., Lei, Q., Keutzer, K., Mahoney, M.W.: Hessian-based analysis of large batch training and robustness to adversaries. In: Advances in Neural Information Processing Systems, pp. 4949–4959 (2018)
27. Zinkevich, M., Weimer, M., Li, L., Smola, A.J.: Parallelized stochastic gradient descent. In: Advances in Neural Information Processing Systems, pp. 2595–2603 (2010)

Supervised Two-Stage Transfer Learning on Imbalanced Dataset for Sport Classification

Tianyu Bi[1,2(✉)], Dmitri Jarnikov[1], and Johan Lukkien[1]

[1] Department of Mathematics and Computer Science, Eindhoven University of Technology, P.O. Box 513, 5600 Eindhoven, MB, The Netherlands
{t.bi.1,d.s.jarnikov,j.j.lukkien}@tue.nl

[2] Irdeto, High Tech Campus 84, 5656 Eindhoven, AG, The Netherlands

Abstract. Sport classification is a crucial step for content analysis in a sport stream monitoring system. Training a reliable sport classifier can be a challenging task when the data is limited in amount and highly imbalanced. In this paper, we introduce a supervised two-stage transfer learning (Two-Stage-TL) method to solve the data shortage problem. It can progressively transfer features from a source domain to the target domain using a properly selected bridge domain. For the class imbalance issue, we compare several existing methods and demonstrate that the log-smoothing class weight is the most applicable way for this specific problem. Extensive experiments are conducted using ResNet50, VGG16, and Inception-ResNet-v2. The results show that Two-Stage-TL outperforms classical One-Stage-TL and achieves the best performance using log-smoothing class weight. The in-depth analysis is useful for researchers and developers in solving similar problems.

Keywords: Multimedia content analysis · Sport classification · Transfer learning · Class imbalance learning

1 Introduction

The online piracy of media content is widespread, especially for sport streams. To combat piracy of sport streams, content protection companies usually apply a sport stream monitoring system. Figure 1 shows the workflow of such a system, which tracks illegal activities, detects pirated sport streams, collects sample data for sport classification and content identification, and finally enforces content rights. With respect to sport classification, traditional systems either need human in the loop, which is not cost-effective and not scalable, or use handcrafted classifiers, which are not robust and lack flexibility. Thus, there is a need to build a better sport classification model for the system.

Automatic sport classification is a sub-topic of multimedia content analysis. Existing approaches can be categorized by the type of data (single image or images/video), or by the algorithms (handcrafted features or deep learning) as shown in Table 1.

© Springer Nature Switzerland AG 2019
E. Ricci et al. (Eds.): ICIAP 2019, LNCS 11751, pp. 356–366, 2019.
https://doi.org/10.1007/978-3-030-30642-7_32

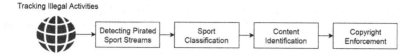

Tracking Illegal Activities

Fig. 1. Workflow of a sport stream monitoring system. For each sport stream, several screenshots are collected as the sample data for further analysis.

Table 1. Existing methods.

	Handcrafted features	Deep learning
Single image	Fisher Kernel [1], Bag-of-features [2]	Deep CNN image classifiers [3–5]
Images/video	Sparse features [6], Dense trajectory [8]	Two-stream [7], C3D [9], LSTM [10]

Since the data collected by the system is single image, we focus on image classification methods. Deep Convolutional Neural Networks (CNN) such as ResNet50 [4] and Inception-ResNet-v2 [5] have shown state-of-the-art performance and outperformed the handcrafted methods. Thus, we decide to build a sport image classification model based on deep learning methods.

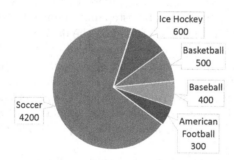

Fig. 2. Pie chart of Live-Sports dataset.

To train our model, we collect a dataset using the sport stream monitoring system and manually label the data. This dataset is called Live-Sports, which has five sport categories as shown in Fig. 2. Due to the dataset limitation, we are facing two challenges. The first challenge is the data shortage problem. Training deep learning models usually require massive amounts of data. However, we only have 6000 images over five sport categories. By training with a limited amount of data, the generalization error of the supervised learning model can be high [11]. The second challenge is the class imbalance problem. As shown in Fig. 2, the dataset is highly imbalanced in categories. Recent study [12] reveals that the class imbalance problem can have a detrimental effect on classification performance especially when the class imbalance ratio is large. Since our target data has a large imbalance ratio, class balancing methods need to be applied to reduce the detrimental effect on the target performance.

To address the first challenge, supervised transfer learning with fine-tuning, can be applied, which reuses the deep learning model or features trained on one task to another related task [13]. For general image classification tasks, a representative way is to use deep learning models that are pretrained on ImageNet and fine-tuned on the target domain [11]. It can be called one stage transfer learning (One-Stage-TL), which transfers features from one source to one target. One-Stage-TL works well for most cases since the earlier layers in the pretrained network extract general features such as edges, colors, and textures, which have high transferability for general image classification tasks [14]. However, the latest findings also reveal that feature transferability drops considerably in the higher layers when there is a large discrepancy between the source and target domains [11]. Thus, One-Stage-TL may not be enough for achieving optimal transferability.

In this work, we suggest an intuitive method that is called supervised two-stage transfer learning (Two-Stage-TL). It establishes knowledge transfer from a source domain to a target domain by using a bridge domain. In this way, it keeps the general features in lower layers, and at the same time, transfers task-related features in higher layers. Feature transferability is enhanced by gradually reducing the domain discrepancy in two stages. Similar ideas have been shown in [15–17]. Our Two-Stage-TL approach is different from theirs as it is designed for deep learning models and it uses a two-step fine-tuning scheme, which fully fine-tunes the CNN model in each step. Based on the defined properties in Sect. 2.1, we find that ImageNet is a good choice for source domain and Sports-1M [18] is a suitable bridge domain. In the experiment, we compare Two-Stage-TL with One-Stage-TL and other training methods using ResNet50 as the model architecture for the sport classification task. We also evaluate the performance of Two-Stage-TL using VGG16 and Inception-ResNet-v2 for comparison. Experimental results show that Two-Stage-TL always achieves better performance than the common One-Stage-TL.

To address the second challenge, existing solutions include oversampling [12], undersampling [12], class weight [12], and imbalance fine-tuning [19]. In this paper, we use a log-smoothing class weight method and compare it with existing methods mentioned above. Experimental results show that the sport classification model achieves the best performance when applying log-smoothing class weight with Two-Stage-TL.

Our contribution consists of three parts. First, we demonstrate that for multi-class classification with a limited number of training data, the Two-Stage-TL method outperforms the One-Stage-TL method if a proper bridge domain is selected. Second, we compared several existing methods for the class imbalance problem and demonstrated that for this specific problem, the log-smoothing class weight is the best way to reduce the impact of class imbalance. Furthermore, extensive experiments are conducted on different CNN models to find the optimal solution considering the tradeoff of accuracy, training time, and model size. Finally, since data shortage and class imbalance are common problems, our in-depth problem analysis and solution are not limited to a specific application and could be helpful to solve similar problems in other applications.

2   Two-Stage Transfer Learning

2.1   Two-Stage Transfer Learning Using Bridge Domain

For image classification tasks, researchers always recommend to pretrain the model on a large-scale publicly available dataset and then fine-tune it on the target dataset. This approach, which is called fine-tuning, has been widely-used for supervised learning tasks. In this paper, we call it one-stage transfer learning (One-Stage-TL), which only transfers knowledge once from a source task to the target task. Here, the source domain and target domain can be denoted by $D_s = (x_i^s, y_i^s)_{i=1}^{n_s}$ and $D_t = (x_j^t, y_j^t)_{j=1}^{n_t}$ respectively, where x_i^s and x_j^t are training samples, y_i^s and y_j^t are labels, and n_s and n_t are the number of samples.

One-Stage-TL can improve the performance on the target task when the source is similar to the target. However, when the source data is quite different, it may lead to very limited performance improvement on the target task due to the low feature transferability. To further improve the target performance, we introduce a very intuitive supervised two-stage transfer learning (Two-Stage-TL) approach. Different from One-Stage-TL, it progressively transfers knowledge from the source to the target by using a bridge domain in the middle. The bridge domain can be denoted by $D_b = (x_k^b, y_k^b)_{k=1}^{n_b}$, where x_k^b represents the training sample, y_k^b represents the label, and n_b is the number of samples.

To guarantee the effectiveness of Two-Stage-TL, the bridge domain should have certain properties. Based on practical experience, we make some assumption with respect to the properties of the bridge domain. First, compared with the task of source t_s, the task of the bridge t_b should be more related to the task of the target t_t. Second, the data distribution of the bridge D_b should be more similar to the target distribution D_t than the source distribution D_s. Third, the bridge dataset X_b should be larger than the target dataset X_t. Finally, since Two-Stage-TL is used for supervised learning tasks, the bridge domain should have labeled data without heavy cleaning work.

Based on our assumption, we find Sports-1M can be a good bridge domain given ImageNet as the source and Live-Sports as the target. Sports-1M [18] is a publicly available dataset, which has approximately 1 million YouTube video links for 487 sport categories. We collect a dataset of Sports-1M with the five sports of interest. We collect 2000 frames extracted from about 100 videos for each sport. Non-sports contents such as commercials or interviews are removed in advance. We find that the dataset is a hybrid of professional sports, user generated contents and remix, while the target dataset contains only professional sports data. Thus, Sports-1M has the same task, and visually different but very similar data compared with the target domain, which meets the requirements of the bridge domain.

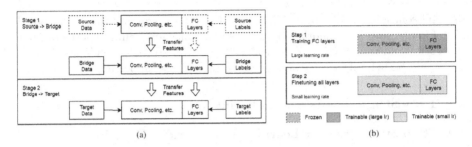

Fig. 3. Two-Stage-TL framework: (a) The Two-Stage-TL approach. Source data is not required if the pre-trained model is available. (b) The two-step fine-tuning scheme. When the target dataset is small, a smaller learning rate is applied in step 2 to avoid overfitting [13].

2.2 Two-Stage-TL Framework

The framework of our Two-Stage-TL approach is shown in Fig. 3. In stage 1, we pretrain the model on the source domain, transfer the features, and fine-tune the model on the bridge domain. To speed up the pretraining step, we can use off-the-shelf features that are pretrained on ImageNet or other benchmarks. In this case, we do not need to collect data and train the model for the source domain. If the bridge has a different task, the model needs modifications on fully-connected (FC) layers. In this case, when we transfer the features from source to bridge, features on FC layers can remain for fine-tuning or be replaced by random initialization. Since FC layers are task-specific with a larger transferability gap [11], it should be fully trained on the new task, while the lower layers, which contain general features, should be gently fine-tuned to further improve the performance [13]. Thus, we use a two-step fine-tuning scheme as shown in Fig. 3(b). In this scheme, the model is trained on FC layers with a large learning rate in step 1 and fine-tuned on all layers with a smaller learning rate in step 2. After training the bridge model, we transfer features of all layers to the target model and fine-tune the model on the target task in stage 2. Similarly, the target model is fine-tuned using the two-step fine-tuning scheme.

2.3 Class Imbalance Learning

We evaluate four class balancing methods including oversampling, undersampling, class weight, and imbalance fitting. Oversampling is a widely-used sampling method proven to be effective in many situations [12]. In our experiment, we choose random minority oversampling, which randomly selects samples from minority classes and applies data augmentation. Undersampling is another sampling method, which is preferable to oversampling in some cases [12]. We choose random majority undersampling that removes randomly selected samples from majority classes.

Class weight is another common approach, which assigns different loss for different classes by giving higher weight to the minority class and lower weight to the majority class. The original class weight is calculated by the equation: $cw_i = n_{majority}/n_i$, where cw_i denotes the class weight for class i, $n_{majority}$ is the number of samples for the majority class, and n_i is the number of samples for class i. Since our dataset is highly imbalanced, the class weight of a minority class can be very large. In this case, we need to smooth the class weight to avoid getting biased on the minority class due to the large weight. Simply dividing the original class weight by a constant value is not enough, since the majority class suffers from a too small weight. We introduce a log-smoothing method that smooths the class weight by a natural logarithm function as follows: $cw_i^{ln} = ln(cw_i) + 1$. In this way, the class weight of minority classes shrinks to a reasonable level, while the class weight of the majority class keeps the same. Both default and log-smoothing class weight methods are evaluated in the experiment.

The last method, which we call imbalance fitting, is inspired by the method in [19]. In our implementation, we first train the network on the balanced data (by undersampling), then fully fine-tune the network with the original dataset. To find the optimal method for our target dataset, we evaluate all of the above methods using different training approaches.

3 Experiments

3.1 Dataset

In our experiment, ImageNet is the source domain and the pretrained features are used for transfer learning in stage 1. Live-Sports and Sports-1M are the target domain and bridge domain. They both have five sport categories: American Football, Baseball, Basketball, Ice Hockey, and Soccer. Live Sports has 6000 images: 100 images for validation, 100 images for testing for each category, and the rest are used for training. Sports-1M has 12500 images: 2000 images for training and 500 images for validation for each category.

For the undersampling method, we create a balanced training set of Live-Sports and each class has the same number of images (100) as the minority class (American Football). The balanced samples are randomly selected from the original training set. For the oversampling method, a balanced training set is created by using data augmentation. Each category has the same number of images (4000) as the majority class (Soccer).

3.2 Experimental Environment and Settings

The experimental environment is a PC with an Intel Xeon E5 CPU and an Nvidia Tesla V100 GPU with 32 GB of memory. We select ResNet50, VGG16, and Inception-ResNet-v2 as the basic CNN models in our experiment, because they are widely used for image classification and have different levels of depth and size. All models used in the experiments are implemented using Keras with TensorFlow as the backend.

362 T. Bi et al.

To preprocess training and testing data, we resize the images to a certain size, which is $224*224$ for ResNet50 and VGG16 and $299*299$ for Inception-ResNet-v2. For real-time data augmentation during training, we use several image processing methods provided by Keras ImageDataGenerator. The image processing methods include rotation ($-90°..90°$), width shift ($-20\%..20\%$), height shift ($-20\%..20\%$), shear ($-0.2°..0.2°$), zoom ($-20\%..20\%$), horizontal flip (*prob* 50%), and vertical flip (*prob* 50%).

We use stochastic gradient descent (SGD) with momentum as the optimization strategy in our experiment. The momentum is set to 0.9, the batch size is set to 32, and the initial learning rate is set to 0.01. For the second step of the two-step fine-tuning scheme, which fine-tunes on all layers, we use a smaller learning rate (0.001) to avoid overfitting to the target domain [13]. For training from scratch, the model is trained by 100 epochs. For transfer learning, the model is trained by 50 epochs in step 1 and 50 epochs in step 2. Instead of running through all the epochs, we stop training when the validation loss does not improve in 10 epochs.

In the test phase, we use classification accuracy and training time as the evaluation metrics.

3.3 Comparison of Different Training Approaches

In this section, we evaluate the performance of Two-Stage-TL and other training methods including Train-From-Scratch, Train-From-Scratch-NoAug (without data augmentation), and One-Stage-TL (using ImageNet as source). Classification accuracy and training time are used to evaluate these methods. Table 2 shows the evaluation results using ResNet50 as the basic network.

Table 2. Classification accuracy and training time of different training approaches.

Approaches	Accuracy	Time (min)
Train-From-Scratch-NoAug	77.8%	19
Train-From-Scratch	79%	35
One-Stage-TL	90.4%	54
Two-Stage-TL	93%	$124+63$

From Table 2, we can see that Train-From-Scratch-NoAug has the lowest classification accuracy, which is only 77.8%. The classification accuracy of Train-From-Scratch increases by 1.2% because of data augmentation. However, it is still quite low (79%), which shows that training from scratch only is not enough for training a reliable sport classifier. One-Stage-TL achieves much higher performance, which is 90.4%. It shows that the pretrained weights on ImageNet are beneficial for our task, sport classification. Compared with other methods, Two-Stage-TL achieves the highest classification accuracy, which is improved by 2.6%

from One-Stage-TL. It demonstrates that using Sports-1M as a bridge between ImageNet and the target can further improve the classification accuracy. The training time of Two-Stage-TL is more than other methods, which is 124 min in the first stage and 63 min in the second stage. The time of the first stage can be ignored, since it is only conducted once and the weights can be reused in the future.

3.4   Comparison of Different Class Balancing Methods

In this section, we evaluate the performance of different class balancing methods including oversampling, undersampling, class weight, and imbalance fitting (Imb-Fit). We use ResNet50 for this experiment because it has a good trade-off between high performance and low training time. From Table 3, we find that oversampling has an enhancement in performance for all training approaches. Compared with other class balancing methods, oversampling enables the highest classification accuracy for Train-From-Scratch and One-Stage-TL. The performance for Train-From-Scratch and One-Stage-TL approaches with the undersampling method drops by 5.2% and 1% respectively compared with the original performance (in Table 2). The reason can be that removing training examples in undersampling affects the generalizability on the test set. For Two-Stage-TL, the undersampling method achieves higher performance than the original setting and oversampling. The default class weight method does not work well on Train-From-Scratch because the model cannot converge under the higher training loss. Two-Stage-TL with log-smoothing class weight achieves better performance, which is 1% higher than using the default class weight method. The imbalance fitting method does not improve the best performance of any training approach. Overall, Two-Stage-TL with log-smoothing class weight is considered as the most applicable approach for our problem.

Table 3. Classification accuracy of different class balancing methods (* log-smoothing).

Approaches	Undersampling	Oversampling	Class weight	Imb-Fit
Train-From-Scratch	72.6%	82.8%	20%	78.6%
One-Stage-TL	89.4%	93.2%	91.6%	91.6%
Two-Stage-TL	94%	93.4%	93% (*94%)	94%

Additionally, we compare the training time of the training approaches with different class balancing methods. From Fig. 4, we can see that for most cases oversampling has the longest training time while undersampling has the shortest training time. This is caused by the different size of the training set, which is 500 for undersampling and 20000 for oversampling. Imbalance fitting and class weight require medium level training time. If training time is crucial, Two-Stage-TL with undersampling is the most applicable one, even though it may lose useful information from training data.

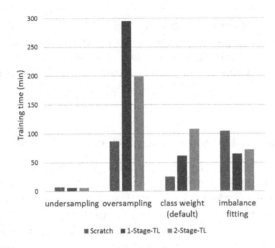

Fig. 4. Training time.

3.5 Comparison of Different CNN Models

In this section, we compare the performance of Two-Stage-TL on different deep CNN models including ResNet50, VGG16, and Inception-ResNet-v2. We use undersampling as the class balancing method for all of them. We evaluate the models using classification accuracy and also compare the model size and the training time in two stages. Table 4 shows the classification accuracy, training time, and model size of three deep CNN models. We find that Inception-ResNet-v2 achieves the best accuracy (96.8%), while ResNet50 achieves a bit lower accuracy (94%) but requires much less training time (136 min) and has much smaller model size (196 MB). For practical implementation, if there is a limitation for training time and model size, ResNet50 is a good choice. Inception-ResNet-V2 is optimal when the classification accuracy is crucial.

Table 4. Classification accuracy, training time, and model size of different CNN models. T1 and T2 refer to the training time in two stages.

Approaches	Accuracy	T1 (min)	T2 (min)	Size (MB)
VGG16	93.8%	270	13	968
ResNet50	94%	130	6	196
Inception-ResNet-v2	96.8%	329	11	428

3.6 Feature Visualization

To demonstrate Two-Stage-TL has better transferability than One-Stage-TL, we visualize Two-Stage-TL features and One-Stage-TL features of test images. The features are extracted from the last hidden layer of the ResNet50 models trained by Two-Stage-TL and One-Stage-TL. We use the t-SNE method to

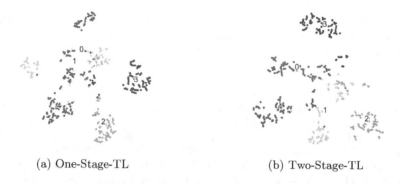

(a) One-Stage-TL   (b) Two-Stage-TL

Fig. 5. Visualization of t-SNE embeddings

reduce dimensions of the features and plot the t-SNE embeddings in a 2D space
for visual analysis. The t-SNE embeddings of Two-Stage-TL and One-Stage-TL
features are shown in Fig. 5, in which the data points of the same class are drawn
in the same color. Our observation is that the test examples with Two-Stage-TL
features are discriminated better compared with One-Stage-TL features. The
samples of each class in Two-Stage-TL features are better clustered with clearer
boundaries. The observation implies that Two-Stage-TL improves the transferability of the features to the target domain. The finding can explain the better
performance of Two-Stage-TL over One-Stage-TL.

4 Conclusion

In this paper, we introduced a supervised two-stage transfer learning (Two-
Stage-TL) method, which improves feature transferability by reducing the
domain discrepancy progressively. To verify its effectiveness, we conducted experiments using three deep CNN models: ResNet50, VGG16, and Inception-ResNet-
v2. To solve the class imbalance problem, we evaluated different class balancing
methods. The experimental results show that the Two-Stage-TL outperforms
the classical One-Stage-TL, and it achieves the best performance using together
with log-smoothing class weight. In future work, we will extend Two-Stage-TL
to Multi-Stage-TL and explore its feasibility in multi-model applications.

References

1. Perronnin, F., Sánchez, J., Mensink, T.: Improving the Fisher Kernel for large-
   scale image classification. In: Daniilidis, K., Maragos, P., Paragios, N. (eds.) ECCV
   2010. LNCS, vol. 6314, pp. 143–156. Springer, Heidelberg (2010). https://doi.org/
   10.1007/978-3-642-15561-1_11
2. Nowak, E., Jurie, F.: Sampling strategies for bag-of-features image classification.
   In: Leonardis, A., Bischof, H., Pinz, A. (eds.) ECCV 2006. LNCS, vol. 3954, pp.
   490–503. Springer, Heidelberg (2006). https://doi.org/10.1007/11744085_38

3. Simonyan, K., Zisserman, A.: Very deep convolutional networks for large-scale image recognition. arXiv preprint arXiv:1409.1556 (2014)
4. He, K., Zhang, X., Ren, S., Sun, J.: Deep residual learning for image recognition. In: Proceedings of the IEEE Conference on Computer Vision and Pattern Recognition, pp. 770–778 (2016)
5. Szegedy, C., Ioffe, S., Vanhoucke, V., Alemi, A.A.: Inception-v4, inception-resnet and the impact of residual connections on learning. In: Thirty-First AAAI Conference on Artificial Intelligence, February 2017
6. Dollár, P., Rabaud, V., Cottrell, G., Belongie, S.: Behavior recognition via sparse spatio-temporal features. In: VS-PETS, Beijing, China, October 2005
7. Simonyan, K., Zisserman, A.: Two-stream convolutional networks for action recognition in videos. In: Advances in Neural Information Processing Systems, pp. 568–576 (2014)
8. Wang, H., Schmid, C.: Action recognition with improved trajectories. In: Proceedings of the IEEE International Conference on Computer Vision, pp. 3551–3558 (2013)
9. Tran, D., Bourdev, L., Fergus, R., Torresani, L., Paluri, M.: Learning spatiotemporal features with 3D convolutional networks. In: Proceedings of the IEEE International Conference on Computer Vision, pp. 4489–4497 (2015)
10. Yue-Hei Ng, J., Hausknecht, M., Vijayanarasimhan, S., Vinyals, O., Monga, R., Toderici, G.: Beyond short snippets: deep networks for video classification. In: Proceedings of the IEEE Conference on Computer Vision and Pattern Recognition, pp. 4694–4702 (2015)
11. Long, M., Cao, Y., Wang, J., Jordan, M.I.: Learning transferable features with deep adaptation networks. arXiv preprint arXiv:1502.02791 (2015)
12. Buda, M., Maki, A., Mazurowski, M.A.: A systematic study of the class imbalance problem in convolutional neural networks. Neural Netw. **106**, 249–259 (2018)
13. Yosinski, J., Clune, J., Bengio, Y., Lipson, H.: How transferable are features in deep neural networks?. In: Advances in Neural Information Processing Systems, pp. 3320–3328 (2014)
14. Ghazi, M.M., Yanikoglu, B., Aptoula, E.: Plant identification using deep neural networks via optimization of transfer learning parameters. Neurocomputing **235**, 228–235 (2017)
15. Pan, S.J., Kwok, J.T., Yang, Q.: Transfer Learning via dimensionality reduction. In: AAAI, vol. 8, pp. 677–682, July 2008
16. Shan, W., Sun, G., Zhou, X., Liu, Z.: Two-stage transfer learning of end-to-end convolutional neural networks for webpage saliency prediction. In: Sun, Y., Lu, H., Zhang, L., Yang, J., Huang, H. (eds.) IScIDE 2017. LNCS, vol. 10559, pp. 316–324. Springer, Cham (2017). https://doi.org/10.1007/978-3-319-67777-4_27
17. Kim, H.G., Choi, Y., Ro, Y.M.: Modality-bridge transfer learning for medical image classification. In: 2017 10th International Congress on Image and Signal Processing, BioMedical Engineering and Informatics (CISP-BMEI), pp. 1–5. IEEE, October 2017
18. Karpathy, A., Toderici, G., Shetty, S., Leung, T., Sukthankar, R., Fei-Fei, L.: Large-scale video classification with convolutional neural networks. In: Proceedings of the IEEE Conference on Computer Vision and Pattern Recognition, pp. 1725–1732 (2014)
19. Havaei, M., et al.: Brain tumor segmentation with deep neural networks. Med. Image Anal. **35**, 18–31 (2017)

Variational Autoencoder Inspired by Brain's Convergence–Divergence Zones for Autonomous Driving Application

Alice Plebe[1][(✉)] and Mauro Da Lio[2]

[1] Department of Information Engineering and Computer Science,
University of Trento, Trento, Italy
`alice.plebe@unitn.it`
[2] Department of Industrial Engineering, University of Trento, Trento, Italy
`mauro.dalio@unitn.it`

Abstract. In the last decades, the research in autonomous vehicles has greatly improved thanks to the success of artificial neural models. Yet, self-driving cars are far from reaching human performances. It is our opinion that would be wise to reflect on why the human brain is so effective in learning tasks as complex as the one of driving, and to try to take inspiration for designing new artificial driving agents. For this aim, we consider two relevant and related neurocognitive theories: the Convergence-divergence Zones (CDZs) mechanism of mental simulation, and the predicting brain theory. Then, we propose an implementation of a semi-supervised variational autoencoder for visual perception, with an architecture that best approximates those two neurocognitive theories.

Keywords: Mental imagery · Deep learning · Autonomous driving ·
Variational autoencoder · Free energy

1 Introduction

In recent years, the kind of artificial neural networks (ANNs) known as *deep learning* [7,20] has revolutionized the field of computer vision, with unprecedented results [12,23,24]. One of the application domains that has definitely benefited from the rise of deep learning is that of autonomous vehicles [1,21]. Despite the great progress reached, autonomous driving is still an unsolved problem, a major challenge for image processing is to achieve an integration with motor commands enough reliable for an acceptable level of safety.

Contrary to common belief, humans are very reliable at driving: in the US there is about one fatality per 100,000,000 miles. Such considerations lead to reflect on why the human brain is so efficient in solving the driving task, and if it is possible to take inspiration from the mechanisms whereby the brain learns to perform such a complex task. This is the aim of the European project Dreams4Cars, where we are developing an artificial driving agent inspired by

© Springer Nature Switzerland AG 2019
E. Ricci et al. (Eds.): ICIAP 2019, LNCS 11751, pp. 367–377, 2019.
https://doi.org/10.1007/978-3-030-30642-7_33

the neurocognition of human driving, for further details refer to [2]. The work here presented is a component of the Dreams4Cars project, addressing the visual information collected by a camera on a vehicle.

Artificial neural networks are not a faithful model of how the brain works just because their basic computational entities are named "neurons", as often supposed. However, in deep convolutional neural networks [12], there is some resemblance between the alternating convolutional and pooling layers and the composition of simple and complex brain cells found in the visual cortex [8]. Still, CNNs adhere to a neat division between the visual process and other cognitive tasks, which is clearly a critical departure from behaviors of living agents, including driving. Our effort is in leveraging on the current most established neurocognitive theories on how the brain develops the ability to drive, in order to derive the neural network architecture here presented.

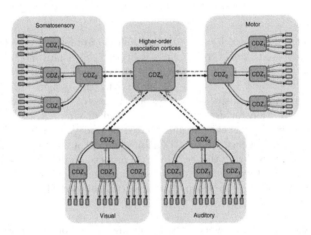

Fig. 1. Schematic representation of the CDZ framework by Meyer and Damasio. Neuron ensembles in early sensorimotor cortices of different modalities send converging forward projections (red arrows) to higher-order association cortices, which, in turn, project back divergently (black arrows) to the early cortical sites, via several intermediate steps. (Color figure online)

2   Simulation, Imagery, and Their Artificial Counterpart

The ability to drive is just one of the many highly specialized human sensorimotor behaviors. What is remarkable in humans (and in part other in other mammals) is the attitude of learning new motor skills without any innate scheme, a capability that involves sophisticated computational mechanisms [5,27]. In principle, ANN models are among the most appropriate artificial tools for replicating this ability, being grounded on a strong empiricist paradigm of cognition [13]. However, for turning this general principle into workable models, many details need to be unfolded.

2.1 Simulation Theory and Convergence-Divergence Zones

A first step can be taken by adopting the proposal of Jeannerod and Hesslow, the so-called *simulation theory of cognition*, dictating that thinking is essentially a simulated interaction with the environment [6,9]. In the view of Hesslow, simulation is a general principle of cognition, explicated in at least three different components: perception, actions and anticipation. Perception can be simulated by internal activation of sensory cortex in a way that resembles its normal activation during perception of external stimuli. Simulation of actions can be performed when activating motor structures, as during a normal behavior, but suppressing its actual execution. The most simple case of simulation is mental imagery, especially in visual modality. This is the case, for example, when a person tries to picture an object or a situation. During this phenomenon, the primary visual cortex (V1) is activated with a simplified representation of the object of interest, but the visual stimulus is not actually perceived [15].

A second step is to identify how, at neural level, simulation can take place. A prominent proposal in this direction has been formulated in terms of convergence-divergence zones (CDZs) [14]. The primary purpose of "convergence" is to record, by means of synaptic plasticity, which patterns of features – coded as knowledge fragments in the early cortices – occur in relation with a specific concept. Such records are built through experience, by interacting with objects. A requirement for convergence zones is the ability to reciprocate feed-forward projections with feedback projections in a one-to-many fashion – the "divergence" path. The convergent flow is dominant during perceptual recognition, while the divergent flow dominates imagery. Convergent-divergent connectivity patterns can be identified for specific sensory modalities, but also in higher order association cortices, as shown in the hierarchical structure in Fig. 1.

2.2 The Predictive Theory

The reason why cognition, according to Hesslow or Jeannerod, is mainly explicated as simulation, is because through simulation the brain can achieve the most precious information of an organism: a prediction of the state of affairs in the environment in the future. The need of predicting, and how it molds the entire cognition, have become the core of a different, but related, theory which has gained large attention in the last decade, made popular under the term "predictive brain", or "free-energy principle for the brain". The leading figure of this theory is Karl Friston [3,4], who argues that the behavior of the brain, and of an organism as a whole, can be conceived as minimization of free-energy. This concept originated in thermodynamics, as a measure of the amount of work that can be extracted from a system. What is borrowed by Friston is not the thermodynamic meaning of the free-energy, but its mathematical form, deriving from the framework of variational Bayesian methods in statistical physics [26]. This basic framework is adapted by Friston for abstract entities of cognitive value, for example, this is his free-energy formulation in the case of perception [4, p. 427]:

$$F_P = \Delta_{\mathrm{KL}}\Big(\breve{p}(c|z)\|p(c|x,a)\Big) - \log p(x|a) \tag{1}$$

where x is the sensorial input of the organism, c is the collection of the environmental causes producing x, a are actions that act on the environment to change sensory samples, and z are inner representations of the brain. The quantity $\breve{p}(c|z)$ is the encoding in the brain of the estimate of causes of sensorial stimuli. The difference between this encoding and the distribution $p(c|x, a)$ in the environment is computed by the Kullback–Leibler divergence Δ_{KL} [26]. The minimization of F_P in Eq. (1) optimizes z.

2.3   Autoencoder-Based CDZs and Free-Energy Models

The CDZ hypothesis has found in the years support of a large body of neurocognitive and neurophysiological evidence, however, it is a purely descriptive model. In our opinion, a computational idea that bears significant similarities with the CDZ scheme is the *autoencoder*. Autoencoder architectures have been the cornerstone of the evolution from shallow to deep neural architectures [7,25], and later exploited for capturing compact information from visual inputs [11]. In this kind of models, the task to be solved by the network is to simulate as output the same picture fed as input. The advantage is that while learning to reconstruct the input image, the model develops a very compact internal representation of the visual scene. Models able to learn such representation are closely connected with the cognitive activity of mental imagery.

A remarkable improvement over the original autoencoders is the concept of *variational autoencoder* [10], where the internal representation is implemented in probabilistic terms, adopting the variational Bayesian framework [26]. The encoder part is held to provide an approximated distribution $\breve{p}_\Phi(z|x)$ of the unknown x, depending on the set of parameters Φ of the encoder. The decoder part has its own set of parameters Θ, and from a fixed internal representation z_0 produces an output $y = d_\Theta(z_0)$. The typical loss function for a variational autoencoder with parameters Φ and Θ can be written as:

$$\mathcal{L}\left(\Phi, \Theta, x\right) = \Delta_{\mathrm{KL}}\big(\breve{p}(z|x)\|p(z)\big) - \log p_\Theta(x|z) \qquad (2)$$

where in the right hand side of the equation the first term is the Kullback–Leibler divergence between the approximate distribution of z produced by the encoder and the prior distribution $p(z)$, while the second term is the elementwise likelihood of the decoder to generate as output the same input data x. It can be easily seen how Eq. (2) has exactly the same form of Friston's "free-energy", shown in Eq. (1), therefore variational autoencoders captures both the CDZ scheme and the idea of predicting by minimization of the free-energy.

3   Implementation

Here we present the implementation of our model of artificial visual imagery, derived from the neurocognitive concepts just described. We implement the model as an artificial neural network with encoder-decoder architecture, choosing Keras with Tensorflow backend as deep learning framework.

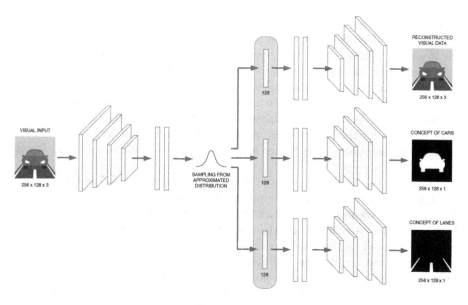

Fig. 2. The architecture of our model. The variational autoencoder has an encoder compressing an RGB image to a compact high-feature representation. Then 3 different decoders map the latent space back to separated output spaces: the decoder on top of the figure outputs into the same visual space of the input; the other two decoders project into conceptual space, producing binary images containing, respectively, *car* entities and *lane marking* entities.

We describe our network as a semi-supervised variational autoencoder with multiple decoding branches. As Fig. 2 shows, the network is composed of a single encoder, which takes as input an RGB image and compresses the information up to a latent space of 128 neurons. Since the images fed to the network have dimension of $256 \times 128 \times 3$, the compression performed by the network is almost of 4 orders of magnitude, a significant achievement compared to similar approaches [19] which limits the compression of the encoder to only 1 order of magnitude. The architecture of the encoder is defined by a stack of 4 convolutions followed by 2 dense layers.

The rest of the network is divided into three separated decoders. The input of each decoder is a tensor of 128, and all decoders have a symmetric architecture with respect to the encoder, with 2 dense layers and 4 stacked deconvolutions. What differs is the output space of each branch.

Similarly to the hierarchical arrangement of CDZs in the brain, autoencoder-based models can be placed at a level depending on the distance covered by the processing path, from the lowest primary cortical areas to the output of the simulation. The first decoder, the one on top of Fig. 2, can be considered as the lowest level the processes that start from the raw image data and converge up to simple visual features. It is trained to reconstruct the same RGB image fed as input, therefore this "visual-space branch" makes up a standard variational autoencoder, which can be trained in a total unsupervised manner.

At an intermediate level, the convergent processing path leads to representations that are no more in terms of visual features, rather in terms of "concepts", where the local perceptual features are pruned, and neural activations code the nature of entities present in the environment that produced the stimuli [16]. In our model we considered two concepts only, that of *cars* and *lane markings*, those essential for the higher level, where the divergent path is in the format of action representations. This higher level is under development [17], and is not the focus of this paper.

Therefore, the output of the two "conceptual-space branches" of the network is a binary image in which white pixels belong to the concept at case (other cars or lane markings), while black pixels represent all the rest of the scene. This is not the case of a standard variational autoencoder, where the model output is trained as the reconstruction of the input. In our case, instead, the conceptual-space decoders are still trained together with the encoder usign RGB images, because this should correspond to the sensorial input information. That is the reason why a semi-supervised training is needed here, we give the network both the input RGB image and the corresponding target binary images for each concept.

The loss functions for the three branches are all derived from the basic Eq. (2). For the two "conceptual-space branches" a variation is introduced for accounting the imbalance of pixels that do not belong to either concepts – with respect to pixels that do belong to. We weighted the second component in Eq. (2), the cross entropy $\log p_\Theta(\boldsymbol{x}|\boldsymbol{z})$, by following [22], assigning the following coefficient to the true value class:

$$P = \left(\frac{1}{NM} \sum_i^N \sum_j^M y_{i,j} \right)^{\frac{1}{k}} \tag{3}$$

where N is the number of pixels in an image, M is the number of images in the training dataset, and P is the ratio of true value pixels over all the pixels in the dataset. The parameter k is used to smooth the effect of weighting by the probability of ground truth, a value evaluated empirically as valid is 4.

4   Results

In our experiments for training and testing the presented model, we adopted the SYNTHIA dataset [18], a large collection of synthetic images representing various urban scenarios. The dataset is realized using the game engine Unity, and it is composed of ∼100k frames of driving sequences recorded from a simulated camera on the windshield of the ego car. We found this dataset to be well suited for our experiment because, despite being generated in 3D computer graphics, it offers a wide variety of illumination and weather conditions, resulting occasionally in very adverse driving conditions. Each driving sequence is replicated on a set of different environment conditions which includes seasons, weather and time

Fig. 3. Samples from the SYNTHIA dataset. All images show the same frame of a driving sequence, but under different environmental conditions. Starting from the top left we have: fall, winter, spring; summer, dawn, sunset; night, winter night, fog; soft rain, rain, night rain.

of the day. Figure 3 gives an example of the variety of data coming from the same frame of a driving sequence. Moreover the urban environment is very diverse as well, ranging from driving on freeways, through tunnels, congestion, "NewYork-like" city and "European" town – as they describe. Overall, this dataset appears to be a nice challenge for our variational autoencoder.

Figure 4 shows the results of our artificial CDZ model for a set of driving sequences. The images produced by the model are processed to better show at the same time the results on conceptual space and visual space. The colored overlays highlight the concepts computed by the network, the cyan regions are the output of the *car* divergent path, and the yellow overlays are the output of the *lane markers* divergent path. These results nicely show how the projection of the sensorial input (original frames) into conceptual representation is very effective in identifying and preserving the sensible features of *cars* and *lane markings*, despite the large variations in lighting and environmental conditions.

Table 1 display the IoU *(Intersection over Unit)* scores obtained by the network over the SYNTHIA dataset. The table shows how the task of recognizing the "car concept" generally ends up in better scores, with respect to the "lane marking concept". An explanation of why the latter task is more difficult can be the very low ratio of pixel belonging to the class of lane markings, over the entire image size. However, the performance of the model are satisfying, exhibiting the best accuracy in the driving sequences on highways, and in the sunniest lighting conditions (spring and summer sequences).

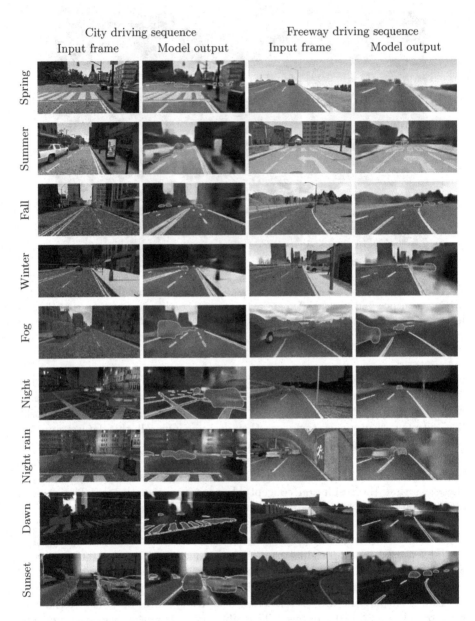

Fig. 4. Results of our model for two driving sequence of the SYNTHIA dataset: city centre and freeway driving, each with 9 different environmental conditions. In the table, odd columns show the input frames, even columns show the outputs of our neural network. In the output images, the background is the result of the visual-space decoder, the output of the *car* conceptual-space decoder is highlighted in cyan, in yellow the output of the *lane markings* conceptual-space decoder. (Color figure online)

To demonstrate the generative capabilities of our model, we verified the result of interpolating two latent space representations. The images on the left and right of Fig. 5 are the two input images, while in the middle there are the images generated from the interpolation of the compact latent spaces of the inputs. Even in the case of very different input images, the interpolation generates novel and plausible scenarios, proving the robustness of the learned latent representation.

Lastly, we would like to stress again that the purpose of our network is not mere segmentation of visual input. The segmentation task is to be considered as a support task, used to enforce the network to learn a more robust latent space representation, which now is explicitly taking into consideration two of the concepts that are fundamental to the driving tasks.

Table 1. IoU scores over the SYNTHIA dataset, grouped into the 5 different driving sequences of the dataset (table on top) and into 9 different environmental and lighting conditions (bottom). The results are given for the two "concepts" of cars and lane markings, and their joint mean.

	all	Highway 1	NewYork 1	European	NewYork 2	Highway 2
Car	0.8566	0.9245	0.9084	0.9037	0.9123	**0.9251**
Lane	0.6627	**0.8161**	0.6900	0.7522	0.6709	0.7493
mIoU	0.7597	**0.8703**	0.7992	0.8280	0.7916	0.8373

	dawn	fall	fog	night	rain	spring	summer	sunset	winter
Car	0.8896	0.8852	0.8872	0.9009	0.9002	0.9201	**0.9264**	0.8978	0.9101
Lane	0.6399	0.7319	0.6509	0.6897	0.7096	**0.7696**	0.7532	0.7247	0.7502
mIoU	0.7648	0.8086	0.7691	0.7953	0.8049	**0.8449**	0.8398	0.8113	0.8302

Fig. 5. Results of interpolation between latent space representations. Images on the extreme left and right are the input, the others are obtained interpolating the two latent spaces of the input images.

5   Conclusions

We presented an artificial neural network inspired by the the neuroscientific foundation of mental imagery, the main form of simulation grounding sensorimotor learning. Specifically, we addressed the two theories of convergence-divergence zones proposed by Meyer and Damasio, and the concept of free-energy minimization purported by Friston. We identified in the variational autoencoder the artificial mechanism closest to these two neuroscientific concepts. In the domain of autonomous driving, we implemented the network as a CDZ, at a level of immediate perception, and at a level of intermediate concepts, of cars and lane markers. The proposed model has been evaluated on the SYNTHIA dataset, proving reliable results over a wide range of driving conditions and illumination. This model is a component inside the Dreams4Cars project, immediately below a higher level model, still based on autoencoder as CDZ, computing motor commands from the conceptual representation of the environment presented in this work.

Acknowledgements. This work was developed inside the EU Horizon 2020 Dreams4Cars Research and Innovation Action project, supported by the European Commission under Grant 731593.

References

1. Bojarski, M., et al.: Explaining how a deep neural network trained with end-to-end learning steers a car. CoRR abs/1704.07911 (2017)
2. Da Lio, M., Plebe, A., Bortoluzzi, D., Rosati Papini, G.P., Donà, R.: A system for human-like driving learning. In: Proceedings of the 25th Intelligent Transport Systems World Congress (2018)
3. Friston, K., Fitzgerald, T., Rigoli, F., Schwartenbeck, P., Pezzulo, G.: Active inference: a process theory. Neural Comput. **29**, 1–49 (2017)
4. Friston, K., Stephan, K.E.: Free-energy and the brain. Synthese **159**, 417–458 (2007)
5. Grillner, S., Wallén, P.: Innate versus learned movements–a false dichotomy. Prog. Brain Res. **143**, 1–12 (2004)
6. Hesslow, G.: The current status of the simulation theory of cognition. Brain **1428**, 71–79 (2012)
7. Hinton, G.E., Salakhutdinov, R.R.: Reducing the dimensionality of data with neural networks. Science **28**, 504–507 (2006)
8. Hubel, D., Wiesel, T.: Receptive fields and functional architecture of monkey striate cortex. J. Physiol. **195**, 215–243 (1968)
9. Jeannerod, M.: Neural simulation of action: a unifying mechanism for motor cognition. NeuroImage **14**, S103–S109 (2001)
10. Kingma, D.P., Welling, M.: Auto-encoding variational bayes. In: Proceedings of International Conference on Learning Representations (2014)
11. Krizhevsky, A., Hinton, G.E.: Using very deep autoencoders for content-based image retrieval. In: European Symposium on Artificial Neural Networks, Computational Intelligence and Machine Learning, pp. 489–494 (2011)
12. Krizhevsky, A., Sutskever, I., Hinton, G.E.: ImageNet classification with deep convolutional neural networks. In: Advances in Neural Information Processing Systems, pp. 1090–1098 (2012)
13. Mareschal, D., Johnson, M.H., Sirois, S., Spratling, M.S., Thomas, M.S.C., Westermann, G. (eds.): Neuroconstructivism: How the Brain Constructs Cognition, vol. I. Oxford University Press, Oxford (2007)

14. Meyer, K., Damasio, A.: Convergence and divergence in a neural architecture for recognition and memory. Trends Neurosci. **32**, 376–382 (2009)
15. Moulton, S.T., Kosslyn, S.M.: Imagining predictions: mental imagery as mental emulation. Philos. Trans. R. Soc. B **364**, 1273–1280 (2009)
16. Olier, J.S., Barakova, E., Regazzoni, C., Rauterberg, M.: Re-framing the characteristics of concepts and their relation to learning and cognition in artificial agents. Cogn. Syst. Res. **44**, 50–68 (2017)
17. Plebe, A., Da Lio, M., Bortoluzzi, D.: On reliable neural network sensorimotor control in autonomous vehicles. IEEE Trans. Intell. Transp. Syst. **early access**, 1–12 (2019)
18. Ros, G., Vazquez, D., Sellart, L., Materzynska, J., Lopez, A.M.: The SYNTHIA dataset: a large collection of synthetic images for semantic segmentation of urban scenes. In: Proceedings of IEEE International Conference on Computer Vision and Pattern Recognition, pp. 3234–3243 (2016)
19. Santana, E., Hotz, G.: Learning a driving simulator. CoRR abs/1608.01230 (2016)
20. Schmidhuber, J.: Deep learning in neural networks: an overview. Neural Netw. **61**, 85–117 (2015)
21. Schwarting, W., Alonso-Mora, J., Rus, D.: Planning and decision-making for autonomous vehicles. Annu. Rev. Control Rob. Auton. Syst. **1**, 8:1–8:24 (2018)
22. Sudre, C.H., Li, W., Vercauteren, T., Ourselin, S., Jorge Cardoso, M.: Generalised dice overlap as a deep learning loss function for highly unbalanced segmentations. In: Cardoso, M., et al. (eds.) DLMIA 2017, ML-CDS 2017. LNCS, vol. 10553, pp. 240–248. Springer, Cham (2017). https://doi.org/10.1007/978-3-319-67558-9_28
23. Szegedy, C., et al.: Going deeper with convolutions. In: Proceedings of IEEE International Conference on Computer Vision and Pattern Recognition, pp. 1–9 (2015)
24. VanRullen, R.: Perception science in the age of deep neural networks. Front. Psychol. **8**, 142 (2017)
25. Vincent, P., Larochelle, H., Lajoie, I., Bengio, Y., Manzagol, P.A.: Stacked denoising autoencoders: learning useful representations in a deep network with a local denoising criterion. J. Mach. Learn. Res. **11**, 3371–3408 (2010)
26. Šmídl, V., Quinn, A.: The Variational Bayes Method in Signal Processing. Springer, Berlin (2005). https://doi.org/10.1007/3-540-28820-1
27. Wolpert, D.M., Diedrichsen, J., Flanagan, R.: Principles of sensorimotor learning. Nat. Rev. Neurosci. **12**, 739–751 (2011)

Hyperspectral Image Classification via Convolutional Neural Network Based on Dilation Layers

Rami Reddy Devaram, Dario Allegra$^{(\boxtimes)}$, Giovanni Gallo, and Filippo Stanco

Department of Mathematics and Computer Science,
University of Catania, Catania, Italy
devaram.ramireddy@studium.unict.it, {allegra,gallo,fstanco}@dmi.unict.it

Abstract. Classification of hyperspectral images is one of the main problem in the research field of Remote Sensing. With the advantage of spectral and spatial information, it is possible to distinguish effectively different materials and terrains. In the last decade, the intensive employing of Convolutional Neural Networks (CNN) for classification and segmentation task led high quality results in the field of Hyperspectral Imaging. In this paper, we propose a novel CNN architecture for HSI pixel-wise classification. In order to improve state-of-art results, the proposed approach focuses on the use of Dilated Convolution. Also, to face dataset imbalance problem we adopt an oversampling strategy which increases the samples in minority classes. To prove the validity of the proposed framework, we tested it on five different HSI datasets and compared the performance with the most successful previous works. Achieved performances prove that our approach is competitive with the state-of-art and exhibits the best results on all the employed datasets.

Keywords: Hyperspectral image · Pixel-wise classification · Dilation layer · Oversampling

1 Introduction

Hyperspectral images (HSI) consist of hundreds of spectral bands and continuous spectral features. Since every pixel of HSI is related to broad-spectrum wavelengths, it includes more information than RGB and Multispectral images. Thanks to the spatial and spectral information, HSI allow to discriminate different terrain or material on Earth surface [13]. For this reason, it has been broadly used in Remote sensing applications (e.g., Land Cover classification). Nonetheless, the huge spectral dimensionality and variability of spectral information involve a high computational burden for Computer Vision tasks [10]. This problem can be prevented through a dimensionality reduction strategy like Principal Component Analysis (PCA) [21]. PCA, is one of the most common methods employed to address high dimensionality issues and to provide representative features with a limited loss of discriminative information.

E. Ricci et al. (Eds.): ICIAP 2019, LNCS 11751, pp. 378–387, 2019.
https://doi.org/10.1007/978-3-030-30642-7_34

Hyperspectral data for the spatial region can be described as set of spectral measurements:

$$x_{i,j} = [s_{i,j}(\lambda_1), s_{i,j}(\lambda_2), \dots, s_{i,j}(\lambda_N)]^T \qquad (1)$$

Where $x_{i,j}$ is the spectral measurement of corresponding spatial region (i, j), **N** is total number of spectral bands and $s_{i,j}(\lambda_N)$ is the spectral band measurement at wavelength λ_N. This means hyperspectral image can be organized as a collection $X = \{x_{i,j} \mid i = 1, 2, \dots, W \quad j = 1, 2, \dots, H\}$, where W and H are image width and height respectively. In a nutshell, HSI is a set of N matrices, one for each wavelength λ_n. In this paper, we focus on deep learning approaches and propose a novel Convolutional Neural Network architecture for HSI pixels classification. The main insight behind this research is the use of Dilated Convolution [27] to systematically aggregate multiscale contextual information without losing resolution. We evaluate the proposed approach on five different datasets and point out that our CNN achieves an overall accuracy higher than 99.20% for all the them. Moreover it outperforms all the most recent and successful state-of-art results on the five benchmark datasets. The rest of the paper is organized as follow: in Sect. 2, we present related works on HSI classification by focusing on deep learning approaches; in Sect. 3, we describe the dataset preparation stage, which includes dimensionality reduction and dataset oversampling; in Sect. 4, we present the proposed network architecture; Sect. 5 reports experimental settings and results; finally, Sect. 6 ends the paper with conclusions and future works.

2   Related Works

In the last years, many strategies for pixel-wise HSI classification have been proposed. However, most of the existing works follow a conventional paradigm which consists of two main steps: (1) handcrafted features extraction; (2) learning a classifier (e.g., SVM, Neural network, etc.). Although some traditional approaches provide high quality results [3,22,24–26] recent works show that strategies based on deep learning paradigm may achieve better performance.

In 2015, Yue et al. [28], proposed a framework which uses PCA, Deep Convolutional Neural Networks (DCNNs) and logistic regression (LR). In 2015, Makantasis et al. [17], used a modified CNN to learn high-level features and a Multi-Layer Perceptron (MLP) for pixel classification. In 2017, Lee et al. [14] introduced a contextual deep CNN to optimally explore local contextual interactions by jointly exploiting local spatio-spectral relationships. Mughees et al. [20] proposed a hyper-voxel auto-encoder that efficiently exploits the spatial contextual features of HSI. Li et al. [16], provided a CNN architecture which uses only 3D Convolutional layers and Fully Connected ones.

In 2018, [5], Gao et al. presented a work where the 1D spectral vectors of hyperspectral data are transformed into 2D spectral feature matrices by emphasizing the difference among samples of different classes. In [15], the authors proposed to use maximum overlap pooling to improve Alexnet performance for

HSI classification. Guo et al. [7], employed an Artificial Neural Network supervised by center-loss (ANNC) for feature extraction; then, they proposed a CNN-based Spatial Feature Fusion (CSFF) strategy to posteriorly integrate the spatial information.

Differently from previous works, we designed a CNN which uses Transposed Convolution and Dilated Convolution.

Transposed Convolution, also know as Deconvolution, was proposed by Zeiler et al. in 2014 [29]. However, it is not the inverse operation of Convolution. Actually, it operates by using convolution to map small set of values to a larger one. It is widely used to perform up-sampling in CNN auto-encoder designed for segmentation tasks (e.g., Segnet [1], U-Net [23]).

Dilated Convolution [27] performs a convolution by considering an area larger then the kernel size. It is like one uses and expanded filter where the empty positions are filling with zeros. However, no expanded filter is created, since the filter elements are matched to distant elements in the input matrix. In CNN architecture this allows an exponential growth of the receptive fields.

We prove validity of the proposed architecture by comparing the achieved performance with state-of-art ones.

2.1 Datasets

The proposed approach has been evaluated on five benchmark datasets, namely University of Pavia, Pavia Center, Botswana, Salinas and Indian Pines. All these datasets are publicly available and employed in many researches in the field. In this section we report the basic information about them.

The **University of Pavia** dataset, has been acquired using Reflective Optics System Imaging Spectrometer (ROSIS) over Pavia, in north Italy. This dataset includes a 610×610 pixels image with 103 bands. Spatial resolution is $1.3\,\mathrm{m}$ per pixel. This area presents 9 different kinds of terrains; hence, each pixel is annotated across 9 classes. Ground truth image in shown in Fig. 1(a).

Similarly, the **Pavia Center** dataset has been acquired by ROSIS and presents the same number of classes. The hyperspectral image consists of with 102 bands; image size is 1096×1096 and spatial resolution $1.3\,\mathrm{m}$. Figure 1(b) depicts the ground truth.

The **Botswana** has been collected by the Hyperion sensor NASA EO-1 satellite over the Okavango Delta in Botswana. This image presents 145 bands of size 1476×256 pixels; spatial resolution is $30\,\mathrm{m}$ per pixel and wavelengths covering $400\,nm$ to $2500\,nm$. It includes 14 distinct land cover types. The ground truth data are shown in Fig. 1(c).

The, **Salinas** data have been collected by AVIRIS sensor with a spatial resolution of $3.7\,\mathrm{m}$. Image size is 512×217 and each pixel is labeled across 16 classes. Ground truth is reported in Fig. 1(d). Original data consisted of 224 bands, but the 20 ones related to water absorption have been discarded. Hence, it includes the 204 remaining bands.

Finally, **Indian Pines** data have been acquired by AVIRIS sensor over the Indian Pines site in North-western Indiana and consists of 145×145 pixels and

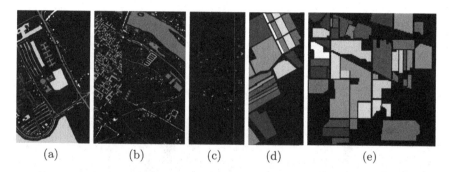

Fig. 1. (a) Ground truth image of Pavia University Dataset; (b) ground truth image of Pavia Center Dataset; (c) ground truth image of Botswana Dataset; (d) ground truth image of Salinas Dataset; (e) ground truth image of Indian Pines Dataset.

224 spectral reflectance bands. This scene is a subset of a larger one. It consists of 16 classes. However, the number of channels have been reduced to 200 by removing bands covering the region of water absorption. We report its ground truth in Fig. 1(e).

3   Data Preparation

To prepare data, we first use Principal Components Analysis to reduce the high dimensionality of original image (i.e., hundreds of spectral bands). PCA is a mathematical procedure to move N-dimensional data in another N-dimensional space where the dimensions are linearly uncorrelated [21]. Additionally, it allows to select the M most representative dimensions. Consequently, a HSI pixel $x_{i,j}$ with N spectral bands, can be reduced to a $\overline{x}_{i,j}$ vector in M-dimensional space, with $M < N$. Then, for each pixel in the reduced space, we extract a $P \times P$ patch to use for its classification. Hence, the pixel-wise dataset for HSI pixels classification includes a collection of patches in the new M-dimensional space.

Secondly, we randomly split the patch dataset in Training, Validation and Test sets. Intuitively, the presence of adjacent patches in both, Training and Test sets, could drive biased classification. Nevertheless, we ignore this fact similarly to the state-of-art works in order to perform a proper comparison with them. To face the problem of imbalanced dataset, we operate an oversampling on the underrepresented classes of Training and Validation sets. To remark the problem of class imbalance, in Fig. 2 we report the percentage distribution across the 16 classes of Indian Pines dataset. It can be noted the severe imbalance: while almost the 25% of the samples belong to the class 11, the classes 1, 7 and 9 includes less then 1% of the samples. The employed oversampling strategy [9], aims to replicate samples in minority classes. If largest class includes S samples, after this process all the classes will include about S samples.

After oversampling on Training and Validation, we train the proposed network. For an unbiased test, oversampling is not used on Test set. Figure 3 shows the pipeline we adopt.

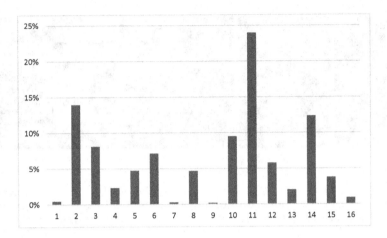

Fig. 2. Distribution of the samples across the 16 classes of Indian Pines dataset. It can be seen the dataset is strongly imbalanced.

4 Proposed Architecture

In this section we describe a new CNN architecture to classify pixels of HSI. Our architecture aims to classify pixel by starting from $P \times P$ patches. The reduced size of the input, drive us to employ Transposed Convolutions layers for up-sampling and the Dilated Convolution layer to exponentially expanding receptive fields without losing resolution or coverage. The architecture consists of six layers. We found out that in the first two layers the network suffered of neurons dying problem, hence we decided to use Exponential Linear Unit (ELU) activation instead of Rectified Linear Unit (ReLU). This problems, also know as "dying ReLU", happens when the neuron get stuck and always outputs 0. Hence, no gradients flow backward through the neuron, and it can be defined "dead". In other words, this stops the learning process of the CNN [2].

The layers which include standard Convolution are followed by Transposed Convolutions layers (proposed by [29] as Deconvolution). Transposed Convolution is the process of going in the opposite direction of a standard convolution. This is done by preserving the connectivity pattern. They aim to densify the sparse activations of Pooling layers and give a dense activation map as output.

In the fourth layer, instead of standard Convolution, we use Dilated Convolution to create a filter that presents spaces between each pixel. In order to not decrease the feature map resolution, we choose Dilated Convolution layer with a dilation factor of 2. Batch Normalization is used to scale the activations and to stabilize the network by normalizing the output of the previous layer. Moreover, to reduce network overfitting, we introduce Drop Out modules with factor 0.5. As in most classification architectures, last layer is Fully Connected and Soft Max units provide the output probability for each class.

Finally, we use ADAM (Adaptive Moment Estimation) optimizer [12] because it presents the advantages of both Adaptive Gradient and Root Mean Square

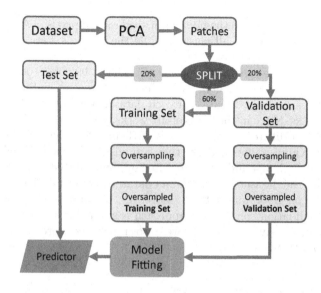

Fig. 3. The proposed framework.

Propagation. We selected the following parameters: learning rate 0.001; $\beta_1 = 0.9$; $\beta_2 = 0.99$. These values control the decay rates of the exponential past gradients and past squared gradients respectively. The proposed architecture is reported in Fig. 4.

5   Experimental Settings and Results

To demonstrate the validity of the proposed approach we perform a 5-Fold Cross validation test on the datasets described in Sect. 2.1. PCA is used to reduce the original number of spectral bands to 30 dimensions, while a patch size of 5×5 is chosen. Then, we randomly select 60% of the patches for Training, 20% for Validation and 20% for Test. Training and Validation set are oversampled and then the network is trained from scratch. As in most of the literature works, we adopted overall accuracy (OA), average accuracy (AA), and kappa coefficient (Kappa) for performance evaluation. OA is the ratio between the number of

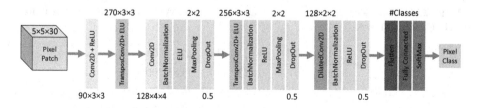

Fig. 4. Proposed CNN architecture

correctly classified pixels and the number of all classified pixels. AA is the average of classification accuracy of all classes, while the Cohen's Kappa coefficient is used to measure the agreement of classification for all the classes.

The results show an overall accuracy of 99.93%, 99.99%, 100.00%, 99.99% and 99.81% for Pavia University, Pavia Center, Botswana, Salinas and Indian Pines dataset respectively. Finally, for each dataset, we report the results of the most recent works. Since in the state-of-art works, not all the datasets have been used, we report a different table for each of them. Moreover, we do not report some AA and Kappa values because they are missing in the original works. As shown in Tables 1, 2, 3, 4 and 5 the proposed approach outperforms all the other methods for all the datasets. In Botswana dataset, we even achieve the 100.00% of performance on Botswana dataset. Moreover, the low standard deviation on 5-Fold Cross validation confirm our approach is stable for each of the datasets.

For a qualitatively evaluation, we also report the predicted classes in Figs. 5(a), (b), (c), (d) and (e).

Table 1. Overall accuracy (OA), Average accuracy (AA) and Kappa coefficient for Pavia University dataset.

Method	[17]	[6]	[19]	[7]	[16]	Our
OA(%)	99.62	99.64	99.18	98.90	99.39	**99.93 ± 0.020**
AA(%)	–	99.61	98.75	98.49	98.85	**99.94 ± 0.028**
KAPPA(%)	–	99.53	98.95	98.52	99.20	**99.91 ± 0.027**

5.1 Discussion

The lack of a common experimental setting in literature makes very time consuming a rigorous comparison with state-of-art approaches. For instance, datasets splitting is often different and this may influence the performances. Moreover, in some works, no validation set is employed. Experimental results undoubtedly prove that the proposed method is competitive. Actually, a stronger argument in this sense, would require a different experimental settings for each state-of-art work or the implementation of all of them. However, this is beyond the scope of this paper and will be considered in future extensions.

Table 2. Overall accuracy (OA), Average accuracy (AA) and Kappa coefficient for Pavia Center dataset.

Method	[17]	[11]	[8]	[7]	[25]	Our
OA(%)	99.91	97.81	99.73	99.75	98.85	**99.99 ± 0.001**
AA(%)	–	92.81	99.25	99.40	98.43	**99.99 ± 0.005**
KAPPA(%)	–	96.88	99.61	99.64	97.90	**99.99 ± 0.002**

Table 3. Overall accuracy (OA), Average accuracy (AA) and Kappa coefficient for Botswana dataset.

Method	[18]	[22]	[26]	[4]	[16]	Our
OA(%)	97.44	88.19	89.44	97.93	99.55	**100.00 ± 0.000**
AA(%)	97.80	89.53	90.60	–	99.60	**100.00 ± 0.000**
KAPPA(%)	–	–	88.57	96.30	99.51	**100.00 ± 0.000**

Table 4. Overall accuracy (OA), Average accuracy (AA) and Kappa coefficient for Salinas dataset.

Methods	[17]	[6]	[15]	[7]	[18]	Our
OA(%)	99.53	98.34	94.76	99.38	99.37	**99.99 ± 0.014**
AA(%)	–	99.33	94.75	99.76	99.67	**99.98 ± 0.009**
KAPPA(%)	–	98.15	94.16	99.30	–	**99.99 ± 0.010**

Table 5. Overall accuracy (OA), Average accuracy (AA) and Kappa coefficient for Indian Pines dataset.

Methods	[17]	[6]	[19]	[20]	[16]	Our
OA(%)	98.88	97.57	96.87	90.08	99.07	**99.81 ± 0.065**
AA(%)	–	98.46	96.75	93.09	98.66	**99.83 ± 0.068**
KAPPA(%)	–	97.23	95.67	88.75	98.93	**99.79 ± 0.074**

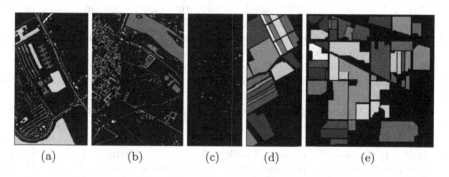

(a)   (b)   (c)   (d)   (e)

Fig. 5. (a) Predicted classes of Pavia University Dataset; (b) predicted classes of Pavia Center Dataset; (c) predicted classes of Botswana Dataset; (d) predicted classes of Salinas Dataset; (e) predicted classes of Indian Pine Dataset.

6   Conclusions

In this work we explore the problem of pixel-wise HSI classification and propose a new framework which includes an oversampling stage to make benchmark datasets balanced, and a new CNN architecture based on Dilated Convolution. Despite the already high performance achieved by state-of-art works, our method outclasses all of them and achieves the best performance for each benchmark dataset. For future works, we are planning to extend our study with an in-depth review of HSI classification literature and perform new tests. We are also considering to use our architecture for similar problems, like pixel-wise semantic segmentation on different domains.

References

1. Badrinarayanan, V., Kendall, A., Cipolla, R.: Segnet: a deep convolutional encoder-decoder architecture for image segmentation. IEEE Trans. Pattern Anal. Mach. Intell. **39**, 2481–2495 (2016). https://doi.org/10.1109/TPAMI.2016.2644615
2. Clevert, D.A., Unterthiner, T., Sepp, H.: Fast and accurate deep network learning by exponential linear units (elus). CoRR abs/1511.07289 (2016)
3. Gao, F., Wang, Q., Dong, J., Xu, Q.: Spectral and spatial classification of hyperspectral images based on random multi-graphs. Remote Sens. **10**, 1271 (2018). https://doi.org/10.3390/rs10081271
4. Gao, H., Lin, S., Yang, Y., Li, C., Yang, M.: Convolution neural network based on two-dimensional spectrum for hyperspectral image classification. J. Sens. **2018**, 1–13 (2018). https://doi.org/10.1155/2018/8602103
5. Gao, H., Yang, Y., Li, C., Zhou, H., Qu, X.: Joint alternate small convolution and feature reuse for hyperspectral image classification. Int. J. Geo-Inf. **7**(9), 349 (2018). https://doi.org/10.3390/ijgi7090349
6. Gao, Q., Lim, S., Jia, X.: Hyperspectral image classification using convolutional neural networks and multiple feature learning. Remote Sens. **10**, 299 (2018). https://doi.org/10.3390/rs10020299
7. Guo, A.J.X., Zhu, F.: A CNN-based spatial feature fusion algorithm for hyperspectral imagery classification. CoRR abs/1801.10355 (2018)
8. Guo, A.J.X., Zhu, F.: Spectral-spatial feature extraction and classification by ANN supervised with center loss in hyperspectral imagery. IEEE Trans. Geosci. Remote Sens. **57**, 1–13 (2018). https://doi.org/10.1109/tgrs.2018.2869004
9. He, H., Garcia, E.A.: Learning from imbalanced data. IEEE Trans. Knowl. Data Eng. **21**(9), 1263–1284 (2009). https://doi.org/10.1109/tkde.2008.239
10. Imani, M., Ghassemian, H.: Binary coding based feature extraction in remote sensing high dimensional data. Inf. Sci. **342**, 191–208 (2016). https://doi.org/10.1016/j.ins.2016.01.032
11. Ju, Y., Li, L., Jiao, L., Zhongle, R., Hou, B., Yang, S.: Modified diversity of class probability estimation co-training for hyperspectral image classification. CoRR abs/1809.01436 (2018)
12. Kingma, D., Ba, J.: Adam: a method for stochastic optimization. CoRR abs/1412.6980 (2014)
13. Landgrebe, D.A.: Signal Theory Methods in Multispectral Remote Sensing. Wiley, Hoboken (2003)
14. Lee, H., Kwon, H.: Going deeper with contextual CNN for hyperspectral image classification. IEEE Trans. Image Process. **26**, 4843–4855 (2017). https://doi.org/10.1109/tip.2017.2725580
15. Li, C., et al.: Hyperspectral remote sensing image classification based on maximum overlap pooling convolutional neural network. Sensors **18**, 3587 (2018). https://doi.org/10.3390/s18103587

16. Li, Y., Zhang, H., Shen, Q.: Spectral-spatial classification of hyperspectral imagery with 3D convolutional neural network. Remote Sens. **9**(1), 67 (2017). https://doi.org/10.3390/rs9010067
17. Makantasis, K., Karantzalos, K., Doulamis, A., Doulamis, N.: Deep supervised learning for hyperspectral data classification through convolutional neural networks. In: International Geoscience and Remote Sensing Symposium, July 2015. https://doi.org/10.1109/igarss.2015.7326945
18. Medjahed, S.A., Saadi, T.A., Benyettou, A., Ouali, M.: A new post-classification and band selection frameworks for hyperspectral image classification. Egypt. J. Remote Sens. Space Sci. **2**, 163–173 (2016). https://doi.org/10.1016/j.ejrs.2016.09.003
19. Mughees, A., Ali, A., Tao, L.: Hyperspectral image classification via shape-adaptive deep learning. In: International Conference on Image Processing, September 2017. https://doi.org/10.1109/icip.2017.8296306
20. Mughees, A., Tao, L.: Hyper-voxel based deep learning for hyperspectral image classification. In: International Conference on Image Processing, September 2017. https://doi.org/10.1109/icip.2017.8296399
21. Pearson, K.: On lines and planes of closest fit to systems of points in space. Phil. Mag. **2**(6), 559–572 (1901)
22. Ranjan, S., Nayak, D.R., Kumar, K.S., Dash, R., Majhi, B.: Hyperspectral image classification: a k-means clustering based approach. In: International Conference on Advanced Computing and Communication Systems, January 2017. https://doi.org/10.1109/icaccs.2017.8014707
23. Ronneberger, O., Fischer, P., Brox, T.: U-Net: convolutional networks for biomedical image segmentation. CoRR abs/1505.04597 (2015)
24. Wang, K., Yong, B.: Application of the frequency spectrum to spectral similarity measures. Remote Sens. **8**(4), 344 (2016). https://doi.org/10.3390/rs8040344
25. Wang, Z., Nasrabadi, N.M., Huang, T.S.: Spatial–spectral classification of hyperspectral images using discriminative dictionary designed by learning vector quantization. IEEE Trans. Geosci. Remote Sens. **52**, 4808–4822 (2014). https://doi.org/10.1109/tgrs.2013.2285049
26. Xia, J., Yokoya, N., Iwasaki, A.: Hyperspectral image classification with partial least square forest. In: International Geoscience and Remote Sensing Symposium, July 2017. https://doi.org/10.1109/igarss.2017.8127790
27. Yu, F., Koltun, V.: Multi-scale context aggregation by dilated convolutions. In: International Conference on Learning Representations (2016)
28. Yue, J., Zhao, W., Mao, S., Liu, H.: Spectral–spatial classification of hyperspectral images using deep convolutional neural networks. Remote Sens. Lett. **6**, 468–477 (2015). https://doi.org/10.1080/2150704x.2015.1047045
29. Zeiler, M.D., Fergus, R.: Visualizing and understanding convolutional networks. Eur. Conf. Comput. Vis. **8689**, 818–833 (2014). https://doi.org/10.1007/978-3-319-10590-1_53

Estimation of Speed and Distance of Surrounding Vehicles from a Single Camera

Mirko Zaffaroni[1,3]($\boxtimes$) (iD), Marco Grangetto[1] (iD), and Alessandro Farasin[2,3] (iD)

[1] Computer Science Department, University of Torino, Turin, Italy
{mirko.zaffaroni,marco.grangetto}@unito.it
[2] Department of Control and Computer Engineering,
Politecnico di Torino, Turin, Italy
alessandro.farasin@polito.it
[3] Fondazione LINKS, Microsoft Innovation Center, Turin, Italy
{mirko.zaffaroni,alessandro.farasin}@linksfoundation.com

Abstract. Deep Learning requires huge amount of data with related labels, that are necessary for proper training. Thanks to modern videogames, which aim at photorealism, it is possible to easily obtain synthetic dataset by extracting information directly from the game engine. The intent is to use data extracted from a videogame to obtain a representation of various scenarios and train a deep neural network to infer the information required for a specific task. In this work we focus on computer vision aids for automotive applications and we target to estimate the distance and speed of the surrounding vehicles by using a single dashboard camera. We propose two network models for distance and speed estimation, respectively. We show that training them by using synthetic images generated by a game engine is a viable solution that turns out to be very effective in real settings.

Keywords: Automotive · Deep Learning · Computer vision · Synthetic dataset

1 Introduction

The availability of large amount of indexed and labeled images is key to the successful design of many complex vision tasks leveraging on powerful Deep Learning (DL) techniques based on Convolutional Neural Networks (CNN). The creation of a large dataset able to correctly represent the target scenario and allowing the trained neural network to generalize in real applications remain a critical design step. Resorting to human visual inspection and manual labeling does not represent a viable solution in many scenarios. In fact, manual labeling does not scale very well to large datasets, except for very simple and repetitive tasks that do not require particular expertise where one can resort to crowdsourcing [3]. Moreover, doubts may arise on the quality of the collected information and potential unexpected bias. Finally for some tasks manual labeling

© Springer Nature Switzerland AG 2019
E. Ricci et al. (Eds.): ICIAP 2019, LNCS 11751, pp. 388–398, 2019.
https://doi.org/10.1007/978-3-030-30642-7_35

is simply not possible as is the case in the automotive scenario targeted in this work, where physical quantities such as distance and speed must be estimated from images. One option in the automotive field is to use special vehicles with ad-hoc, and usually expensive, settings and sensors capable of gathering the information required for training. The set-up and maintenance costs of such real experiments may represent a significant barrier.

In this context the use of computer graphics (CG) simulation is emerging as a powerful source of visual information. CG allows to obtain large sized dataset in a short time and with the usage of cheap resources [11]. In addition, modern video games are getting closer and closer to photorealism, thus promising to bridge the gap between visual simulation and reality that is likely to be the key to training computer vision systems that are effective in real life. Moreover, simulation makes experimental and environmental settings more flexible: i.e. in the automotive field, datasets with heterogeneous driving scenarios can be generated and subjected to different weather and lighting conditions. Higher heterogeneity can significantly improve the trained model in terms of robustness and generalization. As an example by using a simple 3D rendering technique such as Ray-casting in a virtual environment one can get a simulation of a LIDAR scanner [14,15] easily obtaining information on the distance of the elements within the image. Furthermore, it is possible to get data that are normally difficult to obtain, such as measurements of the speed of all the surrounding vehicles speed, that would require a complex setup on the real field.

Clearly, to customize and generate a dataset for visual training one either needs to design a complex CG simulation environment or exploit existing high quality game engines. The second option is viable if one has access to the source code to easily extract information on the entities and the various elements that make up the gaming environment (bounding box, size, distance from the observer, type of entity, etc.). Nowadays, there are few open source simulators that can be used to extract synthetic datasets. In the automotive environment TORCS [1] can be used; however this tool allows the representation of only a few scenarios with limited photorealism. On the other hand, commercial videogames car run very realistic CG and are equipped with intelligent agents to simulate entity actions, e.g. a pedestrian walking. For this reason the research community has recently got interest in Grand Theft Auto V (GTAV) [4,9,12,13], a popular open world videogame that, thanks to the libraries developed by third parties, allows one to extract data from the gaming environment.

In a similar fashion to the work done in [13], in this work we propose two CNN architectures to estimate distance and speed of the surrounding vehicles from a single camera with windshield view (see Fig. 1). Training has been achieved with GTAV simulations and performance validated in real life. The main contributions of this paper lie in:

- a DL model the uses a pre-trained deep CNN to extract semantic features from vehicles images and uses them to predict distance of the surrounding vehicles from a single camera with windshield view;
- a model which uses optical-flow information to predict the speed of surrounding vehicles from pixel motion between pairs of video frames.

- a training framework based on videogame simulation for the creation of training and testing datasets in the automotive field;
- we show that training with synthetic but photorealistic images represents a viable alternative to more expensive experimental data collection, with promising results in the estimation of distance and speed of the vehicles on the road, observed with a single camera.

Dataset, code and pre-trained model are publicly available and can be found at: https://github.com/mirkozaff/DeepGTAPrediction.

2   Methodology

In this section we will introduce the framework used to collect data, preprocess them and the models used to accomplish the vision task.

2.1   Data Collection

Fig. 1. Example of a photorealistic frames extracted from the game environment.

Data have been collected from GTAV thanks to Script Hook V library (SHL), which allows to easily access GTAV native function and extract information about the entities (vehicles) from the game environment. Images and corresponding information have been generated by configuring an in-game agent that drives a vehicle and letting it wander the streets; during the simulation one can collect the required information by queering the game engine through SHL calls. For our goal we built a dataset by collecting, for every vehicle in the range of 30 m from the player, the following items:

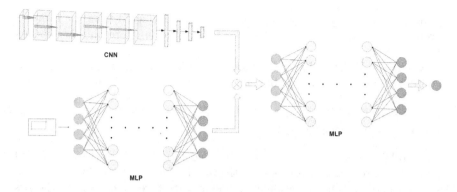

Fig. 2. Prototype architecture of our proposed distance model. A CNN is used to extract semantic features, while the MLP branch is used to learn a spatial representation of the coordinates. Then all these information are merged and decoded into output values trough a last MLP.

- *Frame:* 1920×1080 image captured at 30 Hz, gathered by setting the in-game camera on the dashboard.
- *Entity ID:* identifier of the vehicle to track it in multiple frames.
- *Entity speed, distance:* speed and distance of the vehicle.
- *Entity bounding box:* pair of coordinates that define the *bounding box* B_1 of the vehicle in the captured frame; this is computed by projecting the 3D bounding box obtained from the game engine into 2D screen coordinates.

We noted that the bounding boxes extracted by SHL are often inaccurate and present a drift caused by the delay in the response to each SHL query. To get precise bounding boxes we use pretrained Mask R-CNN [7] model to detect each vehicle in the dumped frame (the same model will be used in the testing phase on real-life images). For each detected vehicle Mask R-CNN output a bounding box B_2. To univocally map B_2 onto previously computed B_1 (and corresponding speed and distance data) we set a threshold on the intersection over union $IoU = \frac{B_1 \cap B_2}{B_1 \cup B_2}$. Only the entities showing $IoU \geq 0.7$ are included in the dataset. The selected threshold has also the effect to filter out some vehicles that cannot be reliably detected due to poor visual conditions.

2.2 Models

Distance. The first model we present is designed to estimate distance from surrounding vehicles using a single camera with windshield view. The input is a single image from which vehicles bounding boxes are detected, e.g. by using Mask R-CNN. As shown in Fig. 2 the architecture is composed by two branches:

- *First branch:* pretrained ResNet50 [8] used to extract semantic features of the target vehicle from the corresponding frame. To this end the classification layers in ResNet50 are removed. The input is a frame crop based on the bounding box B_2. In particular, each vehicle is extracted from the frame by cropping and resizing it at 224×224, that is the input resolution expected by ResNet50.

- *Second branch:* Multi Layer Perceptron (MLP), that is used to encode the coordinate of the bounding box B_2 into a higher multi-dimensional space. We selected the *ELU* activation function [5] for each layer, in place of the classic *ReLU*; we noted that in our scenario *ELU* is very effective to avoid the dead-neuron problem [16].

These two branches are then concatenated and processed through a final MLP responsible of predicting distance from the fused information produced by image pixels and bounding box coordinates. Semantic features provided by the first branch are important because vehicles appearing at the same scale in the image may represent different classes of object; clearly, we cannot base the distance estimation on the sole geometric information, i.e. bounding box dimension and position analyzed by the second branch. In other words, as in real life, we must take into account that cars are smaller than trucks when guessing the corresponding distance.

Speed. The model proposed to estimate the speed of surrounding vehicles is designed with a similar approach using two branches: (i) semantic based on images, (ii) geometrical based on bounding boxes. When speed is regarded one clearly has to consider at least two consecutive images to gather object displacement over time. One option would be to directly process frames. In this paper we propose to use as input the *Optical Flow* (OF) estimated from current (and previous) frame under analysis. OF is a dense vector field that represents the displacement of every pixel, e.g. computed using the Farneback method [6]. Moreover, we use the two bounding boxes of the same vehicle tracked in two consecutive frames (tracking is simply obtained in our GTAV dataset using entity IDs, while it will require additional processing in real setting). The structure of the model for speed estimation is as follows:

- *First branch:* PilotNet [2], a CNN proposed to learn salient points of the road for autonomous driving, is used to process the input OF. The OF vector fields is represented as an image with two bands representing vector magnitude and direction, respectively. The obtained OF image is cropped according to B_2 and resized to 200×66 (the resolution expected by PilotNet). We improved the original PilotNet model by adding batch normalization to the convolutional layer in order to speed up convergence and by using ELU activation function and *Dropout* on the last fully-connected layers.
- *Second branch:* same MLP structure used in previous model to encode in a higher multidimensional space the coordinates of bounding boxes; differently from the distance estimation model, now the input is represented by two bounding boxes associated to the same vehicle tracked in two successive frames.

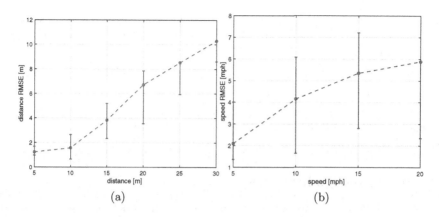

Fig. 3. RMSE on distance (a) and speed (b) estimate.

Finally, the features extracted on the two branches are concatenated and processed by final MLP as already shown in Fig. 2 to estimate speed. Clearly, we adopted a heuristic similar to the one proposed for distance: the lower branch extracts motion features based on bounding box geometrical information and displacement; the Pilonet branch encodes richer features that depend on the OF of all the pixels corresponding to a vehicle and potentially extract also semantic characteristics.

3   Network Training

Using the process presented in Sect. 2.1 it is possible to generate datasets comprising as many vehicles, labeled with distance and speed, as desired. In this work, we employ a training and validation sets with 250,000 and 2,500 samples, respectively to train the distance model. As far as the speed model is regarded, we extract from previous dataset all vehicles visible in two consecutive frames generating a set of 180,000 OF images for training and 1,500 for validation.

The proposed models have been trained using *Mean Squared Error* (MSE) as loss function and *Adam* optimizer with the following parameters: $lr = 0.001$, $\beta_1 = 0.9$, $\beta_2 = 0.999$. In order to avoid over-fitting the training has been stopped as soon as the loss computed on the validation set ceases to decrease; in our experiments this usually happened after about 15 training epochs.

Training of all MLP sub-networks has been done using *Dropout* with parameter $p = 0.4$. In the distance model ResNet50 weights pretrained on *ImageNet* have been kept fixed, while optimizing only the other MLP sub-networks. In the speed model all the network has been trained since no pretrained PilotNet useful in our context was already available.

Training has been run on a PC with Intel(R) Core(TM) i9-7940X CPU, 128 GB RAM and NVIDIA GeForce GTX 1080 Ti (x4). Testing was performed both on the same machine and on a lighter one with Intel(R) Core(TM) i5-6400,

8 GB RAM and NVIDIA GeForce GTX 1050 Ti. This latter has been selected as representative of the hardware that one expects to have on board a vehicle as opposed to the previous higher-end server.

4   Experimental Results

In this section we describe the experimental results obtained in different simulated and real settings.

4.1   Testing on Synthetic Dataset

As a first step, the estimation accuracy of the trained models has been evaluated on synthetic datasets of size 2,500 and 1,800 for distance and speed, respectively. These testing sets have been generated using the GTAV simulation described in Sect. 2.1. It is worth pointing out that training and testing sets have been generated with different random simulations to make them independent.

The proposed models are able to predict distance with a Root MSE (RMSE) of about **2.46** [m] and speed with RMSE of about **2.75** [mph]. In Fig. 1 we provide an example of the obtained visual results. The image shows a car and a truck with labels representing ground truth and predicted distance and speed. For the car the model predicts a distance of 3.8 m versus a real value of 3 m and 9.5 mph speed versus 10.2 mph.

In Fig. 3 we analyze in more details the estimation accuracy. In particular, Fig. 3(a) shows the RMSE on distance as a function of the actual distance range; to this end we compute RMSE (the circle marker) and standard deviation of the estimation error (vertical bars) by binning the collected results in increasing distance ranges of 5 m in the interval $(0, 30)$ m (the top error bar indicates an overestimate, whereas the bottom segment represents an underestimate). It can be noted that, as one may expects, the RMSE increases for larger distances. Overall the distance estimates are quite accurate and unbiased (almost symmetric error bars) within a range of 15 m: as an example the RMSE in the range $(0, 5)$ m is 1.23 m and in the range $(5, 10)$ m is 1.57 m. For farther vehicles the predictions are less accurate and the model tends to underestimate the distance. This can be explained by the fact that at distances greater than 15 m vehicles are represented in the image by fewer pixels limiting the information extraction capabilities of the convolutional layers.

In Fig. 3b we show similar RMSE analysis on the speed estimate as a function of the speed up to 20 mph, that is the maximum value that can be simulated in GTAV. It can be noted that speed RMSE increases as a function of speed. The obtained results shows that the proposed network can guess the speed of the surrounding vehicles at reasonable level by using a single camera view. As an example, in the speed range $(0, 5)$ mph we get RMSE equal to 2.10 mph, and in the range $(5, 10)$ mph we get RMSE equal to 4.15 mph. We expect to be able to improve such results by increasing the number of temporal frames analyzed by the model and using better OF representations.

4.2   Testing on Real Dataset

As already mentioned in Sect. 1 one of the goal of this work is to understand if
CG simulation can be used to effectively train DL models that can be employed
in real settings. To answer this question we need vehicles videos with annotated
data. To this end we used the video sequence provided in [10] and corresponding
distance estimates as an example of real dataset. In Fig. 4 we compare the RMSE
on distance prediction obtained on the real and synthetic datasets subdivided in
2 m ranges (please note that images from [10] are limited to a 6 m range). It can
be noted that the proposed model is quite robust and generalizes well in real
life scenario, even if the actual environment can be significantly different with
respect to GTAV simualtion. Indeed it can be noted that, in the experimented
distance range, the RMSE of the real dataset increases by less than 0.5 m with
respect to the synthetic testing set. Overall the test RMSE was **1.21** on synthetic
data and **1.40** on real data. We would like to perform similar experiment with
speed prediction but unfortunately, to the best of our knowledge, there is no
publicly available dataset that can be employed to this end. Indeed, the setup
of a real road experimentation is quite complex.

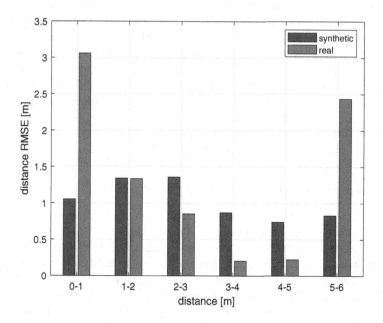

Fig. 4. RMSE on distance estimate (synthetic and real images).

Fig. 5. Example of distance estimate in real environment.

4.3 Testing on the Road

Finally, the model has been tested on a video recorded on the streets around our city using a Go Pro Hero 6 placed on the car dashboard. This last experiment was accomplished in real road environments (both urban and highway) to check the meaningfulness of the obtained predictions. In this case we do not have ground truth data. By analyzing the operations of the proposed system in real live we noted that the predicted distances are plausible and coherent, i.e. vehicles appearing at the same distance are assigned the same value, and approaching vehicles exhibit decreasing distance. As in previous experiment also in this case the model performance is not significantly impaired by the road environment that is very much different with respect the GTAV scenario.

4.4 Computational Cost

In this section we analyze the computational cost of the proposed solutions by measuring the execution time of different algorithmic steps of the two hardware architectures described in Sect. 3; these are meant to be representative of a workstation performing remote computation and lower-end hardware compatible with in vehicle system. In Table 1 we show the average time taken by the calculation of the bounding box, speed and distance estimate for an image with 5 vehicles (on average). It can be noted that to get acceptable delays (compatible with real time requirements of advanced driver-assistance systems) it is necessary to use powerful workstation. As expected the speed estimate represent the slowest module.

Table 1. Execution time of different algorithmic steps.

Work station	
290 ms	Bounding box
15 ms	Distance
45 ms	Speed
120 ms	Latency
500 ms	Total
On board PC	
2 s	Bounding box
280 ms	Distance
880 ms	Speed
3 s	Total

5 Conclusions

In this paper, we proposed two models to accomplish two different tasks: speed and distance prediction using a single camera looking at the road from the driver perspective. Since for such tasks it is either technically difficult or quite expensive to get real video sequences for training CNNs, in this paper we proposed to use simulated data generated by means of a popular game engine. Such an approach allowed us to collect photorealistic driving scenes, where all the visible vehicles can be labeled with distance and speed information. We designed two DL models built around similar ideas: one branch extracts features from the input images, a second one maps vehicles' bounding boxes (dimension and position) to higher dimensional space, and a last MLP network infers distance or speed from all the extracted features. The estimation accuracy has been evaluated on both synthetic and real data showing that the simulated images can be used to effectively train the proposed models. For future work we plan to improve the models by substituting the bounding box detection network with a lighter version and using a DL approach to estimate OF for speed prediction. Moreover, we plan to enrich the input available to the network by including parameters that can be logged on board a car such as throttle, brake and steering data to mention a few.

Acknowledgement. The research leading to these results has received funding from the European Union Horizon 2020 research and innovation programme under grant agreement No 713788 ("optiTruck" project).

References

1. Torcs (2007). http://torcs.sourceforge.net/
2. Bojarski, M., et al.: Explaining how a deep neural network trained with end-to-end learning steers a car (2017). http://arxiv.org/abs/1704.07911

3. Buhrmester, M., Kwang, T., Gosling, S.D.: Amazon's mechanical turk: a new source of inexpensive, yet high-quality, data? Perspect. Psychol. Sci. **6**(1), 3–5 (2011)

4. Chen, C., Seff, A., Kornhauser, A., Xiao, J.: DeepDriving: learning affordance for direct perception in autonomous driving. In: ICCV 2015 (2015)

5. Clevert, D., Unterthiner, T., Hochreiter, S.: Fast and accurate deep network learning by exponential linear units (elus) (2015). http://arxiv.org/abs/1511.07289

6. Farnebäck, G.: Two-frame motion estimation based on polynomial expansion. In: Bigun, J., Gustavsson, T. (eds.) SCIA 2003. LNCS, vol. 2749, pp. 363–370. Springer, Heidelberg (2003). https://doi.org/10.1007/3-540-45103-X_50

7. He, K., Gkioxari, G., Dollár, P., Girshick, R.B.: Mask R-CNN (2017). http://arxiv.org/abs/1703.06870

8. He, K., Zhang, X., Ren, S., Sun, J.: Deep residual learning for image recognition (2015). http://arxiv.org/abs/1512.03385

9. Johnson-Roberson, M., Barto, C., Mehta, R., Sridhar, S.N., Vasudevan, R.: Driving in the matrix: can virtual worlds replace human-generated annotations for real world tasks? (2016). http://arxiv.org/abs/1610.01983

10. Karagiannis, V.: Distance estimation between vehicles based on fixed dimensions licence plates. Ph.D. thesis, University Of Patras (2017)

11. Lin, T.-Y., et al.: Microsoft COCO: common objects in context. In: Fleet, D., Pajdla, T., Schiele, B., Tuytelaars, T. (eds.) ECCV 2014. LNCS, vol. 8693, pp. 740–755. Springer, Cham (2014). https://doi.org/10.1007/978-3-319-10602-1_48

12. Martinez, M., Sitawarin, C., Finch, K., Meincke, L., Yablonski, A., Kornhauser, A.L.: Beyond grand theft auto V for training, testing and enhancing deep learning in self driving cars (2017). http://arxiv.org/abs/1712.01397

13. Palazzi, A., Borghi, G., Abati, D., Calderara, S., Cucchiara, R.: Learning to map vehicles into bird's eye view. In: Battiato, S., Gallo, G., Schettini, R., Stanco, F. (eds.) ICIAP 2017. LNCS, vol. 10484, pp. 233–243. Springer, Cham (2017). https://doi.org/10.1007/978-3-319-68560-1_21

14. Wu, B., Wan, A., Yue, X., Keutzer, K.: Squeezeseg: convolutional neural nets with recurrent CRF for real-time road-object segmentation from 3D lidar point cloud (2017). http://arxiv.org/abs/1710.07368

15. Yue, X., Wu, B., Seshia, S.A., Keutzer, K., Sangiovanni-Vincentelli, A.L.: A lidar point cloud generator: from a virtual world to autonomous driving. In: Proceedings of the 2018 ACM on International Conference on Multimedia Retrieval

16. Zaheer, R., Shaziya, H.: GPU-based empirical evaluation of activation functions in convolutional neural networks. In: 2018 2nd International Conference on Inventive Systems and Control (ICISC)

A Convolutional Neural Network for Virtual Screening of Molecular Fingerprints

Isabella Mendolia[1(✉)], Salvatore Contino[1(✉)], Ugo Perricone[2(✉)], Roberto Pirrone[1(✉)], and Edoardo Ardizzone[1(✉)]

[1] Dipartimento di Ingegneria, Università degli Studi di Palermo, Palermo, Italy
{isabella.mendolia,salvatore.contino01,roberto.pirrone,
edoardo.ardizzone}@unipa.it
[2] Gruppo Drug Design, Fondazione Ri.MED, Palermo, Italy
uperricone@fondazionerimed.com

Abstract. In the last few years, Deep Learning (DL) gained more and more impact on drug design because it allows a huge increase of the prediction accuracy in many stages of such a complex process. In this paper a Virtual Screening (VS) procedure based on Convolutional Neural Networks (CNN) is presented, that is aimed at classifying a set of candidate compounds as regards their biological activity on a particular target protein. The model has been trained on a dataset of active/inactive compounds with respect to the Cyclin-Dependent Kinase 1 (CDK1) a very important protein family, which is heavily involved in regulating the cell cycle. One qualifying point of the proposed approach is the use of molecular fingerprints as a suitable embedding for describing molecules; up to our knowledge there is no Deep Learning approach for VS that makes use of such descriptor. Several kinds of fingerprints are reported in the scientific literature to address different aspects of both the structure and the local properties of a molecule. Both 1D and 2D CNNs have been trained to test the performance of each single descriptor separately, along with suitable ensembles of multiple descriptors for the same compound; the best performing architecture has been used for prediction. The CNN architectures are described in detail, and the results are compared with some recent approaches for Virtual Screening with respect to Cyclin-Dependent Kinase proteins that do not use molecular fingerprints as their descriptor.

Keywords: Deep Learning · Drug design · Molecular fingerprints · Bioactivity prediction · Virtual Screening

Supported by PON "Ricerca e Innovazione" 2014–2020, Azione 1.1: Dottorati innovativi con caratterizzazione industriale.

E. Ricci et al. (Eds.): ICIAP 2019, LNCS 11751, pp. 399–409, 2019.
https://doi.org/10.1007/978-3-030-30642-7_36

1   Introduction

Drug discovery is the very long and complex process leading to the development of a new medication, where several steps and loops are involved. Indeed, one of the most relevant parts in the drug discovery cycle is *drug design* when one already knows the biological target the new compound has to bind to. In general, a biological target is an enzyme or a protein. In a modern drug design setup, many compounds are screened to assess the best matching ones as regards their ability of either inhibiting or activating the target associated to a particular disease. Such a process is also referred to as *Inverse Pharmacology* or *Target-based Drug Design*.

As part of his/her work, the drug designer needs to consult large public or private databases to retrieve information about existing molecules. Such queries can have different nature; particularly, it is necessary to investigate how two molecules can bind with each other according to purely chemical criteria, taking into account biological constraints due to the molecule toxicity for the human organism. From the data point of view, these queries return very heterogeneous information ranging from a whole molecule graph representation to textual and numerical data.

In recent years, computer aided drug design has gained increasing importance to speed up the whole process thus reducing the cost of developing new drugs significantly. *Virtual Screening* (VS) refers exactly to an automated procedure aimed at selecting those molecules that are likely to be active on the desired target. Such procedures range from similarity search to Machine Learning (ML) approaches, and all of them rely on using suitable numerical descriptors of both the structure and some chemical properties of the candidate compound.

Virtual Screening can be regarded as a classification task in the ML perspective; typical approaches are Support Vector Machines and Random Forests. In the Deep Learning era, both Convolutional and Recurrent Neural Networks are used for VS and in other fields of Pharmacology like the prediction of chemical reactions. The reader is referred to [8] for a recent and thorough review.

In this paper a VS procedure based on Convolutional Neural Networks (CNN) is presented, that is aimed at classifying a set of candidate compounds as regards their biological activity on the Cyclin-Dependent Kinase 1 (CDK1) a very important protein family, which is heavily involved in regulating the cell cycle. This work is part of a more wide research oriented to the development of new CDK1 inhibitors starting from natural products, to be used in cancer therapy. The choice of this target is given by the previous experience of the research group in the CDK1 modulators and the fact that canonical VS approaches on CDKs do not respond properly to activity prediction because of high structural similarity between different kinases binding sites. The importance of the target is given by its validation as drug target. It is an archetypal kinase acting as central regulator that drives cells through G2 phase and mitosis. Its importance in tumorigenesis has been demonstrated by the evidence that, unlike other CDKs, loss of CDK1 in the liver confers complete resistance against tumor formation demonstrating its role in the cancer development [4].

The proposed CNN architecture makes use of *molecular fingerprints* as the numerical descriptor of each candidate molecule, and this is quite a novelty as regards DL approaches for biological activity prediction. Several kinds of fingerprints are reported in the scientific literature to address different aspects of both the structure, and the local properties of a molecule. The same fingerprint can be devised also with different sizes. As a consequence, experiments have been performed to test the performance of each single descriptor separately by training 1D CNNs. Also 2D CNNs have been trained on suitable combinations of different equal sized fingerprints for the same compound, to take into account all the diverse information pieces coming from such descriptors at once. As it was expected, multiple fingerprints performed better, and results are reported as regards both the best ensemble and the best size. Moreover, we compared our results with some recent approaches for Virtual Screening with respect to Cyclin-Dependent Kinase proteins that do not use molecular fingerprints as their descriptor.

The rest of the paper is arranged as follows. Section 2 reports a review of the state of te art in ML and DL in drug design, and particularly in VS. Section 3 contains a description of molecular fingerprints along with the details on the datasets, and the CNN architectures. Section 4 contains results and comparisons, while conclusions are drawn in Sect. 5.

2   State of the Art

Clinical candidate molecules selected by drug detection must have a profile responding to different criteria, that are based not only on the effect potency but also on the selectivity, safety as well as the so called *ADMET* properties (Absorption, Distribution, Metabolism, Excretion and Toxicity). Therefore, the design of the optimal compound is a multidimensional challenge involving different aspects of Chemistry and Biology, which is faced using ML. One key aspect for ML approaches gaining success in property prediction is the possibility to access and mining large data sets that contain heterogeneous information. Until recent years, the best performing ML techniques were "shallow" ones [9] that is support vector machines (SVM) and decision trees, particularly ensemble methods like Random Forest (RF). All these ML models should be iteratively refined with new experimental data to increase model reliability and predictive power.

The Kinase protein family presents a huge variety, and contains a very high number of proteins so it provides an amount of data that is well suited for ML approaches oriented to VS for novel kinase inhibitors. In [11] Bayesian models were generated for building Quantitative Structure-Activity Relationship (QSAR) models on different kinases from a large, but sparsely populated data matrix of more than 100,000 compounds. Random Forest has been applied in another case study for predicting kinase activities on hundreds of kinases starting from publicly available data sets integrated with in-house data [12]. In several examples, Random Forest models showed a higher reliability in prediction when compared to other approaches, but they perform worse than deep neural networks.

DNNs have been used for predicting different properties such as biological activity, ADMET properties, and physicochemical parameters demonstrating reliable and robust predictivity capabilities with high sensitivity when used on different targets [7,15]. AtomNet was one of the first CNNs designed for drug discovery to predict bio-activity of small molecules [16]. CNNs have been used also to predict several properties such as the kinetic energy of hydrocarbons as a function of electron density [17]. Several DNN architectures use Simplified Molecular Input Line Entry System (SMILES) as their input data [3,6,14]. SMILES is actually a simple chemical language whose rules allow building string descriptors that can represent both molecular structures and reactions.

The architecture presented in this work relies on CNNs and molecular fingerprints for VS of compounds as regards their biological activity on the CDK1 protein. Up to our knowledge there is no other approach in the literature making use of molecular fingerprints as the data embedding for training a VS deep neural model for bioactivity on CDK1. A detailed description of molecular fingerprints is reported in the next section. As regards CDK-oriented VS, Li et al. [10] propose a least-squares support vector machine (LS-SVM) trained on molecular descriptors to build a Structure-Activity Relationship (SAR) model to classify oxindole-based inhibitors of CDK1 and CDK2. In another study, Pereira et al. [13] present DeepVS a deep learning approach for docking-based virtual screening that has been tested on the data sets included in the Directory of Useful Decoys (DUD) where only CDK2 were used. The results reported in the two previous works were considered to compare the performance of the proposed architecture, computing the fingerprints of the data sets they used. The results of our experiments against DeepVS are reported in Sect. 4, while results reported by the authors of LS-SVM were not useful because they used a very small data set made by 82 compounds referred to by numerical IDs, that was extracted manually from another paper in the literature. As a consequence it was not possible for us to retrieve the original compounds from any chemical database for generating their fingerprints.

3   Materials and Methods

In this section we report a description of molecular fingerprints, the data sets used in our experiments, and the architecture of the proposed CNNs.

3.1   Molecular Fingerprints

Modern approaches in Chemoinformatics have focused on the use of ML techniques applied to fingerprints instead of classical molecular descriptors. The reason is that fingerprints contain information on chemical groups and paths; they provide complete information about molecular complexity thus allowing a more robust comparison between two or more structures than molecular descriptors do. SMILES descriptors also convey information on molecular structures but their inherent string form needs the cycles to be cut, and the description of the same molecule is not unique thus a "SMILES canonicalization" is also needed.

Molecular fingerprints are generated analyzing each atom along with its neighborhood till 6 or 7 bonds away. Such a neighborhood is searched for a set of predefined molecular substructures, the so called *patterns*, that is atom types, bond types, presence of rings, ans so on. After having enumerated all the patterns in the molecule, each of them is used as a seed for a hashing function that outputs in general 4 to 5 index positions whose corresponding bits are set to 1 in the "pattern fingerprint"; such a fingerprint is bit-wise ORed to the molecular one. Actually the hashing function can cause a bit collision so we are not guaranteed of the effective presence of a particular pattern unless at least one of its bits is unique. On the other hand, a molecular substructure is absent if all its bits are set to 0 in the fingerprint. A simplified fingerprint generation procedure is reported in Fig. 1.

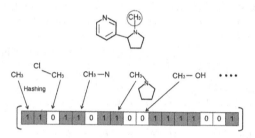

Fig. 1. Simplified fingerprint generation: the hashing function sets just 1 bit per pattern

Molecular fingerprints are generated using different approaches as regards both the neighborhood definition and the size. In our experiments we tested six among the most popular fingerprints: *RDKit, Morgan, AtomPair, Topological Torsion, Layered*, and *FeatMorgan*. All of them differ in the choice of the paths along the molecule to devise patterns, and particularly the *Morgan* and *Feat-Morgan* fingerprint are *circular* that is they generate patterns by going through each atom of the molecule and obtaining all possible paths through this atom with a specific radius. Each unique path is then hashed into the fingerprint: the larger the radius, the larger fragments are encoded. Fingerprints' length can range from 256 to 4K bits; in classical VS, different size fingerprints are compared by "folding" them. The two halves of the longest fingerprint are bit wise OR-ed thus obtaining a new fingerprint whose length is one half of the original one. In our experiments, we tested each kind of fingerprints using three different lengths: 256, 512, and 1024 bits, while the radius of the circular fingerprints was set to 2, that is the conventional value.

From the computational point of view, VS procedures take advantage from the fact that fingerprints are not too sparse bit vectors. Non ML approaches perform different search strategies where some well known similarity measures are used like Tanimoto, Cosine, Dice, Euclid, or Twersky; such measures are computed starting from the number of 1s counted respectively in each fingerprint, and on the number of 1s in common between the two fingerprints.

Fingerprints have been also learnt from molecular graphs using CNNs as reported in [5]. In this work, a single convolutional layer with softmax activation is used in place of the hashing function to produce the bits indexing of a atom neighborhood collected in the same way as circular fingerprints do. Authors report very good performance in predicting both solubility and toxicity from two purposely defined data sets, but the approach suffers from a high computational cost when compared with direct use of circular fingerprints.

3.2   Data Sets

The data used in our experiments where extracted from the well known CheMBL molecular database [1]. Biological activity of the tested compounds was measured using the *half maximal inhibitory concentration* parameter (IC_{50}) that is the amount of substance which is needed to inihibit the target protein (i.e. CDK1) by one half. A molecule has been considered active when $IC_{50} \leq 9\,\mu M$, otherwise it is inactive.

Data preparation was accomplished using the KNIME data analysis platform [2], and a workflow was implemented to prepare both the training and the test set. Activity data for 1830 compounds on the CDK1 target were taken from the *CHEMBL308* ID were CDK1 is considered as a single protein, and the *CHEMBL1907602* ID were it is considered as a protein complex.

At first, incomplete data were deleted; the training set was then made using 1432 samples with a perfect balancing between the two class labels. Particularly, 716 active samples and 662 inactive ones were selected from the *CHEMBL308* ID, while 54 inactive samples were selected from the *CHEMBL1907602* ID. The test set was made as a whole by 175 inactive molecules coming from the *CHEMBL1907602* ID, and 100 active samples coming from the *CHEMBL308* ID.

Data in the two CheMBL IDs were searched for duplicates that were removed to avoid repetitions in both the training and the test set. However it is worth noting that in the same data set there may be two times the same molecule with very different IC_{50} value coming from two different biological assays. We have not used data augmentation because it is not possible to generate molecular fingerprints and predict whether they are active molecules or not in a specific biological assay but we have used 5-cross validation.

3.3   The CNN Architecture

Molecular fingerprint generation acts as a transform on the molecular structure from the spatial domain to a suitable Vector Space Representation. A fingerprint represents the corresponding molecule "as a whole" that is it conveys information about the presence of a particular substructure but not on its exact position or its repetition in different sites of the same molecule. Moreover, we want to perform a binary classification between active and inactive compounds, and biological activity is mostly related to the presence/absence of particular substructures which in turn are well suited to bind to the target protein. As a consequence, a CNN architecture appeared to be the best choice to classify molecular fingerprints.

In this study we present two CNN architectures that have been trained from scratch; the first is a 1D CNN trained on single fingerprints, and a 2D network where each compound was represented by an ensemble of equal length and different kind fingerprints arranged as a bi-dimensional matrix. The second network is aimed at modeling those structural subtleties that can not be represented by any single descriptor alone. In general, different patterns are searched for in each fingerprint kind, and also the same pattern is searched in different ways. Both networks consist of 4 convolutional layers with 512, 256, 128, 64 filters respectively with ReLU activation, each followed by a 2 × 2 Max Pooling, while they differ only in the convolutional kernel dimensions. Classification is achieved through a MLP with 1024, 512, and 256 ReLU units respectively, while the ouput is a sigmoidal unit as we want binary classification. The overall architecture is reported in Fig. 2. Hyperparameters tuning was performed as a grid search in the following sets of values; Convolutional filters tested were $[1024, 512, 256, 128, 64]$ in combination with all Keras padding value; learning rate were multiplied by 10 in the ranges $[10^{-6}, 1; 2 \cdot 10^{-5}, 0.2]$. Dropout probabilities where in the range $[0.2, 0.9]$ with step 0.1, all the available optimizers in Keras were tested. Bi-dimensional tested kernel sizes were $\{(20, 2), (20, 1), (15, 2), (15, 1), (5, 2), (5, 1), (4, 2), (4, 1), (3, 2), (3, 1)\}$, while 1D tested kernels were $\{2, 3, 4\}$. Batch sizes were doubled in the range $[8, 128]$. Early sopping was used to devise training epochs. Table 1 shows the best choices for all the hyperparameters. Due to the low number of samples, small size fingerprints were tested with a number of epochs greater than 55; retraining was performed with 70, 100 and 120 epochs, and the minimum loss was achieved with 100 epochs. No overfitting was encountered with this setup. Hyperparameter optimization took about 150 h to be accomplished on a GPU NVIDIA GTX1060 6 GB, 1280 CUDA Cores, while each experiment took about 20 min.

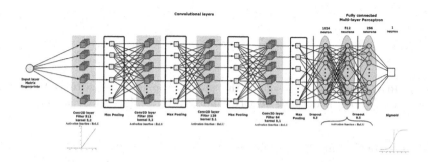

Fig. 2. Bi-dimensional architecture of the network

Table 1. Hyperparameters setting, used in all experiments.

Optimizer	Learning rate	Dropout	Kernel size 2D	Kernel size 1D	Batch size	Epochs	Padding
Adamax	0.0002	0.5	(5,2), (5,1)	3	64	55	Same

4   Results and Discussion

The first set of experiments where devoted to devise the best performing fingerprint type/size in predicting biological activity, and 1D CNN was used. Table 2 reports the best test results for each fingerprint size along with its type. Here and in the following tables, best results are highlighted in bold. The table reports the achieved test accuracy, the F1-score, and the AUC value, which is used commonly when comparing two approaches in the drug design literature. Both a SVM and a Random Forest model were trained on our data sets to validate the performance of our model. The results of such experiment are reported in Fig. 3. As it was expected, ML approaches have a very poor accuracy performance (SVM = 0.9081, RF = 0.9081) if compared to ours best architecture (0.9345), despite the better AUC value shown in Fig. 3.

Table 2. Results of 1D CNN on the test set

Length	Fingerprint	Accuracy	Loss	F1-score	AUC
1024	Layered	0.9100	0.54	0.8700	0.9453
512	**Layered**	**0.9272**	**0.4447**	**0.9000**	**0.9610**
256	Torsion	0.8654	0.5456	0.831	0.9481

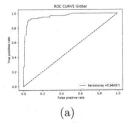 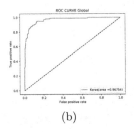 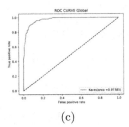

(a)   (b)   (c)

Fig. 3. ROC Curves comparison of the proposed architecture with classical ML approaches; (a) best performing 1D CNN (L-512); (b) SVM; (c) Random Forest.

The second round of experiments was aimed at devising the best fingerprint combination/size for biological activity prediction using 2D CNN. The idea behind this experiments is that different fingerprints for the same molecule contain many different patterns, which in turn describe different molecular substructures. Also different sizes correspond to patterns with variable length.

Table 3. Results of the 2D CNN on the test set with different fingerprint length. Fingerprint types: *(R)DKit, (M)organ, (A)tompair, (T)opological Torsion, (L)ayred,* and *(F)eatMorgan*

(a) 1024 bit fingerprints

Fingerprints	Accuracy	Loss	F1-score	AUC
M,L	**0.9200**	**0.5600**	**0.8800**	**0.9563**
R,M,A	0.900	0.6800	0.8600	0.9527
M,A,L,F	0.9200	0.6000	0.8877	0.9444
R,M,A,L,F	0.9163	0.6082	0.8820	0.9513
R,M,A,T,L,F	0.8945	0.6280	0.8557	0.9494

(b) 512 bit fingerprints

Fingerprints	Accuracy	Loss	F1-score	AUC
M,F	0.8981	0.4463	0.8679	0.9555
M,T,L	**0.9345**	**0.3900**	**0.9117**	**0.9685**
R,M,T,F	0.9418	0.4268	0.9001	0.94
R,A,T,L,F	0.9127	0.4052	0.8867	0.963
R,M,A,T,L,F	0.9236	0.3950	0.9004	0.9774

(c) 256 bit fingerprints

Fingerprints	Accuracy	Loss	F1-score	AUC
L,F	0.9090	0.4087	0.8792	0.9655
R,L,F	**0.9127**	**0.4734**	**0.8846**	**0.9606**
R,A,L,F	0.9054	0.4914	0.8749	0.9572
R,M,T,L,F	0.8909	0.5380	0.8623	0.9624
R,M,A,T,L,F	0.8981	0.5982	0.8679	0.9537

As a consequence, a set of fingerprints arranged as a 2D matrix can act as a better descriptor for molecular substructures than a single one can do. Table 3 reports the overall results for different fingerprint sizes.

As it is reported in Tables 2 and 3, the best performance is achieved with the set of Morgan, Topological Torsion and Layered 512 bit fingerprints (MTL-512). Layered fingerprints are always among the best performing descriptor regardless their size. Moreover, 512 Layered is exactly the best performing descriptor in the 1D CNN architecture. It is trivial to say that 512 bit is the input data size that best suits to the network capacity as it is defined by its architecture. As regards the fingerprint types, it is difficult to devise an exact explanation of the results due to the random process involved in the generation of molecular fingerprints. It is not possible to devise precise patterns in precise positions that are mainly responsible for the network performance. Anyway, we can say that Layered fingerprints have a particular hashing scheme that allows accommodating substructure information with high level of detail so it is reasonable that 1D CNN achieved its best performance using this kind of fingerprint. As regards the 2D CNN's performance, it is worth noting that MTL-512 fingerprints together span all the diverse criteria to search for patterns so it seems quite reasonable that such a triple produced the best result.

We further validated our architecture against the DeepVS network, which is presented in [13], and deals with VS versus CDK proteins even if there are some differences with our work.

DeepVS was trained on the CDK2 protein only; the authors tested their network with a subset of the *CHEMBL301* data set, which is extracted from the DUD-E data set (798 active molecules and 28,329 decoys). At first, the entire *CHEMBL301* data set that consists of 1528 compounds (956 CDK2-active molecules, and 572 inactive ones) was used to test the MTL-512 2D CNN. In this experiment our network achieved $AUC = 0.8030$ that is a very good result when compared with $AUC = 0.82$ achieved by DeepVS, which was trained purposely for CDK2. As some compounds in *CHEMBL301* are also active on CDK1, we removed explicitly all of them to stress the network performance. As a result, we obtained $AUC = 0.678$, which shows an obvious decrease; this still remains a satisfactory result if related to human performances in VS, and also classical ML approaches.

5   Conclusions

A novel CNN architecture has been presented in this work, that is trained on the molecular fingerprints to predict biological activity of candidate medical compounds versus the CDK1 protein target. The main novelty of the paper relies on performing Deep Learning based VS starting from molecular fingerprints for CDK1 that is a very important biological target for its direct implication in the etiology of various cancerous forms. One qualifying point of our approach is that fingerprints capture molecular structures according to different criteria and are already accepted as molecular descriptors by the chemoinformatics society. Another novelty of the approach is the use of fingerprint matrices, in order to keep direct information from single fingerprint and indirect information from the combination of the same. Their shape already makes them an embedding that lends itself perfectly to the intended use. Fine tuning of hyperparameters has been carried on along with several experiments with different fingerprint types and sizes. Early results are satisfactory, and indicate that VS of suitable arrangements of multiple fingerprint types, each addressing different ways of representing molecular substructures, performs better than a single fingerprint approach. Our architecture has been also compared to both classical ML and other state-of-the art DL approaches even if trained on different data, and for a different task. Future work will be oriented to a deep understanding of the relation between particular fingerprints and biological activity prediction, and to build a general architecture for screening compounds with respect to all the CDK family.

References

1. CHeMBL Database. https://www.ebi.ac.uk/chembl/. Accessed 24 Sept 2018
2. Berthold, M.R., et al.: KNIME - the konstanz information miner: version 2.0 and beyond. SIGKDD Explor. Newsl. **11**(1), 26–31 (2009)
3. Bjerrum, E.J.: SMILES enumeration as data augmentation for neural network modeling of molecules. CoRR, abs/1703.07076 (2017)
4. Diril, M.K., et al.: Cyclin-dependent kinase 1 (Cdk1) is essential for cell division and suppression of DNA re-replication but not for liver regeneration. Proc. Nat. Acad. Sci. U.S.A. **109**(10), 3826–3831 (2012)
5. Duvenaud, D.K. et al.: Convolutional networks on graphs for learning molecular fingerprints. In: Advances in Neural Information Processing Systems, pp. 2224–2232 (2015)
6. Fooshee, D., et al.: Deep learning for chemical reaction prediction. Mol. Syst. Des. Eng. **3**, 442–452 (2018)
7. Ghasemi, F., Mehridehnavi, A., Pérez-Garrido, A., Pérez-Sánchez, H.: Neural network and deep-learning algorithms used in QSAR studies: merits and drawbacks. Drug Discovery Today **23**(10), 1784–1790 (2018)
8. Jing, Y., Bian, Y., Hu, Z., Wang, L., Xie, X.-Q.S.: Deep learning for drug design: an artificial intelligence paradigm for drug discovery in the big data era. AAPS J. **20**, 58 (2018)
9. Lavecchia, A.: Machine-learning approaches in drug discovery: methods and applications. Drug Discovery Today **20**(3), 318–331 (2015)
10. Li, J., Liu, H., Yao, X., Liu, M., Hu, Z., Fan, B.: Structure-activity relationship study of oxindole-based inhibitors of cyclin-dependent kinases based on least-squares support vector machines. Anal. Chim. Acta **581**(2), 333–342 (2007)
11. Martin, E., Mukherjee, P., Sullivan, D., Jansen, J.: Profile-QSAR: a novel meta -QSAR method that combines activities across the kinase family to accurately predict affinity, selectivity, and cellular activity. J. Chem. Inf. Model. **51**(8), 1942–1956 (2011)
12. Merget, B., Turk, S., Eid, S., Rippmann, F., Fulle, S.: Profiling prediction of kinase inhibitors: toward the virtual assay. J. Med. Chem. **60**(1), 474–485 (2017)
13. Pereira, J.C., Caffarena, E.R., dos Santos, C.N.: Boosting docking-based virtual screening with deep learning. J. Chem. Inf. Model. **56**(12), 2495–2506 (2016)
14. Segler, M.H.S., Kogej, T., Tyrchan, C., Waller, M.P.: Generating focused molecule libraries for drug discovery with recurrent neural networks. ACS Central Sci. **4**(1), 120–131 (2018)
15. Varnek, A., Baskin, I.: Machine learning methods for property prediction in chemoinformatics: Quo Vadis? J. Chem. Inf. Model. **52**(6), 1413–1437 (2012)
16. Wallach, I., Dzamba, M., Heifets, A.: AtomNet: a deep convolutional neural network for bioactivity prediction in structure-based drug discovery. CoRR, abs/1510.02855 (2015)
17. Yao, K., Parkhill, J.: Kinetic energy of hydrocarbons as a function of electron density and convolutional neural networks. J. Chem. Theory Comput. **12**, 1139–1147 (2016)

Single Image Super-Resolution for Optical Satellite Scenes Using Deep Deconvolutional Network

Sumedh Pendurkar[1]([✉]), Biplab Banerjee[2], Sudipan Saha[3,4],
and Francesca Bovolo[3]

[1] College of Engineering Pune, Pune, India
sumedh.pendurkar@gmail.com
[2] Indian Institute of Technology Bombay, Mumbai, India
bbanerjee@iitb.ac.in
[3] Fondazione Bruno Kessler, Trento, Italy
{saha,bovolo}@fbk.eu
[4] University of Trento, Trento, Italy

Abstract. In this paper, we deal with the problem of super-resolution (SR) imaging and propose a deep deconvolutional network based model for the same. In principle, the SR problem considers the construction of the high-resolution (HR) version of a scene given a number of so-called low-level image instances of the respective scene. Moreover, if there is a single low-resolution (LR) image available, the problem becomes even difficult and ill-posed. We deal with such a scenario and show how the popular deconvolutional network can effectively reconstruct the HR image by learning the functional mapping at the patch level. We evaluate the proposed model on a number of optical remote sensing (RS) images obtained from the UC-Merced dataset. Experimental results suggest that the proposed model consistently outperforms the existing deep and shallow models for single image SR for the RS images.

Keywords: Satellite imaging · Deconvolutional neural networks · Image super resolution · Deep learning

1 Introduction

Rapid developments in RS technologies have contributed to the availability of large quantity of visual data pertaining to the Earth's surface. Satellite images are used in variety of applications ranging from environmental monitoring to homeland security since they reveal a vast amount of intricate details regarding the different geographical locations on ground.

For the sake of extracting accurate information from these images, the quality of the satellite images must be as pristine as possible. Satellite images obtained from sensors are generally affected by different degradation factors and sophisticated image enhancement techniques are needed in order to improve their spatial

© Springer Nature Switzerland AG 2019
E. Ricci et al. (Eds.): ICIAP 2019, LNCS 11751, pp. 410–420, 2019.
https://doi.org/10.1007/978-3-030-30642-7_37

resolution. Among the different approaches, the spatial resolution of an imaging system can be improved using a class of image enhancement algorithms known as SR imaging [16]. Particularly in RS applications including image classification, having higher spatial resolution helps to extract minute features from the respective scenes, thus significantly enhancing the classification results. However, sensors with high spatial resolution are required at the hardware level for obtaining high quality images which is not always feasible. Another challenge in this regard is due to the down-linking of the HR satellite images to ground stations which is often difficult and expensive. All such factors invariably degrade the quality of the satellite images to a considerable extent. As a remedy, SR techniques have become much popular to convert LR satellite images to the corresponding HR versions.

In this regard, the forward model [16] for imaging and motion process can be formulated as

$$Y_k = DB_k M_k X + n_k \tag{1}$$

given the HR scene X, warp matrix M, blur matrix B, down-sampling matrix D, noise vector n and the kth LR image Y_k, respectively. As can be understood, we obtain the LR images because of the degradation caused by warping, blurring and sub-sampling performed to the captured HR scenes due to limitations of cameras. From Eq. 1 it can be affirmed that the process of obtaining the HR images from the LR counterparts is ill-posed nature. Please note that, in this paper, we consider HR scenes as the upscaling of the resolution of available LR images by a factor of 2.

Initially, multi-image SR [17] techniques were followed to generate the HR image from multiple LR observations. As expected, these techniques often face difficulties in registering the LR scenes on the HR grid. This subsequently instigated the research focus on single-image SR. However, the key problem in this respect is the absence of prior knowledge regarding the high frequency details from the images. In this regard, the learning based single image SR techniques such as sparse coding [2,6] are based on an assumption that the sparse representation of the LR image patch over the LR dictionary is same as the corresponding HR patch over the HR dictionary. However, this assumption does not always hold true which leads to restricted performance by these models.

On the other hand, a number of recently introduced deep learning strategies find their application to RS image analysis [3,25]. Recently, deep learning algorithms [5,8,10,19] are used to tackle the SR problem for natural scenes as well as on RS applications. Following the same, we propose a deconvolutional network model for the purpose of single image SR from optical RS data.

The proposed model learns an end-to-end mapping between the LR image and HR image pairs at the patch level. In particular, the images are divided into patches of size 32×32 and then forward-propagated through the network, following which, the reconstruction error is calculated and is subsequently back-propagated. For testing, we consider the standard simulated scenario where the images are upscaled by a factor of 2 and then forward propagated through our network to obtain the predicted HR image.

2   Related Work

2.1   Image Super Resolution

As aforementioned, based on the availability of LR images to be deployed for the SR process, the existing SR algorithms can broadly be classified into two families [1,16]: (i) single image SR, and (ii) multi-image SR.

For multi-image SR, the basic premise is the availability of multiple LR images representing a given scene. These LR images provide different views belonging to the same scene in terms of sub-pixel level shifts. Multi-image SR techniques are broadly classified into: non-uniform interpolation approaches, frequency domain approaches, regularized image reconstruction approaches. Non-uniform interpolation based methods [4] register the LR images on the HR grid. The main problem with registration is the motion estimation with reference to any of the LR images that is required to account for these sub-pixel shifts. Restoration methods such as de-blurring, modeled as spatial averaging operator are used to smoothen the obtained HR image. In contrast, frequency based approaches use the aliasing relationship between continuous Fourier transform of HR image and the discrete Fourier transform of the captured LR images to reconstruct the HR image. Regularization based reconstruction methods are usually used when plenty of LR images are available. Prior knowledge of the solution is used to stabilize the inversion of this ill-posed problem. Either of the deterministic approach or stochastic approaches like Maximum-a-Posteriori (MAP) [17] are used for this purpose.

On the other hand, single-image SR presents more challenging scenario as it involves prediction of the high frequency image details. Some of the early works on single-image SR are documented in [7,22]. Single-image SR techniques are classified into four categories - prediction models, edge based models, image statistical models and exemplar based models [21]. Among them, exemplar based models haven shown to outperform the rest for images of different modalities. Most of these approaches focus on learning a mapping between the LR and HR patch. SR using sparse coding (SCSR) [2,6] are based on regularizing the dictionaries for the HR and LR patches so as to make the dictionary atoms coherent.

2.2   Deep Learning for Image Super Resolution

Convolutional Neural Networks (CNN) have shown high accuracy in image classification [12], object detection [15] and many more. On the other hand, SRCNN [5] is arguably the most popular model for SR from natural images. They propose a 3 layer network consisting of 3 conv layers while the pooling layers are eliminated to avoid loss of pixel information during the reconstruction process.

2.3   Deconvolutional Networks

Likewise, deconvolutional neural networks (deconv-net) are extensively deployed for image denoising, feature extraction, and semantic segmentation [14].

By design, deconv-net follows the encoder-decoder architecture and they have enabled production of highly diverse set of filters beyond the edge primitives [24].

In this paper, deconv-net is used to obtain the HR image from the features extracted by the conv layers in the network for satellite imaging applications. Although it is observed that the deeper networks are proved to be beneficial, however in case of SRCNN the results have saturated at three layers even though the layers are increased. On the other hand, given their ability in efficiently reconstructing images in the decoder stage, deconv-net can incorporate both the deeper structure and learn invariant features which is expected to output better HR versions of the underlying scenes.

3   Deconv-Nets for Single-Image SR

Different stages of the proposed model include pre-processing the image, formulation of the model and training the deconv-net, as detailed in the following:

3.1   Pre-processing

We convert all images into YCbCr color space. All the three channels are upscaled by factor of 2 using bicubic interpolation and the proposed model is applied on the luminance channel following the setup of majority of the existing single-image SR models [18]. Once we obtain the resultant 'Y' channel from the model, the upscaled 'Cb' and 'Cr' are directly stacked to it to obtain the final HR image. For training, we obtain sub-images of 32×32 with a stride of 14 as proposed in [5]. This method is adopted so that we would have training images of fixed sizes for the simplicity of programming. Let us denote the luminance channel after upscaling as Y (not to be confused with 'Y') and the original image sample as X, which is the objective image to be generating by propagating Y through the network.

While deploying the proposed model, we pass the luminance channel of the image without dividing it into patches. This is done to avoid incorporating other methods to stitch the obtained results from patches to form the eventual HR image and handle cases like borders of image-patch, which might result in the poor quality of the obtained image.

3.2   Description of the Proposed Model

The proposed model uses conv layers, each followed by an activation function in order to introduce non-linearities. ReLU [13] is chosen as the activation function since it speeds up the computation and performs relatively good. The deconvolution layers are subsequently used for the reconstruction of the respective HR image. Note that pooling and un-pooling are not incorporated in order to reduce possible information loss as they would reduce the dimensions which is unsuitable for our task. Besides, in case for image SR, feature maps do not require any scale invariance which is generally required for many deep learning tasks.

The block diagram of the proposed deconv neural network based model is shown in Fig. 1. The deconv layers are exactly mirror-like reflection of the conv layers, with same number of layers as in the convolutional part and same filter sizes as that of conv layers.

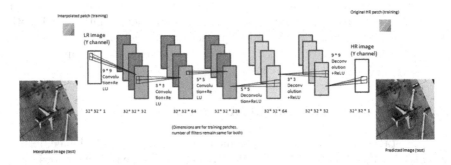

Fig. 1. An illustration of proposed model showing the different layers of the deconvolutional network for image SR.

To summarize, the proposed SR model consists of three stages:

- **Patch extraction:** The first conv layer is used for patch extraction. Larger filters are used to extract patches as well as the basic feature maps from input LR image Y.
- **Feature extraction and Mapping:** The next two conv layers are used to extract high level features and map the LR feature maps into the corresponding HR feature maps.
- **Reconstruction:** The last three deconv layers are used for the construction of the HR image from the feature maps obtained from the conv layers. We choose deconv layers with a stride of 1 over the conv layers as deconv layers are basically transposed conv layers, that work like a backward pass operation which allow reconstruction of original images from the learnt feature maps.

3.3   Training

Using the definitions mentioned in Sect. 3.1, X can be represented as a function of Y given the network parameters θ:

$$X = F(Y; \theta) \tag{2}$$

The standard mean squared error (MSE) over n LR-HR patch pairs given by Eq. 3 is used as the loss function for the proposed model.

$$MSE = \frac{1}{n}(\sum_{i=1}^{n}(F(Y_i; \theta) - X_i)^2 \tag{3}$$

For optimizing MSE, we rely on the Adam's optimizer [11]. The parameter update rule followed in this case is given by:

$$\theta_t = \theta_{t-1} - \frac{\alpha_t \cdot m_t}{(\sqrt{\nu_t} + \hat{\epsilon})} \qquad (4)$$

where m_t is the gradient of MSE with respect to θ, ν_t is the squared gradient, β_1 and β_2 are hyper parameters controlling the moving values of the gradient. On the other hand, a small constant $\hat{\epsilon}$ is used for numerical stability. α_t is the learning rate, which is tuned based on Eq. 5.

$$\alpha_t = \alpha \cdot \frac{\sqrt{1 - \beta_2^t}}{(1 - \beta_1^t)} \qquad (5)$$

3.4 Implementation Details

Given the proposed architecture, the size of filters in the conv layers are 9×9, 3×3 and 5×5 whereas the number of filters considered in each of these layers are 32, 64 and 128, respectively. Note that the number of filters are increased progressively considering that they yield more high-level features, apart from restricting much loss of image details. On the other hand, the deconv layer filters are constructed in opposite fashion compared to the conv layer filters (Fig. 1). In total, the proposed network has $451,969$ parameters. We initialize the weights of the network as per the He uniform initialization [9] as they consider the distribution of outputs after ReLU activation while deciding the variance of the uniform distribution of the weights which makes it easier to train.

We set $\beta_1 = 0.9$ and $\beta_2 = 0.999$ for the Adam's optimizer, inspired by [11]. Learning rate (α) is set to 0.001 with decay of 10^{-6}.

We also pad the output of each layer by zeros for handling the pixels that lie on border. Therefore height and width of feature maps of each layer remain identical (in our case, it is 32×32 for all layers). This is in contrast to SRCNN, which explicitly requires to strip the border pixels for preserving the resolution of the feature maps.

The output of the network is the luminance channel of obtained high resolution image. We interpolate the Cb, Cr channels of the low resolution image and stack the obtained luminance channel on top of it. We convert this resultant YCbCr image, into RGB format to get the final image.

4   Results and Experiments

4.1   Data Set

The model is deployed on the popular UC-Merced optical RS dataset [23] which is extensively used for different RS applications including classification etc. This dataset consists of 21 different scene themes. Each class has a total of 100 images of size 256×256 pixels providing us with total of 2100 images.

50 randomly selected images from each class are used for training while 10 images per class are deployed for cross-validation. The model is tested on 4 images per category. This subsequently generates a total of 205, 520 image patches for mapping the LR to HR patches.

4.2   Metrics

The goodness of the proposed SR model is tested using the standard signal to noise ratio (PSNR) as mentioned in the following:

$$PSNR = 10 \times \log_{10}(255/MSE) \qquad (6)$$

where MSE is obtained according to Eq. 3. Besides, we use the Structural Similarity (SSIM) [20] for measuring the visual similarity at the patch level (between LR and HR patches)

$$SSIM(x,y) = \frac{(2 \times \mu_x \times \mu_y + c_1)(2 \times \sigma_{xy} + c_2)}{(\mu_x + \mu_y + c_1)(\sigma_x + \sigma_y + c_2)} \qquad (7)$$

where x and y represent the LR and HR patches, μ is average value of the luminance channel, σ is standard deviation, σ_{xy} is covariance. Further, $c_1 = (0.01L)^2$, $c_2 = (0.03L)^2$ where L is the dynamic range of the pixel values: $2^{bitsperpixel} - 1$, e.g., in this case $L = 127$.

4.3   Discussions

Fixation of the Network Structure. In order to obtain the optimal architecture, we initially repeat the experiments with varied network structures (in terms of the number of deployed conv and deconv layers). Different combinations used include the 2conv-2deconv model, 3conv-3deconv model and 4conv-4deconv models where 2conv-2deconv implies a model with 2 conv layers followed by 2 deconv layers and so on. From Fig. 2, which is a plot of validation error against epochs, we conclude that 3conv-3deconv layered network performs the best and this architecture is subsequently finalized. From Fig. 3 we conclude that the 2conv-2deconv model underfits the data and fails to establish a relationship between LR and HR images effectively. Whereas, the 4conv-4deconv model's accuracy averaged on the test data is slightly worse as that of 3conv-3deconv model though it performs slightly better on some of the test images. Moreover, it is computationally slower as compared to 3conv-3deconv model as it has more trainable parameters due to addition of more layers. Therefore, the superiority of the 3conv-3deconv model can be validated over the others based on the quality of the obtained HR images in terms of the PNSR measure as well as the computational efficiency.

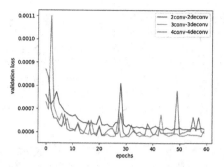

Fig. 2. Validation error versus epochs.

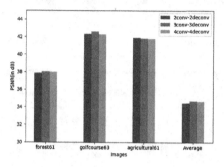

Fig. 3. Comparison of PSNR for different layers.

Empirical Study. The 3conv-3deconv model is also compared with a number of the recent state-of-the-art methods ScSR [21], SRCNN [5] and bicubic interpolation. We have retrained ScSR and SRCNN on the same data set and split as we did for our model to have a fair comparison. Figure 4 shows the HR image generated by state-of-the-art models, our proposed model and the original HR image, respectively for qualitative assessment. On the other hand, Table 1 depicts the accuracy of models based on PSNR and SSIM. From Table 1 it is clear that our proposed model outperforms than state-of-the-art methods for SR on satellite images based on both the considered metrics. Also, from Fig. 4 we can infer that our proposed model recovers more details of HR image as compared to other models.

Table 1. Comparison between Bicubic, ScSR, SRCNN and proposed model

	Bicubic		ScSR		SRCNN		Proposed model	
	PSNR	SSIM	PSNR	SSIM	PSNR	SSIM	PSNR	SSIM
airplane60	33.014	0.923	36.431	0.954	36.503	0.953	37.128	0.955
forest60	32.742	0.952	35.660	0.974	35.369	0.973	35.633	0.975
harbor60	24.044	0.900	26.223	0.940	26.351	0.939	27.652	0.957
parkinglot60	25.800	0.856	27.188	0.898	27.320	0.898	28.121	0.911
Average	31.837	0.883	33.964	0.919	34.095	0.918	34.642	0.924

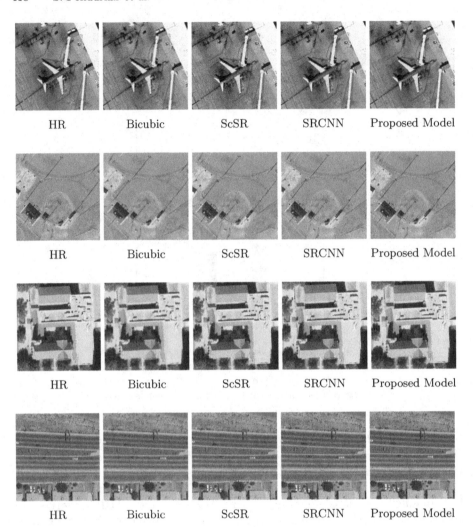

Fig. 4. Qualitative results comparing the images obtained from different algorithms.

5   Conclusions

In this paper, we present an end-to-end deep deconvolutional network based single-image SR model for optical satellite images which is trained on image patches. This is one of the preliminary study in remote sensing regarding the use of deconvolutional network for image SR. Our model produces comparable and even better performance as compared to the existing ad-hoc and deep image SR techniques. Currently, we are interested in exploring the paradigm of zero-shot SR based on deconv-net.

Acknowledgements. Biplab Banerjee was supported by Early Career Research Award from SERB India (File No: ECR/2017/000365). We gratefully acknowledge the support of Intel Corporation for giving access to the Intel®AI DevCloud platform used for this work.

References

1. Bevilacqua, M.: Algorithms for super-resolution of images and videos based on learning methods. Theses, Université Rennes 1, June 2014
2. Candès, E.: Compressive sampling. In: Proceedings of the International Congress of Mathematicians Madrid, pp. 1433–1452. European Mathematical Society Publishing House, August 2006
3. Castelluccio, M., Poggi, G., Sansone, C., Verdoliva, L.: Training convolutional neural networks for semantic classification of remote sensing imagery. In: 2017 Joint Urban Remote Sensing Event (JURSE). IEEE, March 2017
4. Clark, J., Palmer, M., Lawrence, P.: A transformation method for the reconstruction of functions from nonuniformly spaced samples. IEEE Trans. Acoust. Speech Signal Process. **33**(5), 1151–1165 (1985)
5. Dong, C., Loy, C.C., He, K., Tang, X.: Image super-resolution using deep convolutional networks. IEEE Trans. Pattern Anal. Mach. Intell. **38**(2), 295–307 (2016). https://doi.org/10.1109/tpami.2015.2439281
6. Donoho, D.: Compressed sensing. IEEE Trans. Inform. Theory **52**(4), 1289–1306 (2006). https://doi.org/10.1109/tit.2006.871582
7. Glasner, D., Bagon, S., Irani, M.: Super-resolution from a single image. In: 2009 IEEE 12th International Conference on Computer Vision, pp. 349–356, September 2009
8. Haut, J.M., Fernandez-Beltran, R., Paoletti, M.E., Plaza, J., Plaza, A., Pla, F.: A new deep generative network for unsupervised remote sensing single-image super-resolution. IEEE Trans. Geosci. Remote Sens. **56**(11), 6792–6810 (2018). https://doi.org/10.1109/TGRS.2018.2843525
9. He, K., Zhang, X., Ren, S., Sun, J.: Delving deep into rectifiers: surpassing human-level performance on ImageNet classification. In: Proceedings of the 2015 IEEE International Conference on Computer Vision (ICCV), ICCV 2015, pp. 1026–1034. IEEE Computer Society, Washington (2015). https://doi.org/10.1109/ICCV.2015.123
10. Jiang, K., Wang, Z., Yi, P., Jiang, J., Xiao, J., Yao, Y.: Deep distillation recursive network for remote sensing imagery super-resolution. Remote Sens. **10**(11), 1700 (2018). https://doi.org/10.3390/rs10111700
11. Kingma, D.P., Ba, J.: Adam: a method for stochastic optimization. CoRR abs/1412.6980 (2014)
12. Krizhevsky, A., Sutskever, I., Hinton, G.E.: ImageNet classification with deep convolutional neural networks. Commun. ACM **60**(6), 84–90 (2017)
13. Nair, V., Hinton, G.E.: Rectified linear units improve restricted Boltzmann machines. In: Proceedings of the 27th International Conference on International Conference on Machine Learning, ICML 2010, Omnipress, USA, pp. 807–814 (2010)
14. Noh, H., Hong, S., Han, B.: Learning deconvolution network for semantic segmentation. In: 2015 IEEE International Conference on Computer Vision (ICCV). IEEE, December 2015. https://doi.org/10.1109/iccv.2015.178

15. Ouyang, W., et al.: DeepID-net: deformable deep convolutional neural networks for object detection. In: 2015 IEEE Conference on Computer Vision and Pattern Recognition (CVPR). IEEE, June 2015

16. Park, S.C., Park, M.K., Kang, M.G.: Super-resolution image reconstruction: a technical overview. IEEE Signal Process. Mag. **20**(3), 21–36 (2003)

17. Shen, H., Li, P., Zhang, L., Zhao, Y.: A MAP algorithm to super-resolution image reconstruction. In: Third International Conference on Image and Graphics (ICIG), pp. 544–547. IEEE (2004). https://doi.org/10.1109/icig.2004.8

18. Timofte, R., De, V., Gool, L.V.: Anchored neighborhood regression for fast example-based super-resolution. In: 2013 IEEE International Conference on Computer Vision. IEEE, December 2013. https://doi.org/10.1109/iccv.2013.241

19. Tuna, C., Unal, G., Sertel, E.: Single-frame super resolution of remote-sensing images by convolutional neural networks. Int. J. Remote Sens. **39**(8), 2463–2479 (2018). https://doi.org/10.1080/01431161.2018.1425561

20. Wang, Z., Bovik, A., Sheikh, H., Simoncelli, E.: Image quality assessment: from error visibility to structural similarity. IEEE Trans. Image Process. **13**(4), 600–612 (2004). https://doi.org/10.1109/tip.2003.819861

21. Yang, C.-Y., Ma, C., Yang, M.-H.: Single-image super-resolution: a benchmark. In: Fleet, D., Pajdla, T., Schiele, B., Tuytelaars, T. (eds.) ECCV 2014. LNCS, vol. 8692, pp. 372–386. Springer, Cham (2014). https://doi.org/10.1007/978-3-319-10593-2_25

22. Yang, J., Wright, J., Huang, T.S., Ma, Y.: Image super-resolution via sparse representation. IEEE Trans. Image Process. **19**(11), 2861–2873 (2010)

23. Yang, Y., Newsam, S.: Bag-of-visual-words and spatial extensions for land-use classification. In: Proceedings of the 18th SIGSPATIAL International Conference on Advances in Geographic Information Systems - GIS, pp. 270–279. ACM Press (2010). https://doi.org/10.1145/1869790.1869829

24. Zeiler, M.D., Krishnan, D., Taylor, G.W., Fergus, R.: Deconvolutional networks. In: 2010 IEEE Computer Society Conference on Computer Vision and Pattern Recognition. IEEE, June 2010. https://doi.org/10.1109/cvpr.2010.5539957

25. Zhu, X.X., et al.: Deep learning in remote sensing: a comprehensive review and list of resources. IEEE Geosci. Remote Sens. Mag. **5**(4), 8–36 (2017)

Genuine Personality Recognition from Highly Constrained Face Images

Fabio Anselmi[1], Nicoletta Noceti[2(✉)], Lorenzo Rosasco[1,2], and Robert Ward[3]

[1] LCSL, Istituto Italiano di Tecnologia and Massachusetts Institute of Technology, Cambridge, USA
{fabio.anselmi,lorenzo.rosasco}@mit.edu
[2] Università degli Studi di Genova, Genoa, Italy
nicoletta.noceti@unige.it
[3] Bangor University, Bangor, UK
r.ward@bangor.ac.uk

Abstract. People are able to accurately estimate personality traits, merely on the basis of "passport"-style neutral faces and, thus, cues must exist that allow for such estimation. However, up to date, there has been little progress in identifying the form and location of these cues.

In this paper we address the problem of inferring true personality traits in highly constrained images using state of art machine learning techniques, in particular, deep networks and class activation maps analysis.

The novelty of our work consists in that, differently from the vast majority of the current and past approaches (that refer to the problem of consensus personality rating prediction) we predict the genuine personality based on highly constrained images: the target's are self ratings on a validated personality inventory and we restrict to passport-like photos, in which so-called controllable cues are minimized.

Our results show that self-reported personality traits can be accurately evaluated from facial features. A preliminar analysis on the features activation maps shows promising results for a deeper understanding on relevant facial cues for traits estimation.

Keywords: Five-Factor Model · Convolutional neural networks · Class activation maps

1 Introduction

Psychological studies of "thin slices" of behaviour investigate the accuracy of social judgements made by observers on the basis of minimal information, usually nonverbal and unintentional cues emitted by the target person being judged. For example, ratings of university lecturers, made on a basis of silent 2-s video clips, significantly correlated with the lecturers' end-of-semester student evaluations [1]. Of particular interest, observers are able to accurately estimate personality traits on the thinnest of slices, merely on the basis of "passport"-style neutral

© Springer Nature Switzerland AG 2019
E. Ricci et al. (Eds.): ICIAP 2019, LNCS 11751, pp. 421–431, 2019.
https://doi.org/10.1007/978-3-030-30642-7_38

face images [13]. "Accuracy" here refers to the agreement between self-ratings of personality, as made by the targets themselves, and the ratings of observers.

The long-term goal of our work is to gain a deeper understanding on the cues used by observers to make accurate judgements of personality from these highly constrained face images. To date, there has been little progress in identifying the form and location of these cues [21,22]. However, given that observers can make accurate judgements of true personality, these cues must exist, and recent computational advances offer promise. From a computational perspective, before understanding the *what* and *where* of these cues, we need to first assess the feasibility of the underlying task, that is, estimating true personality of people from a single highly constrained image of their face. That is our task here, where, given a set of face images annotated with personality characteristics, we employed a pre-trained model obtained with a well-known convolutional neural network, the VGG16 [16], to extract the relevant features from each image. Then, we trained a fully connected network for personality characteristics regression.

In the experiments, we considered a dataset of still images annotated with the personality scores of the observed subject. Targets were explicitly required to adopt neutral expressions, hair back, cosmetics, glasses and jewelry removed (according to e.g. [13]). The targets' genuine personalities were measured through self-rating with validated five-factor personality inventories, i.e. NEO-IPIP or mini-IPIP (see e.g. [5]).

Our work differs from previous approaches in several ways. First, we are predicting the *true* (or actual, genuine) personality of target persons. The actual personality is defined as the target's self ratings on a validated personality inventory. In contrast, the vast majority of approaches in the computing science fields refer to the problem of *apparent* (or consensus) personality rating prediction [3,7,10,12,19], as made by external observers. While the consensus rating is relatively easy to collect [2], actual personality ratings are generally more laborious and expensive to obtain.

A second aspect of diversity is that, unlike other work (see e.g. [6,18]) we are using highly constrained images, similar to passport photos, in which so-called controllable cues are minimized. Controllable cues include all that aspects of the face image which can be readily modified by the target to create different personality impressions, influencing the consensus personality rating. In this respect, our work shares similarities with [11] who looked for correlation between 3D face structure and personality. However, our stimuli are notably different in that they are 2D and include both shape and surface information.

In summary, to the best of our knowledge, this paper represents the first attempt to address inference of true personality in highly constrained images.

The remainder of the paper is organized as follow. In Sect. 2 we describe our dataset, while in Sect. 3 details on our approach for the personality scores prediction (Sect. 3.1) and on the experimental assessment (Sect. 3.2) are reported, with a preliminar analysis on class activation maps (Sect. 3.3). Sect. 4 is left to a final discussion.

Fig. 1. Average images of a few samples of female (left) and male (right) faces in the dataset.

2 The Data

In this work we employ a dataset acquired in-house consisting of 997 still images depicting the face of a target individual. People have been asked to avoid such cues one can voluntary control – as hairstyle, jewellery, facial expressions, and cosmetics – that in general may affect personality judgements. In Fig. 1 we report two average images of a few samples of female (left) and male (right) faces in the dataset[1] which includes in total 604 female and 393 male faces.

For each target a standard five-factor model [FFM] personality inventory – NEO-IPIP or mini-IPIP – has been proposed, to finally collect a six dimensional vector containing the score for each personality trait plus the information on the gender. To the authors knowledge it is the first time that a dataset with such characteristics is analyzed.

The FFM is defined in terms of five different dimensions (see [9]):

- *Extraversion* vs. *Introversion*, scoring from sociable, assertive, playful to aloof, reserved, shy.
- *Agreeableness* vs. *Disagreeable*, scoring from friendly, cooperative to antagonistic, fault-finding.
- Conscientiousness vs. *Unconscientious* scoring from self-disciplined, organised, to inefficient, careless.
- *Neuroticism* vs. *Emotional stability*, scoring from calm, unemotional to insecure, anxious.
- *Openess* vs *Closed to experience*, scoring from intellectual, insightful to shallow, unimaginative.

Before proceeding with the presentation of our methodology, it is worth discussing some of the properties of the dataset with a brief statistical analysis. A first aspect to be mentioned is the fact that although in principle the range of values that the scores can assume is (1–5) (with maximal resolution of 0.25), the actual distributions of the estimated scores are uneven (see Fig. 2(a)).

---

[1] For privacy issues we can not show the original images.

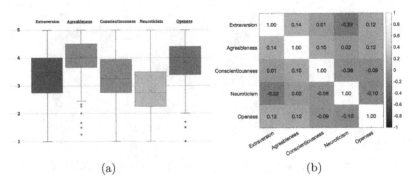

(a)   (b)

Fig. 2. Left: distribution of the FFM traits scores in the dataset. Right: correlation coefficients between the FFM traits.

A second aspect to be considered refers the presence of correlations among the different traits. We evaluated the correlation with the Spearman's Rank Coefficient and report in Fig. 2(b) the results we obtained between the scores of the whole dataset. According to the classification in [8] very weak correlation can be noticed overall among traits, with only one weak correlation between *Extraversion* and *Neuroticism* ($\rho = -0.22, P < 10^{-11}$). Notice however that the null hypothesis (i.e. there is no correlation between a specific pair of traits) can not be rejected at the significance level of 0.05 for the pairs *Extraversion-Conscientiousness* ($\rho = 0.02, P = 0.54$) and *Agreeableness-Neuroticism* ($\rho = 0.02, P = 0.53$).

As it is well known that personality traits may significantly differ in male and female populations, we verified this aspects on the dataset. Performing a statistical comparison between female and male samples using a Two-Sample TTest we assessed that the only trait presenting no significant difference in a statistical sense is *Extraversion* ($P = 0.92$), while for all the others the test reveals a strong separation between the two sample sets (in all cases $P < 10^{-4}$). A visualization of the approximated trait distributions, represented with histograms, is also reported in Fig. 3.

3   Estimating the Five-Factor Model from Images

In this section we discuss the methodology we applied to estimate the scores describing the Five-Factor Model of an individual from a single highly-constrained image of his/her face. To this purpose, we casted the estimation problem to a regression task where we want to learn the mapping between an appropriate representation of the face image and the annotated scores associated with it.

The images in the dataset presented in the previous section have been processed with a face detector [20], to precisely identify the image portion corresponding to the face, and then converted to grayscale. The resulting segmented

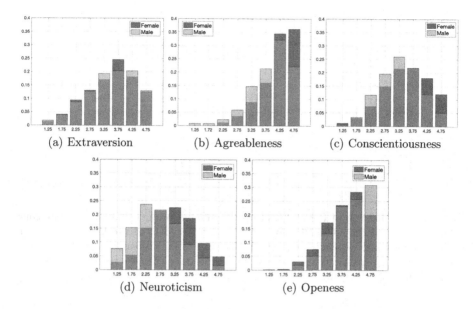

(a) Extraversion   (b) Agreableness   (c) Conscientiousness

(d) Neuroticism   (e) Openess

Fig. 3. Histograms describing the distribution of the 5 personality traits in the female and male samples.

images have finally been resized to a fixed size of 224×224 pixels. Then we extracted the relevant image features using the convolutional part of a pre-trained Neural Network [17]. Finally we used them as input to a fully connected layer to predict the Five-Factor scores for each target individual.

All the computational models are implemented using Keras and Tensor Flow [4].

3.1 Personality Traits Regression with Pretrained VGG16 Network

To extract the relevant features from each image we used the convolutional part of a pre-trained VGG16 convolutional neural network, [17] – pre-trained on the Imagenet dataset [15].

The output of this first part of the architecture is a set of feature vectors of 25088 components that we used to train a fully connected network composed of three dense layers, two of 100 units and a last one with size that depends on the specific task we solve. Indeed, we explored two main regression tasks. With the first, we trained the network to learn the mapping to each trait independently from the others. We refer to this task as "single personality trait regression", and this corresponds to using a last layer composed of a single unit (size $1 \times 1 \times 1$). The second task considers instead the possibility of exploiting possible hidden correlations among traits, by learning them as a whole with a vectorial regression model. We will refer to it as "full personality traits regression", for which the last layer is composed of 6 units (size $1 \times 1 \times 6$). A visual sketch of the deep architecture we finally adopted is reported in Fig. 4.

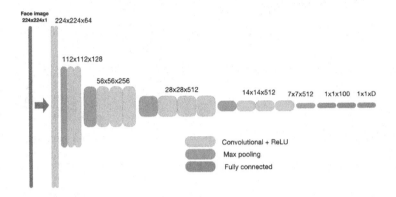

Fig. 4. A visualization of the architecture we adopted in our experiments. The convolutional part of the VGG-16 deep network is followed by dense layers, the latter having different size depending on the specific task to be addressed: $D = 1$ for single personality trait regression, while $D = 6$ for full personality traits regression (see text for details).

The training has been performed on the 80% of the data samples, while the remaining 20% has been employed for evaluation only. At each of the 100 epochs, after a random permutation of the images, the training set was further split into 70% and 30% validation set. To avoid overfitting we used a dropout regularization within the dense layers with rate 0.3. An Adam optimizer was chosen with a batch size of 400 and a learning rate of 0.001 to minimize the mean square error (MSE) loss. The full protocol was replicated 10 times to have a statistics on the MSE on the test set.

3.2 Experimental Assessment

In this section we discuss the results of the experimental analysis we carried out. In Fig. 5 we report the average Mean Square Error (MSE) obtained on the test set for 10 random data splitting, using the architecture depicted in Fig. 4. More specifically, we compare the effects of learning each trait independently from the others (Fig. 5(a)) with the use of a vectorial regression to learn all the traits as a whole (Fig. 5(b)). A first observation refers to the fact that overall the MSEs we obtained are very promising for all the traits (as a reference consider the reported MSE on sex (S) an easy individual characteristic to predict). In this evaluation we implicitly consider the fact that the annotation we use as a reference is result of a quantization from outcomes of self-reported questionnaires, influenced by the individual subjectivity and thus prone to error. The results we obtained are in line with performance reported in works sharing some contacts points with ours although grounding on different motivations (as e.g. [23]).

A visual comparison with the results obtained for the full personality traits regression task highlights uneven effects, in the sense not all the traits seem to benefit from the full vector regression. Table 1 reports in the second and third

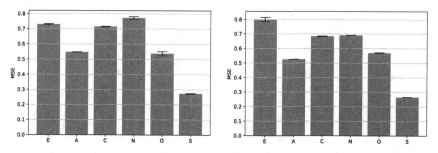

(a) Single personality traits regression and sex (S).

(b) Full vector personality traits regression and sex (S).

Fig. 5. Average mean square error on the test set using the architecture in Fig. 4 with D = 1 (left) and D = 6 (right). Error bars refer to $N = 10$ repetitions.

colums the MSE values for, respectively, single and full traits regression. For each trait, we highlighted in bold the best MSE among the two tasks.

Comparable results have been obtained with a recent kernel-based approach for large-scale datasets [14], an alternative method we used to asses the consistency of our results. The method builds on the use of Kernel Ridge Regression with a gaussian kernel on the same set of features vectors. Figure 6 reports a visual impression of the MSE obtained with the method on the same regression tasks considered above, and the average values are also reported in Table 1 (forth and fifth columns) for a comparison. The values suggest non significant statistical correlation is present among traits. It is in particular interesting to note that the gender of the target individual seems to play a minor role in the score estimate, although statistical evidences that the traits are different in female and male population have been assessed.

The overall results support our methodology and show how self-reported personality traits can be evaluated from single, strongly constrained face images. This result suggests that the features at the basis of the representation may in fact helps in understanding the cues that reveals personality traits. In the next section we thus discuss a preliminary analysis in this direction.

3.3   Activation Maps: A Preliminary Analysis

The assessment of the regression task that proves how it is possible to estimate the Five-Factor model from one single image of an individual, allows us to further investigate on the cues of the face enabling this ability. Since we use highly constrained face images, the effects of controllable cues that might influence the target personality judgment from an observer (and it is fair to assume the same for a computational model) can be neglected. We can thus assume that the visual features showing strong responses for the Five-Factors model estimation are in fact face cues inherently providing essential judgement information.

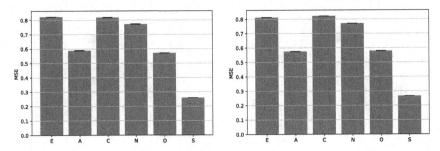

(a) Single personality traits regression and sex (S).

(b) Full vector personality traits regression and sex (S).

Fig. 6. Average mean square error on the test set using the Falkon method [14] (error bars refer to $N = 10$ repetitions).

Table 1. Average mean square errors and standard deviations obtained on the test set for the single and full traits (plus sex (S)) regression models using different approaches (see text for details).

Big5	VGG16 single	VGG16 full	Falkon single	Falkon full
E	**0.7300** ± 0.0035	0.8002 ± 0.0147	0.8377 ± 0.0011	**0.8243** ± 0.0014
A	0.5473 ± 0.009	**0.5261** ± 0.0006	0.5723 ± 0.0010	**0.5654** ± 0.0003
C	0.7145 ± 0.0028	**0.6842** ± 0.0021	**0.8086** ± 0.0002	0.8119 ± 0.0003
N	**0.7731** ± 0.0097	0.9609 ± 0.0006	**0.7529** ± 0.0013	0.7675 ± 0.0004
O	**0.5379** ± 0.0137	0.5690 ± 0.0032	0.5745 ± 0.0006	**0.5733** ± 0.0017
S	0.2719 ± 0.0030	**0.2636** ± 0.0010	**0.2619** ± 6 $\cdot 10^{-5}$	0.2658 ± 9 $\cdot 10^{-5}$

Considering the well-assessed theory about deep features visualization in classification settings [16,24], to the purpose of feature visualization we converted our task to a multi-class classification problem. This choice allowed us to use off the shelf, well tested, algorithms like gradient weighted class activation maps (CAM) for classification (not regression). To this aim we quantized the traits score range into N (in our experiments empirically set to 6) intervals and trained a single fully connected classifier on the same feature vectors dataset as for the regression task. As a consequence, the architecture in Fig. 4 has been slightly modified replacing the very last fully connected layer with a soft-max layer.

To highlight the target image parts on which the network was focusing to make its prediction we used the gradient weighted class activation map (CAM, [16]).

Figure 7 shows the average heatmaps (overlaied to the original images) we obtained for the estimation of high values of the personality scores.

The highlighted regions of maximal signal in the figure show how well defined parts of the individual target faces are selected to score the individual traits. In the case of *Openness* the averaged signal was not significant. Of particular

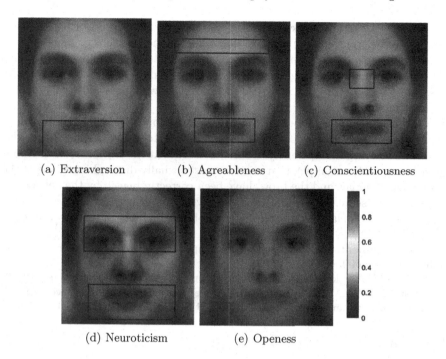

(a) Extraversion   (b) Agreableness   (c) Conscientiousness

(d) Neuroticism   (e) Openess

Fig. 7. Average of superposed heatmaps on each subject correctly predicted for the single trait class. Highlighted zones of maximal signal.

interest are the results for the *Neuroticism* trait, where the two most sexually dimorphic regions of the human face have been tagged: the jaw and the brow. Indeed, it is worth noticing that neuroticism is known to be sexually dimorphic (women higher than men, as also visible from the histograms in Fig. 7(d)), and deserves further study.

4   Discussion

Estimation of personal traits is important for designing personality-aware intelligent systems and the computational model beyond the estimation might allow to make a step towards the understanding and the characterization of the elements of faces to judge social traits. Considering that people are normally able to accurately estimate personality traits, merely on the basis of a "passport"-style neutral face, we hypothesized that cues must exist that allow for such estimation and we addressed the problem of inference of true personality.

To this aim we employed state of art machine learning techniques, in particular, deep convolutional networks and class activation maps analysis, to test our hypothesis and highlight specific face cues upon which personality traits can be inferred.

The novelty of our work consists in the fact that, differently from the vast majority of the current approaches that refer to the problem of apparent (or consensus) personality rating prediction, we predicted the genuine personality of target persons, as the target's self ratings on a validated personality inventory. Also, we focused on highly constrained images, in which so-called controllable cues are minimized.

Our results supported our methodology and hypothesis and show how self-reported personality traits can be accurately evaluated from the facial features. The class activation maps analysis further confirmed the feasibility of our approach showing, for example, that the two most sexually dimorphic regions of the human face, the jaw and the brow, have been correctly tagged by the network to infer the trait score. Our initial results are very promising and a more detailed analysis based on class activation maps will be the subject of further study.

Acknowledgement. This material is based upon work partially supported by the Italian Institute of Technology.

L. R. and F.A. acknowledges the financial support of the AFOSR projects FA9550-17-1-0390 and BAA-AFRL-AFOSR-2016-0007 (European Office of Aerospace Research and Development), and the EU H2020-MSCA-RISE project NoMADS - DLV-777826.

References

1. Ambady, N., Rosenthal, R.: Half a minute: predicting teacher evaluations from thin slices of nonverbal behavior and physical attractiveness. J. Pers. Soc. Psychol. **64**(3), 431 (1993)
2. Biel, J.I., Gatica-Perez, D.: The youtube lens: crowdsourced personality impressions and audiovisual analysis of vlogs. IEEE Trans. Multimed. **15**(1), 41–55 (2013)
3. Celli, F., Bruni, E., Lepri, B.: Automatic personality and interaction style recognition from Facebook profile pictures. In: Proceedings of the 22nd ACM International Conference on Multimedia, pp. 1101–1104. ACM (2014)
4. Chollet, F., et al.: Keras (2015). https://github.com/fchollet/keras
5. Donnellan, M.B., Oswald, F.L., Baird, B.M., Lucas, R.E.: The mini-IPIP scales: tiny-yet-effective measures of the big five factors of personality. Psychol. Assess. **18**(2), 192 (2006)
6. Ferwerda, B., Schedl, M., Tkalcic, M.: Predicting personality traits with Instagram pictures. In: Proceedings of the 3rd Workshop on Emotions and Personality in Personalized Systems 2015, pp. 7–10. ACM (2015)
7. Ferwerda, B., Schedl, M., Tkalcic, M.: Using Instagram picture features to predict users' personality. In: Tian, Q., Sebe, N., Qi, G.-J., Huet, B., Hong, R., Liu, X. (eds.) MMM 2016. LNCS, vol. 9516, pp. 850–861. Springer, Cham (2016). https://doi.org/10.1007/978-3-319-27671-7_71
8. Fowler, J., Cohen, L., Jarvis, P.: Practical Statistics for Field Biology. Wiley, Hoboken (2013)
9. Goldberg, L.R.: The structureof phenotypic personality traits. Am. Psychol. **48**, 26 (1993)
10. Guntuku, S.C., Qiu, L., Roy, S., Lin, W., Jakhetiya, V.: Do others perceive you as you want them to?: Modeling personality based on selfies. In: Proceedings of the 1st International Workshop on Affect and Sentiment in Multimedia, pp. 21–26. ACM (2015)

11. Hu, S., et al.: Signatures of personality on dense 3D facial images. Nat. Rep. **7**, 73 (2017)
12. Junior, J., et al.: First impressions: a survey on computer vision-based apparent personality trait analysis. arXiv preprint arXiv:1804.08046 (2018)
13. Kramer, R.S., Ward, R.: Internal facial features are signals of personality and health. Q. J. Exp. Psychol. **63**(11), 2273–2287 (2010)
14. Rudi, A., Carratino, L., Rosasco, L.: Falkon: an optimal large scale kernel method. In: Advances in Neural Information Processing Systems, vol. 30, pp. 3888–3898. Curran Associates, Inc. (2017)
15. Russakovsky, O., et al.: Imagenet large scale visual recognition challenge. Int. J. Comput. Vis. **115**, 211–252 (2015)
16. Selvaraju, R.R., Cogswell, M., Das, A., Vedantam, R., Parikh, D., Batra, D.: Grad-CAM: visual explanations from deep networks via gradient-based localization. In: 2017 IEEE International Conference on Computer Vision (ICCV), pp. 618–626 (2017)
17. Simonyan, K., Zisserman, A.: Very deep convolutional networks for large-scale image recognition. CoRR abs/1409.1556 (2014). http://arxiv.org/abs/1409.1556
18. Sutherland, C.A., et al.: Personality judgments from everyday images of faces. Front. Psychol. **6**, 1616 (2015)
19. Vinciarelli, A., Mohammadi, G.: A survey of personality computing. IEEE Trans. Affect. Comput. **5**(3), 273–291 (2014)
20. Viola, P., Jones, M.J.: Robust real-time face detection. Int. J. Comput. Vis. **57**(2), 137–154 (2004)
21. Ward, R., Scott, N.J.: Cues to mental health from men's facial appearance. J. Res. Pers. **75**, 26–36 (2018)
22. Ward, R., Sreenivas, S., Read, J., Saunders, K.E., Rogers, R.D.: The role of serotonin in personality inference: tryptophan depletion impairs the identification of neuroticism in the face. Psychopharmacology **234**(14), 2139–2147 (2017)
23. Zhang, C.-L., Zhang, H., Wei, X.-S., Wu, J.: Deep bimodal regression for apparent personality analysis. In: Hua, G., Jégou, H. (eds.) ECCV 2016. LNCS, vol. 9915, pp. 311–324. Springer, Cham (2016). https://doi.org/10.1007/978-3-319-49409-8_25
24. Zhou, B., Khosla, A., Lapedriza, A., Oliva, A., Torralba, A.: Learning deep features for discriminative localization. In: Proceedings of the IEEE Conference on Computer Vision and Pattern Recognition, pp. 2921–2929 (2016)

Evaluation of Continuous Image Features Learned by ODE Nets

Fabio Carrara$^{(\boxtimes)}$ ⬤, Giuseppe Amato ⬤, Fabrizio Falchi ⬤,
and Claudio Gennaro ⬤

Institute of Information Science and Technologies (ISTI),
Italian National Research Council (CNR), Via G. Moruzzi 1, 56124 Pisa, Italy
{fabio.carrara,giuseppe.amato,fabrizio.falchi,
claudio.gennaro}@isti.cnr.it

Abstract. Deep-learning approaches in data-driven modeling relies on learning a finite number of transformations (and representations) of the data that are structured in a hierarchy and are often instantiated as deep neural networks (and their internal activations). State-of-the-art models for visual data usually implement deep residual learning: the network learns to predict a finite number of discrete updates that are applied to the internal network state to enrich it. Pushing the residual learning idea to the limit, ODE Net—a novel network formulation involving continuously evolving internal representations that gained the best paper award at NeurIPS 2018—has been recently proposed. Differently from traditional neural networks, in this model the dynamics of the internal states are defined by an ordinary differential equation with learnable parameters that defines a continuous transformation of the input representation. These representations can be computed using standard ODE solvers, and their dynamics can be steered to learn the input-output mapping by adjusting the ODE parameters via standard gradient-based optimization. In this work, we investigate the image representation learned in the continuous hidden states of ODE Nets. In particular, we train image classifiers including ODE-defined continuous layers and perform preliminary experiments to assess the quality, in terms of transferability and generality, of the learned image representations and compare them to standard representation extracted from residual networks. Experiments on CIFAR-10 and Tiny-ImageNet-200 datasets show that representations extracted from ODE Nets are more transferable and suggest an improved robustness to overfit.

Keywords: Transfer learning · Image representations ·
Continuous neural networks · Ordinary differential equations

This work was partially supported by "Automatic Data and documents Analysis to enhance human-based processes" (ADA), CUP CIPE D55F17000290009, and by the AI4EU project, funded by the EC (H2020 - Contract n. 825619). We gratefully acknowledge the support of NVIDIA Corporation with the donation of a Tesla K40 GPU used for this research.

E. Ricci et al. (Eds.): ICIAP 2019, LNCS 11751, pp. 432–442, 2019.
https://doi.org/10.1007/978-3-030-30642-7_39

1   Introduction

The last decade witnessed the renaissance of neural networks and deep differentiable models for multi-level representation learning known as Deep Learning, that highly improved Artificial Intelligence (AI) and Machine Perception with a special emphasis on Computer Vision. The AI renaissance started in 2012 when a deep neural network, built by Hinton's team, won the ImageNet Large Scale Visual Recognition Challenge [18], and from that, the astonishing results obtained by deep-learning approaches for data-driven modeling produced an exponential-growing research activity on this field. Deep Learning methods have been, and still are, the driving force behind this renaissance, and impressive results have been obtained through the adoption of deep learning in tasks such as image classification [14,18], object detection [26,27], cross-media retrieval [6], image sentiment analysis [31], recognition [1], etc. Being a representation learning approach, the rationale behind deep-learning methods is to automatically discover a set of multi-level representations from raw data that are specialized for the specific task to be solved, such as object detection or classification [19]. Starting from raw data, each level of representation captures features of the input at increasing level of abstraction that are useful for building successive representations. Following this definition, we understand how relevant representations learned in intermediate layers of deep learning architectures are. In the context of visual data modeling, the architectures of models, mostly based on convolutional neural networks, rapidly evolved from simple feed-forward networks to very deep models with complex interactions between intermediate representations, such as residual [15] or densely connected networks [16].

Recently, in the NeurIPS 2018 best paper [9], Chen et al. proposed *ODE Nets*—a novel model formulation with continuous intermediate representations defined by parametric ordinary differential equations (ODEs). This models can be used as a generic building block for neural modeling: the evolution of the activations and the gradients with respect to parameters can be computed calling a generic ODE solver. This formulation provides several benefits, including natural continuous-time modeling, $O(1)$-memory cost, adaptive computation, and tunable trade-off between speed and accuracy at inference time. The authors demonstrated ODE blocks in image classifiers trained on the MNIST dataset, actually creating a continuous and evolving activation space of image representations.

In this work, we analyze the continuous feature hierarchy created by ODE Nets when classifying natural images in terms of generality and transferability, and we compare them to representations extracted with standard neural networks. We investigate multiple architectures in which a different amount of processing is delegated to ODE blocks: we analyze standard residual networks, mixed residual-ODE networks, and finally we also consider ODE-only architectures. Preliminary experiments on CIFAR-10 and Tiny-ImageNet-200 datasets show promising results for continuous representations extracted by ODE Nets outperforming similar-sized standard residual networks on a transfer learning benchmark.

2   Related Work

Neural Image Representations. Ever since the recent breakthroughs in the deep learning field, extracting image representations from deep models, specially convolutional neural networks, has led to unprecedented accuracy in many vision tasks. Early studies explored features extracted from generic object classifiers trained on ImageNet: activations of late fully-connected layers played the role of global descriptors and provided a strong baseline as robust image representations [5,29]. With the definition of more complex networks, the attention shifted to feature maps obtained from convolutional layers. Effective representations can be extracted from convolutional feature maps via spatial max-pooling [3,25,30] or sum-pooling [4,17], or more complex aggregation methods [2,21,24]. Better representation can be obtained by fine-tuning the pretrained networks to the retrieval task via siamese [23] or triplet [2,12] learning approaches. To the best of our knowledge, we are the first to investigate ODE-derived continuous image representations.

ODE-inspired Neural Architectures. Most of current state-of-the art models implements some sort of residual learning [14,15], in which each layer or block computes an update to be added to its input to obtain its output instead of directly predict it. Recently, several works showed a strong parallelism between residual networks and discretized ODE solutions, specifically demonstrating that residual networks can be seen as the discretization of the Euler solution [22,33]. This interpretation sprouted novel residual networks architectures inspired by advanced discretizations of differential equations. [22] and [35] derived residual architectures justified by approximating respectively the Linear Multi-step and Runge–Kutta methods. Comparisons with dynamical systems inspired works on reversibility and stability of residual networks [7,8,13,28]. [9] propose to directly adopt ODE solvers to implement continuous dynamics inside neural networks. Traditional variable-step ODE solvers enable sample-wise adaptive computations in a natural way, while previously proposed methods for adaptive computation on classical networks [8,32] require additional parameters to be trained.

3   ODE Nets

In this section, we review the main concepts about ODE Nets, including their formulation and training approach. For a full detailed description, see [9].

An ODE Net is a neural network that include one or more blocks whose internal states are defined by a parametric ordinary differential equation (ODE). Let $\mathbf{z}(t)$ the vector of activations at a specific time t of its evolution. We define its dynamics by a first-order ODE parametrized by θ

$$\frac{\mathrm{d}\mathbf{z}(t)}{\mathrm{d}t} = f(\mathbf{z}(t), t, \theta).$$

(1)

Given the initial value of the state $\mathbf{z}(t_0)$—the input of the ODE block—we can compute the value of the state at a future time $\mathbf{z}(t_1)$—that we consider the output of the ODE block—via integration of Eq. 1

$$\mathbf{z}(t_1) = \mathbf{z}(t_0) + \int_{t_0}^{t_1} \frac{\mathrm{d}\mathbf{z}(t)}{\mathrm{d}t} \mathrm{d}t = \mathbf{z}(t_0) + \int_{t_0}^{t_1} f(\mathbf{z}(t), t, \theta) \mathrm{d}t . \tag{2}$$

This computation can be efficiently performed by modern ODE solvers, such as the ones belonging to the Runge-Kutta family. Thus, the forward pass of an ODE block is implemented as a call to a generic ODE solver

$$\mathbf{z}(t_1) = \mathrm{ODESolver}(f, \mathbf{z}(t_0), t_0, t_1, \theta) , \tag{3}$$

where f can be an arbitrary function parametrized by θ which is implemented as a standard neural network.

In order to be able to train ODE Nets, we need to adjust the parameters θ in order to implement the correct dynamics of the continuous internal state for our specific task. Thus, given a loss function $\mathcal{L}$, we need to compute its gradient with respect to parameters $\mathrm{d}\mathcal{L}/\mathrm{d}\theta$ to perform a gradient descent step. Although we can keep track of all the internal operations of the specific ODE solver used and use backpropagation, this leads to a huge memory overhead, specially when the dynamics of the internal state are complex, and the ODE solver requires many steps to find the solution. Instead, Chen et al. [9] proposed to adopt the *adjoint sensitivity method*. The adjoint state $\mathbf{a}(t)$ is defined as the derivative of the loss with respect to the internal state $\mathbf{z}(t)$

$$\mathbf{a}(t) = \frac{\partial \mathcal{L}}{\partial \mathbf{z}(t)}, \tag{4}$$

and its dynamics can be described by the following ODE

$$\frac{\mathrm{d}\mathbf{a}(t)}{\mathrm{d}t} = -\mathbf{a}(t) \frac{\partial f(\mathbf{z}(t), t, \theta)}{\partial \mathbf{z}(t)} . \tag{5}$$

The quantity we are interest in—the derivative of the loss with respect to parameters $\mathrm{d}\mathcal{L}/\mathrm{d}\theta$—can be expressed in function of the adjoint $\mathbf{a}(t)$

$$\frac{\mathrm{d}\mathcal{L}}{\mathrm{d}\theta} = \int_{t_0}^{t_1} \mathbf{a}(t) \frac{\partial f(\mathbf{z}(t), t, \theta)}{\partial \theta} \mathrm{d}t, \tag{6}$$

where $\partial f(\mathbf{z}(t), t, \theta)/\partial \theta$ is known and defined by the structure of f. To compute $\mathbf{a}(t)$ and thus $\mathrm{d}\mathcal{L}/\mathrm{d}\theta$, we need to know the entire trajectory of $\mathbf{z}(t)$, but this can be recovered starting from the last state $\mathbf{z}(t_1)$ and by solving its ODE (Eq. 1) backward in time. With a clever formulation, Chen et al. [9] also showed that it is possible to combine the process for finding $\mathbf{z}(t)$, $\mathbf{a}(t)$, and $\mathrm{d}\mathcal{L}/\mathrm{d}\theta$ in a unique additional call to the ODE solver.

Among the properties of ODE Nets, noteworthy benefits are (a) *O(1)-memory cost*, since no intermediate activations are needed to be stored for both forward and backward operations, (b) *adaptive computation*, as modern adaptive ODE solvers automatically adjust the step size required to find the solution depending on the complexity of the dynamics induced by a specific input, (c) *inference-time speed-accuracy trade-off tuning*, as the tolerance of adaptive solvers can be lowered at inference time to obtain less accurate solutions faster or viceversa.

4   Tested Architectures

In this section, we describe the architectures of the image classifiers implemented with ODE Nets that we are going to analyze. We test three architectures in total. The first two are the ones defined by Chen et al. [9], i.e. a standard residual network with 8 residual blocks, and a mixed architecture with two residual blocks and an ODE block. In addition, we analyze an architecture defined by the minimum amount of standard layers, that is thus composed by a single convolutional layer and an ODE block. A detailed description of the architectures follows.

Residual Net. We choose a standard residual network (ResNet) as a baseline image classifier with the same architecture chosen by Chen et al. [9]. Starting from the input, the ResNet is composed by two residual blocks each with a downsample factor of 2, and then by six additional residual blocks. The output of the last residual block is average-pooled and followed by a fully-connected layer with softmax activation that produces the final classification. The formulation of the residual block is the standard one proposed in [15], but the batch normalization operation is replaced with group normalization [34]. Thus, the structure of the residual block is composed by two 3 × 3 256-filters convolutions preceded by a 32-group normalization and ReLU activation, and a last group normalization: GroupNorm-ReLU-Conv-GroupNorm-ReLU-Conv-GroupNorm. For the first two blocks, we used 64-filters convolutions, and we employ 1 × 1 convolutions with stride 2 in the shortcut connections to downsample its input.

Res-ODE Net. The first ODE-defined architecture tested is the one proposed by Chen et al. [9]. They proposed to keep the first part of the architecture as the previously described ResNet and substitute the last six residual blocks by an ODE block that evolves a continuous state $\mathbf{z}(t)$ in a normalized time interval $[0, 1]$. The ODE function f defining its dynamics is implemented using the same network used in the residual blocks. In addition, this module takes the value of the current time t as input to convolutional layers as a constant feature maps concatenated to the other input maps. Similarly to ResNets, the output of the ODE block $\mathbf{z}(1)$ is average-pooled and fed to a fully-connected layer with softmax activation.

ODE-only Net. To fully exploit the ODE block and analyze its internal evolution, we explore an additional architecture only composed by a single convolutional layer and an ODE block. The convolutional layer has 256 4 × 4 filters slided with stride 2 which is not followed by any non-linear activation. The ODE block, defined as in the Res-ODE architecture, takes the output of the convolution as the initial state of the ODE block $z(0)$. As in the other architectures, the final state $z(1)$ is taken as output and fed to the classification layer.

5   Experimental Evaluation

Following [29], we evaluate the effectiveness and generality of learned image representation by measuring its effectiveness in a transfer learning scenario [11]. We learn features extractors for a particular image classification task (source), and we evaluate them by using the learned representations as high-level features for another image classification task with similar domain (target).

For our investigation, we used two low-resolution datasets, that is CIFAR-10 for the source task, and Tiny-ImageNet-200 for the target task. CIFAR-10 [20] is a small-resolution 10-class image classification datasets with 50k training images and 10k test images. Tiny-ImageNet-200[1] is a 200-class classification dataset with 64×64 images extracted from the famous ImageNet subset used for the ILSVRC challenge. Each class has 500 training images, 50 validation images, and 50 test images, for a total of 100k, 10k, and 10k images respectively for training, validation, and test sets.

We train all the models (Residual Net, Res-ODE Net, ODE-only Net) for 200 epochs on the CIFAR-10 dataset, adopting the SGD optimizer with momentum of 0.9, a batch size of 128, a learning rate of 0.1 decreased by a factor 10 when the loss plateaus, and a L2 weight decay of 10^{-4}. We employ commonly used data augmentation techniques for CIFAR-10, that is random cropping, color jittering, and horizontal flipping, and we apply dropout with a .5 drop probability on the layer preceeding the classifier. As ODE solver in ODE Nets, we employ a GPU implementation[2] of the adaptive-step fourth order Runge-Kutta method [10], that performs six function evaluation per step plus the initial and final timestep evalution, i.e. number of function evaluation $= 6 \times$ steps $+ 2$.

Table 1 reports for each model the best test classification error obtained and the complexity in both terms of number of parameters and ODE solver steps. The introduction of ODE blocks in the image classification pipeline drastically reduces the number of parameters of the model but also introduced a slight performance degradation of the overall classification performance. Also note that for ODE Nets, the number of steps required by the ODE solver to compute a forward pass of the network depends on the complexity of the dynamics of internal state induced by a specific input. For Res-ODE models, the ODE solver requires 3 to 4 steps to process an image, indicating that the learned dynamics of hidden state are quite simple, and most of the information extraction process is due to preceding standard layers. On the other hand, in ODE-only networks the ODE block is responsible to model the entire feature extraction process and

---

[1] https://tiny-imagenet.herokuapp.com/.
[2] https://github.com/rtqichen/torchdiffeq.

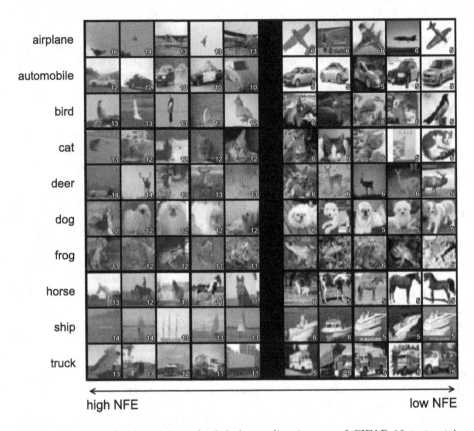

Fig. 1. The most (left) and least (right) demanding images of CIFAR-10 test set in terms of the number of solver steps required by the ODE solver (that is reported near each image).

Table 1. Classification performance on CIFAR-10.

	Test error	Params	Solver steps
Residual Net	7.28%	7.92M	-
Res-ODE Net	7.80%	2.02M	3.8 ± 0.4
ODE-only Net	9.17%	1.20M	7.8 ± 1.5

thus requires to learn more complex dynamics of the hidden state; as a consequence, the mean number of solver step required is higher, but it is more variable depending on the input image. Figure 1 show the top-5 and bottom-5 images of the CIFAR-10 test set in terms of number of solver steps required to make a prediction; we can notice that the more prototypical and easily recognizable images require fewer steps, while additional processing is adaptively employed by the ODE solver when more challenging images are presented.

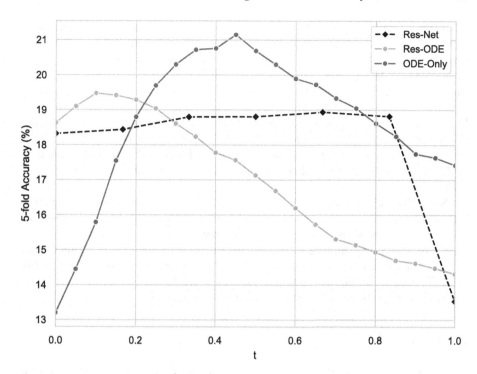

Fig. 2. Accuracy (%) on the Tiny-ImageNet-200 validation set of a linear SVM trained on $\mathbf{z}(t)$. Results obtained using the 7 intermediate layers of the Residual Net are evenly placed between 0 and 1 on the x-axis.

We extract intermediate activations from all the trained models as image representations for the target task (Tiny-ImageNet-200). For Residual Nets, we test the output of the last 7 residual modules before the classifier. For both ODE Nets, there are an infinite amount of intermediate states $\mathbf{z}(t), t \in [0,1]$ that we can extract; we sample $z(t)$ between 0 and 1 with a sample rate of 0.05 and test every sample as image representation for the target task. For all the extracted representations, we apply global average pooling to obtain a spatial-agnostic feature vector.

We train a linear SVM classifier that rely on the extracted features on the validation set of Tiny-ImageNet-200 (for which labels are provided): we perform a grid search of the penalty parameter $C \in \{0.01, 0.1, 1, 10, 100\}$, keeping track of the configuration that obtained the best 5-fold cross-validated accuracy. We then retrain this configuration on the whole set and report its accuracy. In Fig. 2, we report the accuracies obtained by all the SVMs trained on different internal activations of all the tested models. The x-axis indicate the time stamp t used to extract the internal representation of ODE Nets $\mathbf{z}(t)$, while the y-axis indicate the obtained accuracy. For convenience, we place the 7 points obtained from the 7 intermediate layers of the Residual Net evenly spaced in the x-axis between 0 and 1.

In both ODE Nets, we observe a concave trend of the accuracy when using later activations, with a maximum accuracy obtained using intermediate features extracted from the early or mid evolution of the continuous hidden states ($\sim$21% at t = .45 for ODE-only and $\sim$19.5% at t = .1 for Res-ODE). As already suggested by findings in other works [3,5], mid-features seem to be more transferable. Mid-features in Res-ODE are already extracted by preceding standard layers, thus they occur early in the evolution of the continuous hidden state. ODE Nets provide a more general and transferable image representation with respect to Residual Nets that instead provide a lower and practically constant performance on the target task, suggesting a higher degree of overfit to the source task.

Notwithstanding that, the CIFAR-10 dataset is not able to provide enough information about all the classes of the target dataset to obtain competitive accuracies, and a larger and more complex dataset should be used as a source task. Unfortunately, training ODE Nets has currently a high computational cost, as also suggested by the evaluation of their proposers that was limited to the MNIST dataset for image classification. This limits our ability to perform a larger-scale experimentation, that are left for future work.

6   Conclusions

In this paper, we investigated the representations learned by ODE Nets, a promising and potentially revolutionary deep-learning approach in which hidden states are defined by an ordinary differential equation with learnable parameters. We conducted our experiments in a transfer learning scenario: we trained three deep-learning architectures (ODE-only Net, Res-ODE Net and Residual Net) on a particular image classification task (CIFAR-10), and we evaluate them by using the learned representations as high-level features for another image classification task (Tiny-ImageNet-200). The results show that ODE Nets provide a more transferable, and thus more general, image representation with respect to standard residual networks. Considering also other intrinsic advantages of ODE Nets, such as O(1)-memory cost, and adaptive and adjustable inference-time computational cost, this preliminary analysis justifies and encourages additional research on the optimization of this kind of networks and its adoption in image representation learning.

References

1. Amato, G., Falchi, F., Vadicamo, L.: Visual recognition of ancient inscriptions using convolutional neural network and fisher vector. J. Comput. Cult. Heritage (JOCCH) **9**(4), 21 (2016)
2. Arandjelovic, R., Gronat, P., Torii, A., Pajdla, T., Sivic, J.: NetVLAD: CNN architecture for weakly supervised place recognition. In: Proceedings of the IEEE Conference on Computer Vision and Pattern Recognition, pp. 5297–5307 (2016)

3. Azizpour, H., Sharif Razavian, A., Sullivan, J., Maki, A., Carlsson, S.: From generic to specific deep representations for visual recognition. In: Proceedings of the IEEE Conference on Computer Vision and Pattern Recognition Workshops, pp. 36–45 (2015)
4. Babenko, A., Lempitsky, V.: Aggregating local deep features for image retrieval. In: Proceedings of the IEEE International Conference on Computer Vision, pp. 1269–1277 (2015)
5. Babenko, A., Slesarev, A., Chigorin, A., Lempitsky, V.: Neural codes for image retrieval. In: Fleet, D., Pajdla, T., Schiele, B., Tuytelaars, T. (eds.) ECCV 2014. LNCS, vol. 8689, pp. 584–599. Springer, Cham (2014). https://doi.org/10.1007/978-3-319-10590-1_38
6. Carrara, F., Esuli, A., Fagni, T., Falchi, F., Moreo Fernández, A.: Picture it in your mind: generating high level visual representations from textual descriptions. Inform. Retrieval J. **21**(2), 208–229 (2018). https://doi.org/10.1007/s10791-017-9318-6
7. Chang, B., Meng, L., Haber, E., Ruthotto, L., Begert, D., Holtham, E.: Reversible architectures for arbitrarily deep residual neural networks. In: Thirty-Second AAAI Conference on Artificial Intelligence (2018)
8. Chang, B., Meng, L., Haber, E., Tung, F., Begert, D.: Multi-level residual networks from dynamical systems view. In: International Conference on Learning Representations (2018). https://openreview.net/forum?id=SyJS-OgR-
9. Chen, T.Q., Rubanova, Y., Bettencourt, J., Duvenaud, D.K.: Neural ordinary differential equations. In: Advances in Neural Information Processing Systems, pp. 6572–6583 (2018)
10. Dormand, J.R., Prince, P.J.: A family of embedded Runge-Kutta formulae. J. Comput. Appl. Math. **6**(1), 19–26 (1980)
11. Goodfellow, I., Bengio, Y., Courville, A.: Deep Learning. MIT Press, Cambridge (2016)
12. Gordo, A., Almazan, J., Revaud, J., Larlus, D.: End-to-end learning of deep visual representations for image retrieval. Int. J. Comput. Vis. **124**(2), 237–254 (2017)
13. Haber, E., Ruthotto, L.: Stable architectures for deep neural networks. Inverse Probl. **34**(1), 014004 (2017)
14. He, K., Zhang, X., Ren, S., Sun, J.: Deep residual learning for image recognition. In: Proceedings of the IEEE Conference on Computer Vision and Pattern Recognition, pp. 770–778 (2016)
15. He, K., Zhang, X., Ren, S., Sun, J.: Identity mappings in deep residual networks. In: Leibe, B., Matas, J., Sebe, N., Welling, M. (eds.) ECCV 2016. LNCS, vol. 9908, pp. 630–645. Springer, Cham (2016). https://doi.org/10.1007/978-3-319-46493-0_38
16. Huang, G., Liu, Z., Van Der Maaten, L., Weinberger, K.Q.: Densely connected convolutional networks. In: Proceedings of the IEEE Conference on Computer Vision and Pattern Recognition, pp. 4700–4708 (2017)
17. Kalantidis, Y., Mellina, C., Osindero, S.: Cross-dimensional weighting for aggregated deep convolutional features. In: Hua, G., Jégou, H. (eds.) ECCV 2016. LNCS, vol. 9913, pp. 685–701. Springer, Cham (2016). https://doi.org/10.1007/978-3-319-46604-0_48
18. Krizhevsky, A., Sutskever, I., Hinton, G.E.: ImageNet classification with deep convolutional neural networks. In: Advances in Neural Information Processing Systems, pp. 1097–1105 (2012)
19. LeCun, Y., Bengio, Y., Hinton, G.: Deep learning. Nature **521**(7553), 436 (2015)
20. LeCun, Y., Bottou, L., Bengio, Y., Haffner, P., et al.: Gradient-based learning applied to document recognition. Proc. IEEE **86**(11), 2278–2324 (1998)

21. Li, Y., Xu, Y., Wang, J., Miao, Z., Zhang, Y.: MS-RMAC: multiscale regional maximum activation of convolutions for image retrieval. IEEE Signal Process. Lett. **24**(5), 609–613 (2017)

22. Lu, Y., Zhong, A., Li, Q., Dong, B.: Beyond finite layer neural networks: Bridging deep architectures and numerical differential equations. arXiv preprint arXiv:1710.10121 (2017)

23. Radenović, F., Tolias, G., Chum, O.: CNN image retrieval learns from BoW: unsupervised fine-tuning with hard examples. In: Leibe, B., Matas, J., Sebe, N., Welling, M. (eds.) ECCV 2016. LNCS, vol. 9905, pp. 3–20. Springer, Cham (2016). https://doi.org/10.1007/978-3-319-46448-0_1

24. Radenović, F., Tolias, G., Chum, O.: Fine-tuning cnn image retrieval with no human annotation. IEEE Trans. Pattern Anal. Mach. Intell. **41**, 1655–1668 (2018)

25. Razavian, A.S., Sullivan, J., Carlsson, S., Maki, A.: Visual instance retrieval with deep convolutional networks. ITE Trans. Media Technol. Appl. **4**(3), 251–258 (2016)

26. Redmon, J., Divvala, S., Girshick, R., Farhadi, A.: You only look once: unified, real-time object detection. In: Proceedings of the IEEE Conference on Computer Vision And Pattern Recognition, pp. 779–788 (2016)

27. Ren, S., He, K., Girshick, R., Sun, J.: Faster R-CNN: towards real-time object detection with region proposal networks. In: Advances in Neural Information Processing Systems, pp. 91–99 (2015)

28. Ruthotto, L., Haber, E.: Deep neural networks motivated by partial differential equations. arXiv preprint arXiv:1804.04272 (2018)

29. Sharif Razavian, A., Azizpour, H., Sullivan, J., Carlsson, S.: CNN features off-the-shelf: an astounding baseline for recognition. In: Proceedings of the IEEE Conference on Computer Vision and Pattern Recognition Workshops, pp. 806–813 (2014)

30. Tolias, G., Sicre, R., Jégou, H.: Particular object retrieval with integral max-pooling of CNN activations. arXiv preprint arXiv:1511.05879 (2015)

31. Vadicamo, L., et al.: Cross-media learning for image sentiment analysis in the wild. In: 2017 IEEE International Conference on Computer Vision Workshops (ICCVW), pp. 308–317 (Oct 2017). https://doi.org/10.1109/ICCVW.2017.45

32. Veit, A., Belongie, S.: Convolutional networks with adaptive inference graphs. In: Proceedings of the European Conference on Computer Vision (ECCV), pp. 3–18 (2018)

33. Weinan, E.: A proposal on machine learning via dynamical systems. Commun. Math. Stat. **5**(1), 1–11 (2017)

34. Wu, Y., He, K.: Group normalization. In: Proceedings of the European Conference on Computer Vision (ECCV), pp. 3–19 (2018)

35. Zhu, M., Chang, B., Fu, C.: Convolutional neural networks combined with Runge-Kutta methods. arXiv preprint arXiv:1802.08831 (2018)

An UAV Autonomous Warehouse Inventorying by Deep Learning

Antonio De Falco, Fabio Narducci$^{(\boxtimes)}$ (ID), and Alfredo Petrosino (ID)

Department of Science and Technology, University of Naples Parthenope,
Naples, Italy
antonio.defalco2@studenti.uniparthenope.it,
{fabio.narducci,alfredo.petrosino}@uniparthenope.it

Abstract. The use of aerial vehicles for warehouse autonomous inventorying has gained increasingly popularity over recent years. In this work, an approach built around the usage of unmanned aerial vehicles for warehouse scanning and Region-based Convolutional Neural Network (R-CNN) for autonomous inventorying activities is proposed. The experimental results obtained on video acquisitions of a real warehouse environment demonstrated the feasibility of the proposed solution and the possible margins of improvement.

Keywords: Advanced logistics · Autonomous warehouse inventory · Autonomous aerial vehicles · Tags detection and tracking · Faster R-CNN

1 Introduction

The paradigm of Industry 4.0 is prominently changing the warehousing activities as well as the logistics procedures for medium and big vendors. The use of autonomous mobile robots for transportation and delivery [4] or the use of aerial vehicles for autonomous warehouse inventory [13,18] has gained increasingly popularity over recent years. The advances in technology together with the evolution of machine learning and deep learning in computer vision is demonstrating such a field of research being feasible and fruitful. The explosion of e-commerce made the warehouse management a very critical task. Signalling logistics intervention on time and thus avoiding waste of time or inefficiency in delivery of goods becomes the priority of every vendors wants to enter in the electronic markets.

In this work, an autonomous warehousing inventory approach is proposed, which exploits unmanned aerial vehicles thought to perform a continuous check of packages in stocks. The proposed solution is meant to be computationally efficient as well as providing a level of accuracy compliant with an effective warehouse management. It uses light Convolutional Neural Network (CNN) models to detect and recognise on real-time the labels of packages during an aerial scanning of the environment. The aerial vehicle, with onboard environment sensing

© Springer Nature Switzerland AG 2019
E. Ricci et al. (Eds.): ICIAP 2019, LNCS 11751, pp. 443–453, 2019.
https://doi.org/10.1007/978-3-030-30642-7_40

consisting in four common RGB cameras and sufficient computational power, is able to autonomously inspect the warehouse environments and perform the computer vision tasks to track the labels/barcodes of the packages. The experimental results obtained on video acquisitions of a real warehouse environment demonstrated the feasibility of the proposed solution and its reliable usage for the autonomous logistics intervention. It is worth notifying that the proposed approach does not aim to also perform the recognition of text or codes in the packaging labels since well established and reliable procedures are available for that task.

After discussing the related work in the next section, Sect. 3 details the proposed solution and the neural network models used, while Sect. 4 presents the experimental results achieved on a real warehouse scenario. Section 5 draws the conclusion and the future directions of this works. Figure 1 shows example of acquisitions carried out in real warehouse environments and highlights what the proposed solution is meant to recognise as tags and what may represent false positives.

Fig. 1. Frames extracted from video acquisitions of a aerial vehicle during flight. The pictures is an example of a case study of tag detection/recognition in warehouse inventorying. The yellow bounding boxes highlight the real tags while in red ones all other possible false positive labels. (Color figure online)

2   Related Work

Micro aerial vehicles (MAVs) are recently gaining a lot of consideration, both in research and in commercial applications,e.g., surveillance and tracking, aerial photography, inspection, rescue missions and so on [3]. Although the wide range of sensors nowadays available, aerial vehicles (also often referred as *drones*) are still thought to keep significant advantage from the usage of cameras for the tasks of autonomous driving and obstacles avoidance [6,21]. We recently passed from drone models equipping a monocular camera vision system [5] to stereovision cameras [17,20] combined with tiny laser scanners [11,12] that enables a rich acquisition of the scene and its 3D reconstruction. Fossel et al. [7] combined Hector SLAM [14] and OctoMap [10] to build an accurate three-dimensional occupancy model of the environment and thus demonstrating the high efficacy of obstacle avoidance solutions. The works above mentioned, together with the vast literature on autonomous drones, demonstrate the high reliability of indoor autonomous driving of aerial vehicles, which is considered established in this work and not further explored. Rather, the solution discussed in this paper focuses the attention of the task of inventorying the packs in the stock by a real-time localisation and recognition of the packs and the pallets by computer vision techniques. When dealing with warehousing activities, the use of wood pallets for packs transportation and logistics is still considered of utmost importance. The work by Mohamed et al. [16] has proposed a light solution for autonomous forklift that is able to recognise and fork the pallets for transportation, which indeed uses rangefinder-based system. Following their proposed idea, we built a solution completely based on RGB cameras that is able to detect and track the labels of packages (consisting in alphanumeric characters and bar-codes) to enable the autonomous warehouse inventorying. A similar approach has also been presented by Beul et al. [2] which is based on AprilTag detector [22] to locate the packages. Although the high performance of such a solution, it makes the assumption that the operational environment, i.e., the warehouse that may be a very wide indoor space, has to be seamlessly covered by specific tags. These ones consist in special black/white figures, similar to QRCode, by which the aerial vehicle can locate itself and recognise the packs. Such a solution can of course be difficult to scale on increasing size of the warehouse. On the same line, the work by Guérin et al. [9] and Bae et al. [1] presented a novel warehouse inventory based on unmanned aerial vehicles to make the inventory process completely autonomous. In both cases, the drones are meant to scan the goods during the flight by achieving very good results. On the other side, they used the Barcode scanner (the former) and the RFID technology (the latter). Other similar approaches in the literature making usage of RFID technology can be found. Even though they ensure high precision and accuracy, then cannot easily generalise to the all diverse factors affecting how the goods and packs are labelled during the warehousing logistics procedures. What characterise the solution proposed in this paper is that is it totally based on videos acquisitions from RGB camera and therefore, by a proper training stage, can adapt to a huge variety of pack tags and labelling without needing special constraints. Such a choice also makes hard a fair comparison with other approaches in the literature that, as said above, often keep advantage from dedicated sensors. Further, the specialised sensors ease the detection/recognition of tags and labels but also provide a representation of the acquired data that differs from simple RGB images.

3   Tags Detection with R-CNN

As said in the previous section, the work proposed in this paper is inspired to the work by Mohammed et al. [16]. On the other side, rather than using laser scanner, it is totally based on RGB cameras, mounted on the aerial vehicle.

Image processing applications have been demonstrated to keep benefit from Convolutional Neural Networks (CNNs) models [15]. The main component of a CNN is represented by the convolutional layer. It features a local connectivity patterns that forces the network to operate on limited receptive fields. Together with other layers, like pooling, ReLU layers and fully connected layer, the CNN models have become increasingly complex in size and in number of parameters to learn. From one side, that made CNNs more and more performing. On the other side, the computing power needed growth accordingly thus making infeasible to run such neural models on hardware with limited resources. Over recent years, advancements in CNN models led to an alternative version called Region-based Convolutional Neural Networks (R-CNNs) used for object detection and image classification [19,23]. A R-CNN is organised in two steps: (i) a collection of possible bounding boxes containing an object are extracted from the input layer and (ii) the region of interest (ROIs) are then submitted to a classifier to determine if they contain one of the known object to recognise (i.e., the classes of the supervised problem). Inside the family of R-CNN, has gained significant attention the model called Faster R-CNN [8], which is exploited in this work. Faster R-CNNs are characterised from being composed of few convolutional layes followed by a fully connected layer called Region Proposal Network (RPN). The RPN receives as input the convolutional feature maps generated from the previous layers and operates by passing a $n \times n$ sliding window over them. It proposes bounding box candidates (called *anchors*) according to predefined aspect ratios and scales. For each anchor a value of Intersection over Union (IoU) ranging in $[0, 1]$ is computed. It represents the overlap ratio of the anchors and of ground truth bounding boxes (see Definition 1). The ROIs extracted from the input according to the anchors that are above an empirical threshold of IoU, are then provided to a classifier that is in charge of classifying the detected objects. This implies that Faster R-CNNs achieve efficient and fully end-to-end training, as a single CNN is used for region proposal and classification [16].

Definition 1. *Given A be the anchor, B the ground truth bounding box and area(⊙) a function computing the area in pixel of the bounding box ⊙, the Intersection over Union (IoU) is defined as:*

$$IoU = \frac{area(A) \cap area(B)}{area(A) \cup area(B)} \tag{1}$$

The model used in this work is composed by a Faster R-CNN which is divided into three stages: the input layer, the intermediate convolutional stage, and the final fully connected stage. The input layer consists of the input image corresponding to aerial acquisition video frames. The convolutional part of the network model is composed by two convolutional layers, interleaved by two ReLU layers and a final max-pooling layer. The final stage, i.e., the RPN layer, is composed by two fully connected layers ending in a softmax classification layer which determines if the proposed ROIs belong to the class of tags or not. In order to further assess the reliability of the detected tags, a CNN-based classifier is trained to classify the most promising ROIs detected by the Faster R-CNN as tags.

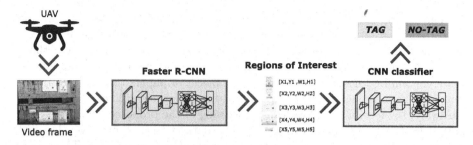

Fig. 2. The overall proposed model consisting in the combination of Faster R-CNN and a shallow CNN.

Table 1. The configuration of the Faster R-CNN model network and the shallow CNN-based classifier.

Faster R-CNN	Shallow CNN
Input layer (32 × 32)	Input layer (250×250)
Conv2D layer(kernel = 3 × 3, filters = 40, stride,padding = 1)	Conv2D layer (kernel = 20 × 20, filters = 25 padding = 1, stride = 1)
ReLU layer	ReLU layer
Conv2D layer (kernel = 3 × 3, filters = 40, stride,padding = 1)	Max-Pooling Layer (kernel = 5 × 5, stride = 2)
ReLU layer	Fully connected layer (neurons = 2)
Max-pooling layer (kernel = 3 × 3, stride = 1)	Softmax layers
Fully connected layer (neurons = 64)	Classification layer
ReLU layer	
Fully connected layer (neurons = 2)	
Softmax layer	
Classification layer	

It consists in a shallow CNN model that takes as input a crop of the full-size original images that contains the ROIs only, therefore it consists in a subset of the entire image containing all the ROIs detected by the Faster R-CNN. The middle layer consists of a single convolutional layer followed by ReLU and max-pooling layers. The final fully connected layer and a softmax layer is in charge of classifying the image. An overall view of the network model is depicted in Fig. 2, it can be noticed that the network is rather shallow, since the objective of the proposed architecture is to perform online recognition on UAVs with limited computational resources and either to avoid overfitting due to the limited number of samples in the dataset.

4   Experimental Results

Before introducing the achieved results and the data used for the experimentation, further details of the network model configuration are provided in Table 1.

448   A. De Falco et al.

The experimentation has been carried out on ad-hoc RGB videos acquired at 720p resolution in real warehouse environments involving the usage of a drone while performing a vertical scanning of the packs on the shelves. From those videos, 292 frames have been extracted. The frames have been selected among those containing tags and containing other pieces of papers that did not represent tags. Even though the training and testing performed offline on commodity hardware, the feasibility of real-time processing of the proposed solution is supported by the results reported in [16]. The dataset is then manually labelled to build the ground truth for classification performance evaluation. The experiments has been performed on both RGB color original images and grayscale converted video frames. Precision/Recall (PR) curves have been used to show the achieved results together with the average precision (AP) metric. We remember that *Precision* is a ratio of true positive instances to all positive instances of objects in the detector, based on the ground truth. *Recall* is a ratio of true positive instances to the sum of true positives and false negatives in the detector, based on the ground truth. *Average precision* is computed over all the detection results and returned as a numeric scalar in range [0, 1].

According to the designed model, we first trained the Faster R-CNN on the training set, which is 70% of the dataset. The number of epochs is set to 10. The PR curves in Fig. 3 show that working with grayscale images introduces a slight improvement in performance, even though the two experiments are about equal each other in terms of average precision (0.87 and 0.85 for grayscale and RGB training respectively).

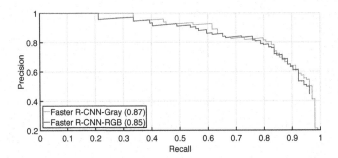

Fig. 3. Training performance of Faster R-CNN on RGB training set and on converted grayscale training set.

Once the Faster R-CNN training is complete and ROIs generated, the shallow CNN-based classifier has been trained on all the extracted ROIs as input. Even in this case the number of epochs is set to 10. In total, 89 ROIs of tags and 131 non-tags have been manually labelled. According to CNN model constraints, the images have been scaled to 250 × 250 resolution and used to train different configurations of the classifier. First of all, it has been used in its designed configuration (as described in Table 1 above) (ConvNet1) and also by adding an extra convolutional layer and ReLU layer (ConvNet2Conv). The starting learning rate has been set to 10^{-3} and a mini-batch size of 50 samples per iteration has been used. Moreover, we also performed data augmentation of the dataset by introducing slight variations in translation, rotation and scaling of the tags. Reducing the learning rate to 10^{-5} and with mini-batch size to 32 samples, the training has been performed on both RGB images (NewConvNet) and grayscale (ConvNetGray) thus resulting in the PR curves shown in Fig. 4. On each plot, the PR curves in different configurations above mentioned have been presented while average precision is reported in figure legend besides each variant of the CNN-based classifier. It results clear how the data augmentation and the lower learning rate significantly improved the recall and precision of the classification.

In the attempt of further improving the average precision of the proposed architecture, we use the weights of the layers from CNN-based classifier trained on grayscale images of ROIs containing the tags (ConvNetGray). Such weights have been used as to initialize the Convolutional layers of the Faster R-CNN and then trained this last model network on input images RGB of the training set. Figure 5 shows how such a solution improved significantly the classification performance.

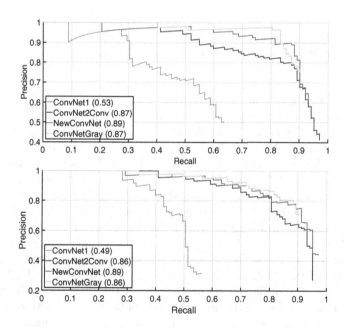

Fig. 4. The PR curves of classification achieved in different configurations for the CNN-based classifier. (Top) the PR curves of classification on training the CNN with RGB images. (Bottom) The classification curves using the CNN trained on grayscale images.

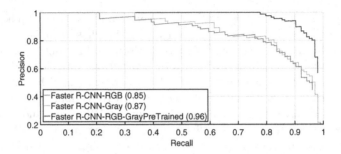

Fig. 5. A comparison of Faster R-CNN performance on different training conditions.

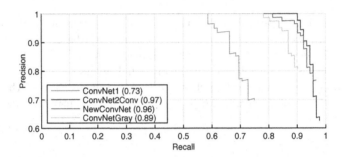

Fig. 6. PR curves obtained by using the Faster R-CNN with pre-training on grayscale images for tags detection and the configurations of the CNN-based classifier for classification. (Color figure online)

Following this intuition, we tested the performance of the Faster R-CNN with pre-trained layers on grayscale images and we again provided the ROIs coming from the CNN-based classifier in all the configuration discussed above. Figure 6 summarises the level of performance achieve in all treatments. We can observe how the pre-training performed on Faster R-CNN introduced a significant increase in PR curves for all the conditions considered. Even though the higher level of performance achieved on using RGB images, working with grayscale images leads to a desirable reduction of computing demand. Since the algorithm has to run on board the aerial vehicles, we chose to test the grayscale configuration (Faster R-CNN pre-trained with grayscale images + CNN on grayscale ROIs) to assess the reliability of the proposed solution. Inspecting the responses of the CNN models, we observed that the Faster R-CNN model reaches a confidence of detection that is most of the time above the threshold of 0.98 both introducing a very negligible rate of false positive. Moreover, when the Faster R-CNN is wrong, i.e., it detects a ROIs as containing a tag when it is does not or vice versa, most of the CNN-based classifier also fails in correctly classifying the tag. This often happens when occlusions or limited field of view of the camera do not allow to unambiguously acquire the tags. This leads to suppose a feasible solution which uses the two-stage approach, i.e. Faster R-CNN + Shallow CNN, only for training while uses the solely Faster R-CNN for detecting and recognising the tags.

5   Conclusions

Warehouse management is commonly associated with complex and dynamic processes presenting critical problems for warehouse managers across industries. Accurate inventorying procedure becomes increasingly challenging on wider and wider warehouse environments. Inaccurate inventory causes problems such as maintaining improper stock levels and buildups of obsolete inventory. Fluctuations in demand on seasonality as well as the speed of purchases in the electronic markets, represents critical issue to face with and proper logistics operations can determine the success or big faults. In this paper a simple solution based on Convolutional Neural Network for warehouse inventorying has been presented. Using unmanned aerial vehicles, the objective is enabling an autonomous warehouse inventorying system according to which the drones are able to localise and recognise the packs in stock and, in case, to signal the missing or the decrease of offer of some products. Even though micro aerial vehicles have received a strong acceleration over recent years, they still suffer from high battery consumption and limited processing power. On the opposite side, machine learning and deep learning techniques for computer vision tasks have achieved considerable high performance at the cost of proportional computational demand, which is far from being compliant with portable computing devices. To such a purpose, the solution proposed in this work is meant to require limited computation power but able to meet the requirements of a precise and accurate autonomous scanning of a warehouse environment. The solution is based on a two-stage learning process, where a Faster R-CNN is used to detect the tags during the aerial check of the packs on the shelves. Once possible tags have been localised, the regions of interest extracted from the video acquisition are promptly sent to a shallow CNN-based classifier which is charge of classifying the right tags and differentiate them from other piece of paper, or residual notes on the packs that do not contribute to the inventory procedures. The experimental analysis carried out on real scenarios by using real video acquisitions in a warehouse facility during a vertical aerial scanning of the stocks have demonstrated the feasibility of the proposed approach. The results achieved in different configurations of the CNN models demonstrate that a high precision can be reached resulting in an average precision above 80%. Observations on CNN behaviour during training led to a round of experiments that showed how to keep advantage for the exclusive usage of the Faster R-CNN model upon the training performed on the shallow classifier and then using those pre-trained layers in the Faster R-CNN. Precision achieved aside, such an attempt demonstrated a computational lightening of the proposed solution which further confirmed the feasibility of the autonomous warehousing inventorying by unmanned aerial vehicles and which can be used for future improvements of the approach proposed in this study.

Acknowledgements. This work has been supported by the Integrated Logistics Platform 4.0 Project (P.L.I 4.0) of the National Operational Programme for Research and Competitiveness 2014–2020

References

1. Bae, S.M., Han, K.H., Cha, C.N., Lee, H.Y.: Development of inventory checking system based on UAV and RFID in open storage yard. In: 2016 International Conference on Information Science and Security (ICISS), pp. 1–2. IEEE (2016)
2. Beul, M., Droeschel, D., Nieuwenhuisen, M., Quenzel, J., Houben, S., Behnke, S.: Fast autonomous flight in warehouses for inventory applications. IEEE Robot. Autom. Lett. **3**(4), 3121–3128 (2018)
3. Beul, M., Krombach, N., Nieuwenhuisen, M., Droeschel, D., Behnke, S.: Autonomous navigation in a warehouse with a cognitive micro aerial vehicle. In: Koubaa, A. (ed.) Robot Operating System (ROS). SCI, vol. 707, pp. 487–524. Springer, Cham (2017). https://doi.org/10.1007/978-3-319-54927-9_15
4. D'Andrea, R.: Guest editorial: a revolution in the warehouse: a retrospective on kiva systems and the grand challenges ahead. IEEE Trans. Autom. Sci. Eng. **9**(4), 638–639 (2012)
5. Elawady, M., Sadek, I., Kidane, H.: Detecting and avoiding frontal obstacles from monocular camera for micro unmanned aerial vehicles. arXiv preprint arXiv:1603.09422 (2016)
6. Flores, G., Zhou, S., Lozano, R., Castillo, P.: A vision and GPS-based real-time trajectory planning for a MAV in unknown and low-sunlight environments. J. Intell. Robot. Syst. **74**(1–2), 59–67 (2014)
7. Fossel, J., Hennes, D., Claes, D., Alers, S., Tuyls, K.: OctoSLAM: a 3D mapping approach to situational awareness of unmanned aerial vehicles. In: 2013 International Conference on Unmanned Aircraft Systems (ICUAS), pp. 179–188. IEEE (2013)
8. Girshick, R., Donahue, J., Darrell, T., Malik, J.: Rich feature hierarchies for accurate object detection and semantic segmentation. In: Proceedings of the IEEE Conference on Computer Vision and Pattern Recognition, pp. 580–587 (2014)
9. Guérin, F., Guinand, F., Brethé, J.F., Pelvillain, H., et al.: Towards an autonomous warehouse inventory scheme. In: 2016 IEEE Symposium Series on Computational Intelligence (SSCI), pp. 1–8. IEEE (2016)
10. Hornung, A., Wurm, K.M., Bennewitz, M., Stachniss, C., Burgard, W.: OctoMap: an efficient probabilistic 3D mapping framework based on octrees. Auton. Robot. **34**(3), 189–206 (2013)
11. Huh, S., Shim, D.H., Kim, J.: Integrated navigation system using camera and gimbaled laser scanner for indoor and outdoor autonomous flight of UAVs. In: 2013 IEEE/RSJ International Conference on Intelligent Robots and Systems, pp. 3158–3163. IEEE (2013)
12. Jutzi, B., Weinmann, M., Meidow, J.: Weighted data fusion for UAV-borne 3D mapping with camera and line laser scanner. Int. J. Image Data Fusion **5**(3), 226–243 (2014)
13. Kayikci, Y.: Sustainability impact of digitization in logistics. Proc. Manuf. **21**, 782–789 (2018)
14. Kohlbrecher, S., Von Stryk, O., Meyer, J., Klingauf, U.: A flexible and scalable slam system with full 3D motion estimation. In: 2011 IEEE International Symposium on Safety, Security, and Rescue Robotics, pp. 155–160. IEEE (2011)
15. LeCun, Y., Bengio, Y., Hinton, G.: Deep learning. Nature **521**(7553), 436 (2015)
16. Mohamed, I.S., Capitanelli, A., Mastrogiovanni, F., Rovetta, S., Zaccaria, R.: Detection, localisation and tracking of pallets using machine learning techniques and 2D range data. arXiv preprint arXiv:1803.11254 (2018)

17. Park, J., Kim, Y.: 3D shape mapping of obstacle using stereo vision sensor on quadrotor UAV. In: AIAA Guidance, Navigation, and Control Conference, p. 0975 (2014)
18. Raptopoulos, A., Damm, D., Ling, M., Baruchin, I.: Transportation using network of unmanned aerial vehicles. US Patent 9,384,668, 5 July 2016
19. Redmon, J., Divvala, S., Girshick, R., Farhadi, A.: You only look once: unified, real-time object detection. In: Proceedings of the IEEE Conference on Computer Vision and Pattern Recognition, pp. 779–788 (2016)
20. Schmid, K., Lutz, P., Tomić, T., Mair, E., Hirschmüller, H.: Autonomous vision-based micro air vehicle for indoor and outdoor navigation. J. Field Robot. **31**(4), 537–570 (2014)
21. Tripathi, A.K., Raja, R.G., Padhi, R.: Reactive collision avoidance of UAVs with stereovision camera sensors using UKF. IFAC Proc. Vol. **47**(1), 1119–1125 (2014)
22. Wang, J., Olson, E.: AprilTag 2: efficient and robust fiducial detection. In: 2016 IEEE/RSJ International Conference on Intelligent Robots and Systems (IROS), pp. 4193–4198. IEEE (2016)
23. Zhang, M., Li, W., Du, Q.: Diverse region-based CNN for hyperspectral image classification. IEEE Trans. Image Process. **27**(6), 2623–2634 (2018)

3D Shape Segmentation with Geometric Deep Learning

Davide Boscaini[(✉)] and Fabio Poiesi

Technologies of Vision, Fondazione Bruno Kessler,
Via Sommarive 18, 38123 Trento, Italy
{dboscaini,poiesi}@fbk.eu

Abstract. The semantic segmentation of 3D shapes with a high-density of vertices could be impractical due to large memory requirements. To make this problem computationally tractable, we propose a neural-network based approach that produces 3D augmented views of the 3D shape to solve the whole segmentation as sub-segmentation problems. 3D augmented views are obtained by projecting vertices and normals of a 3D shape onto 2D regular grids taken from different viewpoints around the shape. These 3D views are then processed by a Convolutional Neural Network to produce a probability distribution function (pdf) over the set of the semantic classes for each vertex. These pdfs are then re-projected on the original 3D shape and postprocessed using contextual information through Conditional Random Fields. We validate our approach using 3D shapes of publicly available datasets and of real objects that are reconstructed using photogrammetry techniques. We compare our approach against state-of-the-art alternatives.

Keywords: 3D semantic segmentation · Geometric deep learning

1 Introduction

Traditional Convolutional Neural Networks (CNNs) use a cascade of learned convolution filters, pooling operations and activation functions to transform image data into feature embeddings processable by fully connected layers that classify the image content [7]. Typically, 3D deep-learning approaches extend traditional 2D methods to non-Euclidean domains as the convolution operation is not well defined in 3D [15]. One of the most challenging researched topic related to 3D deep learning is the semantic segmentation of 3D shapes as it is key to support computer graphics applications such as shape editing [24] and modelling [4]. Challenges to segment 3D shapes include dealing with different topologies, handling noisy geometries and different resolutions, and modeling semantic representations for different segments.

3D segmentation can be performed through multi-view [10,22], volumetric [23] or intrinsic [15,18] deep learning-based approaches. Multi-view and volumetric approaches use Euclidean structures, such as 2D or 3D grids, respectively, to process 3D shapes with 2D CNNs [10,22,23]. In particular, multi-view

This research has been partially funded by the European Union's Horizon 2020 research and innovation programme under grant agreement number 687757.

E. Ricci et al. (Eds.): ICIAP 2019, LNCS 11751, pp. 454–465, 2019.
https://doi.org/10.1007/978-3-030-30642-7_41

approaches simplify the representation of a 3D model using a set of rendered depth images taken from different viewpoints around the model, thus making the segmentation independent of the 3D-model polygon density [10, 22]. Multi-view approaches cannot fully exploit the geometric properties of the 3D shape (e.g. face normals) because geometric information can be lost when data are projected in 2D. Volumetric approaches approximate the 3D shape using voxels which could overshadow geometric details of the object [23]. Intrinsic approaches can be further divided into point-based and convolution-based approaches. Point-based approaches define feature extractors directly on the shape vertices [18], whereas convolution-based approaches extend the traditional convolution operations from grid-like structures to triangular meshes [15]. Point-based approaches mostly process each vertex of the shape independently and loosely exploit local information [18]. The additional structures used by conventional convolution-based approaches increase the shape representation complexity hence prohibiting the processing of high-density polygon models [15]. Typically, 3D segmentation approaches validate their performance on datasets collected in controlled scenarios, and they mostly lack of an evaluation carried out on 3D models reconstructed using photogrammetric techniques [16].

In this paper we propose a novel 3D segmentation approach that retains both the advantages of view-based [10] and intrinsic approaches [15] by building 3D augmented views from multiple viewpoints around a 3D shape. 3D augmented views are a projection of 3D shape portions on 2D regular grids, where each cell of the grid encodes the information about depth and normal of the corresponding projected portion. This allows us to significantly reduce the number of parameters to learn and to perform 3D segmentation of shapes with diverse mesh topology (e.g. polygon structure and/or density). We evaluate our approach on synthetic 3D shapes from publicly available datasets, and on 3D shapes of objects we captured with a smartphone and reconstructed using photogrammetry techniques. Results show that the proposed approach can achieve state-of-the-art accuracy by using only 1% of the parameters used by the alternative approaches.

2   Our Approach

2.1   Problem Formulation

Given a 3D shape $\mathcal{X} \subset \mathbb{R}^3$ composed of vertices $x \in \mathcal{X}$, we design a neural-network based approach $\boldsymbol{p}(x) = \boldsymbol{\Gamma}_{\Theta}(x)$ that outputs a probability distribution $\boldsymbol{p}(x)$ over the label space $\mathcal{L} = \{1, \dots, L\}$, where L is the number of segmentation labels. The output segmentation of $\mathcal{X}$ is computed as

$$h(x) = \underset{\ell=1,\dots,L}{\operatorname{argmax}} \, \boldsymbol{p}(x),$$

where $h(x)$ is a label defining the segment class of the vertex x.

The neural network $\boldsymbol{\Gamma}_{\Theta}$ can be defined as a a parametric function in the set of learnable parameters (i.e. weights) $\boldsymbol{\Theta}$. $\boldsymbol{\Gamma}_{\Theta}$ is composed of four modules, namely

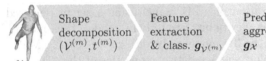

Fig. 1. Our approach outline. 3D augmented views from different viewpoints are computed from the 3D shape (shape decomposition). Point-wise features (i.e. coordinates and surface normals) are extracted from these 3D views and classified to obtain segmentation predictions. Predictions are re-projected and aggregated on the original shape, and refined through a Conditional Random Field for local prediction consistency.

shape decomposition, feature extraction and classification, feature aggregation and prediction refinement. *Shape decomposition* transforms the input 3D shapes into 3D augmented views, or *3D views.* Each 3D view is processed by a *feature extraction and classification* network, namely *ViewNet*, that predicts the class of each vertex. *Prediction aggregation* re-projects the predictions of ViewNet of each 3D view onto the original 3D shape. *Prediction refinement* improves class prediction using contextual information on the original shape. Figure 1 depicts the block diagram.

2.2 Shape Decomposition

We simplify the 3D shape representation (e.g. triangular meshes, quad meshes, CAD models) by decomposing the input shape into several components. Shape decomposition can be performed by clustering shape vertices [8], by using geometrical primitives [9], or by generating range scans from different viewpoints [10]. We use a similar approach to the latter in order to process the 3D shape regardless its 3D representation, resolution and vertex topology.

Given $\mathcal{X}$ in the form of a triangular mesh with vertices $\boldsymbol{X} = (\boldsymbol{x}_1, \dots, \boldsymbol{x}_N)$, $\boldsymbol{x}_n \in \mathbb{R}^3$, $n = 1, \dots, N$, we simplify $\mathcal{X}$ by building 3D views from M different viewpoints. Let $\mathcal{I}(u, v; \boldsymbol{w}_m) = (u, v, d(u, v))$ be a range scan that is captured from the mth viewpoint $\boldsymbol{w}_m$, where (u, v) is the coordinate of a pixel, $d(u, v)$ is the depth value of the 3D shape, and $m = 1, \dots, M$. Let $\mathcal{V}^{(m)}$ be the mth 3D view whose vertices $\boldsymbol{V}^{(m)} = (\boldsymbol{v}_1, \dots, \boldsymbol{v}_{N^{(m)}})$ are obtained by registering the coordinates $(u, v, d(u, v))$ of the range scan to the coordinates of the vertices $\boldsymbol{X}$. The faces of the 3D view are obtained by connecting depth values using the typical regular grid pattern of 2D images. For each vertex $\boldsymbol{v}_n \in \boldsymbol{V}^{(m)}$ we compute the surface normal $\boldsymbol{n}(\boldsymbol{v}_n) \in \mathbb{R}^3$ to define the signal on the 3D view as $\boldsymbol{f}(\boldsymbol{v}_n) = (\boldsymbol{v}_n, \boldsymbol{n}(\boldsymbol{v}_n))$. The relation between a 3D view and the input 3D shape is defined by the correspondence function $t^{(m)} \colon \mathcal{V}^{(m)} \to \mathcal{X}$ that assigns the vertices of the mth 3D view to the corresponding vertices of the 3D shape.

Fig. 2. Example of 3D augmented views. Left-hand side: a synthetic 3D shape from the FAUST dataset [2]. Right-hand side: examples of the 3D augmented views extracted by the shape decomposition module. 3D views have an uniform vertex density and capture the underlying geometry even at a lower resolution.

2.3 Feature Extraction and Classification

The feature extraction and classification module processes the M 3D views in parallel to learn features through a set of deep neural networks, namely ViewNets, with shared weights. Formally, each ViewNet is a non-linear parametric function $g(v_n) = \Phi_{\Theta_{\mathrm{cla}}}(f(v_n))$ that takes vertex-wise features $f(v_n)$ as input and produces the probability distribution $g(v_n) = (g_1(v_n), \ldots, g_L(v_n))$ as output, where L is the number of segmentation classes and $\Theta_{\mathrm{cla}} \subset \Theta$ is the set of ViewNet learnable weights. Let $g_{\mathcal{V}^{(m)}} \in [0,1]^{N^{(m)} \times L}$ be the matrix containing the pdfs of all vertices of $\mathcal{V}^{(m)}$.

A ViewNet module is defined as the composition of *Intrinsic Convolutional* (IC), *Fully Connected* (FC) and *Softmax* layers. FC and Softmax are standard layers, whereas the IC layer replaces the convolutional layer used in traditional Euclidean CNNs to perform convolution operations on 3D views [15]. The convolution at $x \in \mathcal{X}$ using IC layers requires additional information, in the form of a local coordinate frame and a set of weighting functions that maps the signal of the local neighbourhood of x to a fixed grid.

2.4 Prediction Aggregation

Predictions inferred from each 3D view are re-projected and aggregated on the 3D shape $\mathcal{X}$ in order to transfer the segmentation result on the original input. We name this operation ProjNet. ProjNet employs a pooling operation that takes the ViewNet predictions $g_{\mathcal{V}^{(m)}}$ on $\mathcal{V}^{(m)}$ as input and the correspondence function $t^{(m)}: \mathcal{V}^{(m)} \to \mathcal{X}$ for any m, to produce a single confidence map $g_{\mathcal{X}}$ defined on $\mathcal{X}$. The pooling operation is defined as

$$g_{\mathcal{X}}(x_n) = \frac{1}{|\Omega(n)|} \sum_{\tilde{m} \in \Omega(n)} g_{\mathcal{V}^{(\tilde{m})}}(v_{\tilde{n}}),$$

where $\Omega(n) = \{m : t^{(m)}(\tilde{n}) = n\}$ is the set of 3D view indices relative to the vertex $\boldsymbol{x}_n \in \mathcal{X}$, and $\boldsymbol{g}_{\mathcal{Y}^{(\tilde{m})}}(\boldsymbol{v}_{\tilde{n}})$ is the probability distribution over the segmentation classes associated to vertex $\boldsymbol{v}_{\tilde{n}}$ of the $\tilde{m}$th 3D view.

2.5   Prediction Refinement

The output of ProjNet is a point-wise prediction, i.e. the label prediction of each vertex is estimated independently from its neighbors, thus leading to likely local label inconsistencies. Moreover, some vertices of the input 3D shape may not have been projected on any of the 3D views, thus leading to vertices with undefined label predictions on $\mathcal{X}$. Therefore, we impose local label consistency by using a surface-based Conditional Random Field (CRF) approach [10,25] that exploits contextual information to produce structured and dense predictions.

For each vertex $\boldsymbol{x}_n \in \boldsymbol{X}$, let $y_n : \boldsymbol{x}_n \to \mathcal{L}$ be a random variable that assigns a label $\ell \in \mathcal{L}$ to it, and let $\boldsymbol{y} = (y_1, \ldots, y_N)$ be the set of the random variables associated to the N vertices of $\boldsymbol{X}$. The CRF energy associated to $\boldsymbol{y}$ is defined as:

$$E(\boldsymbol{y}) = \sum_{n=1}^{N} \psi_{\text{unary}}(y_n) + \sum_{n=1}^{N} \sum_{\tilde{n}=n+1}^{N} \psi_{\text{pairwise}}(y_n, y_{\tilde{n}}), \tag{1}$$

where the unary term $\psi_{\text{unary}}(y_n)$ quantifies the assignment cost of y_n to vertex $\boldsymbol{x}_n$ and the pairwise term $\psi_{\text{pairwise}}(y_n, y_{\tilde{n}})$ quantifies the joint assignment cost of $y_n, y_{\tilde{n}}$ to vertices $\boldsymbol{x}_n, \boldsymbol{x}_{\tilde{n}}$ [14]. Because $\boldsymbol{g}_{\mathcal{X}}(\boldsymbol{x}_n)$ measures the cost of assigning the vertex $\boldsymbol{x}_n$ to $\mathcal{L}$, we define the unary term as $\psi_{\text{unary}}(y_n) = -\log(\boldsymbol{g}_{\mathcal{X}}(\boldsymbol{x}_n))$.

The pairwise potential is instead defined as the weighted sum of three Gaussian kernels:

$$\psi_{\text{pairwise}}(y_n, y_{\tilde{n}}) = \mu(y_n, y_{\tilde{n}}) \bigg(w_{\text{near}} \, k_{\text{near}}(y_n, y_{\tilde{n}}) - w_{\text{far}} \, k_{\text{far}}(y_n, y_{\tilde{n}})$$

$$+ w_{\text{feat}} \, k_{\text{feat}}(y_n, y_{\tilde{n}}) \bigg),$$

where

$$k_{\text{near}}(y_n, y_{\tilde{n}}) = \exp\left(-\frac{d_{\mathcal{X}}(\boldsymbol{x}_n, \boldsymbol{x}_{\tilde{n}})}{\sigma_{\text{near}}}\right),$$

$$k_{\text{far}}(y_n, y_{\tilde{n}}) = 1_{\mathcal{X}} - \exp\left(-\frac{d_{\mathcal{X}}(\boldsymbol{x}_n, \boldsymbol{x}_{\tilde{n}})}{\sigma_{\text{far}}}\right),$$

$$k_{\text{feat}}(y_n, y_{\tilde{n}}) = \exp\left(-\frac{\|\boldsymbol{f}(\boldsymbol{x}_n) - \boldsymbol{f}(\boldsymbol{x}_{\tilde{n}})\|_2}{\sigma_{\text{feat}}}\right),$$

$d_{\mathcal{X}}(x, \tilde{x})$ is the geodesic distance between the vertices $x, \tilde{x} \in \mathcal{X}$, $1_{\mathcal{X}}$ is the identity function on $\mathcal{X}$, and $\mu(y_n, y_{\tilde{n}})$ is a label compatibility term.

Similarly to [10,25], k_{near} favors local spatial consistency, while k_{feat} promotes the assignment of similar labels to vertices with similar properties. The third kernel k_{far} is novel and is introduced to disambiguate symmetries. Because symmetric parts are likely to be located far from each other (e.g. arms and legs

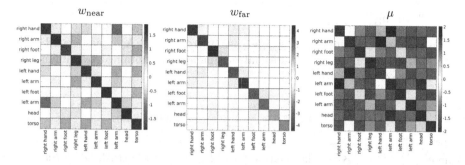

Fig. 3. Example of Conditional Random Field (CRF) learned weights (w_{near}, w_{far}, μ) in the case of human 3D shapes.

in a human shape) we designed k_{far} to avoid distant points to have similar labels. The set of CRF learnable parameters is defined as $\Theta_{CRF} = \{\mu, w_{near}, w_{far}, w_{feat}\}$, $\Theta_{CRF} \subset \Theta$. Figure 3 shows how CRF learns the relationships among segments through an example of learned parameters (i.e. w_{near}, w_{far} and μ) on human 3D shapes. In w_{near} we can observe that the head weights suggest that there is a strong relationship between head and torso rather than between head and right foot/right arm. Similarly, the torso weights suggest that there is a strong relationship between torso and arms/legs rather than between torso and feet/hands.

The most probable pdf configuration of y for $\mathcal{X}$ is obtained by minimizing the energy $E(y)$ defined in Eq. 1. The exact inference of the CRF distribution is intractable, thus we use a mean-field approximation [10,14]. The iterative algorithm for approximate mean-field inference can be implemented as a Recurrent Neural Network (RNN) by rephrasing each step of the algorithm as a CNN layer [25].

3   Results

3.1   Experimental Setup

We evaluate our 3D segmentation approach through two different experiments. Firstly, we use data from the publicly available Princeton Shape Benchmark (PSB) dataset [20] that contains synthetic shapes of several objects and animals; in particular, the rigid shapes of the Airplane class, and the non-rigid shapes of the Ant, Four Leg and Teddy classes. The segmentation labels of each object are defined as in [20]. Secondly, we use data of non-rigid human shapes; in particular, (i) synthetic people with different poses (FAUST dataset [2]), (ii) real people acquired with depth sensors (SCAPE dataset [1]) and with structured light 3D body scanners (SHREC14 dataset [5]), and (iii) real people that we acquired with a smartphone and reconstructed using the photogrammetry pipeline COLMAP [19]. We manually labelled the ground truth for FAUST and SCAPE datasets and used their training data to learn the neural network model for the human shapes. We have used this model to test our approach on all the other human shapes of FAUST, SCAPE, SHREC14 and COLMAP datasets. The segmentation labels for the non-rigid human shapes are: $\mathcal{L} = \{$head, torso, right arm, right hand, right leg, right foot, left arm, left hand, left leg, left foot$\}$.

3.2   Training

Given a labelled training set, where each vertex $x_n \in X$ is associated to a ground-truth label $h(x_n)$, the optimal parameters are obtained by minimizing the *categorical cross-entropy* loss,

$$c(\delta_{h(x_n)}, \Gamma_\Theta(x)) = -\sum_{n=1}^{N} \delta_{h(x_n)} \log(\Gamma_\Theta(x_n)),$$

where $\delta_{h(x_n)}$ is the Kronecker delta defined for the ground-truth label $h(x_n)$.

Our approach is trained end-to-end and from scratch. We use $M = 10$ 3D views (Sect. 2.2, Fig. 2) taken from equi-spaced viewpoints around the shape. For training we use the Adam optimizer [13] with a learning rate of 0.001. The CRF weights are initialized with identity matrices, i.e. each segment class is only in relationship with itself.

3.3   Evaluation

PSB Dataset: Table 1 shows the quantitative results of our approach on a subset of PSB's 3D shapes. We compare the accuracy of our approach with ShapeBoost [11], Guo et al. [6] and ShapePFCN [10]. The first two approaches use classifiers that are learned from hand-crafted features, whereas the latter is an end-to-end deep learning approach similar to ours (i.e. features are also learned). We can observe that the accuracy of our approach is similar to that of state-of-the-art methods. However, compared to ShapePFCN [10] that is based on the VGG16 architecture [21], which uses 134M parameters, our neural network uses 14K parameters, i.e. 1% of ShapePFCN's parameters [10]. Figure 4 shows examples of segmentation results that are obtained on the Airplane category. The uncertainty map next to each segmentation result showed that the highest level of uncertainty is located where different segments intersect. Qualitatively, the results are very accurate and show only minor errors on the rudder region.

Table 1. Segmentation mean accuracy (the higher the better [10]) on the Princeton Shape Benchmark dataset [20].

Category	Hand-crafted features		End-to-end	
	ShapeBoost [11]	Guo et al. [6]	ShapePFCN [10]	Ours
Airplane	96.1	91.6	93.0	94.1
Ant	98.7	97.6	98.6	94.8
Four leg	83.3	82.4	85.0	94.5
Teddy	98.7	97.3	97.7	92.8

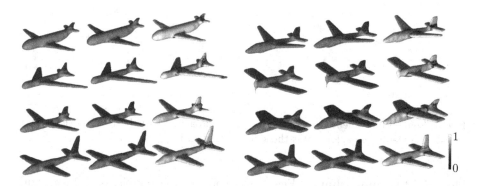

Fig. 4. Semantic segmentation results of our approach on PSB Airplane test shapes. Segmentation color key: green = body, blue = wings, purple = engine, yellow = stabilizer, and red = rudder. Each segmentation result (center) is accompanied by its ground-truth (on its left) and a confidence map (on its right) showing the uncertainty (entropy) of the network prediction over the 3D shape. The darker the color the higher the uncertainty. (Color figure online)

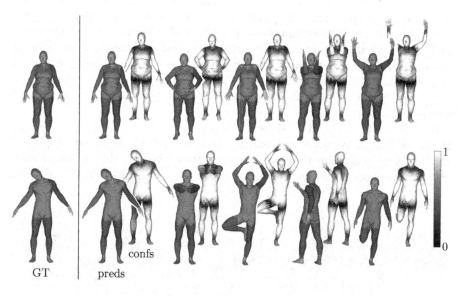

Fig. 5. Semantic segmentation results of our approach on a subset of FAUST's test shapes. Segmentation color key: colour code: yellow = head, green = torso, blue = right arm, light blue = right hand, orange = right leg, yellow = right foot, red = left arm, light red = left hand, purple = left leg, light purple = left foot. Each segmentation result (left) is accompanied by a confidence map (right) showing the uncertainty (entropy) of the network prediction over the 3D shape. The darker the color the higher the uncertainty. (Color figure online)

Fig. 6. Semantic segmentation results of our approach on a subset of SCAPE's test shapes. Segmentation color key is the same as that in Fig. 5.

Non-rigid Human Shapes: Figs. 5, 6, 7 and 8 show examples of segmentation results that are obtained on the non-rigid human shapes. Beside each segmented shape we can observe their associated entropy map. The smaller the entropy the higher the uncertainty. As expected, the largest level of uncertainty is located at the joints between two segments, that is where transition is not well defined. Because we have annotations for FAUST and SCAPE, we quantified the accuracy [10] and Intersection over Union (IoU) [18] of the segmentation results. In FAUST we achieved an accuracy of 93.8% and IoU of 88.5% while in SCAPE we achieved an accuracy of 72.1% and IoU of 58.7%. This accuracy and IoU differences are due to the unbalanced number of training samples of the two datasets. FAUST annotations are much more numerous than those of SCAPE. A few of the poses of FAUST's training shapes are also present in the test set. This does not occur in the case of SCAPE, where poses are only present once. Figure 6 shows examples of the segmentation errors occurred in SCAPE test, e.g. on the right-hand block we can see that the legs of the shape in the middle have been segmented with inverted labels.

Results in Figs. 7 and 8 show that the method can generalize also to 3D shapes that have not been used for training. Interestingly, our approach can effectively generalize the mesh representation through the 3D augmented views and produce a reliable segmentation in the case of COLMAP's shapes.

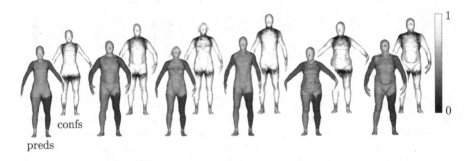

Fig. 7. Semantic segmentation results of our approach on a subset of SHREC14's shapes. Trained on FAUST and SCAPE training sets. Segmentation color key is the same as that in Fig. 5.

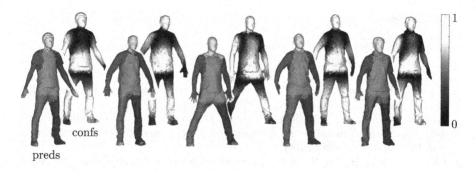

Fig. 8. Semantic segmentation results of our approach on a subset of COLMAP's shapes. Trained on FAUST and SCAPE training sets. Segmentation color key is the same as that in Fig. 5.

Note that the mesh topology of COLMAP's shapes is different from those used in training. This is because the meshing operation based on Poisson reconstruction of COLMAP produces highly irregular polygons [12]. However, it is also clear that COLMAP's shapes are more challenging than SHREC14's ones by looking at the respective confidence maps. Overall, results show that our approach can effectively segment 3D shapes of different subjects, despite their different pose.

4 Conclusions

We presented an approach to segment 3D shapes efficiently regardless their mesh topology. To achieve this we decomposed the segmentation problem into sub-segmentation problems by using 3D augmented views generated from the underlying 3D shape. This enabled us to train a neural network with 1% of the parameters used by alternative state-of-the-art solutions, while maintaining similar accuracy performance. We showed that our approach is generic and can be used to segment 3D shapes with arbitrary mesh topologies, like those computed with photogrammetry reconstruction techniques (e.g. Poisson reconstruction [12]) that have a high density of polygons and that are distributed irregularly. Moreover, our approach also showed evidence of being flexible to segment other categories of 3D shapes (e.g. airplanes) other than human ones.

Future research directions include an extensive analysis of the results, evaluating the impact of a multi-scale approach applied on the 3D augmented views and exploring next-best-view approaches [17] to select the most suitable 3D views of the object of interest. We will also exploit the structured output of the CRF to build models for surface matching between 3D shapes [3] and explore attention mechanisms to make the prediction of our approach robust to the clutter present on the 3D shape (i.e. untrained segmentation classes).

References

1. Anguelov, D., Srinivasan, P., Koller, D., et al.: SCAPE: shape completion and animation of people. In: Proceedings of the ACM Trans. Graph. **24**(3), 408–416 (2005)
2. Bogo, F., Romero, J., Loper, M., et al.: FAUST: dataset and evaluation for 3D mesh registration. In: Proceedings of the CVPR (2014)
3. Boscaini, D., Masci, J., Rodolà, E., et al.: Learning shape correspondence with anisotropic convolutional neural networks. In: Proceedings of the Neural Information Processing Systems (2016)
4. Chen, X., Zhou, B., Lu, F., et al.: Garment modeling with a depth camera. ACM Trans. Graph. **34**(6), 1–12 (2015)
5. Giachetti, A., et al.: SHREC'14 track: automatic location of landmarks used in manual anthropometry. In: Proceedings of the 3DOR (2014)
6. Guo, K., Zou, D., Chen, X.: 3D mesh labeling via deep convolutional neural networks. ACM Trans. Graph. **35**(1), 3:1–3:12 (2015)
7. He, K., Zhang, X., Ren, S., et al.: Deep residual learning for image recognition. In: Proceedings of the CVPR (2016)
8. Hua, Z., Huang, H., Li, J.: Mesh simplification using vertex clustering based on principal curvature. Int. J. Multimed. Ubiquit. Eng. **10**(9), 99–110 (2015)
9. Kaiser, A., Ybanez, Z., Alonso, A., et al.: A survey of simple geometric primitives detection methods for captured 3D data. Comput. Graphi. Forum. **38**(1), 167–196 (2019)
10. Kalogerakis, E., Averkiou, M., Maji, S., et al.: 3D shape segmentation with projective convolutional networks. In: Proceedings of the CVPR (2017)
11. Kalogerakis, E., Hertzmann, A., Singh, K.: Learning 3D mesh segmentation and labeling. ACM Trans. Graph. **29**(4), 102:1–102:12 (2010)
12. Kazhdan, M., Bolitho, M., Hoppe, H.: Poisson surface reconstruction. In: Proceedings of the SGP (2006)
13. Kingma, D., Ba, J.: Adam: a method for stochastic optimization. In: Proceedings of the ICLR (2015)
14. Krahenbuhl, P., Koltun, V.: Efficient inference in fully connected CRFs with Gaussian edge potentials. In: Proceedings of the NIPS (2011)
15. Monti, F., Boscaini, D., Masci, J., et al.: Geometric deep learning on graphs and manifolds using mixture model CNNs. In: Proceedings of the CVPR (2017)
16. Nocerino, E., Lago, F., Morabito, D., et al.: A smartphone-based pipeline for the creative industry - the REPLICATE project. In: International Archives of Photogrammetry, Remote Sensing and Spatial Information Sciences (2017)
17. Potthast, C., Sukhatme, G.: A probabilistic framework for next best view estimation in a cluttered environment. J. Vis. Commun. Image Represent. **25**(1), 148–164 (2014)
18. Qi, C., Su, H., Mo, K., et al.: PointNet: deep learning on point sets for 3D classification and segmentation. In: Proceedings of the CVPR (2017)
19. Schonberger, J., Frahm, J.M.: Structure-from-motion revisited. In: Proceedings of the CVPR (2016)
20. Shilane, P., Min, P., Kazhdan, M., et al.: The Princeton shape benchmark. In: Proceedings of Shape Modeling International, June 2004
21. Simonyan, K., Zisserman, A.: Very deep convolutional networks for large-scale image recognition. In: Proceedings of the ICLR (2015)
22. Su, H., Maji, S., Kalogerakis, E., et al.: Multi-view convolutional neural networks for 3D shape recognition. In: Proceedings of the ICCV (2015)

23. Wu, Z., Song, S., Khosla, A., et al.: 3D ShapeNets: a deep representation for volumetric shapes. In: Proceedings of the CVPR (2015)
24. Yu, Y., Zhou, K., Xu, D., et al.: Mesh editing with poisson-based gradient field manipulation. ACM Trans. Graph. **23**(3), 644–651 (2004)
25. Zheng, S., Jayasumana, S., Romera-Paredes, et al.: Conditional random fields as recurrent neural networks. In: Proceedings of the ICCV (2015)

Within-Network Ensemble for Face Attributes Classification

Sara Atito Ali Ahmed$^{(\boxtimes)}$ ⓘ and Berrin Yanikoglu ⓘ

Sabanci University, 34956 Istanbul, Turkey
{saraatito,berrin}@sabanciuniv.edu

Abstract. Face attributes classification is drawing attention as a research topic with applications in multiple domains, such as video surveillance and social media analysis. In this work, we propose to train attributes in groups based on their localization (head, eyes, nose, cheek, mouth, shoulder, and general areas) in an end-to-end framework considering the correlations between the different attributes. Furthermore, a novel ensemble learning technique is introduced within the network itself that reduces the time of training compared to ensemble of several models. Our approach outperforms the state-of-the-art of the attributes with an average improvement of almost 0.60% and 0.48% points, on the public CELEBA and LFWA datasets, respectively.

Keywords: Face attributes classification · Deep learning · Multi-task learning · Multi-label classification · Ensemble learning

1 Introduction

Attribute classifiers have been drawing attention in zero-shot or few-shot learning problems where classes share attributes among them and can thus be recognized with zero or a few samples. Face attribute in particular has been a focus [5–7,13,17], as describing facial attributes has useful applications such as attribute-based search. Previously, work on face attribute classification approaches were based on handcrafted representations, as in [3,11,12]. This kind of approaches are prone to failing when presented different variations of face images and in unconstrained backgrounds. Recently, researchers tackle this task using deep learning, which has resulted in huge performance leaps in several domains [13, 16,18,19,21,22]. Liu et al. [13] use two cascaded convolutional neural networks (CNNs), for face localization (LNet) and attributes prediction (ANet). Each attribute classifier is trained independently where the last fully connected layer is replaced with a support vector machine classifier. Similarly in Zhong et al. [21], attribute prediction is accomplished by leveraging different levels of CNNs.

Lately, the task is shifted to be a multi-task learning (MTL) problem by training attributes in groups, mainly to speed up the training process and reduce overfitting. Yet, only few works address the relationship between different facial attributes [1,6,7]. Hand and Chellapa's work divides the attributes into nine

© Springer Nature Switzerland AG 2019
E. Ricci et al. (Eds.): ICIAP 2019, LNCS 11751, pp. 466–476, 2019.
https://doi.org/10.1007/978-3-030-30642-7_42

groups and train a CNN consisting of three convolutional sub-networks and two multi-layer perceptrons [7]. The first two convolutional sub-networks are shared for all of the classifiers and the rest of the network is independent for each group. They also compare their results to the results of classifiers trained independently for each attribute and show the advantage of grouping attributes together. Atito and Yanikoglu use the multi-task learning paradigm, where attributes that are grouped based on their location, share separate layers [1]. Learning is done in two-stages: first by directing the attention of each network to the area of interest and then fine-tuning the networks. In Han et al. [6], attributes are grouped into ordinal vs. nominal attributes, where nominal attributes usually have two or more classes and there is no intrinsic ordering among the categories, like race and gender. The attributes are jointly estimated by training a convolutional neural network that consists of some shared layers among all the attributes and category-specific layers for heterogeneous attributes.

In this work, we propose an end-to-end network where all of the attributes are trained at once in a multi-label learning scenario. An extra layer along with a combined objective function are added to the network to capture the relation between the attributes. Furthermore, a novel ensemble technique is introduced.

The main contributions are summarized as follows. (1) We use an end-to-end deep learning framework for face attribute classification, capturing the correlation among attributes with an extra layer that is trained at the same time with the first one. (2) We propose a novel within-network ensemble technique. (3) We obtain state-of-the-art results on both the CELEBA and LFWA datasets.

2   Proposed Approach

In this paper, we approached the face attributes classification problem in a multi-label/multi-task fashion using an end-to-end framework. In Sect. 2.1, we trained our base system in a multi-label fashion by sharing the network layers among all of the attributes. While in Sect. 2.2, we introduced groups and attributes specific layers for distinct feature extraction. In Sect. 2.3, an extra layer is embedded to the architecture to capture the relation between different attributes. Finally, in Sect. 2.4, a novel ensemble approach within the architecture itself is introduced.

Training a large deep learning network from scratch is time consuming and needs tremendous amount of training data. Therefore, all of our proposed architectures are based on fine-tuning a pre-trained model, namely the ResNet-50 network [8] which is the first place winner of the (ILSVRC) 2015 classification competition with top-5 error rate of 3.57%, trained on a dataset with 1.2 million hand-labeled images of 1,000 different object classes.

2.1   Base System

Multi-Task learning has already shown a significant success in different applications like face detection, facial landmarks annotation, pose estimation, and traffic flow prediction [10,14,15,20].

In this work, we use MTL such that all the attributes are trained at once, using the same shared layers. To match the output of ResNet-50 network with our task, the output layer is replaced with 40 output units (one for each attribute) and use the cross-entropy loss function to measure the discrepancy between the expected and actual attribute values.

The multi-task approach not only saves on the training time, but the shared network is also more robust to overfitting, according to our experimental results. Intuitively, the model is forced to learn a general representation that captures all of the specified tasks which less the chance of overfitting. Similar findings are also reported in [2] and attributed to the regularization effect obtained by sharing weights for multiple tasks.

Table 1. Grouping attributes based on their relative location.

Group	Attributes
Head	(1) Black Hair (2) Blond Hair (3) Brown Hair (4) Gray Hair (5) Bald (6) Bangs (7) Straight Hair (8) Wavy Hair (9) Receding Hairline (10) Hat
Eyes	(11) Arched Eyebrows (12) Narrow Eyes (13) Bushy Eyebrows (14) Bags Under Eyes (15) Eyeglasses
Nose	(16) Big Nose (17) Pointy Nose
Mouth	(18) Big Lips (19) Smiling (20) Mustache (21) Wearing Lipstick (22) Mouth Slightly Open
Cheek	(23) 5 O-clock Shadow (24) Rosy Cheeks (25) Goatee (26) High Cheekbones (27) No Beard (28) Sideburns
Shoulder	(29) Double Chin (30) Wearing Necklace (31) Wearing Necktie
General	(32) Attractive (33) Blurry (34) Chubby (35) Young (36) Male (37) Pale Skin (38) Oval Face (39) Heavy Makeup, (40) Earrings

2.2 Multi-task Learning with Attribute Grouping

When all the layers are shared in a simple multi-task learning approach, the resulting network may be overly constrained. Therefore, we added a residual block for each group of attributes, after the last residual network block (res5b), as well as few layers for each attribute. This architecture is shown in the dashed part of Fig. 1.

For grouping, the 40 attributes defined for the CELEBA and LFWA datasets are divided into 7 groups based on their localization (head, eyes, nose, cheeks, mouth, shoulder, and general areas) as shown in Table 1.

In the rest of the paper, we discuss our improvement to the multi-task learning network described thus far.

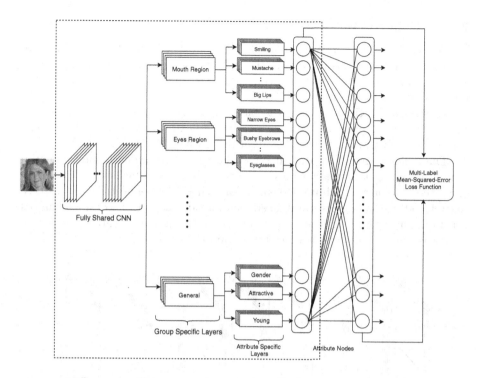

Fig. 1. End-to-end architecture for face attributes classification.

2.3 End-to-End Network

Neither the basic, nor the multi-task architectures so far take into account the correlations among attributes.

In previous work, correlations among facial attributes are learned and exploited by using a separate network or learning phase. In this work we add another fully connected layer with 40 output nodes to the network described in Sect. 2.2, for simplicity and end-to-end training. The resulting architecture is shown in Fig. 1, where the last layer aims to pick the most suitable predictions based on the predictions in the previous layer, by learning the correlations between the attributes.

The multi-label mean-squared-error loss used in this network consists of two terms, one for each of the last two layers. Specifically, for a given input image and A attributes, the loss function is denoted as shown in Eq. 1, where $\hat{y}_1[a]$ and $\hat{y}_2[a]$ denote the output for attribute a, in the last two layers:

$$loss = \sum_{a=1}^{A} \left(y[a] - \hat{y}_1[a]\right)^2 + \left(y[a] - \hat{y}_2[a]\right)^2 \tag{1}$$

In this architecture, mean-squared-error loss is used instead of cross-entropy loss, with target values of $\{-1, 1\}$, since we aim to capture attribute correlations with the last layer weights.

2.4   Within-Network Ensemble

Ensemble approaches are very important in reducing over-fitting and they are used more and more to improving the performance of deep learning systems. However, forming ensembles from deep learning systems is very costly, as training often takes long hours or days.

To reduce the time to build the base classifiers forming the ensemble and inspired by the improved results with the end-to-end architecture with two output layers, we trained an ensemble all at once, within a single network.

The architecture illustrated in Fig. 2 shows the main idea behind our approach. Assuming that we have a classification/regression task with N outputs (here the 40 binary attribute nodes), we branch a fully connected layer with N output nodes after every several layers and include their error in the global loss function. During testing, the outputs of these branches are treated as separate base classifier outputs and averaged to obtain the final output.

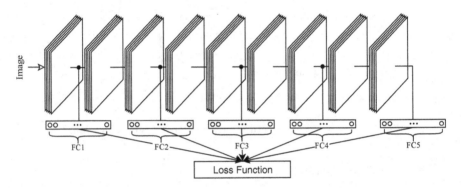

Fig. 2. A basic architecture of within-network ensemble approach, with 5 output layers.

In this work, we have constructed the ensemble with 5 such branches, each with 40 output nodes. The training of the network for one epoch on the LFWA dataset took approximately 18 min, compared to 16 min with the end-to-end network.

Notice that the base classifiers formed in this fashion use progressively more complex features and the training is much faster compared to training several separate network as base classifiers. On the other hand, while these base classifiers are not independent from each other, they show complementary behaviour, based on our experimental findings. More implementation details are discussed in Sect. 3.3.

3   Experimental Evaluation

We evaluated the effectiveness of our approach using the widely used CELEBA and LFWA datasets, described in Sect. 3.1. Data augmentation techniques used while training are presented in Sect. 3.2. In Sect. 3.3, the network and implementation details are explained. Finally, in Sect. 3.4, the performance of our proposed method is evaluated along with a comparison with several state-of-the-art techniques.

3.1   Datasets

Our experiments are conducted on two well-known datasets for face attributes classification to assess our proposed method, CELEBA and LFWA [13].

CELEBA [13] consists of $202,599$ images of $10,177$ different celebrity faces identities. The first $8k$ identities are set for training (in total around 160k images), while the remaining images are used for validation and testing (around 20k images each). The dataset provides 5 landmark locations (both eyes, nose, and mouth corners), along with ground-truth for 40 binary attributes for each image.

LFWA [13] is originally constructed for face identification and verification [9], but recently, it is annotated with the same 40 binary attributes. The annotated dataset contains 13,143 images of 5,749 different identities. The dataset has a designated training set portion of 6,263 images, while the rest is reserved for testing. LFWA is one of the challenging datasets with large variations in pose, contrast, illumination and image quality.

3.2   Data Augmentation

Deep networks typically have large number of free parameters on the order of several millions, which makes the networks prone to overfitting. One way to combat overfitting is to use data augmentation. Recently, several advanced methods for face data augmentation have been developed and automated as in [4].

In this work, we want to show the effectiveness of our stand-alone architecture without using sophisticated data augmentation or pre-processing techniques. Therefore, we only use the following simple, but effective data augmentation techniques: (1) Rotation: training images are rotated using a random rotation angle between $[-5, +5]$ around the origin. (2) Scaling: images are scaled up and down with a random scale factor up to a quarter of the image size. (3) Contrast: by converting the color space of the images from RGB to HSV and randomly multiplying the S and V channels with a factor range between $[0.5, 1.5]$. In addition, blurring with two different filter size (3×3 and 5×5) and histogram equalization are performed.

At every iteration, we randomly decide whether to apply a transformation to the input image and then pick its parameter randomly. Thus, an input image may undergo a combination of multiple transformations, during one presentation.

3.3   Network Details and Implementation

As mentioned in Sect. 2.3, ResNet-50 is used as our base model in this work, chosen due to its relatively small size and good performance.

All of the layers of ResNet-50 are shared among all of the attributes, up until the last residual block, namely res5b. Then, seven forks are branched from the res5b layer, one for each group of attributes. Each group's shared layers are similar to the layers in the last residual block of ResNet-50, which are as following: a dropout layer followed by a three consecutive blocks of convolutional layer, batch normalization, scaling and ReLU layer.

After every group block, several forks are branched, one for each attribute: a dropout layer, pool layer, followed by a fully connected layer with one unit. The output coming from all of the branches are then concatenated to form a vector of 40 units and a hyperbolic tangent ($tanh$) activation layer is applied after this layer. Finally, a fully connected layer with 40 units is added at the end, followed by $tanh$ activation layer, to learn the correlations among attributes.

For the within-network ensemble, 5 base classifiers are branched after the res2c, res3c, res4a, res4d and res5a layers of the network. The whole network is trained at once, with 7 terms in the loss function (5 coming from the extra branched layers and 2 from the last two fully connected layers).

The implementation is done using the ResNet-50 models provided in the Matlab deep learning toolbox. Throughout this work, we set the batch size equal to 32 and the initial learning rate as 10^{-3} with a total of 20 epochs with stochastic gradient descent for parameters optimization.

The training of the three models effectively took the same amount of time. Specifically, training ResNet-50 model using LFWA dataset for one epoch was performed in 15.52 min with the multi-task learning network, 16.02 min with the end-to-end network and 18.28 min with the within-network-ensemble approach.

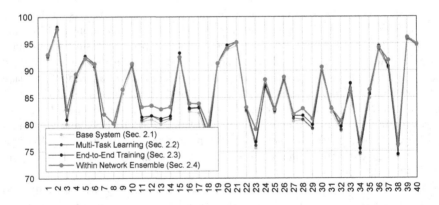

Fig. 3. Obtained accuracies on LFWA dataset from the increasingly complex networks described in Sect. 2. Best viewed in color. (Color figure online)

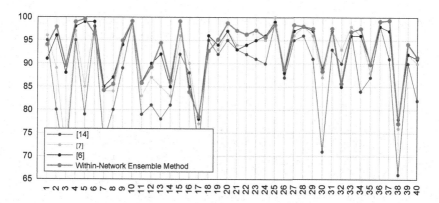

Fig. 4. State-of-the-art accuracies on CELEBA dataset compared with our proposed approach. Best viewed in color. (Color figure online)

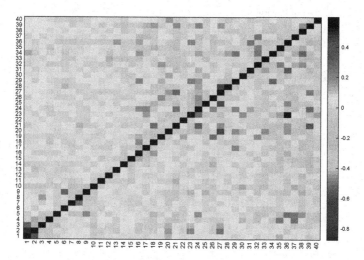

Fig. 5. Learned weights of the last hidden layer that capture the relation between attributes (attributes order is same as in Table 1).

3.4 Results and Evaluation

A comparison between our proposed methods that are described in Sect. 2, is shown using the LFWA dataset in Fig. 3. We have obtained an average accuracy of 85.15% using the base system approach; 85.66% with the multi-task network using attribute grouping; 85.92% after embedding an extra layer to capture the relation between the attributes; and finally 86.63% using our novel within-network ensemble technique. Our approach outperforms the state-of-the-art results on LFWA ([6]) by 0.48%.

In Fig. 4, our within-network ensemble approach is compared with the state-of-the-art accuracies obtained on the larger CELEBA dataset. We obtained an

Table 2. State-of-the-art accuracies on CELEBA dataset compared with the results obtained in this work, using the within-network ensemble. Bold figures indicate the best results.

#	Attribute	Baseline	[13]	[7]	[6]	This work
Head group						
1	Black Hair	72.84%	95%	**96%**	91%	94.00%
2	Blond Hair	86.67%	80%	89%	96%	**97.89%**
3	Brown Hair	82.03%	68%	71%	88%	**89.61%**
4	Gray Hair	96.81%	95%	97%	98%	**98.96%**
5	Bald	97.88%	79%	85%	99%	**99.57%**
6	Bangs	84.43%	98%	**99%**	**99%**	96.32%
7	Straight Hair	79.01%	73%	84%	**85%**	84.21%
8	Wavy Hair	63.60%	80%	84%	**87%**	85.53%
9	Receding Hairline	91.51%	89%	94%	94%	**94.90%**
10	Wearing Hat	95.80%	99%	99%	99%	**99.13%**
Eyes group						
11	Arched Eyebrows	71.56%	79%	83%	**86%**	85.79%
12	Narrow Eyes	85.13%	81%	87%	**90%**	89.21%
13	Bushy Eyebrows	87.05%	78%	85%	92%	**94.41%**
14	Bags Under Eyes	79.74%	81%	83%	85%	**86.33%**
15	Eyeglasses	93.54%	92%	96%	99%	**99.13%**
Nose group						
16	Big Nose	78.80%	88%	**90%**	85%	83.86%
17	Pointy Nose	71.43%	72%	77%	78%	**78.54%**
Mouth group						
18	Big Lips	67.30%	95%	**96%**	**96%**	92.70%
19	Smiling	49.97%	92%	93%	94%	**95.15%**
20	Mustache	96.13%	95%	97%	97%	**98.75%**
21	Wearing Lipstick	47.81%	93%	94%	93%	**97.11%**
22	Mouth Slightly ...	50.49%	92%	94%	94%	**96.27%**
Cheek group						
23	5 o'Clock Shadow	90.01%	91%	95%	95%	**97.18%**
24	Rosy Cheeks	92.83%	90%	95%	**96%**	95.66%
25	Goatee	95.42%	99%	100%	99%	98.41%
26	High Cheekbones	51.82%	87%	88%	88%	**88.69%**
27	No Beard	14.63%	95%	96%	97%	**98.36%**
28	Sideburns	95.36%	96%	98%	98%	**98.05%**
Shoulder group						
29	Double Chin	95.43%	91%	96%	97%	**97.56%**
30	Wearing Necklace	86.21%	71%	87%	**89%**	88.32%
31	Wearing Necktie	92.99%	93%	97%	97%	**97.58%**
General						
32	Attractive	50.42%	90%	**93%**	85%	85.68%
33	Blurry	94.94%	97%	**98%**	96%	96.84%
34	Chubby	94.70%	84%	96%	96%	**97.54%**
35	Young	24.29%	87%	88%	**90%**	89.84%
36	Male	61.35%	98%	98%	98%	**99.13%**
37	Pale Skin	95.79%	91%	97%	97%	**99.35%**
38	Oval Face	70.44%	66%	76%	**78%**	77.07%
39	Heavy Makeup	59.50%	90%	92%	92%	**94.19%**
40	Wearing Earrings	79.34%	82%	90%	91%	**91.34%**
	Average	76.87%	87.30%	91.32%	92.60%	**93.20%**

average accuracy of 93.20% that surpasses the state-of-the-art obtained in [6], by 0.60%. Note that improvements are small due partly to the already high accuracy rates for this problem and the fact that some of the binary attributes are in fact continuous attributes (e.g. smile).

By visualizing the learned weights of the last hidden layer (Fig. 5), we found that the relationship between attributes are nicely captured. For instance, the learned weights show a high negative correlation between "No Beard" attribute and "Mustache", "Goatee", and "Side Burns" attributes. Contrarily, there is a high positive correlation between "Heavy Makeup" attribute and "Wearing Lipstick", "Rosy Cheeks", and "No Beard" attributes.

State-of-art results on the CELEBA dataset and those obtained with the within-network ensemble are shown in Table 2.

4   Conclusion

We present an end-to-end multi-task framework for face attribute classification that considers attribute location to reduce network size and correlation among attributes to improve accuracy.

We also introduce a novel ensemble technique that we call within-network ensemble, by branching output nodes from different depths of the network and computing the loss over all these branches. As the network is shared, this branching results in very little computational overhead. To the best of our knowledge, this ensemble technique has not been suggested before, while it brings non-negligible improvements (0.71% points accuracy improvement over the end-to-end network). Our results surpass state-of-the-art on both LFWA and CELEBA datasets, with 86.63% and 93.20% average accuracies, respectively.

Acknowledgements. We gratefully acknowledge NVIDIA Corporation with the donation of the Titan X Pascal GPU used in this research.

References

1. Aly, S.A., Yanikoglu, B.: Multi-label networks for face attributes classification. In: IEEE International Conference on Multimedia and Expo Workshops (ICMEW), pp. 1–6. IEEE (2018)
2. Baxter, J.: A Bayesian/information theoretic model of learning to learn via multiple task sampling. Mach. Learn. **28**(1), 7–39 (1997)
3. Bourdev, L., Maji, S., Malik, J.: Describing people: a poselet-based approach to attribute classification. In: International Conference on Computer Vision (ICCV), pp. 1543–1550. IEEE (2011)
4. Cubuk, E.D., Zoph, B., Mane, D., Vasudevan, V., Le, Q.V.: Autoaugment: learning augmentation policies from data. arXiv:1805.09501 (2018)
5. Ehrlich, M., Shields, T.J., Almaev, T., Amer, M.R.: Facial attributes classification using multi-task representation learning. In: IEEE Conference on Computer Vision and Pattern Recognition Workshops, pp. 47–55 (2016)

6. Han, H., Jain, A.K., Wang, F., Shan, S., Chen, X.: Heterogeneous face attribute estimation: a deep multi-task learning approach. IEEE trans. Pattern Anal. Mach. Intell. **40**(11), 2597–2609 (2018)
7. Hand, E.M., Chellappa, R.: Attributes for improved attributes: a multi-task network utilizing implicit and explicit relationships for facial attribute classification. In: 31st AAAI Conference on Artificial Intelligence (2017)
8. He, K., Zhang, X., Ren, S., Sun, J.: Deep residual learning for image recognition. In: IEEE conference on Computer Vision and Pattern Recognition (CVPR), pp. 770–778 (2016)
9. Huang, G.B., Ramesh, M., Berg, T., Learned-Miller, E.: Labeled faces in the wild: a database for studying face recognition in unconstrained environments. Technical repot, 07–49, University of Massachusetts, Amherst, Technical Report, October 2007
10. Huang, W., Song, G., Hong, H., Xie, K.: Deep architecture for traffic flow prediction: deep belief networks with multitask learning. IEEE Trans. Intell. Transp. Syst. **15**(5), 2191–2201 (2014)
11. Kumar, N., Berg, A.C., Belhumeur, P.N., Nayar, S.K.: Attribute and simile classifiers for face verification. In: IEEE 12th International Conference on Computer Vision (ICCV), pp. 365–372. IEEE (2009)
12. Li, Y., Wang, R., Liu, H., Jiang, H., Shan, S., Chen, X.: Two birds, one stone: jointly learning binary code for large-scale face image retrieval and attributes prediction. In: IEEE International Conference on Computer Vision (ICCV), pp. 3819–3827 (2015)
13. Liu, Z., Luo, P., Wang, X., Tang, X.: Deep learning face attributes in the wild. In: IEEE International Conference on Computer Vision (ICCV), pp. 3730–3738 (2015)
14. Luo, Y., Tao, D., Geng, B., Xu, C., Maybank, S.J.: Manifold regularized multitask learning for semi-supervised multilabel image classification. IEEE Trans. Image Process. **22**(2), 523–536 (2013)
15. Ranjan, R., Patel, V.M., Chellappa, R.: Hyperface: a deep multi-task learning framework for face detection, landmark localization, pose estimation, and gender recognition. arXiv:1603.01249 (2016)
16. Rozsa, A., Günther, M., Rudd, E.M., Boult, T.E.: Are facial attributes adversarially robust? In: 23rd International Conference on Pattern Recognition (ICPR), pp. 3121–3127. IEEE (2016)
17. Rudd, E.M., Günther, M., Boult, T.E.: MOON: a mixed objective optimization network for the recognition of facial attributes. In: Leibe, B., Matas, J., Sebe, N., Welling, M. (eds.) ECCV 2016. LNCS, vol. 9909, pp. 19–35. Springer, Cham (2016). https://doi.org/10.1007/978-3-319-46454-1_2
18. Sharif Razavian, A., Azizpour, H., Sullivan, J., Carlsson, S.: CNN features off-the-shelf: an astounding baseline for recognition. In: IEEE Conference on Computer Vision and Pattern Recognition Workshops, pp. 806–813 (2014)
19. Song, F., Tan, X., Chen, S.: Exploiting relationship between attributes for improved face verification. Comput. Vis. Image Underst. **122**, 143–154 (2014)
20. Yi, S., Jiang, N., Feng, B., Wang, X., Liu, W.: Online similarity learning for visual tracking. Inform. Sci. **364**, 33–50 (2016)
21. Zhong, Y., Sullivan, J., Li, H.: Face attribute prediction using off-the-shelf CNN features. In: International Conference on Biometrics (ICB), pp. 1–7. IEEE (2016)
22. Zhu, Z., Luo, P., Wang, X., Tang, X.: Multi-view perceptron: a deep model for learning face identity and view representations. In: Advances in Neural Information Processing Systems (NIPS), pp. 217–225 (2014)

Visual and Textual Sentiment Analysis of Daily News Social Media Images by Deep Learning

Andrea Felicetti[1,2], Massimo Martini[1,2], Marina Paolanti[1,2(✉)],
Roberto Pierdicca[1,2], Emanuele Frontoni[1,2], and Primo Zingaretti[1,2]

[1] Dipartimento di Ingegneria Civile, Edile e dell'Architettura,
Università Politecnica delle Marche, Via Brecce Bianche 12, 60131 Ancona, Italy
{m.paolanti,r.pierdicca,e.frontoni,p.zingaretti}@univpm.it
[2] Dipartimento di Ingegneria dell'Informazione, Università Politecnica delle Marche,
Via Brecce Bianche 12, 60131 Ancona, Italy

Abstract. In recent years, following the exploding spread of Social Networking platforms, more and more people have started to share large quantities of data on Internet where they express personal opinions, ideas or emotional states regarding any kind of topic. With the increasing amount of these type of data, finding a way to analyzing it has become a need for major companies, political parties or whatever organization based on its own customers' feedback. This paper proposes a new case of study that has seen a limited assortment of similar proposals in the current state-of-art: in particular, we propose an innovative approach for analyzing both visual and textual features of Social Media images using Deep Convolutional Neural Networks (DCNNs), in order to collect more accurate results than the single analysis of both type can do alone. The deep learning approach estimates the overall sentiment of daily news-related pictures from social media based on both visual and textual clues. The proposed approach was applied and tested on a new public dataset with more than 9.000 annotated Instagram images. Experimental results confirmed the effectiveness of the approach, showing high values of accuracy.

1 Introduction

Nowadays, publishing or sharing a thought, an image or a video is an easy and quite intuitive task that most of people performe normally during the day. Posts about own ideas on surrounding events, rating of products, places and companies' services are published in a large amount on a daily basis. For this reason, an increasing need to somehow control, analyzing and collecting data from them has become crucial and fundamental for the organizations that rely on their customers' support: being able to determine if a product is having success, if people are discontent about a political reform or if a certain restaurant has enough standards for you are typical examples showing their important role for

© Springer Nature Switzerland AG 2019
E. Ricci et al. (Eds.): ICIAP 2019, LNCS 11751, pp. 477–487, 2019.
https://doi.org/10.1007/978-3-030-30642-7_43

marketing policies and politics carried on by the major financial and commercial organizations.

This study, in particular, focuses its attention on image content: a lot of different approaches were proposed to resolve these needs in the most efficient way, most of them based on visual analysis or textual analysis, singularly. With the increasing popularity of social networks and image sharing platforms [5] more and more opinions are expressed by an image format. Several researchers have now started to propose solutions for the sentiment analysis of visual content. It is important to notice, however, that a multitude of user' pictures does not only include visual elements, but also textual elements. For example, people take pictures of advertisement posters or more frequently, use any image-editing software to add some words or sentences on them. In order to estimate the overall sentiment of a picture, then, it is essential to not only analyze the sentiment of the visual elements but also to correctly understand the meaning of the included text and to analyze it accordingly. As in retail [24,25], it can happen that identical images have an opposite meaning since their textual content is exactly the opposite. If we do not consider the text, we could determine a wrong sentiment. In this paper, it is improved and extended the approach which has already been described in [23]. The sentiment of a picture is identified by a machine learning classifier based on visual and textual features, extracted from two specially trained Deep Convolutional Neural Networks (DCNNs). In particular, we focus on sentiment analysis for both visual and textual information of daily news-related pictures taken from Instagram.

For the visual feature extractor, VGG-16 net [29], AlexNet [17], CaffeNet [14], GoogLeNet [30], and ResNet [11] with 50 layers and ResNet with 101 layers were used and applied to the whole image, trained by fine-tuning a model pre-trained on the ImageNet dataset. For the textual feature extractor, the DCNN architecture was used, proposed by [40] and created by fine-tuning a model that has been previously trained on synthesised social media images. The model first had to detect and recognise text before extracting features. With reference to these features, six state-of-the-art classifiers, i.e., kNearest Neighbors (kNN) [1], [32], Support Vector Machine (SVM) [8], Decision Tree (DT) [27], Random Forest (RF) [2], Naive Bayes (NB) [28], and Artificial Neural Network (ANN) [20], were evaluated to classify the overall sentiment.

The approach has been applied to a newly collected dataset "SocIal Media PictureS News-related" (SIMPSoN) Dataset of daily news pictures from Instagram. Both visual and textual elements concerning daily news were present in the dataset with a total of 9.247 images.

Ground truth has been manually evaluated by three human annotators to make it more reliable. The SIMPSoN Dataset is publicly available[1] for research purposes. The application of our approach to this dataset showed good results in terms of precision, recall, and F1-score, which demonstrated the effectiveness of the proposed approach.

---

[1] http://vrai.dii.univpm.it/content/simpson-dataset.

The main contributions of this paper, aside from extending the system and the analysis presented in [23], are (i) the collection and analysis of an Instagram pictures dataset for deep learning purposes that is public to all researchers with more than 9.000 social media images, (ii) the proposal of a novel method that evaluates the visual and textual content of an image simultaneously, and (iii) performance comparison of data collection for social media pictures classification.

The paper is organised as follows: Sect. 2 is an overview of the research status of textual and visual sentiment analysis; Sect. 3 introduces more specifically our approach, describing also the visual features extractor, the textual features extractor, and the overall sentiment classifier; Sect. 4 presents the results; and Sect. 5 discusses the conclusions and future works.

2   Related Works

The Sentiment Analysis is a wide field that contains a lot of different approaches and methods that can be used according to the particular case of study. Sentiment analysis is applied to a large set of applications, that come from political election prediction [7,33] stock market predicting [10,18], product evaluation [9,31] and movie boxoffice performance [35].

Taking into account data sources, an important distinction for sentiment analysis approaches is the division into unimodal and multimodal [3]: while unimodal approaches consider only one data source, multimodal models consider several types of data sources when determining the sentiment. According to [12], mainly in the last years the multimodal approach has an increasing attention. This because often, an only one source of information can be ambiguous and so not sufficient to detect the real sentiment of an emotion. For multimodal sentiment, three types of combination methods exist: early fusion [22,26], late fusion [34,35], and intermediate fusion [6,37].

In the early fusion, multiple sources of data are integrated to form a single feature vector. In [26], the authors use deep convolutional neural networks to extract features from visual and textual sources and then fuse all the features with a multiple kernel learning classifier.

Late fusion aggregate decisions derived from multiple sentiment classifiers. Each classifier is trained considering different modalities, that are independent in the features space. Late fusion is employed in [4,34], that combines the prediction results using text and images for sentiment analysis.

Finally, the last approach is intermediate fusion that refers to the use of artificial neural networks, where the fusion process occurs in an intermediate layer of the networks. In the study [38], the authors employ both images and text to determine the sentiment by fine-tuning a CNN for image sentiment analysis and by training a paragraph vector model for textual sentiment analysis. Furthermore, in [39], the authors employ deep learning approaches to analyze the sentiment of Chinese micro-blogs posts from both textual and visual contents. In recent years, the use of methods based on Deep learning is increased in the sentiment analysis field. For example, in [15], the authors use a Convolutional

Neural Network (CNN) to extract features from sentences and perform sentiment analysis of Twitter messages; in [21], an ensemble system to detect the sentiment of a text document from a data set of IMDB movie reviews and ratings. CNNs have also been applied to the visual part of sentiment analysis. For example, in [36] visual sentiment prediction framework is introduced: it performs transfer operations learning from a pre-trained CNN with millions of parameters.

3   Materials and Methods

The approach presented in [23], i.e., the combination of the visual and textual features, has been used and extended for the development of the proposed framework. The framework for joint visual and textual analysis, as well as the novel social media dataset (SIMPSoN Dataset) used for evaluation, was comprised of three main components: the visual feature extractor, the textual feature extractor, and the overall classifier (see Fig. 1). Two trained DCNNs were used for visual and textual feature extraction. Then, the two features were combined and fed into the fusion classifier. To estimate the overall content of the image, state-of-art machine learning algorithms were compared. Further details on the visual and textual feature extractor and overall classifier are given in the following sections.

The framework is comprehensively evaluated on the "SIMPSoN" Dataset, publicity available, collected for this work. The details of the data collection and ground truth labeling are discussed in Subsect. 3.4.

3.1   Description of Visual Feature Extractor

The visual feature extractor provides information about the visual part of the picture. For this task, it is trained with image labels that indicate the visual category of the images. The training is performed by fine-tuning a DCNN. Different DCNNs were tested to chose the ones with the best performance: VGG-16 net [29], an AlexNet [17], a CaffeNet [14], a GoogLeNet [30], and a ResNet [11] with 50 layers, and a ResNet with 101 layers. The DCNNs have been pre-trained on the ImageNet dataset [17] to classify images into 1,000 categories. The fine-tuning is performed by cutting off the final classification layer and replacing it with a fully connected layer that has three outputs (one for each category class); the learning rate multipliers are increased for that layer. Loss and accuracy layers are adapted to take the input from the newly created final layer. The output of the next to last layer is passed to the fusion classifier (fc7 layer for VGG-16, AlexNet, and CaffeNet; pool5 for GoogLeNet and ResNet50). The image feature extractor is implemented using standard Keras tools[2]. The dataset was initially subjected to a phase of preprocessing to be able to be used: images was cropped at the center and resized to 224×224 pixels. Furthermore the training was improved by using data augmentation techniques: images of the dataset was randomly flipped (Left-to-Right, Top-to-Down) and rotated ($90°$, $180°$, $270°$).

---

[2] http://keras.io/.

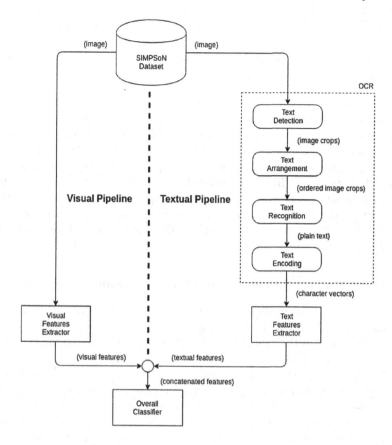

Fig. 1. Workflow of the multimodal sentiment evaluation.

3.2 Description of the Textual Feature Extractor

The textual feature extractor provides information about the textual category of a picture. It is trained with image labels that indicate the textual category of the images. Multiple components make up the textual feature extractor. The central component is a character-level CNN [40], extended for this analysis by one additional convolution layer. This extra layer, inserted before the last pooling layer, has a kernel size of three and produces 256 features. The text must be transformed into characters before being processed by the character-level DCNN, since it is embedded in the picture as pixels. For this reason, the following steps have been performed:

1. *Text Detection*: Individual text boxes are detected in an image with the TextBoxes Caffe model [19].
2. *Text Arrangement*: Detected text boxes are put in order based on a left-to-right, top-to-bottom policy, thus forming logical lines.

3. *Text Recognition*: Each text box is processed by the OCR model [13] to transcribe the text of the box.
4. *Text Encoding*: The recognised text is encoded into one-hot vectors based on the alphabet of the character-level DCNN.

The textual features of the next to last layer of the character-level DCNN are passed to final fusion classifier.

The performance of a Dictionary based model is also evaluated. Each phrase is mapped into a real vector domain, a technique that is called "word embedding" when working with the text. This is a technique where words are encoded as real-valued vectors in a high dimensional space; the similarity between word meanings translates to closeness in the vector space [16]. The sequence length (number of words) in each phrase varies, so we constrained each phrase to be 20 words, truncating long phrases and padding the shorter phrases with zero values. Results were compared with those of character-level DCNN.

3.3 Description of the Overall Sentiment Classifier

Fusion classifier estimates the overall content of an image on the basis of the visual and textual features. Thus, the visual and textual features extracted from DCNN were pooled in the predictor vector and the machine learning classifier it is trained with indicated the overall sentiment of the images. Based on all features, six state-of-the-art classifiers—k-Nearest Neighbor (kNN), Support Vector Machine (SVM), Decision Tree (DT), Random Forest (RF), Naive Bayes (NB), and Artificial Neural Network (ANN)—were compared to recognise the overall content of the images. For what concerns the kNN, we employed the euclidean distance as metric function. The Gaussian kernel was used for SVM. We selected the optimal hyper-parameters for the machine learning methods (i.e., kNN: number of neighbours, SVM: kernel scale and box constraint, RF: number of weak classifiers, ANN: number of hidden layers), implementing a grid-search and optimising the F1-score in five-fold cross-validation within the training set. The testing performances were evaluated in terms of precision, recall, and F1-score.

3.4 SIMPSoN Dataset

In order to evaluate the performance of the implemented system we used a purposely created dataset comprising 9247 images. The sentiment of the images was labeled manually. Since our goal is to conduct a visual sentiment analysis, we have based our work on Instagram, the most famous image sharing social network. Through profiles, hashtag and location, it is possible to search the images related to recent news. The true content has been manually estimated to provide a more precise and less cluttered dataset. All pictures are annotated with respect to their visual, textual, and overall content.

Figure 2 shows three examples of pictures in the SIMPSoN Dataset. As can be seen, the overall content depends not just on the visual content of the picture, but also on the textual content. The current dataset is used to test and deploy the proposed methodology and compare different approaches. Further details will be presented in the results section.

(a) Positive   (b) Neutral   (c) Negative

Fig. 2. Images from our data set. (a) is an example of positive image, (b) represents an image with neutral sentiment, and (c) is a picture with negative sentiment.

As we can see, we have considered "positive" the images showing solidarity, friendship, and in general all the ethical positive facts; for the negatives, we chose to include in this category all the pictures showing violence, racism and excessive vulgar statements.

4   Results and Discussion

In this section, we report the results of the experiments conducted on SIMPSoN Dataset. The performance of the overall classifier is presented, with the performance of the visual and textual classifiers (based on the visual and textual feature extractors) being the key indicators to the overall classification. For the experimental analysis, the labelled dataset has been split into a training set and a test set. Each classifier was trained solely through the training set, while the test set was used for all test purposes. The considered dataset is split into two randomly selected sub-sets: 80% for training images and 20% for test images, accounting for all permutations of overall, visual, and textual annotations.

The performance of the visual classification is reported in Table 1.

Table 1. Visual classification results.

DCNN	Accuracy	Precision	Recall	F1-score
VGG16	**74.57**	**72.10**	**74.03**	**73.06**
AlexNet	70.08	71.35	71.10	71.22
CaffeNet	69.14	71.80	70.13	70.96
GoogleNet	71.22	70.14	71.08	71.61
ResNet50	73.54	69.63	71.10	70.36
ResNet101	69.18	70.40	68.02	69.21

As shown above, high values of precision and recall can be achieved. In Table 2, the precision, recall, and F1-score of the textual classification is presented. From the results we can see that for this type of dataset and based on a classification of a few classes, the VGG16 has better performance than a much deeper network like the ResNet. The latter is usually better performing with classification problems on many classes, for example with the 1000 classes of ImageNet dataset. The textual classification performance is mainly good, but lower than the visual classification performance. While the classification of visual and textual image content is equally difficult for humans, the classification of the text in the picture is much more challenging for machines, as it needs to be detected and recognised before it can be classified.

Table 2. Textual classification results.

OCR	DCNN	Accuracy	Precision	Recall	F1-score
Char based	Kim [16]	66.13	68.59	59.37	58.26
	Zhang [40]	57.15	54.10	53.07	52.73
Dict based	Kim [16]	**68.05**	**67.34**	**63.53**	**63.68**
	Zhang [40]	56.34	55.67	53.55	52.80

The features vectors (visual and textual) are extracted from the last layer before the last fully connected of the best models (visulal an textual). Than the 4096 visual and 1024 textual features are concatenated in a unique vector that is the imput of final classifiers. To train the final classifiers the feature vectors were balanced between the classes based on the overall ground truth. Therefore 2898 samples, equal to the number of the minority class, were selected from each class. For each class 2318 samples are used for training and the remaining 580 used for the test (split 80–20%). Finally, the results about the Overall Sentiment Classification are shown in Table 3.

The best classifier in our study was the SVM, followed by k-NN and RF.

Table 3. Overall classification results.

Classifier	Accuracy	Precision	Recall	F1-score
DT	74.22	75.55	73.14	74.34
RF	76.12	76.07	77.10	76.58
kNN	77.80	78.90	77.22	78.06
NB	73.81	72.90	73.12	73.01
ANN	74.74	72.10	71.45	71.77
SVM	**79.70**	**78.12**	**79.45**	**78.78**

5   Conclusion

Multimodal sentiment analysis of social media pictures represents a challenging task useful to estimate user opionion on several fields. In this paper, we introduce a deep learning approach for recognizing the sentiment of daily news social media pictures by taking visual as well as textual information into account. The sentiment of a picture is identified by a machine learning classifier based on visual and textual features extracted from two especially trained DCNNs. By combining DCNNs with machine learning classifiers such as kNN, SVM, DT, RF, NB, and ANN, the approach is able to learn a high level representation of both visual and textual content and to achieve good precision and recall for sentiment classification. The experiments on the SIMPSoN Dataset yield high accuracies and demonstrate the effectiveness and suitability of our approach. Further investigation will be devoted to improve our approach by employing a larger dataset and by comparing the performance of other networks, such as LSTM (Long Short Term Memory). Moreover, we will extend the evaluation by comparing our visual and textual classifiers with other existing systems for visual and textual sentiment analysis.

References

1. Bø, T.H., Dysvik, B., Jonassen, I.: Lsimpute: accurate estimation of missing values in microarray data with least squares methods. Nucleic Acids Res. **32**(3), e34–e34 (2004)
2. Breiman, L.: Random forests. Mach. Learn. **45**(1), 5–32 (2001)
3. Cambria, E., Poria, S., Bisio, F., Bajpai, R., Chaturvedi, I.: The CLSA model: a novel framework for concept-level sentiment analysis. In: Gelbukh, A. (ed.) CICLing 2015. LNCS, vol. 9042, pp. 3–22. Springer, Cham (2015). https://doi.org/10.1007/978-3-319-18117-2_1
4. Cao, D., Ji, R., Lin, D., Li, S.: A cross-media public sentiment analysis system for microblog. Multimed. Syst. **22**(4), 479–486 (2016)
5. Chang, Y., Tang, L., Inagaki, Y., Liu, Y.: What is Tumblr: a statistical overview and comparison. ACM SIGKDD Explor. Newsl. **16**(1), 21–29 (2014)
6. Chen, M., Wang, S., Liang, P.P., Baltrušaitis, T., Zadeh, A., Morency, L.P.: Multimodal sentiment analysis with word-level fusion and reinforcement learning. In: Proceedings of the 19th ACM International Conference on Multimodal Interaction, pp. 163–171. ACM (2017)
7. Chung, J.E., Mustafaraj, E.: Can collective sentiment expressed on twitter predict political elections? In: Twenty-Fifth AAAI Conference on Artificial Intelligence (2011)
8. Cortes, C., Vapnik, V.: Support-vector networks. Mach. Learn. **20**(3), 273–297 (1995)
9. Cui, H., Mittal, V., Datar, M.: Comparative experiments on sentiment classification for online product reviews. In: AAAI, vol. 6, p. 30 (2006)
10. Feldman, R., Rosenfeld, B., Bar-Haim, R., Fresko, M.: The stock sonar–sentiment analysis of stocks based on a hybrid approach. In: Twenty-Third IAAI Conference (2011)

11. He, K., Zhang, X., Ren, S., Sun, J.: Deep residual learning for image recognition. In: IEEE Conference on Computer Vision and Pattern Recognition, pp. 770–778 (2016)
12. Huang, F., Zhang, X., Zhao, Z., Xu, J., Li, Z.: Image-text sentiment analysisvia deep multimodal attentive fusion. Knowl.-Based Syst. **167**, 26–37 (2019)
13. Jaderberg, M., Simonyan, K., Vedaldi, A., Zisserman, A.: Reading text in the wild with convolutional neural networks. Int. J. Comput. Vis. **116**(1), 1–20 (2016)
14. Jia, Y., et al.: Caffe: convolutional architecture for fast feature embedding. In: 22nd International Conference on Multimedia, pp. 675–678. ACM (2014)
15. Kim, Y.: Convolutional neural networks for sentence classification. arXiv preprint arXiv:1408.5882 (2014)
16. Kim, Y., Jernite, Y., Sontag, D., Rush, A.M.: Character-aware neural language models. In: Thirtieth AAAI Conference on Artificial Intelligence (2016)
17. Krizhevsky, A., Sutskever, I., Hinton, G.E.: ImageNet classification with deep convolutional neural networks. In: Advances in Neural Information Processing Systems, pp. 1097–1105 (2012)
18. Li, X., Xie, H., Chen, L., Wang, J., Deng, X.: News impact on stock price return via sentiment analysis. Knowl.-Based Syst. **69**, 14–23 (2014)
19. Liao, M., Shi, B., Bai, X., Wang, X., Liu, W.: TextBoxes: a fast text detector with a single deep neural network. arXiv preprint arXiv:1611.06779 (2016)
20. Lippmann, R.: An introduction to computing with neural nets. IEEE Assp mag. **4**(2), 4–22 (1987)
21. Mesnil, G., Mikolov, T., Ranzato, M., Bengio, Y.: Ensemble of generative and discriminative techniques for sentiment analysis of movie reviews. arXiv preprint arXiv:1412.5335 (2014)
22. Morency, L.P., Mihalcea, R., Doshi, P.: Towards multimodal sentiment analysis: harvesting opinions from the web. In: Proceedings of the 13th International Conference on Multimodal Interfaces, pp. 169–176. ACM (2011)
23. Paolanti, M., Kaiser, C., Schallner, R., Frontoni, E., Zingaretti, P.: Visual and textual sentiment analysis of brand-related social media pictures using deep convolutional neural networks. In: Battiato, S., Gallo, G., Schettini, R., Stanco, F. (eds.) ICIAP 2017. LNCS, vol. 10484, pp. 402–413. Springer, Cham (2017). https://doi.org/10.1007/978-3-319-68560-1_36
24. Paolanti, M., Romeo, L., Martini, M., Mancini, A., Frontoni, E., Zingaretti, P.: Robotic retail surveying by deep learning visual and textual data. Robot. Auton. Syst. **118**, 179–188 (2019)
25. Paolanti, M., Sturari, M., Mancini, A., Zingaretti, P., Frontoni, E.: Mobile robot for retail surveying and inventory using visual and textual analysis of monocular pictures based on deep learning. In: 2017 European Conference on Mobile Robots (ECMR), pp. 1–6. IEEE (2017)
26. Poria, S., Chaturvedi, I., Cambria, E., Hussain, A.: Convolutional MKL based multimodal emotion recognition and sentiment analysis. In: 2016 IEEE 16th International Conference on Data Mining (ICDM), pp. 439–448. IEEE (2016)
27. Quinlan, J.R.: Induction of decision trees. Mach. Learn. **1**(1), 81–106 (1986)
28. Rish, I.: An empirical study of the naive bayes classifier. In: IJCAI 2001 Workshop on Empirical Methods in Artificial Intelligence, vol. 3, pp. 41–46. IBM New York (2001)
29. Simonyan, K., Zisserman, A.: Very deep convolutional networks for large-scale image recognition. arXiv preprint arXiv:1409.1556 (2014)
30. Szegedy, C., et al.: Going deeper with convolutions. In: Conference on Computer Vision and Pattern Recognition (2015)

31. Tang, D., Qin, B., Liu, T.: Learning semantic representations of users and products for document level sentiment classification. In: Proceedings of the 53rd Annual Meeting of the Association for Computational Linguistics and the 7th International Joint Conference on Natural Language Processing (Volume 1: Long Papers), vol. 1, pp. 1014–1023 (2015)

32. Troyanskaya, O., et al.: Missing value estimation methods for DNA microarrays. Bioinformatics **17**(6), 520–525 (2001)

33. Tumasjan, A., Sprenger, T.O., Sandner, P.G., Welpe, I.M.: Predicting elections with Twitter: what 140 characters reveal about political sentiment. In: Fourth international AAAI conference on weblogs and social media (2010)

34. Wang, M., Cao, D., Li, L., Li, S., Ji, R.: Microblog sentiment analysis based on cross-media bag-of-words model. In: Proceedings of International Conference On Internet Multimedia Computing and Service, p. 76. ACM (2014)

35. Wöllmer, M., et al.: Youtube movie reviews: sentiment analysis in an audio-visual context. IEEE Intell. Syst. **28**(3), 46–53 (2013)

36. Xu, C., Cetintas, S., Lee, K.C., Li, L.J.: Visual sentiment prediction with deep convolutional neural networks. arXiv preprint arXiv:1411.5731 (2014)

37. You, Q., Cao, L., Jin, H., Luo, J.: Robust visual-textual sentiment analysis: when attention meets tree-structured recursive neural networks. In: Proceedings of the 24th ACM International Conference on Multimedia, pp. 1008–1017. ACM (2016)

38. You, Q., Luo, J., Jin, H., Yang, J.: Joint visual-textual sentiment analysis with deep neural networks. In: Proceedings of the 23rd ACM International Conference on Multimedia, pp. 1071–1074. ACM (2015)

39. Yu, Y., Lin, H., Meng, J., Zhao, Z.: Visual and textual sentiment analysis of a microblog using deep convolutional neural networks. Algorithms **9**(2), 41 (2016)

40. Zhang, X., Zhao, J., LeCun, Y.: Character-level convolutional networks for text classification. In: Advances in Neural Information Processing Systems, pp. 649–657 (2015)

Deep Compact Person Re-Identification with Distractor Synthesis via Guided DC-GANs

Víctor Ponce-López$^{(\boxtimes)}$ ⓘ, Tilo Burghardt, Yue Sun, Sion Hannuna, Dima Damen ⓘ, and Majid Mirmehdi ⓘ

Department of Computer Science, University of Bristol, Bristol BS8 1UB, UK
v.poncelopez@bristol.ac.uk

Abstract. We present a dual-stream CNN that learns both appearance and facial features in tandem from still images and, after feature fusion, infers person identities. We then describe an alternative architecture of a single, lightweight ID-CondenseNet where a face detector-guided DC-GAN is used to generate distractor person images for enhanced training. For evaluation, we test both architectures on FLIMA, a new extension of an existing person re-identification dataset with added frame-by-frame annotations of face presence. Although the dual-stream CNN can outperform the CondenseNet approach on FLIMA, we show that the latter surpasses all state-of-the-art architectures in top-1 ranking performance when applied to the largest existing person re-identification dataset, MSMT17. We conclude that whilst re-identification performance is highly sensitive to the structure of datasets, distractor augmentation and network compression have a role to play for enhancing performance characteristics for larger scale applications.

Keywords: Person Re-ID · GANs · Distractor synthesis · Deep face analysis

1 Introduction

Visual person re-identification (Re-ID) is tasked with linking people's identities across multiple acquisition scenarios usually comprising disjoint fields of view. Given this highly variable operational environment, real-world Re-ID constitutes a particularly challenging sub-domain in computer vision due to inherent viewpoint and illumination changes, partial occlusions, limitations on resolution, and significant appearance alterations, such as changes in clothing [9,14]. These exigent visual conditions and the presence of facial occlusions render unimodal approaches, such as face recognition systems, *on their own* inadequate – and that is despite their human-level performance on favourable, well-known datasets, *e.g.* [16,33].

© Springer Nature Switzerland AG 2019
E. Ricci et al. (Eds.): ICIAP 2019, LNCS 11751, pp. 488–498, 2019.
https://doi.org/10.1007/978-3-030-30642-7_44

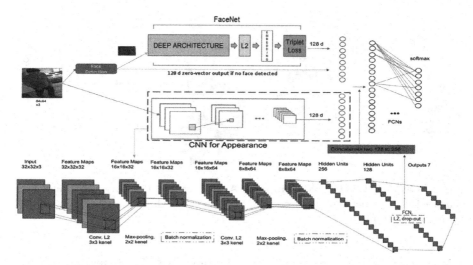

Fig. 1. Utilised Dual-Stream Architecture. Dual-stream CNN subdivided into appearance and facial feature streams using late feature fusion to map from frames to person identities. The appearance CNN network is based on LeNet-5 [15].

The emergence of deep learning techniques such as Convolutional Neural Networks (CNNs), streamed network designs, and large scale datasets [3, 30, 35] all have significantly evolved the field of Re-ID and addressed some of the issues mentioned above, with significant impact on applications including outdoor CCTV surveillance [7] and indoor e-health systems [1]. Whilst CNN-based representation learning excels at generating discriminative feature stacks that map inputs to compact identity clusters in embedding space, obtaining cross-referenced ground truth over long term [27], realising deployment of inexpensive inference platforms, and establishing visual identities from very limited data, remain challenging. In particular, the dependency of most deep learning paradigms on high computational requirements and on vast annotated training data pools appear as significant challenges to the field of person Re-ID.

In this paper, we explore the problem of ineffective training and heavy network footprints by proposing a generative-discriminative framework that generates images of a distractor class for enhancing the training of a discriminative ID-network – one which is lightweight and compact to deploy.

Initially, we describe a traditional two-stream CNN architecture (see Fig. 1) split into appearance and facial feature streams that map in a conventional way, after late feature fusion, from still images to person identities. This network follows a regular streaming architecture deploying one visual task per stream before combined inference. Then, we propose to utilise the facial stream of this architecture to aid a setup where a single compact CondenseNet [11] is trained to perform Re-ID. Critically, training data is enhanced via a Deep Convolutional Generative Adversarial Network (DC-GAN) [20] generating a large set of distractor images semantically guided by facial semantics (see Fig. 2). Note that

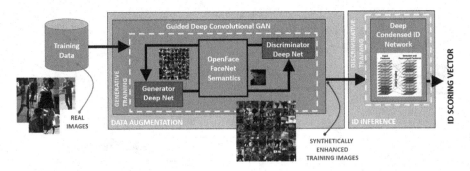

Fig. 2. Guided DC-GAN Compact Architecture. CondenseNet training is enhanced via distractor data generated by a DC-GAN which is semantically guided by a face detector.

synthesised distractor person images are generated by training input from across all identities; the synthesised content is thus *not* identical to given images of *any one* identity. Conceptually, adding such a distractor class as an extra identity to the given identities for training the identification network enforces differentiation of persons from visually nearby distractors.

For evaluation, we introduce Facial-LIMA (FLIMA), which is an extension of the Long-term Identity-aware Multi-target multi-camerA dataset (LIMA) [14], by way of added frame-wise annotations of occurrence of faces. For an evaluation in a second, very different scenario, comparative experiments on the large Multi-Scene Multi-Time (MSMT17 [30]) person Re-ID dataset are presented. This comparison includes the dual-stream architecture and different settings of the proposed Guided DC-GAN trained compact CondenseNet against other reported results of the state-of-the-art on this dataset. Due to differences in the standard evaluation protocols, to sensitivity to the presence of detectable faces, and to resolution differences, we report on the varying efficacy of the tested approaches.

2   Related Work

The transition from hand-crafted features and small-scale evaluation to deep learning systems [36] with large-scale training datasets has fundamentally changed the way Re-ID systems are designed and operated. Looking back, early sliding window algorithms that made use of Histograms of Oriented Gradients (HOG) [6] or Haar-like Features [29] together with Eigenfaces [23] or Support Vector Machines (SVM) [5] were used to first detect and then classify persons or faces based on finding and categorizing a relevant image patch. However, these approaches' reliance on manually crafted features render them suboptimal in many application scenarios.

Deep Learning – Deep representation learning, on the other hand, avoids manual feature crafting entirely and has achieved significant improvements in image classification tasks compared to traditional methods. Space Displacement Neural Networks (SDNN) [15] demonstrated that neural nets can be effective for scale-invariant object detection too as shown, for instance, for face location [28], and detection and tracking [18] in videos. More recently, object detection has been addressed by region-focussed architectures such as R-CNN, Fast R-CNN, and Faster R-CNN [21] by integrating region proposal generation and classification by sharing convolutional features. With respect to person Re-ID, various CNN-centered approaches have been introduced recently, *e.g.* [24,31], including two-stream Siamese CNNs [4] providing pairwise class equivalences. Often, however, it is not the network design alone, but the availability of a large, learning-relevant training data corpus that makes the difference in effective network training.

Adversarial Synthesis – Generative Adversarial Networks (GANs) [8] have been applied widely and successfully to create large, learning-relevant training data via augmentation – building on their ability to construct a latent space that underpins the sparser training data, and then to sample from it to produce further training information. DC-GANs [20] pair the GAN concept with compact convolutional operations to synthesise visual content more efficiently. The DC-GAN's ability to organise the relationship between a latent space and an actual image space associated to the GAN input has been shown in a variety of applications, including face and pose analysis [17,20]. In these and other domains, latent spaces have been constructed that can convincingly model and parameterise object attributes, and hence dramatically reduce the amount of data needed for conditional generative modeling of complex image distributions. Some recent examples are face frontalisation [32] and identity preservation via generative modelling [26,34]. For instance in [34], Dual-Agent GANs (*i.e.* DA-GANs) were introduced to synthesise profile face images with varying poses.

Despite the deep learning revolution, the utilisation of *both* facial and person appearance features has remained a fundamental challenge in long-term monitoring [14,19]. Thus, in Sect. 4.1 we employ a two-stream CNN architecture (see Fig. 1) split into appearance and facial feature streams. We then compare it in Sect. 4.2 to a single compact CondenseNet [11], which has access to both facial and overall appearance information, where training data is enhanced via a DC-GAN [20] performing distractor image generation. These models are then explored and results are presented and discussed in Sect. 5. We begin by introducing the datasets used.

3   Datasets: LIMA, FLIMA and MSMT17

The LIMA dataset [14] consists of 188,427 frames of 7 manually labeled identities associated to person bounding box tracklets estimated by OpenNI NiTE. Identities refer to 6 person identities and 1 'unknown' label, which represents one distractor class that acts as an umbrella to capture any non-identity including

Fig. 3. FLIMA Data Annotation. (a) Examples of challenging face annotations and one example **(b)** where 2 faces are contained in the bounding box.

noise or multiple people in the same bounding box tracklet. The whole dataset is recorded in various indoor environments and split into 13 sessions. According to previous works for long-term analysis [14,19], one fundamental evaluation protocol is to perform a leave-one-out performance evaluation with a train-test ratio of 12 : 1 to validate the generalization capability over the different periods.

The FLIMA[1] dataset extends LIMA and assigns to every person bounding box an additional tag indicating the presence or absence of a face. Note that if a bounding box contains more than one face, the box will still just be labelled as 'face'. In general, well resolved frontal-to-profile facial occurrences are labeled as a 'face'. By contrast, faces that are mostly occluded or non-visible are considered as 'non-face'. Figure 3 provides some examples from the FLIMA dataset. Overall, $60,939$ bounding boxes are annotated as containing faces.

Beyond FLIMA, we also consider the MSMT17[2] dataset [30], as it is the largest person Re-ID dataset available. It contains $126,441$ bounding boxes of $4,101$ identities taken by 15 cameras during 4 days.

4   Proposed Methods

4.1   Dual-Stream Architecture

We propose a two-steam network as shown in detail in Fig. 1. The fundamental design contains two separate streams for full person and facial appearance, respectively, which are combined through a fully connected layer that utilises Softmax activation plus a categorical cross-entropy cost function. Adam [13] is used as optimizer for network training.

The first stream deals with overall person appearance and a modified version of the LeNet-5 [15] architecture is utilised to implement it. Different to the standard implementation, (i) the input tensors are reshaped to $s = 64{\times}64{\times}3$, (ii)

---

[1] FLIMA dataset will be made available at https://data.bris.ac.uk/data.
[2] MSMT17 dataset is online at https://www.pkuvmc.com/publications/msmt17.html.

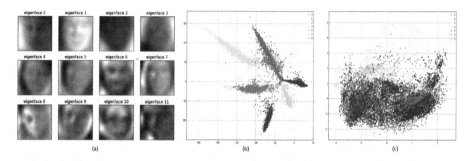

Fig. 4. Facial Feature Representation. (a) Eigenface components, (b) CNN features, (c) Eigenface features.

additional batch normalization layers [12] are introduced after the max-pooling layers to speed-up training, and (iii) L2-regularization and drop-out are added to the last fully connected layers in order to reduce over-fitting and stabilize training.

The second stream deals with facial information exclusively. It starts out by applying a face detector [21] to the input patch containing a detected person. If a face is found then the facial region is fed into FaceNet [22] based on Open-Face [2], which is adjusted to output a 128-D feature vector (or all zeros if no face is found). These OpenFace features separate identities significantly better than traditional approaches, such as Eigenfaces [10] in tandem with a Radial Basis Function Support Vector Machine (RBF-SVM) and grid-search. Figure 4 illustrates the supremacy of deep features over the traditional approach on FLIMA face data. The experiments of our dual-stream network lasted 36 h for training 1000 epochs on the FLIMA dataset with a Geforce Quadro K4100M running on 4GB RAM. We stabilised the training using the same parameters as in [15], but with a learning rate of 0.001 and a dropout probability of 0.4.

4.2 DC-GAN Trained Compact CondenseNet

We argue that, instead of a classic dual-stream solution, a single compact CondenseNet [11] can perform Re-ID equally well or better as long as synthetic training can be effectively leveraged. The idea is to semantically guide an adversarial generative process that utilises the facial stream of the dual-stream architecture as a guidance network. As described in the original DC-GAN paper [20], a discriminator D and a generator G network are trained in tandem, the former learning to distinguish between generated and real input, the latter learning to produce outputs ever closer to the real inputs. The adversarial training loss of this process is, in agreement with [8]:

$$min_G \max_D V(D,G) = \mathbb{E}_{\mathbf{x} \sim p_{data}(\mathbf{x})}[\log(D(\mathbf{x}))] + \mathbb{E}_{\mathbf{z} \sim p_{\mathbf{z}}(\mathbf{z})}[\log(1 - D(G(\mathbf{z})))],$$

$$(1)$$

where the data space in $\mathbf{x}$ and latent space in $\mathbf{z}$ are sampled for optimisation. One can understand (1) as a combination of losses, such that the global discriminator loss for the real and generated images is:

$$\mathcal{L}_D = \mathcal{L}_{D_{\mathbf{x}}} + \mathcal{L}_{D_{\mathbf{z}}},$$

$$(2)$$

where $\mathcal{L}_{D_{\mathbf{x}}}$ is the discriminator loss for real images and $\mathcal{L}_{D_{\mathbf{z}}}$ the discriminator loss for the generated images, as:

$$\mathcal{L}_{D_{\mathbf{x}}} = \frac{1}{m} \sum_{i=1}^{m} \left[\log \left(D\left(\mathbf{x}^{(i)} \right) \right) \right],$$

$$(3)$$

$$\mathcal{L}_{D_{\mathbf{z}}} = \frac{1}{m} \sum_{i=1}^{m} \left[\log \left(1 - D\left(G\left(\mathbf{z}^{(i)} \right) \right) \right) \right].$$

$$(4)$$

Based on this fundamental layout, we design a training regime that gives particular emphasis to high quality real training images – those which are well resolved and thus contain detectable facial features. These should ideally be modelled as producing a smaller discriminator loss compared to other training images. Following this paradigm, we introduce a penalisation term to our adversarial training loss for all training images where faces are *not* detected, and modify the discriminator losses from Eqs. (3) and (4) to be:

$$\mathcal{L}'_{D_{\mathbf{x}}} = \frac{1}{m} \sum_{i=1}^{m} \left[\log \left(D\left(\mathbf{x}^{(i)} \right) \right) + \lambda_1 \left(\Delta\left(\mathbf{x}^{(i)} \right) \right) \right],$$

$$(5)$$

$$\mathcal{L}'_{D_{\mathbf{z}}} = \frac{1}{m} \sum_{i=1}^{m} \left[\log \left(1 - D\left(G\left(\mathbf{z}^{(i)} \right) \right) \right) - \lambda_2 \left(\Delta\left(G\left(\mathbf{z}^{(i)} \right) \right) \right) \right],$$

$$(6)$$

where $\Delta(.) = 1$ when there is no face detectable in the argument, and $\Delta(.) = 0$ otherwise. The two constants $\lambda_{1,2}$ are penalisation factors. Note that practically, this penalisation factor will be multiplied by $n \le m$ according to n face-detected images within the current batch of m images.

Once the training procedure ends, $48,000$ synthetic training images are generated by the DC-GAN and used as an additional (distractor) class for training (see Fig. 5). We follow the framework of [19] to train a CondenseNet as a person ID-inference network, using 100 epochs for training the DC-GAN and $1,500$ epochs for the CondenseNet training processes, respectively. We use the same parameters as [19] and different values for the penalisation factors, *e.g.* $\lambda_1, \lambda_2 = [0, 0.025, 0.05]$, of the discriminator and generator, respectively.

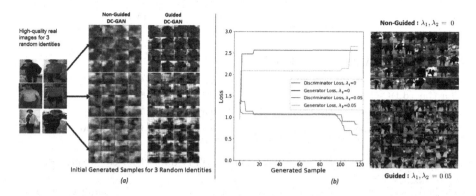

Fig. 5. Augmentation with Guided DC-GANs. (*a*) Augmentation samples after training DC-GANs with and without face detector guidance on FLIMA instances (3 individual identities shown). Note the improved quality of samples with guidance. (*b*) Training of the DC-GAN process on all identity samples of the MSMT17 dataset as used for the generation of distractors. We plot the loss values for the initial generated samples. We also show samples of global distractors for different $0 \leq \lambda_{1,2} \leq 0.05$ values. Again, note improvements when activating the guidance with a value above 0.

5   Results

5.1   FLIMA Results

Table 1 shows results of the application of various architectures to the FLIMA dataset. The first row reports the Re-ID performance when only the $4,531$ facial patches detected by Faster RCNN are processed by an RBF-SVM applied to Eigenfaces. Both precision and recall are poor due to the method's reliance on a basic methodology and well-resolved facial features. In contrast, the second row shows comparative results of the method in [19], which utilises full person imagery. The third row depicts performance details of the DC-GAN trained CondenseNet. The fourth row gives the recognition performance of the LeNet5 stream of the dual-stream architecture that deals with person appearance features only. The final row shows a considerably increased performance for Recall when deploying the full dual-stream architecture. Here, in a dataset with a small number of individuals and good facial resolution, a dual stream approach is advantageous, noticing similar F1-scores for appearance-only CNN stream and an appearance-based CondenseNet approach.

5.2   MSMT17 Results

Comparative performance measures, on what is currently the largest person Re-ID dataset (MSMT17), are provided in Table 2. This dataset has lower resolution facial content than FLIMA, uses a different evaluation scheme [31], and deals with far greater numbers of identities. We apply two metrics to quantify performance: correct classification rate of the top ranked individual (Rank@1)

Table 1. Recognition performance on FLIMA

Method	# Test Images	Precision	Recall	F1-score
RCNN and RBF-SVM-Eigenface (Faces only)	4,531	0.56	0.52	0.47
Selective Augmentation Approach [19]	14,494	0.75	0.74	0.74
Our Guided DC-GAN trained CondenseNet	14,494	0.85	0.85	0.85
Our Appearance-Stream only	14,494	0.92	0.81	0.86
Our Full Dual-Stream	14,494	**0.93**	**0.90**	**0.91**

Table 2. Person Re-ID performance on MSMT17 dataset for single queries.

Method	Rank@1	mAP
Dual-Stream Architecture	4.89	5.91
GoogLeNet [25]	47.6	23.0
PDC [24]	58.0	29.7
GLAD [31]	61.4	**34.0**
Selective Augmentation Approach [19]	61.5	15.01
Our Guided DC-GAN ($\lambda_1, \lambda_2 = 0.05, 0.025$) trained CondenseNet	**63.85**	16.64
Our Guided DC-GAN ($\lambda_1, \lambda_2 = 0.05, 0$) trained CondenseNet	**65.51**	18.57

and mean Average Precision (mAP). Our dual-stream architecture and DC-GAN trained CondenseNet results are shown alongside four other approaches, *i.e.* GoogLeNet [25], a Pose-driven Deep Convolutional model (PDC) [24], a Global-Local-Alignment Descriptor approach (GLAD) [31], and the Selective Augmentation Approach [19]. It can be seen that whilst GLAD outperforms all other methods with respect to mAP performance, our DC-GAN trained CondenseNet approach provides a significant improvement in Rank@1 performance for single-queries. This is a 4% performance increase above the next best performing method and 27% over GoogLeNet without using expensive and time-consuming training of very-deep multi-stream networks that benefit the mAP metric. Further, one has to consider that this increment is achieved with a significantly smaller footprint of the inference network – the produced CondenseNet carries 8× fewer parameters.

Given its very simple appearance CNN streams, the dual-stream architecture relies on features extracted from the facial stream. Compared to FLIMA, MSMT17 contains lower resolution facial patches and, most importantly, it has an evaluation scheme where the training set contains all different identity-classes to those from the test set. This renders the learning of specific identities completely ineffective and explains the poor performance of the dual-stream approach bound to learned facial features. The increased performance results with our guided DC-GAN trained compact CondenseNet on MSMT17 are based on leveraging distractor synthesis which remains highly relevant in this setting.

6   Conclusion

In this paper we investigated potential approaches for person Re-ID based on the exploitation of facial and person appearance representations, as well as an integration that semantically guides the image synthesis of DC-GAN training. First, we presented a traditional dual-stream architecture to learn *both* relevant appearance and facial features in combination from still images to infer person identities. We then described a second alternative architecture of a single, lightweight ID-CondenseNet, where a DC-GAN is used to generate distractor person images for enhanced training guided by the face detector leveraged from the face stream of our dual-stream CNN architecture. We introduced the FLIMA dataset with well-resolved facial content where we showed that the dual-stream approach performs superior. However, we then reported improvements in top-1 ranking performance compared to all tested state-of-the-art architectures on MSMT17 when using our proposed CondenseNet system. We therefore conclude that re-identification performance is highly sensitive to the structure of datasets and evaluation metrics. As shown on MSMT17, distractor augmentation and network compression may nevertheless have a role to play for enhancing performance characteristics.

Acknowledgements. This work was performed in the SPHERE IRC funded by the UK Engineering and Physical Sciences Research Council (EPSRC), Grant EP/K031910/1.

References

1. Acampora, G., Cook, D.J., Rashidi, P., Vasilakos, A.V.: A survey on ambient intelligence in healthcare. Proc. IEEE **101**(12), 2470–2494 (2013)
2. Amos, B., Ludwiczuk, B., Satyanarayanan, M.: OpenFace: A General-Purpose Face Recognition Library with Mobile Applications. Technical report, CMU-CS-16-118 (2016)
3. Barbosa, I.B., Cristani, M., Caputo, B., Rognhaugen, A., Theoharis, T.: Looking beyond appearances: synthetic ttraining data for deep CNNs in re-identification. CVIU **167**, 50–62 (2018)
4. Chung, D., Tahboub, K., Delp, E.J.: A two stream siamese convolutional neural network for person re-identification. In: ICCV (2017)
5. Cortes, C., Vapnik, V.: Support-vector networks. Mach. Learn. **20**(3), 273–297 (1995)
6. Dalal, N., Triggs, B.: Histograms of oriented gradients for human detection. In: CVPR, vol. 1, pp. 886–893 (2005)
7. Filković, I., Kalafatić, Z., Hrkać, T.: Deep metric learning for person Re-identification and de-identification. In: MIPRO, pp. 1360–1364 (2016)
8. Goodfellow, I., et al.: Generative adversarial nets. In: NIPS, pp. 2672–2680 (2014)
9. Haghighat, M., Abdel-Mottaleb, M.: Low resolution face recognition in surveillance systems using discriminant correlation analysis. In: FG, pp. 912–917 (2017)
10. Halko, N., Martinsson, P., Tropp, J.: Finding structure with randomness: probabilistic algorithms for constructing approximate matrix decompositions. SIAM Rev. **53**(2), 217–288 (2011)

11. Huang, G., Liu, S., van der Maaten, L., Weinberger, K.: CondenseNet: An Efficient DenseNet using Learned Group Convolutions. CoRR abs/1711.09224 (2017)
12. Ioffe, S., Szegedy, C.: Batch normalization: accelerating deep network training by reducing internal covariate shift. ICML **37**, 448–456 (2015)
13. Kingma, D.P., Ba, J.: Adam: a method for stochastic optimization. In: ICLR (2015)
14. Layne, R., et al.: A dataset for persistent multi-target multi-camera tracking in RGB-D. In: CVPR Workshops, pp. 1462–1470 (2017)
15. Lecun, Y., Bottou, L., Bengio, Y., Haffner, P.: Gradient-based learning applied to document recognition. Proc. IEEE **86**(11), 2278–2324 (1998)
16. Lu, C., Tang, X.: Surpassing human-level face verification performance on LFW with Gaussian face. In: AAAI, pp. 3811–3819 (2015)
17. Ma, L., Jia, X., Sun, Q., Schiele, B., Tuytelaars, T., Van Gool, L.: Pose guided person image generation. In: NIPS, pp. 406–416 (2017)
18. Nowlan, S.J., Platt, J.C.: A convolutional neural network hand tracker. In: NIPS, pp. 901–908 (1995)
19. Ponce-López, V., Burghardt, T., Hannuna, S., Damen, D., Masullo, A., Mirmehdi, M.: Semantically selective augmentation for deep compact person re-identification. In: ECCV Workshops, pp. 551–561 (2018)
20. Radford, A., Metz, L., Chintala, S.: Unsupervised representation learning with deep convolutional generative adversarial networks. In: ICLR (2015)
21. Ren, S., He, K., Girshick, R., Sun, J.: Faster R-CNN: towards real-time object detection with region proposal networks. TPAMI **39**(6), 1137–1149 (2017)
22. Schroff, F., Kalenichenko, D., Philbin, J.: FaceNet: a unified embedding for face recognition and clustering. In: CVPR, pp. 815–823 (2015)
23. Sirovich, L., Kirby, M.: Low-dimensional procedure for the characterization of human faces. JOSA-A **4**(3), 519–524 (1987)
24. Su, C., Li, J., Zhang, S., Xing, J., Gao, W., Tian, Q.: Pose-driven deep convolutional model for person re-identification. In: ICCV, pp. 3980–3989 (2017)
25. Szegedy, C., et al.: Going deeper with convolutions. In: CVPR (2015)
26. Tran, L., Yin, X., Liu, X.: Disentangled representation learning GAN for pose-invariant face recognition. In: CVPR (2017)
27. Twomey, N., et al.: The SPHERE Challenge: Activity Recognition with Multi-modal Sensor Data. CoRR abs/1603.00797 (2016)
28. Vaillant, R., Monrocq, C., Le Cun, Y.: Original approach for the localization of objects in images. IEE-VISP **141**(4), 245–250 (1994)
29. Viola, P., Jones, M.: Rapid object detection using a boosted cascade of simple features. In: CVPR, vol. 1, pp. I-511–I-518 (2001)
30. Wei, L., Zhang, S., Gao, W., Tian, Q.: Person transfer GAN to bridge domain gap for person re-identification. In: CVPR (2018)
31. Wei, L., Zhang, S., Yao, H., Gao, W., Tian, Q.: GLAD: Global-Local-Alignment Descriptor for Pedestrian Retrieval. CoRR abs/1709.04329 (2017)
32. Yin, X., Yu, X., Sohn, K., Liu, X., Chandraker, M.: Towards Large-Pose Face Frontalization in the Wild. In: ICCV, October 2017, pp. 4010–4019 (2017)
33. Yu, S.I., Meng, D., Zuo, W., Hauptmann, A.: The solution path algorithm for identity-aware multi-object tracking. In: CVPR, pp. 3871–3879 (2016)
34. Zhao, J., et al.: Dual-agent GANs for photorealistic and identity preserving profile face synthesis. In: NIPS, pp. 66–76 (2017)
35. Zheng, L., Shen, L., Tian, L., Wang, S., Wang, J., Tian, Q.: Scalable person re-identification: a benchmark. In: ICCV (2015)
36. Zheng, L., Yang, Y., Hauptmann, A.G.: Person Re-Identification: Past, Present and Future, CoRR (2016)

Dimensionality Reduction Using Discriminative Autoencoders for Remote Sensing Image Retrieval

Mohbat[(✉)], Tooba Mukhtar, Numan Khurshid, and Murtaza Taj

Computer Vision and Graphics Lab, Department of Computer Science,
Lahore University of Management Sciences, Lahore, Pakistan
{16060073,19100210,15060051,murtaza.taj}@lums.edu.pk

Abstract. Advancements in deep learning techniques caused a paradigm shift in feature extraction for image perception from hand-crafted methods to deep methods. However, these deep features if learned through unsupervised methods bear large memory footprints and are prone to the curse of dimensionality. Traditional feature reduction schemes involving aggregation of these learned visual descriptors may lead to loss of essential information necessary for their obvious discrimination. Therefore, this research studies various feature reduction techniques for remote sensing image features. We also propose an deep discriminative network with dimensionality reduction (DAE-DR), exploiting stacked autoencoder based solution to abbreviate unsupervised features without significantly affecting their discriminative and regenerative characteristics. It is observed that the spatial dimensions encoded in the feature vector are more important than increasing the number of network filters for efficient image reconstruction. Validation of our approach has been tested for remote sensing image retrieval (RSIR) problem. Results demonstrate that our proposed network achieves 25 times reduction in feature size with only 0.8 times depletion of retrieval score.

Keywords: Unsupervised features ·
Remote sensing image retrieval (RSIR) · Deep learning · Deep features

1 Introduction

Developments in imaging technology resulted in the extremely large datasets, however, learning any useful information from these datasets, particularly using modern deep learning architectures, require large amount of annotations. Although initiatives such as ImageNet challenge and those related to autonomous vehicles provide such annotated data, they are only limited to street level imagery. In many areas, such as remote sensing, there is a dearth of annotated datasets [6]. Thus, there is a dire need of a method that allows unsupervised learning of features that are distinctive, posses reconstruction capability and are effectively compact.

© Springer Nature Switzerland AG 2019
E. Ricci et al. (Eds.): ICIAP 2019, LNCS 11751, pp. 499–508, 2019.
https://doi.org/10.1007/978-3-030-30642-7_45

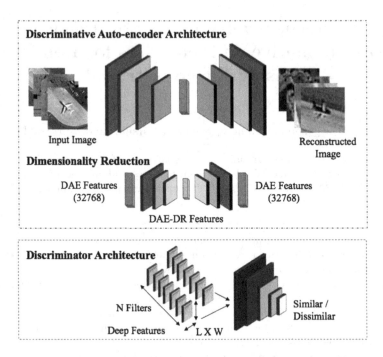

Fig. 1. DAE-DR framework in which the feature learning and reduction step is explained in the upper part of the figure while the process of discriminating reduced features set is presented in the lower part of the figure.

To cultivate distinctiveness among unsupervised features, we adopted discriminative autoencoder network inspired from Generative Adverserial Networks (GANs) [4] and Siamese Networks [8] in our previous work [11]. However, these learned features are high dimensional with large memory footprints which require huge storage capacity for big data applications, such as remote sensing image retrieval.

Dimensionality reduction could be considered as one of the possible solutions, employed through feature aggregation (by using global sum-pooling, max-pooling, and scaled sum-pooling) or selection of kernels from the activations of the learned network [5,12]. However, these methods have two important limitations. Firstly, theses methods fail to perform on features learned through unsupervised learning approaches. Secondly, they require an unbounded set of experiments still, they do not guarantee compact feature representation.

In our previous work we proposed a Discriminative Autoencoder (DAE) architecture that takes high-dimensional features from the depth layer of autoencoder as an input and projects them onto a space that separates similar images from non-similar images (see Fig. 1) [11]. This work demonstrates a step-wise procedure to abbreviate the features acquired through deep autoencoder network without significantly effecting their discriminative and regenerative characteristics.

Our approach leverages from the fact that autoencoders with linear activation are mathematically equivalent to Linear Principle Component Analysis (PCA) and those with non-linear activation (such as sigmoid) are equivalent to non-linear PCA. To prove the efficacy, we evaluated our approach on RSIR problem using benchmark datasets including University of California Merced Land Use/Land Cover (LandUse) [13] and High-resolution Satellite scene (SatScene) [3] containing 2100 and 1050 images, respectively.

2 Preliminaries

2.1 Discriminative Autoencoder (DAE)

For the dataset X containing n images such that X $= \{x_1, x_2, \cdots, x_n\}$, our network transforms the given input image, x_i onto the feature space generating feature f_i through deep learning network $f_i = h_\theta(x_i) = r(Wx_i + b)$.

Similarly, it then reconstructs the output image x'_i from the input feature f_i using $x'_i = g_{\theta'}(f_i) = t(W'f_i + b')$. Where, h and g are encoder and decoder functions, respectively. Similarly, $\theta = \{W, b\}$ are encoder parameters and $\theta' = \{W', b'\}$ are decoder parameters for r and t being non-linear activation functions. By employing the mean squared error $L(x_i, x'_i) = \|x_i - x'_i\|_2$ as loss function, we optimize the parameters θ and θ' as follows:

$$\theta^*, \theta'^* = \arg\min_{\theta, \theta'} \frac{1}{N} \sum_{i=1}^{N} L(x_i, x'_i) \tag{1}$$

A pair of these image features (f_q, f_t) are then concatenated and given to the discriminator network $y' = d((f_q, f_t), \theta_d)$ to compute the Bernoulli probabilities (match or unmatched), where d is a discriminator model and y' is classification probability. The parameters of d are optimized by using cross entropy loss function $L_d(y, y') = -\sum_{q,t} y log y'$ as given in Eq. (2).

$$\theta_d^* = \arg\min_{\theta_d} \sum_{q,t} [L(y_i, d(h_\theta(x_q) * h_\theta(x_t)))] \tag{2}$$

In our previous work [11], it has been demonstrated that the features f learned using residual autoencoder coupled with the discriminative metric learning scheme outperforms supervised features based approaches. However, these features are prone to the curse of dimensionality.

2.2 Autoencoder vs PCA Relationship

We aim to obtain a transformation Φ that transform f to subspace $\tilde{f}$ as $\tilde{f} = \Phi_{\tilde{\theta}}(f, \tilde{W})$ and then from $\tilde{f}$ we aim to reconstruct the output $\tilde{x}$ as $\tilde{x}' = g_{\tilde{\theta}}(\tilde{f}) = t(\tilde{W}\tilde{f} + \tilde{b})$ and compute similarity as $\tilde{y}' = d(\{\tilde{f}_q, \tilde{f}_t\}, \tilde{\theta}_d)$. $\tilde{f}$ should be such that it is a compact representation of f without any significant loss of information.

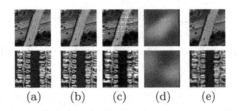

(a)   (b)   (c)   (d)   (e)

Fig. 2. Visualization of reconstructed images from (a) Input (b) $8 \times 8 \times 512$ dimensional features of DAE (c) 1063 PCA basis (d) $1 \times 1 \times 1024$ dimensional encoder features (DAE-DR 1D) (e) $8 \times 8 \times 20$ dimensional encoder features (DAE-DR 2D).

In order to introduce energy conservation the transform should also be unitary i.e.

$$\|\tilde{f}\|^2 = \tilde{f}^H \tilde{f} = \Phi_{\hat{\theta}}(f, \tilde{W})^H \Phi_{\hat{\theta}}(f, \tilde{W}) = \|f\|^2 \tag{3}$$

where f^H is the hermitian conjugate of f. One such unitary transform is Eigen matrix of auto-correlation $R_{ff} = ff^H$ which form the basis of Principle Component Analysis (PCA). In order to learn the optimal feature vector, we exploited the relationship between PCA and auto-encoder basis. Mathematically, a linear autoencoder is defined as:

$$f_1 = W_1 \times X + b_1 \tag{4a}$$

$$\tilde{X} = W_2 \times f_1 + b_2 \tag{4b}$$

Where, W_1 and W_2 are weights, X is input and $\tilde{X}$ is reconstructed output. Minimizing the mean square cost function (Eq. 5) with respect to W_1, W_2, b_1, b_2, the problem reduces to optimization with respect to W_2 only, as given in Eq. (6).

$$min_{W_1,W_2,b_1,b_2} = \|X - (W_2(W_1 X + b_1) + b_2)\|^2 \tag{5}$$

$$min_{W_2} = \|X^* - W_2 W_2^\dagger X^*\|^2 \tag{6}$$

where, X^* is obtained by subtracting mean image from each image in data as $X^* = X - \bar{x}1_N^T$. Thus, by singular decomposition of W_2, it can be proven that the singular vectors of W_2 are actually the principle components of X. Consequently, PCA is equivalent to linear autoencoder whereas typical deep neural network based autoencoder with non-linear activation functions would be analogous to non-linear version of the PCA [2]. Therefore, the deep CNN autoencoder would learn feature space much better than PCA where PCA would help us to compute the optimal dimension of the space.

3   Methodology

3.1   Dimensionality Reduction in DAE via PCA

PCA helps to find the optimal dimension of space spanned by data but the challenge is the auto-correlation matrix which is computationally expensive. So, instead of computing f as $f = \Phi^H x$ where $\Phi = \xi(R_{XX})$, and $\xi(.)$ returns the Eigen vectors, we compute Φ as $\Phi = F\xi(R_{F^H F})$ (using Sirovich and Kirby method [10]), i.e. by computing Eigen vectors of inner product of depth features instead of raw images, where $F = \{f_1, f_2, \cdots\}$. $\tilde{f}$ is then computed as:

$$\tilde{f} = \Phi^H f \tag{7}$$

Therefore, we compute the auto-correlation $R_{\tilde{f}^H \tilde{f}}$ of $\tilde{f}$ to identify the basis vectors that contain the maximum amount of energy. By reducing the feature dimension using PCA, from analysis of DAE features (32768 dimensions) on LandUse dataset, it has been found that 95% of the information lies in only 1063 principle components.

3.2 Dimensionality Reduction via DAE-DR Network

We modified our existing DAE architecture to DAE-DR network to learn the features with compact dimensions. The following three ways demonstrate the achieved modification for conversion of features from DAE to DAE-DR.

Pruning Spatial Dimensions of Filters. By the introduction of 3 additional residual blocks in autoencoder, spatial dimension is reduced to 1 × 1 while increasing the number of filters to 1024, resulting in a 1D fine-grained feature vector (DAE-DR 1D). Nonetheless, as compared to PCA neither regeneration nor retrieval score were encouraging. It is quite obvious from Fig. 2(d) that reduction of spatial dimension of activation's results in loss of structural information and outputs a degraded reconstructed image, hence, confirming the idea presented in [11].

Table 1. Regeneration loss: Averaged MSE on test set where training hyper-parameters were same for all models. PSNR averaged over 21 classes of LandUse.

Model/Scheme	Feature Size	MSE Loss	PSNR (dB)
DAE [11]	$(8, 8, 512)$	97.7	29.89
DAE (PCA)	1280	1114.34	6.150
DAE-DR 1D	$(1, 1, 1024)$	2179.32	16.541
DAE-DR 2D	$(8, 8, 20)$	636	21.192

Pruning Temporal Dimensions of Filters. Filters could also be pruned by adapting "Try and learn" learning approach [7], converting DAE to DAE-DR. However, this method takes a lot of training time which exponentially increases with the complexity of network. Another way is to introduce a stack of layers which reduces the dimensions depth wise while keeping the spatial dimensions unchanged throughout. This technique ensures that the structural information is stored in the spatial dimension. However, the addition of depth in the network architecture produces a blurred regeneration.

Fig. 3. Qualitative evaluation of RSIR for *harbour, building, intersection, and forest* class from *LandUse* with query image (*on the left most side*) and its respective first ten retrieved images in each row. It also includes some misclassification results for *intersection* class.

Modification of Existing DAE Network. Another way is to modify the hidden layers of the original autoencoder network by manipulating the number of filters to produce the desired dimensional features. This approach yields the 2D compact features (DAE-DR 2D) with significant improvement in reconstruction as illustrated in Fig. 2(e).

The discriminator network for each of the three scenarios mentioned above has been modified in such a way that it accommodates the input feature dimension, preserving the overall architecture of the network.

4   Results and Discussion

4.1   Training and Evaluation

In order to evaluate the performance of reduced features with our previous results, all the training hyper-parameters were maintained as discussed in [11]. Data augmentation enabled the discriminator network to be robust to scaling, illumination and transnational invariances. For evaluation of all the approaches proposed in Sect. 3, standard metrics discussed in [9] for remote sensing image matching were computed and a brief analysis has been provided in this section.

4.2   Analysis of Image Reconstruction

We trained three variants of auto-encoder networks and compared the regenerated images with [11]. Qualitative visual results demonstrated in Fig. 2 show that the reconstruction of DAE-DR 2D features is smoother than reconstruction from PCA basis vectors. Moreover, the spatial compression of features results in the loss of structural information which degrades the reconstruction of the image. For quantitative evaluation, we compare the reconstruction MSE loss and Peak Signal to Noise Ration (PSNR). From Table 1, it can also be noticed that the MSE loss of DAE-DR 1D feature is almost 20 times higher than the

Table 2. Comparative evaluation of our proposed approach for feature dimension reduction where it should be noted that despite having smaller feature size, our approach outperform hand-crafted features and is comparable with supervised deep features.

Feature type	Features	Feature size	ANMRR↓
LandUse dataset			
Hand-crafted	LBP RGB [9]	54	0.751
	SIFT (VLAD) [14]	25600	0.649
	SIFT (FV) [9]	40960	0.639
Deep-supervised	NetVLAD [1]	4096	0.406
	SatResNet-50 [9]	2048	0.239
Deep-unsupervised	DAE	32768	0.090
	DAE (PCA)	1063	0.591
	DAE-DR 1D	**1024**	0.495
	DAE-DR 2D	1280	**0.417**
SatScene dataset			
Hand-crafted	LBP RGB [9]	54	0.664
	SIFT (VLAD) [14]	25600	0.649
	SIFT (FV) [9]	40960	0.552
Deep-supervised	NetVLAD [1]	4060	0.371
	SatResNet-50 [9]	2048	0.207
Deep-unsupervised	DAE	32768	0.060
	DAE (PCA)	**804**	**0.473**
	DAE-DR FG 1D	1024	0.495
	DAE-DR 2D	1280	0.50

loss of DAE. It can also be clearly analyzed that with the decrease in the feature dimension, the quality of the reconstructed images is impaired. Hence, for an effective reconstruction of the images local spatial information is crucial.

4.3 Analysis of Remote Sensing Image Matching

In order to evaluate the performance of the proposed approach, we provide quantitative as well as qualitative evaluation. Subjective evaluation by observing Fig. 3 clearly shows that the top 10 retrieved images mostly belong to the same class, however, the retrieved images are sometimes confused with visually similar images of different classes e.g. forest with rivers and over-head with highway class. For quantitative evaluation on metrics used for remote sensing image matching, we computed the values of Average Normalized Modified Retrieval Rank (ANMRR) and Mean Average Precision (mAP) [9]. The previously proposed unsupervised features outperforms supervised features in terms of lower

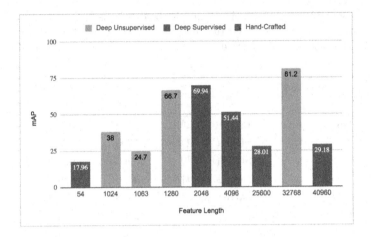

Fig. 4. Comparison between different feature sizes and their mAP scores for **LandUse** dataset.

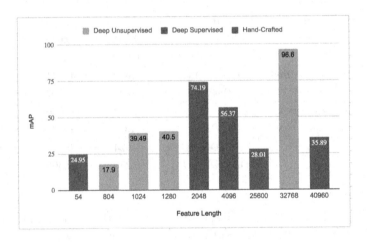

Fig. 5. Comparison between different feature sizes and their mAP scores for RS **SatScene** dataset.

ANMRR and higher mAP values which is evident from Table. 2 and a comparative analysis of features represented in Fig. 4 and Fig. 5. In our case, even with 25 times reduction in feature size, the performance is still comparable to hand-crafted approaches and competing with other supervised approaches e.g. NetVLAD [1]. As described in Table 2, the ANMRR value of DAE is comparatively better as compare to other DAE-DR unsupervised feature approaches for LandUse dataset. Furthermore, our approach outperforms other hand-crafted approaches in terms of ANMRR and feature size. Such significant differences in metric values demonstrates the effectiveness and superiority of our proposed feature size for the problem of RSIR using unsupervised features. By exploiting the local spatial and global semantic information, the proposed feature length outperforms the baseline sizes.

5 Conclusion

This paper introduces a novel unsupervised dimensionality reduction network after thoroughly studying some of the systematic methods of reducing unsupervised feature dimension including PCA. Through experiments we have shown that our proposed network DAE-DR 2D is able to achieve comparable content based image retrieval results from a significantly smaller feature vector. While a larger number of feature maps are required to obtain accurate retrieval results, we show that by retraining the spatial information and discarding the redundant filters it is possible to produce an optimal size image descriptor employing discriminative autoencoder.

References

1. Arandjelovic, R., Gronat, P., Torii, A., Pajdla, T., Sivic, J.: NetVLAD: CNN architecture for weakly supervised place recognition. In: Proceedings of the IEEE Conference on Computer Vision and Pattern Recognition, pp. 5297–5307 (2016)
2. Bourlard, H., Kamp, Y.: Auto-association by multilayer perceptrons and singular value decomposition. Biol. Cybern. **59**(4–5), 291–294 (1988)
3. Dai, D., Yang, W.: Satellite image classification via two-layer sparse coding with biased image representation. IEEE Geosci. Remote Sens. Lett. **8**(1), 173–176 (2011)
4. Goodfellow, I., et al.: Generative adversarial nets. In: Ghahramani, Z., Welling, M., Cortes, C., Lawrence, N.D., Weinberger, K.Q. (eds.) Advances in Neural Information Processing Systems, vol. 27, pp. 2672–2680. Curran Associates, Inc. (2014). http://papers.nips.cc/paper/5423-generative-adversarial-nets.pdf
5. Gordo, A., Almazán, J., Revaud, J., Larlus, D.: Deep image retrieval: learning global representations for image search. In: Leibe, B., Matas, J., Sebe, N., Welling, M. (eds.) ECCV 2016. LNCS, vol. 9910, pp. 241–257. Springer, Cham (2016). https://doi.org/10.1007/978-3-319-46466-4_15
6. Haklay, M., Weber, P.: OpenStreetMap: user-generated street maps. IEEE Pervas. Comput. **7**(4), 12–18 (2008)
7. Huang, Q., Zhou, K., You, S., Neumann, U.: Learning to prune filters in convolutional neural networks. arXiv preprint arXiv:1801.07365 (2018)
8. Koch, G., Zemel, R., Salakhutdinov, R.: Siamese neural networks for one-shot image recognition. In: Deep Learning Workshop, International Conference on Machine Learning, Lille, France (2015)
9. Napoletano, P.: Visual descriptors for content-based retrieval of remote-sensing images. Int. J. Remote Sens. **39**(5), 1–34 (2018). https://doi.org/10.1080/01431161.2017.1399472
10. Sirovich, L., Kirby, M.: Low-dimensional procedure for the characterization of human faces. J. Opt. Soc. Am. **4**(3), 519–524 (1987)
11. Tharani, M., Khurshid, N., Taj, M.: Unsupervised deep features for remote sensing image matching via discriminator network. arXiv preprint arXiv:1810.06470 (2018)

12. Xia, G.S., Tong, X.Y., Hu, F., Zhong, Y., Datcu, M., Zhang, L.: Exploiting deep features for remote sensing image retrieval: a systematic investigation. arXiv preprint arXiv:1707.07321 (2017)
13. Yang, Y., Newsam, S.: Bag-of-visual-words and spatial extensions for land-use classification. In: Proceedings of the 18th SIGSPATIAL International Conference on Advances in Geographic Information Systems, pp. 270–279. ACM (2010)
14. Zhou, W., Newsam, S., Li, C., Shao, Z.: Learning low dimensional convolutional neural networks for high-resolution remote sensing image retrieval. Remote Sens. **9**(5), 489 (2017)

Multiple Organs Segmentation in Abdomen CT Scans Using a Cascade of CNNs

Muhammad Usman Akbar[1,2(✉)], Shahab Aslani[1,2], Vitorio Murino[1,3], and Diego Sona[1,4]

[1] Pattern Analysis and Computer Vision, Istituto Italiano di Tecnologia, Genova, Italy
muhammad.akbar@iit.it
[2] Department of Electrical, Electronics and Telecommunication Engineering and Naval Architecture, Università degli Studi di Genova, Genoa, Italy
[3] Department of Computer Science, Università di Verona, Verona, Italy
[4] Neuroinformatics Laboratory, Fondazione Bruno Kessler, Trento, Italy

Abstract. Automatic organ segmentation is a vital prerequisite of many clinical application in radiology. The anatomical variability of organs in the abdomen makes it difficult for many methods to obtain good segmentations for all organs. In this paper, we present a particular ensemble of convolutional neural networks, combining technologies that analyze the images with either a local or a global perspective. In particular, we implemented a cascade of models combining the advantages of using local and global processing. We have evaluated our proposed system on CT scan of 30 subjects in a nested cross-validation framework, showing a significant performance improvement if compared with state-of-the-art methods.

Keywords: Deep learning · Ensemble learning ·
Convolutional neural networks · Medical imaging · Segmentation ·
Abdomen organs

1 Introduction

Accurate segmentation of abdominal organs is an important preliminary task in many clinical applications, such as computer aided diagnosis systems, computer assisted surgery systems, radiotherapy systems, etc. Manual segmentation is still a standard practice in radiology that is performed slice-by-slice and organ-by-organ. This makes manual segmentation time consuming and a possible source of errors due to both the variability of human expertise and the inherent subjectivity of the expert. For this reason, there exist many semi-automated segmentation tools, which however still require an interaction with an expert that can introduce biases or unacceptable variability.

To overcome this problem various automated techniques were introduced. Most of the approaches were based either on statistical shape models or on

© Springer Nature Switzerland AG 2019
E. Ricci et al. (Eds.): ICIAP 2019, LNCS 11751, pp. 509–516, 2019.
https://doi.org/10.1007/978-3-030-30642-7_46

atlases. Statistical shape models work with an estimation of the distribution of target shapes and have proven to be a successful approach [2,11]. Atlas-based approaches try to segment the images based on registered atlases [4,8,10]. Recently, deep convolutional neural networks (CNNs) have proven to be very effective in many tasks including segmentation, outperforming many state-of-the-art traditional approaches.

In general, all deep learning methods work with two different approaches, either they process the full image (in 3D or slice by slice) [1] or they work with a patch based approach where multiple small patches (in 2D or 3D) are processed separately and results are concatenated to reconstruct the segmentation at the original size [10]. Both approaches enjoy pros and cons. The first approach, thanks to its global processing, is good in locating the organs in the whole space while being less precise on the edges of the segmented areas and on small objects. The second approach instead works on local information, having no perception of the overall objects location while being more able in the segmentation of smaller structures and edges.

Our aim is therefore to create a pipeline of different models combining the two above approaches in order to enjoy the advantages of both frameworks. We propose, therefore, an approach based on the combination of three different CNNs resulting in an improved segmentation where each single approach fails.

Organs segmentation is a difficult task because of the complex anatomical variability of all organs. Due to this variability, machine learning approaches would require datasets with a large number of examples, which is an uncommon condition in medical imaging. For this reason, the most recent CNN based approaches to medical imaging segmentation are limited to single specific organs (usually liver). The proposed method, instead, has been tested on a task requiring the segmentation of 13 different organs, controlling the overfitting through a nested cross-validation

The paper is organized as follows. The proposed system is first explained in Sect. 2, together with a description of the used dataset and the experimental setup. In Sect. 3 results of the experiments will be given and discussed comparing the proposed model with state-of-the-art solutions. Finally, some conclusion will be drawn in Sect. 4.

2 Data and Methods

2.1 Abdomen Organ Segmentation Dataset

We used a publicly available dataset[1] [5] which consist of 30 healthy subjects. The data was hand-labeled with 13 classes corresponding to 13 different abdomen organs with various sizes (Spleen, R. Kidney, L. Kidney, Gallbladder, Esophagus, Liver, Stomach, Aorta, Inferior Vena Cava, Portal Vein and Splenic Vein, Pancreas, R Adrenal Gland, L Adrenal Gland). The data is available in Nifty volumes. We unified the axial spacing to 3 mm. For this purpose, interpolation algorithm was used to interpolate the CT and gold standards to unify

---

[1] https://www.synapse.org/#!Synapse:syn3193805/wiki/217789.

the axial spacing. Gray value was truncated between -350 and 350 because of the complex boundaries of different organs and size was re-sampled to 256×256 while maintaining the voxel spacing of 3 mm. Extra parts of the image with no organ labels present were cropped for image pre-processing. The average number of slices per subject was 140.

2.2 Proposed System

The proposed system consists of three models incorporated in a simple framework. We connected the three models in such a way that first 2 models, exploiting respectively the global and the local information, produce segmentations that are used together with the input image by a third model. In an ensemble learning perspective, instead of using traditional approaches to combine the outcome of multiple models (e.g. majority vote), we learn how to combine the outcome using a further deep model, which exploits the predictions of the two previous models together with the input data to generate a refined segmentation. This model learns how to use the two previous segmentations according to how much trustable they are on each sub-structure of the whole image. For this reason, since the reliability of segmentations is based on the location of all substructures, the third model must be selected among those processing the full image exploiting the global information. The flow diagram of the proposed architecture can be seen in Fig. 1. In the pipeline the three models are referred as P1, P2 and P3 respectively.

In other words, the first two models, exploiting respectively the global and the local information, are used to generate the auxiliary information which is then used by a third model to generate the final prediction. The models used to generate the auxiliary information, are respectively the Fully Convolutional Network (FCN) [9] and the 3D-UNet patch-based model [7]. The segmentation's from these two models are concatenated together with the original input forming a three-channels image, which is then used as input to a third model FC-DenseNet103 [3] to generate the final segmentation.

FCN Model (P1). We used DLTK implementation [7] with residual block consisting of ReLU activation function followed by 3D convolution layer to extract the features. To handle the stride convolution, we added pooling to the input before the addition in the residual unit. For all convolution layers, Kernel size is 3×3 with stride 1 and padding size 1. In the decoder stage, fully convolutional layers were used to target the output probabilities. Features maps learned at each layer were up sampled to the original size and then fed to the up-score unit where the features from encoder are learned to produce the sparse feature map. The kernel size used for up score unit was 1^3 and finally a soft-max layer was used to produce the segmentation.

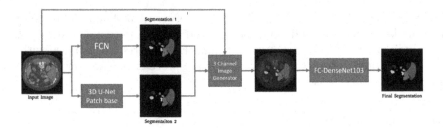

Fig. 1. The entire processing pipeline composed by three CNNs. Input: 256 × 256 gray scale image; Segmentation 1: prediction from FCN model; Segmentation 2: prediction from 3D U-Net Patch Base Model; RGB 3 Channel Image: combination of Segmentation 1, Segmentation 2 and input forming an RGB image; Final Segmentation : prediction from FC-DenseNet103 with the three RGB channels in input.

3D-UNet Patch-Based Model (P2). We used the 3D U-Net patch-based version publicly available[2]. Patch size of 64 is used. Max-pooling operations were performed to reduce the spatial size and high level features were extracted while the bottom block was providing information to the output of the encoder. In the decoder stage two deconvolutional blocks were used to resume the spatial size for the segmented output. In the last stage, convolution and soft-max layers were used to reduce the number of feature maps and to get the probability maps for target objects.

FC-DenseNet103 Model (P3). The input to the last model in the pipeline was a three-channel image composed by P1 and P2 predictions and the original input image. We used the FC-DenseNet103 provided in [3], feature maps are extracted in dense block of transition down layer and use pre-activation layer, where ReLU, convolution, max pooling and Batch normalization were performed on the input slice of 256 × 256. Up-sampling was performed in transition up layer where input was up sampled and concatenated with the skip connections and finally segmentation was calculated using soft-max layer.

2.3 Experimental Setup

FCN model was trained for 20000 iterations with batch size of 8 with tensor-flow. Training was done using Adam optimizer with learning rate of 0.0001. Similarly, 3D-UNet model was trained for 800000 iterations with patch size of 64. Again, Adam Optimizer was used with a learning rate of 0.00001. The last prediction model (FC-DenseNet103) using auxiliary data was trained for 20 epochs with batch size of 8 and tensor-flow as backend. RMSPropOptimizer was used with a learning rate of 0.0001. The proposed system was implemented on NVidia GTX 1080. FCN and FC-DenseNet103 took on average five hours for training while 3d-Unet took on average fifteen hours for training.

---

[2] https://github.com/zEttOn86/3D-Unet.

For the sake of comparisons we also trained and tested FC-DenseNet103 only using the input images to evaluate the performance improvement due to the auxiliary information. All the mentioned models were evaluated performing a training from scratch, using nested cross-validation with 24 subjects used for training, 2 subjects used for validation and 4 subjects used for testing. For evaluation purpose, we used Dice score to measure the intersection between resulting segmentation and ground truth:

$$DSC = \frac{2|X \cap Y|}{|X| + |Y|} \tag{1}$$

3 Results and Discussion

The average results (dice scores) for all models are shown in Table 1. The results were determined for all models only using the input image (P1, P2, and P3) and for FC-DenseNet103 also using the auxiliary information (P4). Moreover, the table shows the dice score of four other state-of-the-art methods (IMI, CLS, CNN-sw, FCN), which were top-ranked in the MICCAI challenge providing the dataset [6].

Table 1. Result of varius CNNs. Dice score obtained with Eq. (1) is shown for all models used in our pipeline (P1 is the FCN, P2 is the 3D Unet patch-based, and P3 is the FC-DenseNet103 when considered alone or P4 when considered in the pipeline proposed by the paper. Results of state-of-the-art models (IMI, CLS, CNN-sw and FCN) [6] determined on the same dataset are provided for comparison.

Class	P1	P2	P3	P4	IMI	CLS	CNN-sw	FCN
Spleen	0.856	0.817	0.913	**0.953**	0.919	0.911	0.930	0.936
R. Kidney	0.907	0.902	0.854	**0.934**	0.901	0.893	0.866	0.897
L. Kidney	0.890	0.897	0.813	**0.941**	0.914	0.901	0.911	0.911
Gallbladder	0.543	0.574	0.319	**0.719**	0.604	0.375	0.624	0.613
Esophagus	0.594	0.578	0.624	**0.784**	0.692	0.607	0.662	0.588
Liver	0.920	0.927	0.942	**0.968**	0.948	0.940	0.946	0.949
Stomach	0.757	0.779	0.739	**0.942**	0.805	0.704	0.775	0.764
Aorta	0.840	0.796	0.812	**0.884**	0.857	0.811	0.860	0.870
Inferior Vena Cava	0.782	0.757	0.661	**0.870**	0.828	0.760	0.776	0.758
Portal & Splenic Veins	0.674	0.624	0.498	0.752	**0.754**	0.649	0.567	0.715
Pancreas	0.606	0.613	0.431	**0.832**	0.740	0.643	0.602	0.646
R. Adrenal Gland	0.542	0.513	0.353	**0.752**	0.615	0.557	0.631	0.630
L. Adrenal Gland	0.471	0.462	0.146	**0.702**	0.623	0.582	0.583	0.631

From Table 1, it can be seen that the proposed cascade of CNNs (column P4) performs much better than any other solution, including the state-of-the-art methods top-ranked in the challenge. It clearly indicates the positive effect of auxiliary information provided as further input channels. The effect is reflected by the difference between column P3 and P4 where the same model was used respectively without and with auxiliary information. The results showed significant improvements for some organs, especially small ones like adrenal glands, pancreas, veins, esophagus. This is due to the particular combination of models. Indeed, FCN (P1) and Unet (P2) work at different granularity. The first model works mostly on the global information of the whole image, hence, it better locates the specific organs, while the second model works with local information, being more able to segment on smaller structures and edges. The FC-DenseNet103 model while being a weaker model, thanks to the auxiliary information, it can learn how to use the segmentations provided by the two previous models, refining its own segmentation based on the input images. From an alternative perspective, the FC-DenseNet103 model learns how to cleverly combine the results coming from the ensemble of two other models. In another way, it can be considered an advanced voting approach integrated by the original input as auxiliary information.

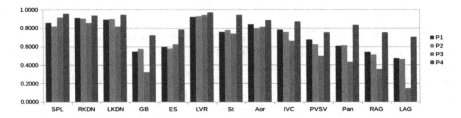

Fig. 2. Comparison of different models average dice used in proposed technique for all class labels.

The bar chart in Fig. 2 is a graphical representation of the results in Table 1 showing the dice score for all elements in the proposed cascade. It can be seen that the entire pipeline (P4), i.e., FC-DenseNet103 with auxiliary information is dominating all classes while the same model (P3) without auxiliary information has sometimes very poor performance. Thus, providing the auxiliary information to the model proved to be beneficial. In order to have a clearer understanding of the processing, the sample results depicted in Fig. 3 show that predictions of P1 and P2 are sometimes affected by small mistakes worsening the performance. However, the third model provided with auxiliary information is able to identify and correct the mistakes producing more accurate predictions. Interestingly, a collateral result is that the processing time of the third model with auxiliary information is reduced as the model is able to learn easily and quickly as compared to when it is not provided with auxiliary information.

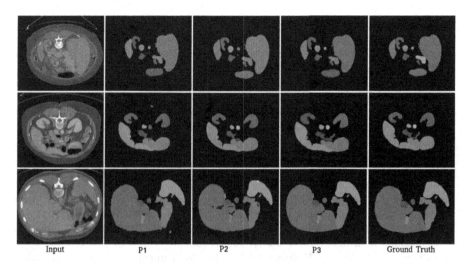

Input   P1   P2   P3   Ground Truth

Fig. 3. Examples of Resulting Predictions for three different subjects with Ground Truth

4 Conclusion

In this paper, we proposed an architecture built upon the combination of three different models solving quite efficiently a segmentation task. The three models are connected in such a way that first two models help the third one to produce better segmentation. This is obtained providing the preliminary segmentation from the first two models as auxiliary information to the third one. The relevant component here is the difference in the approaches used by the first two models. The first one segments the organs processing the whole window in one step. This makes the model aware of the location of different organs, losing the precision on small structures and edges. The second method on the contrary is patch-based, hence, it works on local information, making it better when processing small structures and edges.

Giving the outcome of these two models as auxiliary information to a third model helps the system to preserve the positive aspects of all segmentations while ignoring the negative traits. This can be observed from the results in Sect. 3 where it is evident that adding the auxiliary information results in a significant improvement of the segmentation accuracy.

References

1. Aslani, S., et al.: Multi-branch convolutional neural network for multiple sclerosis lesion segmentation. NeuroImage **196**, 1–15 (2019)
2. Heimann, T., Meinzer, H.P.: Statistical shape models for 3D medical image segmentation: a review. Med. Image Anal. **13**(4), 543–563 (2009)

3. Jégou, S., Drozdzal, M., Vazquez, D., Romero, A., Bengio, Y.: The one hundred layers tiramisu: fully convolutional densenets for semantic segmentation. In: In Proceedings of the IEEE Conference on Computer Vision and Pattern Recognition Workshops, pp. 11–19 (2017)

4. Karasawa, K., et al.: Multi-atlas pancreas segmentation: atlas selection based on vessel structure. Med. Image Anal. **39**, 18–28 (2017)

5. Landman, B., et al.: Multi-modal learning from unpaired images: application to multi-organ segmentation in CT and MRI. In: 2015 MICCAI Multi-Atlas Labeling Beyond the Cranial Vault - Workshop and Challenge (2015) https://doi.org/10.7303/syn3193805

6. Larsson, M., Zhang, Y., Kahl, F.: Robust abdominal organ segmentation using regional convolutional neural networks. Appl. Soft Comput. **70**, 465–471 (2018)

7. Pawlowski, N., et al.: DLTK: state of the art reference implementations for deep learning on medical images. In: Medical Imaging Meet NIPS Workshop (2017)

8. Tong, T., et al.: Discriminative dictionary learning for abdominal multi-organ segmentation. Med. Image Anal. **23**(1), 92–104 (2015)

9. Valindria, V.V., et al.: Multi-modal learning from unpaired images: application to multi-organ segmentation in CT and MRI. In: IEEE Winter Conference on Applications of Computer Vision (WACV). IEEE (2018)

10. Wang, Z., et al.: Geodesic patch-based segmentation. In: Golland, P., Hata, N., Barillot, C., Hornegger, J., Howe, R. (eds.) MICCAI 2014. LNCS, vol. 8673, pp. 666–673. Springer, Cham (2014). https://doi.org/10.1007/978-3-319-10404-1_83

11. Wimmer, A., Soza, G., Hornegger, J.: A generic probabilistic active shape model for organ segmentation. In: Yang, G.-Z., Hawkes, D., Rueckert, D., Noble, A., Taylor, C. (eds.) MICCAI 2009. LNCS, vol. 5762, pp. 26–33. Springer, Heidelberg (2009). https://doi.org/10.1007/978-3-642-04271-3_4

Multiview Geometry and 3D Computer Vision

Performance Evaluation of Learned 3D Features

Riccardo Spezialetti[(✉)], Samuele Salti, and Luigi Di Stefano

Viale del Risorgimento 2, Bologna, Italy
{riccardo.spezialetti,samuele.salti,luigi.distefano}@unibo.it

Abstract. Matching surfaces is a challenging 3D Computer Vision problem typically addressed by local features. Although a variety of 3D feature detectors and descriptors has been proposed in literature, they have seldom been proposed together and it is yet not clear how to identify the most effective detector-descriptor pair for a specific application. A promising solution is to leverage machine learning to learn the optimal 3D detector for any given 3D descriptor [15]. In this paper, we report a performance evaluation of the detector-descriptor pairs obtained by learning a paired 3D detector for the most popular 3D descriptors. In particular, we address experimental settings dealing with object recognition and surface registration.

Keywords: 3D Computer Vision · Surface matching · 3D features

1 Introduction

Surface matching is an ubiquitous task in 3D Computer Vision, where it helps to tackle major applications such as object recognition and surface registration. Nowadays, most surface matching methods follow a *local* paradigm based on establishing correspondences between 3D patches referred to as *features*. The typical *feature-matching pipeline* consists of three steps: *detection, description* and *matching*.

Although over the last decades many 3D detectors and descriptors have been proposed in literature, it is yet unclear how to effectively combine these proposals to create an effective pipeline. Indeed, unlike the related field of *local image features*, methods to either detect or describe 3D features have been designed and proposed separately, alongside with specific application settings and related datasets. This is also vouched by the main performance evaluation papers in the field, which address either repeatability of 3D detectors designed to highlight geometrically salient surface patches [14] or distinctiveness and robustness of popular 3D descriptors [2].

More recently, however, [9] and [15] have proposed a machine learning approach that allows for learning an optimal 3D keypoint detector for any given 3D descriptor so as to maximize the end-to-end performance of the overall

© Springer Nature Switzerland AG 2019
E. Ricci et al. (Eds.): ICIAP 2019, LNCS 11751, pp. 519–531, 2019.
https://doi.org/10.1007/978-3-030-30642-7_47

feature-matching pipeline. The authors show that this approach provides effective pipelines across diverse applications and datasets. Moreover, their object recognition experiments show that, with the considered descriptors (*SHOT* [13], *Spin Image (SI)* [4], *FPFH* [8]), learning to detect specific keypoints leads to better performance than relying on existing general-purpose handcrafted detectors (*ISS* [17], *Harris3D* [10], *NARF* [11]).

By enabling an optimal detector to be learned for any descriptor, [15] sets forth a novel paradigm to maximize affinity between 3D detectors and descriptors. This opens up the question of which learned detector-descriptor pair may turn out most effective in the main application areas. This paper tries to answer this question by proposing an experimental evaluation of learned 3D pipelines. In particular, we address object recognition and surface registration, and compare the performance attained by learning a paired feature detector for the most popular handcrafted 3D descriptors (*SHOT* [13], *SI* [4], *FPFH* [8], *USC* [12], *RoPS* [3]) as well as for a recently proposed descriptor based on deep learning (*CGF-32* [5]).

2   3D Local Feature Detectors and Descriptors

This section reviews state-of-the-art methods for detection and description of 3D local features. Both tasks have been pursued through *hand-crafted* and *learned* approaches.

Hand-Crafted Feature Detectors. Keypoint detectors have traditionally been conceived to identify points that maximize a saliency function computed on a surrounding patch. The purpose of this function is to highlight those local geometries that turn out repeatedly identifiable in presence of nuisances such as noise, viewpoint changes, point density variations and clutter. State-of-the-art proposals mainly differ for the adopted saliency function. Detectors operate in two steps: first, the saliency function is computed at each point on the surface, then *non-maxima suppression* allows for sifting out saliency peaks. *Intrinsic Shape Signature (ISS)* [17] computes the eigenvalue decomposition of the scatter-matrix of the points within the supporting patch in order to highlight local geometries exhibiting a prominent principal direction, *Harris3D* [10] extends the idea of image corners by deploying surface normals rather than image gradients to calculate the saliency (i.e. *Cornerness*) function. *Normal Aligned Radial Feature (NARF)* [11] first selects stable surface points, then highlights those stable points showing sufficient local variations. This leads to locate keypoints close to depth discontinuities.

Learned Feature Detectors. Unlike previous work in the field, Salti *et al.* [9] proposed to learn a keypoint detector amenable to identify points likely to generate correct matches when encoded by the *SHOT* descriptor. In particular, the authors cast keypoint detection as a binary classification problem tackled by a Random Forest and show how to generate the training set as well as the feature representation deployed by the classifier. Later, Tonioni *et al.* [15] have demonstrated that this approach can be applied seamlessly and very effectively to other popular descriptors such as *SI* [4] and *FPFH* [8].

Hand-Crafted Feature Descriptors. Many hand-crafted feature descriptors represent the local surface by computing geometric measurements within the supporting patch and then accumulating values into histograms. *Spin Images (SI)* [4] relies on two coordinates to represent each point in the support: the radial coordinate, defined as the perpendicular distance to the line trough the surface normal at the keypoint, and the elevation coordinate, defined as the signed distance to the tangent plane at the keypoint. The space formed by this two values is then discretized into a 2D histogram.

In *3D Shape Context (3DSC)* [1] the support is partitioned by a 3D spherical grid centered at the keypoint with the north pole aligned to the surface normal. A 3D histogram is built by counting up the weighted number of points falling into each spatial bin along the radial, azimuth and elevation dimensions. *Unique Shape Context (USC)* [12] extends *3DSC* with the introduction of a unique and repeatable canonical reference frame borrowed from [13].

SHOT [13], alike, deploys both a unique and repeatable canonical reference frame as well as a 3D spherical grid to discretize the supporting patch into bins along the radial, azimuth and elevation axes. Then, the angles between the normal at the keypoint and those at the neighboring points within each bins are accumulated into local histograms. *Rotational Projection Statistics (RoPS)* [3] uses a canonical reference frame to rotate the neighboring points on the local surface. The descriptor is then constructed by rotationally projecting the 3D points onto 2D planes to generate three distribution matrices. Finally, a histogram encoding five statistics of distribution matrices is calculated. *Fast Point Feature Histograms (FPFH)* [8] operates in two steps. In the first, akin to PFH [7], four features, refereed to as SPFH, are calculated using the Darboux frame and the surface normals between the keypoint and its neighbors. In the second step, the descriptor is obtained as the weighted sum between the SPFH of the keypoint and the SPFHs of the neighboring points.

Learned Feature Descriptors. The success of deep neural networks in so many challenging image recognition tasks has motivated research on learning representations from 3D data. One of the pioneering works is *3D Match* [16], where the authors deploy a siamese network trained on local volumetric patches to learn a local descriptor. The input to the network consists of a Truncated Signed Distance Function (TSDF) defined on a voxel grid. In [5], the authors deploy a fully-connected deep neural network together with a feature learning approach based on the *triplet ranking loss* in order to learn a very compact 3D descriptor, referred to as *CGF-32*. Their approach does not rely on raw data but on an hand-crafted input representation similar to [1], canonicalized by the local reference frame presented in [13].

3   Keypoint Learning

In order to carry out the performance evaluation proposed in this paper, for most local descriptors reviewed in Sect. 2 we did learn the corresponding optimal detector according to the *keypoint learning* methodology [15]. We provide here a brief overview of this methodology and refer the reader to [9,15] for a detailed description.

The idea behind keypoint learning is to learn to detect keypoints that can yield good correspondences when coupled with a given descriptor. To this end, keypoint detection is cast as binary classification, *i.e.* a point can either be a good candidate or not when used to create matches by means of the given descriptor, and a Random Forest is used as classifier. Training of the classifier requires to define the training set, *i.e.* both positive (good) and negative (not good) points, as well as the feature representation.

As for positive samples, the method tries to sift out those points that, when described by a chosen descriptor, can be matched correctly across different 2.5D views of a 3D object. Thus, starting from a set of 2.5D views $\{V_i\}, i = 1, \ldots, N$ of an object from a 3D dataset, each point $p \in V_i$ in each view V_i is embedded by the chosen descriptor. Then, for each view V_i, a subset of overlapping views is selected based on an overlap threshold τ. A two-step positive samples selection is performed on V_i and each overlapping view V_j. In the first step, a list of correspondences between descriptors is created by searching for all descriptors $d \in V_i$ the nearest neighbor in the descriptor space between all descriptors $g \in V_j$. A preliminary list of positive samples P_i^j for view V_i is created by taking only those points that have been correctly matched in V_j, *i.e.* the points belonging to the matched descriptors in the two views correspond to the same 3D point of the object according to threshold ϵ. The list is then filtered removing *non-maxima* local extrema within ϵ_{nms} using the descriptor distance as saliency. In the second step, the list of positive samples is refined by keeping only the points in V_i that can be matched correctly also in those others overlapping views that have not been used in the first step. Negative samples are then extracted on each view, sampling random points among those points which are not included in the positive set. A distance threshold ϵ_{neg} is used to avoid a negative being too close to a positive and to other negative samples, and also to balance the size of the positive and negative sets.

As far as the representation input to the classifier is concerned, the method relies on histograms of normal orientations inspired by *SHOT* [13]. However, to avoid computation of the local Reference Frame while still achieving rotation invariance, the spherical support is divided only along the radial dimension so as to compute a histogram for each spherical shell thus obtained. [15] showed that, although inspired by SHOT, such representation can be used to learn an effective detector also for other descriptors.

4   Evaluation Methodology

The performance evaluation proposed in this paper aims to compare different learned detector-descriptor pairs while addressing two main application settings, namely object recognition and surface registration. In this section, we highlight the key traits and nuisances which characterize the two tasks, present the datasets and performance evaluation metrics used in the experiments and, finally, provide the relevant implementation details.

4.1   Object Recognition

In typical object recognition settings, one wishes to recognize a set of given 3D models into scenes acquired from an unknown vantage point and featuring an unknown arrangement of such models. Peculiar nuisances in this scenario are occlusions and, possibly, clutter, as objects not belonging to the model gallery may be present in the scenes. In our experiments we rely on the following popular object recognition datasets:

- *UWA* dataset, introduced by Mian *et al.* [6]. This dataset consists of 4 full 3D models and 50 scenes wherein models significantly occlude each other. To create some clutter, scenes contain also an object which is not included in the model gallery. As scenes are scanned by a Minolta Vivid 910 scanner, they are corrupted by real sensor noise.
- *Random Views* dataset, based on the Stanford 3D scanning repository[1] and originally proposed in [14]. This dataset comprises 6 full 3D models and 36 scenes obtained by synthetic renderings of random model arrangements. Scenes feature occlusions but no clutter. Moreover, scenes are corrupted by different levels of synthetic noise. In the experiments we consider scenes with Gaussian noise equal to $\sigma = 0.1$ mesh resolution units.

To evaluate the effectiveness of the considered learned detector-descriptor pairs we rely on descriptor matching experiments. Specifically, for both datasets, we run keypoint detection on synthetically rendered views of all models. Then, we compute and store into a single kd-tree all the corresponding descriptors. Keypoints are detected and described also in the set of scenes provided with the dataset, $\{S_j\}, j = 1, \ldots, N_S$. Eventually, a correspondence is established for each scene descriptor by finding the nearest neighbor descriptor within the models kd-tree and thresholding the distance between descriptors to accept a match as valid. Correct correspondences can be identified based on knowledge of the ground-truth transformations which bring views and scenes into a common reference frame and checking whether the matched keypoints lay within a 3D distance ϵ. Indeed, denoting as $(k_j, k_{n,m})$ a correspondence between a keypoint k_j detected in scene S_j and a keypoint $k_{n,m}$ detected in the n-th view of model m, as $\mathbf{T}_{j,m}$ the transformation from S_j to model m, as $\mathbf{T}_{n,m}$ the transformation

---

[1] 3 http://graphics.stanford.edu/data/3Dscanrep/.

from the n-th view and the canonical reference frame of model m, the set of correct correspondences for scene S_j is given by:

$$C_j = \{(k_j, k_{n,m}) : \|\mathbf{T}_{j,m}k_j - \mathbf{T}_{n,m}k_{n,m}\| \leq \epsilon\} \tag{1}$$

From C_j, we can compute True Positive and False Positive matches for each scene and, by averaging them across scenes, for each of the considered datasets. The final results for each dataset are provided as *Recall vs. 1-Precision* curves, with curves obtained by varying the threshold on the distance between descriptors.

4.2 Surface Registration

The goal of surface registration is to align into a common 3D reference frame several partial views (usually referred to as scans) of a 3D object obtained by a certain optical sensor. This is achieved through rather complex procedures that, however, typically rely on a key initial step, referred to as *Pairwise Registration*, aimed at estimating the rigid motion between any two views by a *feature-matching pipeline*. Differently from object recognition scenarios, the main nuisances deal with missing regions, self-occlusions, limited overlap area between views and point density variations. In our experiments we rely on the following surface registration dataset:

- *Laser Scan* dataset, recently proposed in [5]. This dataset includes 8 public-domain 3D models, *i.e.* 3 taken from the AIM@SHAPE repository (*Bimba, Dancing Children* and *Chinese Dragon*), 4 from the Stanford 3D Scanning Repository (*Armadillo, Buddha, Bunny, Stanford Dragon*) and *Berkeley Angel* According to the protocol described in [5], training should be carried out based on synthetic views generated from *Berkeley Angel, Bimba, Bunny* and *Chinese Dragon*, while the test data consists of the real scans available for the remaining 3 models (*Armadillo, Buddha* and *Stanford Dragon*).

Thus, given a set of M real scans available for a test model, we compute all the possible $N = \frac{M(M-1)}{2}$ view pairs $\{V_i, V_j\}$. For each pair, we run keypoint detection on both views. Due to partial overlap between the views, a keypoint belonging to V_i may have no correspondence in V_j. Hence, denoted as $\mathbf{T}_i$ and $\mathbf{T}_j$ the ground-truth transformations that, respectively, bring V_i and V_j into a canonical reference frame, we can compute the set $\mathcal{O}_{i,j}$ that contains the keypoints in V_i that have a corresponding point in V_j. In particular, given a keypoint $k_i \in V_i$

$$\mathcal{O}_{i,j} = \{k_i : \|\mathbf{T}_i k_i - \mathcal{NN}(\mathbf{T}_i k_i, \mathbf{T}_j V_j)\| \leq \epsilon_{ovr}\}, \tag{2}$$

where $\mathcal{NN}(\mathbf{T}_i k_i, \mathbf{T}_j V_j)$ denotes the nearest neighbor of $\mathbf{T}_i k_i$ in the transformed view $\mathbf{T}_j V_j$. If the number of points in $\mathcal{O}_{i,j}$ is less than 20% of the keypoints in V_i, the pair (V_i, V_j) is not considered in the evaluation experiments due to insufficient overlap. Conversely, for all the view pairs (V_i, V_j) exhibiting sufficient overlap, a list of correspondences between all the keypoints detected in

V_i and all the keypoints extracted from V_j is established by finding the nearest neighbor in the descriptor space via kd-tree matching. Then, given a pair of matched keypoints (k_i, k_j), $k_i \in V_i, k_j \in V_j$, the set of correct correspondences, $\mathcal{C}_{i,j}$, can be identified based on the available ground-truth transformations by checking whether the matched keypoints lay within a certain distance ϵ in the canonical reference frame:

$$\mathcal{C}_{i,j} = \{(k_i, k_j) : \|\mathbf{T}_i k_i - \mathbf{T}_j k_j\| \leq \epsilon\} \tag{3}$$

Then, the *precision* of the matching process can be computed as a function of the distance threshold ϵ [5]:

$$precision_{i,j}(\epsilon) = \frac{|\mathcal{C}_{i,j}|}{|\mathcal{O}_{i,j}|} \tag{4}$$

The *precision* score associated with any given model is obtained by averaging across all view pairs. We also average across all test models so as to get the final score associated to the *Laser Scan* dataset.

Table 1. Parameters for object recognition datasets.

Dataset	$r_{desc}(mm)$	$r_{det}(mm)$	τ	$\epsilon(mm)$	$\epsilon_{nms}(mm)$	$\epsilon_{neg}(mm)$	$r_{nms}(mm)$	$s_{min}(mm)$
UWA	40	20	0.85	7	4	2	4	0.8
Random Views	40	20	–	7	–	–	4	0.8

4.3 Implementation

For all handcrafted descriptors considered in our evaluation, we use the implementation available in the PCL library. For *CGF-32*, we use the public implementation made available by the authors [5]. As for the *Keypoint Learning* (KPL) framework described in Sect. 3, we use the publicly available original code for the generation of the training set[2]. During the detection phase, each point of a point cloud is passed through the Random Forest classifier which produces a score. A point is identified as a keypoint if it exhibits a local maximum of the scores in a neighborhood of radius r_{nms} and the score is higher than a threshold s_{min}. For each descriptor considered in our evaluation, we train its paired detector according to the KPL framework. As a result, we obtain six detector-descriptor pairs, referred to from now on as *KPL-CGF32, KPL-FPFH, KPL-ROPS, KPL-SHOT, KPL-SI, KPL-USC*.

In object recognition experiments, the training data for all detectors are generated from the 4 full 3D models present in the *UWA* dataset. According to the KPL methodology [9,15], for each model we render views from the nodes of an icosahedron centered at the centroid. Then, the detectors are used in the scenes of the *UWA* dataset as well as in those of the *Random Views* dataset. Thus,

---

[2] http://github.com/CVLAB-Unibo/Keypoint-Learning.

Table 2. Parameters for surface registration dataset.

Model name	$r_{desc}(mm)$	$r_{det}(mm)$	τ	$\epsilon(mm)$	$\epsilon_{nms}(mm)$	$\epsilon_{neg}(mm)$	ϵ_{ovr}	$r_{nms}(mm)$	$s_{min}(mm)$
Angel	40	20	0.85	7	4	2	–	–	–
Bimba	40	20	0.85	7	4	2	–	–	–
Bunny	40	20	0.65	7	4	2	–	–	–
Chinese Dragon	40	20	0.65	7	4	2	–	–	–
Armadillo	40	20	–	7	–	–	2	4	0.5
Buddha	40	20	–	7	–	–	2	4	0.5
Stanford Dragon	40	20	–	7	–	–	2	4	0.5

similarly to [9,15], we do not retrain the detectors on *Random Views* in order to test the ability of the considered detector-descriptor pairs to generalize well to unseen models in object recognition settings. A coherent approach was pursued for the *CGF-32* descriptor. As the authors do not provide a model trained on the *UWA* dataset, we trained the descriptor on the synthetically rendered views of the 4 *UWA* models using the code provided by the authors and following the protocol described in the paper in order to generate the data needed by their learning framework based on the *triplet ranking loss*. Thus, *KPL-CGF32* was trained on *UWA* models and, like all other detector-descriptor pairs, tested on both *UWA* and *Random Views* scenes.

In surface registration experiments we proceed according to the protocol proposed in [5]. Hence, detectors are trained with rendered views of the train models provided within the *Laser Scan* dataset (*Angel, Bimba, Bunny, Chinese Dragon*) and tested on the real scans of the test models (*Armadillo, Buddha, Stanford Dragon*). As *CGF-32* was trained exactly on the abovementioned train models [5], to carry out surface registration experiments we did not retrain the descriptor but used the trained network published by the authors[3].

The values of the main parameters of the detector-descriptor pairs used in the experiments are summarized in Tables 1 and 2. As it can be observed from Table 1, train parameters for *Random Views* dataset are not specified as we did not train KPL detectors on this dataset. For surface registration, since models belong to different repositories, we report parameters grouped by model. Test parameters for *Angel, Bimba, Bunny* and *Chinese Dragon* are not reported as they are only used in train. Similarly, we omit train parameters for *Armadillo, Buddha* and *Stanford Dragon*. Due to the different shapes of the models in the dataset, τ is tuned during the train stage so that the number of overlapping views remains constant across all models.

---

[3] https://github.com/marckhoury/CGF.

5 Experimental Results

5.1 Object Recognition

Results on the *UWA* dataset are shown in Fig. 1. First, we wish to highlight how the features based on descriptors which encode just the spatial densities of points around a keypoint outperform those relying on higher order geometrical attributes (such as, *e.g.*, normals). Indeed, *KPL-CGF32*, *KPL-USC* and *KPL-SI* yield significantly better results than *KPL-SHOT* and *KPL-FPFH*. These results are coherent with the findings and analysis reported in the performance evaluation by Guo *et al.* [2], which pointed out the former feature category being more robust to clutter and sensor noise. It is also worth observing how the representation based on the spatial tessellation and point density measurements proposed in [1] together with the local reference frame proposed in [13] turn out particularly amenable to object recognition, as it is actually deployed by both features yielding neatly the best performance, namely *KPL-CGF32* and *KPL-USC*. Yet, learning a dataset-specific non-linear mapping by a deep neural network on top of this good representation does improve performance quite a lot, as vouched by *KPL-CGF32* outperforming *KPL-USC* by a large margin. Indeed, the results obtained in this paper by learning both a dataset-specific descriptor as well as its paired optional detector, *i.e.* the features referred to as *KPL-CGF32*, turn out significantly superior to those previously published on *UWA* object recognition dataset (see [9] and [15]).

In [15], the results achieved on *Random Views* by the detectors trained on *UWA* prove the ability of the KPL methodology to learn to detect general rather than dataset-specific local shapes amenable to provide good matches alongside with the paired descriptor, and even more effectively, in fact, than the shapes found by handcrafted detectors. Thus, when comparing the different features, we can assume here that descriptors are feed by detectors with optimal patches and focus on the ability of the former to handle the specific nuisances of the *Random Views* dataset. As shown in Fig. 1, *KPL-FPFH* and *KPL-SHOT* perform slightly better than *KPL-USC*, *KPL-CGF32* and *KPL-SI*. Again, this is coherent with previous findings reported in literature (see [2] and [15]), which show how descriptors based on higher order geometrical attributes turn out more effective on *Random Views* due to the lack of clutter and real sensor noise. As for *KPL-CGF32*, although it performs still overall better than the other descriptors based on point densities, we observe quite a remarkable performance drop compared to the results on the *UWA* dataset, much larger, indeed, than that observed for *KPL-USC*, which shares with *KPL-CGF32* a very similar input representation. This suggests that the non-linear mapping learned by *KPL-CGF32* is highly optimized to tell apart the features belonging to the objects present in the training dataset (*i.e.* *UWA*) but turns out quite less effective when applied to unseen features, like those found on the objects belonging to *Random Views*. This *domain shift* issue is a peculiar wick trait of learned features, which may cause them to yield less stable performance across diverse datasets than handcrafted representations.

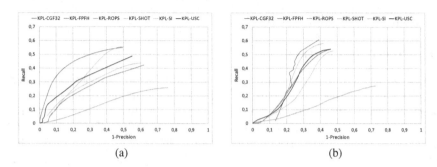

Fig. 1. Quantitative results on object recognition. Column a: *UWA* dataset. Column b: *Random Views* dataset.

5.2 Surface Registration

First, it is worth pointing out how, unlike in object recognition settings, in surface registration it is never possible to train any machine learning operator, either detector or descriptor, on the very same objects that would then be processed at test time. Indeed, should one be given either a full 3D model or a set of scans where ground-truth transformations are known, as required to train 3D feature detectors (*i.e. KPL*) or descriptors (e.g. *CGF-32*), there would be no need to carry out any registration for that object. Surface registration is about stitching together several scans of a new object than one wishes to acquire as a full 3D model. As such, any learning machinery is inherently prone to the domain shift issue.

As mentioned in Subsect. 4.2, our experiments rely on the *Laser Scan* dataset [5] and follow the split into train and test objects proposed by the authors. As shown in Fig. 2, when averaging across all test objects, the detector-descriptor pair based on the learned descriptor *CGF-32* provides the best performance. This validates the findings reported in [5], where the authors introduce *CGF-32* and prove its good registration performance on *Laser Scan*, also in our experimental setting where an optimal detector is learned for every descriptor.

6   Conclusion and Future Work

Object recognition settings turn out quite amenable to deploy learned 3D features. Indeed, one can train upon a set of 3D objects available beforehand, *e.g.* due to scanning by some sensor or as CAD models, and then seek to recognize them into scenes featuring occlusions and clutter. These settings allow for learning an highly specialized descriptor alongside its optimal paired detector so to achieve excellent performance. In particular, the learned pair referred to in this paper as *KPL-CGF32* sets the new state of the art in descriptor matching on the *UWA* benchmark dataset. Although the learned representation may not exhibit comparable performance when transferred to unseen objects, in object recognition it is always possible to retrain on the objects at hand to improve

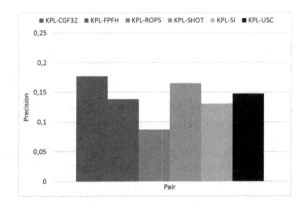

Fig. 2. Surface registration results on the *Laser Scan* dataset.

performance. An open question left to future work concerns whether the input parametrization deployed by *CGF-32* may enable to learn an highly effective non-linear mapping also in datasets characterized by different nuisances (*e.g.* *Laser Scan*) or one should better try to learn 3D representations directly from raw data, as vouched by the success of deep learning from image recognition. Features based on learned representations, such as *KPL-CGF32*, are quite effective also in surface registration, although this scenario is inherently more prone to the domain shift issue and, indeed, features based on handcrafted descriptors, like in particular *KPL-SHOT* and *KPL-USC*, turn out very competitive.

We believe that these findings may pave the way for further research on the recent field of learned 3D representations, in particular in order to foster addressing domain adaptation issues, a topic investigated more and more intensively in nowadays deep learning literature concerned with image recognition. Indeed, 3D data are remarkably diverse in nature due to the variety of sensing principles and related technologies and we wittness a lack of large training datasets, *e.g.* at a scale somehow comparable to ImageNet, that may allow learning representations from a rich and varied corpus of 3D models. Therefore, how to effectively transfer learned representations to new scenarios seems a key issue to the success of machine/deep learning in the most challenging 3D Computer Vision tasks.

Finally, *KPL* has established a new framework whereby one can learn an optimal detector for any given descriptor. In this paper we have shown how applying *KPL* to a learned representation (*CGF-32*) leads to particularly effective features (*KPL-CGF32*), in particular when pursuing object recognition. Yet, according to the *KPL* methodology, the descriptor (*e.g. CGF-32*) has to be learned before its paired detector: one might be willing to investigate on whether and how a single end-to-end paradigm may allow learning both component jointly so as to further improve performance.

References

1. Frome, A., Huber, D., Kolluri, R., Bülow, T., Malik, J.: Recognizing objects in range data using regional point descriptors. In: Pajdla, T., Matas, J. (eds.) ECCV 2004. LNCS, vol. 3023, pp. 224–237. Springer, Heidelberg (2004). https://doi.org/10.1007/978-3-540-24672-5_18

2. Guo, Y., Bennamoun, M., Sohel, F., Lu, M., Wan, J., Kwok, N.M.: A comprehensive performance evaluation of 3D local feature descriptors. Int. J. Comput. Vision **116**(1), 66–89 (2016)

3. Guo, Y., Sohel, F., Bennamoun, M., Lu, M., Wan, J.: Rotational projection statistics for 3D local surface description and object recognition. Int. J. Comput. Vision **105**(1), 63–86 (2013)

4. Johnson, A.E., Hebert, M.: Using spin images for efficient object recognition in cluttered 3D scenes. IEEE Trans. Pattern Anal. Mach. Intell. **21**(5), 433–449 (1999)

5. Khoury, M., Zhou, Q.Y., Koltun, V.: Learning compact geometric features. In: Proceedings of the IEEE Conference on Computer Vision and Pattern Recognition, pp. 153–161 (2017)

6. Mian, A., Bennamoun, M., Owens, R.: On the repeatability and quality of keypoints for local feature-based 3D object retrieval from cluttered scenes. Int. J. Comput. Vision **89**(2–3), 348–361 (2010)

7. Rusu, R.B., Blodow, N., Marton, Z.C., Beetz, M.: Aligning point cloud views using persistent feature histograms. In: IEEE/RSJ International Conference on Intelligent Robots and Systems, IROS 2008, pp. 3384–3391. IEEE (2008)

8. Rusu, R.B., Bradski, G., Thibaux, R., Hsu, J.: Fast 3D recognition and pose using the viewpoint feature histogram. In: 2010 IEEE/RSJ International Conference on Intelligent Robots and Systems (IROS), pp. 2155–2162. IEEE (2010)

9. Salti, S., Tombari, F., Spezialetti, R., Di Stefano, L.: Learning a descriptor-specific 3D keypoint detector. In: Proceedings of the IEEE International Conference on Computer Vision, pp. 2318–2326 (2015)

10. Sipiran, I., Bustos, B.: Harris 3D: a robust extension of the harris operator for interest point detection on 3D meshes. Vis. Comput. **27**(11), 963 (2011)

11. Steder, B., Rusu, R.B., Konolige, K., Burgard, W.: NARF: 3D range image features for object recognition. In: Workshop on Defining and Solving Realistic Perception Problems in Personal Robotics at the IEEE/RSJ International Conference on Intelligent Robots and Systems (IROS), vol. 44 (2010)

12. Tombari, F., Salti, S., Di Stefano, L.: Unique shape context for 3D data description. In: Proceedings of the ACM Workshop on 3D Object Retrieval, pp. 57–62. ACM (2010)

13. Tombari, F., Salti, S., Di Stefano, L.: Unique signatures of histograms for local surface description. In: Daniilidis, K., Maragos, P., Paragios, N. (eds.) ECCV 2010, Part III. LNCS, vol. 6313, pp. 356–369. Springer, Heidelberg (2010). https://doi.org/10.1007/978-3-642-15558-1_26. http://dl.acm.org/citation.cfm?id=1927006.1927035

14. Tombari, F., Salti, S., Di Stefano, L.: Performance evaluation of 3D keypoint detectors. Int. J. Comput. Vision **102**(1–3), 198–220 (2013)

15. Tonioni, A., Salti, S., Tombari, F., Spezialetti, R., Di Stefano, L.: Learning to detect good 3D keypoints. Int. J. Comput. Vision **126**(1), 1–20 (2018)

16. Zeng, A., Song, S., Nießner, M., Fisher, M., Xiao, J., Funkhouser, T.: 3DMatch: learning local geometric descriptors from RGB-D reconstructions. In: 2017 IEEE Conference on Computer Vision and Pattern Recognition (CVPR), pp. 199–208. IEEE (2017)
17. Zhong, Y.: Intrinsic shape signatures: a shape descriptor for 3D object recognition. In: 2009 IEEE 12th International Conference on Computer Vision Workshops (ICCV Workshops), pp. 689–696. IEEE (2009)

3DMM for Accurate Reconstruction of Depth Data

Claudio Ferrari$^{(\boxtimes)}$ ⓘ, Stefano Berretti ⓘ, Pietro Pala ⓘ,
and Alberto Del Bimbo ⓘ

Media Integration and Communication Center, University of Florence, Florence, Italy
claudio.ferrari@unifi.it

Abstract. In this paper, we propose a framework to derive accurate reconstructions of the 3D face surface from low resolution depth frames by means of a 3D Morphable Model (3DMM). By using a 3DMM specifically designed to support local and expression-related deformations of the face, we propose a two-steps 3DMM fitting solution: initially the model is warped based on landmarks correspondences; subsequently, it is iteratively refined by means of a mean-square optimization on the nearest-neighboring vertices. Preliminary results show that the proposed solution is able to derive faithful 3D models of the face, both for low- and high-resolution scans; quantitative results also evidence the higher accuracy of our approach with respect to methods that use one step fitting based on landmarks. In addition, we employed the 3DMM fitting to learn expressions specific coefficients, that can be further applied to the deformed models so as to generate subject-specific expressive scans, while the fitting procedure allows maintaining unaltered the general surface topology of the original scans.

Keywords: 3DMM construction · 3DMM fitting · 3D face analysis

1 Introduction

Recent advances in 3D scanning technologies make it possible to acquire registered RGB and depth frames at affordable cost. For instance, cameras with such capability are the Microsoft Kinect, the Asus Xtion and the Intel RealSense. These devices can operate at 30 fps or even more, but their depth resolution is modest, and individual frames are badly affected by noise that prevents the accurate reconstruction of the 3D geometry of the observed scene. This is particularly true for non-planar object surfaces, such as in the case of reconstructing the 3D geometry of faces. In the last few years, several 3D face reconstruction approaches have been proposed, also in truly uncooperative, *in the wild*, conditions [6]. However, a common trait of these approaches is that reconstruction of the 3D face model from data observed in a generic image or video frame is finalized to reproduce realistic renderings of the observed face in a different pose (*e.g.*, frontal pose) for the purpose of boosting the accuracy of person or facial expression recognition. In these solutions, smoothness of the reconstructed 3D face model is privileged with respect to fitting to the actual 3D geometry of the face. Indeed, this yields pleasant and realistic face renderings, but may prove

© Springer Nature Switzerland AG 2019
E. Ricci et al. (Eds.): ICIAP 2019, LNCS 11751, pp. 532–543, 2019.
https://doi.org/10.1007/978-3-030-30642-7_48

inadequate to provide a precise reconstruction of the 3D geometry of the face and its deformations in the presence of voluntary and involuntary expressions.

Motivated by these considerations, in this paper we propose a novel face modeling approach that starting from an RGB-D low-resolution sequence of the face is capable of reconstructing an accurate 3D face model over time also in the presence of facial expressions and generic facial deformations. This opens the way to the fine grained analysis of 3D local face deformations between expressive and neutral models. For example, this can have applications in face rehabilitation, where a subject at home (*e.g.*, a patient recovering after a stroke or a face surgery) can be instructed to perform some facial deformations in front of a camera. In our proposed solution, we start by the idea of using a 3DMM that also includes modes of deformation associated to facial expression variations and is specifically designed to account for local changes of the face. This is possible thanks to a dictionary learning framework that gives the atoms of the dictionary the capability of producing local deformations of the average model of the face. The model is then fit to a point cloud as captured by a low-resolution scanner (*e.g.*, Kinect) through a coarse-to-fine solution: the initial fitting is driven by the correspondence of a set of landmarks; the coarsely deformed model is then refined by an iterative closest points reassignment that minimizes the mean square error between corresponding points in an ICP like manner. The use of a dataset that includes both neutral and expressive face models for constructing the dictionary of deformation components favors the identification of identity-specific and expression-specific components. By changing the weights that control the former components the resulting 3DMM is deformed in such a way that the identity of the represented subject is altered. Differently, by changing the weights that control the latter components the resulting 3DMM preserves the identity of the represented subject yet changing the facial expression. This feature of the DL-3DMM model has been exploited to learn the set of weights (and their values) that are most correlated to some basic facial expressions. Experiments have been performed to measure the reconstruction error between the 3D models derived by fitting the 3DMM to the target scans of two large face datasets and the target scans themselves used as ground truth. In addition, our 3DMM has been compared against the 3D model that the Kinect toolkit fits on the target face. Finally, we also show that the 3D face models reconstructed with the proposed approach can be also used to synthesize new face models with varying expressions, while preserving the identity of the subject. Potentially, this opens the way to the application of the proposed method to a large category of applications, including data augmentation for the training of deep neural networks.

2   Related Work

In general, methods capable of reconstructing a 3D model of the face from low-resolution depth data can be categorized as either *driven by the data* or based on *fitting a 3D (morphable) model*.

Methods in the first category build a 3D face model by integrating tracked live depth images into a common final 3D model. For example, a method to produce laser scan quality 3D face models from a freely moving user with a low-cost, low-resolution depth camera was proposed in [9]. The model is initialized with the first depth image, and then each subsequent cloud of 3D points is registered to the reference using a GPU implementation of the ICP algorithm. This registration rejects poor alignment due to facial expressions, occlusions, or a poor estimation of the transformation. One evident limitation of this approach is that it is not capable of reconstructing expressive models of the face. In [14], the Kinect Fusion approach was proposed to fuse all of the depth data streamed from a Kinect sensor into a single global implicit surface model of the observed scene in real-time. To this end, the current pose of the sensor is obtained by tracking the live depth frame relative to the global model using a coarse-to-fine ICP algorithm, which uses all of the observed depth data available. In [10] the method was extended by considering dynamic actions of the foreground. Though the Kinect Fusion approach is general, its application to 3D face reconstruction results into models that reduce the noise with respect to individual frames, but still show a quite visible gap with respect to high-quality scans. In [2], a method was presented for producing an accurate and compact 3D face model in real-time using an RGB-D sensor like the Kinect camera. To this end, after initialization, Bump Images are updated in real time by using every RGB-D frame with respect to the current viewing direction and head pose; these latter are estimated using a frame-to-global-model registration strategy.

Though this method takes a live sequence of RGB-D images streamed from a fixed consumer sensor with unknown head pose, it is assumed the relative movement of the head between two successive frames to be small, and that the facial expression does not change during reconstruction. The work in [19] presents a combined hardware/software solution for marker-less reconstruction of non-rigidly deforming objects with arbitrary shape. First, a smooth template model of the subject while moving rigidly is scanned. This geometric surface prior is used to avoid strong scene assumptions, such as a kinematic human skeleton or a parametric shape model. Next, a GPU pipeline performs non-rigid registration of live RGB-D data to the smooth template using an extended non-linear as-rigid-as-possible framework. High-frequency details are fused onto the final mesh using a linear deformation model. However, this solution relies on a specific stereo matching algorithm to estimate real-time RGB-D data.

Methods in the second category, *i.e.*, methods that use a 3DMM to reconstruct a face model from depth data, are few. The method described in [18] employed a 3DMM that is fit to the depth images obtained from an RGB-D camera. The template mesh and the incoming frame are aligned using features detected in the RGB image as a coarse alignment step. The template is then aligned non-rigidly to the incoming frame, and the 3DMM is fit to the template. Unfortunately, this approach produces results that are biased towards the template. The work in [11] contributes a real time method for recovering facial shape and expression from a single depth image. The output is the result of minimizing the error in reconstructing the depth image, achieved by applying a set of identity and expression blend shapes to the model.

A discriminatively trained prediction pipeline is used that employs random forests to generate an initial dense, but noisy correspondence field. Then, a fast ICP-like approximation is exploited to update these correspondences, allowing a quick and robust initial fit of the model. The model parameters are then fine tuned to minimize the true reconstruction error using a stochastic optimization technique. However, none of these solutions can reconstruct fine details of expressive faces using a 3DMM.

3   3D Morphable Face Model

The work in [4] first presented a complete solution to derive a 3DMM by transforming the shape and texture from a training set of 3D face scans into a vector space representation based on PCA. The 3DMM was further refined into the Basel Face Model in [15], and subsequent evolutions but expressive scans were not part of the training set in all these solutions. Indeed, two aspects have a major relevance in characterizing the different methods for 3DMM construction: (1) the human face variability captured by the model; (2) the capability of the model to account for facial expressions. Both these feature directly depend on the number and heterogeneity of training scans. One of the few 3DMM in the literature that exposes both these features is the Dictionary Learning based 3DMM (DL-3DMM) proposed in [8]. Since we mainly develop on this model, below we first describe the peculiar features that make the DL-3DMM suitable for our purposes, then we focus on the proposed fitting procedure.

DL-3DMM Construction. Differently from works in the literature that either use optical-flow [4] or the non-rigid ICP algorithm [15], the dense alignment of the training data for the DL-3DMM was obtained with a solution based on face landmarks detection. These landmarks are then used for partitioning the face into a set of non-overlapping regions, each one identifying the same part of the face across all the scans. Re-sampling the internal of the region based on its contour, a dense correspondence is derived region-by-region and so for all the face. Such method showed to be robust also to large expression variations as those occurring in the Binghamton University 3D Facial Expression (BU-3DFE) database [17]. This dataset was used in the construction of the DL-3DMM.

Once a dense correspondence is established across the training data, these are used to estimate a set of M deformation components $\mathbf{C}_i$, usually derived by PCA, that will be linearly combined to generate novel shapes $\mathbf{S}$ starting from an average model $\mathbf{m}$:

$$\mathbf{S} = \mathbf{m} + \sum_{i=1}^{|M|} \mathbf{C}_i \alpha_i \, . \tag{1}$$

In the DL-3DMM, a dictionary of deformation components is learned by exploiting the *Online Dictionary Learning for Sparse Coding* technique [12]. Learning is performed in an unsupervised way, without exploiting any knowledge about the data (*e.g.*, identity or expression labels). The average model is deformed using the atoms $\mathbf{D}_i$ in place of $\mathbf{C}_i$ in Eq. (1). More details on the dictionary learning procedure can be found in [8]. The model $\mathbf{m}$, the dictionary $\mathbf{D}$ and the atoms weight $\mathbf{w}$, constitute the DL-3DMM.

3DMM Fitting. The 3DMM was originally designed with the goal of reconstructing the 3D shape of a face from single images [5]; the different techniques to fit the 3DMM to a face image can be divided in two main categories: *analysis-by-synthesis*, and *geometric based.* Methods in the former category perform a complex iterative procedure aimed at generating a synthetic image as similar as possible to the input one, optimizing with respect to the 3DMM (shape and texture) and rendering (*e.g.*, camera or illumination) parameters. Despite their complexity, the resulting reconstructions are rather accurate. Nonetheless, given a textured rendering, it is hard to discern if the retrieved shape resembles the real geometry of the face; this because the same rendering might be the result of different combinations of the many involved parameters. Alternatively, methods in the geometric-based category try to deform the 3DMM so as to match some geometrical features detected on the image, like facial landmarks or edges [3]. These approaches exploit the fact that human faces are composed of muscles—hence facial movements involve an extended surface rather than a single point—that are constrained to fixed anthropometric proportions and limited variability. Thus, when trying to deform the 3DMM to fit a set of sparse landmarks, the surrounding surfaces will smoothly follow the deformation in a statistically plausible way. This motivates the coarse reconstruction of the shape of the whole face based only on few control points. Obviously, the resulting reconstruction will be a coarse, but smooth approximation of the real surface.

The proposed method attempts to fill this gap; it builds upon the geometric approaches and extends the fitting based on facial landmarks to a whole point cloud. This extension implies a 3D scan corresponding to the face image to be available, which changes the context and the objective. In this configuration, the goal becomes deforming a generic face shape to match a target one, both represented as point clouds; indeed, the problem can be seen as the non-rigid registration of point clouds, which is a well-known problem in computer vision for which many solutions have been proposed [1,13]. All the literature solutions, however, are intended to work with generic point clouds representing arbitrary objects, while in this case the problem is bounded to human faces. The main difficulty is that faces are highly deformable objects, which often makes such approaches fail in matching the two shapes. On the opposite, we can exploit this prior to leverage a statistical tool such as the 3DMM to bound the deformation.

The proposed approach, first performs a similarity transformation to map the target shape into the average model space, accounting for 3D rotation, translation and scale (*SimilarityTransform* in Algorithm 1). This is achieved by means of 49 landmarks $\mathbf{L}_t \in \mathbf{R}^{49 \times 3}$, which are detected on the face image and back-projected to the mesh.

To initialize the approach and account for large shape differences that might impair the subsequent steps, we apply the DL-3DMM fitting using the landmarks similarly to [8]. The average model $\mathbf{m} \in \mathbf{R}^{p \times 3}$ is deformed on the target shape

---

Algorithm 1: Point Cloud Fitting (PCF)

Input: Average Model $\mathbf{m}$, Dictionary $\mathbf{D}$, Weights $\mathbf{w}$, Target Shape $\mathbf{t}$,
            Landmarks $\mathbf{L}_t, \mathbf{m}(\mathbf{I}_l)$, Error Threshold τ, Iterations Limit $MaxIter$
Output: Deformed Model $\hat{\mathbf{m}}$

$\tilde{\mathbf{t}} = \text{SimilarityTransform}(\mathbf{L}_t, \mathbf{t}, \mathbf{m}(\mathbf{I}_l))$;
$\hat{\mathbf{m}} = \text{LandmarkFitting}(\mathbf{L}_t, \mathbf{m}(\mathbf{I}_l), \mathbf{D}, \mathbf{w})$;
$i = 0$;
while $i < MaxIter \,\|\, err > \tau$ **do**
    | $\text{ICP}(\tilde{\mathbf{t}}, \hat{\mathbf{m}})$;
    | $\tilde{\mathbf{t}} = \text{VertexAssociation}(\tilde{\mathbf{t}}, \hat{\mathbf{m}})$;
    | $\hat{\mathbf{m}} = \text{ShapeFitting}(\tilde{\mathbf{t}}, \hat{\mathbf{m}}, \mathbf{D}, \mathbf{w})$;
    | $err = \text{ComputeEuclideanError}(\tilde{\mathbf{t}}, \hat{\mathbf{m}})$;
    | $i = i + 1$

$\tilde{\mathbf{t}} \in \mathbf{R}^{k \times 3}$ minimizing the Euclidean distance of the landmarks, whose indices on $\mathbf{m}$ are indicated as $\mathbf{I}_l \in \mathbf{N}^{49}$ (*LandmarkFitting* in Algorithm 1). Differently from [8], the fitting is performed directly in the 3D space and projection on the image plane is avoided. The deformation coefficients $\boldsymbol{\alpha}$ are computed using the dictionary atoms $\mathbf{d}_i$ as:

$$\min_{\alpha} \left\| \mathbf{L}_t - \mathbf{m}(\mathbf{I}_l) - \sum_{i=1}^{|\mathbf{D}|} \mathbf{d}_i(\mathbf{I}_l)\alpha_i \right\|_2^2 + \lambda \left\| \boldsymbol{\alpha} \circ \hat{\mathbf{w}}^{-1} \right\|_2 . \tag{2}$$

In the equation above, $\mathbf{d}_i(\mathbf{I}_l)$ indicates that, for each dictionary atom, only the elements associated to the vertices corresponding to the landmarks are involved in the minimization. The solution is found in closed form and the average model $\mathbf{m}$ is deformed using Eq. (1) to obtain an initial estimate $\hat{\mathbf{m}}$. Then, we perform a rigid ICP registration between $\hat{\mathbf{m}}$ and $\tilde{\mathbf{t}}$ to refine the alignment, and compute the per-vertex distance between the two meshes. We subsequently associate each vertex of $\hat{\mathbf{m}}$ to its nearest neighbor in $\tilde{\mathbf{t}}$, obtaining a re-parametrization (*VertexAssociation* in Algorithm 1) of p indices of $\tilde{\mathbf{t}}$. Note that $k \neq p$ in general, thus a vertex of $\hat{\mathbf{m}}$ might be associated with multiple vertices of $\tilde{\mathbf{t}}$; even if $p = k$, this can still happen because of points that share the same nearest neighbor. Once the association is done, the DL-3DMM is fit minimizing the Euclidean distance between each pair of associated points, using a least squares solution. The fitting method reported in [8] uses a regularized formulation (Eq. (2)), which is necessary to avoid uncontrolled deformations. In our case, we use all the vertices to fit the target shape; thus the usefulness of the regularization becomes marginal and the minimization of Eq. (2) becomes:

$$\min_{\alpha} \left\| \tilde{\mathbf{t}} - \hat{\mathbf{m}} - \sum_{i=1}^{|\mathbf{D}|} \mathbf{d}_i\alpha_i \right\|_2^2 . \tag{3}$$

The procedure is repeated until the error between subsequent iterations is lower than a threshold τ or the maximum number of iterations if reached. Algorithm 1 reports the pseudo-code of the proposed Point Cloud Fitting procedure (PCF).

Note that the procedure can be applied either to single independent frames or sequences without any change to the algorithm; indeed, the model at frame t can be obtained either starting from the average model $\hat{\mathbf{m}}$ or the fitted model at frame $t-1$.

3.1   Learning Expression Coefficients

Given the DL-3DMM as described above, the result of the fitting procedure is a set of coefficients $\boldsymbol{\alpha} = \{\alpha_1, \ldots, \alpha_{|D|}\}$ that are used to deform the average model using Eq. (1). Considering a generic face image, these coefficients codify the global shape deformation (*i.e.*, the identity) along with other deformations (*i.e.*, expressions). To derive the set of coefficients that control the expressions, we first need to isolate the identity component from the deformation. To this aim, we first fit the DL-3DMM to a face image in neutral expression to account for the identity and obtain the coefficients $\boldsymbol{\alpha}_{id}$ (Eq. (1) after replacing PCA components $\mathbf{C}_i$ with dictionary elements $\mathbf{d}_i$); subsequently, the fitted model is used in place of the average model to fit an expressive face image of the same subject. In this way, we obtain a set of coefficients $\boldsymbol{\alpha}_{expr}$ that encode the expression. The procedure is depicted in Fig. 1. The final and crucial step is to find a recurrent pattern in the $\boldsymbol{\alpha}_{expr}$ coefficients, separately for each expression. To this end, we investigated and compared the appropriateness of different methods using statistical indicators and regressors. Results are reported in [7].

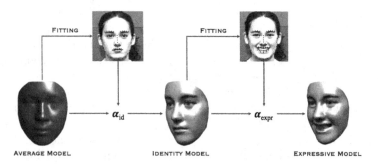

Fig. 1. Extraction of the expression-specific deformation coefficients from the DL-3DMM fitting.

4   Experimental Results

We evaluated the proposed approach based on DL-3DMM and PCF in the task of accurate 3D face reconstruction. The experiments are conceived to demonstrate that RGB-D data, even if affected by noise and provided by low resolution scanners, can be processed through PCF to reconstruct the 3D face shape. We also show that previously learned expressions can be effectively transferred to the 3D reconstructed models.

To quantitatively evaluate the reconstruction accuracy, we used two benchmarks of 3D facial scans, namely, the Binghamton University 3D Facial Expression database (BU-3DFE) [17] and the Face Recognition Grand Challenge database (FRGC) [16]. The BU-3DFE dataset has been largely employed for 3D expression/face recognition; it contains scans of 44 females and 56 males, with age ranging from 18 to 70 years old, acquired in a neutral plus six different expressions: anger, disgust, fear, happiness, sadness, and surprise (2,500 scans in total). The subjects are distributed across different ethnic groups or racial ancestries. This dataset has been used to train the DL-3DMM and a fully registered version of 1,779 out of the 2,500 scans is available. The FRGC dataset is composed of 466 individuals, for a total of 4,007 scans collected in two separate sessions. Approximately, the 60% of such are in neutral expression, while the others show spontaneous expressions. For the experiments, we used the "fall2003" session, comprising 1,729 scans. In the following, we first present and discuss results on BU-3DFE and FRGC, then for some Kinect scans. For all the reported experiments, the regularization term λ of Eq. (2) has been fixed to 0.01; the error threshold τ and the maximum number of iterations in Algorithm 1 have been fixed to 0.001 and 50 respectively.

Table 1. Reconstruction error (in mm) for the landmark fitting (FL) and full point cloud fitting (FL + PCF) with both DL and PCA based 3DMM.

Dataset	FL	FL + PCF
BU-3DFE (DL)	4.507 ± 2.809	0.802 ± 0.235
BU-3DFE (PCA)	4.979 ± 2.766	1.015 ± 0.254
FRGC (DL)	8.272 ± 4.939	0.455 ± 0.282
FRGC (PCA)	7.512 ± 4.756	0.728 ± 0.375

Reconstruction Accuracy. Here, we evaluate the accuracy of the vertices association by computing, for each vertex of the 3DMM, its distance to the closest vertex of the 3D point cloud. To highlight the potential of the proposed solution, values of the mean accuracy are computed with reference to two distinct cases: (i) DL-3DMM fitting based on facial landmarks (FL), and (ii) DL-3DMM fitting based on facial landmarks and PCF (FL + PCF). Further, we also report results obtained using the standard PCA-based 3DMM solution. Recently, in order to deal with multimodal variations, i.e., identity and expressions, the most widely used 3DMM formulations employ a multilinear model made up of two 3DMM components; one modeling the identity and the other modeling facial expressions. Here, we wish to demonstrate the appropriateness and advantages of the selected DL-3DMM formulation, that can effectively account for both the properties in a single model. The mean error and standard deviation across all the models for the BU-3DFE and FRGC datasets are reported in Table 1.

In Fig. 2, accuracy values are reported at a higher level of detail, showing for each model of the BU-3DFE and FRGC datasets the error obtained by using FL (in blue), and FL + PCF (in red). Results demonstrate a noticeable improvement is obtained with the proposed procedure. To provide a qualitative yet representative description of the accuracy of 3D face reconstruction, Fig. 3 reports some heat-maps obtained by encoding with a chromatic value the error associated with each vertex of the reconstructed model; it can be appreciated how the real surface is accurately reconstructed and fine details of regions where landmarks are missing are accurately replicated, while maintaining a smoother surface. The higher accuracy of the proposed solution is demonstrated by the presence of large regions with blue/cyan colors (low error values) for models reconstructed using FL + PCF compared to regions with red/yellow colors (high error values) for models reconstructed using FL.

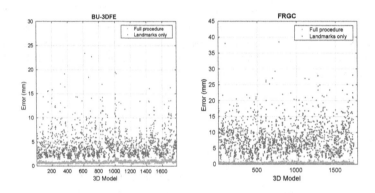

Fig. 2. Comparison between landmark fitting (FL, in blue), and full point cloud fitting (FL + PCF, in red). BU-3DFE (left) and FRGC (right). (Color figure online)

Kinect Data Reconstruction. Our approach has been experimented also on Kinect data. To this end, we collected a few sequences to qualitatively test our method on. Reconstruction of the face surface using the proposed approach is compared to the reconstruction supported by the native libraries of the Microsoft's Kinect Face API that enables the extraction of a HD face model for each face detected in the RGB-D stream. The average error obtained in such sequences is 35.89, 1.70 and 58.40 mm, respectively, for the FL, the FL + PCF and the Kinect reconstruction, demonstrating the effectiveness of the approach even for low-resolution data and also compared to the Microsoft's Kinect Face API. From Fig. 3, we can appreciate that the sole landmarks were not sufficient to reproduce the real shape, *e.g.*, the nose, but it could only coarsely capture the expression.

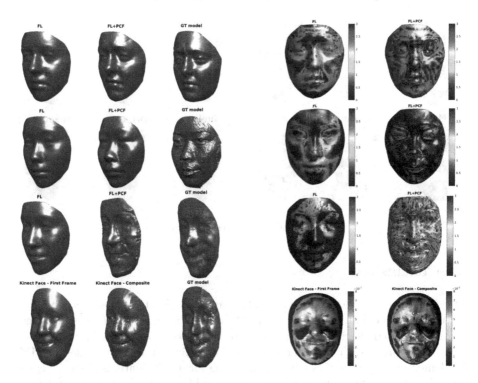

Fig. 3. Comparison between DL-3DMM fitting based on facial landmarks (FL) and facial landmarks plus PCF (FL + PCF). Three leftmost columns: reconstructions and ground truth (GT) models; two rightmost columns: error heat-maps. From top to bottom; the first two rows report sample models from, respectively, BU-3DFE, FRGC; the last two rows, show the reconstruction of raw Kinect depth frames using our method in comparison with the Microsoft's Kinect Face API. (Color figure online)

4.1 Generation of Expressive Models

In order to derive qualitative results, we fitted the DL-3DMM to some neutral faces of the dataset and applied the estimated deformation coefficients α_{est} so as to generate expressive scans for each expression. The expressive models generated from the neutral 3DMM according to the learned deformation vectors are rendered for qualitative evaluation. Some examples can be appreciated in Fig. 4; starting from the neutral expression, we can effectively generate expressive renderings applying the expression-specific parameters separately. The last column in the same figure shows another interesting application of our method, that is the generation of complex, mixed expressions by combining the parameters of the single prototypical expressions. This feature allows us to mix an arbitrary number of expressions and further demonstrates the meaningfulness of the estimated parameters. The examples in Fig. 4 are generated using a combination of 3 basic expressions.

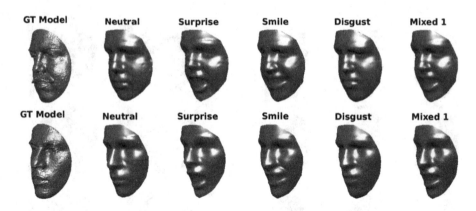

Fig. 4. Synthetic expressions transfer.

5   Conclusions

In this paper, we have proposed a 3DMM based solution to reconstruct a highly-detailed 3D model of the face from depth frames or sequences. This is obtained by the combined effect of two specific algorithmic solutions for 3DMM construction and fitting: on the one hand, we used a dictionary learning based 3DMM implementation that makes possible modeling local deformations of the face; on the other, the model is fit to a target point cloud by a two steps approach, where the 3DMM is first deformed under the effect of the correspondence between a limited set of landmarks, and subsequently refined by an iterative local adjustment of point correspondences. Preliminary results have been reported that show as the proposed framework provides superior results with respect to a landmark-based solution. Further, we successfully learned and applied expression-specific deformation to the fitted scans, while maintaining the accurate subject-specific topology of the face surface unaltered.

References

1. Amberg, B., Romdhani, S., Vetter, T.: Optimal step nonrigid ICP algorithms for surface registration. In: IEEE Conference on Computer Vision and Pattern Recognition, pp. 1–8 (2007)
2. Anasosalu, P.K., Thomas, D., Sugimoto, A.: Compact and accurate 3-D face modeling using an RGB-D camera: let's open the door to 3-D video conference. In: IEEE International Conference on Computer Vision Workshops, pp. 67–74 (2013)
3. Bas, A., Smith, W.A.P., Bolkart, T., Wuhrer, S.: Fitting a 3D morphable model to edges: a comparison between hard and soft correspondences. In: Chen, C.-S., Lu, J., Ma, K.-K. (eds.) ACCV 2016. LNCS, vol. 10117, pp. 377–391. Springer, Cham (2017). https://doi.org/10.1007/978-3-319-54427-4_28
4. Blanz, V., Vetter, T.: A morphable model for the synthesis of 3D faces. In: ACM Conference on Computer Graphics and Interactive Techniques, pp. 187–194 (1999)

5. Blanz, V., Vetter, T.: Face recognition based on fitting a 3D morphable model. IEEE Trans. Pattern Analy. Mach. Intell. **25**(9), 1063–1074 (2003)
6. Booth, J., et al.: 3D reconstruction of 'in-the-wild' faces in images and videos. IEEE Trans. Pattern Anal. Mach. Intell. **40**(11), 2638–2652 (2018)
7. Ferrari, C., Berretti, S., Pala, P., Del Bimbo, A.: Rendering realistic subject-dependent expression images by learning 3DMM deformation coefficients. In: Leal-Taixé, L., Roth, S. (eds.) ECCV 2018. LNCS, vol. 11130, pp. 441–455. Springer, Cham (2019). https://doi.org/10.1007/978-3-030-11012-3_34
8. Ferrari, C., Lisanti, G., Berretti, S., Del Bimbo, A.: A dictionary learning-based 3D morphable shape model. IEEE Trans. Multimedia **19**(12), 2666–2679 (2017)
9. Hernandez, M., Choi, J., Medioni, G.: Laser scan quality 3-D face modeling using a low-cost depth camera. In: European Signal Processing Conference (EUSIPCO), pp. 1995–1999 (2012)
10. Izadi, S., et al.: Kinectfusion: Real-time 3D reconstruction and interaction using a moving depth camera. In: ACM Symposium on User Interface Software and Technology, pp. 559–568 (2011)
11. Kazemi, V., Keskin, C., Taylor, J., Kohli, P., Izadi, S.: Real-time face reconstruction from a single depth image. In: IEEE International Conference on 3D Vision, vol. 1, pp. 369–376, December 2014
12. Mairal, J., Bach, F., Ponce, J., Sapiro, G.: Online dictionary learning for sparse coding. In: International Conference on Machine Learning, pp. 689–696 (2009)
13. Myronenko, A., Song, X.: Point set registration: coherent point drift. IEEE Trans. Pattern Anal. Mach. Intell. **32**(12), 2262–2275 (2010)
14. Newcombe, R.A., et al.: Kinectfusion: real-time dense surface mapping and tracking. In: IEEE International Symposium on Mixed and Augmented Reality, October 2011
15. Paysan, P., Knothe, R., Amberg, B., Romdhani, S., Vetter, T.: A 3D face model for pose and illumination invariant face recognition. In: IEEE International Conference on Advanced Video and Signal Based Surveillance (AVSS), pp. 296–301 (2009)
16. Phillips, P.J., et al.: Overview of the face recognition grand challenge. In: IEEE Workshop on Face Recognition Grand Challenge Experiments, pp. 947–954, June 2005
17. Yin, L., Wei, X., Sun, Y., Wang, J., Rosato, M.J.: A 3D facial expression database for facial behavior research. In: IEEE International Conference on Automatic Face and Gesture Recognition, pp. 211–216 (2006)
18. Zollhöfer, M., Martinek, M., Greiner, G., Stamminger, M., Süßmuth, J.: Automatic reconstruction of personalized avatars from 3D face scans. Comput. Animation Virtual Worlds **22**(2–3), 195–202 (2011)
19. Zollhöfer, M., et al.: Real-time non-rigid reconstruction using an RGB-D camera. ACM Trans. Graph. **33**(4), 156:1–156:12 (2014)

The Effects of Data Sources: A Baseline Evaluation of the MoCA Dataset

Elena Nicora, Gaurvi Goyal, Nicoletta Noceti[✉], and Francesca Odone

DIBRIS - Università degli Studi di Genova, Genoa, Italy
{elena.nicora,gaurvi.goyal,nicoletta.noceti,
francesca.odone}@dibris.unige.it

Abstract. In this work we discuss the action classification performance obtained with a baseline assessment of the MoCA dataset: a multimodal, synchronised dataset including Motion Capture data and multi-view video sequences of upper body actions in a cooking scenario. To this purpose, we setup a classification pipeline to manipulate the two data type. For the MoCap, we employ a representation based on the use of 3D+t histograms modelling the space-time evolution of an action, classified using a classical Support Vector Machine with a linear kernel. As for the videos, we learn the representation using a variant of the Inception 3D model, followed by a Single Layer Perceptron as a classifier. Discussing the experimental analysis will be the opportunity to observe the diversity of MoCap and video data at work in two scenarios of uneven complexity, i.e. on streams of data describing regular repetitions of the same action, or when actions are part of a more complex and structured activity where actions influence each other.

Keywords: Action classification · Motion Capture · Videos

1 Introduction

Classifying actions from visual data is paramount for a number of applications, ranging from robotics and human-machine interaction, to industry and entertainment. Over the last decades, research activities rode the wave of technological advances in the visual devices, comfortably bouncing from the use of one specific data source to another. Videos and Motion Capture devices are undoubtedly two backbones of the research in recent years, and the numerous surveys published so far on action understanding topics, e.g. [2,5,11] just to name a few, report detailed discussions on the peculiarities of the two. While stating which data source may be considered the best choice from a general standpoint is not trivial, it may be speculated that videos and skeleton data can be considered as complementary information carriers, characterized by uneven amount of signal-to-noise ratios. On one hand, Motion Capture data can provide precise but sparse 3D representations of actions; on the other, videos are more rich but also harder to analyse and affected by perspective projection issues.

© Springer Nature Switzerland AG 2019
E. Ricci et al. (Eds.): ICIAP 2019, LNCS 11751, pp. 544–555, 2019.
https://doi.org/10.1007/978-3-030-30642-7_49

In this paper, we discuss the action classification performance obtained with a baseline assessment of the MoCA (MultimOdal Cooking Actions) dataset, with specific focus of the effect of data sources. To this purpose, we setup a classification pipeline that, starting from the same "data portions" (provided by data annotation), is suitably instantiated to manipulate Motion Capture or video data. For the first, we employ a representation based on the use of 3D+t histograms modelling the space-time evolution of an action, classified using a classical Support Vector Machine with a linear kernel. As for the latter, we learn the representation using a variant of the Inception 3D model [1], followed by a Single Layer Perceptron as a classifier.

Exploiting the MoCA dataset, we compare the classification of upper-body cooking actions in two scenarios of different complexity: (i) on streams of data describing regular repetitions of the same action, (ii) when actions are part of a more complex and structured activity, and thus, although performed more naturally, are influenced by other actions occurring in the temporal neighborhood.

The reminder of the paper is organized as follow. In Sect. 2 we introduce the dataset and its characteristics, followed by Sects. 3 and 4 where we present the methodologies of representation and classification for, respectively, Motion Capture and video data. Sect. 5 discusses the experimental assessment, while Sect. 6 is left to conclusions.

2   The MoCA Dataset

The MoCA (MultimOdal Cooking Actions) dataset [10] is a multimodal, synchronised dataset in which we collect Motion Capture (henceforth referred to as MoCap) data and video sequences acquired from multiple views of upper body actions in a cooking scenario[1]. It has been collected with the specific purpose of investigating view-invariant action properties in both biological and artificial systems, and in this sense it may be of interest for multiple research communities in the cognitive and computational domains. Beside addressing classical action recognition tasks, the dataset enables research on different nuances of action understanding, from the segmentation of action primitives robust across different sensors and viewpoints, to the detection of action classes depending on their dynamic evolution or the goal.

We report in Table 1 the list of 20 cooking actions included in the dataset. The range of actions presents significant diversity in terms of motion granularity, since actions may involve the movement of fingers, hands or the entire arms. Also, they may involve the use of one or two arm(s) of the volunteer, and possibly the use of tools might require application of a variety of forces.

The acquisition setting (see Fig. 1(a)) included a motion capture system composed by six VICON infrared cameras, each one equipped with an infrared strobe capturing the light emitted by six reflective markers placed on relevant joints of the right arm of the actor: shoulder, elbow, wrist, palm, index finger and little

---

[1] The dataset is available for download at https://github.com/nicolettanoceti/CookingDataset.

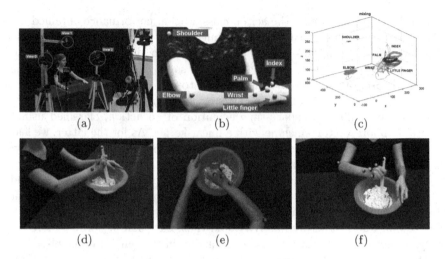

Fig. 1. A visualization of the acquisition setting. (a) An overall image of the setup, (b) a detailed view of the markers of the right arm of the volunteer, (c) sample trajectories, color coded with respect to the marker, for one entire unsegmented sequence of action *Mixing in a bowl* (with 17 instances). Sample frames of the corresponding video acquisitions are reported in (d) View 0, (e) View 1 and (f) View 2.

finger (Fig. 1(b)). Markers were calibrated in order to share the same coordinate system and the final trajectories were recorded synchronously at a rate of 100 Hz/s. An example of the acquired trajectories for the action *Mixing in a bowl* is reported in Fig. 1(c). For what concerns the video data, three identical high resolution IP cameras were employed. The cameras observe the scene from three different viewpoints: a lateral view (View 0), an egocentric view (View 1; obtained with a camera mounted slightly above the subject's head), and a frontal

Table 1. The list of 20 cooking actions included in the MoCA dataset. Below, a description of the activities in the *scene* sequences are reported.

Shredding a carrot	Cutting the bread
Cleaning a dish	Eating
Beating eggs	Squeezing a lemon
Mincing with a mezzaluna	Mixing in a bowl
Open a bottle	Turn the frittata in a pan
Pestling	Pouring water in multiple containers
Pouring water in a mug	Reaching an object
Rolling the dough	Washing the salad
Salting	Spreading cheese on a slice of bread
Cleaning the table	Transporting an object

view (View 2). Figure 1, bottom row, reports sample frames for the action *Mixing in a bowl* acquired from V0, V1, and V2.

For each action a training and a test sequence is available, containing an average of 25 repetitions of the action. Furthermore, acquisitions of more structured activities – we called scenes – are included, in which the actions are performed in sequence for a final, more complex goal of action recognition in more structured activities.

The dataset is accompanied by an annotation, which comprises the segmentation of single action instances in terms of time instants in the MoCap reference frame. A function then allows mapping the time instants to the corresponding frame in the video sequences (acquired at 30 fps). In addition, functionalities to load, segment, and visualize the data are also provided.

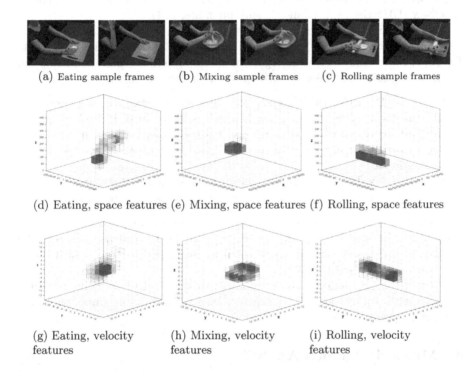

(a) Eating sample frames   (b) Mixing sample frames   (c) Rolling sample frames

(d) Eating, space features (e) Mixing, space features (f) Rolling, space features

(g) Eating, velocity features   (h) Mixing, velocity features   (i) Rolling, velocity features

Fig. 2. Example of 3D+t histograms for 3 different actions. Above: sample frames to show the evolution of actions. Middle: histograms of action positions. Below: histograms of instantaneous velocities. All histograms refer to the *palm* joint.

3   MoCap Data Analysis

Methods for action representation from MoCap data are mostly based on the geometrical relationships among joints and their orientation in space [8], often aggregating information from different joints or body parts [7,15]. It is worth notice that in general the amount of markers needed to succeed in a classification task strongly depends on the granularity of the action itself, and if in some cases the sparsity of the MoCap may represent a problem, in others it helps to focus on the essential yet relevant action units.

Considering the variability of the actions included in our dataset, we compose action descriptors combining different joints and their variations over time. More specifically, we represent the space-time evolution of action instances from Motion Capture data using 3D+t equally-binned histograms, collected by partitioning the volume of positions and instantaneous velocities (i.e. the displacements between two time-adjacent positions) of actions. Histograms are built using 4 out of the 6 joints available. In detail, after a visual inspection of the trajectories (see an example in Fig. 1(c)), we selected the most descriptive joints, i.e. elbow (E), wrist (W), palm (P) and index finger (I).

Following this procedure, for each action instance $\mathbf{x}$, we collected a total of 8 vectorial descriptors, i.e. $H_j^f(\mathbf{x})$ where $j \in \{E, W, P, I\}$ denotes the joint, while $f \in \{s, v\}$ represents the feature (space or velocity) used to build the histogram.

In the experiments, we will consider different histograms aggregations:

- $H^f(\mathbf{x}) = [H_E^f(\mathbf{x})H_W^f(\mathbf{x})H_P^f(\mathbf{x})H_I^f(\mathbf{x})]$, i.e. concatenating the histograms of all joints for a certain feature. The length is 6084 for space-based histograms, and 8788 for velocity-based descriptors. These options will allow us to explore the representation capability of space and velocity features, if employed independently.
- $H(\mathbf{x}) = [H^s(\mathbf{x})H^v(\mathbf{x})]$, i.e. concatenating the histograms at the previous point (final length 14872), to fully exploit the potential of the representation.

In Fig. 2 we report a visualisation of the histograms we obtained for 3 different actions, i.e. *Eating*, *Mixing*, and *Rolling*. It can be noticed how, despite the apparent simplicity of the representation, meaningful peculiarities of each action can be appropriately encoded.

As for the actual action classification, we trained a multi-class Support Vector Machine with a linear kernel[2], which is known to be suitable when employing histograms (see e.g. [3]).

4   Multi-view Video Analysis

The availability of pre-trained models enabled, in the last years, a diffusion and solid assessment of deep architectures for image understanding tasks. The same could not be said for the analysis of dynamic information until very recently due to lack of datasets of appropriate size. Despite the significant improvements that deep architectures provide with respect to state-of-art [5,13], only very recent datasets made available to the research community [6] opened the possibility of fully exploring the potential of pre-trained models when applied to different temporal tasks or datasets.

---

[2] We employed the LinearSVC implementation available in Python.

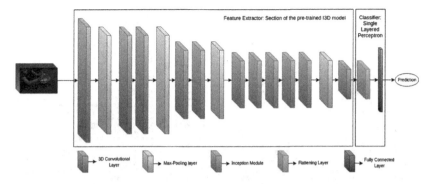

Fig. 3. SpatioTemporal 3D Convolutional Neural Network derived by using a section of the Inception 3D [1] as a feature extractor followed by a flattening layer and a single fully connected layer as a classifier. Batch Normalization and Dropout layers are not shown.

Taking inspiration from the above, in order to analyse the video streams, we used learnt intermediate level features from a pre-trained neural network, and employed this learnt representation as input to a multi-class classification architecture. To learn the representation we consider a variant of the Inception 3D or I3D model [1], derived from the InceptionV1 [12]. It is a two-stream Inflated 3D ConvNets model, originally including two streams, RGB and Optical flow, jointly combined with a late fusion model. Conversely, we use only the flow stream of the network, also less prone to overfitting. The model is pre-trained on ImageNet dataset [4] and on Kinetics-400 [6]. Once trained, the network may be seen as a multi- resolution representation of image sequences.

Figure 3 summarizes the actual network we incorporate in our work, including both the feature extractor derived from the pre-trained I3D network and the classifier. For a given multi-class classification task, segmented video clips of the actions are used as inputs to the recognition pipeline. From them, the optical flow is extracted, using the TV-L1 algorithm [14], and fed to the trained Inception 3D model, from which we derive the activations of learnt intermediate spatio-temporal features (a matrix of size $\{8,7,7,832\}$). The point of extraction of the features was found empirically as one tolerant to changes in the specific classification dataset.

As for the classifier, we considered the Single Layered Perceptron (SLP), a single fully connected neural network layer, without non-linear activation. The features learnt from the optical flow are flattened, and after a random dropout they are fed into the SLP layer, followed by a batch normalization layer, to promote regularization of the solution.

5   Experimental Evaluations

In this section we thoroughly discuss the experiments we performed on the MoCA dataset. The analysis has the potential of being a baseline for the dataset, but at the same time allows us to unfold the effects of data sources and their nature on the classification results.

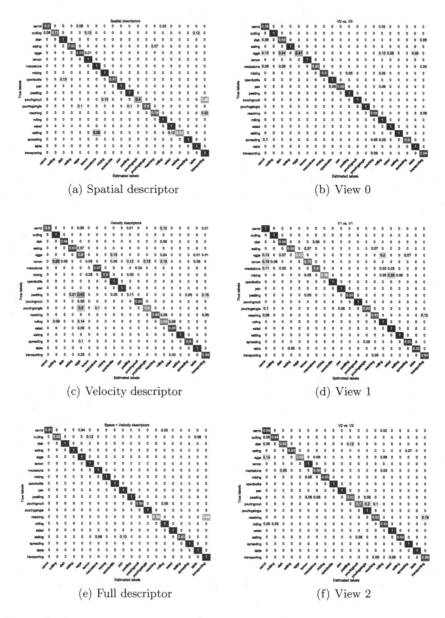

(a) Spatial descriptor

(b) View 0

(c) Velocity descriptor

(d) View 1

(e) Full descriptor

(f) View 2

Fig. 4. Confusion matrices corresponding to the classifiers. Left column: MoCap data considering, from top, space only, velocity only, and the combination of the two. Right column: video data using, from top, View 0, View 1, or View 2.

Table 2. Average classification accuracy on the MoCA dataset using MoCap and video data in different configurations (see text for details)

Method	Avg. Acc. ± Std. Dev.
MoCap (Space) + Linear SVM	0.92 ± 0.19
MoCap (Velocity) + Linear SVM	0.82 ± 0.27
MoCap (Space + Velocity) + Linear SVM	0.95 ± 0.11
2D V0-V0 + SLP	0.93 ± 0.14
2D V1-V1 + SLP	0.90 ± 0.14
2D V2-V2 + SLP	0.91 ± 0.10

5.1 Cooking Actions Recognition: An Assessment

We start the discussion on the experimental analysis by reporting the results we obtained on the recognition tasks of visual data streams with each stream describing repetitions of the same action (i.e. using the test sequence acquired similarly to the training, where the volunteer repeats a certain action for, on average, 25 times, see Sect. 2). In both the classification pipelines (i.e. based on MoCap and video data) the models are learnt on the training sequences and evaluated on the test sequences. As for the SVMs, parameters have been selected with K-fold Cross Validation (K = 5) coupled with a grid-search approach.

We report in Table 2 the average classification accuracies and standard deviations obtained for different combinations of the MoCap histograms, and for the different views for the video data. As expected, the MoCap data, when fully exploited, leads to the best results, slightly superior but comparable to the performance obtained with the videos, which are influenced by the viewpoint. As a reference, we mention that a state-of-art method for action recognition from skeleton data [9], based on the aggregation of displacement vectors describing the joints configuration over time, provides an accuracy of 0.98.

A closer look to the accuracies of each action reveals uneven performances. To comment on this, we report in Fig. 4 the confusion matrices for all the cases we considered. At first glance, it is easy to confirm what was already argued from the accuracy in the table, i.e. the confusion matrices for the classification of videos, regardless the specific viewpoint, and for the MoCap data when the full descriptor is employed, are very close to being diagonal. Meanwhile, the remaining two cases, especially the one corresponding to the use of velocity only, display a higher variance of the results. In fact, in the majority of cases the performance of the full descriptor is higher than both spatial and velocity based representations, or comparable to the best of the two. The remaining failures can be attributed to the simplicity of the classifier. A deeper investigation on the misclassified examples also reveal that the misclassified actions are different when looking at the space or at the velocity, as expected. As for the videos, in case of all viewpoints, two actions, i.e. *Beating Eggs* and *Mincing with a mezzaluna* tend to be misclassified most often.

Comparing the performance of the two classification pipelines, we observe that videos, carrying richer and more redundant information, perform better on more structured and complex actions, like *Cutting the bread* and *Salting*, where the skeleton data are too poor. On the other hand, if an action is too simple – meaning its dynamic is not enough informative – as in the case of *Reaching*, the MoCap fails to convey the appropriate amount of information, while the videos compensate with the appearance the lack in dynamic evidences. In case the action is characterized by a high frequency or is spatially circumscribed, as *Beating eggs*, the video data provides noisier representations, thus the sparser but precise measures of the MoCap perform better.

5.2   Classifying Action Sequences

As observed in the previous section, the regularity of the movements that the volunteer attains when performing repeatedly the very same task favours the overall uniformity of the replicas, thus facilitating the classification despite the apparent diversity of action complexity. Conversely, the execution of an action when part of a mixed sequence – i.e. when appearing as an element of a more structured activity – is highly influenced by the context, the other movements occurring in the sequence, and their goal. To quantitatively assess such complexity, we consider the sequences of the MoCA dataset we called *scenes*, in which the actor simulates the preparation of a meal in a more natural way, and apply the same trained models we adopted in the previous experiments. Table 3 reports a brief description of the activity represented with the *scene* sequences, the number of actions and the accuracies obtained using the MoCap data with full descriptor, and the 3 video sequences. A dramatic gap with respect to the results obtained on actions repetitions can be observed, proving the strong influence of the contextual actions on the classification of each sub-part.

Table 3. Accuracy obtained on each *scene* sequence.

#Scene	Instances	Mocap	V0	V1	V2
1	36	0.72	0.33	0.08	0.08
2	20	0	0.42	0.47	0.58
3	26	0	0.04	0.04	0.04
4	17	0	0.06	0.19	0.25
5	22	0.32	0	0.05	0.05

We propose in Table 4 a closer look to the actions involved in the *scenes*, reporting the number of instances and how many of them have been correctly classified. In a further column we highlight the number of samples for which the classification of the corresponding video clips was deterred due to the short length of the segmented clips, lower than the minimum required by the model.

Table 4. An analysis on the classification of each action present in the *scene* sequences (see text for details).

Action	#Instances	MoCap	V0	V1	V2	Non-class
Carrot	17	0	7	8	10	0
Cutting	1	0	0	0	0	1
Eating	4	0	0	1	1	0
Eggs	28	26	0	0	0	28
Lemon	5	1	0	0	0	0
Mixing	17	0	0	0	0	0
Openbottle	1	0	0	0	0	0
Pouringsingle	2	0	1	0	0	0
Reaching	13	0	0	0	0	2
Salting	1	0	1	0	0	0
Spreading	6	0	0	0	0	0
Table	10	6	0	0	0	0
Transporting	16	0	6	6	6	1
Total	121	34	15	15	17	32
Overall Acc.	–	0.27	0.12	0.12	0.14	–

Two main observations are in order. The first refers to the fact the complexity of the *scenes* does not influence a particular type of actions – e.g. repetitive or sporadic actions – but rather affects the classification task in general. Actions like *Reaching* and *Transporting an object* are certainly characterised by a high variability in space – depending on the starting and ending point of an action – and in velocity, influenced by the weight of the specific object to be moved. The latter aspect affects more in general the manipulation of objects, a type of action that in the *scenes* has been in some cases instantiated slightly differently than in the training and test sequence (e.g. in the action *grating* a piece of cheese is used instead of a carrot). It is interesting to note that when attenuating the complexity of the classification task the performance are only partially influenced. To this purpose, we evaluated the classification results considering a lower number of actions classes – more specifically considering only the ones actually present in one of the scenes: while the accuracy of the MoCap increases to the 0.70, the videos presents, on average, an accuracy of 0.25. This clearly shows that the problem of the *scene* classification is inherently complex.

A second main observation is related to the fact the two sources of data show complementary abilities, in the sense that when an action instance is recognised this happens with just one of the two. This suggests that a multimodal approach may be beneficial to solve ambiguities.

6 Discussion

In this work we discussed the action classification performance obtained with a baseline assessment of the MoCA dataset, a multimodal synchronised dataset including Motion Capture data and multi-view video sequences of upper body actions in a cooking scenario. We instantiated two classification pipelines to manipulate the two data modalities. For the MoCap, we employed 3D+t histograms modelling the space-time evolution of an action, classified using a classical Support Vector Machine with a linear kernel. As for the videos, we learned the representation using a variant of the Inception 3D model, followed by a Single Layer Perceptron as a classifier. We experimentally evaluated the classification on streams of visual data describing regular repetitions of the same action, or when actions are part of a more complex and structured activity where actions influence each other. The critical discussion on the results we obtained highlighted the diversity of MoCap and video data at work, showing they provide equally relevant and complementary abilities to characterize actions. Our future efforts on the dataset will be aimed at exploiting this complementarity with inherently multi-modal action representations.

Acknowledgements. The authors would like to express their gratitude to Alessandra Sciutti, Francesco Rea and Alessia Vignolo, for their help in acquiring the dataset and the helpful discussions over the entire course of this research.

References

1. Carreira, J., Zisserman, A.: Quo vadis, action recognition? a new model and the kinetics dataset. In: CVPR 2017, pp. 4724–4733 (2017)
2. Cheng, G., Wan, Y., Saudagar, A.N., Namuduri, K., Buckles, B.P.: Advances in human action recognition: a survey. arXiv preprint arXiv:1501.05964 (2015)
3. Dalal, N., Triggs, B.: Histograms of oriented gradients for human detection. In: CVPR 2005, vol. 1, pp. 886–893. IEEE Computer Society (2005)
4. Deng, J., Dong, W., Socher, R., Li, L.J., Li, K., Fei-Fei, L.: Imagenet: a large-scale hierarchical image database. In: CVPR 2009, pp. 248–255. IEEE (2009)
5. Herath, S., Harandi, M., Porikli, F.: Going deeper into action recognition: a survey. Image Vis. Comput. **60**, 4–21 (2017)
6. Kay, W., et al.: The kinetics human action video dataset. arXiv preprint arXiv:1705.06950 (2017)
7. Kulić, D., Takano, W., Nakamura, Y.: Incremental learning, clustering and hierarchy formation of whole body motion patterns using adaptive hidden markov chains. Int. J. Robot. Res. **27**(7), 761–784 (2008)
8. Lillo, I., Carlos Niebles, J., Soto, A.: A hierarchical pose-based approach to complex action understanding using dictionaries of actionlets and motion poselets. In: CVPR 2016, pp. 1981–1990 (2016)
9. Luvizon, D.C., Tabia, H., Picard, D.: Learning features combination for human action recognition from skeleton sequences. Pattern Recogn. Lett. **99**, 13–20 (2017)
10. Malafronte, D., Goyal, G., Vignolo, A., Odone, F., Noceti, N.: Investigating the use of space-time primitives to understand human movements. In: Battiato, S., Gallo, G., Schettini, R., Stanco, F. (eds.) ICIAP 2017. LNCS, vol. 10484, pp. 40–50. Springer, Cham (2017). https://doi.org/10.1007/978-3-319-68560-1_4

11. Poppe, R.: A survey on vision-based human action recognition. Image Vis. Comput. **28**(6), 976–990 (2010)
12. Szegedy, C., Vanhoucke, V., Ioffe, S., Shlens, J., Wojna, Z.: Rethinking the inception architecture for computer vision, pp. 2818–2826 (2016)
13. Tran, D., Bourdev, L., Fergus, R., Torresani, L., Paluri, M.: Learning spatiotemporal features with 3D convolutional networks. In: ICCV 2015, pp. 4489–4497 (2015)
14. Zach, C., Pock, T., Bischof, H.: A duality based approach for realtime TV-L^1 optical flow. In: Hamprecht, F.A., Schnörr, C., Jähne, B. (eds.) DAGM 2007. LNCS, vol. 4713, pp. 214–223. Springer, Heidelberg (2007). https://doi.org/10.1007/978-3-540-74936-3_22
15. Zinnen, A., Blanke, U., Schiele, B.: An analysis of sensor-oriented vs. model-based activity recognition. In: 2009 International Symposium on Wearable Computers, pp. 93–100. IEEE (2009)

Author Index